The G.I. Joe Roster

ALSO BY THERESA BANE
AND FROM MCFARLAND

Encyclopedia of Mythological Objects (2020)
Encyclopedia of Beasts and Monsters in Myth, Legend and Folklore (2016)
Encyclopedia of Giants and Humanoids in Myth, Legend and Folklore (2016)
Encyclopedia of Spirits and Ghosts in World Mythology (2016)
Encyclopedia of Imaginary and Mythical Places (2014)
Encyclopedia of Fairies in World Folklore and Mythology (2013)
Encyclopedia of Demons in World Religions and Cultures (2012)
Encyclopedia of Vampire Mythology (2010, paperback 2020)

The G.I. Joe Roster
Characters of the Toy and Media Universe

THERESA BANE

McFarland & Company, Inc., Publishers
Jefferson, North Carolina

All photographs are of Tom Wyckoff's collection and were taken by Thomas K. Prater.

LIBRARY OF CONGRESS CATALOGING-IN-PUBLICATION DATA

Names: Bane, Theresa, 1969– author.
Title: The G.I. Joe roster : characters of the toy and media universe / Theresa Bane.
Description: Jefferson : McFarland & Company, Inc., Publishers, 2024. | Includes index.
Identifiers: LCCN 2024007865 | ISBN 9781476693040 (paperback : acid free paper) ∞
ISBN 9781476651767 (ebook)
Subjects: LCSH: G.I. Joe figures. | G.I. Joe (Fictitious character) | Action figures (Toys) | BISAC: PERFORMING ARTS / Television / Reference | PERFORMING ARTS / Animation (see also Film / Genres / Animated)
Classification: LCC NK8475.M5 B36 2024 | DDC 688.7221—dc23/eng/20230306
LC record available at https://lccn.loc.gov/2024007865

BRITISH LIBRARY CATALOGUING DATA ARE AVAILABLE

ISBN (print) 978-1-4766-9304-0
ISBN (ebook) 978-1-4766-5176-7

© 2024 Theresa Bane. All rights reserved

*No part of this book may be reproduced or transmitted in any form
or by any means, electronic or mechanical, including photocopying
or recording, or by any information storage and retrieval system,
without permission in writing from the publisher.*

Front cover illustration © 2024 CSA-Printstock

Printed in the United States of America

*McFarland & Company, Inc., Publishers
Box 611, Jefferson, North Carolina 28640
www.mcfarlandpub.com*

To all servicemen, past and present,
who inspired the toyline
that inspires generations

Table of Contents

Preface 1

Introduction 5

Section One: G.I. Joe — 13

G.I. Joe 13
Continuity 16
Marvel Comics Universe 18
Image Comics 20
The Animated Series 20
Action Force 21
Sigma 6 22
Chain of Command and Rank Organization 22
Bases and Holdings 25
G.I. Joe Character Field Guide 27

Section Two: Cobra — 173

Cobra Command 173
Marvel Comics Universe 174
The Animated Series 176
Action Force 176
Sigma 6 176
Cobra High Command 176
Major Reoccurring Cobra Characters 177
Rank and File 179
Bases and Holdings 179
Cobra Character Field Guide 181

Index 259

Preface

As an author, I am always working on something. Most of the research and writing are typically filed away for "someday," as I become inspired by a new idea. Documents are finished, put into a folder, carefully named, and then, filed away for "another time," that magical day when I will get back to it. I have scores of jump drives, nearly 100 discs, and three laptops filled with Word documents waiting for "one day" to roll around. It seems so futile, except that for one project, all was not in vain.

Years ago, I had, for reasons I cannot now recall, begun to compile a list of the G.I. Joe characters. This was so long ago that I could not jump on the internet and Google the answer. The list was neatly typed up, filed, and put away for future reference. I had no idea what I was going to do with it, but I had it.

A few years later I cared for my mother in her final months. During this time, on my very first laptop, a large and heavy machine, I worked on a book about the history of the haunted historic locations in the city of Greensboro, North Carolina. Oddly, at night rather than sleeping, I found my mind drifting back to that list of G.I. Joe characters. When time permitted, I revisited the list, which had by now developed into a document. I even went so far as to rummage through my brothers' toys they thought they had safely secured and stored in my parents' basement. After my mom passed and the history book was completed, the G.I. Joe document was again saved, filed, and forgotten.

Years passed. Laptops and projects came and went.

But then fate stepped in. My husband was going to celebrate a milestone birthday. Of course, I wanted to gift him something special, but what? And then, it came to me. I would make a G.I. Joe field guide, one of a kind, just for him. I dug through my archive of electronic research projects and eventually found the file. It was nearly 25 years old and on a read/write CD by a company no longer in existence. I held my breath and put it in my drive. And wonders will never cease: the data were still viable. All the information was there. It took some work, but I wrangled it into a reference book I thought he would enjoy, and he did. He showed it off to his friends and fellow G.I. Joe fans, a one-of-a-kind, original, limited-edition field guide made just for him.

The following year we found ourselves at a toy convention and happened upon a G.I. Joe cosplay group, the Blue Ridge Marauders (facebook.com/BlueRidgeMarauders/). They were selling art prints to raise money for an amazing cause, K9s for Warriors (k9sforwarriors.org). I met Tommy Wyckoff, a cosplayer with the Southeast's largest collection of G.I. Joe action figures. It is his figures that were photographed for the book by Thomas K. Prater (thomaskprater.com). My husband showed Tommy his book, and they discussed the pros and cons of its features as it stood then. Wanting to improve upon it, I reached out to other Joe collectors, showing them some sample pages, and asking for their input. I took their cheers and jeers to heart and adjusted.

It was during this stage that I was approached by McFarland to see if I had anything in the works. I presented them with the G.I. Joe manuscript. I am sure it shocked them, as it is a far cry from my usual subject matter of folklore, legends, and mythology, but after some suggestions were made and a quick rewrite completed, the book was finally finished.

What started off as a lark in 1995, became a busy project in 2004, and evolved into a novelty gift in 2020 finally reached its full potential after almost 30 years as a fully developed character field guide.

This particular book is different from my others not only in subject matter but in presentation as well. I learned from my discussions with collectors that they want information fast, not hidden away in paragraphs. This is why I chose to go with a field guide format. As some characters in the G.I. Joe multiverses are more developed than others, you'll see that not all entries are fully fleshed out.

After the name comes the series and year the action figure first appeared. Collectors usually specialize in clusters of years, but the toys were made from 1982 through 1994. I also list their real name—as characters tend to refer to one another by their code names nearly exclusively. Also listed are their aliases and their prototype names, when known. As the toyline was a global success, the spelling and actual names of the characters varied by region; so I included the various regional spellings of their names.

Naturally, name, rank, and serial number are included as well as gender, place of birth, and service branch.

When discernible, also listed are the bases and locations where they were stationed. As a global anti-terrorist fighting unit, G.I. Joe needed to have outposts all over the world. After all, there was no telling where Cobra would strike next.

Primary and secondary military occupational specialties, hereafter abbreviated to MOS, are included as well. All of the Joes have this listed, while Cobra operatives, being less disciplined and trained, are not so concerned with such matters.

There is a brief physical description of each action figure as it first appeared. When the character appeared in other formats, such as comics or cartoons, I also included those descriptions.

It may seem odd to list each character's faction, but within G.I. Joe and Cobra there are sub-teams and organizations as well as mercenary outfits and proactive private citizens. You will discover that some characters are members of many such units and have switched sides as well!

The heading called Background Information is just that; each action figure had a brief bio on the back of his or her packaging. The information found here did not properly fit into any of the other headings but was still important.

Each of the action figures came with an accessory, or three, typically some sort of gun, helmet, or even an animal companion. The series or manufacturing and packaging location often decided what accessories the figure was equipped with. Most often there was uniformity in the item itself, but the color and quality of the plastic varied wildly.

With so many cartoon episodes produced by different animation studios and 155 comics issued, it is small wonder readers and fans alike feel a connection to the characters. In spite of the many writers, directors, and editors involved over the years, the characters have maintained a startling consistency not found with other product lines. This is why I feel that my Abilities and Conditions headings are accurate for each.

Abilities simply supply a list of skills and talents the character has *demonstrated*. This can also be something mentioned by the character or said of him by another. Abilities are always an asset.

Conditions are the physical and mental limitations characters have and must overcome or fall victim to. Whenever possible, I used phrases from the source itself. Because these are, for the sake of this product, non-quantifiable, I have listed them alphabetically rather than by my perception of their strength.

Nearly every Joe and Cobra action figure had a quote on his or her packaging material. This was occasionally something the character said, but most often it was something said about him or her by an unnamed commanding officer or teammate. This information had to be included; often these quotes paint a vivid portrait of the character's personality. These quotes are taken as they appeared on the packaging; I did not correct grammar, spelling, or typos. They also appear in quotation marks.

The last of the entries is Notes. This general catchall is where any last bits of

Case 2.

Case 3.

information about the character that are important to know but do not easily fit into one of the other headings are placed.

Apart from the comics, cartoons, and fun facts sent to me by fans, once word of the development of this book began to spread, I found the internet to be a viable resource. Of note, I found the websites *gijoe.fandom.com*, *goarmy.com*, and *yojoe.com* to be very useful in not only confirming facts but also discovering new ones. Thank you to Tommy Wyckoff, who opened up his home to us and let us photograph his collection, twice (and for letting us play with some of our favorite figures). Thank you to Thomas K. Prater, my photographer, and his artful eye. And above all, I want to thank my husband, T. Glenn Bane. He is supportive of all my endeavors, no matter how wacky. I will be so happy to present this book to him. Again.

There you have it, the origin story of this G.I. Joe character field guide. And now you know, and knowing is half the battle. Yo Joe!

Introduction

Welcome to the multiverse of G.I. Joe. It's a truly amazing place to be. It's a world filled with larger-than-life heroes a child of the eighties could admire and villains so vile and heinous they united a generation in wishing for their downfall. It's easy to tell the white hats from the black hats in this multiverse, as it's a very polarized world. Nevertheless, whenever entering a new sphere, the wizened traveler will seek out a guidebook companion.

Congratulations, you've found the book you always wanted and never knew you needed. A book dedicated solely to your childhood, of lying on your bedroom floor and pretending to be the hero saving America and the free world from the evil and tyranny of those who would oppress everything that makes our country great. A book of American mythology for the adolescent. And within these pages is all the information you will ever need on every one of those characters, white hats and black hats alike. Some of the information you may remember well, as it relates to your favorite action figures; some of it may have been long forgotten but remembered anew after reading it (a lovely *oh yeah* moment); and then there will be those tidbits of information you may have never known at all. How exciting!

I know this was the case for me when I began writing the book. With each character I wrote about came a swell of memories, of times spent playing for hours with my brothers and our G.I. Joe action figures. Admittedly, we did mix in some other action figures we had amassed, but in the end G.I. Joe won out. They were, I suppose, the most relatable to us. And it didn't hurt that one of the characters had the same first and last name as one of my brothers. But the backstories that were squeezed onto their file cards (a.k.a. the back of their packaging) told us where they went to school, where they were from, what their hobbies were, and even their trademark quote. These windows into their world were relatable because we had heard of these places, maybe even been to them, or shared the same hobby. They were from here, not some distant galaxy far away.

And also, the toys had more points of articulation and better accessories.

There's no denying it: we all love G.I. Joe. Even now as you read this, your brain is playing the opening credit music in the back of your head; before long, you're no longer subconsciously humming it, but singing along, smiling because what a great time it was to be a kid. Every day after school our entire generation was glued to the television set, the home appliance that dominated the family's living room. It was maybe the best 30 minutes of our day. Which characters would appear in today's episode? What crazy plot did Cobra Commander have to take over the world this time? Would Destro and the Baroness betray him or help? And remember how you flipped out when there was a two-part episode? I sure do. Tomorrow literally could not come soon enough, and it was all we talked about in school the next day. Those were great times.

Anyone reading this book would, I imagine, have at the very least a passing familiarity with G.I. Joe. But I would like to remind present-day readers of the time and place in which G.I. Joe thrived. It was a different world back then, and I suspect that modern children would not recognize the world we knew and grew up in.

The time when I and many other kids connected with G.I. Joe was the 1980s—and to some that may spell it out enough. It was a time when toylines reigned supreme. If there was a cartoon on the air, rest assured it also had an accompanying toyline and breakfast cereal. Toys for boys were hyper-masculine, toys for girls uber-feminine. Anything that could be used by either gender was something innocuous and usually played with outside, like a Frisbee or backyard waterslide.

Ronald Reagan was president of the United States of America; the country was a world power both financially and militarily. The country's military strength was unchallenged, even by our greatest enemy of the time—Russia. Reagan took an aggressive stance on them even as the Cold War was ending. World politics was a very black-and-white place; it was simply us against them. The only thing preventing them from dropping the bomb on us (assuming, of course, that our "Star Wars" satellite didn't intercept and save us from nuclear annihilation) was their fear of the unstoppable retaliation America would launch in her death throes.

The stress of living under the constant worry of nuclear detonation over your hometown may seem like too much trauma for a child to deal with, but we did. We grew up with it and we were used to it. In a psychological study I read, I discovered that children play games such as "war" and "monsters" to sample emotions safely and protectively. It lets them experience otherwise frightening emotions in a safe environment where they control the narrative. And what better way to explore the imagined horrors of war and helplessness promised by our parents' evening news than to become the military hero, the savior the G.I. Joe franchise promised us in their original lineup: Breaker, Flash, Grunt, Rock 'n Roll, Scarlett, Short-Fuze, Snake Eyes, Stalker, and Zap.

The G.I. Joe toyline was founded with the idea of America's military might in mind—the product line's song tells us pretty much everything we needed to know: "He'll fight for freedom! Wherever there's trouble, G.I. Joe is there! G.I. Joe (A Real American Hero)."

And fight they did—a lot. Everything that was happening in the real world at the time, G.I. Joe was also confronting (often before it was even on the news), be it in the animations or in the comics. Joe was all about conservatism and a free market economy; nationalism and the desire for maintaining democracy were the order of the day. So, naturally, the Cobra organization was about establishing a dictatorship with its own devalued currency. The world was so much larger to us kids because there were all of these seemingly sudden government uprisings, terror attacks, and coups in countries we had never heard of before happening on the other side of the world. Civil discontent was everywhere outside of America. Places with names like Afghanistan, El Salvador, Falkland Islands, Grenada, and Tiananmen Square in Beijing, China. Fortunately, G.I. Joe was indefatigable. As the song promised, "He never gives up! He's always there! Fighting for freedom over land and air!" I would guess that about half of the storylines involved the Joes traveling "overseas" to fight the good fight against Cobra. To be certain, there was trouble on the home front as well, as Cobra had sleeper cell agents planted in small towns across America. But they were never successful, as evil always turns on itself and, when the Joes arrive, it's all over for Cobra Commander except for the crying.

Technology was booming throughout the eighties. At the start of the decade phones were firmly attached to walls in our homes, and the answering

Gung Ho in Marine dress uniform.

machine—if you were lucky enough to have one—was gigantic. As the decade ended, cell phones were making their debut. They were huge, required a battery pack, and were wildly expensive to both purchase and use, but that particular genie was out of its bottle. Computers, something only NASA had to launch rockets into space at the beginning of the decade, were appearing in civilian homes. Art imitated life: the Joes were computer savvy, and computers themselves were everywhere, used by all the characters at some point or another. High-tech weaponry, gadgets, and armor were common to both the Joes and Cobra alike. The real world was working hard on genetics and would eventually clone Dolly the sheep. Yawn. Dr. Mindbender had already mastered genetic cloning and created three lines of special operatives—the Snow Wolves, the Sand Scorpions, and the Swamp Rats—and managed to gather the DNA of at least 35 of history's most brilliant, ruthless, and successful military leaders and tacticians who ever existed to create Serpentor!

While natural disasters such as the eruption of Mount St. Helens, Hurricane

Hugo, and El Niño filled the news, the Joes were busy doing everything they could to stop Cobra's Weather Dominator.

While the image of a deep-fried egg became the symbol of our brain on drugs and we were told to "Just Say No!" to drugs by First Lady Nancy Reagan, the Joe's Drug Elimination Force confronted Headman, a fedora- and spats-wearing drug kingpin. This character was so nocuous even Cobra felt they needed to team up with their sworn enemy to assist in getting him off the streets.

So long as G.I. Joe ruled the marketplace, there was nothing the nightly news could present to us kids that we had to worry about; G.I. Joe was going to be there and stay until the fight was won, as the jingle promised.

In writing this book, I strived to make it as complete as possible, not just in making sure that every character was represented but also presented in the way that made the most sense. Typically, when I write a book such as this, I would use an encyclopedic approach. I would carefully write out detailed descriptions in paragraph format citing my sources at the end of each entry. It worked well in my other books, but it would have failed for this topic. Fans of G.I. Joe want the information they seek quickly; they don't want to be bothered reading paragraphs to find out one bit of information. I turned to the fans for their opinion, and they were overwhelmingly in support of a field guide format. I had to agree with them. Not only was the information there in just a line or two, but also it was sort of reminiscent of the file cards that were dutifully printed on the back of each figure's packing material. I made a master template of what facts would be important to present for every character in the multiverse. I suspected there would be some characters who did not have every line filled out, and I was correct. Most often the Joes produced for sale in countries outside the United States had the least amount of information to draw from. Naturally, characters who were popular or figured prominently in the fiction are fleshed out more thoroughly. Overall, I am pleased with the formatting of the book and I feel fans will be as well.

In this book, I have attempted to list and write up every character in the G.I. Joe multiverse. I assure you, this was no small undertaking. In addition to the legion of action figures produced over the years by Hasbro and licensed manufacturers, there were also characters who appeared, typically only once, in the animation. I wanted to be sure I included them. One-off though they may have been, they were created to be an integral part of that particular storyline. That same diligence was applied to finding and listing all characters who made an appearance in the 155 comics issues published by Marvel and the additional 43 comics issues published by Image.

I did not include characters and one-off characters who appeared only in crossovers. For instance, although Megatron did appear in the Transformers/G.I. Joe crossover, he, along with all the Autobots and Decepticons, would be better suited to appear in their own book. Having them here would only dilute the purpose of this work. For the same reason, I did not include the Ponies from the My Little Pony crossover.

I also excluded the characters who appeared in the live-action G.I. Joe films (*G.I. Joe: The Rise of Cobra*, 2009; *G.I. Joe: Retaliation*, 2013; and *Snake Eyes: G.I. Joe Origins*, 2021). Originally, I considered their inclusion but was never comfortable with the idea.

I felt that the characters portrayed in the films were too unlike the originals to qualify as G.I. Joe characters. To make sure my rationale for exclusion was sound and valid, I consulted a few online fan groups. I explained my reason for asking the question as well as my thoughts on the matter. The fans, as ever, were supportive, agreed with my explanation, and were excited about the idea of the forthcoming book.

All of the existing collector guides on the market available to Joe enthusiasts focus exclusively on action figures. I even have one collector's book that focuses solely on the accessories of the original 12-inch Joe. These works differ mostly on the years and series they cover. Some give more information about the figures than others, but it is all presented more or less in the same paragraph lump of information. Color photographs of the figures are common and repetitive. A few mention the current price a figure may be worth on the market, but I always find that highly distracting. Prices fluctuate, the value of the dollar changes, popularity and desirability are impossible to predict, and nothing dates material faster than having to convert then prices to today's.

This book is different. To begin, it uses a field guide presentation to deliver the relevant information fans clamor for. And it is unique not only in the manner the information is presented to the reader but also in the amount of information about the character amassed in one location. Everything there is to know about any character in the G.I. Joe multiverse is in one place. It covers all G.I. Joe characters, beyond the action figures. Characters who were present only in the comics and animations are represented. Also, I included characters that appeared in Hasbro-approved novelization of fan fiction. I dug deep into my research, not wanting to leave any Joe behind.

Four versions of Sgt. Slaughter.

Author photo with B.A.T.

Author photo 1.

To be certain I included everyone in the multiverse, I had to rewatch the cartoon series as well as the animated movies. There were some great books I pored over, fan groups I consulted, and websites I visited. The fandom for this franchise is wide and deep.

Interestingly, the Hasbro website was not a source for research. It was, however, where I and anyone could go download an app called Selfie Series that would walk you through the process of scanning your face into a 3D image and becoming a full-fledged member of G.I. Joe. The app has since been discontinued.

Once you have scanned and approved the image, you upload it to the site. First, you select Snake Eyes or Scarlett for the body type. There are numerous eye and skin colors and hairstyles to choose from. I selected Scarlett, which, in some way, I

Author photo 2.

like to believe makes me a member of G.I. Joe. The way I see it, this is accomplished in one of three ways. I am either (a) Scarlett in some alternative universe yet to be discovered who changes her code name to Daystar; (b) Daystar (my code name) is a stand-alone character now that I have been uploaded into the G.I. Joe universe via its app; or (c) Daystar is a Reservist, of which Duke himself speaks so highly (see entry "Reservist" for full, flattering details).

If you're a fan of G.I. Joe, either a hardcore collector or just someone who wants to recapture a little bit of your youth and walk down memory lane, you need this book. Go ahead and buy it; you won't have any regrets. Let your inner kid come out and play for a while.

Section One

G.I. Joe

G.I. Joe

> "G.I. Joe is a highly-skilled, on-demand, international, special missions force of men and women from around the globe, selected for their elite abilities in their chosen disciplines. Officially, G.I. Joe doesn't exist, and very few know the truth: these heroes fight a secret war, as the first and last line of defense against forces that seek to plunge our world into chaos."—
> Official Hasbro Description

Making its debut in 1964, G.I. Joe was a male, 12-inch-tall, jointed doll. Based on real-life heroes, its face was a conglomeration of Congressional Medal of Honor winners. The first line consisted of Action Marine, Action Pilot, Action Sailor, and G.I. Joe. They are considered to be the first "action figure." In the mid-1970s, Hasbro was forced to reduce the size of the figure to eight inches due to the rising prices of petroleum, but the production line came to an end in the late 1970s. A Joe figure of this size would not be seen again until its comeback in the 1990s.

In 1982 Hasbro relaunched G.I. Joe, this time as a 3.75-inch figure; it was a smash hit, and the size was in production until 1994. The product catalog, titled "Legend of G.I. Joe," read: "The forces of evil are on the rise, the enemy army of Cobra Command (an international, paramilitary, terrorist force) wants to conquer the world! Only one group of heroic, dedicated, fighting soldiers can stop them. Code name.... G.I. Joe!" The toys were made for the Australian, Canadian, Chinese, European, Japanese, Korean, South African, and United States markets. Typically, each toy was marked with a "made in" Hong Kong, China, or Indonesia stamp on the small of its back.

The 3.75-inch line of figures was originally intended to be the accessories to the vehicle line of toys. Project manager H. Kirk Bozigian made sure parents could buy their child every single action figure, vehicle, and weapon system from the 1982 line for less than $100 (about $300 in today's market).

In 1983 (series two) 16 figures were released with the new two-handed swivel arm battle grip. Adding two extra points of articulation to the figure enabled them to be posed in more realistic stances. The fragility of the thumbs was also addressed. It should also be noted that the belt buckle on figures that year is highly reminiscent of the Hasbro logo.

A new size and line were introduced—Sgt. Savage in 1994 and G.I. Joe Extreme in 1995—but neither line was a success. The 3.75-inch line returned in 1997.

Vehicle gear.

Figures in Series 14, the *Real American Hero* line, were released in three-packs in 1997; this was overseen by the Hasbro holding Kenner. The plastic was clearly an inferior quality, and the O-rings, the part holding the upper part of the figure to the lower part, would break with startling ease—often while still in the packaging.

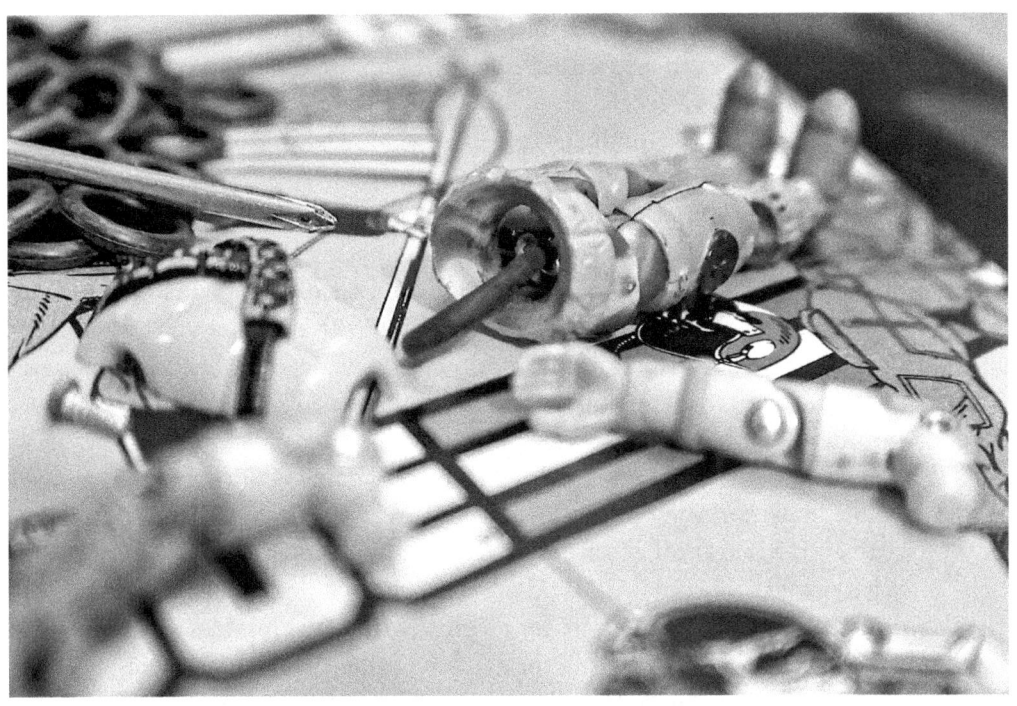

Disassembled Joe for O-ring repair 2.

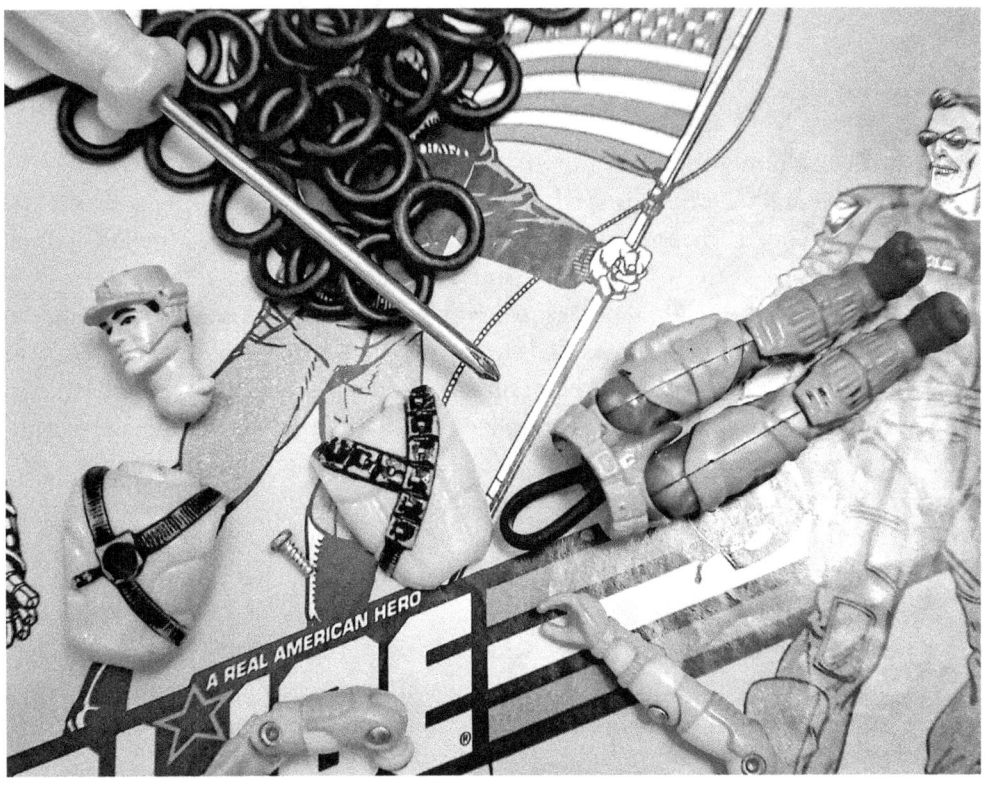

O-ring repair 3.

The Oktober Guard was released in 1998, series 15, alongside the Cobra Infantry team. While Oktober Guard excited fans by releasing long-sought-after figures, the Cobra soldiers were less well received.

Series 17 was released in 2000. The big change here was figures were now being sold in packs of two rather than three. This reduction in price boosted sales.

Only 24 figures were released in 2001, mostly re-paints of existing molds, but fans were accepting of it because they were eagerly anticipating the 12 new sculpts due to come out in 2002. This was a new G.I. Joe versus Cobra series. What fans were not prepared for was the new scale and removal of the O-ring. This not only greatly limited leg movement and reduced the range of motion of the waist but also made the arms look too large and long for the body. The fans complained so intently that Hasbro stopped the line and redesigned the series.

Spy Troops were released in 2003; this two-pack had one G.I. Joe member and one Cobra member. Each had some sort of disguise accessory, and the file cards explained how they came to be one another's archrivals.

Valor vs. Venom came out in 2004. There was a science-fiction element to this line; the concept was that Cobra, desperate for an edge, infused animal DNA into some of its operatives. This created Snow Wolf, the Sand Scorpions, and Swamp Rat.

In 2005, Hasbro announced that series 21 would begin selling directly to consumers, although some chains would still carry the product line for a short while. This was done to spare the cost of distribution to retail outlets and stores.

Continuity

As a rule of thumb, the continuity of G.I. Joe is lovingly inconsistent, especially true for the action figures. For instance, some characters have multiple code names, and some of the code names are even shared by members of both G.I. Joe and Cobra. The prefix of a rank, such as "Sgt." or "Agent," was added to some names when Hasbro lost the rights to the original names. An "s" was added to the end of other names to change them while keeping them as close to the originals as possible, as in the case of Viper, who became Vipers. The more popular a character is, the more versions of that character were produced. Some were simple repaints while other versions were original new sculpts. This causes debate among collectors as to how many versions of a particular character there are. Easily, there are at least eight for the Baroness alone.

To confound matters, stylistic variations occurred depending on where the toy was made. Some had logos drawn on while others were stenciled; there were "long" and "short" neck versions of some figures; eye and hair color, although matching, were not what the file card read; there were wide color variations in the equipment they were packaged with as well as the color of their uniforms' base and trimmings. Then there were convention exclusives and mail-in-only line productions.

Opposite, top: Roadblock variations. *Bottom:* Three versions of the mail-in custom G.I. Joe.

Production quality assurance was not always stellar. There are numerous occasions when a figure was shown with a particular set of equipment on the packaging but was equipped in its packaging differently. Most often this was done by swapping out one type of firearm or helmet for another. There were also occasions when the characters were in twin packs. The illustration art on the packaging showed them with their equipment, but, beneath the plastic, the toys were brandishing their opponents' accessories. Whether it was an error or a decision made due to the allowance of space remains uncertain.

Two versions of Scarlett.

Then, there were the exclusive lines available only at particular stores. BJ's, K-Mart, Kay-Bee, Toys "R" Us, and Walmart were most often selected, but there was also a Dollar General and Family Dollar single packs release.

Another problem was all of the unauthorized figures that have been produced. Many are done by collectors making improvements on existing characters, creating their ideal Joe, or making a Joe who exists in one of the storylines but was never produced. The ease of accessibility to spare parts and 3D printers has made customization incredibly easy. Aside from the fans, there are also unauthorized figures created by toy manufacturers that are not considered to be a part of the Joe universe.

Honestly, it is difficult to say with certainty exactly how many authentic individual G.I. Joe characters exist, but, if pressed for an answer, I would conservatively put the number around 1,400.

Marvel Comics Universe

Most stories involved the G.I. Joe team battling against their enemy, Cobra Command, while focusing on the inter-relationships and background stories of the characters. The main writer for the series was military historian Larry Hama; he also developed the characters' individual histories and wrote nearly all of the file card information. In addition, he authored the short-lived G.I. Joe spin-off series *G.I. Joe*

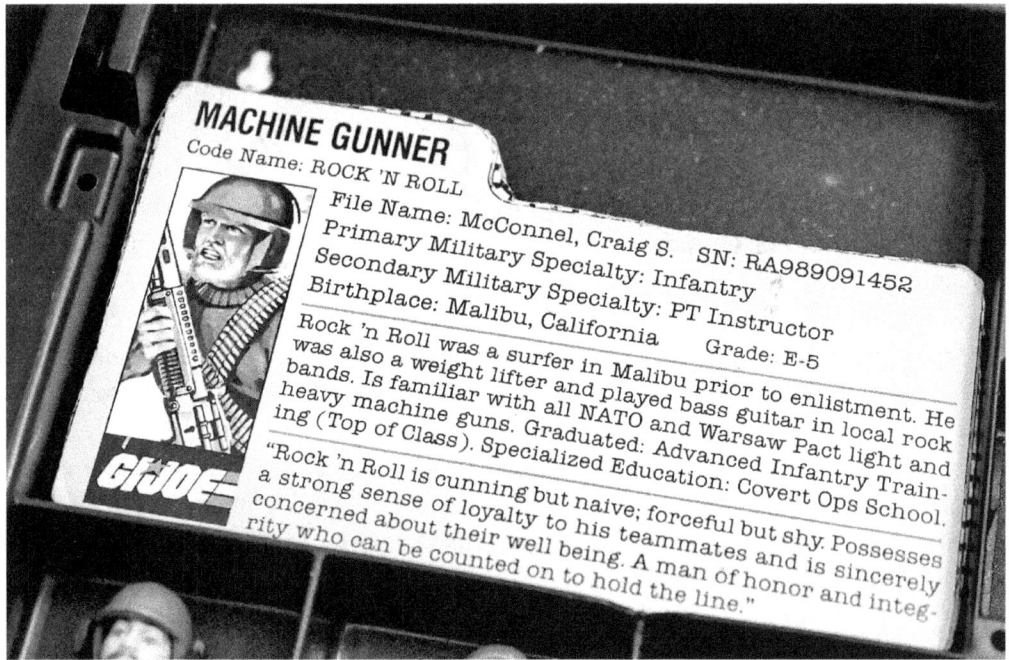

Rock 'n Roll file card.

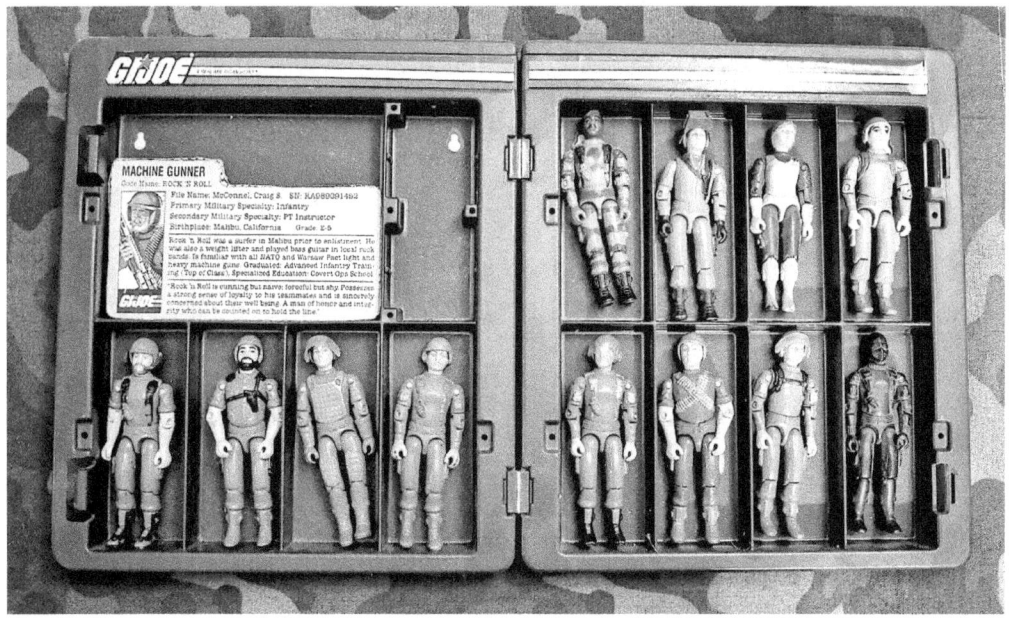

Original G.I Joe lineup.

Special Missions. Hama gave the comics a sense of realism not seen before in a comic: there was humor—not slapstick—realistic military references, and intelligent storylines. Over the course of 12 years, there were 155 issues and a four-issue miniseries crossover with the Transformers.

In the first issue, it is revealed that the team's official moniker is "Special Counter-Terrorist Unit Delta." It featured an ensemble cast, the original 13 characters being Breaker, Clutch, Flash, Grand Slam, Grunt, Hawk, Rock 'n Roll, Scarlett, Short Fuze, Snake Eyes, Stalker, Steeler, and Zap.

Early issues introduced basic concepts of the Joe universe, such as the base under a motor pool and the iconic "original 13" Joe Team members. It introduced two recurring villains, Cobra Commander and the Baroness; Destro was introduced about 10 issues later.

Many storylines involved the machinations and power struggles between Destro, Cobra Commander, and the Baroness. Issue #11 established a pattern for the series in which every so often Marvel would publish an issue introducing a group of characters and vehicles that represented the new year's toy offerings.

The series was praised for its attention to detail and realism in the area of military tactics and procedures. In style and plot structure, the comic often made use of overlapping story threads. It was a completely character-driven storyline.

Image Comics

Image comics published *Devil's Due* from October 2001 to June 2005, 43 issues in all; the storyline picks up seven years after the Marvel Comics series ended. It also used some elements from the animated TV series. Fans often refer to this comic series as *A Real American Hero* vol. 2 or *G.I. Joe: Reinstated*, after the name of the four-issue mini-arc.

The Animated Series

"G.I. Joe is America's elite military strike force—the most fearsome rapid-deployment team of all, standing ready to fight the ruthless criminal organization Cobra ... anywhere, anytime, anyway!"

The toy industry in the 1980s was predatory. Toylines were developed, and then the companies made a cartoon about the toy, basically creating a 30-minute commercial. What made the G.I. Joe cartoon stand apart was that it was good. It had a suspenseful storyline and managed to bypass the network's stringent standards for violence. It was syndicated in 1985, running Monday through Friday; the focus was on action, inside jokes, and social satire.

Between 1983 and 1992 there were 144 animated episodes, six five-part mini-series, and 10 two-part episodes. Sunbow/Marvel Productions ran the show *G.I. Joe: A Real American Hero* from September 12, 1983, to October of 1987. It had 95 episodes.

1984 gave us *G.I. Joe II: The Revenge of Cobra* (*The Weather Dominator* in later airings); it involved the Joes and Cobras traveling around the world to recover the scattered fragments of Cobra's new weather-controlling weapon, the Weather Dominator.

Frostbite and two versions of Lifeline.

G.I. Joe: The Movie was released on VHS in 1987 and was split into a five-part series for television syndication. It follows up on the events of Season 2, revealing Cobra Commander to be an agent of Cobra-La led by a half-serpent being named Golobulus. The same organization is revealed to have had a hand in the creation of Serpentor. Additionally, two new sub-teams were introduced to the Joes: the Rawhides and the Renegades.

DiC presented *Operation Dragonfly* in 1989. Two additional series were created and aired in 1990 and 1991; they did not fare as well as the previous series as they lacked both the quality and sophistication to which fans had grown accustomed.

Action Force

Action Force was based on the *Action Man* toyline. It was used to introduce the *G.I. Joe : A Real American Hero* toyline to the European market. Several publishing companies produced comic books based on the figures.

The figures are a mixture of historical military figures (e.g., Desert Rat, German Stormtrooper) and more contemporary soldiers (e.g., Arctic and Naval Assault). In contrast to the American-centric G.I. Joe figures, the Action Force figures were a mixture of international figures, including British, German, Australian, and American soldiers. The first figures were not accompanied by file cards giving backstories or names, nor were they featured in comic books. Eventually, the G.I. Joe storyline merged with Action Force (which by then had become "Battle Action Force"), and the two storylines merged into one.

Sigma 6

This is the reimagining of the characters from the 1980s toyline *G.I. Joe: A Real American Hero.* The new series offered a streamlined story and characters, stripping away old continuity and "rebooting" the franchise with younger versions of the cast, rendered in the anime style.

"Sigma 6" is the code name for a new group of G.I. Joe heroes with highly specialized capabilities they use to protect the world from the Cobra Commander and his evil forces.

It's now the twenty-first century, and G.I. Joe is fighting to prevent Cobra from taking over the world. They are equipped with Sigma suits. Designed by G.I. Joe member Hi-Tech, these bodysuits protect the Joes from Cobra's laser blasts and enhance their abilities. The Joes are code-named "Sigma 6."

Chain of Command and Rank Organization

The lowest rank a member of a Delta unit can be is a Sergeant (E-5); therefore, all full members of G.I. Joe have at least that rank. Corporals and provisionary members are specialists and support members, although, in the loose Joe command structure, few are treated with anything less than respect for their contributions and skill. For example, Stalker could give Falcon an order and expect it to be followed: experience and expertise matter more than rank and pay grade.

Rank and leadership are not fixed in any of the Joe universes; this is only an approximation of the chain of command.

Army General Hollingsworth and Army General G.I. Joe would be the two highest-ranking officers in the organization with a rank of 10/O-10; they are Senior Advisors.

Commanding Officers would be:

Army Lieutenant General Hawk (10/O-9)
Navy Vice Admiral Keel-Haul and Admiral Ledger (9/O-9) (Retired Advisors)
Army Major General Austin (Retired Advisor) (9/O-8)
Army Brigadier General Flagg III and Natalie Poole (SAS) (9/O-7)
Executive Officer: Army Chief Warrant Officer Flint (9/CW5)
Naval Operations Commander: Navy Chief Warrant Officer Wet Down (9/CW5)
Field Commander: Army Command Sergeant Major Duke (9/E-9)
Command Sergeant Major: Altitude, Beach Head, Mercer, Scarlett, Stalker (9/E-9)
Marine Sergeant Major: Gung Ho (9/E-9)
Marine Master Gunnery Sergeant: Lowdown (9/E-9)

Chain of Command and Rank Organization

Stars and Stripes Forever in box.

Air Force Colonel Air Support/Space Cos: Ace, Payload (Space Command)
Lieutenant Colonel: Skystriker (Air Support XO), Sure Fire
Major: Ghostrider
Captain: Countdown, Freestyle, Gears, Slipstream, Space Shot, Wraith
1st Lieutenant: Bambi, Dogfight, Evac, Sub-Zero, Tomahawk

Army

Colonel: Courage (Retired)
Lieutenant Colonel: Surefire (Former Chief of Pit Security—discharged)
Major (7/O-4): Altitude, Bullet-Proof, Barrage, Mayday, Steeler
Captain (6/O-3): Budo, Claymore, Doc (Greer), Falcon (Special Forces Commander),

Hawk, General Hawk Talking Commando, General Hawk astronaut, Long Arm.

Grid-Iron, Lady Jaye, Lifeline, Nightingale, Psyche-Out, Rapid-Fire, Robo-J.O.E., Sci-Fi, Spirit, Spitfire, Stitches, Updraft

First Lieutenant (6/O-2): Subzero, Thunderwing

2nd Lieutenant (6/O-1): Digger, Grand Slam, Grunt, Freefall, Hard Drive, Trakker, Super Trooper

Chief Warrant Officer 4 (5/W-4): Wild Bill

Chief Warrant Officer 2 (5/W-2): Lift-Ticket

Warrant Officer 1 (5/W-1): Tollbooth

Master Sergeant: (4/E-8): Airwave, Big Brawler, Blizzard, Clutch, Dial Tone, Dojo, Double Blast, Drop Zone, Mace, Roadblock, Savage (retired), Skydive, Snake Eyes

Sergeant First Class (3/E-7): Airborne, Cold Front, Cross Country, Crossfire, Dodger, Hot Seat, Long Range, Recondo, Rock 'n Roll, Rumbler, Salvo, Shockwave, Side Track, Snow Job, Static Line, T'Jbang, Zap

Staff Sergeant (2/E-6): Cover Girl, Dart, Effects, Hi-Tech, Iceberg, Law, Low Light, Pathfinder, Repeater, Side Track, Sightline, Snow Storm, Starduster, Tripwire, Tunnel Rat, Whiteout, Windchill

Sergeant (1/E-5): Airtight, Alpine, Ambush, Armadillo, Backblast, Barbecue, Barrel Roll, Barricade, Bazooka, Blowtorch, Bullhorn, Bushido, Chameleon, Chance, Chuckles, Dial Tone, Dusty, Faces, Flash, Footloose, Fridge, Frostbite, Hacker, Hardball, Hardtop, Heavy Duty, Hit and Run, Ice Cream Soldier, Jinx, Kamakura, Kickstart, Lifeline, Long Arm, Long Range 2, Med Alert, Muskrat, Mutt, Nunchuk, Outback, Ozone, Quarrel, Recoil, Red Dog, Red Spot, Redmack, Rip Cord, Short

Fuze, Sideswipe, Skidmark, Sneak Peek, Sparks, Steam-Roller, Stiletto, Stretcher, Switch Gears, Taurus, Wide Scope

Advisor/Probationary Member/Specialist (0/E-4): Ashiko, Backstop, Banzai, Big Lob, Cannonball, Charbroil, Checkpoint, Cloudburst, Cross Hair, Downtown, Fast Draw, Greenshirts, Helix, Lightfoot, Mayday, Mouse, Paquette, Red Zone, Rollbar, Rook, Salvo, Sandstorm, Scoop, Shaz, Snapdragon, Steel Brigade, T'Gin-Zu, Tiger Claw, Wildcard, Wreckage

Marines

Colonel (8/O-6): Sharp
Captain (6/O-3): Mainframe
2nd Lieutenant (6/O-1): Bombstrike, Crimson Rain
Gunnery Sergeant (3/E-7): Leatherneck, Sgt. Slaughter
Staff sergeant (2/E-6): Mirage
Sergeant (1/E-5): Ice Storm
Corporal (0/E-4): Blast-Off

Navy/Coast Guard

Commander (8/O-5): Naval Operations CO Cutter
Lieutenant Commander (7/O-4): Marissa Faireborn
Lieutenant (6/O-3): Link
Chief Warrant Officer (5/W-4): Torpedo
Senior Chief Petty Officer (4/E-8): Shipwreck
Chief Petty Officer (3/E-7): Cold Shot, Deep Six
Petty Officer First Class (2/E-6): Cookie, Topside, Wet Suit
Petty Officer First Class (1/E-5): Depth Charge, Night Fox
Petty Officer Third Class (0/E-4): Felino, Rampart
Seaman Apprentice (0/E-2) Mara

Bases and Holdings

Arashikage Martial Arts Academy: Located in San Francisco, CA, it was owned and operated by Tommy Arashikage (Storm Shadow); he opened it after having spent several months in Snake Eyes's cabin in the High Sierras. The address for the academy was 4498 Zoe Avenue; the phone number was 555-5277, no zip code given. The academy was abandoned after Zartan and a band of Red Ninjas attacked it looking for Storm Shadow. G.I. Joe's Budo and Dojo are stationed there.

The Pit 1: This is G.I. Joe's command center. Located beneath the Chaplain's Assistant School's motor pool in Fort Wadsworth, Staten Island, New York, it is a five-level fortress of "steel, radiation shielded concrete, and alloy armor." It is under the command of Army Lieutenant General Hawk (O-9). Only the elite G.I. Joes and a privileged few are privy to knowledge of its existence. The Pit became a matter of interest to

Four versions of Storm Shadow.

Four versions of Keel-Haul.

Cobra, and they made several attempts to ascertain its true location. The Pit was often seen in the Sunbow animations but seldom in the Marvel Comics Universe.

The Pit 2: Eventually Cobra discovered the Pit; when the battle was over, the Army took the opportunity to completely revamp the base, creating The Pit 2. It was under the command of General Austin. It too was eventually destroyed by Cobra.

The Pit 3: Under the command of Army General G.I. Joe (O-10) and Army Brigadier General Flagg III (O-7); it is located in a remote area of Utah.

The Pit 4: In the IDW Universe, Pit 4 is located somewhere in the Nevada desert; it appears to be nothing more than a simple exercise camp with only a water tower and a number of Quonset huts. The lone guard on duty is a hologram; actual security is performed by closed-circuit cameras placed in covert and readily visible locations. The headquarters itself is accessible via an elevator in one of the Quonset huts. Rather than several levels, the Pit is a vast underground cavern spacious enough to have several small standing buildings. Several pillars stand supporting the cavern ceiling.

USS *Flagg*—A U.S. Navy aircraft carrier commanded by Admiral Ledger (animated continuity). The original USS *Flagg* (CVN-99) was a straightforward Nimitz-Class Supercarrier, but it was sunk. In the *G.I. Joe: Resolute* timeline, the *Flagg* had been extensively retrofitted to include a very pronounced prow and two extremely prominent catapults. The deck island design is now basically circular and has been pushed partially off the deck to make more area for aircraft. While these changes are substantial, they are not unprecedented. The *Flagg* appears to be serving as the supreme G.I. Joe Command Headquarters.

G.I. Joe Character Field Guide

Ace 1

Series: Two (1983)
Real Name: Brad J. Armbruster. According to the prototype card, his name is Wendall.
Place of Birth: Providence, Rhode Island; according to prototype card, Seattle, Washington
Gender: Male
Grade/Rank: O-3 or 8/O-6: Colonel; Air Support (Air CO)
SN: AF 335986725
Service Branch: Air Force
Faction(s): Battle Corps
Primary MOS: Fixed-wing pilot, single, and multiple-engine
Secondary MOS: Intelligence operations
Appearance: Red hair. Wears a segmented flight suit with red pads on the shirt and waist with dark gray wristbands, belt, boots, and stripes on legs. He also wears a white helmet with a clear, domed front; a black air mask; a black vest; and blue goggles.
Other Known Appearances (Cartoon): Black hair
Accessories: Clear, domed helmet
Background Information: "Worked three after-school and weekend jobs during high school to pay for flying lessons. Earned his civilian single-engine, fixed-wing papers at age nineteen."
Abilities: Movie stunt pilot, Pilot; Poker player, Qualified Operator: XP-14 (a derivative of the F-14 Tomcat); Qualified Weapons Expert: F-5E, F-15, F-16, XP-14/F; Senior instructor USAF Fighter Weapons Squadron "The Aggressors" (pilot combat training school)
Conditions: Cutthroat poker player; Hobby

Skill: poker; Predilection for gambling; Wisecracker; Would rather be flying

Notes: In 1986 Ace, one of the original G.I. Joes, was replaced by Slip Stream. The original file card squadron was code-named Top Gun, after a real-world military school.

Ace, Version 2

Series: Eleven (1992)
Alias/Variations: Brad
Real Name: Wendell L. Armbruster
Place of Birth: Seattle, Washington
Gender: Male
Grade/Rank: O-4 (Air Force major)
SN: 533-4902-RT81
Service Branch: Air Force
Primary MOS: Battle copter pilot
Secondary MOS: Ordnance officer
Appearance: Red hair. He wears a blue, open-collar jacket with a blue-green vest and black gloves; a black air mask with a hose attached to the chest; black boots; blue pants with a blue-green belt and leggings; and a white helmet with neon green goggles.
Accessories: Submachine gun
Abilities: Daring aerobatic maneuvers, Fighter-pilot, Graduate of the Combined Services Escape and Evasion school
Conditions: Fighter-pilot jock, Seeking the ultimate challenge for his flying skills
Quote/Motto: "Flying a modern fly-by-wire jet is like flying a computer with wings. Piloting a Battle Copter into a fast-rising thermal with the control surfaces vibrating through your sticks and harness—that's flying!"

Action Force

Based on the *Action Man* toyline, Action Force was a European line of action figures used to introduce G.I. Joe to Europe. Because of the shifting nature of the characters in the toyline, the corresponding Action Force spin-off material had a highly complicated continuity. The franchises merged into *G.I. Joe and the Action Force*. The storyline explained that the merger was to better fight Cobra. After a couple of years, the suffix "...*and the Action Force*" was dropped.
Alias/Variations: AF; Action Force: International Heroes, Battle Action Force, G.I. Joe and the Action Force
Subteams: Q Force: allied ocean-based team; SAS Force: allied special operations team; Space Force: allied space operations team; Z Force: allied infantry and artillery-based unit
Purpose: An international band of soldiers who fought the Red Shadows, Cobra, and the Nazis. The Action Force series gradually took over the second generation of Action Force and the Z Force, Q Force, Space Force, and SAS teams.
Leader: Duke
Members: Ace, Airborne, Blowtorch, Breaker, Cutter, Deep Six, Doc, Dolphin, Duke, Flash, Grunt (available by mail-in only), Gung Ho, Moondancer, Mutt and Junkyard, Recondo, Rip Cord, Roadblock, Scarlett, Snow Job, Stalker, Ton Up, Torpedo, Tripwire
Quote/Motto: "To confront and defeat the forces of the terrorist organization, Cobra Command."

Action Man

Series: Twenty (2004)
Real Name: CLASSIFIED
Place of Birth: CLASSIFIED
Gender: Male
Grade/Rank: CLASSIFIED
SN: CLASSIFIED
Service Branch: British intelligence
Faction(s): G.I. Joe
Primary MOS: International counterespionage
Secondary MOS: Hand-to-hand combat
Appearance: Black hair, blue eyes
Accessories: Two side arms
Quote/Motto: "Quick and imaginative thinking can get you into and out of any situation."
Notes: In the comics, he was assassinated by a Red Shadow agent while walking on a beach holding a surfboard.

Aguia Commando

Series: Eleven (1994)
Gender: Male
Faction(s): G.I. Joe, Patrulha Do Ar ("Sky Patrol")
Appearance: Black boots, black helmet with open face, padded blue shirt, silver gloves, silver pants, silver vest
Accessories: Backpack, parachute, two guns
Conditions: Undertakes the most dangerous military missions in the world

Air Commandos

Series: Ten (1991)
Purpose: Glider specialists trained for recon and quick-strike missions

Leader: Spirit
Members: Cloudburst, Skymate

Air Raid

Series: Two (1983); Twenty-Five (2009)
Alias/Variations: Sgt. Airborne
Real Name: Franklin E. Talltree
Place of Birth: Navajo reservation, Arizona
Gender: Male
Grade/Rank: E-5 Sergeant
SN: 030-44-TT62; RA030446233
Faction(s): G.I. Joe
Primary MOS: Airborne infantryman
Secondary MOS: Helicopter gunship gunner
Accessories: Helmet, parachute pack, pistol, rifle
Background Information: Passed Arizona state bar exams; Graduated top of his class from Fort Benning Airborne School
Abilities: Air assault trooper; Airborne Qualified combat officer; Experienced; Helicopter gunship gunner; Highly skilled; Professional Skill: Lawyer; Professional Skill: Helicopter Assault Trooper; Qualified Expert Operator: Sky Sweeper Jet; Qualified Weapon Expert: Hughes helicopter chain gun; Qualified Weapons Expert: M-16, M-60; Qualified Weapons Expert: M-1911A auto pistol; Quick-thinking; Skydiving; Wealthy: Parents own oil fields
Preferred Weapon: 820 selective-fire long-range full automatic assault rifle

Air Raid 2

Series: Thirty-Two (2016)
Alias/Variations: Airraid, Air Raid
Real Name: Benjamin R. Thomas
Place of Birth: Annapolis, Maryland
Gender: Male
Grade/Rank: O-4 Major
SN: 221-9198-BD84
Service Branch: Air Force
Faction(s): G.I. Joe
Primary MOS: Flight test officer
Secondary MOS: Operations research analyst
Background Information: Officer Training School program at Maxwell Air Force Base, Montgomery, Alabama, and continued with Advanced Flight Training School
Abilities: Analytical skills; Aviator; Evasion skills; Highly adaptive pilot; Tests and evaluates experimental aircraft and aerospace weapon systems
Conditions: Knows the risks; No stranger to using the ejection seat
Quote/Motto: "It's time to step up and soar."
Notes: He is currently assigned to fly the Sky Patrol Sky Striker (XP-26), an experimental stealth upgrade of the preeminent combat jet.

Airborne

Series: Two (1983)
Alias/Variations: Air Raid
Real Name: Franklin E. Talltree
Place of Birth: Caughnawaga, Quebec, Canada (Naples, Italy for European distribution)
Gender: Male
Grade/Rank: 3/E-7: Sergeant first class
SN: RA030446233
Service Branch: Army
Faction(s): G.I. Joe, member of an unnamed highly trained airborne unit specializing in advanced stealth technology and laser weaponry used to neutralize Cobra's aerial assaults. Leader is Skydive and members include Airborne, Airwave, Altitude, Drop Zone, and Static Line.
Stationed: Trained to be paratrooper at Fort Benning; Trained repelling out of helicopters at Fort Campbell
Primary MOS: Helicopter assault trooper, air assault
Secondary MOS: Helicopter gunship gunner, RTO operator
Accessories: Assault pack, helmet, XM-16 attack rifle (1983). His parachute has a cross on the inside and is a rare collector's find.
Background Information: "Subject's parents are oil-rich Navahos who indulged their eldest son with skydiving lessons in the mistaken belief that the panache associated with the daring sport would be an asset to his political career once he finished law school." Upon passing the Arizona state bar exams, he joined the Army and opted for Airborne training, commenting "I would rather jump out of airplanes than write legal briefs."
Abilities: Paratrooper; Helicopter pilot; Privileged background; Psychic bond with his brother; Rappelling out of helicopters
Conditions: Disquieting presence
Quote/Motto: "He's not like us. Oh, he jokes around with the rest of the guys and seems to get loose, but every once in a while, you catch his eye and he's not looking at you, he's looking right through you. Weird. Navaho Shamans got a word for it. Translates something like, 'the Far-Seeing Look.'" Quote given by G.I. Joe member, Stalker.

Notes: He was the first Native American to join the G.I. Joe team. The 1983 version of Airborne is not the character from the 1990 Sky Patrol; they are two different individuals.

Airborne 2
Series: Nineteen (2003)
Alias/Variations: Rigger
Real Name: Robert M. Six
Place of Birth: Lake Geneva, Wisconsin
Gender: Male
Grade/Rank: E 7
SN: 501-2232-DP65
Service Branch: Army
Faction(s): G.I. Joe, Sky Patrol
Primary MOS: Sky Patrol parachute assembler
Secondary MOS: Battlefield medic
Appearance: Yellow hair. Dark grey gloves, belt, and boots; dark grey vest; grey shirt; pants with beige camouflage; silver shoulder guards and kneepads.
Accessories: Backpack/parachute case, helmet, rifle, parachute
Abilities: Combat medic; Master Rigger; Parachutes assembler; There when you need him!
Conditions: Brave; Dedicated; Popular in Sky Patrol; Priority is health and safety of his comrades; Reputation: No one knows more about U.S. T-10 parachutes; Someone you can rely on
Quote/Motto: "Airborne is one of the most popular guys on the patrol; you have to like him. He makes sure your parachute opens every time you make a jump. Airborne is also the individual who has to go out, usually under heavy fire, and save you from an unfortunate encounter with a bullet, or a run-in with a landmine. Through thick and thin, Airborne is always there when you need him." Quote by unnamed G.I. Joe team member.
Notes: The first Joe to inherit a code name, he is the second Airborne.

Airtight
Series: Four (1985)
Alias/Variations: Ar Puro (Brazil); Gasmasker (Holland); Oxygene (Belgium)
Real Name: Kurt Schnurr
Place of Birth: New Haven, Connecticut (Munich, Bavaria, Germany for European distribution)
Gender: Male
Grade/Rank: 1/E-5: Sergeant
SN: 307-42-4683
Service Branch: Army
Faction(s): G.I. Joe, Anti-Venom Task Force
Primary MOS: Hostile environment specialist, CBR (Chemical, Biological, and Radiological warfare)
Secondary MOS: Ordnance
Appearance: Black face mask; green helmet with two black stripes; green vest, gloves, and belt; yellow shirt and pants. The vest has a black control panel on it.
Other Known Appearances (Cartoon): Brown hair. Dark green belt, gloves, and vest; pale-yellow shirt and pants.
Accessories: Compressor pack, sniffer, two air hoses
Abilities: Can hold his breath for long periods; Qualified Operator: Hypodermic jet, JUMP, LCV Recon Sled, motorcycle, Silver Mirage, Sky Hawk, SkyStriker
Conditions: Collects plastic toy dinosaurs; Reputation: Weird kid who became a strange adult; Respected by peer group; Unreformed practical joker
Quote/Motto: "Airtight is an unreformed practical joker; sneezing powder, plastic barf, whoopee cushion—the whole bit!! No prank is too low for him. You'd think that other Joes would hate his guts, but they don't. Because when the bad guys escalate the firefight and start playing dirty, it's old Airtight who suits up and wades into the thick of it." Quote by an unnamed G.I. Joe team member.
Notes: Handles anything toxic, hazardous, or weird; he is NOT a member of the Eco Warriors with Barbecue, Deep Six, and Flint.

Airwave
Series: Nine (1990)
Real Name: Cliff V. Mewett
Place of Birth: Louisville, Kentucky
Gender: Male
Grade/Rank: 4/E-8: Master sergeant; E-8 (Army first sergeant)
SN: 450-1941-CS49
Service Branch: Army, Ranger, Sky Patrol
Faction(s): G.I. Joe, member of an unnamed highly trained airborne unit specializing in advanced stealth technology and laser weaponry. They neutralize Cobra's aerial assaults. Leader Skydive. Members include Airborne, Airwave, Altitude, Drop Zone, and Static Line. Sky Patrol communications specialist; Signal Corps Adjutant to the Joint Chiefs of Staff (JCS).

Primary MOS: Sky Patrol audible frequency specialist
Secondary MOS: Signal Corps Adjutant for JCS
Appearance: Yellow hair. Brown belt, boots, and wristbands; dark yellow shirt and pants with brown panels; pale yellow leg holsters, shoulder guards, and vest with brown pipes; and pale yellow-blue gloves.
Accessories: Full-head helmet with detachable visor; machine gun/grenade launcher with the magazine on top and grenade feed on the bottom; parachute in a parachute pack
Abilities: Always able to gain a signal; Audible frequencies specialist; Field practical skills; Improvise equipment on the fly; Repair circuits; Sky Patrol communications
Conditions: Belief: Knowledge and skills aren't theoretical; Belief: The job is not defined by equipment but by problems and solutions; Die-hard mentality; Reputation: Gets a signal where others can't
Quote/Motto: "Once, on a simulated artillery spotting mission in a deserted industrial complex, Airwave's radio was totaled by enemy machine gunfire. The squad immediately wanted to scrub the mission and call it a day, but not Airwave. As mock shells exploded all around, this die-hard maneuvered his way towards a semi-destroyed telephone booth. When inside, he adjusted the phone's circuitry and called his own artillery battery to relay the target coordinates on enemy positions. He believes that his job is not defined by his equipment, but by problems and their solutions!" Quote by unnamed G.I. Joe team member.
Notes: Shares the same name as Colonel Courage.

Aisha

Real Name: Aisha Hauser
Place of Birth: The Trucial States
Gender: Female
Faction(s): G.I. Joe
Stationed: Fort Bragg; North Shore Hospice in Oyster Bay, Long Island, New York
Primary MOS: Arabic instructor
Abilities: Arabic instructor
Conditions: Wife of Duke
Notes: Married to Duke; she suffered a traumatic and catastrophic brain injury

Albatroz

Series: Eleven (1992)
Alias/Variations: ("Albatross")
Gender: Male
Faction(s): G.I. Joe, Brazilian exclusive Sky Patrol: Patrulha Do Ar ("Sky Patrol")
Accessories: Backpack, helmet, parachute, two guns
Conditions: Feels invincible; Tempts fate; Undertakes the most dangerous missions
Notes: The Albatross is one of the most superstition-laden birds in the world. Samuel Taylor Coleridge's "The Rime of the Ancient Mariner" paints the albatross as a symbol of burdens, regret, and a severed relationship with God, making it an odd code name for a Joe.

Alpine

Series: Four (1985)
Real Name: Albert M. Pine
Place of Birth: Snake River Plain, Minidoka, Idaho (Grenoble, France for European distribution)
Gender: Male
Grade/Rank: E-4 Corporal; 1/E-5: Sergeant
SN: 237-51-3844
Service Branch: Army
Faction(s): G.I. Joe, Strike Team: Charlie, and Tiger Force
Stationed: Ranger School, Fort Benning
Primary MOS: Mountain trooper
Secondary MOS: Finance Clerk
Appearance: African American; black hair and mustache. Black belt and goggles; brown pants; brown wristbands; green and black cap and jacket; green boots and gloves; white shirt; yellow rope across the chest.
Other Known Appearances (Cartoon): Brown shirt under his vest; symbol on the front of his cap; white goggle frames
Accessories: Axe, backpack, Baretta SMG-12, grappling hooks, GRB-88 Grappling Launch Line, pickaxe
Abilities: Accountant, Degree in finance; Mountain climbing; Qualified Operator: A.W.E. Striker; Qualified Weapons Expert: M-16, M-14, M-60, M-1911A1
Conditions: Child of Algerian immigrants (European); Friends with Bazooka; Makes wisecracks; Tries to escape his past
Quote/Motto: "Every time Alpine scales a sheer cliff piton by piton, overcoming granite and gravity with muscle and persistence, he is symbolically climbing out of the quagmire of his past. That's why we send him up first

on vertical assaults. He doesn't take to being knocked down too easily." Quote by unnamed G.I. Joe team member.
Notes: Frequently paired with Bazooka. He owns a home in Delhi Hills, Ohio, and enjoys drinking at the local bar.

Altitude

Series: Nine (1990)
Real Name: John-Edward O. Jones
Place of Birth: Cambria, California
Gender: Male
Grade/Rank: 7/O-4: Major; 9/E-9: Sergeant Major
SN: 782-6901-VT52
Service Branch: Army Ranger
Faction(s): G.I. Joe, Sky Patrol, and Strike Team: Charlie
Primary MOS: Sky Patrol Recon Scout
Secondary MOS: Combat artist
Appearance: Black flat-top hair; belt, brown gloves, green shirt and pants with gold gray half-vest, holster, orange sleeves, and leg coverings
Accessories: Helmet with visor, parachute with parachute pack, three-piece rocket pistol
Abilities: Drawing; Photographic memory; Professional Skill: Animator; Wilderness survival; Stealth
Conditions: Belief: Has a lot to live up to; Celebrity: Son of a famous Hollywood stuntman
Quote/Motto: "The principal job of a scout is to bring back information. The more detailed the information, the better. Altitude can sneak up on an enemy installation, thoroughly observe it for a few days, and not even be spotted. After he has gathered enough information, he quietly leaves his observation post to return to headquarters. Once there, he uses his recall abilities to sketch the installation in exact detail. He is so good that the Sky Patrol uses his sketches instead of maps because they're that precise." Quote by unnamed G.I. Joe team member.
Notes: He is a full-blooded Apache.

Amber

Real Name: Amber (surname Unknown)
Gender: Female
Service Branch: None
Faction(s): G.I. Joe
Appearance: Long blonde hair
Abilities: College student, Dancing, Martial arts
Conditions: Lack of judgment; Makes bad decisions; Sleeps through baseball; "Wants to make a difference"
Notes: She is dating Quick Kick. Her best friend, Sandy, has short red hair.

Ambush

Series: Twenty (2004)
Alias/Variations: Aaron "Ambush" McMahon
Real Name: Aaron McMahon
Place of Birth: Walnut, California
Gender: Male
Grade/Rank: E-3 (Army private first class)1/E-5: Sergeant
SN: 849-1343-AM97
Service Branch: Army Ranger
Faction(s): G.I. Joe, Dino Hunters, and Desert Patrol Squad
Primary MOS: Concealment specialist
Secondary MOS: Infantry
Appearance: Red hair and mustache. Black boots; dark brown sleeves; green belt and diagonal strap across chest; light brown pants with a crisscross pattern; yellow shirt
Other Known Appearances: Hair varies between dark and light red
Accessories: Backpack with clips on the bottom for a rifle and tabs on the top for poles; four interlocking tent poles; pistol with a substantial portion behind grip and trigger guard; submachine gun with a scope, stock, and magazine behind the grip; safari helmet; two nets
Background Information: As a child, he once played hide-and-seek and remained hidden for three days; it took the National Guard to find him under his mother's front porch.
Abilities: Advanced recon training; Camouflage; Delta Force training; Evasive skills; Friends with Captain Grid-Iron; Friends with Pathfinder; Infiltration skills; Qualified Operator: Battle Wagon; Stealth
Conditions: Disappears when he doesn't want to be found; Friend named Evy, a female Range-Viper; Frenemies with Pathfinder; Nothing he won't do to accomplish the mission
Quote/Motto: "When this guy goes on assignment, expect the unexpected! There's nothing he won't do to accomplish his mission. Once, he concealed himself as a shrub, tumbled into a heavily guarded Cobra weapons depot, captured their base commander, then safely delivered him to G.I. Joe headquarters for interrogation! To this day, we still can't figure out

how he pulled it off!" Quote by unnamed G.I. Joe team member.

Notes: Ties Robo-J.O.E. as the lowest-ranking member of G.I. Joe

Ansatsusha

Alias/Variations: Billy
Real Name: William
Place of Birth: Cobra Island
Gender: Male
Grade/Rank: Special Advisor
Service Branch: Arashikage clan
Faction(s): G.I. Joe, Arashikage clan
Primary MOS: Martial arts
Secondary MOS: Swordsmanship
Appearance: Caucasian with an American accent
Background Information: Born the son of a spiritual leader, Father Cobra, he was raised in a town-size commune; his father preached against the establishment and had a strong desire to topple big business and the government. He rejected his father's ways and joined an anti-Cobra underground organization.
Abilities: Camouflage; Hand-to-hand; Knowledge Skill: Ways of the Arashikage ninja; Martial arts, Professional Skill: Ninja; Stealth; Sword expert; Weapon Skill: Katana
Conditions: Attempts to learn from Snake Eyes; Attempts to supplant Snake Eyes as G.I. Joe's Ichiban Ninja; Dislikes fighting face-to-face; Grudge against Destro; Lost an eye to Destro; Mysterious; Prefers to kill from the shadows; Professes a hatred of Cobra; Secretive; Seeks the leadership of the Arashikage clan
Quote/Motto: "You talk of honor? Ninjas have no honor. That's why you hire us—to kill those you lack the honor to fight yourself."
Notes: Ansatsusha is one of the Joes who traveled across the rift to the Transformers Universe; he hunts down G.I. Joes who have gone AWOL.

Anti-Venom Task Force

Series: Twenty (2004)
Alias/Variations: AVTF
Purpose: To track down and restore innocent citizens who have been mutated into dangerous monsters, V-troops, by Doctor Mindbender's use of Cobra's venom. These Joes spray victims with a serum that changes them back to normal.
Leader: Duke
Members: Barricade, Charbroil, Lifeline, Mutt and Junkyard, and Roadblock

Appearance: Black boots and gloves; dark green upper body armor, tan camouflage pants. The helmet has the character's name printed across the front.
Notes: Airtight was a late addition to the team.

Arashikage Clan

Purpose: The Arashikage is a ninja clan based in Japan with members all over the world. Members exist inside both G.I. Joe and Cobra; some chose to remain neutral.
Leader: None stated
Members: Banzai, Billy Arboc, Blind Master, Budo, Dojo, Firefly (Faceless Master), Gorky, Hard Master, Jinx, Kamakura, Middle Master, Nunchuk, Slice, Snake Eyes (Silent Master), Soft Master, Storm Shadow (Young Master), Tiger Claw, T'Jbang
Notes: Jinx is the only member of the Clan to train under all the Masters, except Faceless Master.

Arctic Attack Force

Purpose: A special unit assignment for specific Joes to work in Arctic Missions
Leader: None specified, default to rank
Members: Dee-Jay, Stalker, Sub-Zero, and Snow Serpent

Armadillo

Series: Seven (1988)
Alias/Variations: Rumbler (most commonly used by friends), Gila, and Sand-Turtle
Real Name: Philo R. Makepeace
Place of Birth: Fort Huachuca, Arizona
Gender: Male
Grade/Rank: 1/E-5: Sergeant; E-7 (Army sergeant first class)
SN: 319-52-4887
Service Branch: Army
Faction(s): G.I. Joe
Notably Served At: The Battle of Benzheen; Cobra Island; Sierra Gordo; Sao Cristobel
Primary MOS: Armored assault vehicle driver
Secondary MOS: Advanced reconnaissance
Appearance: Black eyes, grim-faced, hair color unknown as he never takes off helmet. Light green boots, helmet, and vest; orange-brown pants, silver belt buckle; and white wristbands.
Accessories: None
Abilities: Experienced driver; Knowledge Skill: Land assault technologies; Qualified

Operator: Rolling Thunder; Skilled long-distance trucker
Conditions: Aggressive driver; Humorless when driving; Never takes off his helmet; Reputation: Most reliable driver in the motor pool; Sense of humor
Quote/Motto: "Armadillo is no fun to ride with! You put him behind the wheel of anything with big tires and he just plain loses his sense of humor! His only concern becomes accomplishing his objective and getting to his destination. He used to make good time driving big rigs, but he just left too many people pulled over to the side of the interstate with their teeth rattling. Nobody complains about the way he drives the Rolling Thunder. He gets you there, right?" Quote by unnamed G.I. Joe team member.
Notes: Not to be confused with Rumbler.

Ashiko
Series: Twenty-Eight (2012)
Alias/Variations: Unknown
Real Name: N. Kaeru
Place of Birth: Unknown
Gender: Male
Grade/Rank: O/E-4: Advisor specialist
SN: 482-16-NK88
Service Branch: Army
Faction(s): Arashikage, G.I. Joe, and Ninja Force
Stationed: Unknown
Notably Served At: Frusenland
Primary MOS: Unknown
Secondary MOS: Unknown
Appearance: Asian. Black and gray contact armor
Accessories: Helmet, knife, pistol, sheath backpack, sheath, sword, armor, three rifles, two submachine guns, two gauntlets, and a Vehicle-Integrated Sub-Compact Weapon System (transforming robotic motorcycle)
Abilities: Arashikage ninja, Instructor; Martial arts expertise; Motorbike stunt skills; Professional Skill: Motorcycle stunt rider; Professional Skill: Martial arts instructor at a community school in Spanish Harlem, New York; Qualified Expert Operator: Vehicle-Integrated Sub-Compact Weapon System (transforming robotic motorcycle)
Conditions: Arashikage clan drama; Cares about the community

Avalanche
Series: Six (1987)
Real Name: Ian M. Costello
Place of Birth: Madawaska, Maine
Gender: Male
Grade/Rank: E-5 (Army sergeant)
SN: 512-89-8788
Service Branch: Army
Faction(s): G.I. Joe and Battleforce 2000
Notably Served At: The Battle of Benzheen, Bering Strait
Primary MOS: Armored vehicle driver
Secondary MOS: Cold weather survival driver
Appearance: Brown hair and eyes. Belt and boots, silver ammo belt on chest; silver shoulder guards, and white helmet and snowsuit with brown camouflage
Accessories: Squarish mic attaching to the helmet; laser rifle with disc-like piece near muzzle; Dominator snow tank
Abilities: Boot-legging; Field tests experimental equipment and state-of-the-art prototypes; Poacher; Qualified Operator: Dominator Snow Tank; Smuggler; Wilderness survival: Cold-weather
Conditions: Never caught on to military discipline
Quote/Motto: "As part of a survival exercise, Avalanche and twenty other trainees were left in the wilds with a knife and a compass apiece. Most of the others staggered in haggard and worn after a week. They found Avalanche a month later and two hundred miles away, lounging in a motel and spending the money he had made from the furs he brought in...." Quote by unnamed G.I. Joe team member.
Notes: KIA while maneuvering through an oil field during the Battle of Benzheen when it was bombed by Cobra Commander. He is buried in Arlington National Cemetery. There is no connection between him and the vehicle of the same name.

Backblast
Series: Eight (1989)
Alias/Variations: Leontor (Brazil)
Real Name: Edward J. Menninger
Place of Birth: New York City, New York
Gender: Male
Grade/Rank: 1/E-5: Sergeant
SN: 000-6648-YO11
Service Branch: Army
Faction(s): G.I. Joe, Battle Corps, and Winter Operations
Stationed: Joe's Utah headquarters

Notably Served At: Battle of Benzheen, Cobra Island, Punta del Mucosa, Sierra Gordo
Primary MOS: Security CO, air defense artillery
Secondary MOS: Signal corps
Appearance: Black mustache. Black backpack straps, boots, gloves, holster, wristband with knife holder, and sleeveless T-shirt with yellow "GO ARMY" on chest; green pants with white panel on the left leg; helmet.
Accessories: Serrated knife with jagged handle; missile launcher with three tubes and detachable base with handles; rough monocular with strap; three tapered missiles with fins near the front; and elliptical ammo belt
Background Information: He grew up in a house next to one of the most popular airports in the world. His bedroom was directly under the landing path of incoming jets. When asked about his job preferences he asked, "Where can I go to shoot airplanes out of the sky?"
Abilities: Anti-aircraft soldier
Conditions: Hates airplanes
Quote/Motto: "You get your best shot at a ground attack aircraft when it's coming straight at you. Unfortunately, it usually fires everything it has in your direction. It's the job of the air-defense specialist to stand in the open with his launcher aimed at the incoming aircraft and wait for the lock-on signal before he can fire. I'm glad it is his job and not mine!" Quote by unnamed G.I. Joe team member.

Backstop

Series: Six (1987)
Alias/Variations: Back Stop, Back-Stop; prototype names were Box Car, Hardball, and No Guff.
Real Name: Robert A. Levin
Place of Birth: Montreal, Quebec
Gender: Male
Grade/Rank: 0/E-4: Advisor/Probationary Member/Specialist/Reservist*
Service Branch: Army
Faction(s): G.I. Joe, British Action Force (alternate continuity)
Stationed: Utah Quonset hut base
Notably Served At: Canada, Frusenland
Primary MOS: Persuader driver; armor
Secondary MOS: Mechanized infantry
Appearance: Black hair. Green shirt with gray chest and shoulder armor; red and black boots; red gloves; white belt and holsters; and yellow pants; sculpted holsters on each leg
Accessories: Included with the Persuader; full-head helmet with cut-out portion over face; revolver with trigger far from the grip
Background Information: Family moved from Canada to Detroit, where he grew up
Abilities: Greco-Roman wrestler, Golden Glove boxer, Professional Skill: Demolition derby driver; Professional Skill: Junior League Hockey player; Qualified Operator: Persuader; Strong; Strong-willed
Conditions: Aggressive; Reputation: "Don't mess with him"; History of broken bones, ripped tendons, and severed arteries
Quote/Motto: Quote by unnamed G.I. Joe team member: "Don't mess with Backstop. Even though he's had more broken bones, ripped tendons, and severed arteries than anyone else in the Joe Team, he's still strong enough and strong-willed enough to break, rip, or sever something of yours." A quote taken from the Peer Personality Profile prototype dossier: "There's nothing wrong with Backstop that a straight-jack and a set of leg-irons won't cure ... temporarily that is. It would be nice to say that deep inside he's a gentle soul who is kind to little furry animals, but it simply wouldn't be true. He'd just bite their heads off."
Notes: One of two Joes without a rank/pay grade (the other being Storm Shadow). Currently, he is a reserve member of the current Joe team assigned to domestic operations in the United States. *All reservists can be called back into action if a mission calls for it.

Ballistic

Series: One (1995)
Alias/Variations: Eagle Eye
Real Name: Albert Salviatti
Gender: Male
Grade/Rank: None given
SN: 4KJT8M6J
Service Branch: Army
Faction(s): G.I. Joe and Team Extreme
Primary MOS: Pinpoint Sharp-Shooter
Appearance: Black hair, long sideburns. Black boots, one blue gauntlet, gray pants, red shoulder guards, yellow shirt
Accessories: Armor, backpack, missile, missile launcher, two guns
Abilities: Cool under fire; Heightened perception; Natural talent; Sharpshooter; Skilled marksman
Conditions: Reputation: "The guy who never

misses"; Contact: Julia Rossi, ballistics expert; Rivalry with former comrade-in-arms, the Silencer; Shuns technology

Bambi

Real Name: Alabama Cassidy
Place of Birth: Unknown
Gender: Female
Grade/Rank: 5/O-2: 1st Lieutenant
Service Branch: Air Force
Faction(s): G.I. Joe
Primary MOS: Fixed-wing pilot
Secondary MOS: Cargo hauler
Appearance: Short brown hair. White Air Force uniform
Abilities: Combat piloting; Deadly with a pistol; First aid; Piloting, Qualified Operator: C130 Hercules aircraft; Search-and-rescue experience; Trains search and rescue dog; Tougher than nails
Conditions: Accepted as "one of the guys"; Always has her crossbreed dog at her side; Easy sense of humor; Hides her feminine side (except with closest friends); Hopeless with a rifle; Loves to sing but terrible at it
Quote/Motto: "Per ardua ad astra."
Notes: Obtained her pilot's license at 16; graduate of the Royal Military College in Quebec, Canada

Banzai

Series: Twelve (1993)
Real Name: Robert J. Travalino
Place of Birth: Hartsdale, New York
Gender: Male
Grade/Rank: 0/E-4: Specialist (Army corporal)
SN: 452-H89-0678
Service Branch: Army; currently a reserve member*
Faction(s): G.I. Joe, Ninja Force
Notably Served At: Philippines; Tibet
Primary MOS: First-strike commando
Secondary MOS: Nunchaku instructor
Appearance: Yellow hair. Black and purple spotted pants, black boots and gloves; shirtless; purple and black diagonal strap; purple face mask with yellow sash
Accessories: Battle-ax; knife; sickle sword; sword; and two Y-shaped dueling knives
Abilities: Always ready to defend himself; Blind fighting; Commando; Lethal slam technique "Suzushi Slam"; Meditation; Ninja; Nunchaku instructor; Wilderness Survival: Hostile mountain climate
Conditions: Aggressive; Blood brother of Bushido; Proud; Reputation: Never caught off guard; Reputation: One of the world's premier nunchaku masters; Rising Sun ninja
Quote/Motto: "To get in touch with my inner self, I always practice nunchakus with my eyes closed."
Notes: Trained with a reclusive ninja master in Tibet. *All reservists can be called back into action if a mission calls for it.

Barbecue

Series: Four (1985)
Alias/Variations: Gabriel A. Garibaldi (Action Force alternate continuity, comics)
Real Name: Gabriel A. Kelly
Place of Birth: Boston, Massachusetts; (Naples, Italy for European distribution)
Gender: Male
Grade/Rank: 1/E-5: Sergeant, E-4 Corporal
SN: 321-61-4231
Service Branch: Army; reserve status* for special missions
Faction(s): G.I. Joe, Eco-Warriors, and Slaughter's Marauders
Notably Served At: The Assault on Springfield, Cobra Island, Gulf of Mexico
Primary MOS: Firefighter
Secondary MOS: Infantry
Appearance: Curly red hair with green eyes. Air tank, belt, boots; dark gray helmet with silver face mask; gloves, and pants with dark gray shoulder pocket, holster, orange-red shirt, the silver emblem on the right arm, and wristbands
Other Known Appearances: Dark blond hair. The edge of his ax is painted with silver highlights; his Slaughter's Marauder version is not painted.
Accessories: Extinguisher pistol; fire ax; foam tanks, frame backpack red tanks; hose
Abilities: Carousing; Combat ready; Firefighter; Qualified Operator: Dragonfly, Falcon Glider, FLAK, motorcycles, Silver Mirage, and Snow Cat
Conditions: Adrenaline junkie; Insensitive; Often at odds with Stalker; Party animal; Sarcastic comments; Sense of civic duty; Reputation: Cool customer outside his job; Wild tendencies
Quote/Motto: "Barbecue is what you call your basic party animal. He can open bottles with his teeth, pick up quarters with his ears, and wrap his lips completely around the bottom

of a quart Coke bottle. You may well ask how all this affects his function as the G.I. Joe Firefighter.... It doesn't. It simply makes him a more interesting fellow to have around." Quote by an unnamed G.I. Joe team member.

Notes: Before joining G.I. Joe, he was the seventh Kelly in his direct line in the Boston Fire department. *All reservists can be called back into action if a mission calls for it.

Barracuda

Real Name: Jean-Luc Bouvier
Place of Birth: Marseille, France
Gender: Male
Faction(s): Action Force, Special Anti-Terrorist Squad
Primary MOS: Underwater assault
Secondary MOS: Stunner mines
Abilities: Champion swimmer; Close combat expert; Explosives expert; Professional Skill: Exploration diver; SCUBA diver
Conditions: Courageous; Fearless; Highly dedicated; Mind of his own

Barrel Roll

Series: Nineteen (2003)
Real Name: Dwight E. Stall
Place of Birth: Cincinnati, Ohio
Gender: Male
Grade/Rank: 1/E-5: Sergeant
SN: 299-06-BR69
Service Branch: Army
Faction(s): G.I. Joe
Primary MOS: Marksmanship instructor
Secondary MOS: Fixed-wing aircraft pilot
Appearance: Brown hair. Black armbands and boots, blue shirt with rolled-up sleeves; gray and black gloves; light blue chest pads and pants with blue kneepads
Accessories: Sniper's rifle; Cobra pilot disguise (full-head helmet with Cobra emblem over face; chest plate with red stripes; leg armor with red stripes); a specially modified Cobra personal glider
Abilities: Calculates trajectories on the fly; Can remain motionless for hours; Crack shot; Fixed-wing aircraft pilot; Hang glider; High-altitude sniper; Marksmanship instructor; Math whiz; Skilled halo jumper; Skilled pilot; Sniper; Stealth
Conditions: Practices daily on the sniper range
Quote/Motto: "With me, it's not so much wanting to hit the bulls-eye as really hating to miss."
Notes: The brother of both G.I. Joe Bombstrike and Cobra operative Black Out

Barricade

Series: Eleven (1992)
Real Name: Philip M. Hoslinger
Place of Birth: Pittsburg, Kansas
Gender: Male
Grade/Rank: 1/E-5: Sergeant
SN: 434-8713-VW99
Service Branch: Army
Faction(s): G.I. Joe, NTI-Venom Task Force, and Battle Corps
Primary MOS: Bunker buster (penetrating hard targets)
Secondary MOS: Badger driver
Appearance: Black hair. Blue pants with gold waist and leg armor; blue shirt with gold armor on the chest and shoulders; gold boots and gloves
Accessories: Battering ram launcher with top-mounted handle and trigger; battering-ram missile; frame backpack; helmet with red trim and visor with built-in infrared heat source sensors; suit of flexible composite, laminate armor; Z-99 battlefield sidearm
Abilities: Heightened reflexes; Knowledge Skill: Urban assault; Nerves of steel; Qualified Operator: Badger driver; Specialist: Bunker buster; Specialist: Urban combat specialists
Quote/Motto: "Never kick down a door that you can blow down with a Satchel Charge!"
Notes: Fellow Joe member Roadblock is sometimes called Barricade

Battle Commanders

Alias/Variations: Talking Battle Commanders
Purpose: The leading charter members of G.I. Joe return to the battle lines to lead troops into combat.
Leader: Hawk
Members: Hawk, Sgt. Stalker
Quote/Motto: "Eat lead, Cobra!," "Yo, Joe!," "Move out!" attributed to Hawk. "Blitz 'em!," "Attack!," "Let's party!" attributed to Sgt. Stalker

Battle Corps

Series: Twelve (1993)
Purpose: The most combat-ready and therefore first line of defense utilized against Cobra
Leader: General Flagg
Members: Ace, Backblast, Barricade, Bazooka, Beach Head, Bullet-Proof, Colonel Courage,

Cross Country, Cutter, Dial Tone, Duke, Flint, Frostbite, Gung Ho, Ice Cream Soldier, Iceberg, Keel-Haul, Law, Leatherneck, Lifeline, Long Arm, Mace, Muskrat, Mutt and Junkyard, Outback, Roadblock, Shipwreck, Snow Storm, Stalker, Wet Suit, Wild Bill, and Windchill

Equipment: Blockbuster tank, Ghoststriker X-16 jet, Manta-Ray raft, Mudbuster jeep, Razor-Blade helicopter, and the S.H.A.R.K. 9000 boat

Battleforce 2000

Series: Six (1987)
Purpose: A military testing and research team who tried out experimental equipment and state-of-the-art prototypes
Leader: Maverick
Members: Avalanche, Blaster, Blocker, Dodger, and Knockdown. Dee Jay and Pulverizer were late additions to the group.
Stationed: Frusenland
Notably Served At: The Battle of Benzheen
Equipment: The Dominator tank, specially designed for use in freezing weather conditions (Avalanche); Vindicator, an advanced hovercraft (Blaster); Eliminator, a jeep-like assault vehicle (Blocker); Marauder, a high-tech battle cycle (Dodger); Sky-Sweeper, a mobile anti-aircraft platform (Knockdown); Vector, a VTOL jet fighter (Maverick); and a mobile laser cannon platform called Pulveriser, the only vehicle on the team with no primary designated operator—any qualified Joe can operate it.
Notes: Except for Dodger, the entire special force was killed during the Battle of Benzheen; they are laid to rest at Arlington National Cemetery. Dodger was reassigned to Sonic Force.

Bazooka

Series: Four (1985)
Alias/Variations: Sergeant Bazooka. Prototype names included Armor Hammer, Hard Line, Heat Man, Long Shot, Rough Tackle
Real Name: David L. Katzenbogen
Place of Birth: Hibbing, Minnesota
Gender: Male
Grade/Rank: 1/E-5: Sergeant
SN: 112-40-0577
Service Branch: Army Ranger
Faction(s): G.I. Joe, Battle Corps, and Tiger Force
Stationed: El-Hassim military base in Iraq
Notably Served At: "Third Horde" (Third Armored Division); Advanced Infantry School, Fort Benning; Armor School, Fort Knox
Primary MOS: Armor-defeating weapons systems
Secondary MOS: Tank driver
Appearance: Black hair and mustache. Dark gray boots; green wristbands, pants, and belt; red football shirt with blue "14" on front and blue collar
Other Known Appearances (Cartoon): Beige helmet and pants; brown wristbands
Accessories: Helmet with brim strap, missile launcher with sling; missile rack
Abilities: Advanced infantry; Certified Operator: Abram's tank; Certified Operator: Helicopters; Decisive; Fast thinker; Qualified: EOD (Explosive Ordnance Disposal); Qualified Expert: All Warsaw Pact RPG systems, Dragon Anti-Tank Missile, LAW rocket, LAW System, Milan System, Recoilless rifle; Security guard; Strong; Survivor instincts; Tenacious
Conditions: Always chewing gum; Anti-armor expert; Dreads driving tanks; Hobby Skill: Fishing; Lovable goof; Minnesota accent; Rarely speaks in complete sentences; Reputation: A little slow; Reputation: Usually works with Alpine
Notes: The jersey he wears is from former Patriots quarterback Steve Grogan. Later in the series, he gained weight, went bald, and was released from duty as he could not meet the physical requirements. After returning to shape, he rejoined the Joes. He was murdered in both the comics and animated series.

Beach Head

Series: Five (1986)
Alias/Variations: Beachhead or Beach-Head; prototype names included Ambush, Cool, Mr. Bones
Real Name: Wayne R. Sneeden
Place of Birth: Auburn, Alabama (Auckland, New Zealand for European distribution)
Gender: Male
Grade/Rank: E-6 (1986); E-7 (2002); E-9: Sergeant Major (2007)
SN: 902-46-SW14; RA 011-60-9231; 90K-LI-014
Service Branch: Army Ranger
Faction(s): G.I. Joe, Battle Corps, Strike Team: Alpha, and Tiger Corps
Stationed: El-Hassim military base in Iraq;

Airborne and Ranger school Fort Benning, Georgia; The Pit, Utah, located beneath Fort Wadsworth
Notably Served At: Battle of Springfield; Blackwater Prison Escape; Cobra Island; Sierra Gordo
Primary MOS: Infantry
Secondary MOS: Small Arms Armorer
Appearance: Black backpack straps, gloves, belt, pockets, and boots; dark green pants and kneepads; light green face mask and shirt. In India there were several variations of Beach Head; most wore a bright green mask and shirt, red trim, with a yellow vest. Between 1986 and 2014 there were 17 different versions of the character released as an action figure. In the Sunbow animation, he was seen without his mask for a few moments and had reddish-brown hair. He was voiced with a deep Southern accent, presented with a gruff demeanor, and wore the outfit of his 1986 action figure. In the Reel FX, he was made to be a California surfer and wore his action figure's 2003 outfit.
Accessories: 9-mm XF-7 Wasp submachine gun, ammo case, utility backpack
Abilities: Advisor to Central America operations; Amphibious and Airborne Assault Trooper; Determined; Green Beret; High pain threshold; Highly motivated; Keen mind; Lane instructor; Qualified Drill Sergeant; Qualified Expert: Explosive ordnance disposal; Qualified Expert: Suppression fire; Qualified Weapons Expert: All NATO and former Warsaw Pact Small Arms; Unwavering discipline
Conditions: Bullied as a child; Considered a legend among the Joes; Consummate professional; Daily 10-mile run; Intolerant of slackers; Likes to be the first one out of the helicopter; Low tolerance for under-achievers; Moderate temperament; Overachiever; Raised in abject poverty; Rumored to have a collection of spike-knuckled trench knives; Ruthless; Seeking the next challenge; Short-tempered; Unwavering patience on and off the battlefield; Vigorous daily physical training
Quote/Motto: "Getting angry is a total waste of time and energy. I'd rather get the job done first and worry about assigning the blame after the firefight is over." "I don't use deodorant." (see Note below) "Most folk will get mad on occasion or at least get irritable—not Beach Head. He thinks anger is a waste of time and energy. Rage clouds the vision and pollutes logic. Fury impairs judgment and makes you careless. The results of anger are totally unacceptable to Beach Head. He doesn't get angry ... he gets even." Quote by an unnamed G.I. Joe team member.
Notes: Beach Head is fifth in charge of G.I. Joe. He is authorized to wear the Master Explosive Ordnance Disposal Badge, the Combat Infantryman's Badge, and the Good Conduct Medal with oak leaf clusters. Beach Head's claim of not using deodorant has one of three hotly debated explanations: (1) It was a joke, as in he never worries and therefore never sweats. (2) He has less than admirable personal hygiene habits, but it is a tactical preventative measure, as scented deodorant could be a dead giveaway if he were dropped into a close combat war zone without prior notice. Finally, (3) he has a disdain for scented and unscented types of deodorant stemming from a skin allergy caused by a compound common in most brands.

Beaver

Series: Two (1983)
Real Name: Jacques-Peter Smith
Place of Birth: Province of Ontario, Canada
Gender: Male
SN: AF 342746
Faction(s): Action Force, Canadian Special Forces
Primary MOS: Waterborne sabotage
Secondary MOS: Night attack
Appearance: An all-black uniform
Accessories: Kayak and paddle, life jacket, rifle, skullcap
Abilities: Kayak whitewater rapids; Knowledge Skill: Rivers; Knowledge Skill: Watercrafts; Stealth; Swimming; Undercover patrol
Quote/Motto: "They seldom see Beaver come; they never see him go."

Big Bear

Series: Eleven (1992)
Alias/Variations: Bigbear
Real Name: Grigori Ivanovich Rostoff
Place of Birth: Archangel, Russia
Gender: Male
Grade/Rank: E-5 (Army Sergeant [Serzhant] equivalent)
Faction(s): G.I. Joe ally, Oktober Guard
Notably Served At: The elite 103rd Guards Air Assault Division

Primary MOS: Air Assault
Appearance: Red hair, beard. Black boots, gray furred cap with a red star, green pants and shirt, brown belt
Accessories: AK-88 fully automatic rifle; AK-S74U assault rifle with stock and sling; pouch backpack; Chest-mounted anti-personnel stiletto; dual barreled bazooka launcher; Field artillery trajectory indicator, double missile launcher; MB-02 bunker-busting hand grenade; Soviet Army field pack; two missiles; Z2EE4-O0 Shinokof surface-to-air missile
Abilities: Specialist: Anti-armor; Specialist: Heavy weapons
Conditions: "Can be meaner than a Siberian wolf with its leg caught in a steel trap"; "Can be wilder than a Murmansk fur merchant"; His way of doing things; Resents being referred to as the "Russian equivalent of G.I. Joe"; Savors every moment before destroying fortified bunkers, tanks, and other mechanized infantry vehicles
Quote/Motto: "You G.I. Joes! Airborne troops afraid to fall without parachutes! No guts!" "You've got to have the guts to stand and fight before you can see any glory!" "In all our lives, there comes a time when the power of evil becomes so threatening to world peace that global leaders must join together to stop its impending danger; Cobra is just such an evil. That's when they send Big Bear into the fight alongside the G.I. Joe team." Quote taken from G.I. Joe personnel files.
Notes: He is often incorrectly thought to be a fellow Oktober Guard member, Horror Show.

Big Ben

Series: Ten (1991)
Alias/Variations: David J. Bennett (-2001)
Real Name: David J. Bennet
Place of Birth: Burford, England
Gender: Male
Grade/Rank: E-7 (Equivalent); E-6 (Army Staff Sergeant)
Service Branch: British Special Air Service (SAS)
Faction(s): G.I. Joe, temporary exchange program; International Action Force (alternate continuity); member of the 22nd Regiment of the British Special Air Service
Stationed: Bradbury Barracks in Hereford; NATO Long Range Recon Patrol School in West Germany
Notably Served At: Cobra Island, Trans-Carpathia

Primary MOS: Infantry
Secondary MOS: Subversive operations
Appearance: Black hair, brown eyes. Black boots and microphone, gold ammo belts on chest; gray and green hat; green-brown camo pants, light brown jacket with green straps
Accessories: Ammo bandolier, backpack, explosives pack and strap, large pouch backpack, M-203 grenade launcher, M-60E machine gun with bipod, M-67 hand grenades (two), machete, shovel, sniper's rifle, TNT satchel charge, XMLR-3A laser rifle
Abilities: Commando skills
Conditions: Admires Americans for their iron-fisted courage; Belief: Americans have strange accents; Belief: Americans have strange ways of doing things
Quote/Motto: "I'm here to teach the bad guys that the fight for freedom and justice knows no borders."
Notes: He was briefly involved with U.S. Senator Dr. Deborah Carday, who was in truth Zarina in disguise. She tricked him into falling in love with her before being discovered.

Big Brawler

Series: Seventeen (2001), Twenty (2004)
Real Name: Brian K. Mulholland
Place of Birth: New York City, New York
Gender: Male
Grade/Rank: 4/E-8: Master Sergeant
Service Branch: Army
Faction(s): G.I. Joe, Tiger Force
Primary MOS: Counterintelligence and espionage
Secondary MOS: Jungle survival expert
Appearance: Black hair and soul patch beard. Black belt, boots, and gloves; green camouflage pants and T-shirt with "ARMY" on front
Other Known Appearances: Red hair and a full red beard
Accessories: AK-S74U assault rifle, backpack, flashlight
Abilities: Army intelligence; Counterintelligence; Espionage; Liaison to the U.S. Army Intelligence and Security Command (INSCOM), Hand-to-hand combat expert, Psychological warfare expert; Specialist: Jungle missions; Superior intelligence-gathering and infiltration skills; Wilderness Survival: Jungles
Conditions: Can't resist the urge to pound Cobra on sight; Changes the mission without permission or warning; Prefers to remain on

the front lines; Quick-tempered; Refuses all officer-level promotions; Reputation: A loose cannon

Billy Arboc

Alias/Variations: William Kesler (Alias)
Real Name: William Arboc
Place of Birth: Springfield, Illinois
Gender: Male
Service Branch: Civilian, Honorary Joe
Faction(s): G.I. Joe, Arashikage
Notably Served At: Borovia; Cobra Island; Fort Meade; Los Angeles; San Francisco; Scotland; Springfield, Illinois; the Silent Castle
Primary MOS: Ninja apprentice
Secondary MOS: Covert operations
Appearance: Brown hair; square jaw, lithe build; Brown boots, drab green pants; short-sleeved scoop neck shirt; *I Ching* hexagram tattoo on the right arm
Accessories: Grappling hook with string, submachine gun, sword, web gear
Abilities: Arashikage martial artist; Apprentice to Storm Shadow; Contact: Anti-Cobra Underground Resistance; Contact: Jinx; Contact: Kamakura; Contact: Scarlett; Contact: Spirit; Contact: Zap; Heightened Willpower; Ninjutsu; Tenacity; Well-traveled
Conditions: Ashamed of his father; Lost right eye; Prosthetic right cybernetic leg; Lives in the shadow of his father; Loyal to his adoptive Arashikage family; Rebellious spirit; Son of Cobra Commander; Survived many "corrective sessions" from Cobra; Survived intense interrogation by the Brainwave Scanner; Unhinged from torturous brainwashing sessions; Wants to rescue Storm Shadow
Quote/Motto: "I have issues with my father, but my training has allowed me to no longer feel any animosity toward him."
Notes: Bill, attempting to assassinate his father, was shot in the neck with a poison dart by Cobra Commander, who had his body hoisted up a flagpole with a message that no one is untouchable. In another continuity, Billy is killed during a battle against the cyborg team, Blue Ninjas, a group that despises the Arashikage. Snake Eyes and Storm Shadow take his body to Cobra Commander, who buries him.

Big Lob

Series: Twenty-Six (2010)
Real Name: Bradley J. Sanders
Place of Birth: Chicago, Illinois
Gender: Male
Grade/Rank: 0/E-4: Specialist Corporal, Africa, Uganda
Service Branch: Army, Reservist member of G.I. Joe*
Faction(s): G.I. Joe, Rawhides
Notably Served At: Africa, Uganda
Primary MOS: Grenade thrower
Secondary MOS: Infantry
Appearance: African American. Brown boots and cargo pants, red T-shirt with the number 14 in yellow.
Accessories: Bandolier, pistol, multi-shot grenade launcher; an arsenal of high explosive, flechette, incendiary, chemical compounds, and smoke grenades
Abilities: Athletic; Conditioning; Outstanding physical prowess; Professional Skill: Basketball player; Speed; Strength; Throwing hand grenades at specified targets; Toughness
Conditions: Speaks in sports commentator jargon; Talks about himself in the third person, Talks in sports metaphors; Well-liked by his teammates
Quote/Motto: "When Big Lob makes his move, he always shoots to score the big win!"
Notes: Became a reservist to remain close to home. *All reservists can be called back into action if a mission calls for it.

Biologico

Series: Five (1985)
Place of Birth: Brazil
Gender: Male
Grade/Rank: E-4 Specialist
Service Branch: Army
Faction(s): G.I. Joe, Forca Eco ("Eco-Warriors")
Primary MOS: Medical infectologist
Secondary MOS: Microbiology
Accessories: Rifle, water-firing backpack
Abilities: Medical infectologist; microbiology

Biomassa

Series: Four (1985)
Alias/Variations: Biomass
Place of Birth: Brazil
Gender: Male
Grade/Rank: E-4 Specialist
Service Branch: Army
Faction(s): G.I. Joe, Forca Eco ("Eco-Warriors")
Primary MOS: Energy specialist
Appearance: Orange helmet, purple and orange water-firing backpack, and a purple rifle

Accessories: Helmet, rifle, water-firing backpack
Abilities: Energy specialist

Biosfera
Series: Four (1985)
Place of Birth: Brazil
Gender: Male
Grade/Rank: E-4 Specialist
Service Branch: Army
Faction(s): G.I. Joe, Forca Eco ("Eco-Warriors")
Primary MOS: Environmental engineer
Secondary MOS: Communications, information analysis
Accessories: Mortar with stand; water cannon with a backpack
Abilities: Communications; Environmental engineer; Information analysis

Black Dragon
Series: Nineteen (2003)
Real Name: Kang Chi Lee
Place of Birth: Hong Kong
Gender: Male
SN: 78IL490K
Faction(s): G.I. Joe, Team Extreme
Primary MOS: Ninja Warrior
Appearance: Blond hair, blue-eyed, Chinese
Accessories: Two swords, nunchuks, multi-flail weapon
Abilities: Knowledge Skill: Criminal organization; Martial artist; Ninja; "Sixth Sense" for tracking; Night missions specialist; Stealth; Stealth mission expert; Tracking; Wise
Conditions: Has history with a crime family from Hong Kong; Rivals of the Arashikage; Stoic
Notes: There is a spy organization called Black Dragon as well as a VTOL copter.

Black Dragon, Organization
Series: Nineteen (2003)
Purpose: The Black Dragon organization has existed since before the Cold War, providing services to whatever world power it deemed most important to its own long-term goals. Their island headquarters in the South Atlantic was thought destroyed by the original G.I. Joe team over 30 years ago, but the sole survivor declared himself the new Supreme Leader and has since built an impregnable fortress deep beneath those same ruins, far from the eyes of any world power. Under his unbending will, this group has risen to become the foremost source of espionage agents in the world. Their true purpose, however, is revenge—and the Black Dragon Leader will stop at nothing short of the destruction of the G.I. Joe team.
Leader: Black Dragon Leader
Members: Followers of Black Dragon Leader

Blades
Series: Twenty-Five (2009)
Real Name: Herbert J. Rotweiler
Place of Birth: Riverside, Iowa
Gender: Male
Grade/Rank: W-2 Army warrant officer, second class
SN: 342-22-1530
Service Branch: Army
Faction(s): G.I. Joe, Special Action Force
Primary MOS: Helicopter pilot
Secondary MOS: Intelligence analyst
Appearance: Black bodysuit, blue visor/goggles; gray boots, plate, and helmet; yellow "SAS" logo on his chest.
Accessories: Belt, knife, rifle
Abilities: Aerial recon; Helicopter pilot; Renowned air strike pilot; Tracks shipments of gold and uranium sales in the UK; Works with Royal Military Police
Conditions: Hobby Skill: Sci-Fi movies and TV shows; Natural piloting ability; Recovering "mamma's boy"; Renowned air strike pilot; Vowed to never be tied down to any location
Quote/Motto: "He who dares to challenge Cobra, wins!"
Notes: Action Force (alternate continuity)

Blast-Off
Series: Twelve (1993)
Real Name: Jeffrey D. Thompson
Place of Birth: Kirkwood, Missouri (Sydney, Australia for European distribution)
Gender: Male
Grade/Rank: 0/E-4: Corporal or E-4 (Marine sergeant)
SN: J8675-30-9
Service Branch: Marine
Faction(s): G.I. Joe, Mega-Marines
Primary MOS: Flamethrower
Secondary MOS: Firefighter
Appearance: Blue shirt with red "2" on chest; dark gray pants, vest, and wristbands; red boots, gloves, and head covering; moldable bio-armor
Accessories: Bio-armor mold; knife; laser rifle; submachine gun; missile launcher with a

trigger; soft, full-head helmet; super-charged flamethrower; two missiles
Abilities: Firefighter
Conditions: Courageous; One standing order: "burn those Mega-Monsters like marshmallows in a campfire!"; Persistent; Reputation: Best firefighter in the state of Missouri
Quote/Motto: "When I blast into battle with a flame thrower and a tank full of fuel, things REALLY get hot!"

Blast-Off 2

Real Name: Greg Taggart
Place of Birth: Sydney, Australia
Gender: Male
SN: AF 934102
Service Branch: Air Force
Faction(s): Action Force, Space Force
Primary MOS: Weaponry
Secondary MOS: Free-fall aerobatics
Background Information: Trained by the Australian Air Force; Parachute Training School; NASA Free Fall Space training course
Abilities: Free-fall aerobatics; Patroller; Weaponry
Conditions: Diamond in the rough; Drinks nothing but milk and fresh juice
Quote/Motto: "Blast-Off is a rough diamond type of guy. He drinks nothing but milk and fresh juice."

Blaster

Series: Six (1987)
Real Name: Brian R. David
Place of Birth: Panama City, Florida
Gender: Male
Grade/Rank: E-5 Sergeant
SN: 641-05-7835
Service Branch: Army
Faction(s): G.I. Joe, Battleforce 2000
Stationed: Frusenland
Notably Served At: The Battle of Benzheen
Primary MOS: Ground-effect vehicle operator
Secondary MOS: Microwave technician
Appearance: Black belt; black glove on right hand; blue glove and wristband on left hand; green helmet with blue trim; green pants; green short-sleeved shirt with yellow and dark green camouflage chest panel; yellow and dark green camouflage boots
Accessories: Boxy laser gun with a handle on top; face mask over nose and mouth
Abilities: Certified Operator: Vindicator (an advanced hovercraft); Designs hovercrafts; Ground-effect vehicle operator; Microwave technician
Conditions: Fan of loud rock and roll music; Loves to design hovercrafts; Single-minded
Quote/Motto: "OK, so he's a little single-minded, maybe even a bit obsessed—but how many of the Joes aren't? The plus side is that he's willing to push his hovercraft to the limit and beyond, just to prove its worth. The result is faster and better support for the ground pounders—something they don't mind at all...."
Notes: KIA during the Battle of Benzheen when it was bombed by Cobra Commander. He is buried in Arlington National Cemetery.

Blind Master

Series: Twenty-Nine (2013)
Gender: Male
Grade/Rank: Leader of the Arashikage ninja clan
Faction(s): Arashikage ninja clan
Notably Served At: Borovia; Denver; Grenada; Marseille, France; San Francisco, California
Appearance: African American
Other Known Appearances (Cartoon): He is only referenced once in passing by Jinx.
Accessories: Bladed shield that doubles as a hat; mask, sash, flute, nine-ring sword, a two-piece bladed bamboo staff, flying saw with a handle
Abilities: Instructor; Knife fighter; Knowledge Skill: Secret ninja arts; Martial Artist; Professional Skill: Business owner (Dojo in Denver, Colorado); Qualified Weapons Expert: Bladed shield, flying saw, legendary nine-ring sword; Skilled with multiple weapons; Student: Billy Arboc; Teacher; Thrown; Wise
Conditions: Blind; Belief: Living without sentiment or love is to be devoid of weakness; Mysterious; Reputation: Sees what others can't; Reputation: Greatest teacher in the ways of ninjutsu; Reputation: Toughest of the masters; Reputation: Trained Kim Arashikage; Reputation: Trained Snake Eyes; Reputation: Trained Storm Shadow; Tattoo: Arashikage clan; Wants to avenge the Hard Master's death
Notes: He was killed by Zartan. Following his death, the Blind Master's soul became part of the Master Sword wielded by Snake Eyes.

Blizzard

Series: Seven (1988)

Alias/Variations: Ventisca ("Blizzard" Spain)
Real Name: Gregory M. Natale
Place of Birth: Wolfboro, New Hampshire (Leipzig, Austria for European distribution; Juneau, Alaska, for Spanish distribution)
Gender: Male
Grade/Rank: E-7 (Army sergeant first class); 4/E-8: Master sergeant
Service Branch: Army
Faction(s): G.I. Joe, Tiger Force
Stationed: Thule, Greenland
Primary MOS: Cold weather operations/Arctic warfare training instructor
Secondary MOS: Infantry
Appearance: Red hair. Black kneepads and pockets; dark gray belt; gray backpack straps; orange-brown boots and gloves; stripe on chest; white coat and pants
Other Known Appearances: Goggles and helmet
Accessories: Sled/backpack with two detachable handles and holes for footwear; two skis; two spiked snowshoes; helmet with engraved earmuffs and goggles; wrapped pistol with textured grip; wrapped rifle with long grip and L-shaped stock
Abilities: Arctic attack soldier
Conditions: Careful, Hard, Mean
Quote/Motto: "The Arctic is totally unforgiving. You make one little mistake, you've had it. The cold makes you tired, and being tired makes you careless, and being careless makes you a statistic. Blizzard doesn't make mistakes and doesn't get careless; he wants to make the other guy the statistic."

Blocker

Series: Six (1987)
Real Name: David B. McCarthy
Place of Birth: Boston, Massachusetts
Gender: Male
Grade/Rank: E-5 (Army sergeant)
SN: 500-63-0163
Service Branch: Army
Faction(s): G.I. Joe, Battleforce 2000
Stationed: Frusenland
Notably Served At: Aberdeen Proving Grounds, the Battle of Benzheen
Primary MOS: Mechanized recon
Secondary MOS: Special services
Appearance: Black gloves; black helmet and pants with orange camouflage; black shirt with silver straps and orange armor on arms; orange and black boots
Accessories: Laser pistol with strap on back and handle on top
Background Information: As a cabbie, he survived seven armed robberies, three backseat births, and one near-fatal plunge through a collapsing roadway.
Abilities: Eliminator driver; Professional Skill: Taxi driver; Qualified Expert Operator: Every wheeled vehicle in the Army; Qualified Operator: Eliminator; Test Driver for prototype vehicles
Conditions: Distinctive Feature: Boston accent; Does not like safety equipment
Quote/Motto: "I've seen him go over into a complete roll at high speed, recover, and keep on going. He takes on the slalom minimally at 85 mph and doesn't tip nary a cone. The skidpad? Don't even ask. All that and he does it with vehicles built to military specs. Amazing!" Quote by an unnamed G.I. Joe team member.
Notes: KIA during the Battle of Benzheen when it was bombed by Cobra Commander. He is buried in Arlington National Cemetery.

Blowtorch

Series: Three (1984)
Alias/Variations: Antorcha (for distribution in Mexico); Tocha (for distribution in Spain); Hot-Foot, Pyro
Real Name: Timothy P. Hanrahan
Place of Birth: Tampa, Florida (Toulouse, France in the European version)
Gender: Male
Grade/Rank: 1/E-5 Sergeant; E-4, E-6 (Staff Sergeant, 2002)
SN: RA527341209
Service Branch: Army
Faction(s): G.I. Joe
Primary MOS: Infantry special weapons
Secondary MOS: Small-arms armorer
Appearance: Several: Red hair; dark eyes and eyebrows and a short neck; light eyes and eyebrows matching his hair and a short neck, and light eyes and eyebrows with a longer neck. Yellow bodysuit with red knee, arm, shoulder pads, and a red chest pad; yellow shirt, pants, gloves, belt, and boots with orange-red pads on chest, arms, legs, and feet. There were also two variations in his helmet, one had a peg hole on each side and the other did not; neither version is considered rarer than the other. It is assumed the holes were meant to hold a clear visor.

Accessories: Helmet, M-7 flamethrower; M-7 manpack, oxygen mask

Abilities: Advanced degrees in structural and chemical engineering; Knowledge Skill: All military incendiary devices, flame projection equipment, pyrotechnics, and heat-projection devices; Knowledge Skill: Chemical engineering; Knowledge Skill: Structural engineering; Qualified Weapons Expert: M-7 Flamethrower, M-16, and the M1911A1 Auto Pistol

Conditions: Burn scars on his body; Cigarette smoke drives him crazy; Distinctive Feature: Irish accent; Pyrophobic; No fear of fire; Refuses to live anywhere where he can't safely jump out the windows; Sits near the exit in movie theaters; Sleep near a smoke detector

Quote/Motto: "He has ... made a study out of fire...[and] knows [its] effect on known construction materials, vegetation, protective shield and explosives. To Blowtorch, the use of fire in warfare is a science that predates the bow and arrow." Quote taken from his prototype file card.

Bombardier

Series: Thirty (2014)
Real Name: Connor D. Tree
Place of Birth: Coalville, United Kingdom
Gender: Male
Grade/Rank: OR-5 (E-5 equivalent)
SN: AF 318008
Service Branch: Army (U.K.)
Faction(s): G.I. Joe, Action Force (alternate continuity)
Stationed: Defense Science and Technology at Porton Down
Primary MOS: S.A.F. Experiential Weapons
Secondary MOS: Experimental ordnance
Appearance: Light brown hair and eyebrows, dark eyes. Black belt; gloves; gray bodysuit, yellow arm-, chest-, and thigh-pads; gray boots
Accessories: Belt, helmet, mini-drone, missile, missile launcher, two rifles, visor
Abilities: Creates robotic drones; Excels in weapons programs
Conditions: Episodes of fear; Episodes of paranoia; Episodes of rage; Held captive and forced to work for the Black Major; Remaining family member is a sleeper agent at large; Witnessed all but one family member tortured and executed
Quote/Motto: "Bombardier bears the psychological scars of his incarceration. He has managed to pass every medical examination, but there have been fleeting moments of rage, paranoia, or fear. Although there have been several requests to attach him to other units, I want to be there to help him if the situation arises." Taken from the files of Captain Skip.
Notes: Would-be graduate of Imperial College London, but he obliterated half of the William Penny Laboratory in an after-hours project.

Bombstrike

Series: Twenty-One (2005)
Alias/Variations: Bombshell, Cadet Bombshell
Real Name: Alyssa Renee Stall
Place of Birth: Cranston, Rhode Island
Gender: Female
Grade/Rank: E-4 Corporal; 6/O-1: 2nd Lieutenant
SN: 448-34-AS77
Service Branch: Marine and Air Force (sources conflict)
Faction(s): G.I. Joe
Notably Served At: Istanbul, Turkey
Primary MOS: Forward air control
Secondary MOS: Counterintelligence
Appearance: Thick, short yellow hair. Belt, boots; green camo pants with gray gloves; green pads on shoulders; kneepads; light brown shirt with Joe logo on chest
Accessories: Radio with two antennas; rectangular pouch backpack, rifle with stock attached to handle; wrist communicator
Abilities: Always hits her target; Calculates air raid strikes in her head; Heightened perception; Hobby Skill: Soccer
Conditions: Gracious loser; Plays to win; Focused intensity; Uncompromising courage
Quote/Motto: "Some people think a great view means a serene mountain scene. Mine is a clear line to the enemy and an open path from bomb to bunker."
Notes: Sister of the G.I. Joe high altitude sniper Barrel Roll and Cobra sniper Black Out; the latter kidnapped her during a mission, and she has not been seen since.

Bon Appetit

Alias/Variations: B.A. LaCarr; District Attorney LaCarr; Judge B.A. LaCarr; Sherriff B.A. LaCarr
Gender: Male
Service Branch: Former Cobra Air Force

Faction(s): G.I. Joe
Stationed: Trawler Cobra Heli-carrier; USS *Flagg*
Primary MOS: Mess hall cook
Secondary MOS: Soldier
Appearance: Bushy gray beard and mustache, nearly bald; brown eyes; short, stocky, barefooted; Large round black glasses; tattered Cobra uniform, white apron with Cobra insignia
Abilities: Blow to the head restores sanity; Electrical engineering; Hydro engineering; Kelp farming; Knowledge Skill: Anti-matter device operations; Knowledge Skill: Daily operations of LaCarr City; Professional Skill: Cook; Reprogramming of B.A.T.S.; Robot repair; Seaweed farming; Survival Skill: Sunken ship; Underwater city construction
Conditions: Belief: The last member of Cobra; Elderly, Former member of Cobra, Intolerant of rude and rowdy behavior; Mentally unstable
Quote/Motto: "Bon Appetit. They call me that just because of a few Cobra Strato Vipers got ptomaine poisoning. But these B.A.T.s don't mind my cooking."
Notes: He was aboard the Trawler Cobra Heli-carrier when it sunk to the bottom of the ocean in the Sunbow animation episode titled "Computer Complications." He only appeared in season 2 episode 20, "Raise the Flagg!" After being rescued, he asked to join G.I. Joe and was welcomed into the fold.

Boulder

Series: Three (1984), 8" commando scale, twenty-three (2007)
Real Name: Greg M. Donahue
Gender: Male
Grade/Rank: E-5 Sergeant
Faction(s): G.I. Joe, Sigma 6
Notably Served At: World War III, Kazakhstan
Primary MOS: Mountain scout
Secondary MOS: Mountain climbing
Appearance: African American. Black gloves and pants, green T-shirt, lace-up brown boots, red bandana.
Accessories: Binocular strap, binoculars, bipod, blaster, grappling hook, knife, large dog tag, pickaxe, sheath, small dog tag, three grappling hook prongs, two grenades, two weapons crate handles, two weapons crate latches, and a two-part weapons case
Abilities: Mountain climbing; Mountain scout; Scout enemy camp

Notes: Boulder is currently listed as a reserve member of the Sigma 6 team assigned to domestic operations in the United States. *All reservists can be called back into action if a mission calls for it.

Breaker

Series: One (1982)
Alias/Variations: Alvin "Breaker" Kibbey; Topson (Argentina, "Roger"), and Falcon (Brazil)
Real Name: Alvin R. Kibbey
Place of Birth: Gatlinburg, Tennessee (Munich, Germany and later, Milan, Italy in European release)
Gender: Male
Grade/Rank: E-4 (corporal)
SN: RA757793518
Service Branch: Army
Faction(s): G.I. Joe, Stars and Stripes Forever, and Z Force
Primary MOS: Communications officer RTO (Radio Telephone Operator)
Secondary MOS: Communications technology
Appearance: Brown hair and beard. Black boots; dark green belt and pants with silver pockets; olive drab short-sleeved shirt with black straps
Other Known Appearances: He does not have a beard or helmet in the comic; the outfit is the same but dark green, sometimes with an open collar, and no chest straps.
Accessories: Helmet, radio headset, TV-radio backpack (1982–83)
Background Information: Breaker is the link between the battlefield and headquarters and can call in an airstrike, provide artillery coordinates, request a medevac, or find an extraction site. Also, he provides situation reports to the command center.
Abilities: (CLASSIFIED: Speaks Seven Languages); Codebreaking; Communications officer; Covert electronics; Knowledge Skill: All NATO and Warsaw Pact communication gear; Green Beret; Jam enemy transmissions; Qualified Weapons Expert: M-16; M-1911A1; MAC-10 (Ingram); Qualified Operator: JUMP, Sky Hawk, VAMP Mark II, and SHARC prototype; Specialized Education: Signal school; Uncanny ability to turn adverse situations to his favor
Conditions: Chews bubble gum; Constantly monitors all radio frequencies; Efficient; Renown: Carries an M-16 and blowing bubbles; Self-assured; Southern accent; Well-liked by teammates

Quote/Motto: "He's efficient and self-assured and has an uncanny ability to turn adverse situations to his favor." Quote by an unnamed G.I. Joe team member.
Notes: Crazylegs, Quick Kick, and Breaker died in a vehicle explosion while escaping in a stolen Cobra Rage tank in Trucial Abysmia. Cross Country, Duke, and Falcon managed to escape. The 1982 Breaker figure was produced straight-armed. In 1986 Breaker, one of the original G.I. Joes was replaced by Dial-Tone.

Budo

Series: Seven (1988)
Alias/Variations: Katana, Daito, and Slasher
Real Name: Kyle A. Jesso
Place of Birth: Sacramento, California (Osaka, Japan for European distribution)
Gender: Male
Grade/Rank: 6/O-3 Captain, E-5 (Army sergeant)
SN: 083-4810-JK09
Service Branch: Army
Faction(s): G.I. Joe
Stationed: Arashikage Martial Arts Academy, San Francisco, California
Primary MOS: Infantry
Secondary MOS: Hand-to-hand combat instructor
Appearance: Short black hair. Brown boots, vest, and wristbands; gray belt, kneepads, and shirt; hook on the waist for a sword; olive green pants
Accessories: Curved sword with a ring on side of the hilt; helmet with scarab-like antennae; sai with a ring on the end of the hilt; sword with a long hilt and angled tip
Background Information: Father was an orthodontist in Oakland, grandfather was a farmer in Fresno, great-grandfather was a track worker on the Rocky Mountain Line, and great-great-grandfather was a fencing master in one of the last great samurai warrior families of Japan. On his eighteenth birthday he was given the family swords and a haiku written by his ancestor: "The great sword unsheathed/Glitters brightly in the dark/Unseen and at rest."
Abilities: Fifth-degree black belt in *Iaido* (art of the live blade) and similar rank in three other martial arts; Infiltrating skills, Recruiter; Samurai warrior; Undercover skills
Conditions: Affinity for his chopped, pan-head Harley; Loves heavy metal music

Quote/Motto: "The man has a fifth-degree black belt in Iaido (the art of the live blade), and similar rank in three other martial arts. He could have even higher rankings if he didn't spend so much time working on his chopped, pan-headed Harley and listening to heavy metal." Quote by an unnamed G.I. Joe team member.
Notes: Had a romantic relationship with the ninja, Jinx

Bullet-Proof

Series: Eleven (1992)
Alias/Variations: Tiro Certo (Brazil)
Real Name: Earl S. Morris
Place of Birth: Chicago, Illinois
Gender: Male
Grade/Rank: 7/O-4 Major
SN: 696-5214-ES66
Service Branch: Army
Faction(s): G.I. Joe, Battle Corps, and the Drug Elimination Force (Leader)
Notably Served At: Broca Beach, The Caribbean, Central America, and the Golden Triangle
Primary MOS: Drug Elimination Force Leader
Secondary MOS: Federal Marshall
Appearance: African American; black flat-top hair; green shirt and pants with beige urban camo; beige diagonal strap, gloves, and boots
Accessories: 9-mm sidearm with tear-proof holster; ammo clip battle pouch; canteen; combat-ready backpack, chemical warfare mask; curved magazine; delayed blast, shrapnel grenade; double-barreled cannon with a black trigger; fully automated GP-88 field rifle; gas mask; pouch backpack; heat-seeking surface-to-surface missile; heavy artillery operator's helmet; leg compartment for binoculars; missile launching bullet gun; missile; submachine gun with long, hollow stock; tall helmet and curved mouthpiece; ZP99 leather bandolier
Abilities: Federal Marshal; Qualified Expert Operator: G.I. Joe AH-74 Desert Apache pilot
Conditions: Belief: Luck does not exist; Dedicated to the eradication of illegal narcotics; Practices shooting every day; Reputation: Never took a shot in the field; Urban commando
Quote/Motto: "I don't believe in any magic charms. I'm just really careful and I practice shooting every day!"

Bullhorn

Series: Nine (1990)

Real Name: Stephen A. Ferreira
Place of Birth: Providence, Rhode Island
Gender: Male
Grade/Rank: 1/E-5 Sergeant
SN: 780-5287-FR33
Service Branch: Army
Stationed: F.B.I. Academy in Quantico, Virginia
Primary MOS: Intervention specialist
Secondary MOS: Armor
Appearance: Black hair, eyes, eyebrows. Black cap; brown face paint; a gray-green shirt with dark gray straps and grenades on chest; brown pants with gray belt, holster
Accessories: Backpack case with slots for a rifle; gas mask with visor; machine gun with large guard and scope, and magazine behind grip; three-piece rifle (stock, muzzle, and scope); two-piece bullhorn
Abilities: Accurate shot; Charismatic; Effective crisis negotiator; Good friends with Pathfinder; Good listener; Hand-to-hand combat instructor; Hostage negotiator; Professional Skill: Negotiator
Conditions: Choirboy looks; Compassionate personality; Extremely calm individual; Steely coolness; Reckless driver
Quote/Motto: "Everyone is willing to talk to Bullhorn! And why shouldn't they be? He has the looks of a choirboy and is a good listener. This guy has more finesse than the slickest diplomat, using it to convince his adversaries that he actually CARES about their problems. That's when they discover the folly of messing with a former hand-to-hand combat instructor from Quantico who is also a contender for the national practical pistol title!" Quote by an unnamed G.I. Joe team member.
Notes: A contender for the "National Practical Pistol" title

Bushido

Series: Twelve (1993)
Real Name: Lloyd S. Goldfine
Place of Birth: Hollis, Queens, New York
Gender: Male
Grade/Rank: 1/E-5: E-5 (Army sergeant)
SN: 452HEA-0079
Service Branch: Army
Faction(s): G.I. Joe, Ninja Force
Stationed: Iceland
Primary MOS: Cold weather specialist
Secondary MOS: Strategist
Appearance: Light blue and white traditional Samurai helmet with white horns; a light blue shirt with white straps and gloves; orange details on straps; light blue pants fading to white, with white belt and boots; gauze-wrapped forearms; high-top sneakers
Accessories: 9-mm Beretta; battle-ax; knife; leather bandolier suspenders; Nago Teppo smoke grenades, Shinobi throwing dagger; sickle; sidearm storage pouches; suit of inviso-armor (changes color when exposed to light and water); sword; twin dueling knives
Abilities: Heightened sense of awareness; Heightened discipline; Snow ninja
Conditions: Blood brother to Banzai; Distinctive Feature: Wears an ancient samurai helmet; Great respect for tradition and family pride; Likes to practice martial arts skills in freezing temperatures; Reputation: Cool and calculating in the heat of battle
Quote/Motto: "Like a pointed crystal, I am as clean as I am dangerous." "Like an invisible razor, I cut swift and unseen."
Notes: His father was also a warrior.

Candy Apple

Alias/Variations: Bongo the Balloon Bear
Real Name: Candy Apple
Place of Birth: Possibly, Staten Island, New York
Gender: Female
Service Branch: None
Faction(s): Civilian
Appearance: Tall with wavy shoulder-length blonde hair; ankle boots, clutch purse, large clunky jewelry, loudly patterned flimsy blouse, mini skirt
Abilities: Driving, Professional Skill: Delivery person (balloons to carnivals and parties)
Conditions: Crush on Rip Cord; Will not wear the Bongo Bear costume
Notes: Her father, who lives in Staten Island, is one of the Fred series; she was unaware of this until informed by the Joes. Candy was killed by Scrap-Iron while assisting the Joes on a mission she became entangled in. In the vehicle with her at the time of her death was Billy Arboc.

Cannonball

Series: Twenty-One (2005)
Real Name: John Warden
Place of Birth: Sioux Falls, South Dakota
Gender: Male
Grade/Rank: 0/E-4: Advisor/Probationary Member/Specialist
SN: 234-55-GI89

Service Branch: Army
Faction(s): G.I. Joe
Primary MOS: Transportation
Secondary MOS: Infantry
Appearance: Dark brown soul-patch beard and Winfield-style mustache; powerfully developed upper body. Black gloves; gray pants with a black belt, kneepads, and boots; a white short-sleeved shirt with yellow padded chest straps; yellow bandana
Accessories: R.H.I.N.O. (Rapid Heli-Integrated Neutralizing Offensive Vehicle)
Abilities: Lucky; Professional Skill: Test driver for trucks, retired; Professional Skill: "Human cannonball" stuntman, retired; Qualified Operator: R.H.I.N.O.
Conditions: Fearless enthusiasm; Reputation: Always walks away from a wreck without a scratch; Wild-and-crazy driver/helicopter pilot
Quote/Motto: "You want the slow lane? Don't look at me. I only know one way to drive: eating up the road with a full-throttle and a screaming engine."
Notes: He wears a bandana on his head as a helmet

Captain "Eagle" Buckingham

Real Name: Charles Richard Buckingham
Place of Birth: Middlesex, England
Gender: Male
Grade/Rank: Captain
SN: AF34698
Service Branch: Army
Faction(s): G.I. Joe ally; Action Force (alternate continuity)
Primary MOS: Guerrilla warfare
Secondary MOS: Commando assault
Abilities: Familiar with guerrilla tactics; Former Army; Inspires loyalty; Natural leader; Nobility, Weapons familiarity
Conditions: Seeks adventure; His men are fiercely loyal to him; Leads from the front
Notes: Son of an earl; education from Cambridge, Eton, and Sandhurst; won the Sword of Honor

Captain Skip

Series: Thirty-Three (2017)
Alias/Variations: Skip
Real Name: Grant J. Campbell
Place of Birth: Edinburgh, Scotland
Gender: Male
Grade/Rank: O-3 (equivalent) Army (U.K.)
SN: 6-04 and AF 39696, sources conflict
Faction(s): Special Action Force/Z Force
Stationed: Second Battalion Parachute Regiment (2 Para)
Primary MOS: Military strategy
Secondary MOS: Artillery troop officer
Appearance: Black hair, black eyes; green camos, red beret
Accessories: British flag, flagpole bracket, flagpole mount, pulley flagpole, rifle, submachine gun, web gear, zip-line handle
Background Information: Graduated first at Officer Training College
Abilities: Inspire; International Playboy; Leadership; Professional Skill: Head of a worldwide corporation; Z Force: Oversees armor, artillery operations, and infantry
Conditions: Comes from a long family line of success in business and government; Fights alongside his troops; Wants to prove his worth beyond family name
Quote/Motto: "As a fellow commanding officer, I know that Captain Skip gets results by not accepting second best from any of his soldiers." From Captain "Eagle" Buckingham's files.

Chameleon

Series: Sixteen (2000)
Real Name: Erika La Tene
Place of Birth: CLASSIFIED
Gender: Female
Grade/Rank: 1/E-5: Sergeant
Service Branch: Army
Faction(s): G.I. Joe
Primary MOS: Intelligence
Secondary MOS: Computer technologies
Appearance: Long black hair; glasses. Black plated armor suit, gloves, and thigh-high boots, all with red detailing; red Cobra insignia on the chest
Accessories: Small, angular, backpack with large, engraved Cobra emblem; high-density laser rifle; walkie-talkie
Abilities: Acting; Assassination, Hand-to-hand combat; Deep-cover agent; Infiltration; Military skills; Mimicry; Sabotage; Secret agent; Trained by French Revolutionaries
Conditions: Illegitimate half-sister of Cobra's Baroness; passing resemblance to Jinx; Respects Chuckles
Notes: Chameleon is not to be confused with The Chameleon [Swamp Skier] vehicle ridden by Zartan. Her action figure is strikingly

similar in appearance to the Baroness; the file card reveals they are half-sisters.

Chance

Alias/Variations: Greenshirt 910, Steel-Brigadier 910
Real Name: Michael Cunningham
Place of Birth: Lexington, Kentucky
Gender: Male
Grade/Rank: 1/E-5: Sergeant EOD
Service Branch: Army
Faction(s): G.I. Joe, Greenshirt, Steel Brigade, and Strike Team: Alpha
Notably Served At: Afghanistan, Palestine, The Pit* Evacuation, the USS *Flagg*, the Battle of the Great Flood of 2011, Trucial Abysmia
Primary MOS: Demolitions
Secondary MOS: Infantry
Appearance: Helmet and equipment cover his body
Abilities: Burrito bomb expert; Cool under fire; Familiarity: Rifles; Hand-to-hand combat; Magnet mines expert; Rolls with blows; Small Arms: Pistols; Undercover operations; Weight trainer; Years of combat experience
Conditions: Difficult to enrage; Extensive family; Impulsive drive to help others; Proud of his military family history; Raising his six-year-old niece; Second- and third-degree burns on his body
Quote/Motto: "Sometimes, the best thing to do is just follow your heart or your gut."
Notes: Fifth-generation military; Chance is the code name his grandfather had during World War II. * The Pit, Utah, located beneath Fort Wadsworth.

Charbroil

Series: Seven (1988)
Real Name: Carl G. Shannon
Place of Birth: Blackduck, Minnesota
Gender: Male
Grade/Rank: 0/E-4: Specialist
SN: 247-4041-SC09
Service Branch: Army
Faction(s): G.I. Joe, Anti-Venom Task Force, and Strike Team: Charlie
Primary MOS: Flame weapons specialist
Secondary MOS: Small arms armorer
Appearance: Red hair, black or orange eyes. Asbestos suit. Orange-brown shirt with yellow shoulder guards and silver chest armor and wristbands; orange-brown pants with yellow stripes on outside legs; red belt; silver kneepads
Accessories: Large backpack, antenna, handle, and hose; flamethrower with handle and jagged forward grip; full-head helmet with red eyes; thick hose; thermo-insulated oxygenated helmet, a pressurized thermochemical backpack (with a hologram glued on), flamethrower, and a large thick "flame-retardant" hose
Abilities: Knowledge Skill: Water pipes; Knowledge Skill: Home heating systems; Professional Skill: Mill blast furnace worker
Conditions: Reputation: Pretty nice guy
Quote/Motto: "Flame weapons are scary to the max. Why do you think he wears that asbestos suit? That tank on his back is full of jellied gasoline. Know what happens if a hot tracer round hits that? You wanna be standing next to him? For a flamethrower specialist, he's a pretty nice guy but with that thing on his back, he isn't going to win a popularity contest in the middle of a firefight." Quote by an unnamed G.I. Joe team member.

Checkpoint

Series: Twenty-Two (2006)
Real Name: Jared Wade
Place of Birth: Springboro, Ohio
Gender: Male
Grade/Rank: 0/E-4: Corporal, Advisor/Probationary Member/Specialist
SN: 849-77-WJ59
Service Branch: Army
Faction(s): G.I. Joe, Steel Brigade
Primary MOS: Security CO, military police
Secondary MOS: Carpenter
Appearance: Short, light brown hair; light blue long-sleeve shirt, light brown cargo pants, green kneepads, black boots
Accessories: Flak vest, helmet, missile, missile launcher, missile launcher shield, tonfa stick
Abilities: Greco-Roman wrestling; Martial arts; Weapon Skill: Missile launcher; Powerfully built
Conditions: Distinctive Feature: Narrow/squinting eyes; Huge ego; Imposing; Professional rivalry with Major Barrage; Reputation: Only one to defeat Barrage in a wrestling match
Quote/Motto: "When the big man says your perimeter's secure, you can bet there won't be any nasty surprise showing up in the doorway behind you." Quote by an unnamed G.I. Joe team member.

Chuckles

Series: Six (1987)
Real Name: Philip M. Provost
Place of Birth: Little Rock, Arkansas
Gender: Male
Grade/Rank: 1/E-5: Sergeant
SN: 299-58-5214
Service Branch: Army; CIA
Faction(s): G.I. Joe
Notably Served At: Chomo-Lungma, Cobra Unity, Qabdat Khafia base; Western Asia
Primary MOS: Criminal investigations division
Secondary MOS: Intelligence
Appearance: Blond hair; blue, short-sleeved, open-collar Hawaiian shirt with pink flowers and green leaves; green pants with beige belt, brown holster, and black boots
Other Known Appearances: White shirt with thin-petaled yellow and pink flowers; dark blue pants
Accessories: Colt Combat Commander .45; Quickdraw shoulder harness
Abilities: Expert at faking his death; Hotwire vehicles; Man's man; Naturally likable; Perseverance; Physically strong (can lift and throw a missile); Qualified Operator: Dreadnok Swampfire, H.A.V.O.C., Tomahawk Helicopter; Professional Skill: Undercover agent
Conditions: Belief: He can fight his way out of any situation; Belief: Owes his main allegiance to Southeastern Insurance Group, Fort Lauderdale (where his career started); Confident; Conscientious about his "cover"; Every CID's favorite companion; Former Operative of a "rival" intelligence agency; Gregarious nature; Jocular personality; Occasional bouts of isolation and depression; Will take any missions no matter how big or small
Quote/Motto: "Chuckles' natural likeability is his greatest asset. He can sit around all day with a bunch of Cobras, grinning, cracking jokes, and punching shoulders, all the while wearing a miniature transmitter that's being homed in on by the Joe Team. Chuckles is aware of the consequences of being found out.... He's also confident of his ability to fight his way out of any situation." Quote by an unnamed G.I. Joe team member.
Notes: Possibly slain by Coil agent, Overlord, during the second invasion of Cobra Island; uncertainty remains because he was supposed to use the battle to fake his death. His name is part of a memorial to fallen Joes located in Arlington.

Claymore

Series: Five (1986)
Alias/Variations: Captain Claymore
Real Name: John Zullo
Place of Birth: Manchester, Vermont
Gender: Male
Grade/Rank: O-3 (Army captain); by special assignment only
SN: MH 009-40-3277
Service Branch: Army
Faction(s): G.I. Joe, Special Mission: Brazil
Notably Served At: Brazil, Southeast Asia
Primary MOS: Anti-terrorist specialist/covert operations
Secondary MOS: Martial Arts
Appearance: Black hair and black cop-style mustache; yellow, brown-spotted short-sleeved shirt with a green padded vest; brown belt, brown pockets, and gloves; yellow, brown-spotted pants with a brown belt and green boots
Accessories: Helmet and submachine gun
Background Information: Born the son of an immigrant who came to America to work in the marble quarries of Vermont. Graduate of Dartmouth College in New Hampshire, he finished at the top of his class with a major in Eastern Philosophies. He enlisted in the U.S. Army and served three back-to-back hitches somewhere in Southeast Asia. His mission was, and still is, "CLASSIFIED."
Abilities: Green Beret; Language Skill: Chinese, Japanese, Portuguese, Vietnamese; Knowledge Skill: Eastern Philosophy; Proficient in all forms of martial arts; Qualified Weapons Expert: All NATO and Warsaw Pact explosive devices, all NATO long-range sniper rifles, all NATO small arms
Conditions: Reputation: Respected by all branches of the Armed Services; Reputation: A soldier
Quote/Motto: "The name John Zullo does not identify any known living person." Quote by an unnamed G.I. Joe team member.
Notes: He led a team of specialists to recover a military satellite from Cobra territory in the Brazilian jungle: Dial Tone, Leatherneck, Mainframe, and Wet Suit. He is a graduate of Dartmouth College in New Hampshire; he attended Airborne and Ranger school.

Clean-Sweep

Series: Ten (1991)
Alias/Variations: Anti-Tox

Real Name: Daniel W. Price
Place of Birth: Elizabeth, New Jersey
Gender: Male
Grade/Rank: E-4 (Army corporal)
SN: 225-7836-DP74
Service Branch: Army
Faction(s): G.I. Joe, Eco-Warriors
Primary MOS: Chemical operations specialist
Secondary MOS: Combat engineer
Appearance: Brown hair and "copstash" mustache; a yellow shirt with neon green tubing and brown gloves; yellow pants with neon green belt and brown boots; clothes change color in water
Accessories: Soft full-head helmet with visor and trim; small tech backpack with control panel arm; long, futuristic pistol with trigger distinct from grip; large tread robot with a plunger
Abilities: Chemical warfare expert; Extensive array of data identifying chemicals and their counteragents; Persistence; Laser pistol expert
Conditions: Feels more than just a sense of duty to sanitize the affected area
Quote/Motto: "You might think it's a cushy job, sitting back in a climate-controlled, solvent-resistant suit while operating the remote-controlled sludge-sucking robot. But if that robot's tracks get stuck or the sludge pump backs up, Clean-Sweep is the one who has to slog out into the toxic waste pool and duck Cobra laser blasts while he's trying to get it going again." Quote by an unnamed G.I. Joe team member.

Cloudburst

Series: Ten (1991)
Real Name: Chuck Ram
Place of Birth: San Diego, California
Gender: Male
Grade/Rank: O/E-4: E-4 (Army corporal) Specialist; ensign
SN: 036-4848-RG31
Service Branch: Army
Faction(s): G.I. Joe, Air Commandos
Primary MOS: Aeronautics
Secondary MOS: Infantry
Appearance: Brown hair and eyes; yellow helmet with chinstrap; a yellow shirt with a black vest and yellow straps; white gloves; white pants with yellow shin coverings, pink pads on sides of legs
Accessories: Hang glider; machine gun with short, L-shaped stock and grip with long, angled magazine; transparent visor with nose notch
Abilities: Designs gliders; Professional Skill: Aeronautics; Qualified Expert Operator: USN helo-pilot; Specialist: Gliders
Conditions: Constantly updating his equipment; Won't settle for "almost"
Quote/Motto: "Cloudburst won't settle for almost or pretty good. He is constantly updating his gliders and redesigning his flight gear to cut down on drag and radar signature. He knows that his services will be called upon when all other methods for covert troop insertion are deemed impractical, and that can happen only if the situation is hairy to the max." Taken from G.I. Joe personnel files.

Clutch

Series: One (1982); Three (1984)
Alias/Variations: Double Clutch
Real Name: Lance J. Steinberg
Place of Birth: Asbury Park, New Jersey
Gender: Male
Grade/Rank: 4/E-8: E-4 (Corporal) (1982), E-5 (Sergeant) (2007)
SN: RA757340802
Service Branch: Marine/Army (sources conflict)
Faction(s): G.I. Joe, Mega-Marines, and Strike Team: Bravo
Stationed: Philadelphia Naval Base
Notably Served At: Al-Awai; Libyan desert; Broca Beach; Brazil; Canada
Primary MOS: Transportation, VAMP driver
Secondary MOS: Infantry
Appearance: Black hair, beard, and mustache in pointed Van Dyke style; olive drab or tan uniform with tan, or green, belt, holster, and boots. Series 3 is referred to as the Tan Clutch as it is the exact mold as the previous, but with a tan paint scheme.
Other Known Appearances: Five o'clock shadow
Accessories: A green helmet (1982–83). Came with the VAMP Mark 2
Abilities: Advanced Infantry Training; Covert ops; Driving expert; Hobby Skill: Races street machines; Professional Skill: Executive bodyguard; Professional Skill: Mechanic for the Indy League Racing Circuit; Professional Skill: Transportation specialist; Qualified Expert Operator: Monster blaster A.P.C., VAMP battle jeep, VAMP; Mark II driver; Qualified

Weapon Expert: M14, M16; M1911A1, M3A1, M79 and M60; Ranger
Conditions: Complicit with trickery; Crude behavior; Inherent decency; Oversexed chauvinist; Predictably reliable; Takes little seriously; Unabashed skirt chaser; Wild card
Quote/Motto: "He greases his hair with motor oil, rarely shaves, and chews on the same toothpick for months." Clutch still calls women "chicks." Taken from G.I. Joe personnel files.
Notes: The 1982 Clutch figure was produced straight-armed.

Cold Front

Series: Nine (1990)
Alias/Variations: Big Chill, Cold Steel, Cold War, Cold Wave, Perma-Frost, Sub-Zero
Real Name: Charles Donahue
Place of Birth: Fort Knox, Kentucky
Gender: Male
Grade/Rank: 3/E-7: Sergeant first class
SN: 834-1956-TH56
Service Branch: Army
Faction(s): G.I. Joe, 3rd Armored Division
Primary MOS: Cold weather operations; Avalanche driver
Secondary MOS: Fire control technician
Appearance: Red hair. White helmet; white snowsuit with gray fur collar and gloves; gray straps and belt; brown gloves and thigh-high boots
Accessories: Transparent visor; bent, white mic attaching to the helmet; medium-sized white pistol with a distinct trigger guard and sound suppressor
Abilities: Knowledge Skill: Tactics and strategies; Qualified Expert Driver: Avalanche, Arctic Tank/Hovercraft; Tank driver
Conditions: Distinctive Features: Big, noisy, and ugly; Obsession with tanks; Will destroy any car he drives
Quote/Motto: "Cold Front cannot allow himself to drive a car because he'll destroy it. A well-built station wagon lasts about two weeks in his hands and is usually not salvageable for parts. After he was pried out of the wreckage of his last civilian vehicle, he remarked, 'I keep forgetting they're not tanks!'" "He likes everything about tanks because they are just like him: big, noisy, and ugly!"
Notes: His vehicle, the Avalanche, should not be confused with the Battleforce 2000 character Avalanche.

Cold Shot

Real Name: Not Given
Place of Birth: Alaska
Gender: Male
Grade/Rank: 3/E-7: Chief petty officer
SN: Custom Model
Service Branch: Army
Faction(s): G.I. Joe
Stationed: Naval Amphibious Base Coronado, California
Accessories: Backpack, rifle (modified with scope and barrel), snowshoes
Background Information: Taught his wilderness survival skills by his father. He saved Blizzard from a Cobra attack and was recruited by him to join the Joes.
Abilities: Arctic survival; First aid
Conditions: First shot is always a warning shot; the second shot is a precise headshot
Notes: A custom Joe; recruited by Blizzard

Colonel Brekhov

Series: Fifteen (1999)
Real Name: Ivan Nikolevich Brekhov
Place of Birth: Odesa, Ukraine
Gender: Male
Grade/Rank: O-6 (Army colonel equivalent)
SN: CLASSIFIED
Service Branch: Army (Soviet/Russian)
Faction(s): Oktober Guard
Notably Served At: Sierra Gordo
Primary MOS: Command and strategy
Secondary MOS: Infantry
Appearance: Light brown hair; light green jacket with rolled-up sleeves; light brown straps; light green pants; gray boots; always has a cigar
Accessories: AK-103, backpack (antenna is removable), belt of ammo (connects to the chain gun and backpack), chain gun (with two removable barrels), hat, knife
Abilities: Command; Commando; Infantry; Leadership; Oktober Guard Commander; Old war-horse; Strategy; Superb strategist; Tactical mind
Conditions: Belief: Women have no place on the battlefield (Diana notwithstanding); Fearless in battle; Genuinely cares about the welfare of the Soviet Union and its people; Hates Cobra; Military is his life; Quintessential Soviet soldier; No love for Americans; Not above setting aside political differences; Reputation: Distinguished commander; Smokes cigars
Quote/Motto: "Brekhov is what some would call

an 'old war-horse.' The military is his life and it's really all he knows. He's the quintessential Soviet soldier through and through and has no great love for Americans. But he hates Cobra even more. I can respect an attitude like that." Quote by General Hawk.

Notes: He was the original commander of the Oktober Guard; he was KIA in Sierra Gordo while attempting to save his friends and allies.

Colonel Courage

Series: Twelve (1993)
Alias/Variations: Coronel Coragem (Brazil)
Real Name: Cliff V. Mewett
Place of Birth: Boston, Massachusetts
Gender: Male
Grade/Rank: 8/O-6: Colonel (Retired); O-6—Colonel, Africa
SN: T67-981-243
Service Branch: Army
Faction(s): G.I. Joe, Battle Corps
Primary MOS: Administrative strategist
Secondary MOS: Patriot driver
Appearance: African American, black hair and short box beard; "Fritz" styled green helmet with colonel ensign on it; off-white shirt with rolled-up sleeves; neon green straps and belt; black holster; green legs and brown boots; officer accessory harness; J2J pineapple grenade; colt 45 Quickdraw pistol, G.I. Joe officer issue dress tie; armor-piercing assault gun; standard-issue 9-mm; standard issue officer machine gun
Accessories: Knife, laser, machete, machine gun, pistol, spring-loaded launcher
Abilities: Attention to detail; Bureaucracy; Dapper; Disciplined; Efficient work ethic; Intelligence; Knowledge Skill: Armor-piercing weapons; Knows how to push his subordinates; Knowledge Skill: Abilities of his subordinates; Leadership; Organizational skills; Qualified Expert Operator: Patriot; Qualified Weapons Expert: Machine gun; Strategic commander
Conditions: Jumps at the opportunity for combat duty; Strict about discipline; Strict about proper dress; Works to transform a "bad seed" into a "clean, mean, efficient fighting machine"; Works hard to instill dress and discipline in his subordinates
Quote/Motto: "I'll never surrender when wearing a tie 'cause I can't be beat when I'm neat!"
Notes: Shares the same name as Airwave

Cool Breeze

Real Name: Elijah F. Green
Gender: Male
Grade/Rank: Unknown
Service Branch: Army
Faction(s): G.I. Joe
Notably Served At: Emirate of Benzheen
Primary MOS: Reconnaissance specialist
Appearance: African American, clean-shaven; appears to wear round tinted spectacles and multi lenses optic headgear; In some panels, it appears he has two cybernetic arms.
Accessories: Radio jamming equipment
Abilities: Reconnaissance specialist
Conditions: Belief: He and the team cannot be beaten; Displays of hubris; Risk-taker; Selfless
Notes: He was KIA by a prisoner during a reconnaissance mission in the Emirate of Benzheen; he was given a hero's funeral at Arlington National Cemetery.

Countdown

Series: Eight (1989)
Real Name: David D. Dubosky
Place of Birth: Plainfield, New Jersey
Gender: Male
Grade/Rank: 6/O-3: Captain
SN: 111-8866-DD66
Service Branch: Air Force
Faction(s): G.I. Joe, Star Brigade
Notably Served At: Trucial Abysmia
Primary MOS: Astronaut/fighter pilot
Secondary MOS: Electronics engineer
Appearance: Black hair, dark eyes, olive skin; white spacesuit with green padding on sides of torso and legs; blue piping on chest and gloves; blue belt, holster, and kneepads; silver boots
Accessories: Full-head helmet with face shield, grappling hook, jet pack with rotating jets, machine pistol with a small magazine
Abilities: Electronics engineer; Multi-tasker; NASA astronaut; Physically tough; Qualified Expert Operator: Space shuttle *Defiant*; Qualified Operator: F-16 Fighter Pilot; Ranked chess master
Conditions: Reputation: Boring personality
Quote/Motto: "I don't care if he can take a five-gee turn without blacking out, and never get queasy in zero-gravity! I know that he can fly a fighter plane with burned-out instruments through extreme turbulence with one hand while repairing instruments with the other hand and simultaneously playing three

games of chess in his head! None of it makes him any less boring!" Quote by an unnamed G.I. Joe team member.

Cover Girl

Series: Two (1983)
Alias/Variations: Agent Courtney Krieger, Agente Secreta: Sparta (Brazil); Covergirl; Sparta (Argentina). Her prototype Code name was Hurricane Helga.
Real Name: Courtney A. Krieger; prototype name was Ariana Krieger
Place of Birth: Peoria, Illinois
Gender: Female
Grade/Rank: 2/E-6 Staff sergeant
SN: RA 973244860
Service Branch: Army
Faction(s): G.I. Joe
Stationed: Survival School at Fort Bragg; Western Hemisphere Institute for Security Cooperation; Governor's Island, Leumeria (underwater base)
Notably Served At: Patagonia; Castle Destro; London; Republic of Baranique; Warrenton, Ohio; the Pit*; Hohhot; Mount Cotopaxi in Ecuador
Primary MOS: Heavy armor driver (Wolverine driver)/special weapons expert
Secondary MOS: General special forces
Appearance: Long blonde hair, blue eyes, dresses in regular green military fatigues
Other Known Appearances (Cartoon): Cut hair shorter, orange/auburn coloring (resembling Scarlett's in style), brownish eyes, and a mostly beige uniform with a brown leather jacket. She also becomes distinctly more tomboy-ish.
Accessories: None
Abilities: Beautiful; Camouflage skills; Celebrity; Demolitions; Gifted athlete; Highly intelligent; Highly skilled combatant; Infiltration; Mechanical know-how; Professional Skill: Supermodel; Qualified Operator: Heavy machines, Ranger hummer, Wolverine; Sharpshooter; Wealthy
Conditions: Constantly hit on by other Joes; Dating Shipwreck; Disgusted and repulsed by Clutch; Docile personality; Driven to master distinctly unfeminine traits; Enjoys fighting; Fondness for operating heavy machinery; Has a crush on Duke; Loves blowing things up; Needs to prove she's not just a pretty face; Reputation: Former model; Reputation: Tank jockey; Seeks out challenges; Tomboy-ish (in the Marvel Comics Universe)
Quote/Motto: "A prime example of denial. She finds herself to be so beautiful that she must work against it. She is compelled to learn and master decidedly un-feminine disciplines, but in the end—the self-assurance this provides only makes her more alluring and compliments her already stunning good looks with a maddening charismatic attraction that reduces most men to stuttering fools." Quote given Colonel A. Goodwin, USMC.
Notes: *The Pit, Utah, Joe team's base, is located beneath the Chaplain's Assistant motor pool at Fort Wadsworth. There is another Joe with the code name Sparta, but she is not to be confused with Cover Girl.

Crankcase

Series: Four (1985)
Alias/Variations: Alternate code names were Fast-Lane and Roll-Bar
Real Name: Elwood G. Indiana
Place of Birth: Lawrence, Kansas
Gender: Male
Grade/Rank: E-4 Sergeant
SN: 451-61-5102
Service Branch: Army
Faction(s): G.I. Joe
Stationed: Ranger School and Desert Warfare School; Special Air Service Tactical Driving School
Notably Served At: Trucial Abysmia
Primary MOS: Motor Vehicle Driver
Secondary MOS: Armor
Appearance: Orange-red hair and "copstash" mustache; a green short-sleeved shirt with beige collar and brown backpack straps; black gloves; beige pants with brown belt and boots
Other Known Appearances (Comic): Brown gloves; Never spoke in the comics
Accessories: Helmet with flared brim; large assault rifle with open stock and oversized magazine
Abilities: Builds street machines; Motor vehicle driver expert; Qualified Operator: A.W.E. Striker; Qualified Weapon Expert: M-16, M1911A1, M-60, and TOW; Races street machines; Ranger vehicle driver
Conditions: Constantly ticked off; Not happy unless he's driving
Quote/Motto: "There are several ways to get from one place to another in Kansas and driving fast is most of them." "Ever get irritable when you're standing in a line that just doesn't seem to be moving at all? Well, the

whole [world] seems to be moving in slow motion to Crankcase—all the time! That's why he's constantly ticked off. He's just not happy unless he has a wheel in one hand, a shifter in the other, and the wind in his face." Quote by an unnamed G.I. Joe.

Notes: Crankcase died along with Doc, Thunder, and Heavy Metal while being held captive; it was due to an unfortunate misunderstanding of Cobra Commander's orders by bloodthirsty S.A.W. Viper, Robert "Overkill" Skelton. Doc is shot first; Crankcase, Thunder, and Heavy Metal are killed next.

Crazylegs

Series: Six (1987)
Alias/Variations: Alado (Argentina)
Real Name: David O. Thomas
Place of Birth: Fort Dodge, Iowa (Rouen, France for European distribution)
Gender: Male
Grade/Rank: E-4 Corporal
SN: 870-28-9277
Service Branch: Army Ranger
Faction(s): G.I. Joe, Night Force
Notably Served At: Trucial Abysmia
Primary MOS: Infantry/assault trooper
Secondary MOS: Parachute rigger
Appearance: Dark eyes; red helmet with black goggles; gray flight suit; red-scaled vest, shoulder guard, and stripes on the inside of legs; beige gloves; black boots
Accessories: EM 4 assault rifle with stock; parachute backpack
Abilities: Airborne Ranger; Forward artillery observer; Organist
Conditions: Hums Johann Sebastian Bach's music in combat; Reputation: Would have been the world's greatest pianist if his fingers weren't too short
Quote/Motto: "We can be storming a hardened position, right into the teeth of an enfilade-green tracer so thick in the air you can smell the magnesium, AP (Anti-Personnel) mines going off with intersecting cones of fire, bouncing Bettys ... the works! Crazylegs comes ducking and weaving through all this with a weird light in his eyes and humming a selection from Johann Sebastian Bach!" "The Airborne Rangers don't care how perfectly you can play Bach's *Toccata and Fugue in D Minor*, they're only concerned with your willingness to jump out of a helicopter into a hot LZ with nothing but a rifle, a couple of grenades, and the best wishes of your commanding officer." Quotes taken from transcripts of taped Peer Personality Profile review, given by fellow, unnamed G.I. Joe team members.

Notes: Crazylegs, Quick Kick, and Breaker died in a vehicle explosion while escaping in a stolen Cobra Rage tank in Trucial Abysmia. Cross Country, Duke, and Falcon managed to escape.

Cross Country

Series: Five (1986)
Alias/Variations: (Name): Prototype name was Rhine
Real Name: Robert M. Blais; prototype name was Arlen W. Slaughter
Place of Birth: Greensboro, North Carolina
Gender: Male
Grade/Rank: 3/E-7: Sergeant first class
SN: RA 555-38-6214
Service Branch: Army
Faction(s): G.I. Joe, Battle Corps, and Strike Team: Charlie
Primary MOS: Armor
Secondary MOS: Heavy equipment operator
Appearance: Brown hair, brown gloves; Confederate flag belt buckle, Confederate kepi cap with black goggles, dark gray pants with a brown belt; gray wristbands; light green vest with black diagonal strap; red pockets; white short-sleeved shirt; white wrap over brown boots
Other Known Appearances (Cartoon): Same, but with white cap and light brown vest; he sported a mustache in India
Accessories: Included with the H.A.V.O.C.
Abilities: Affinity for heavy machinery; Cool under fire; Qualified Expert Operator: H.A.V.O.C; Qualified Operator: H.A.V.O.C., LCV Recon Sled; Ranger Hummer; Qualified Weapon Expert: Heavy Laser Cannon, M-16A2, M-2 50 cal. MG, .45 Auto-Pistol; Sense the most favorable route; Sense of direction
Conditions: Distinctive Feature: Southern accent; Fearless; Loves country music
Quote/Motto: "Crank-Case might be a wild man behind the wheel of his A.W.E. Striker, but Cross Country will steer that H.A.V.O.C. of his across terrain that would break both axles of the RTV. Of course, a tracked vehicle has natural advantages, but it is Cross Country's talent for sensing the most favorable grade,

the shallowest mud, and the firmest sand that makes the difference." Quote by an unnamed G.I. Joe team member.

Notes: Crazylegs, Quick Kick, and Breaker died in a vehicle explosion while escaping in a stolen Cobra Rage tank in Trucial Abysmia. Cross Country, Duke, and Falcon managed to escape.

Cross Hair

Series: Nineteen (2003)
Real Name: Don G. Fardie
Place of Birth: Brockton, Massachusetts
Gender: Male
Grade/Rank: 0/E-4: E-4 (Army corporal) specialist
SN: 774-95-CD82
Service Branch: Army Ranger
Faction(s): G.I. Joe, Tiger Force
Primary MOS: Infantry
Secondary MOS: Marksmanship instructor
Appearance: Light brown hair; green paint-wiped shirt and pants; shades of brown trim; gray gloves and boots
Accessories: AK-S74U assault rifle; backpack, camo net, jungle hat, knife, M-16/203, pistol, sniper rifle with large scope and curved stock attached to grip, waist belt with an attached knife; web vest
Abilities: Camouflage; Heightened perception; Knowledge Skill: Targets, studies intensely; Knowledge Skill: Teammates; Professional Skill: Sniper
Conditions: Always blends into the background; Always studying his teammates
Quote/Motto: "When I'm in full under-cover mode you can forget about the needle in the haystack; I become just another piece of straw in the haystack." "I didn't miss. Is it my fault he was wearing body armor?"

Crossfire

Series: Seventeen (2001)
Real Name: Bill White
Place of Birth: Long Island, New York
Gender: Male
Grade/Rank: 3/E-7: Sergeant first class
SN: None given
Service Branch: Army
Faction(s): G.I. Joe
Primary MOS: Heavy weapons operator
Secondary MOS: Demolitions
Appearance: Light brown hair, black eyes; green-grey shirt, camo green pants, twin brown bandoliers, tan boots
Accessories: Rifle
Abilities: Assemble/disassemble small weaponry in the dark; Demolitions expert: Heavy weapons expert; Knowledge Skill: Heavy weapon ordinance; Machine gunner
Conditions: Always keeps his temper in check; Overly interested in how machines work; Persistent
Notes: He was personally trained from a young age by a sergeant major at Fort Bragg. Crossfire is not to be confused with the vehicle of the same name driven by Rumbler.

Curtis Letson

Real Name: Curtis Letson
Gender: Male
Faction(s): G.I. Joe, Greenshirt
Notably Served At: New Moon, Colorado
Notes: KIA in New Moon, Colorado, when fellow Greenshirt Thomas Stall broke cover calling attention to their location.

Cutter

Series: Three (1984)
Alias/Variations: Cuchilla ("Knife" Spain); Cruiser, Drydock, Hurricane, Speed-boat
Real Name: Skip A. Stone
Place of Birth: Kinsley, Kansas (Auckland, New Zealand for European distribution)
Gender: Male
Grade/Rank: 8/O-5: Commander—Naval Operations CO or O-4-Lieutenant Commander (LCDR)—Naval Operations XO; O-2 Lieutenant, junior grade, sources conflict
SN: RA403540688
Service Branch: Coast Guard
Faction(s): G.I. Joe, Battle Corps, and Drug Elimination Force
Stationed: Naval Amphibious Base Coronado, California
Primary MOS: Hovercraft captain
Secondary MOS: Special services: Annapolis women's swimming team coach
Appearance: Red hair and mustache (eyebrows and mustache matching the hair or darker); blue baseball cap with red "B"; a light blue short-sleeved shirt with open collar; orange life jacket; dark blue bell-bottom pants; green belt, holster, and watch; black shoes
Other Known Appearances (Cartoon): Same, but with brown gloves; The figure came with many different shades of facial hair.
Accessories: Included in the Killer W.H.A.L.E. hovercraft. Electronic battle-flash grappling

hook launcher; flashlight (attached to his leg), grappling hook, string, submachine gun, tripod for the grappling hook launcher
Abilities: Expert in intercepting drug-runners in coastal waters; Knowledge Skill: Coastal waters ways; Qualified Expert Operator: Barracuda, Killer W.H.A.L.E. hovercraft; Skipper of a high-speed drug interceptor craft
Conditions: Badgers until he gets what he wants; Cocky smart-aleck; Continually on the nerves of his teammates; Contrary nature; Distinctive Feature: Wears a Boston Red Sox ball cap; Distinctive Feature: Slightly exaggerated Bostonian accent (on the Sunbow cartoon); Loves to take down drug dealers; Tactlessly shoots off his mouth; Truly bizarre sense of humor; Wants a life at sea; Willpower
Quote/Motto: "Nothing makes my day like taking down a big dealer. Seeing the look on his face when he realizes the high times are over and it's off to the Federal Pen for the rest of his miserable life! What a satisfying feeling!"
Notes: In the comics, Cutter was one of the fatalities in Storm Shadow's attack on the USS *Flagg*. He was impaled in the upper chest, denying Storm Shadow his sword. Cutter was the first Coast Guard member of the G.I. Joe team.

D-Day

Series: Fourteen (1995)
Real Name: David X. Brewi
Gender: Male
Grade/Rank: E-5
Service Branch: U.S. Army
Faction(s): G.I. Joe, Savage Eagles
Abilities: Boxer; Highly trained; Heavy Weapons specialists
Conditions: Reputation: Former Golden Gloves champion; Undisciplined

Daemon

Real Name: Jeff Lacefield
Place of Birth: Cincinnati, Ohio
Gender: Male
Grade/Rank: Special agent
Service Branch: Army
Faction(s): G.I. Joe
Notably Served At: Cobra Island
Appearance: Blond hair, blue eyes, slender build
Abilities: Develops computer viruses; Follower: Firewall; Master computer programmer; Nano-mite technology; Knowledge Skill: Comic books, science fiction, and video games; Trained soldier
Conditions: Banters with Firewall as they work; Immature; Inability to take a joke; Inherent awkwardness; Relentlessly bullied as a child for being small
Notes: Daemon is killed when his neck is snapped by Serpentor during a battle with The Coil. His name was added to the memorial dedicated to the fallen members of the G.I. Joes at Arlington National Cemetery.

Daina

Series: Twenty-One (2005)
Alias/Variations: Dinah; Diana; Oktober Guard One, Volga (1995), Vorona (1988)
Real Name: Diana L. Janack
Place of Birth: Prague, Czechoslovakia
Gender: Female
Grade/Rank: O-1 (equivalent) Lieutenant
Service Branch: Army (Czechoslovakia/Czech Republic)
Faction(s): G.I. Joe
Notably Served At: Afghanistan; Iran
Primary MOS: Marksman
Secondary MOS: Helicopter pilot
Appearance: Blonde hair, blue eyes, exceptionally beautiful
Accessories: Drum grenade launcher, knife, rifle, submachine gun
Abilities: Brilliant tactician (second only to Brekhov); Can pilot any vehicle in the Soviet arsenal; Cool under fire; Expert marksman; Exceptionally skilled with all Warsaw Pact Weapons; Intelligent; Knowledge Skill: Fixed-wing pilot; Multitude of talents; Qualified Operator: Fixed-wing vehicles; Small arms specialist; Sniper; Weapons expert
Preferred Weapon: Snaiperskaya Vintovka Dragunova (Dragonuv sniper rifle)
Conditions: Beautiful; Compelled to do twice as much; Driven to extremes; Easy to underestimate; Has to prove her worth repeatedly; Target for chauvinistic insults; Patient; Reputation: Chronic bad temper; Rough edge; Trademark hat
Quote/Motto: "You want charm, go somewhere else. I'm here to fight, and to win." "I'm never sure what to make of her. I've never liked the idea of women in combat in the first place. If it had been up to me, Volga would fly us to the mission and then leave. But how do you tell someone not to fight who's so good at it?" Taken from Colonel Brekhov's files.

Dart

Series: Eighteen (2002)
Real Name: Jimmy Tall Elk
Place of Birth: White Earth Indian Reservation, Minnesota
Gender: Male
Grade/Rank: 2/E-6: Staff Sergeant
SN: 146-23-EK09
Service Branch: Army
Faction(s): G.I. Joe
Primary MOS: Recon
Secondary MOS: Infantry/refrigeration repair technician
Appearance: Black pants; brown belt, leg straps, and boots; golden eagle medallion
Accessories: Backpack, camo net, knife, pistol machine gun
Abilities: Combat Infantryman's badge; Covert reconnaissance; Lore Skill: Knowledge handed down from his grandfather, father, and uncles; Professional Skill: Hunting guide; Qualified to wear both Airborne wings and Ranger tabs; Hobby Skill: Woodcraft
Conditions: Personal grudge against Cobra CLAWS (the elite COBRA troopers)
Quote/Motto: "Nothing mystical or psychic about what I do. I just know what to look for and I have a lot of patience."

Dee-Jay

Series: Eight (1989)
Alias/Variations: Abutre Negro, Corrosao (Brazil)
Real Name: Thomas R. Rossi III
Place of Birth: Providence, Rhode Island
Gender: Male
Grade/Rank: Sp-4 (Army specialist 4)
SN: 553-0935-GA56, 553-0935-RT56 (sources conflict)
Service Branch: Army
Faction(s): G.I. Joe, Arctic Attack Force, and Battleforce 2000
Stationed: Frusenland
Notably Served At: The Battle of Benzheen
Primary MOS: Radio telephone operator
Secondary MOS: Infantry
Appearance: African American; white helmet with goggles and a red bar on the forehead; an olive-green shirt with white armor vest and gloves; blue pants with silver codpiece, white boots, and dark gray leggings and holster
Accessories: Short antenna with tip attaching to the helmet; tall tech backpack; futuristic laser rifle with severely angled trigger guard; hose with hose caps attaching to helmet and shoulder
Abilities: Communications expert; Communications repair expert; Professional Skill: Disc jockey
Conditions: Chatterbox; Popular DJ in Boston; Reputation: Hottest disc jockey in Boston
Quote/Motto: "Simulated ground-wave transmitters and ultra-fast burst encoders are complicated pieces of electronic hardware. If you're pinned down and need a medivac extraction or old-fashioned air support, you're just whistling in the wind if your radio is down for the count. His teammates can count on Dee-Jay to get the message out, even if he has to rebuild a transmitter from parts. Once he's on the air, it's his chatter that they can do without." Quote by an unnamed G.I. Joe team member.
Notes: He was killed in the Battle of Benzheen, with massive amounts of shrapnel taken to the lower chest area.

Deep Six

Series: Three (1984)
Alias/Variations: Deep-Six
Real Name: Malcolm R. Willoughby
Place of Birth: Baltimore, Maryland (Cork, Eire, Ireland for European distribution)
Gender: Male
Grade/Rank: 3/E-7: Chief petty officer; Navy petty officer 2nd class (master diver's rating)
SN: RA226960917
Service Branch: Navy
Faction(s): G.I. Joe, Eco Warriors
Notably Served At: Battle in the Gulf of Mexico; coast of Algeria
Primary MOS: Diver (master diver's rating)
Secondary MOS: Small craft pilot/motorized
Appearance: Red hair, light or dark eyebrows; clear dome helmet; large gray diving suit with yellow trim and dark gray shoulders, gloves, knee joints, and shoes
Other Known Appearances (Cartoon): Hair lighter than on the figure, sandier brown than red; grill on left chest is usually not colored
Accessories: Included with the S.H.A.R.C. flying submarine; Large air pump bellows with a clear hose attached to a peg in the figure's back

Abilities: Animal Companion: dolphin named Finback; Can hold his breath for an incredible length of time; Navy diver; Qualified Operator: S.H.A.R.C.
Conditions: Aloof, solitary; Hobby Skill: Bottle cap collector; Hobby Skill: *New York Times* crossword puzzles; Loner; Recluse; Soft-spoken
Quote/Motto: "Down in the depths where light doesn't reach, and the water pressure can crush you like an eggshell—that's where Deep Six likes it!" Quote by fellow G.I. Joe team member Torpedo.

Depth Charge

Series: Nineteen (2003)
Real Name: Nick H. Langdon
Place of Birth: Pittsburgh, Pennsylvania
Gender: Male
Grade/Rank: 1/E-5: Petty officer first class
SN: 975-23-BD29
Service Branch: Navy Seal
Faction(s): G.I. Joe
Stationed: Naval Amphibious Base Coronado, California
Primary MOS: UDT
Secondary MOS: Bandsman (glockenspiel)
Appearance: Blond hair, brown eyes; blue bodysuit with white piping
Accessories: Breathing apparatus, flippers, goggles, helmet, and spear gun
Abilities: Reputation: Best scores in the history of the UDT Program; SEAL; Specializes in clearing mines and other devices in the water; Underwater demolitions expert
Conditions: Hates the water; Loves his job
Quote/Motto: "Want to know why I am so enthusiastic about running up on the beach and clearing Cobra off of it? Because if Cobra wasn't there, I wouldn't have to jump into the water, to begin with!"

Desert Patrol Squad

Purpose: "A special G.I. Joe Desert Patrol Squad heads into the desert to conduct routine training exercises geared for this harsh environment. They expect plenty of heat, sand, and scorpions, what they don't expect is to find a large force of Cobra Venom Troopers, who immediately attack them! There's no time for practice as a real, all-out battle between the heroic G.I. Joe team and the evil Cobra enemy explodes."
Members: Ambush, Dusty, Gung Ho, Scarlett, Stalker, Snake Eyes, Switch Gears, Tunnel Rat

Desert Wolf

Series: Three (1984), 8" Commando scale, twenty-three (2007)
Real Name: Lance M. Langdon
Gender: Male
Service Branch: U.S. Army Ranger
Faction(s): G.I. Joe, Sigma 6
Notably Served At: World War III
Primary MOS: Ranger
Secondary MOS: Reconnaissance
Appearance: African American, short-sleeved golden body armor, black boots, and gloves
Accessories: Ammo belt, grenade launcher, helmet, large dog tag, long-distance barrel rifle, small dog tag, two grenades, two-part weapons case with handles and latches
Abilities: Ranger; Reconnaissance specialists; Wilderness Survival: Desert
Notes: Desert Wolf is currently a reserve member of the Sigma 6 team assigned to domestic operations in the United States. *All reservists can be called back into action if a mission calls for it.

Dial Tone

Series: Five (1986)
Alias/Variations: Dialtone, Dial-Tone, Kiestoon (Holland), Transistor (Belgium); prototype names were Hot-Line and Squelch
Real Name: Jack S. Morelli
Place of Birth: Eugene, Oregon (Milan, Italy for European distribution)
Gender: Male
Grade/Rank: Sergeant, E-4 (Army corporal) 1986; E-6: Master sergeant 2002
SN: 428-7133-BA60; 428-713-BA60; 858-9142-92KH; 858-91-KH92RA 428-71-3360
Service Branch: Army
Faction(s): G.I. Joe, Battle Corps, Sonic Fighters, Sound Attack, Special Mission: Brazil (1986), and Tiger Force
Primary MOS: Radio telecommunications
Secondary MOS: Infantry
Appearance: Black beret; black gloves and pants, brown belt, brown hair and mustache; green boots, green kneepads, green vest with black straps; a pale beige shirt with open collar
Other Known Appearances (Cartoon): Bright yellow shirt; green pants with black boots and kneepads. The 1986 Special Mission: Brazil Toys "R" Us exclusive box play set had black beret, black collared shirt, black gloves, brown vest, green boots, green knee pads, red pants, tan belt, twin green bandoliers. The set

also included Claymore, Leatherneck, Mainframe, and Wet Suit. The 1990 Sonic Fighter action figure had black belt, black beret; black boots, black gloves, black kneepads, black vest with silver straps, blue pants, brown hair and mustache, gray shirt with open collar. 1994 Battle Corps wore a black belt, black boots, black knee pad on left knee, blue helmet, blue short-sleeved shirt, green suspenders, neon yellow abdominal pad, olive drab pants, neon yellow goggles. The 2000 figure wore a forest green beret and camos with black boots and combat webbing with silver (or brown) grenades on his chest. The 2002 B.J.'s exclusive Sound Attack boxed set wore forest green beret and camos, gray boots, gray combat webbing with grenades, gray kneepads, and gray gloves. The box set also included the A.W.E. Striker, Fast Blast Viper, Firefly, Roadblock, Snake Eyes, Storm Shadow, Undertow, and Wet-Suit. The 2003 Tiger Force figure wore a black bandolier, black beret, black gloves, olive-drab pants, royal blue long sleeved shirt, silver belt, tiger striped vest, tiger stripped boots, and tiger stripped kneepads.

Accessories: Anti-scrambler communications backpack; 9-mm Parabellum submachine gun pistol with short stock and slots on the muzzle (or a HK53 compact assault rifle with silencer and long grip, sources conflict). 1986 "Special Mission: Brazil" included a light gray anti scramble communication pack with (barely) removable mouthpiece and a 9-mm Parabellum submachine gun with silencer. The 1990 Sonic Fighter action figure came with a black flamethrower, black grenade launcher and chamber, black laser pistol, black sonic backpack with radar dish, and a black submachine gun. 1994 Battle Corps action figure came with a blue high-tech helmet with attached mic and neon yellow visor, neon yellow figure stand, neon yellow knife, neon yellow machine gun, neon yellow pistol, neon yellow rifle, silver gun-shaped spring missile launcher with long grip and neon yellow trigger, and two neon yellow spring missiles. The 2000 figure came with a black backpack, black figure stand, black submachine gun and stock, and black walkie-talkie. The 2002 B.J.'s exclusive Sound Attack boxed set came with a black backpack, silver bandolier, silver rifle, and a silver RPG (with Sound Attack tab). 2003 Tiger Force came with a black backpack and black rifle.

Background Information: "…built his own crystal set (a rudimentary radio) when he was 10 … had his own ham station by the time he was 16 … making all his equipment, buying parts with quarters earned bagging groceries."

Abilities: Build communication equipment; Communications expert; Knowledge Skill: Fixed ground station communications; Knowledge Skill: Mobile station communications; Knowledge Skill: Space stations communications; Knowledge Skill: Temporary field stations communications; Owns a ham station; Part of a CB network; Qualified Expert Operator: Conquest, Devilfish, Falcon Glider, H.A.V.O.C., Killer W.H.A.L.E., and LCV Recon Sled

Conditions: Danger Hound; Distinctive Feature: Northern accent; Reputation: Engineering prodigy; Seeks the adrenaline rush; Techno-nerd

Quote/Motto: "One of the scariest things that can happen to you out in the field is to lose contact with your base. That means you are ALONE. No artillery support, no airstrikes, no medevac, no extraction, no NOTHING! The cavalry ain't comin' until the man with the radio tells 'em to."

Notes: According to the video game *G.I. Joe: The Rise of Cobra* he is the sibling of Jill S. Morelli, Dial Tone 2.

Dial Tone 2

Series: Twenty-Five (2009)
Real Name: Jill S. Morelli
Place of Birth: Eugene, Oregon
Gender: Female
Grade/Rank: E-4 Specialist
SN: 428-71-JM33
Service Branch: Marine
Faction(s): G.I. Joe
Stationed: The Pit*, the USS *Flagg*
Primary MOS: Telecommunications
Appearance: Beige and brown desert camo, brown kneepads, knee-high black boots, short brown hair and blue eyes
Other Known Appearances (Cartoon): Blue eyes, black heels, light brown hair, tan military blouse and skirt. In the IDW comics, her hair is blonder, and she wears glasses to read.
Accessories: Black display stand, black rifle, and a silver laptop
Background Information: Originally just one of the "*fobbits*" staffing The Pit, her

telecommunications skills have made her an invaluable member of the fighting force. Her data file states that she took over her brother's post on the team after he disappeared on a mission.

Abilities: Counter electronic attacks; Counter electronic sabotage; Knowledge Skill: Latest technology; Combat communication specialist

Conditions: Distinctive Feature: An 820 selective-fire long-range fully automatic assault rifle; Reputation: Works well with Scarlett; Young up-and-coming marine

Quote/Motto: "They gave me several [code names] to choose from, and I chose Dial Tone because it amused me."

Notes: To date, no background information has been revealed about this character. No mention has been made of the Jack S. Morelli character in this series. *The Pit, Utah, Joe team's base, is located beneath the Chaplain's Assistant motor pool at Fort Wadsworth. According to the video game *G.I. Joe: The Rise of Cobra* she is the sibling of Jack S. Morelli, Dial Tone.

Digger

Real Name: Percy R. Trench
Place of Birth: Exmouth, Western Australia
Gender: Male
Grade/Rank: 6/O-1: 2nd lieutenant
SN: 026-3425-RG9
Service Branch: Australian Army Corps; Army
Faction(s): G.I. Joe International Ops Team
Primary MOS: Ophiology; desert reconnaissance
Appearance: Australian accent; blond hair, thick blond mustache; uniform appearance
Accessories: Knapsack, piston, rifle
Abilities: Determination; Guts; Intelligence gathering; Wilderness Survival: Desert
Conditions: Rival: Major Bludd; Uses Australian slang
Quote/Motto: "Bein' a Joe isn't always Vegemite on toast. Ya neva know when Cobra gunna strike next."

Dino Hunters

Series: Twelve (1993)
Purpose: "Dinosaurs have been unearthed from deep inside Cobra Island and the evil organization was going to turn them loose on the world. It is up to these Joes to capture the creatures and save them from the hands of Cobra."
Leader: None stated, default to rank
Members: Ambush (camouflage specialist) and Low Light (dinosaur night spotter)
Quote/Motto: "Trying to capture a dinosaur is like trying to wrestle a whale in a fish tank!" "Ambush." "I predict a successful mission … so long as the dinosaurs aren't hungry!" Quote by Low Light.
Notes: The team utilized their own vehicle: All-Terrain Dinosaur Reconnaissance Vehicle. They utilize a "dino-stun" tranquilizer gun with a scope.

Doc

Series: Two (1983)
Alias/Variations: S.O.S. (Argentina)
Real Name: Carl W. Greer
Place of Birth: Concord, Massachusetts (Kingston, Jamaica for European distribution)
Gender: Male
Grade/Rank: E-4 Specialist on prototype dossier; O-3 Captain
SN: RA367221097
Service Branch: Army
Faction(s): G.I. Joe
Notably Served At: Trucial Abysmia
Primary MOS: Medical doctor
Secondary MOS: Chaplain's assistant
Appearance: African American. Green sunglasses, a beige open-collared shirt with rolled-up sleeves and a red cross on the right shoulder; beige pants with a red belt and brown shoes; white undershirt
Other Known Appearances (Cartoon): The belt is usually brown instead of red, and without white pouches; often seen without a helmet
Accessories: Flare launcher with a sling to mark landing zones, helmet with molded flares on sides, stretcher
Background Information: Harvard Medical School graduate with a residency at John Hopkins
Abilities: Airborne, Mountaineering, and Desert training; Medical doctor; Qualified Operator: Killer W.H.A.L.E., Sky Hawk, TROC's mirror trucks
Preferred Weapon: 820 selective-fire long-range fully automatic assault rifle
Conditions: Avowed pacifist
Quote/Motto: "The G.I. Joe team is the best we have. We send them into the worst situations imaginable because that's where we need them most. When the going gets rough, they need something more than a pill roller. I'm

their main man!" A note posted anonymously as a disclaimer to Doc's Peer Personality Profile: "Why would an avowed pacifist with a medical degree want to join the army and serve in the field with its most elite combat team? See excerpt below from subject's initial enlistment review [for explanation]." The excerpt reads: "When I read about the G.I. Joe team, I said to myself, these fine young men and women are the best we have. And we send them into the worst situations imaginable because that's where we need them. When the going gets rough, they're going to need someone more than a pin-roller. And I think I'm the man for the job."

Notes: Doc died along with Crankcase, Thunder, and Heavy Metal while being held captive; it was due to an unfortunate misunderstanding of Cobra Commander's orders, by bloodthirsty S.A.W. Viper, Robert "Overkill" Skelton. Doc is shot first; Crankcase, Thunder, and Heavy Metal are killed next.

The Doc

Series: Twenty-six (2010)
Real Name: Sven Inglesen
Place of Birth: Tronsk, Norway
Gender: Male
SN: AF 396047
Faction(s): G.I. Joe, Z Force
Primary MOS: Field combat medicine
Secondary MOS: Arctic survival
Accessories: Mortar or flare launcher (depending on issue) and first aid kit
Background Information: Studied medicine in Vienna
Abilities: Hobby Skill: Trapper; Language Skill: Speaks five (unspecified) languages fluently; Medic; Runs five miles a day
Conditions: Compassionate; Oldest member of Z Force (45 years old); Tough

Doc 2

Series: Thirty-Two (2016)
Real Name: Carla P. Greer
Place of Birth: Concord, Massachusetts
Gender: Female
Grade/Rank: O/3-Army
Service Branch: Army
Faction(s): G.I. Joe
Primary MOS: Medical doctor
Secondary MOS: Chaplain's assistant
Appearance: Black leather boots, brown webbing and belts to hold her gear, khaki jacket with medical insignia in a variety of locations, khaki trousers, white holster for her tranquilizer gun
Accessories: First aid kit, tranquilizer gun
Abilities: Highly intelligent; Knowledge Skill: High tech equipment; Medical doctor; Qualified weapons expert: Modern firearms; Raw gumption! Self-defense martial arts; Standard military training
Conditions: Courageous; Lives in awe of Doc's reputation; Reputation: Niece of the original Doc; Pacifist

Dr. Adele Burkhart

Gender: Female
Occupation: Primary: Nuclear physics; Secondary: Humanitarian
Faction(s): G.I. Joe
Appearance: Blonde hair
Abilities: Brilliant nuclear physicist; Political activist
Conditions: Completely uncompromising; Critical stance on the military; Deep sense for humanity; Distrust of the military; On a mission to promote education for women; Periodically kidnapped by Cobra; Principled; Rejects all violence; Reputation: One of the world's top nuclear physicists; Self-sacrificing; Staunch anti-military pacifist; Strongly opinionated; Weepy ingrate

Dodger

Series: Six (1987)
Real Name: Richard Renwick
Place of Birth: South Bend, Indiana
Gender: Male
Grade/Rank: 3/E-7: Sergeant first class
SN: 439-67-9256
Service Branch: Army
Faction(s): G.I. Joe, Battleforce 2000, Sonic Force
Stationed: Frusenland
Notably Served At: The Battle of Benzheen
Primary MOS: Communications
Secondary MOS: None listed
Appearance: Green helmet with gray chinstrap; an orange sleeveless shirt with green pockets and gray straps; green half-gloves; green pants with gray urban (t-shaped) camo; green boots with gray kneepads. Sonic Fighter Uniform: blue-green helmet with chinstrap; a blue-green sleeveless shirt with red pockets and gold straps; brown half-gloves; olive

green pants with brown boots and gray knee-pads

Accessories: Large mic attaching to the helmet; ultra-sonic photon rifle with a spiked guard on rear grip, handle and scope on top Sonic Fighter Equipment: Large sonic backpack with a detachable antenna, laser rifle, photon rifle, submachine gun

Abilities: Cook; Electronics; Guts and instinct!; Laser demolitions; Maintenance expert; Qualified Operator: Armored vehicle operation, Hi-tech battle cycle; Marauder driver; Qualified Weapons: General purpose laser weapon, Laser pistol, Marauder; M-A2 S.A.W. 5.56-mm machine gun, 9-mm Beretta auto pistol

Conditions: Fascination with the latest in armored fighting technology; Relies on guts and instinct; Techno-nerd

Quote/Motto: "This guy was driving tracked vehicles before they had any of these fancy new gadgets. If he has to, he unbuttons the hatch, sticks his face out the window, and drives by instinct and guts. Sure, he's an expert with all the new equipment, but who knows if it's all going to work when the chips are down? Dodger isn't dependent on them and that makes him someone you can count on." Quote by an unnamed G.I. Joe team member.

Notes: He served as the cook for the Battleforce 2000 team; he is the only surviving member. After the war, he was moved and assigned to another Joe team, the Sonic Fighters.

Dogfight

Series: Eight (1989)
Real Name: James R. King
Place of Birth: Providence, Rhode Island
Gender: Male
Grade/Rank: O-2 (Air Force first lieutenant)
SN: 882-0041-RT87
Service Branch: Air Force
Faction(s): G.I. Joe
Notably Served At: Benzheen
Primary MOS: Mudfighter Pilot
Secondary MOS: Electronics Technician
Appearance: Red hair and mustache; brown cap with silver wing pin; silver sunglasses and headphones; white shirt; brown open jacket with a silver circle on chest; dark blue pants with a black belt, holster
Accessories: Long pistol with scope
Abilities: Powerful throwing arm; Precise hand-eye coordination; Qualified Expert Operator: Mudfighter; Uncanny depth perception
Conditions: Permanently banned from every carnival and fair in the state of Alabama
Quote/Motto: "The Cobras hear the Mudfighter first. That big-bladed un-ducted fan makes a racket like a giant mutant lawnmower. Chances are good that Dogfight will be diving out of the sun with his thumb dancing a fandango on his bomb release trigger with all the Mudfighter's guns blazing. By that time, it's far too late for evasive action or return fire!" Quote by an unnamed G.I. Joe team member.

Dojo

Series: Eleven (1992)
Alias/Variations: The Talkative One
Real Name: Michael P. Russo
Place of Birth: San Francisco, California
Gender: Male
Grade/Rank: 4/E-8: Master sergeant
SN: 761-3893-MF04
Service Branch: Army
Faction(s): G.I. Joe, Ninja Force
Stationed: Arashikage Martial Arts Academy, San Francisco, California
Primary MOS: Silent weapons ninja
Secondary MOS: Kung-fu instructor
Appearance: Tanned skin; bald with a black ponytail, Fu Manchu mustache, goatee; blue and yellow boots; a blue shirt with yellow straps, half-gloves, reinforced titanium wrist guards; sash on waist; steel-encased shin protectors; tear gas smoke grenades on the belt; throwing stars; white pants; yellow goggles
Accessories: Sickle, sword with a long hilt and angled tip
Abilities: Hand-to-hand combat instruction; Martial arts; Qualified Operator: Brawler; Weapons Master: Chain and sickle, three-section staff, sai, and throwing dirk; Secret combat techniques; Silent weapons expert
Conditions: Immutable integrity; Prefers to drive the "Brawler"; Reputation: Once the secret pupil of a ninja master in hiding (Soft Master); Reputation: Uses "Patter" to distract his opponents; The most talkative of the Ninja Force Fighters; Unbeatable skills
Notes: Recruited by Storm Shadow.

Dolphin

Series: Twenty-Six (2010)
Alias/Variations: Lt. Dolphin

Real Name: Gareth Morgan
Place of Birth: Cardiff, Wales
Gender: Male
Grade/Rank: O-1 (Equivalent)
SN: AF 934332
Service Branch: Navy (British)
Faction(s): Special Action Force, Q Force (Commander)
Primary MOS: Submarine commander/underwater solo attack
Secondary MOS: Deep sea exploration
Appearance: Short black hair, black eyes
Accessories: Sealion; helmet, kayak, kayak arm, kayak counterweight, knife, machine gun mounted on the kayak, paddle, rifle with bipod
Abilities: Cartography; Command; Commander of a Royal Navy sub; De facto expert of the waterways of Europe; Excellent Knowledge Skill: all Action Force underwater weapons; Expert in deep-sea exploration; Hobby Skill: Boating; Instruction; Knowledge Skill: Polar ice caps; Leadership; Tough as nails; Underwater operations expert; Welshman
Conditions: Welshman; Young
Quote/Motto: "Want to take on Q Force boys? Go blow some bubbles!"
Notes: Q Force Commander; Action Force (alternate continuity)

Double Blast

Series: Seventeen (2001)
Real Name: Charles L. Griffith
Place of Birth: Dayton, Ohio
Gender: Male
Grade/Rank: 4/E-8: Master sergeant
SN: 215-9885-LC38
Service Branch: Army
Faction(s): G.I. Joe
Primary MOS: Heavy machine gunner
Secondary MOS: Electrical engineering
Appearance: African American; bald with black mustache and goatee; light and dark green camouflage vest with black belt and straps; bare arms; green gloves and holster; rust-orange pants; black boots
Accessories: Backpack with attached ammo box; helmet (no holes); M-2 and tripod
Abilities: Field strip and reassemble a weapon in less than 60 seconds in the dark; Can fix anything with whatever!; Jack of all trades; Knowledge Skill: Handheld weapons; Qualified Weapons: Heavy machine gunner
Conditions: Relies on the element of surprise in attack strategy; Rookie, Young kid straight from the Marines
Quote/Motto: "I'll pour on the firepower until the enemy retreats!"
Notes: Often confused with Road Block because the name, birthplace, MOS, and personal background are identical

Double Clutch

Series: Nineteen (2003)
Alias/Variations: Clutch
Real Name: Lance J. Steinberg
Place of Birth: Asbury Park, New Jersey
Gender: Male
Grade/Rank: E-4 (Marine sergeant)
SN: 757-34-LJ82
Service Branch: Marine
Faction(s): G.I. Joe
Primary MOS: Transportation
Secondary MOS: Infantry
Appearance: Brown hair and beard; dark green cap and short-sleeved shirt; silver vest; dark green pants; black gloves, belt, and boots
Abilities: Advanced infantry training; Covert ops; Executive bodyguard; Hobby Skill: Racing street machines; Knowledge Skill: High-tech devices for vehicles; Mechanic; Qualified Expert Operator: Coyote vehicle; Qualified Operator: Any ground vehicle; Ranger
Quote/Motto: "Aside from knowing how to operate all the high-tech devices on these vehicles, it takes a real driver to be able to wheel into the hot spots and out again, while the enemy is still trying to shift into second gear."
Notes: Double Clutch was originally called Clutch.

Downtown

Series: Eight (1989)
Real Name: Thomas P. Riley
Place of Birth: Cleveland, Ohio (Luton, Bedfordshire, England, for European distribution)
Gender: Male
Grade/Rank: 0/E-4: Advisor/Probationary Member/Specialist
SN: 131-78-0476, 131-7804-RT76, and 131-7831-RT76, three versions
Service Branch: Army Ranger
Faction(s): G.I. Joe
Notably Served At: Cobra Island
Primary MOS: Infantry
Secondary MOS: Special operations
Appearance: Yellow hair; a blue-green shirt

with black pockets, orange straps, and green padding on the stomach; light brown pants with a black belt, brown boots, and orange shin guards

Accessories: Soft helmet; large backpack with pouches on sides and slots on the back for shells; large revolver with trigger guard; large three-piece mortar (tube, sight, and stand); six mortar shells with grooves and fins near back

Abilities: Judges range and trajectory by eyesight; Professional Skill: Basketball Player; Reputation: Never misses a foul shot

Conditions: Sometimes hand color matches face, other times it's yellow

Quote/Motto: "If Downtown sets up his mortar in the parking lot of a ballpark, and had a spotter sitting in the bleachers, he could put a round on the second base bag within two attempts! Downtown picked up his name playing high school basketball. He didn't have the height for slam dunks, but he had a reputation for never missing a foul shot!" Quote by an unnamed G.I. Joe team member.

Dragonsky

Series: Twenty-One (2005)
Real Name: Andrei Freisov
Place of Birth: Moscow, Russia
Gender: Male
Grade/Rank: Starshina ("Master Sergeant"); E-8 (equivalent)
Service Branch: Army (Soviet/Russian)
Faction(s): Oktober Guard
Primary MOS: Infantry/special weapons (flamethrower)
Secondary MOS: Mechanical engineer
Appearance: Short orange/blond hair or bald; purple head covering; gray camo shirt with purple padded vest and black gloves; gray camo pants with black belt and boots
Accessories: Backpack; cutting torch with red flame; helmet
Background Information: Joined the Soviet Army at a young age and had a long and successful military career. He was trained by a brilliant commander who went insane and became General Mayhem.
Abilities: Experienced!; Infantry; Incendiary weapons expert; Intuition!; Knowledge Skill: Fire control; Knowledge Skill: Flamethrower; Knowledge Skill: Latest in military pyro-technology; Knowledge Skill: the Military; Mechanical engineer; Qualified Operator: Armored vehicles; Qualified Weapon Expert: Flamethrower; Qualified Weapon: Latest military pyro-technology; Special weaponry expert
Conditions: Always ready to protect his comrades; Belief: The odds don't matter! Dedicated; Distinctive Feature: Wears a special flame-retardant suit; Honored to be a member of the Oktober Guard; Loyal; One of the oldest members of the Oktober Guard; Personal Nemesis: General Mayhem
Quote/Motto: "Even in Siberia, I make sure things get really hot!" "Whenever the enemy tries to make the situation hot for me, I make it ten times hotter for them."
Notes: The Oktober Guard is the Russian/Warsaw Pact Equivalent of the G.I. Joe Team. His greatest honor came with the invitation to join the elite Oktober Guard.

Drop Zone

Series: Nine (1990)
Real Name: Samuel C. Delisi
Place of Birth: Poteau, Oklahoma
Gender: Male
Grade/Rank: 4/E-8: Master Sergeant
SN: 675-4109-SG54
Service Branch: Army
Faction(s): G.I. Joe, Sky Patrol
Primary MOS: Sky Patrol weapons specialist
Secondary MOS: Special forces advisor
Appearance: Black hair; dark orange suit with a gray vest and brown wristbands and leg coverings; brown belt; brown and gray boots
Accessories: Full-head helmet with detachable visor; handheld, double-barreled cannon with shoulder harness; parachute in parachute pack.
Abilities: Paratrooper; Weapons specialist
Conditions: Belief: Duty and honor have meaning; Loves his job; Patriotic; Relishes the smell of gun oil and nitro solvent; Volunteers for every hazardous assignment
Quote/Motto: "Just because he volunteers for every hazardous assignment doesn't qualify him for a special commendation. This guy is fully aware of all the cruel realities that accompany a battle. His main concern is to successfully complete the mission to the best of his ability. Drop Zone is a true G.I. Joe dogface. He believes that duty and honor still have meaning in today's complex society and that Cobra is lower than pond scum!" Quote by an unnamed G.I. Joe team member.

Drug Elimination Force

Series: Eleven (1992)
Alias/Variations: DEF
Purpose: "This is a team of law enforcement specialists dedicated to stopping Headhunter and his ambitious drug cartel." "Drug-Fighting G.I. Joes battle Headman and his gang of drug thugs for control of 'Main Street U.S.A.!'" "Each drug enforcement agent and villain utilize a Battle-Flash weapon to elevate this conflict to new heights of danger!"
Leader: Bullet-Proof
Members: Cutter, Mutt and Junkyard, and Shockwave

Duke

Series: Two (1983), three (1984)
Alias/Variations: Original name was Carl Hauser
Real Name: Conrad S. Hauser
Place of Birth: St. Louis, Missouri
Gender: Male
Grade/Rank: Master sergeant in 1983 mail-in exclusive; first sergeant E-8 (1984); 9/E-9: command sergeant major; field commander and second-in-command of the G.I. Joe
SN: RA213757793
Service Branch: Army
Faction(s): G.I. Joe, Anti-Venom Task Force, Battle Corps, Heavy Assault Squad, Star Brigade, Strike Team: Alpha (Leader), and Tiger Force (Leader)
Stationed: Airborne School, Fort Benning; U.S. Army Special Language School; the Pit*,
Notably Served At: South Vietnam, Springfield, Trucial Abysmia
Primary MOS: Airborne infantryman
Secondary MOS: Artillery, small-arms armorer
Appearance: Yellow hair; a beige shirt with rolled-up sleeves; gold eagle on right chest; green diagonal strap; green belt and pants; brown boots
Other Known Appearances (Cartoon/Comic/Movie): Blond hair and blue eyes. Belts and chest straps brown, meeting in the back in the manner seen on the Cobra figure; slightly brighter pants, and usually black boots. Rarely wore his helmet. Some of the 1984 series 3 figures had cuffed sleeves, similar to series 2 Stalker. Cuffed sleeve variant is more difficult to find.
Accessories: (1983) American flag sticker, assault pack, binoculars, helmet, M-32 Submachine gun. (1984) Assault pack, binoculars, helmet (variant with or without holes on the side), M-32 submachine gun
Background Information: Original file card said he came from a bilingual home and was fluent in both French and German. He enlisted in the Army at the age of 18 in 1960 and graduated from Special Language school. He went into Special Forces in 1963 and did his first tour in the Republic of Vietnam working with and training the Montagnard to fight the Viet Cong. His 1984 prototype dossier read: "Current grade: Major O-4. Battlefield Commission in 1967. Captured by the NVA [North Vietnamese Army] in 1969. Escaped six months later. Ran special ops school at Langley [did not specify if it was the Air Force base or the CIA Headquarters]. Advisory Commission on Special Warfare. Chairman, Combined Anti-Terrorist neutralization unit."
Abilities: Black ops; Command; Language Skill: English, French, German, Han Chinese, and Southeast Asian dialects; Qualified Operator: Armadillo, A.W.E. Striker, Conquest, Dragonfly, H.A.V.O.C., JUMP, Mauler, RAM, Silver Mirage, SHARC prototype, Sky Hawk, SkyStriker, Snow Cat, the H.I.S.S., Viper Glider, Water Moccasin; Special forces
Conditions: Belief: A commander's place is with his troops; Command; Distinctive Feature: Scar on his right cheek; Hard-charging man of action; Personality does not fit with the role of a master sergeant; Romantically paired with Scarlett
Quote/Motto: "They tell me that an officer's job is to impel others to take the risks—so that the officer survives to take the blame in the event of total catastrophe. With all due respect, sir … if that's what an officer does, I don't want any part of it." This statement was in Duke's personnel file after declining a commission.
Notes: Crazylegs, Quick Kick, and Breaker died in a vehicle explosion while escaping in a stolen Cobra Rage tank in Trucial Abysmia. Cross Country, Duke, and Falcon managed to escape. *The Pit, Utah, G.I. Joe base located beneath the Chaplain's Assistant motor pool at Fort Wadsworth

Dusty

Series: Four (1985)
Real Name: Ronald W. Tadur
Place of Birth: Las Vegas, Nevada (Alice Springs, Australia for European distribution)

Gender: Male
Grade/Rank: 1/E-5: Sergeant
SN: 371-11-4605
Service Branch: Army
Faction(s): G.I. Joe, Desert Patrol Squad, and Tiger Force
Stationed: Basic training at Fort Bliss, Texas
Notably Served At: Invasion of Benzheen
Primary MOS: Desert trooper
Secondary MOS: Refrigeration and air-conditioning maintenance
Appearance: Chocolate-chip (desert) camouflage BDU (battle dress uniform) and hooded desert headgear; wears a light-yellow shirt and light-yellow pants with brown splotches and a light-yellow beret
Accessories: Backpack, bipod, FAMAS assault rifle
Abilities: Animal companion: Sandstorm; Desert trooper; Excellent tracker; Instruction; Knowledge Skill: Desert ecology; Language Skill: Arabic, Hebrew, Kazakh, and the Oirat-Khalkha languages of Central Asia; Leadership; Professional Skill: Air conditioning and refrigeration repair; Qualified Operator: Night Rhino, Sand Razor; Qualified Weapons Expert: M-14, M-16, M-16A2, M-60, M-1911A1 Auto Pistol, M-203 40-mm Grenade Launcher; Stealth
Conditions: Deep friendship with Sneak-Peek; Reputation: Patient
Quote/Motto: "Dusty loves the desert. It is clean, pure, and unforgiving. Unlike Vegas which is always willing to give you a second chance." Quote by an unnamed G.I. Joe team member.
Notes: Once, he was falsely accused of treason. This was the first member of G.I. Joe to be environmentally suited for a specific environment. Dusty's surname is a nod to the artist who developed the design for all the G.I. Joe action figures from 1982 to 1987, Ronald Rudat.

Dynamite

Series: Fourteen (1995)
Real Name: Hector J. Garrido
Place of Birth: Argentina, 1922
Gender: Male
Grade/Rank: E-5
Service Branch: U.S. Army
Faction(s): G.I. Joe, Savage Eagles
Abilities: Chemist, Demolitions expert; Highly trained
Conditions: Love for explosives; Undisciplined

Eco-Warriors

Alias/Variations: E-Force; EF
Purpose: "An emergency unit assembled to prevent Cobra forces from bringing down civilization through environmental damage." "Cobra has unleashed a crushing blow to the earth, dumping tons of hazardous toxic sludge into the environment in their quest for world domination. G.I. Joe and Cobra are armed with all-new, sophisticated water-launching armaments with exciting color-change Eco-suits! Even now the future of the earth hangs in the balance!" From the toy catalog.
Leader: Flint
Members: Barbecue, Clean-Sweep, Deep-Six and Finback, Ozone
Vehicles: Eco-Striker (1992, based on A.W.E. Striker)

Effects

Series: Thirteen (1994)
Real Name: Aaron Beck
Place of Birth: Fort Worth, Texas
Gender: Male
Grade/Rank: 2/E-6: Staff sergeant
Service Branch: Army
Faction(s): G.I. Joe, Star Brigade
Stationed: Space Station Delta
Primary MOS: Explosives/munitions ordnance
Secondary MOS: Special effects coordinator
Appearance: Yellow hair, dark eyes; light blue jacket with black collar; blue pants with black belt and boots
Accessories: Full-head space helmet with face shield; machine gun; three-piece catapult with a rubber band and two globe "flame" projectiles
Abilities: Creates explosives with mesmerizing special effects

Escorpiao Voador ("Flying Scorpion")

Series: Pre 1986
Gender: Male
Faction(s): G.I. Joe, Patrulha Do Ar ("Sky Patrol")
Appearance: Dark-skinned with short black hair
Accessories: Backpack, handgun, helmet, parachute, rifle

Evac

Real Name: Jason Morera

Gender: Male
Grade/Rank: 5/O-2: 1st Lieutenant
Service Branch: Air Force
Faction(s): G.I. Joe, Strike Team: Bravo
Stationed: Pit on Staten Island
Notably Served At: Afghanistan; Canada; Quintesson Invasion
Primary MOS: Parajumper
Secondary MOS: Medic
Background Information: Washed out of the SEAL training program, transferred to the Air Force
Abilities: Associate degree in Survival and Rescue; Bachelor of Science Degree in Emergency Medical Services; Extensive medical training; Field medic; Hobby Skill: Guitar; National Registry of Emergency Medical Technicians-Paramedic (NREMT-P) certification; Parajumper; Soldier
Conditions: Dedicated medic and soldier; Distinctive Feature: Carries several small arms; Fascinated with medicine; Laid back; Love of music; Will defend wounded with force if necessary; Will fight his way to a downed soldier
Quote/Motto: "That others may live."
Notes: He is a character from the Transformers Universe, MUX

Faces

Series: Nineteen (2003)
Real Name: Michelino J. Paolino
Place of Birth: Parma, Ohio
Gender: Male
Grade/Rank: 1/E-5: Sergeant
SN: 783-78-MJ41
Service Branch: Army
Faction(s): G.I. Joe
Primary MOS: Intelligence
Secondary MOS: Language instructor
Appearance: Dark hair, mustache, and beard; white T-shirt, brown leather jacket, jeans, black boots
Accessories: Bag, two guns, a Crimson Guard Commander mask, a Doctor Mindbender mask, and a strap
Abilities: Acting; Advanced makeup and disguise techniques; Creates prostheses; Espionage; Infiltration; Makeup artist; Mimicry; Sculpts masks
Conditions: Jokes and teases with brutally accurate impression; Impersonates his superiors; Uses skills to gain extra shore leave
Quote/Motto: "I'm only successful if I'm undetected. Even if I do get caught out, I can remain undercover as long as I best the Cobra who caught me to the draw—and that's a given."
Notes: Sent to a top-secret intelligence school to learn the tricks of cloak and dagger

Falcon

Series: Six (1987)
Alias/Variations: Lieutenant Falcon, after 1988
Real Name: Vincent R. Falcone
Place of Birth: Fayetteville, North Carolina (Glastonbury, Somerset, England, for European distribution)
Gender: Male
Grade/Rank: 6/O-3: Captain (Special Forces commander)
SN: 035-38-2264
Service Branch: Army; Green Beret
Faction(s): G.I. Joe, Night Force, Sonic Fighters, and 5th SFGA "Blue Light" counter-terrorist unit
Notably Served At: 5th Special Forces Group Airborne "Blue Light" counter-terrorist unit; Benzheen; Badhikistan; Cobra Island; Cobra-La; Trucial Abysmia
Primary MOS: Infantry
Secondary MOS: Medic
Appearance: Green beret; brown hair; olive green and black camouflage short-sleeved shirt and pants; green neckerchief; light green backpack straps and belt; olive green and black boots
Other Known Appearances (Cartoon): Black hair; brown chest straps and belt; brown instead of black on camo. In the 1987 G.I. Joe: The Movie by Sunbow, Falcon was voiced by actor Don Johnson; it was revealed in the movie that he is the half-brother to Duke. In the movie, he is portrayed as being irresponsible, the opposite of what was written on his file card.
Accessories: 12-gauge pump action shotgun with long grip and stock; Bowie survival knife, Special Forces communication pack (with engraved rope and two canteens) with detachable antenna and clips on the side for a knife
Background Information: Second generation Green Beret; his father "served in the 10th Special Forces Group Airborne from its beginnings at Fort Bragg's Smoke Bomb Hill."
Abilities: Demolitions; Green Beret; Language Skill: Spanish, French, Arabic, and Swahili; Heightened perception; Mentally Agile; Physically Tough; Professional Skill: Military

consultant for various Hollywood productions; Qualified Weapons Expert: NATO and Warsaw Pact small arms; Winning personality

Conditions: Budding relationship with Jinx; Cocky; Disregard for military security; Does not follow protocol; Faces challenges head-on; Half-brother of Duke; Irresponsible misfit redeemed through Sgt. Slaughter's training; Reckless; Reputation: Exemplifies the Green Berets; Second-generation Green Beret; Succumbs to drugs

Quote/Motto: "Green Berets are specialists in training and leading native insurgents. Native insurgents are usually primitive tribal peoples who respond to two types of leadership. You can bully and overwhelm them with superior firepower and technology … or you can bite the head off a snake, chug-a-lug the local beverage, and yell, 'Follow me!' Falcon is a snake-biter if I ever saw one." Quote by an unnamed G.I. Joe team member.

Notes: Crazylegs, Quick Kick, and Breaker died in a vehicle explosion while escaping in a stolen Cobra Rage tank in Trucial Abysmia. Cross Country, Duke, and Falcon managed to escape. In the comics, it is heavily implied he is the son of Hawk.

Fast Draw

Series: Six (1987)
Alias/Variations: Prototype name was Backfire
Real Name: Eliot Brown
Place of Birth: Collierville, Tennessee (Bracknell, Berkshire, England, for European distribution)
Gender: Male
Grade/Rank: 0/E-4 Corporal specialist
SN: 667-01-0350
Service Branch: Army Ranger
Faction(s): G.I. Joe, Rapid Deployment Force, and Battleforce 2000 (only in Brazil)
Primary MOS: Ordnance/mobile missile specialist
Secondary MOS: Clerk typist
Appearance: Red helmet with green chinstrap; green shirt and pants; gray padded vest, leggings, and boots; blue backpack straps and belt; red gloves and kneepads
Accessories: Face shield with visor and voice-activated link-up; segmented air tube; missile launcher backpack with hole for air tube; two gun-shaped activators; two short-finned missiles; two hoses

Abilities: Qualified Weapons Expert: FAFNIR missile system; Qualified Weapons Expert: Mobile missile; Teams well with Repeater and Shockwave; Unshakable

Conditions: Arrogant; "Come-and-get-it!" mindset; Thinks himself an Old West gunslinger

Quote/Motto: "Fast Draw thinks of himself as an old-west gunfighter. A whole squadron of Cobra Stuns could be rumbling across the landscape at him and he just stands there with a missile rack in each hand and that 'Come-and-Get-it' look in his eyes. You might call him arrogant but at least he has the firepower to back him up." Quote by an unnamed G.I. Joe team member.

Notes: The FAFNIR [Fire and Forget Non-tube-launched Infantry Rocket] missile system target acquisition and homing devices are all self-contained in the missile itself, allowing the operator to take cover immediately after launch. Target lock-on displays are projected on the interior of the helmet faceplate as well as threat and malfunction warnings. The missile is extremely fast and resistant to ECM jamming. Fast Draw was named after Marvel Comics artist Eliot Brown.

Feedback

Alias/Variations: One
Gender: Female
Grade/Rank: Recruit
Faction(s): G.I. Joe, Greenshirt
Appearance: Green bodysuit, light gray padded armor, oval black goggles, large helmet
Notes: Recruits are usually given joke nicknames until they earn their Joe code name.

Felino

Series: Thirty-one (2015)
Alias/Variations: "The Terror of the Amazon," Tigre Da Selva ("Tiger of the Forest"), The Feline
Real Name: Joao Kayapo
Place of Birth: Altamira, Brazil
Gender: Male
Grade/Rank: 0/E-4: Petty officer third class, specialist
Service Branch: Navy
Faction(s): G.I. Joe, Comandos Em Acao ("Commandos in Action"), and Tiger Force
Stationed: Escolar Naval ("Navy School")
Notably Served At: Brazil
Primary MOS: Riverine patrol boat operator

Secondary MOS: Counter-piracy operations
Appearance: Jungle camo
Accessories: Backpack, bazooka, goggles, harness, helmet, rifle with removable bipod, RPG
Abilities: Knowledge Skill: Cobra customs and traditions; Qualified Operator: Riverine patrol boat; Qualified Operator: Tiger Shark
Conditions: Endless enthusiasm; Hates Cobra
Quote/Motto: "If you only get one shot, use a rocket launcher."
Notes: Brazilian release only

Firewall

Real Name: Michelle LaChance
Place of Birth: Virginia Beach, Virginia
Gender: Female
Grade/Rank: Special agent
Service Branch: Army
Faction(s): G.I. Joe, not a field operative
Stationed: Las Vegas
Primary MOS: Computer technology
Appearance: Black hair kept in ponytails; light tan leather jacket, jeans
Abilities: Knack for computers; Knowledge Skill: Computer systems; Knowledge Skill: Military computers; Professional Skill: CLASSIFIED; Professional Skill: Hacking government systems; Received basic military training
Conditions: Friends with Daemon; Hates uncaring braggarts; Immature acting when working with Daemon; Justifies using skills to ruin an enemy's life; Served time in a Federal Prison; Watched by Mainframe
Notes: She is under Flint's command, a member of one of his special units.

Flagg (1)

Series: Eleven (1992)
Real Name: Lawrence J. Flagg
Place of Birth: Philadelphia, Pennsylvania
Gender: Male
Grade/Rank: Brigadier general
SN: RA 818-50-1673
Service Branch: Army
Faction(s): G.I. Joe
Primary MOS: Infantry commander
Secondary MOS: Field artillery
Appearance: Carries excess weight; physically resembles General Aaron "Iron Butt" Austin
Background Information: He was responsible for creating Special Counter-Terrorist Group Delta, code-named G.I. Joe, in response to rising terrorist threats, especially the evil Cobra Command organization. He was the first commander of the G.I. Joe team but often spent time in an administrative role.
Abilities: "Bag of dirty tricks!"; Bureaucracy; Captain of army pistol team; Knowledge Skill: General Austin; Knowledge Skill: His personnel; Knowledge Skill: Right person for the job; Leadership (in advisory capacity); Logistics; Military operations; Qualified Weapons Expert: Pistols; Works closely with General Austin
Conditions: Carries excess weight; Hard-working man; Honorable; Martyr; Physically resembles General Austin; Never arrogant; Protective of children; Reputation: His "bag of dirty tricks" is legendary; Trusts Hawk; Relies on the advice of Sparks; Under no delusions about his abilities; Won't risk innocent or civilian lives
Quote/Motto: "Don't just take the high ground, take it all!"
Notes: He was killed by Major Bludd during Cobra's first attack on Joe headquarters, the Pit. The aircraft carrier the USS *Flagg* was named in his honor. The *Flagg* became the main naval vessel used by the G.I. Joe team. General Flagg is buried in Arlington Cemetery.

Flagg (3)

Series: Thirty-three (2017)
Alias/Variations: General Flagg
Real Name: James Longstreet Flagg III
Place of Birth: Alexandria, Virginia
Gender: Male
Grade/Rank: O-7 (Army brigadier general)
SN: 212-9820-GU95
Service Branch: Army
Faction(s): G.I. Joe, Battle Corps (Leader)
Primary MOS: Chief strategic commander
Secondary MOS: General commander
Appearance: Brown hair; brown jacket with yellow collar and cuffs; black belt and gloves; light green pants with black boots
Other Known Appearances: The original G.I. Joe commander in the comic series
Accessories: Large bomb with fins and slot for catapult; officer's cap with an eagle on front; rifle with a grenade launcher, ribbed grip, long magazine, and short scope; rubber band for catapult, three-piece light bomb catapult (base, arm, and black switch)
Background Information: He's the son of the original G.I. Joe Commanding General (after whom the USS *Flagg* aircraft carrier was

named). General Flagg is a graduate of the Virginia Military Institute, as were the five preceding generations of Flaggs; he won the Medal of Valor and countless decorations.
Abilities: Contacts: Virginia Military Institute Graduates; Reputation: Son of the original G.I. Joe Commanding General; Tenacious; Wards off machinations of administrators who'd interfere with G.I. Joe operations
Conditions: Carries devastating personal weapons; Likes to be in the thick of it
Quote/Motto: "I didn't reach the rank of General by standing in the shadows. I got out and earned it on the front lines."

Flash

Series: One (1982)
Real Name: Anthony S. Gambello
Place of Birth: Lodi, California (Birmingham, Somerset, England, for European distribution)
Gender: Male
Grade/Rank: 1/E-5: Sergeant
SN: RA607432985
Service Branch: Army
Faction(s): G.I. Joe, Strike Team: Bravo
Stationed: Electronics School, Chemical School, Covert Electronics; Aberdeen Proving Ground
Notably Served At: Cobra Island, Springfield; Easter Island; K-12
Primary MOS: Infantry laser rifle trooper
Secondary MOS: Electronics, CBR
Appearance: Brown hair, olive drab shirt with a silver red-padded vest; brown gloves; dark green belt and red-padded pants over brown boots
Other Known Appearances (Cartoon/Comic): Flash's chest padding was divided into six rectangular segments without the silver frame. He always wore his visor, which was tinted blue.
Accessories: Clear visor; helmet; XMLR-1A laser rifle with cord; powerpack with hole for cord (1982–83)
Abilities: CBR (Chemical, Biological, and Radiological) expert; Chemical schooling; Contacts: Autobots; Covert electronics; Friends with Breaker; Electronics expert; Highly educated; Highly skilled in electronic technology; Knowledge Skill: Covert electronics; Knowledge Skill: Operating, maintaining, and supervising the use of nuclear, biological, and chemical detection and decontamination equipment; Master's Degree in electronic engineering; Qualified Weapons Expert: M-16; M-1911A1; XMLR-1A (shoulder-fired laser rifle); Repair equipment in the field; Specialized Education: Electronics
Conditions: Innate and unshakable faith in the order of the universe; Methodical, Persistent
Quote/Motto: "Flash is methodical and persistent. Has an innate and unshakable faith in the order of the universe. He's working on his master's degree in electronic engineering (nights)."
Notes: Flash was KIA during the second invasion of Cobra Island; his name was added to a G.I. Joe memorial at Arlington National Cemetery. His last words were "Mission Accomplished." The 1982 Flash was produced straight-armed. The "XM" in his laser rifle stands for "eXperimental Model."

Flint

Series: Four (1985)
Alias/Variations: David Faireborn, his UK Action Force (alternate continuity) "real name." His intended surname was to be Fairbairn, as in the Fairbairn-Sykes Commando Knife.
Real Name: Dashiell R. Faireborn (–1988); Dashiell R. Faireborne (1991–)
Place of Birth: Wichita, Kansas (Lincoln, Lincolnshire, England, for European distribution)
Gender: Male
Grade/Rank: E-6 Staff sergeant; WO-1: Chief warrant officer
SN: 307-62-4107
Service Branch: Army green beret
Faction(s): G.I. Joe, Battle Corps, Eco-Warriors, and Tiger Force
Stationed: Airborne School, Ranger School, Special Forces School, Flight Warrant Officers School
Notably Served At: Dozens of blackout missions
Primary MOS: Infantry
Secondary MOS: Helicopter pilot
Appearance: Black beret with a red emblem; black hair; black shirt with green ammo belts; green and brown camo pants with brown belts and gloves; green and black boots
Other Known Appearances (Cartoon): Dark green shirt with reddish-brown straps; camo on pants consisted of wavy stripes of dark green and reddish-brown. In the cartoon version of Flint, he was down-to-earth and level-headed.

Accessories: Backpack with angled canteen and dynamite engraved on back; riot shotgun

Background Information: A former Rhodes Scholar pursuing a postgraduate degree in English literature at Oxford University in England, he became bored with the "groves of Academe."

Abilities: Airborne, Ranger, and Special Forces training; Command; Concentration; English Literature; Green Beret; Has the goods to back up his attitude!; Qualified Operator: Helicopters; Rhodes Scholar; Rugged; Tactical planner; Tactician

Conditions: Arrogant; Brave; Brutal; Charismatic; Cocky; Distinctive Feature: Black beret; Distinctive Feature: Lop-sided grin; Ego sometimes gets in the way of his relationship with Lady Jaye; Facial scars due to his aggressive approach in battle; Refuses to be intimidated; Romantically paired with Lady Jaye; Self-confident; Steadfast; Tenacious

Quote/Motto: "We had thought COBRA had us in the stinking dungeon for good—so we didn't know what was going down when we heard that chopper comin' in and all the heavy hardware going off like the Fourth of July. Then somebody kicked down the door to our cell and when the smoke cleared, there was Flint with that lop-sided grin sayin' 'C'mon boys, we're going home.'" Quote by an unnamed G.I. Joe team member.

Notes: Recruited by Duke; he is third in command. He has a daughter named Marissa Faireborn. He had written a book about his experiences in G.I. Joe; his marriage to Lady Jaye mellowed him out. After her death, he becomes a sullen and brooding man who rarely speaks (when he does, it is to suggest maximum force against any size threat) and trains to become a better warrior at the cost of his humanity.

Footloose

Series: Four (1985)
Alias/Variations: Prototype names were Action, Bravo, and Grunt
Real Name: Andrew D. Meyers
Place of Birth: Gary, Indiana (Dundee, City of Bantor, Scotland for European distribution)
Gender: Male
Grade/Rank: 1/E-5: Sergeant
SN: 039-44-9036
Service Branch: Army Ranger
Faction(s): G.I. Joe, Slaughter's Marauders
Stationed: Basic and AIT at Fort Benning
Primary MOS: Infantry
Secondary MOS: Special services (basketball coach)
Appearance: Brown hair and mustache; open-collar, short-sleeved, green and brown camo shirt and pants; light green backpack straps and belt; dark gray and green boots
Other Known Appearances (Cartoon): Black hair; light brownish-gray camo on the darker green outfit; light beige straps and backpack
Accessories: Backpack (with engraved canteen and grenade), wider on the bottom than on top; M-16 with sling; M73-A1 LAW missile launcher with sling
Background Information: Valedictorian of his high school class, captain of the track team, and Eagle scout
Abilities: All-American boy; Camouflage; Desert training; Infantry trooper; Jump school; Qualified Operator: Armadillo, A.W.E. Striker, JUMP, LCV Recon Sled, Mauler, Sky Hawk, Snow Cat, Cobra Stinger, cargo planes, motorcycles; Qualified Weapons Expert: All NATO and Warsaw Pact small arms; Qualified Weapons: Heavy Artillery
Conditions: Dropped out of society for three years after high school
Quote/Motto: "Some of the Joes think Footloose is out there, but all he's trying to do is find himself. He's an All-American Boy who got lost on the way to the fair and he's simply trying to go home any which way he can. Most folks think they know who they are and where they're going.... They're the dangerous ones!" Quote by an unnamed G.I. Joe team member.
Notes: His dossier for his inspiration for joining the army: "He was standing on the boardwalk in Venice [Beach, California], pondering something cosmic when the utter pointlessness of his existence hit him between the eyes like a runaway freight train. 'I think I'll join the Army,' he said and promptly did."

Fox Hunt

Purpose: "Fox Hunt was a reconnaissance and Black Ops kill squad. Meant to be the first line of defense against the enemies of the United States. Each member of the unit was to be one member of an individual field in the United States Marine Corps.: a Sniper, A Demolitions Specialist, a Scout, a Heavy Weapons Specialist, and a Captain, who could be

whichever role he chose, but needed powerful leadership skills. They were most prominent in Afghanistan, where they eliminated multiple HVTs that were terrorist ring leaders."
Leader: None stated, default to rank
Members: Pulled as needed by assignment

Freefall

Series: Nine (1990)
Alias/Variations: Free Fall, Jumpmaster, Spc. Altitude
Real Name: Philip W. Arndt
Place of Birth: Downers Grove, Illinois
Gender: Male
Grade/Rank: Sergeant (E-5); 6/O-1: 2nd lieutenant
SN: 664-2781-BS10
Service Branch: Army Ranger
Faction(s): G.I. Joe
Stationed: Ranger Indoctrination course; Airborne Ranger school
Primary MOS: Paratrooper
Secondary MOS: Infantry
Appearance: Yellow hair; orange flight suit with green camouflage; dark gray straps on chest, arms, and legs; dark gray gloves and boots
Accessories: Air mask with a peg for hose, goggled helmet, pouch backpack with gas canisters on sides, standard hose, submachine gun with short stock and long magazine and forward grip
Abilities: Determination; High and far jumps; Eastern Philosophy expert; Paratrooper; Ranger; Runs fast; Unparalleled technical skill
Conditions: Boundless energy; Determined; Highly motivated; Honest to a fault; Large ego
Quote/Motto: "Here is a trooper who exemplifies the very best we can produce. Someone who is highly motivated and possesses an unparalleled degree of technical skill and boundless fonts of energy and determination. He can run faster, jump higher, and do more push-ups than any soldier who has ever survived Ranger School. He has a master's degree in Eastern Philosophy and is honest to a fault. His only problem is that his ego is about as big as the Grand Canyon!" Quote by an unnamed G.I. Joe team member.

Freestyle

Series: Twenty-nine (2013)
Real Name: Jocelyn De La Vega
Place of Birth: Bronx, New York
Gender: Female
Grade/Rank: 6/O-3: Captain
SN: 134-10-1109
Service Branch: Air Force
Faction(s): G.I. Joe, Night Force
Stationed: Advanced flight training
Primary MOS: Fixed-wing pilot
Secondary MOS: Intelligence operations
Appearance: Short black hair; fighter pilot uniform
Accessories: Pistol, submachine gun, two helmets, web gear
Background Information: First generation immigrant from the Dominican Republic, daughter of a New York City cab driver
Abilities: Cooking expert; Qualified Expert Operator: Fighter jets; Quick reflexes
Conditions: Eclectic love of music; Hotshot fighter pilot; Reckless and fearless flying techniques
Quote/Motto: "Freestyle is known for her reckless and fearless flying techniques. Lucky for us, these unique skills are crucial to giving Night Force control of both the air and ground. On those rare occasions during off-hours when she lets her guard down, she shares her exceptional cooking abilities and eclectic love of music with the unit." Taken from the files of Falcon.

Freight

Series: Fourteen (1995)
Real Name: Omar K. Diesel
Gender: Male
SN: 66TYHDR2
Service Branch: Army
Faction(s): G.I. Joe, Team Extreme
Primary MOS: Cutting-edge demolitions expert
Appearance: African American, a bulky giant of a man; red bandana for a helmet; green pants, green boots with black straps, gray chest armor, cross bandoliers
Accessories: Glove, knife, mace
Abilities: Demolitions expert; Professional Skill: Football player; Hand-to-hand combat; Head-butts
Conditions: Over-the-top aggressive; Throws his weight around

The Fridge

Series: Six (1986)
Alias/Variations: William "The Refrigerator" Perry

Real Name: William Perry
Place of Birth: Aiken, South Carolina
Gender: Male
Grade/Rank: 1/E-5: Sergeant
SN: None
Service Branch: Army
Faction(s): G.I. Joe
Primary MOS: Physical training instructor
Secondary MOS: Special services
Appearance: African American; black hair and mustache; gap in teeth; sleeveless blue football shirt with white "72" on front; red, white, and blue wristbands; green pants with a brown belt, red pockets, and white boots with gray kneepads; white Super Bowl ring
Accessories: A football attached to a chain
Background Information: A member of the NFL's 1985 Chicago Bears Super Bowl–winning football team
Abilities: Physical training instructor; Professional Skill: Defensive Lineman for the Chicago Bears; Strategy
Conditions: Major character flaw: Celebrity; Distinctive Feature: Gap in front teeth, Super Bowl ring on his finger; More bulk than skill
Quote/Motto: "If lacrosse is the little brother of war, football must be the rich uncle. Note the similarities: Strategy (offensive and defensive), teamwork, violence, camaraderie, television coverage, parades for the victors, and humiliation for the defeated. Using the Fridge to train the Joes is logical and practical. Besides, the Fridge likes to see the looks on their faces when they look up from the mud and see who they have to get past—to pass the course!" Quote by an unnamed G.I. Joe team member.
Notes: This was a mail-in exclusive through Hasbro. Buyers needed to collect the correct number of coupons (Combat Pay dollars) included in vehicle packages. The buyer needed to call a number and obtain a special code (PTI, Physical Training Instructor), which needed to be written on the coupon to be redeemed.

Frostbite

Series: Four (1985)
Alias/Variations: Prototype names were Iceberg and Thin-Ice
Real Name: Farley S. Seward
Place of Birth: Galena, Alaska
Gender: Male
Grade/Rank: 1/E-5: Sergeant
SN: 215-58-9136
Service Branch: Army
Faction(s): G.I. Joe, Battle Corps, Tiger Force, and Winter Operations
Stationed: Transportation school at Fort Eustis; Armored school at Fort Knox; Fort Greely Cold Regions Test Center
Notably Served At: Alaska's Bering Strait; Russia
Primary MOS: Arctic special operations commander/Snow Cat driver
Secondary MOS: Vehicle specialist
Appearance: Brown hair and beard; large black goggles; white hood; green snow jacket over blue shirt; white snow pants; brown belt; black gloves and boots
Accessories: Included with the Snow Cat; rifle
Abilities: Professional Skill: Lineman on the pipeline; Qualified Expert Operator: All forms of transportation; Qualified Operator: Snow Cat; Qualified Operator: Tiger Cat; Qualified Weapons Expert: M-16, M-1911A1, M-2 50-caliber machine gun, M-60 7.62-mm machine gun
Conditions: Distinctive Feature: Big grin; Distinctive Feature: Steely eyes; Grudge against the Neo-Viper troops for harming Arctic lands; Lives for the promise of endless challenges; Prefers frigid conditions
Quote/Motto: "The cold north teaches you to always keep your cool, whether you're facing a wall of ice or a wall of Cobra troops." "Frostbite was born in a place where summer is a myth and a crowd consists of two people standing in the same acre." Quote by an unnamed G.I. Joe team member.

Gaucho

Series: Twenty-Six (2010)
Alias/Variations: Chico Gonzalles
Real Name: Rico Gonzalles
Place of Birth: Mexico City, Mexico (the *Distrito Federal*, Mexico for European distribution)
Gender: Male
Grade/Rank: OR 6 Sergeant
SN: AF 395452
Service Branch: Army (Mexico)
Faction(s): G.I. Joe, Z Force
Primary MOS: Mechanic
Secondary MOS: Combat engineer
Appearance: Thick, black handlebar mustache; black cap, red T-shirt, green army shirt, cross bandoliers
Accessories: Backpack, grenade launcher, machete

Abilities: Bodybuilder; Brilliant mechanic; Military training; Professional Skill: Circus strongman; Reputation: Strongest soldier in Action Force (alternate continuity); Seldom needs power tools
Conditions: Boasts he can fix anything; Frequently works out
Quote/Motto: "Hey, hombre, I can fix anything."

Gears
Series: Thirteen (1994)
Real Name: Joseph A. Morrone
Place of Birth: Westerly, Rhode Island
Gender: Male
Grade/Rank: 6/O-3: Captain
SN: None
Service Branch: Air Force
Faction(s): G.I. Joe, Star Brigade
Primary MOS: Chief engineer (special projects)
Secondary MOS: Research and Development
Appearance: Black hair, blue body armor with silver padded joints
Accessories: Helmet
Abilities: Inductee in the National Inventors Hall of Fame; Invention technician; Technological genius
Conditions: On Cobra's top-10 hit list
Notes: Responsible for the innovations integrating human muscles and brain waves with Robotic Battle Armor and computer circuitry creating Robo-J.O.E.

General Austin
Alias/Variations: Iron Butt
Real Name: Aaron B. Austin
Place of Birth: CLASSIFIED
Gender: Male
Grade/Rank: 9/O-8 Major General
SN: CLASSIFIED
Service Branch: Army, (retired advisor)
Faction(s): G.I. Joe
Stationed: Pentagon, Washington, D.C.
Notably Served At: CLASSIFIED
Primary MOS: G.I. Joe Commander
Secondary MOS: Anti-terrorist operations
Appearance: Red-brown hair, pencil mustache; traditional green general uniform
Abilities: Sees viewpoints from all sides; Thorough understanding of politics
Conditions: Overall declining health; Reputation: Tough and demanding
Notes: Smokes a pipe. He retired due to having suffered a massive heart attack caused by stress and his overall declining health.

General Crowther
Real Name: Thurston Crowther
Gender: Male
Grade/Rank: General
Service Branch: U.S. Army
Faction(s): Jugglers
Stationed: Washington, D.C.
Abilities: Contact: Mercenary Major Bludd
Conditions: Enraged by implied threats; Resents the top-secret elite teams of the military
Notes: One of the various leaders of the secret committee of Generals is known as "the Jugglers"

General Philip Rey
Real Name: Philip A. Rey
Place of Birth: Springfield Museum of Antiquities
Gender: Male
Grade/Rank: General, reserve*
Service Branch: Army
Faction(s): G.I. Joe
Notably Served At: Europe; Jordan
Primary MOS: CLASSIFIED
Secondary MOS: CLASSIFIED
Appearance: 6'1", white hair, blue eyes, 200 pounds, a variety of small scars on his face. Uniform consists of a brown shirt (with camouflaged sleeves) beneath the gray chest and shoulder plates, brown trousers, gray boots, gray knee and wrist pads, gray gloves, and a gray helmet with a red visor attached that covers his eyes and his nose. Wears partial combat armor at all times, including a helmet, chest plate, shoulder pads, etc. Joe-Com, long blade knife; several semi-automatic pistols
Background Information: Doctor Mindbender altered his growth patterns and features to hide his connection to the Cobra Emperor; Crystal Ball constructed his personality and Zandar inserted him as a U.S. military general, to make him Cobra's most insidious sleeper agent. Years of service time with G.I. Joe helped him shake off Cobra's control. His past remains CLASSIFIED, known only to Duke and General Colton.
Abilities: Expert knife fighter; Hand-to-hand combat; Leadership; Military officer; Programmed military experience; Qualified Weapons: Modern firearms; Willpower
Conditions: Always wears some armor; Aware he feels compelled to follow orders despite misgivings; Clone of super-soldier;

Confident; Distinctive Feature: Small scars on his face; Former laboratory experiment; In therapy with psychiatrist Scott Stevens; Mental blocks keep him from remembering; One of the dozen original clones produced during Cobra's development of Serpentor; Past is CLASSIFIED; Programmed military experience; Proud; Rarely question orders; Reputation: The man who cut off Major Bludd's hand; Unaware of his past; Violent nightmares after questioning orders; Wants to prove he's an exemplary soldier; Willful

Quote/Motto: "My name is Philip Rey."

Notes: Currently, he is a reserve member of the current Joe team assigned to domestic operations in the United States. *All reservists can be called back into action if a mission calls for it.

Ghostrider

Series: Seven (1988)
Alias/Variations: Ghostwing, Blipless, No-Show, Silent Knight, Slinker, Wraithwing
Real Name: Jonas S. Jeffries
Place of Birth: Chicago, Illinois
Gender: Male
Grade/Rank: 7/O-4: Major; Major, USAF O-4
SN: 112-30-7140
Service Branch: Air Force
Faction(s): G.I. Joe
Notably Served At: Benzheen; Cobra Island; Stealth Fighter base in South America (destroyed)
Primary MOS: Stealth fighter pilot
Secondary MOS: Aeronautical engineer
Appearance: Silver helmet with green goggles; a gray shirt with black flight jacket and gloves; gray pants with brown holster and black boots; green map of Ohio on the right leg
Accessories: Cloth scarf
Abilities: Aeronautical engineer; Conscientiously works on not being noticed; Qualified Expert Operator: Phantom X-19 Stealth Fighter; Qualified Expert Operator: Stealth fighter
Conditions: Accepts no one can remember his code name; Has the nerve to fly "Nap-of-the-earth" at high speeds; No one on the Joe team can remember his name
Quote/Motto: "Ghostrider has been working on not getting noticed since the second grade. He may have been the only person to make it through the Chicago public school system without ever cleaning an eraser or washing a blackboard. Teachers never noticed him, not because he was dull or lackluster, but because he consciously worked on not being noticed. That's how he is in the cockpit of a stealth fighter. He's WILLING himself to be invisible!" Quote by an unnamed G.I. Joe team member.
Notes: His name was never actually said by any other Joes, or even used in narration.

G.I. Jane

Series: Twenty-two (2006)
Alias/Variations: Nurse
Real Name: Jane Ann Martelle
Place of Birth: Cumberland, Rhode Island
Gender: Female
Grade/Rank: E-5 Sergeant
SN: 413-51-AM61
Service Branch: Army
Faction(s): G.I. Joe
Stationed: A secret Strategic Defense Initiative installation in New York City
Primary MOS: Particle physics
Secondary MOS: Combat nurse
Appearance: Short wavy blonde hair, short-sleeved gray T-shirt with G.I. Joe logo on it; green combat fatigues, green boots, green fingerless gloves
Accessories: Knife, pistol, rifle
Abilities: Combat medic; Medical skills; Physicist; Scientific expertise; PhD in physics
Quote/Motto: "It takes all kinds of soldiers to fight Cobra, I battle them by developing scientific technology. Of course, when I am up to my ears in Cobra thugs, just throw me an M16 and get out of my way."

G.I. Joe

Series: Thirteen (1994)
Real Name: Joseph B. Colton
Place of Birth: Central Falls, Rhode Island
Gender: Male
Grade/Rank: O-2 (1st lieutenant) (1964); O-10 (general) (1994)
SN: 1033-1027-HAS93 (1994); 103-31-HA27 (2006)
Service Branch: Army
Faction(s): G.I. Joe, Adventure Team
Stationed: Head of a secret Strategic Defense Initiative installation in New York City, the Chrysler Building (renamed in the comics as the Studebaker Building due to licensing issues); the Strategic Defense Initiative (SDI); The Rock
Notably Served At: His missions were "ultra" CLASSIFIED

Primary MOS: G.I. Joe X-O (Executive Officer); Strategic and Tactical Operations
Secondary MOS: Combat infantry (training and intelligence)
Appearance: Green beret; black hair grayed at the temples; brown eyes; green shirt and pants with brown belt and boots
Accessories: Heavy machine gun
Abilities: Combat infantry (training and intelligence); Expert marksman; Innate combat skills; Green Beret; Qualified Weapon Expert: Heavy machine gun; Qualified Weapons: All modern weapons; Strategic and tactical operations; Warrior's heart!
Conditions: Courageous; Destined for military glory; Reputation: The most decorated battlefield soldier the world had ever known; Reputation: The most feared battlefield soldier the world had ever known
Quote/Motto: "Duty, Honor, Country! Not just words … a way to live your life!"
Notes: Graduated in 1960 from the United States Military Academy at West Point, receiving the academy's highest possible honors

Glenda

Series: Four (1985)
Real Name: Jane Mullighan
Gender: Female
Grade/Rank: E-7 (Sgt 1st class, Army)
SN: RG 666-34-8210
Service Branch: Army
Faction(s): G.I. Joe
Primary MOS: Test pilot
Secondary MOS: Intelligence
Appearance: Straight blonde hair she wears pulled back into a tight bun. Electric blue bodysuit, silver chest plate, silver gloves, and boots
Accessories: Headset, laser rifle
Background Information: She was flying super-sophisticated helicopters at six years old. After her father died heroically, Glenda swore to continue fighting for his noble cause.
Abilities: Air intelligence officer; Helicopter copilot in high-risk missions; Heightened intelligence; Master instructor; Test pilot
Conditions: Swore to continue fighting for her father's noble cause
Notes: The first woman to become Master Instructor of the Action Force (alternate continuity) and the first woman to become Master Instructor of Heroic Commands. She was killed by Red Shadow agents.

Gorky

Series: Fifteen (1998)
Real Name: Mikhail P. Gorky
Place of Birth: Arkhangelsk, Russia
Gender: Male
Grade/Rank: O-2 (Army first lieutenant equivalent) Lieutenant
SN: CLASSIFIED
Service Branch: Navy (Soviet/Russian)
Faction(s): Oktober Guard
Primary MOS: Naval commando
Secondary MOS: Infantry
Appearance: Gray furred cap with red star; red hair and beard; a gray shirt with light brown straps; gray pants with a light brown belt and dark gray boots
Accessories: AK-S74U assault rifle, backpack
Background Information: Went to Oktober Guard from the Black Sea regiment of the Naval Infantry, the Soviet equivalent of the Navy SEALs
Abilities: Commando; Extensive experience in land, sea, and air operations; Infantry; Naval commando; Tough; Versatile fighter; Wilderness Survival: Any
Conditions: Crush on Lady Jaye; Despises Cobra; Get the job done!; Frequently treated like an inexperienced youngster; Grew a beard to appear more mature; Utterly fearless
Quote/Motto: "So I am sent this kid with a reputation for being the best the Naval Infantry has to offer. I am not impressed. Then I see him against Cobra, and not just the troops, but tanks and helicopters. He stands his ground. Now I am impressed." Taken from Colonel Brekhov's files.
Notes: Diana and Gorky helped the joint forces of G.I. Joe and Cobra rescue the Baroness and Flint, but Gorky betrayed them and was riddled by an AGP driven by Destro.

Grand Slam

Series: One (1982)
Alias/Variations: Red Pads
Real Name: James J. Barney
Place of Birth: Chippewa Falls, Wisconsin
Gender: Male
Grade/Rank: Sergeant E-5 (1982), 6/O-1: 2nd Lieutenant
SN: RA379541044
Service Branch: Army
Faction(s): G.I. Joe
Stationed: Graduated: Special Weapons School

(top of class). Specialized Education: Artillery School; Advanced Tech School
Primary MOS: Laser artillery; laser jet pack soldier (1983)
Secondary MOS: Electronics engineer
Appearance: Brown hair; a dark-green shirt with a silver red-padded vest; black gloves; dark green belt and fatigues with red-padded pants over black boots
Other Known Appearances (Cartoon): Similar, but with dark brown gloves and no padding on pants. The 1983 version was olive-drab fatigue with silver pads.
Accessories: Dark green helmet; visor (Prototype visor was black) (1982–83)
Abilities: Calm; Cover fire expert; Estimate distances and plot trajectories; Laser artillery soldier; Highly Intelligent; Proficient with HAL (Heavy Artillery Laser); Qualified Weapons Expert: M-16; M-1911A1
Conditions: Hobby Skill: Escapist fantasy (science fiction novels and comics); Introvert; Questions his sanity; Shy; Soft-spoken; Uncomfortable in social situations; Vacant stare
Quote/Motto: "He's soft-spoken and calm—just a bit shy. Intelligent. Loves to read escapist fantasy (science fiction and comic books)." Quote by an unnamed G.I. Joe team member.
Notes: The 1982 Grand Slam figure was produced straight-armed. The 1983 figure with silver pads is a rare find as the silver paint application wore off extremely easily.

Greenshirt

Purpose: Greenshirt is a term applied to the generic-looking soldiers from the cartoon. They are the equivalent of "extras," serving the story as background characters; they have no speaking parts. They are used to supplement the Heavy Assault Squad. In the comics, the Greenshirts were soldiers used as support troops for the main G.I. Joe team. They are broken into three types: infantry, navy, and air force. Some Greenshirts have been given personalities and play slightly larger roles; a rare few become members of the team. Many Greenshirts die in combat. Greenshirt training is all live fire, to work together to accomplish their goals, and also how to ride the fine line of disobeying direct orders.
Leader: None given; default to rank
Notes: Recruits are given joke or satirical nicknames until they earn their Joe code name.

Grid-Iron

Series: Nine (1990)
Real Name: Terrence Lyndon
Place of Birth: Evergreen Park, Illinois
Gender: Male
Grade/Rank: 6/O-3: Captain; O-3 Captain, Africa; reservist*
SN: 903-5221-YY07
Service Branch: Army
Faction(s): G.I. Joe
Primary MOS: Hand-to-hand combat specialist
Secondary MOS: Infantry
Appearance: Light brown hair; a light green shirt with dark green urban camo; green vest; yellow pants with gray belt and holster
Accessories: Football helmet with clear visor; four missiles with two slots on each; long gun-shaped missile launcher with large scope and second grip on front; shotgun with trigger guard and no stock; small backpack with roll and tab for grenade; three football-shaped grenades
Abilities: Friends with Pathfinder and Ambush; Infantry; Quarterback of the West Point football team; Hand-to-hand combat specialist
Conditions: Determination to be "where the action is!"; Distinctive Feature: Wears a football helmet into battle; Does John Wayne imitations—a lot; Speech peppered with football terminology; Tries hard to be likable
Quote/Motto: "The other G.I. Joes were a bit put off by this West Pointer when he first showed up, but he turned out to be bearable to the point that nobody tried to 'lose' him on his first mission. If he would only stop trying so hard to be likable and put a halt to his John Wayne [classic Hollywood tough guy] imitation, they might let him play quarterback at the annual G.I. Joe Fish Fry Football Game!" Quote by an unnamed G.I. Joe team member.
Notes: *All reservists can be called back into action if a mission calls for it.

Grill

Series: Fourteen (1995)
Real Name: Darren K. Filbert
Place of Birth: Warren, Ohio, 1925
Gender: Male
Grade/Rank: E-5 Sergeant
Service Branch: U.S. Army
Faction(s): G.I. Joe, Savage Eagles
Notably Served At: Syria in the Middle East; World War III
Appearance: African American

Abilities: Creator of the Eagle's arsenal and vehicles; Genius in mechanics; Highly trained
Conditions: Undisciplined

Grunt

Series: One (1982)
Alias/Variations: Sokerk (Argentina), Estopim (Brazil)
Real Name: Robert W. Graves
Place of Birth: Columbus, Ohio
Gender: Male
Grade/Rank: E-4 (Army corporal); member of the reserves*
SN: RA52779623
Service Branch: Army; Leader of the Greenshirts
Faction(s): G.I. Joe, Greenshirts, and Stars and Stripes Forever
Primary MOS: Infantry
Secondary MOS: Small arms armorer
Appearance: Brown hair, dark green shirt with brown straps and light green pockets on shoulders; dark green pants with brown boots; gray combat bodysuit
Other Known Appearances (Cartoon): Often missing light green pockets on his shoulders. "Tan Grunt" has tan fatigues and a tan helmet.
Accessories: Combat pack, helmet; M-16 assault rifle (1982–83)
Abilities: Advanced infantry training; Cool under fire; Engineering; Infantry trooper; Qualified Operator: A.W.E. Striker and Falcon Glider; Qualified Weapons Expert: M-14, M-16, M-1911A1 (Auto-Pistol); Qualified Weapons: All NATO and Warsaw Pact small arms, Domestic civilian arms
Conditions: Girlfriend: Lola; Highly motivated; Stand-up guy
Quote/Motto: "Grunt is a highly motivated, systematic individual. He's a stand-up guy who doesn't blow his cool in a firefight." Quote by an unnamed G.I. Joe team member.
Notes: *All reservists can be called back into action if a mission calls for it. The 1982 Grunt figure was produced straight-armed. In the Marvel Comics Universe, Grunt retired from G.I. Joe and received a degree in engineering from Georgia Tech.

Gung Ho

Series: Two (1983); six (1987)
Alias/Variations: Gung-Ho
Real Name: Ettienne R. LaFitte
Place of Birth: Fer-de-Lance, Louisiana
Gender: Male
Grade/Rank: E-7 (Gunnery Sergeant) (1983); E-9 (Sergeant Major) (1992)
SN: MC56488390
Service Branch: Marine
Faction(s): G.I. Joe, Battle Corps, Desert Patrol Squad, Mega-Marines, and Strike Team: Alpha
Stationed: Honor graduate from Marine Corps Recruit Depot Parris Island; Airborne School, Recondo School, Marine Ordnance School, Administration School at Camp Johnson
Notably Served At: Sierra Gordo; Cobra Island; Trans-Carpathia; Florida Everglades
Primary MOS: Recondo
Secondary MOS: Jungle warfare training instructor
Appearance: Well-muscled, bald, large black handlebar mustache; dark green hat; bald with brown mustache; open light blue vest; blue Marine tattoo on chest; green/light blue camouflage pants; gray boots; black headband; green vest with an open collar and black stripes; ammo belt on chest; black right armband; beige pants with a brown belt, holster, and boots. Series Six (1987): Traditional Marine Dress Uniform; white military cap with gold Marine emblem and black bill; bald with brown mustache; dark blue Marine dress jacket with red trim; white gloves; white belt and hook for a sword; blue slacks with red stripes on outside legs; black shoes
Accessories: XM-76 grenade launcher (1983). Fairly large pouch backpack with sculpted rope and canteen; huge machine gun with a handle on top, single grip, and triangular stock; spring-loaded missile launcher with shoulder rest and trigger; missile with extra-thick tip; United States flag on a flagpole. Series Six (1987): Non-combat decorative dress saber; sticker sheet of campaign ribbons and rank insignia for each arm. With some effort, the cap is removable and may be considered an accessory.
Background Information: "Subject was born into a large back-water swamp Cajun clan and entered into the family poaching business at the age of 13. By 17 he had moved to New Orleans and won a reputation as a bare-knuckled brawler to be reckoned with and a knife fighter to be avoided. Joined the Marines when he was 18."
Abilities: Bare-knuckle brawler; Cajun; Esprit-de-Corps attitude is infectious;

Knowledge Skill: Swamps of Louisiana; Knife fighter; Part of a large Cajun clan; Qualified Weapons Expert: All NATO infantry small arms, Warsaw Pact infantry weapons, and the XM-76 grenade launcher; Strength and perseverance; Trades insults

Conditions: Brave; Cajun; Distinctive Feature: USMC tattoo on his Chest; French Cajun ancestry; Kid sister who is a successful child model; Mother scolds him for not visiting enough; Part of a large Cajun clan; Proud Marine through and through; Reputation: Tough brawler and knife-fighter in New Orleans; Reputation: Craziest and scariest Jarhead to come out of Parris Island; Reputation: Lack of fear on the battlefield; Reputation: Legendary feats of near-superhuman strength; Speaks in a French Cajun Accent; Talks to his gun; Treats his gun as a child

Quote/Motto: "Look, *all* Marines is crazy. They're the assault troops, right? They're a hairy, scary, crazy outfit! So the big brass decide that the G.I. Joe teams need a representative from the esteemed USMC. They tell us they sending the best the Corps has got. Well, all that means to me is they sent us the hairiest, scariest, craziest jarhead that ever scratched, kicked, and bit his way out of that hole-in-the-swamp they call Parris Island!" Quote from a transcript of a taped Peer Personality Profile review, given by fellow G.I. Joe team member Zap.

Notes: His mother once beat up the Baroness. In 1986 Gung Ho, one of the original G.I. Joes, was replaced by Leatherneck.

Hacker

Series: Nineteen (2003)
Real Name: Jesse E. Jordan
Place of Birth: Emmetsburg, Iowa
Gender: Male
Grade/Rank: 1/E-5: Sergeant
SN: 885-64-JJ76
Service Branch: Army
Faction(s): G.I. Joe
Stationed: Fort Leonard Wood
Primary MOS: Computer technology/information retrieval
Secondary MOS: Radio telecommunications
Appearance: Short brown hair, bright blue eyes; light gray pants and shirt; dark gray straps, gloves, belt, kneepads, and shoes; light blue panel on the right leg
Accessories: Submachine gun with short rear-mounted scope, hollow stock, and angled magazine; knife; grappling hook and string; Firefly disguise (goggled ski mask; vest with Cobra emblem; leg armor with Cobra emblems on kneepads); grappling hook with cord, rifle, shin pads, mask, Sound Attack submachine gun, Cobra vest
Abilities: Hand-to-hand combat; Knowledge Skill: Cobra protocol; Computer specialist; Information retrieval specialist
Conditions: Arrogant
Quote/Motto: "If it's digital and in-memory someplace, I can get it. If that means putting on a Cobra suit and going where they live, then that's fine by me."

Hammer Team

Purpose: A top-secret military unit created to capture Firefly. It was believed there was a traitor on the team, but Duke went forward with the mission, which proved to be a disaster. Firefly killed most of the Hammer Team including Ophelia, the apprentice of Snake Eyes.
Leader: Duke and Chuckles
Members: Mikhail Derenko, Sean Collins (Kamakura), Ophelia, Snake Eyes, and others unnamed
Notes: Mikhail Derenko was the traitor.

Hard Drive

Series: Twenty (2004)
Real Name: Martin A. Pidel
Place of Birth: Yonkers, New York
Gender: Male
Grade/Rank: E-4 Corporal
SN: 865-22-GJ46
Service Branch: Army; reserve member*
Faction(s): G.I. Joe
Stationed: MIT graduate (age 17)
Notably Served At: Russia
Primary MOS: Combat computer technology
Secondary MOS: Special services
Appearance: Black hair; light green cap with silver monocle and headset; black shirt with tan holsters and belt; gray gloves; light green pants; tan boots
Accessories: G-36 assault rifle; tech backpack with antenna; wrist monitor; wrist communicator
Abilities: Can fix anything or anyone in the field; Linear equations; Greco-Roman wrestling; Medic; Qualified Weapons: Small arms armorer; Specialist: Battlefield computer;

Specialist: Communications; Tech-savvy guru; Uses a fighting system that is a complex integration of weapons, optics, communications, and sensors; Video game expert
Conditions: History with the Baroness
Quote/Motto: "Combat is the ultimate 'Boss Battle,' so I like to make sure I have plenty of 'Power-Ups' on hand in the form of carbs, energy bars, and soda!"
Notes: Holds 27 patents; *All reservists can be called back into action if a mission calls for it.

Hard Master

Series: Twenty-four (2008)
Real Name: Unknown
Place of Birth: Japan
Gender: Male
Grade/Rank: Leader of the Arashikage clan of ninjas
Faction(s): Arashikage clan
Primary MOS: Ninja master
Appearance: Asian; bald; white headband, red ghee with white trim, and boots
Accessories: Arrow, bow, headband, mask, sword, sheath with string
Abilities: Arashikage martial arts; Imitation; Leader of the Arashikage ninjas; Martial arts techniques: Arashikage mindset; Martial arts techniques: Cloak of the Chameleon; Martial arts techniques: Darkened Room; Martial arts techniques: Ear That Sees; Martial arts techniques: Sleeping Phoenix; Ninja master; Professional Skill: Family business; Recognizes natural ability
Conditions: Elderly; Favored Snake Eyes as a student; Nephew: Storm Shadow; Overconfident
Quote/Motto: "You have done well, acolyte. You will meet with more lessons on your journey, and each one will further temper the steel to make the blade stronger than it was before."
Notes: Hard Master was the president and chairman of the Arashikage clan of the ninja's board. His brother, the Soft Master, served as vice president (finance); the third member of the board was their nephew Tommy Arashikage, the "Young Master," a junior partner. His murder by Zartan drove Storm Shadow to Cobra and Snake Eyes to join G.I. Joe.

Hardball

Series: Seven (1988)
Alias/Variations: Thumper, High-Pop, Line-Drive, Lob-Shot
Real Name: Wilmer S. Duggleby
Place of Birth: Cooperstown, New York
Gender: Male
Grade/Rank: E-4 (Army corporal)
SN: 075-0948-DW76
Service Branch: Army
Faction(s): G.I. Joe
Primary MOS: Infantry
Secondary MOS: Special services
Appearance: African American; blue baseball cap; white baseball shirt with blue trim and red "G.I. Joe" on right chest; gray undershirt sleeves; black half-gloves; orange-brown pants with light green belt and holster; black boots
Accessories: Grenade launcher with two grips and removable rotating barrel; large backpack (with engraved "U.S.") full of grenades
Abilities: Athletic prowess; Deliberate; Infantry; Heightened reflexes; Judge distances accurately; Professional Skill: Centerfield in the minor leagues; Special services; Team-player
Quote/Motto: "Grenade launchers are fitted with adjustable, graduated sights, calibrated in 25-meter increments. In a firefight, nobody wants to start readjusting sights—especially the blooper man. Hardball can drop a 40 mm frag into a bucket from 75 meters, simply by eyeballing it. The man's a natural." Quote by an unnamed G.I. Joe team member.
Notes: While on assignment in South America, Hardball, along with Rampart and Glenda, is killed by the Red Shadows.

Hardtop

Series: Six (1987)
Alias/Variations: Hard Top, Hard-Top
Real Name: Nicholas D. Klas; prototype name was Floyd R. Pincus
Place of Birth: Chicago, Illinois
Gender: Male
Grade/Rank: 1/E-5: Sergeant
SN: 284-10-MC75
Service Branch: Army
Faction(s): G.I. Joe, Tiger Force
Primary MOS: Heavy equipment operator/crawler driver
Secondary MOS: Electronics
Appearance: White hardhat; a blue shirt with white backpack straps with red trim; blue pants with a white belt, holster, pad
Accessories: Included with the Defiant: Space Vehicle Launch Complex; bent mic attaching to the helmet; pistol with diagonal grooves on the side

Abilities: Designer/driver of the Crawler; Doesn't question orders; Electronics; Frequently works with Payload; Get the job done!; Knowledge Skill: Braking systems; Knowledge Skill: Computers; Knowledge Skill: Engines; Knowledge Skill: Exhaust systems; Knowledge Skill: Hydraulics; Knowledge Skill: Vehicle's defensive weapon systems; Liaison to the National Space Agency; Professional Skill: Heavy equipment operator; Qualified Operator: Crawler, Space Vehicle Launch Operator; Superior intelligence; Supervises repairs and upgrades
Conditions: Don't get in his way; One of Cobra Commander's most wanted prisoners; Own set of priorities; Silent type; Superior Commitment
Quote/Motto: "A nod and a handshake say I'll take that job." "You might say he was the strong silent type, emphasis on the silent. His idea of a long conversation is a nod and a handshake. It's not that he's unfriendly, he simply has his own priorities, and talking isn't one of them." Quote by an unnamed G.I. Joe team member.
Notes: Some of the sealed figures of Hardtop did not have the gun included, making this accessory highly desirable to collectors.

Harpoon

Series: Fourteen (1995)
Real Name: Jose Montalvo
Gender: Male
Grade/Rank: E-4 Specialist
SN: 20L3JF8I
Service Branch: Navy
Faction(s): G.I. Joe, Team Extreme
Primary MOS: Aquatic operations coordinator
Appearance: Dark-skinned, straight black hair, gray boots, skin-tight royal blue bodysuit with most of his chest exposed; baby blue vest and codpiece combination, silver necklace, a silver gauntlet on the right hand, silver and orange suspender webbing
Accessories: Two guns, the larger of which could shoot water
Abilities: Aquatic operations coordinator; Covertly delivers SEALs to places subs can't reach; Hostage rescue mission expert; Nautical expert; Professional Skill: (retired) Navy SEAL; Qualified Expert Operator: DEVGRU operator, SDV
Conditions: Comic relief; Rather go fishing than fight; Spends time with Rock 'n Roll and Mariner

Hashtag

Real Name: Aruna Singh
Place of Birth: Fort Lewis, Tacoma, Washington
Gender: Female
Grade/Rank: Corporal
SN: None
Service Branch: Army
Faction(s): G.I. Joe
Stationed: Journalism at Fordham University; Reserve Officers' Training Corps
Notably Served At: Warrenton; North Africa
Primary MOS: Telecommunications systems
Secondary MOS: Public relations
Appearance: Spiky, pixie style black hair; slender, pink shirt, pink socks, white sneaker/boots, green vest
Abilities: Blogger; Decent shot; Public relations; Social media guru; Communications specialist; Telecommunications systems
Conditions: Disillusioned by military intelligence; Disliked by her teammates (Duke's strike team); Embedded with the Joes for PR purposes; Fan of Courtney Krieger and Project: Runway; Initially didn't believe in guns; Makes poor combat decisions; Traumatized (had to shoot to kill to save Cover Girl's life)
Notes: At some point, Aruna left the military, becoming a civilian journalist. She covered the induction of Earth into the Council of Worlds alongside the Cybertronian reporter, Circuit.

Hawk

Series: One (1982), Five (1986)
Alias/Variations: General Hawk, later in his career; General Abernathy, General Tomahawk
Real Name: Clayton M. Abernathy
Place of Birth: Denver, Colorado (Warminster, Wiltshire, England, for European distribution)
Gender: Male
Grade/Rank: O-6 Colonel (1982); O-7 Brigadier General (1986); Advisor when Duke assumed leadership of the Joes; Active Reservist*
SN: RA 212-75-4036
Service Branch: Army
Faction(s): G.I. Joe, Star Brigade
Stationed: The Pit, Utah, located beneath Fort Wadsworth
Notably Served At: Battle of Benzheen; North Atlantic range Command

Primary MOS: Artillery missile commander
Secondary MOS: Radar
Appearance: Crew cut blond hair and blue eyes; brown jacket with black holster; light and dark green camouflage pants with black belts, holster. The 1986 figure wears a black belt, black chest holster, B3 sheepskin bomber jacket, jungle camo pants, and now has brown eyes and hair. This figure was also offered as a Hasbro mail-in offer in 1992, but the accessories were not included.
Other Known Appearances (Cartoon): Black hair and brown eyes; opaque, white-lensed goggles on helmet; brown boots
Accessories: Helmet, visor (1982–83); backpack with a canteen on back; goggled helmet; pistol. Variations include: helmet, helmet with goggles; submachine gun. The 1986 figure was released with a green field pack, green helmet, and black Walther PPK 9-mm short pistol.
Background Information: Comes from a wealthy family, graduated top of his class from West Point. He was the original field commander before he got his general's star and was "booted upstairs" to honcho the entire G.I. Joe operation.
Abilities: Advisor; Artillery; Keenly intelligent; Leadership; Mentor to Duke; Missile commander; Perceptive; Qualified Operator: A.W.E. Striker, Conquest, H.A.V.O.C., JUMP, LCV Recon Sled, Mauler, Snow Cat, and Tomahawk; Quiet; Radar operations; Wealthy
Conditions: Distinctive Feature: Wears sunglasses; Greaves his deceased wife; Intense hatred for Cobra Commander; Obsessed with the capture of Cobra Commander; Paralyzed below the waist (gunshot delivered by Zartan); Selfless; Teenage son, Scott (computer expert); Undergoing physiotherapy
Quote/Motto: "Hawk's the type of commander who goes out and gets shot at like everyone else. Troops respect that. They know he won't ask them to do anything he isn't willing to do himself. And that's why they are willing to do anything Hawk tells them." Quote by an unnamed G.I. Joe team member.
Notes: *All reservists can be called back into action if a mission calls for it. The 1982 Hawk figure was produced straight-armed.

Hawkwind

Real Name: Lars Elsund
Place of Birth: Stockholm, Sweden
Gender: Male
SN: AF 934103
Service Branch: Air Force
Faction(s): Action Force, Space Force
Primary MOS: Security trooper
Secondary MOS: Hand-to-hand combat
Appearance: Blond hair, blue eyes, tall
Background Information: NATO Armed Forces Unit; Chief instructor in hand-to-hand combat. Received his space training at a special school funded by both the U.S. and Russian Space Command
Abilities: Freefall diving; Hand-to-hand unarmed combat expert; Instructor; Judo; Karate; Paratrooper; Running; Security trooper; Singing; Tough; Wrestling
Conditions: No-nonsense soldier; Proud of being Swedish; Sings when cheerful
Quote/Motto: "Hawkwind is a tough, no-nonsense soldier. Proud of being Swedish. Breaks out into song when in a cheerful mood." Quote by an unnamed G.I. Joe team member.
Notes: He won Olympic gold in both Judo and Karate; he also won the Freefall Combat Chevron Award.

Head Banger

Series: Fourteen (1995)
Real Name: Kevin M. Kaye
Gender: Male
Grade/Rank: E-5 Sergeant
Service Branch: U.S. Army
Faction(s): G.I. Joe, Savage Eagles
Abilities: Highly trained; Knack for communications systems; Knowledge Skill: Heavy metal music
Conditions: Heavy rocker; Undisciplined

Heavy Assault Squad

Purpose: These Joes, known as the Heavy Assault Squad, specialize in using heavy weapons; they are supplemented by Greenshirts.
Leader: Duke, Roadblock, and Snake Eyes
Members: Greenshirts
Quote/Motto: "We're the good guys and they're the bad guys. The job of the good guys is to put the bad guys out of business." Quote given by Duke.

Heavy Duty

Series: Ten (1991)
Alias/Variations: Hershel Dalton
Real Name: Lamont A. Morris

Place of Birth: Chicago, Illinois; Biloxi, Mississippi (sources conflict)
Gender: Male
Grade/Rank: E-5 Sergeant
SN: 807-0246-LM65
Service Branch: Army Ranger
Faction(s): G.I. Joe, Star Brigade
Stationed: The Pit, Utah, located beneath Fort Wadsworth
Notably Served At: The Pit; Istanbul, Turkey
Primary MOS: Laser weapons systems operator
Secondary MOS: Indirect fire infantryman
Appearance: African American; black hair and mustache; neon green cap; an off-white sleeveless torn shirt with black strap; red tattoo on left arm; dark pants with neon green triangles; black belt and boots
Accessories: Small, tech backpack with clip for cannon support; large handheld support with detachable double-barreled cannon and two detachable spring-loaded missile launchers, L-shaped eyepiece attaching to backpack; two missiles with fins at middle and front
Abilities: Classical guitarist; Culturally refined; Exceptional hand-eye coordination; Extremely strong; Heavy ordnance trooper; Highly dexterous; Hobby Skill: Home-based recording studio; Indirect fire infantryman; Knowledge Skill: Advanced weapon systems; Machine gunner; Multi-tasks on complex operations; Professional Skill: Laser weapons systems operator; Qualified Operator: Mobile battle bunker; Right- and left-hand independence
Conditions: Ashamed of his Southern heritage (Mississippi background); Generic personality; Loves explosives; Passion for classical guitars and Bach; Passion for cooking but not the skills; Passion for metropolitan living; Preoccupied; Speaks in rhymes; Unafraid of heavy enemy fire
Quote/Motto: "Let's say you zap a laser-guided missile at a tank. You try to keep your laser-guided designator dot on that tank for the entire run of the missile while that tank commander is popping caps at you. If you move, the laser dot disappears from the tank and your missile wanders away. Heavy Duty carries enough extra firepower to shut down the enemy while his missiles are running. And Heavy Duty doesn't duck for ANYBODY!" Quote by an unnamed G.I. Joe team member.
Notes: He is Roadblock's cousin, but there are bad feelings between them from a past rift. He is usually paired with teammate, Tunnel Rat.

Heavy Metal

Series: Four (1985)
Alias/Variations: Walter A. McDaniel, Rampage, Comando Avancado (Brazil). Prototype names include Bogie Wheel, Fast Track, Road Iron, and Rolling Jack
Real Name: Sherman R. Guderian
Place of Birth: Brooklyn, New York (Liverpool, Merseyside, England, for European distribution)
Gender: Male
Grade/Rank: E-4 Army corporal
SN: 632-45-6200
Service Branch: Army
Faction(s): G.I. Joe
Stationed: Finance School, Fort Belvoir
Primary MOS: Armor/Mauler M.B.T. tank driver
Secondary MOS: Finance
Appearance: Tanker's uniform: a leather jacket over non-catch overalls; Confederate soldier's belt buckle prominent on his gun belt; Green helmet with chin strap and black goggles; dirty face; As Rampage, the same, but with brighter colors and five o'clock shadow
Other Known Appearances (Cartoon): White lenses on goggles; the vest is brown. As Rampage, the same but with brighter colors and a five o'clock shadow
Accessories: Mauler M.B.T. Tank. Long mouthpiece/microphone attaching to a hole in helmet; rifle with trigger guard and sling
Background Information: He "enlisted to go to finance school, his ultimate goal to become a CPA. But one day at Fort Belvoir he watched a column of tanks roll by and was never the same again."
Abilities: Armor; Finance; Qualified Operator: Mauler M.B.T., Armadillo; Qualified Weapon Expert: M-16, M-1911A1, M-2 50-caliber MG, and M-60 MG
Conditions: Aspires to be middle-class; Dreams of being a CPA; Loves tanks
Quote/Motto: "Many people find comfort in order and discipline. Mathematics reduces the complexities of the world to manageable sums. Heavy Metal likes tanks. They are immutable statements in iron." "Heavy Metal likes order. When a page-long column of figures adds up correctly, that's order. When a long column of tanks line up to face the enemy, that's order on another scale." Quotes

are taken from transcripts of a taped Peer Personality Profile review, given by unnamed G.I. Joe team members.

Notes: Heavy Metal died along with Crankcase, Doc, and Thunder, while being held captive; it was due to an unfortunate misunderstanding of Cobra Commander's orders, by bloodthirsty S.A.W. Viper Robert "Overkill" Skelton. Doc is shot first; Crankcase, Thunder, and Heavy Metal are killed next. The Heavy Metal mouthpiece/microphone is the rarest and most difficult to find of all G.I. Joe accessories.

Hector Ramirez

Alias/Variations: Jose Riviera
Real Name: Hector Ramirez
Gender: Male
Faction(s): Civilian; host of the TV show *Twenty Questions*
Appearance: Mexican; black hair, large black mustache, three-piece suit. First depicted with a thin mustache and black hair parted to the side then depicted with a bushy mustache and gray hair parted; then went back to his original design for his subsequent appearances and storyboards for *G.I. Joe: The Movie*. The DiC *G.I. Joe* gave him a new outfit (a brown cargo vest and green turtleneck sweater) while maintaining his facial appearance, albeit with brown hair parted to the side and a mustache that was thin and then bushy. In *Jem*, Ramirez has a thin mustache and black slicked-back hair. In *Inhumanoids*, Ramirez sported a bushy mustache and black hair parted to the side. Ramirez's appearance in *Transformers* is mostly consistent with his *Inhumanoids* appearance, having a bushy mustache and hair parted to the side, though his hair is brown rather than black.
Abilities: Celebrity; Discovers a person's weak spot; Dumb Luck; Gets the interview!; Host of *Twenty Questions*; Intern: Sofía Orozco; Lulls people into a false sense of security; Professional Skill: Journalist; Professional Skill: Reporter; Professional Skill: TV personality; Tenacity; Weaseling
Conditions: Always looking for a scoop; Belief: He'll win an Emmy, Pulitzer, or both; Credibility is questionable; Easily bamboozled; Engages in sensationalism; Frequently in unnecessarily dangerous situations; Full of misguided bravado; Thrives on "hard-hitting" controversy more than factual accuracy; Vapid

Notes: Appeared in *G.I. Joe*, *The Transformers*, *Inhumanoids*, and *Jem and the Holograms*. He was killed by Red Shadow agents after informing Joe Colton of their existence. The cab he left the meeting in exploded. In the twenty-second century, Hector's great-nephew Lester Black, carries on his work.

Helix

Series: Twenty-five (2009)
Alias/Variations: Agent Helix
Real Name: CLASSIFIED
Place of Birth: CLASSIFIED
Gender: Female
Grade/Rank: O/E-4: Specialist
SN: CLASSIFIED
Service Branch: Civilian
Faction(s): G.I. Joe
Stationed: Governor's Island
Primary MOS: Covert operations officer
Appearance: Blue eyes, short hair bob, black with blonde streaks; skintight yellow upper bodysuit, skintight black lower bodysuit; black combat webbing, corset, thigh-high boots
Accessories: Missile launcher, machete, missile with a net, rifle, two pistols
Abilities: Advanced martial arts training; Competed in both official and underground tournaments around the world (some to the death); Covert operations officer; Distinctive Feature: "Whirlwind attack" (overpowering combinations of kicks and firepower); Expert marksman; Identifies and solves complex physical calculations quickly; Olympic-class gymnast; Practitioner of many different fighting styles; Tactical minded; Total organic battlefield awareness*
Preferred Weapon: Dual 10-mm auto pistols
Conditions: Abilities are considered disconcerting; *Everything has a data set (example: knows the number of miles remaining before a car will run out of gas or ammo count in the bad guy's guns); Reputation: Can master a fighting style after encountering it once; Reputation: Only person to spar Snake Eyes to a stalemate

Hep Cat

Real Name: Kevin M. Kaye
Place of Birth: Clarinda, Iowa, in 1904
Gender: Male
Grade/Rank: E-5 Sergeant

Service Branch: U.S. Army
Faction(s): G.I. Joe, Savage Eagles
Abilities: Communications systems; Highly trained; Knowledge Skill: Music
Conditions: Music lover; Undisciplined

Hi-Tech

Series: Twenty (2004)
Real Name: David P. Lewinski
Place of Birth: St. Paul, Minnesota
Gender: Male
Grade/Rank: E-4; 2/E-6: Staff sergeant specialist
SN: 711-60-KLJL
Service Branch: Army Special Forces
Faction(s): G.I. Joe
Primary MOS: Armament Research & Design
Secondary MOS: Telecommunications
Appearance: Lots of flowing yellow hair; black headset on the left cheek; a gray shirt with red straps and pockets; black half-gloves; blue pants with red belt and pockets; black boots with gray armor
Accessories: Knife, missile launcher with a detachable stand, missile with long fins, pistol with T-shaped stock, shield, wrist communicator
Abilities: Armament research and design; Communications; Computer hacking; Decoding; Specialist: Operations support; Technological genius; Telecommunications; Works on developing technology that can remove the animal hybridization venom
Conditions: Repair on the fly; Can't "No"; Dependable; Good-natured soul; Listens to rock music; Prefers a soldering gun over a pistol; Reputation: Inventor of the MIRC (Mind Interface Remote Control); Reputation: Nothing he can't hack or decode; Spends downtime fixing teammates' personal electronics and vehicles
Quote/Motto: "If it isn't alive or art, I can fix it."

Hit and Run

Series: Seven (1988)
Alias/Variations: Alpinista (Brazil and Argentina)
Real Name: Brent Scott; Bryan Scott (UK Action Force, alternate continuity)
Place of Birth: Sioux City, Iowa (Basildon in Essex, England, UK Action Force, alternate continuity)
Gender: Male
Grade/Rank: E-4 (Army corporal)
SN: 345-75-8126, later changed to 345-7581-SB26
Service Branch: Army Delta Force
Faction(s): G.I. Joe, Tiger Force in Europe
Notably Served At: Cobra Island; Sierra Gordo
Primary MOS: Infantry
Secondary MOS: Mountaineering
Appearance: Green helmet with red goggles; green camo paint with black stripes on face and arms; green and black camouflage shirt and pants; black web straps and belt; black boots
Accessories: Grappling hook; knife with a ribbed hilt and S-shaped Quillen; parachute pack; short submachine gun with jagged triangular stock and long magazine (resembles the XM-15); two-piece duffel bag with clips on the side for a knife
Abilities: Climbs sheer walls; Hostage negotiations; Knowledge Skill: Hostage situations; Light infantryman; Mountaineering; Night vision; Tirelessly runs for miles
Conditions: Grew up in a county institution; Hates drunk drivers; Orphaned at the age of three
Quote/Motto: "Infantrymen don't march. They run. They run to get to the battle, they run during the battle, and they run to get away from the battle. The Army doesn't call it running. They call the first 'advancing,' the second, 'maneuvering,' and the last, 'disengaging.' Hit and Run calls it all running, and he's real good at it." Quote by an unnamed G.I. Joe team member.

Hollingsworth

Alias/Variations: General Hollingsworth
Real Name: (first name unknown) Hollingsworth
Gender: Male
Grade/Rank: O-10 General; adviser to Hawk and the G.I. Joe team
Service Branch: Army; on the committee of generals that oversees the Joes—the Jugglers for a short time
Faction(s): G.I. Joe
Stationed: Pentagon
Primary MOS: Pentagon Oversight of the G.I. Joe Team
Appearance: African American, a little pudgy, mostly bald but some black hair, thin black mustache on upper lip; green dress uniform

Hollow Point

Series: Twenty-three (2003)
Real Name: Max W. Corey

Place of Birth: Quitman, Arkansas
Gender: Male
Grade/Rank: E-6 (Marine technical sergeant)
SN: 828-0924-DD02
Service Branch: Marine Corps scout
Faction(s): G.I. Joe, Marine Expeditionary Unit
Stationed: Quantico
Primary MOS: Marksmanship instructor/range officer
Secondary MOS: Helicopter recon
Appearance: Dark red cap; yellow hair and beard; dark blue shirt and gloves; dark green vest with cream pockets; dark green pants, belt, kneepads, and boots; "Lego" posts on wrists and ankles
Other Known Appearances: Dark blue vest that was the same color as the shirt
Abilities: Advises mission teams on the optimal use of terrain, firing points, and choice of ammo; Helicopter recon; Instructor; Intuitive skill for the proper handling and maintenance of any weapon; Marksmanship instructor; Pinpoint accuracy; Professional Skill: Safari park operations; Qualified Operator: LOCUST; Quickly reads the situation, Range officer; Scout; Sniper; Taught the range officer course at Quantico; Trains Joes in the use of new weapons
Conditions: Puts himself in danger
Quote/Motto: "Cobra forces are a nasty bunch, but their techniques are bad. It's my job to make sure we're better trained and more disciplined."
Notes: Recruited by Duke.

Honda Lou West

Real Name: Honda Lou West
Gender: Female
Service Branch: Civilian
Faction(s): G.I. Joe
Primary MOS: Owner/Operator of Wild West Haulin'
Appearance: Feathered blonde hair, blue eyes, freckles, brown boots, vest, gloves, jeans, purple shirt, brown cowboy hat, big gold buckle, and belt
Abilities: Professional Skill: Owner/operator of a trucking company
Conditions: Fearless; Gets the job done!; Grumpy; Unappreciative
Quote/Motto: "Cobra's truck my hushpuppies! These are MY trucks, mister. Ever'one of 'em loaded and paid for by yours truly, Honda Lou West. President and manager of Wild West Haulin'!"

Horror Show

Series: Twenty-one (2005)
Alias/Variations: Horrorshow
Real Name: Stepan Drukersky
Place of Birth: Tbilisi, Georgia, Soviet Union
Gender: Male
Grade/Rank: Unknown
Service Branch: Army (Soviet/Russian)
Faction(s): Oktober Guard
Notably Served At: Afghanistan; Iran; Sierra Gordo
Primary MOS: Weapons expert
Secondary MOS: Infantry
Appearance: Brown cap; black handlebar mustache; green long-sleeved jacket with beige belt and sleeves. Beige pants with green kneepads and black boots
Accessories: Backpack, rifle, Soviet RPG-7V rocket-propelled grenade launcher with PG-7VL rocket
Abilities: Acting; Brute force; Deep-sea diver; Disregard personal injuries; Easily fist-fights three opponents; Deceptive speed and strength; Get the job done!; Fighting skills; Infantry; Longtime friend of Colonel Brekhov; Physically large; Small arms; Strong; Trooper; Weapons expert
Preferred Weapon: Shoulder-mounted RPG
Conditions: Clumsy gait; Doesn't ask questions; Likes to fight; Likes "the challenge"; Knows he's not the smartest; Not the brightest mind; Reputation: From a well-known theater family; Stout
Quote/Motto: "I fight until I am the only one left standing. That is what I do."
Notes: According to Russian reports, Horror Show is as strong as a polar bear. While trying to save "El Jefe," Horror Show, along with Colonel Brekhov, Schrage, and Stormavik went on a suicide run trying to clear a Cobra Razorback tank from the road, driving a small jeep with only a handful of weapons. In his final moments, Horror Show laughed off the intense barrage of bullets that had shredded Colonel Brekhov and himself. He drove the explosive-filled jeep into the tank, destroying both.

Hot Jets

Real Name: Yuri Ivanovich Asimov
Place of Birth: Leningrad, Russia

Grade/Rank: Unknown
SN: AF 934100
Service Branch: Air Force
Faction(s): Action Force, Space Force
Primary MOS: Space astrogation
Secondary MOS: Pilot instructor
Background Information: Trained at Soviet Military Complex, Baikonur; two-year training program with NASA
Abilities: Hand-to-hand armed combat; Instructor; Lunar pilot; Pilot instructor; Pilot; Satellite repair; Space astrogation; Suborbital piloting; Zero gravity training
Conditions: Reputation: The best space pilot; Respected by Soviet and American space commands
Quote/Motto: "Hot Jets is the best space pilot there is. Highly respected by both Soviet and American space Commands." Quote by an unnamed G.I. Joe team member.

Hot Seat

Series: Eight (1989)
Real Name: Michael A. Provost
Place of Birth: Pawtucket, Rhode Island (Bath, England, for European distribution)
Gender: Male
Grade/Rank: E-7 (Army sergeant first class)
SN: 442-56-DI96
Service Branch: Army
Faction(s): G.I. Joe
Primary MOS: Raider driver
Secondary MOS: Drill instructor
Appearance: Gray hair; a beige shirt with a green vest; orange pants; black gloves, belt, and boots
Accessories: Helmet covering one eye and with attached mic
Abilities: Drill instructor; Heightened reflexes; Powerful left jab; Professional Skill: Heavyweight contender; Qualified Operator: Raider; Tactical mind
Conditions: Consciously works at attaining a sense of "oneness" with his vehicle; Disliked boxing as a profession; Fearful of permanent brain stem damage
Quote/Motto: "The Raider is a fast, heavily armed, all-terrain, armored fighting vehicle that is perfect for modern, behind-the-lines confrontations! But a fighting machine, no matter how sophisticated, is only as effective as its operator. Hot Seat consciously works at attaining a sense of 'oneness' with his vehicle. He strives to make it respond to his will, in order to accomplish those feats which others consider to be impossible." Quote by an unnamed G.I. Joe team member.
Notes: Works well with long-time Joe allies Oktober Guard and the Tucaros

Ice Cream Soldier

Series: Thirteen (1994)
Real Name: Tom-Henry Ragan
Place of Birth: Providence, Rhode Island
Gender: Male
Grade/Rank: E-5 (Army sergeant)
SN: XL9-11-87
Service Branch: Army
Faction(s): G.I. Joe, Battle Corps
Primary MOS: Fire operations expert
Secondary MOS: Barbecue chef
Appearance: Orange helmet with black visor; orange shirt with neon yellow diagonal straps and gloves; orange pants with a black belt; neon yellow leg bands and boots
Accessories: Auto-pistol; flamethrower; machete; missile launcher with a trigger; submachine gun; two missiles
Abilities: Fire operations expert; Flamethrower commando; Knowledge Skill: Fire; Professional Skill: Barbecue chef
Conditions: Joes don't like to go into battle with him; Joes don't like to talk to him; Likes people making fun of his code name; Reputation: A lunatic; Wants people to underestimate him
Quote/Motto: "Eating ice cream without hot fudge is like fighting without ammunition."
Notes: His equipment can deliver streams of flame up to 75 feet.

Ice Storm

Series: Twenty-seven (2011)
Real Name: Nolan M. Ligotke
Place of Birth: Elyria, Ohio
Gender: Male
Grade/Rank: E-4 Specialist
SN: 280-84-JW75
Service Branch: U.S. Coast Guard, Navy
Faction(s): G.I. Joe
Stationed: Ellesmere Island Research Base in Qikiqtaaluk, Canada
Primary MOS: Cold weather rescue
Secondary MOS: Naval VBSS
Appearance: Black pants and boots, red and black Arctic coat, black skullie
Accessories: Clear IV tube, goggles, harness, and rifle; IV bag module, kneepads, medic

pack, pistol, rope bundle, silencer, strap for trauma board, submachine gun, trauma board, two shock paddles, vest, Z+ tank with a clear oxygen mask

Abilities: Cold weather rescue; Hobby Skill: Designs action figures of team members; Hobby Skill: Drawing; Hobby Skill: Model making; Professional Skill: Snow crab fisherman; Qualified Operator: S.H.A.R.C. Submarine; Qualified Weapon Expert: 820 selective-fire long-range fully automatic assault rifle, VBSS Unit (Visit, Board, Search, and Seizure)

Conditions: Always on duty; Not afraid of cold weather; Yearns to explore frozen wastelands

Quote/Motto: "They tease me a lot, but in another life, I could have been one heck of a toy designer."

Iceberg

Series: Five (1986)
Alias/Variations: Prototype names included: Chill, Cool Breeze, Ice-Man, and Winter
Real Name: Clifton L. Nash
Place of Birth: Brownsville, Texas
Gender: Male
Grade/Rank: E-5 (Army sergeant)
SN: 271-65-5660
Service Branch: Army
Faction(s): G.I. Joe, Battle Corps
Stationed: Apogee Base in Greenland
Primary MOS: Infantry
Secondary MOS: Cold weather survival instructor
Appearance: African American; white hat with green goggles; white snowsuit, blue vest, and green backpack and belt; dark green gloves and white boots
Other Known Appearances (Cartoon): White vest instead of light blue
Accessories: XM60E37.62-mm machine gun
Background Information: "Iceberg hates hot weather. In Brownsville, Texas, in the summer you can spit on the sidewalk and watch it sizzle. While other kids saves up for bicycles, Iceberg saves up for an air conditioner."
Abilities: Cold weather survival instructor; Infantry; Qualified Operator: Dreadnok Swampfire; Qualified Operator: JUMP; Qualified Weapons Expert: M-16A2, M-79, M-60, and M-1911A1; Snow trooper; Wilderness Survival: Arctic
Conditions: Hates hot weather; Loves ultra-cold climates; Slight Jamaican accent
Quote/Motto: "We have plenty of cold-weather specialists that can stand the cold well enough but very few that like it. Iceberg's just not happy until the mercury dips below zero. This is not to say he's unaware of the dangers of cold weather or that he is impervious to the lethal effects of hypothermia. Rather, his love for ultra-cold climates has forced him to learn every aspect of arctic survival." Quote by an unnamed G.I. Joe team member.
Notes: Iceberg is not to be confused with Cold Breeze. Iceberg was offered as a mail-in offer in 1992 and came with a rectangular file card but rather than his long, white rifle, he came with a large, tan Heckler and Koch PSG-1.

Inferno

Series: Three (1984), 8" Commando Scale (2007)
Place of Birth: Possibly Hawaii
Gender: Male
Faction(s): G.I. Joe, Sigma 6
Notably Served At: World War III
Primary MOS: Firefighting specialist
Appearance: Red full-coverage body armor
Accessories: Ax, backpack, belt, chest harness, helmet, hose, oxygen tank, two gauntlets
Abilities: Knowledge Skill: Intimate knowledge of fires (how they start, stop, spread, move, burn, etc.); Specialist: Firefighting
Notes: His ax is supercooled and can snuff flames on contact. The is also an Inferno who is a member of S.K.A.R.

International Action Force

Series: Twelve (1993)
Purpose: This is a special unit assignment. "There comes a time when the power of evil becomes so threatening to world peace that global leaders must join together to stop its impending danger; Cobra is just such an evil. An international force of G.I. Joe combat specialists has been called upon to hit Cobra and hit them hard! Russia is represented by Big Bear, an anti-armor specialist who loves to blow up Cobra tanks. From England comes Big Ben, an expert in subversive operations and enemy infiltration. Japan has sent Budo, one of its greatest samurai warriors who plans on slicing Cobra into tiny pieces of snake meat. Spirit, a Native American, also joins the team from his home in Arizona, where he was called for duty to track down and eliminate Cobra Dreadnoks. World peace must be upheld, and Cobra's evil must be stopped.... TODAY!"

Leader: None listed, defer to rank
Members: Big Bear, Big Ben, Budo, and Spirit
Notes: The file card included refers to the formation of the Joe team's members from around the world to infiltrate Cobra's Montana wilderness hideout and "stop them cold" (from the insert) in their plot to disrupt communications worldwide.

Iron Bear

Series: Twenty-eight (2012)
Real Name: CLASSIFIED (General Artur Vaskovia)
Place of Birth: Saint Petersburg, Russia
Gender: Male
Grade/Rank: O-7 (equivalent) General
Service Branch: Army (Soviet/Russian)
Faction(s): Oktober Guard General
Primary MOS: Operations commander
Secondary MOS: Counterintelligence
Appearance: Brown Russian long coat and uniform, young face, dark hair, dark eyes
Accessories: Baton, hat, knife, rifle with ammo drum
Abilities: Command; Experienced war veteran; Knowledge Skill: Armaments; Knowledge Skill: Battles; Knowledge Skill: Locations; Knowledge Skill: Military strategies; Knowledge Skill: Noteworthy soldiers; Knowledge Skill: Vehicles; Leadership; One step ahead of the enemy; Secret headquarters; Wise
Conditions: Confident; Humble around his soldiers; Rumor: Amassed a sizable collection of war memorabilia; Young-looking face
Quote/Motto: "Knowledge is of no value unless you put it into practice."

Jammer

Series: Twenty-six (2010)
Real Name: Calvin Mondale
Place of Birth: New York City, New York
Gender: Male
Grade/Rank: E-7 (Equivalent) Sergeant
SN: AF 396618
Service Branch: Army (British)
Faction(s): S.A.F. (Special Action Force)/Z Force
Primary MOS: Communication engineer
Secondary MOS: Electronic warfare
Appearance: African American, red beret, wears one of three outfits: entirely green fatigues, dark green camouflage stripes fatigues, or a black camouflage stripes fatigues version
Accessories: Antenna, backpack, GPS locator, hose, microphone, pistol, radio, red beret, rifle, submachine gun
Abilities: Brilliant electronic engineer; Communication engineer; Developed Z Force command center communication system; Electronic warfare; Jams insurgent communication systems; Leading computer designer; Monitors insurgent communication systems; PhD from UCLA; Relays space force satellite surveillance to Z Force for heavy artillery bombardments
Conditions: Delights in improving electronic devices; Ex-Pat (American living in England); Finds corporate life tedious; Reputation: Leading computer designer
Quote/Motto: "I'll have the bad guys' signals jammed and on the run in no time." "Subject is a master of improvised signal disruption devices, but won't hesitate to go on the offensive with long range acoustic devices of his own design." Quote by Captain Skip.
Notes: Action Force (alternate continuity)

Jinx

Series: Six (1987)
Alias/Variations: Agent Jinx
Real Name: CLASSIFIED (Kimi Arashikage, "Kimi" is a nickname)
Place of Birth: Los Angeles, California; (Cardiff, Wales for European distribution)
Gender: Female
Grade/Rank: E-5 Sergeant
SN: 037-42-4683
Service Branch: Army
Faction(s): G.I. Joe, Ninja Force, Rawhides, and Tiger Force
Notably Served At: Cobra-La
Primary MOS: Ninja/intelligence
Secondary MOS: Finance clerk
Appearance: Asian, short black hair, looks young; red mask; red shirt and pants with a dragon emblem on left chest; black cuffs and belt; red shoes and fingernails
Accessories: Naginata staff; pouch backpack with two slots for swords; two medium-length ninja swords with textured hilts and angled tips
Background Information: Bryn Mawr graduate (liberal arts college in Pennsylvania); underwent training with the Blind Master
Abilities: Blind fighting; Bounty hunter in Tokyo; Detect deception; Fast; Finance clerk; Infiltration skills; Martial arts expert; Ninja;

Reputation: Bad luck; Reputation: Blind luck; Intelligence specialist; Stealth; Willpower

Conditions: Easy to underestimate her; Fights best blindfolded; Likes to rib teammate; Often blamed for any unlucky occurrences; Often partnered with Kamakura; Teammate Budo is her lover; Teammate Falcon is a former lover; Trains intensely

Quote/Motto: "Don't underestimate Jinx. She has been to the Secret Mountain and studied the Seven Silent Forms with the Blind Master. She has the 'Eye That Pierces,' the 'Iron Hand' and the 'Heart That Waits.' She can see through your deception, batter aside your defenses, and dazzle you with the strength of her will." Quote by an unnamed G.I. Joe team member.

Notes: She is the cousin of Storm Shadow (Tommy Arashikage); recruited into G.I. Joe by Snake Eyes. She was KIA by Chuckles to protect his undercover status.

The Jugglers

Alias/Variations: The official name for this group is unknown; they're called the Jugglers because they make everything balance in the end and manage to look good doing it.

Purpose: A top-secret committee of generals who oversaw many units, G.I. Joe being only one of the units under their jurisdiction. They were a hindrance to the Joes for years. They meet in secret behind unmarked doors in the Pentagon.

Leader: The first leader was General Malthus; his personal "army" was called the Domestic Operations Agency. The next leader was General Thurston Crowther.

Members: At one point, Hawk became a member of the Jugglers, hoping to weed out the corruption from the inside; once the Joe team was reinstated, he vowed to shield the team from Juggler political meddling and keep their power in check. The known members are Admiral Dyson, General Abernathy "Hawk" (DDP), General Austin, General Crowther, General Curtis, General Gibbs (chairman of the Jugglers), General Harring, General Hollingsworth, General Malthus, General Ryan, General Winters

Julie Haun

Real Name: Julie Haun
Gender: Female
Service Branch: Army
Faction(s): G.I. Joe, Greenshirt
Notably Served At: New Moon, Colorado
Notes: KIA in New Moon, Colorado, when fellow Greenshirt Thomas Stall broke cover and called attention to their location.

Junko Akita

Real Name: Junko Akita
Gender: Female
Background Information: Yakuza member Ryjui Hyata killed her parents when she was 15.
Abilities: Apprentice to Storm Shadow; Ninjutsu; Trained geisha
Conditions: Lover to Storm Shadow; Vowed revenge on Ryjui Hyata
Notes: She was tortured and brainwashed by the Red Ninja Clan to fight Storm Shadow; he tried to break the control on her, but in a moment of clarity she committed suicide rather than fight and risk killing him.

Kamakura

Series: Nineteen (2003)
Alias/Variations: The "Green Power Ranger" (so-called by General Hawk); Throwdown
Real Name: CLASSIFIED (Sean Collins [Broca])
Place of Birth: CLASSIFIED (Roseville, California)
Gender: Male
Grade/Rank: E-5 Sergeant
SN: CLASSIFIED
Service Branch: Army
Faction(s): G.I. Joe Reservist member status*; Greenshirts, Sigma 6 team Reservist member status*; Strike Team: Bravo, and Hammer Team
Stationed: Fort Wadsworth; the Pit III
Notably Served At: Afghanistan; Olliestan; Trans-Carpathia
Primary MOS: Infantry
Secondary MOS: Intelligence
Appearance: Short brown hair and brown eyes
Accessories: Ninja weapons; Uzi machine gun
Background Information: He is the son of the original Fred Broca, a Crimson Guardsman who looked exactly like the rest of the "Fred series." His father was killed and replaced by Fred II, who was revealed to be Wade Collins, a war buddy of Snake Eyes and Stalker.
Abilities: Apprentice to Snake Eyes; Ninja; Member of the Arashikage clan; Magical Sword: Possess mystical properties and only someone with exceptional skill and focus can use it; Willpower

Conditions: Apprentice to Snake Eyes; Assumed the Snake Eyes identity; Clan tattoo on his arm; Face is scarred; Face not revealed; Seeks to avenge Hammer Team by killing Firefly; Sole survivor of Hammer Team; Son of the original Fred Broca

Notes: *All reservists can be called back into action if a mission calls for it. Sean Collins (Broca) has been declared deceased and is buried at Arlington National Cemetery with full honors. He was given a sword named "Tatsuwashi" by Snake Eyes.

Keel-Haul

Series: Four (1985)
Real Name: Everett P. Colby
Place of Birth: Charlottesville, Virginia
Gender: Male
Grade/Rank: 9/O-9: Vice Admiral (VADM) Keel-Haul
SN: 672-38-4202
Service Branch: Navy (Retired)
Faction(s): G.I. Joe, Battle Corps
Stationed: Pentagon, Washington, D.C.
Notably Served At: USS *Intrepid*; Battle of Benzheen, Cobra Island
Primary MOS: Command (USS *Flagg*)
Secondary MOS: Pilot
Appearance: White and black sailor's cap; black hair and mustache; an open-collared blue shirt with dog tag; maroon jacket with gold medals and black gloves; beige pants with black belts, holster. There is a white patch painted on his right shoulder, stars painted on his blue collar.
Other Known Appearances: The mail-in exclusive did not have the white patch or gold stars and frequently arrived without the pistol.
Accessories: Included with the USS *Flagg* playset; silver Walther PPK pistol with textured grip
Background Information: Graduated from Annapolis and Navy Flight School; Naval War College in Newport, Rhode Island; Armed Forces Staff College; Holder of the Navy Cross, DFC, and Air Medal
Abilities: Command; Leadership; Qualified Operator: Phantom F-4; Respected military historian; Nationally rated chess player; Pilot
Conditions: World's worst clarinet player; Reputation: Highly decorated seaman; Reputation: Recipient of the Air Medal; Reputation: Recipient of the Flying Cross medal; Reputation: Recipient of the Navy Cross

Quote/Motto: "Keel-Haul was always cool. He could set an F-4 down on a carrier deck at night with half his instruments out and walk away whistling. You know what it's like to land on a carrier at night? Try jumping on a moving skateboard while blindfolded." Quote by an unnamed team member.

Notes: He is the highest-ranking G.I. Joe officer, outside of General Joseph Colton (O-10), outranking General Hawk by two pay grades, and serves as head of the Joe team when they operate out of the *Flagg*.

Kickstart

Series: Twenty-six (2010)
Real Name: Joseph A. Rivera
Gender: Male
Grade/Rank: E-5 Sergeant
SN: 947-88-JR60
Service Branch: Army
Faction(s): G.I. Joe
Appearance: Short brown hair, brown eyes; solid green army fatigues, black knee pads
Accessories: 820 selective-fire, long-range fully automatic assault rifle, helmet with night-vision goggles, vest
Background Information: Caltech Alumnus
Abilities: Bioengineering expert; Computer technology expert; Electronic engineering expert; Qualified Operator: Steel marauder
Conditions: Die-Hard gamer

Kiwi

Real Name: Scott Walters
Place of Birth: Christchurch, New Zealand
Gender: Male
SN: AF 934777
Faction(s): Action Force, Space Force
Primary MOS: Computer Engineering
Secondary MOS: Freefall combat
Appearance: Cybernetic right hand
Background Information: PhD Graduate from MIT
Abilities: Computer engineering; Cybernetic right hand; Computer security expert; Freefall combat; Knowledge Skill: Space hardware
Conditions: Brave; Lost right hand
Quote/Motto: "Kiwi typifies the spirit and bravery of all Action Force." Quote by an unnamed Action Force team member.
Notes: He has received three citations for bravery.

Knockdown

Series: Six (1987)
Real Name: Blain M. Gonsalves
Place of Birth: San Francisco, California
Gender: Male
Grade/Rank: E-5 Sergeant
SN: 501-32-4065
Service Branch: Army
Faction(s): G.I. Joe, Battleforce 2000
Stationed: Aberdeen Proving Grounds; Frusenland
Notably Served At: The Battle of Benzheen
Primary MOS: Infantry
Secondary MOS: Microwave technician
Appearance: Short brown hair and eyes; blue shirt, black pants, brown padded vest, silver wristband, black glove on right hand and blue glove on left hand, ribbed green boots.
Other Known Appearances: Red hair; a blue shirt with a beige vest and left armband; gloves blue on the left hand, black on the right hand; black pants with beige and brown boots
Accessories: Flexible helmet with monocular; large "experimental ground-to-air pistol"
Abilities: Electronic detection systems expert; Hobby Skill: Lepidopterist (collects butterflies and moths); Hobby Skill: Skeet-shooting; Infantry; Infrared sensors expert; Knowledge Skill: Air disasters; Knowledge Skill: Infrared sensors; Knowledge Skill: Radar systems; Knowledge Skill: Target tracking computers; Marksman; Microwave technician; Qualified Operator: Sky-Sweeper; Repair radar systems; Target tracking computers expert
Conditions: Fear of flying; Reputation: Authority on air disasters
Quote/Motto: "Knockdown likes to go skeet-shooting with a bolt-action rifle. He thinks it's more sporting. According to him, anybody can hit a clay pigeon with a shotgun! He collects butterflies and moths—just plucks them out of the air with his fingers. Knockdown is also an authority on air disasters—maybe to replace his morbid fear of flying." Quote by an unnamed G.I. Joe team member.
Notes: He was KIA during the Battle of Benzheen when it was bombed by Cobra Commander. He is buried in Arlington National Cemetery.

Lady Jaye

Series: Four (1985)
Alias/Variations: Lady J. Prototype names were Lady Shea, Lady Shay, Shady Lady, Sprite
Real Name: Alison R. Hart-Burnett. Prototype surname was Hart-Smyth
Place of Birth: Martha's Vineyard, Massachusetts (Cork, Eire, Ireland for European distribution)
Gender: Female
Grade/Rank: 6/O-3: Captain
SN: 853-71-6749
Service Branch: Army intelligence
Faction(s): G.I. Joe, Slaughter's Marauders
Stationed: Fort Lewis, Seattle to guard Power Station Alpha; the Pit*; Trans-Carpathia
Notably Served At: Springfield; Scotland; New York; Gulf of Mexico
Primary MOS: Intelligence/covert operations
Secondary MOS: Personnel clerk
Appearance: Brown hair; black hat with a silver circle on front; green open-collared, short-sleeved shirt and pants; brown backpack straps and belt; black gloves and boots
Other Known Appearances (Cartoon): No hat; dark green gloves and pants, with brown boots; knife strapped to the chest on the left side, attaching to diagonal chest strap; backpack was a dark green cylindrical quiver filled with javelins. In a later era, she has blonde and approximately shoulder-length hair. In the Sunbow cartoon, they did not use her Gaelic accent.
Accessories: Power javelin; square backpack; surveillance camera with strap
Background Information: Graduated from Bryn Mawr; graduate work at Trinity College in Dublin, Ireland; intelligence school Fort Holabird, Baltimore, Maryland.
Abilities: Airborne qualified; Covert operations specialist; Cryptological linguistics (signals intelligence and electronic interception analysis); Impersonation: voice and mannerisms; Infantry fieldwork; Knowledge Skill: Cultures of Afghanistan, France, Germany, Italy, Poland, Portugal, Russia, Spain; Linguist: Easily pass as a native in Afghanistan, France, Germany, Italy, Poland, Portugal, Russia, Spain; Personnel clerk; Professional Skill: Actress; Professional Skill: Mime; Qualified Operator: Armadillo, A.W.E. Striker, Conquest, Dragonfly, Falcon Glider, Killer W.H.A.L.E., LCV Recon Sled, MANTA, Polar Battle Bear, RAM, SHARC, Silver Mirage, Sky Hawk, Sky-Striker, Snow Cat, Tomahawk, VAMP, Cobra Moray, Cobra Night Raven, Cobra Stun, the Ghost jet, jeep, motorcycle, and Cobra sub; Qualified Weapon Expert: M-16, M1911A1, and reflex crossbow; Ranger

Preferred Weapon: Signature Weapons: Variety of specialized throwing javelins featuring unique properties like energy projectors, a pure diamond head for cutting through hard materials, one that released nets for capturing enemies, rescue flares, and one that generated a protective force field–like bubble letting her and another person breathe underwater and include small propulsion units that could carry them to the surface

Conditions: Belief: "Less is more"; Distinctive Feature: Faint Gaelic accent; Enjoys grunt duty; Eschews complicated makeup and rubber masks; Famed romance with Flint; Married Flint; Mellow and level-headed; Occasional temper; Related to Destro; Romantically linked to Grid-Iron; Undertakes field tests of both new equipment and new Joes

Quote/Motto: "Lady Jaye doesn't go in for that phony wig and rubber mask brand of disguise like those jokers on Mission Impossible.... She becomes the subject: body language, subtle gestures, correct shading of dialect—the right look in the eye. Cloaked and sandaled, she can squat down with a basket of oranges in any Middle Eastern marketplace and blend in perfectly." Quote by an unnamed G.I. Joe team member.

Notes: She has a daughter by Flint named Marissa Faireborn. Lady Jaye was killed by Red Shadows member Dela Eden while trying to save Flint. * The Pit, Utah, located beneath Fort Wadsworth

Law and Order

Series: Six (1987)
Real Name: Christopher M. Lavigne
Place of Birth: Houston, Texas (Streatham, London, England, for European distribution)
Gender: Male
Grade/Rank: E-4 (Army corporal)
SN: 044-56-8883
Service Branch: Army
Faction(s): G.I. Joe, Battle Corps, Rawhides, and Sonic Fighters
Primary MOS: Military police/K-9
Secondary MOS: Intelligence
Appearance: Brown hair; orange short-sleeved shirt with "MP" on left arm; open light blue vest with black holster; olive green pants with black belt and boots
Other Known Appearances (Cartoon): Noticeably darker shirt, vest, and pants. Order was larger than the toy's scale with light and dark gray areas.
Accessories: Bomb-sniffing German shepherd, Order; helmet with flared brim and "M.P." on front; 9-mm Uzi; black M.P. truncheon; spiked leash
Background Information: Walked a beat in Houston's Fifth Ward for two years before the pair enlisted for the M.P.'s
Abilities: Airborne; Attention to detail; Canine companion; Developing and maintaining G.I. Joe security protocols; Knowledge Skill: Police culture; Knowledge Skill: Prison culture; Natural affinity for animals; Professional Skill: Military policeman; Professional Skill: Policeman; Professional Skill: Prison guard; Trained dog handler
Conditions: Good-natured; Reputation: Fiercer than his dog; Reputation: No-nonsense procedure and attention to detail
Quote/Motto: "M.P.'s are responsible for the security of an installation. That may sound like a cushy job if all they are guarding is a garrison full of clerks, cooks, and accountants, but it's another matter altogether when they're acting as the defensive line for an elite unit like the Joes. The bad guys are going to send in the best they have and that's not good enough to get past Law & Order. You don't want to mess with him and that dog of his. Chew your leg right off, he will. After that, you still have to deal with the dog!" Quote by an unnamed G.I. Joe team member.

Leatherneck

Series: Five (1986)
Alias/Variations: Prototype names were Gunny, Gyrene, Jar Head, Semper-Fi
Real Name: Wendell A. Metzger
Place of Birth: Stromsburg, Nebraska (Berchtesgaden, Germany for European distribution)
Gender: Male
Grade/Rank: E-7 Marine gunnery sergeant
SN: RA 368-10-0025
Service Branch: Marine
Faction(s): G.I. Joe, Battle Corps, and Special Mission: Brazil (1986)
Stationed: Camp Lejeune; Parris Island Military Academy; Vietnam; Gitmo; the CEC Military Academy
Notably Served At: Springfield, Cobra Island
Primary MOS: Infantry/rifleman
Secondary MOS: Drill sergeant
Appearance: Black hair and mustache; green

cap, shirt, and pants with brown "bird's foot" camouflage; beige vest with dark green pads; black belt, holsters

Other Known Appearances (Cartoon): Standard blotchy green/yellow camo pattern, with darker green than on figure; gray backpack straps. The 1986 Special Mission: Brazil, Toys "R" Us exclusive wears a brown belt, brown boots, tan camos, two-tone dark brown vest, tan marine hat, and a wristwatch on left hand. The set also included Claymore, Dial Tone, Mainframe, and Wet Suit.

Accessories: Small backpack (with engraved roll and canteen); "over/under" M-16/203 rifle with a grenade launcher. The 1986 Special Mission: Brazil, Toys "R" Us exclusive came with a gray M-16 "over-under" rifle and a field pack.

Abilities: A man you can trust!; Always the traditional soldier; An insurmountable obstacle to the enemy; Badass; Qualified Operator: Devilfish, Falcon Glider, LCV Recon Sled, Mauler, Silver Mirage, and the Dreadnok cycle; Works well with Wet Suit

Conditions: Always applies suntan lotion when at the beach; Hot-headed; Ill-tempered; Irrational grudge against those who don't fit his definition of "worthy"; No patience with dishonesty, indecisiveness, and lazy people; Obnoxious; Opinionated; Overbearing; Reputation: Hardest gunny at Camp Lejeune; Reputation: Meanest corporal in Gitmo; Reputation: Roughest tech sergeant of the 1st Recon Battalion in Vietnam; Reputation: Toughest drill sergeant on Parris Island; Trades insults with Wet Suit about their respective branches of service; Trustworthy; Uncouth

Quote/Motto: "He is uncouth, opinionated, and overbearing. And he has no patience at all with the indecisive, the lazy, and the dishonest. Not a man you can like, but one you can trust."

Ledger

Alias/Variations: Admiral Ledger
Real Name: Warren D. Ledger
Gender: Male
Grade/Rank: Vice Admiral (O-9)
Service Branch: Navy
Faction(s): G.I. Joe
Stationed: Aircraft carrier USS *Flagg*
Primary MOS: Commander of the USS *Flagg*
Secondary MOS: Training

Appearance: Full, thick, gray beard
Background Information: Naval Academy; Navy Flight School; Naval War College; Armed Forces Staff College
Abilities: Keeps his ship running efficiently
Conditions: Braggart; Old-school mariner; Professional; Proud, Traditional maritime superstitions
Quote/Motto: "I've been at sea so long, whales ask me for directions."

Leviathan

Real Name: Jamie Hugh McLaren
Place of Birth: Glasgow, Scotland
Gender: Male
Grade/Rank: Commander
SN: AF 93403
Service Branch: Navy
Faction(s): Action Force, Q Force
Primary MOS: Naval battle tactics
Secondary MOS: Gunnery
Background Information: Royal navy
Abilities: Commander of a destroyer; Deep-sea diving; Experienced diver; Gunnery; Naval battle tactics; Quick-thinking; Sheer ability!
Conditions: Blue-collar family (shipyard workers); Slow moving
Quote/Motto: "Leviathan is a slow-moving but quick-thinking man. This has got him out of many tight spots." Quote by an unnamed Action Force member.

Lifeline

Series: Five (1986)
Real Name: Edwin C. Steen
Place of Birth: Seattle, Washington
Gender: Male
Grade/Rank: E-5 sergeant
SN: RA 128-03-2496
Service Branch: Army
Faction(s): G.I. Joe, Battle Corps, and Tiger Force
Primary MOS: Medic/rescue trooper
Appearance: Red and white helmet with silver goggles; black hair; green sunglasses; a red open-collar shirt with white pockets and silver backpack straps; red pants with a white belt, pockets, and boots; "Rescue" on the left leg
Other Known Appearances (Cartoon): No weapons on the uniform; pockets on chest often absent
Accessories: Browning double-action 9-mm pistol, EMS kit with air mask and hose, relay backpack with antenna

Abilities: Black belt in Aikido; Paramedic; Qualified Operator: Conquest, JUMP; Steely gaze

Conditions: Belief: Rescue personnel are never off-duty; Girlfriend: Brittany "Bree" Van Mark; Principled pacifist; Minister's son; Sympathizes with Dr. Adele Burkhart

Quote/Motto: "Troops have to know that if something really heavy comes down on them and they're in no condition to walk out of the mess, somebody is going to have the heart to wade in and extract them. That somebody is Lifeline." Quote by an unnamed G.I. Joe team member.

Notes: The first of two characters code-named Lifeline. The 1991 Rice Krispies mail-in exclusive has Lifeline without his sculpted black side arm holster on his left leg or his 9-mm pistol; rather he came with a flare gun.

Lifeline 2

Series: Eighteen (2002)
Real Name: Greg Scott
Place of Birth: Spring Valley, New York
Gender: Male
Grade/Rank: E-5 Sergeant
Service Branch: Army
Faction(s): G.I. Joe, Anti-Venom Task Force, and reserve member
Stationed: Walter Reed Medical Center
Primary MOS: Medic
Secondary MOS: Rescue trooper
Appearance: Light brown hair, eyes, and five o'clock shadow. White shirt, short-sleeved vest festooned with pouches and medical gear; black pants and boots
Accessories: Carry case medkit
Abilities: Combat rescue ready; Straightforward medic
Notes: The second of two characters code-named Lifeline. Currently, he is a reserve member of the Joe team assigned to domestic operations in the United States. *All reservists can be called back into action if a mission calls for it.

Lift-Ticket

Series: Five (1986)
Real Name: Victor W. Sikorski
Place of Birth: Lawton, Oklahoma (Wimborne, Dorset, England, for European distribution)
Gender: Male
Grade/Rank: 5/W-2: Chief warrant officer 2
SN: 675-51-5671
Service Branch: Army
Faction(s): G.I. Joe, Strike Team: Alpha
Notably Served At: Australian Outback; Vietnam, Grave Island, Mekong Delta; Latin America; Sao Cristobel
Primary MOS: Tomahawk pilot; rotary wing aircraft pilot; VTOL (Vertical Take-Off and Landing) and V/STOL (Vertical/Short Take-Off and Landing) pilot
Secondary MOS: Fixed-wing and rotary-wing aircraft pilot
Appearance: Red helmet with black goggles and chinstrap; green shirt and pants with a beige vest; red shoulder guards and kneepads; black pockets, gloves, belt, and boots
Other Known Appearances (Cartoon): Same, but with dark brown pockets, gloves, and boots
Accessories: Included with the Tomahawk helicopter; helmet, mic attaching to the helmet, rifle, two radio headsets, vest
Background Information: Joined the Army to get out of his hometown; West Point Prep., O.C.S. (Officer Candidate School); Flight Warrant Officer School
Abilities: "Bulletproof!"; Cool under fire; Expert pilot; Extraction expert; Lucky; Persistent; Qualified Expert Operator: Eaglehawk Helicopter, LCV Recon Sled, Silver Mirage, Tomahawk Helicopter; Stubborn persistence
Conditions: Downplays his abilities; Reputation: One of the best helicopter pilots in the army; Reputation: Notable for his extraction missions
Quote/Motto: "Getting into a target area is comparatively easy—you wait until dark and get sneaky. Now, getting out after some caps have been popped and a can o' firefight's been opened; well, that's another story. All you can do is squat on the LZ [landing zone] and hope that whoever's driving the extraction chopper is skillful, persistent, lucky, and bulletproof. Lift-Ticket satisfies the first three requirements, and he's working on the fourth!" Quote by an unnamed G.I. Joe team member. "You don't just fly into an LZ expecting the weapons fire to somehow miss you. You've got to have a whole lot of skill, plenty of stubbornness, and a fistful of luck if you want to get you and your team out of there in one piece."

Lightfoot

Series: Seven (1988)
Alias/Variations: Chain-Fire, Hotfoot, Nitro

Real Name: Cory R. Owens
Place of Birth: Wichita, Kansas
Gender: Male
Grade/Rank: 0/E-4: Corporal, specialist
SN: 075-09-4876, changed to 075-0948-OC76
Service Branch: Army
Faction(s): G.I. Joe, Night Force, Strike Team: Charlie
Notably Served At: Trucial Abysmia, New York City, New York; Sierra Gordo
Primary MOS: Explosives; demolitions
Secondary MOS: Artillery coordinator
Appearance: Brown hair; yellow shirt with black vest, armbands, and gloves; green stripe on top of the vest; yellow pants with black belt, boots, and horizontal stripes on the outside legs
Other Known Appearances (Night Force Uniform): Brown hair; brown shirt with black vest, armbands, and gloves; blue stripe on top of the vest; brown pants with black belt and boots; all the same equipment but in black
Accessories: Backpack with holo-sticker; flat, bright segmented cable; helmet with two antennae on rear and red eyepieces; tread robot with holo-sticker; two-handled, cross-shaped remote control
Abilities: Artillery coordinator; Demolitions expert; Heightened perception; Heightened sense of smell; Knowledge Skill: Foreign forces and other non-military applications; Knowledge Skill: Explosive detonators; Knowledge Skill: Terrorists' favorite detonators; Memorized all the conversion tables for foreign and non-military explosives; Memorized all mathematical tables for calculating explosives; Memorized all the mathematical tables for cutting structural steel, timber, and breaching various forms of bunker material; Memorized all the mathematical tables in military manuals for explosives; Memorized all the mathematical tables of power requirements for firing circuits; Memorized all the mathematical tables of safe firing distances; Teammates feel better when he is on the mission
Conditions: Careful; Cracks under integration; Suffers from old torture injuries; Takes twice as long to clear an area of tripwires and traps
Quote/Motto: "Lightfoot has elevated being careful to an art form. You might say he's a Zen fussbudget. His eyes sweep the ground before him in measured quadrants, alert for tripwires, signs of digging, and out-of-place vegetation. He sniffs the air for that tell-tale plastic explosive smell of 'dead rubber.' Lightfoot may take twice as long to clear an area, but at least you won't get any nasty surprises." Quote by an unnamed G.I. Joe team member.

Link

Series: Twenty (2004)
Alias/Variations: Dr. Link Talbot
Real Name: Lincoln B. Talbot
Place of Birth: Clarksburg, Massachusetts
Gender: Male
Grade/Rank: E-4 (Navy petty officer, 3rd class)
SN: 845-B4-LT57
Service Branch: Navy
Faction(s): G.I. Joe
Primary MOS: Veterinarian/scientist
Secondary MOS: Special operations
Appearance: African American; rows of short, black hair; a white sleeveless shirt with yellow shoulder pads; black gloves and belt; red pants with yellow and gray padding; gray boots
Accessories: Grenade launcher; harpoon rifle; wrist communicator
Background Information: Championship-winning martial arts skills; SEAL School; PhD from University of Pennsylvania School of Veterinary Medicine (VMD)
Abilities: Combat-trained soldier; Martial arts expert; Navy SEAL; Professional Skill: Chief veterinarian at the National Zoo; Professional Skill: Vet; Scientist; Steel discipline
Conditions: Paranoid: Personally investigates when DNA is taken from zoo; Third-generation vet; Views his animal charges as priceless natural treasures
Quote/Motto: "Being back in action feels good. I get a chance to help out and protect anyone—animal or human—who is threatened by COBRA."

Lockdown

Series: Three (1984), 8" Commando Scale (2007)
Gender: Male
Faction(s): G.I. Joe, Sigma 6
Notably Served At: World War III
Primary MOS: SWAT
Appearance: Simple blue and black uniform includes folds, buttons, pouches, and belt
Accessories: Dog tags, helmet, impact shield, Jolt-Volt Battering Ram, power cuffs, submachine gun
Abilities: Extensive experience capturing criminals; Knowledge Skill: Codes; Knowledge Skill:

Entry into fortified structures/strongholds; Knowledge Skill: Procedures; Military law enforcement experience; SWAT; Urban tracking; Urban warfare tactics; Weapons expert

Conditions: Distinctive Feature: Golden sunglasses; Distinctive Feature: Ridiculously chunky submachine gun with a silver and black deco and some blue and green accents; Looks like "one tough customer"

Long Arm

Series: Twelve (1993)
Alias/Variations: Longarm
Real Name: Thomas P. Mangiaratti
Place of Birth: Boulder Creek, California
Gender: Male
Grade/Rank: 1/E-5: Sergeant
SN: 69-428-LIK4
Service Branch: Army
Faction(s): G.I. Joe, Battle Corps, Drug Elimination Force
Stationed: El-Hassim Military Base in Iraq to assist in a training program for the Kurdish rebels operating in Al-Alawi with demolitions
Primary MOS: Initial assault; version 2: Bomb disposal robotic system operator
Secondary MOS: Offensive tactician; version 2: Explosive ordnance specialist
Appearance: African American; orange protection suit with hood; gold details on chest; black gloves and boots
Accessories: Knife, laser rifle, machine gun, round full-head helmet with clear visor, shield, spring-loaded missile launcher, two missiles
Abilities: Bomb disposal robotic system operator; Close-quarter combat tactics; Dodges bullets; Explosive ordnance specialist; First strike specialist; Hits hard!; Knowledge Skill: Munitions; Munitions disposal; Sharp eye; Strong; SWAT bomb detector
Conditions: Always wears a specialized suit; Charges ahead; Danger hound; Kicks doors off their hinges; Long history of taking risks; Potential death wish; Reputation: First man in, last one out
Quote/Motto: "I'm always the first one into the firefight, but I wouldn't have it any other way." "If you see me running, something is about to go BOOM!"

Long Range

Series: Eight (1989)
Alias/Variations: Knock-Out Man
Real Name: Karl W. Fritz (89)
Place of Birth: Warwick, Rhode Island
Gender: Male
Grade/Rank: 3/E-7: Sergeant first class (SFC)
SN: 909-6655-BN23
Service Branch: Army
Faction(s): G.I. Joe
Notably Served At: Olliestan
Primary MOS: Artillery machine operator
Secondary MOS: Artillery
Appearance: Red hair and full, thick beard; light green shirt with gray vest and gloves; dark green pants with light green belt, and gray thigh-high boots
Accessories: Complex, thick black pistol with trigger guard; helmet covering one eye and with lights on sides
Abilities: Genius intellect; Qualified Expert Operator: Thunderclap; Trigonometry, applied trigonometry, and calculus expert
Conditions: Likes to be impressed; Never grasped simple arithmetic; Reputation: Hits targets with pinpoint accuracy; Reputation: Child prodigy
Quote/Motto: "Long Range can drop a round on a dinner plate at a range of 15 miles, in one attempt, given a topological map and up-to-the-minute wind and barometric pressure readings. In layman's terms, that means he can fire a round from the outfield of Giants Stadium in the New Jersey Meadowlands and it will land directly on second base in Shea Stadium in Flushing, New York! Incredible!" Quote by an unnamed G.I. Joe team member.

Long Range 2

Series: Twenty-one (2005)
Real Name: Alejandro Garcia (05)
Place of Birth: Monterrey, Mexico
Gender: Male
Grade/Rank: E-5 (Sergeant)
SN: 452-86-WS45
Service Branch: Army
Faction(s): G.I. Joe, Sigma 6
Primary MOS: Transportation expert, Rolling Operations Command Center (R.O.C.C.)
Secondary MOS: Infantry, rifleman
Background Information: A naturalized U.S. citizen.
Abilities: Qualified Expert Operator: Rolling Operations Command Center (R.O.C.C.); Studies philosophy (Aristotle, Zeno, and Diogenes); Sniper
Conditions: Won't let anything stop him from completing his objective

Quote/Motto: "Aristotle said that law is order, and good law is good order. I intend to make Cobra learn what good law and order is. If they have to learn it the hard way, so be it."

Notes: He is a reserve member of the current Joe team assigned to domestic operations in the United States. *All reservists can be called back into action if a mission calls for it.

Low Light

Series: Five (1986)
Alias/Variations: Lowlight
Real Name: Cooper G. MacBride
Place of Birth: Crosby, North Dakota; Crosby, New Mexico ('89 and '93 cards had error)
Gender: Male
Grade/Rank: 2/E-6: Staff sergeant
SN: RA 827-48-5037
Service Branch: Army
Faction(s): G.I. Joe, Dino Hunters, and Slaughter's Marauders
Stationed: Instructor at the Army marksmanship program in Fort Benning, Georgia
Notably Served At: Southeast Asia; Frankfurt, Germany; Sierra Gordo; Sao Cristobel; New York City, the Battle of the Statue of Liberty; the Battle of Cobra-La
Primary MOS: Infantry/night spotter
Secondary MOS: Marksmanship instructor
Appearance: Black gloves, black ski-cap, dark gray jacket with a red pad on the right shoulder, dark gray pants with a black belt, red goggles; yellow hair. 1989, Slaughter's Marauders: curly blond hair, with no facial hair. He wore a black belt, blue cap, and goggles, blue gloves, jacket with brown, yellow-green, and dark green stripes; pad on right shoulder; pants striped dark green, yellow-green, dark green, and brown. Third release: short, straight, black hair, and a full beard. Fourth Release, Dino Hunter: blond hair and beard. Fifth release: featured black hair and beard. Sixth, seventh, and eighth release: with blond hair and no beard. All versions include a visor (either red or blue) over his eyes.
Other Known Appearances (Cartoon): No gloves
Accessories: 7.62-mm model 85 sniper rifle with bipod, backpack, Uzi submachine gun
Background Information: From an abusive household; his father forced him to spend the night in a county dump with instructions not to come home without 20 dead rats. He was lost on a hunting trip and found three weeks later. He went from being afraid of the dark to being a bogeyman.
Abilities: Camouflage; Expert on image intensification; Heavy artillery; Maintains position and is still for hours; Makes his own image-intensification goggles; Qualified Operator: A.W.E. Striker, Devilfish, Falcon Glider, JUMP; Night Spotter; SWAT Sharpshooter; Stealth expert; Sniper; Wilderness survivalist expert
Conditions: Abused by father as a child; Afraid of rats; Afraid of the dark; Avoids conversations with teammates; Belief: Scoop is a Cobra spy; Extremely private person; Maintains his night-vision equipment; Regularly suffers from nightmares; Suspicious of Scoop; Talks only when necessary
Quote/Motto: "The Joes like to have Low Light along for the ride. They know that if something gets really heavy, and that's bound to happen sooner or later, all they have to do is wait until dark ... it doesn't matter what field of fire the bad guys control—the night belongs to Low Light." Quote by an unnamed G.I. Joe team member.
Notes: He is a reserve member of the current Joe team assigned to domestic operations in the United States. *All reservists can be called back into action if a mission calls for it.

Lowdown

Gender: Male
Grade/Rank: 9/E-9: Master gunnery sergeant (MGySgt)
Service Branch: Marines
Faction(s): G.I. Joe, Strike Team: Charlie
Stationed: The USS *Flagg*
Notably Served At: Los Angeles Quintesson Spiral
Primary MOS: Parasniper
Background Information: Crew chief of Strike Team: Charlie
Abilities: Cardsharp; Hobby Skill: Poker; Marine; Qualified Expert Operator: CheyTac Intervention LRRS, the Barrett M107, Steyr Scout Tactical, the AMP TS DSR-1; Qualified Weapon Expert: M16A2, M249, M240G, M2, M203, and AT-4; Sniper
Conditions: Cool and calculating demeanor; Enjoys kicking back and sharing a few cold ones with friends; Made peace with the fact that the next jump might be his last
Quote/Motto: "Hey, I can hit your house from here."
Notes: During the attack on Los Angeles, he rescued Synergy from Starlight Music. Lowdown

is a character from the Transformers Universe, MUX.

Mace

Series: Twelve (1993)
Alias/Variations: Cerebro (Brazil)
Real Name: Thomas S. Bowman
Place of Birth: Denver, Colorado
Gender: Male
Grade/Rank: 4/E-8: Master sergeant
SN: 463-NH-739D
Service Branch: Marine
Faction(s): G.I. Joe, Battle Corps, and D.E.F.
Primary MOS: Undercover surveillance
Secondary MOS: Intelligence
Appearance: Yellow hair; yellow shirt; black jacket with yellow holster; black gloves; beige pants with black belt and shoes
Accessories: Full-head helmet with a thick antenna on the side and cut-out for one eye, knife, pistol, spring-loaded missile launcher with a trigger, submachine gun, two Law missiles, XM-15
Background Information: Feeds information to Battle Corp members who then make the resulting raids and arrests
Abilities: Contacts: High-level criminals; The trust of high-level criminals; Undercover operative
Conditions: Always ready to fight for what's right!, Belief: No risk is too great in the war against crime; Need to protect the innocent; Spent years undercover
Quote/Motto: "I always have the last laugh on Cobra criminals, right after I lock them up!"

Magda

Alias/Variations: The Bareback Rider
Real Name: Magda (surname unknown)
Place of Birth: Borovia
Gender: Female
Faction(s): Civilian political activist
Notably Served At: Borovia
Appearance: Blonde hair, blue eyes
Abilities: Equestrian bareback rider; Political activist
Conditions: Enemies; Husband: The White Clown; Speaks out against the Borovian government
Notes: She "disappeared" after speaking out against the Borovian government. Once captured, she was promised a fair trial by the president of Borovia but Cobra Commander executed her and her husband himself.

Mainframe

Series: Five (1986)
Alias/Variations: Dataframe, Data Frame; prototype names were Chip, Big Byte, and Relay
Real Name: Blaine L. Parker
Place of Birth: Phoenix, Arizona
Gender: Male
Grade/Rank: 6/O-3: Captain
SN: RA 818-50-1673
Service Branch: Army Airborne, Marine
Faction(s): G.I. Joe, Special Mission: Brazil (1986)
Stationed: Parris Island, South Carolina; Pentagon, Washington, D.C.
Notably Served At: South-East Asia; the space shuttle *Defiant*, the USS *Flagg*; Battle of Benzheen; Cobra Island; Rio de Janeiro; Vietnam
Primary MOS: Computer technology
Secondary MOS: Infantry
Appearance: Black helmet; gray short-sleeved shirt; black diagonal strap and gloves; gray pants with a black belt, holster
Other Known Appearances (Cartoon): Dark gray pants; black or dark gray collar on the shirt. Special Mission: Brazil (1986) Toys "R" Us Exclusive wears black gloves, gray boots, red bandolier with black pouches, red belt with gold buckle, red helmet, red holster with sculpted gun on left side, red pants, and a tan short-sleeved shirt. The set also included Claymore, Dial Tone, Leatherneck, and Wet Suit.
Accessories: BP75E field transmitter-receiver unit, hose, portable combat-ready computer system, walkie-talkie. The 1986 Special Mission: Brazil, came with a black hose, black walkie-talkie, gray BP75E field transmitter-receiver unit, and a gray portable combat-ready computer system
Background Information: Combat Infantryman's Badge. After leaving the army, he got his degree from MIT and worked in Silicon Valley before boredom took its toll and he joined the Marines. He underwent a reverse-aging process.
Abilities: Athlete; Communications expert; Designs computer viruses; Hacker; Highly Intelligent; Infantry; Protege: Firewall; Qualified Operator: Conquest, H.A.V.O.C., LCV Recon Sled, and Silver Mirage; Scholar; Specialist: Computers; Trusted field commander; Wealthy
Conditions: Distinctive Feature: Gray short-sleeved uniform; Ex-wife and children;

Rather learn about computers than do anything else; Reputation: Long and sordid career; Romantically paired with Zarana ("Carol Weidler")

Quote/Motto: "Too much of the modern battlefield is computer coordinated not to have a computer specialist right out there in the field with you. Problem is, that most hackers don't exactly fit the combat profile. Mainframe is the exception. He was ten years older than the next oldest trainee at Parris Island and he still finished in the top ten of the class. He's got brains—but he's hard." Quote by an unnamed G.I. Joe team member. "Mainframe enlisted in the Army Airborne at the age of 17 and made it over to Southeast Asia for the last year of hostilities, just in time to get his Combat Infantryman's Badge. He left the army to get his degree from MIT on the GI Bill and did a stint toiling in the antiseptic corridors of Silicon Valley making big bucks and fighting off boredom with a stick. Luckily, the Marines were looking for a few good men with just his qualifications, the proper papers were signed, and Mainframe was back in uniform."

Notes: He is killed in action during the second invasion of Cobra Island; his name was added to a G.I. Joe memorial at Arlington National Cemetery. The action figure did not come with a weapon despite his uniform having a combat infantryman's badge.

Major Altitude

Series: Ten (1991)
Alias/Variations: Air-Cav, Updraft, Whirlwind
Real Name: Robert D. Owens
Place of Birth: Rumford, Rhode Island
Gender: Male
Grade/Rank: WO-2 (Army chief warrant officer)*
SN: 038-8729-AT01
Service Branch: Army
Faction(s): G.I. Joe
Stationed: G.I. Joe Headquarters
Primary MOS: Battle copter pilot
Secondary MOS: Fuselage art designer
Appearance: Brown hair and mustache; a dark green shirt with brown zipper and gloves; neon green diagonal straps; dark green pants with a brown belt; neon green padding on legs; brown and neon green boots
Accessories: Helmet; machine gun
Background Information: Top of the class in Aviator School and Flight Warrant Officer School
Abilities: Battle copter pilot; Determination; Extremely popular with the other Joes
Conditions: Intensity; Never quits; Reputation: The most determined Joe
Quote/Motto: "Major Altitude is no genius, he's not the strongest G.I. Joe, but he's certainly the most determined. Every goal he sets for himself, no matter how trivial, is attacked with the same level of intensity. This has made him extremely popular with the other G.I. Joes. Let's face it. If you're pinned down in an inaccessible box canyon by a heavily armed company of Cobra Vipers, wouldn't you prefer it if the guy who was sent in to rescue you wasn't a quitter?"
Notes: *"Major" is part of the character's code name, not his rank. There is also a Joe with the code name Updraft.

Major Barrage

Series: Twenty-one (2005)
Real Name: David Vennemeyer
Place of Birth: Victoria, Texas
Gender: Male
Grade/Rank: 7/O-4: Major
SN: 468-22-DV56
Service Branch: Army
Faction(s): G.I. Joe
Primary MOS: Artillery
Secondary MOS: Physical fitness instructor
Appearance: Black hair and goatee, handsome; white T-shirt with blue tattoo on right arm; gray gloves; green pants with thick brown camo stripes; dark green belt; brown boots
Accessories: Soft plastic vest with rings on front; two thin tech-enhanced shotguns with long stock
Background Information: 6'8" and 300 pounds; ex-collegiate Division I wrestler
Abilities: Artillery commander; Bad to the bone!; Close quarters combat; Fast-bashing fists; Incredible endurance; Intelligent; Two tech-enhanced shotguns; Wrestling skills
Conditions: Fast temper; Reputation: Can take down a squadron in battle and keep on going; Thoughtful off the battlefield
Quote/Motto: "I don't mind taking a hit or two if it means I can get close enough to a Cobra trooper to wrap my hands around his neck and give a little squeeze."

Major Storm

Series: Nine (1990)
Real Name: Robert G. Swanson
Place of Birth: Providence, Rhode Island
Gender: Male
Grade/Rank: 7/O-4: Major
SN: 765-2113-GE00
Service Branch: Army
Faction(s): G.I. Joe
Primary MOS: Long-range artillery officer
Secondary MOS: Intelligence analyst (96B)
Appearance: Yellow hair; a green shirt with beige camouflage; green pants; beige chest strap, belt, and holster; black gloves and boots
Accessories: Helmet covering one eye, with a star on the front and attached mic; machine pistol; long machine pistol with severely angled grip
Abilities: Battle-hardened; Brilliant strategic tactics; Commander of mobile headquarters; Deciphers the General's systems; Extensive battlefield experience with armored vehicles; Long-range artillery officer
Conditions: Reputation: The only one who can decipher some of the General's systems; the General is his pride and joy
Quote/Motto: "From the commander seat of the General, he can scan the battlefield with an amazing array of sensors, including third-generation image intensifiers, infrared detectors, pulse–Doppler radar, and laser range finders. All this electronic hodge-podge is controlled by an advanced computer-guided system that only the Major can decipher. The General boasts more firepower than an entire 155 mm howitzer battery and its anti-aircraft defense system is second to none! To the dismay of the crew who keep it rumbling, Major Storm refers to it as 'his tank'!"
Notes: He is the commander of the General, a large, armored vehicle with multiple types of offensive weaponry.

Malyenkiy

Alias/Variations: Malenkiy
Real Name: Evaldas Malenkiy
Gender: Male
Grade/Rank: Unknown
Service Branch: Army (Russian)
Faction(s): Oktober Guard
Notably Served At: Benzheen; Trucial Abysmia
Primary MOS: Tank driver
Appearance: Sandy brown hair, brown eyes, brown Russian uniform
Abilities: Tank driver
Conditions: Always has vodka on hand; Always has something to eat on him; Loves good food; Loves strong vodka; Lust for life; Youngest member of Oktober Guard

Mangler

Gender: Male
Faction(s): G.I. Joe, Greenshirt, probationary status
Notably Served At: Trucial Abysmia, Africa
Appearance: Blond hair, 19 years old; simple fatigues
Abilities: Athletic; Strong
Conditions: Arrogant, Brash, Blurts out information; Courageous; Not a team player; Young
Quote/Motto: "I'll buy us some time."
Notes: He was killed during a secret raid in the country of Trucial Abysmia.

Manleh

Series: Twenty-five (2009)
Alias/Variations: Sgt. Manleh
Real Name: Jason Kavanagh
Place of Birth: Buenos Aires, Argentina
Gender: Male
Grade/Rank: E-5 (Sergeant, equivalent)
SN: RA384072331
Service Branch: Army (Argentine)
Faction(s): Comandos Heroicos (Heroic Commandos)
Primary MOS: Paratrooper
Secondary MOS: Air transportation
Appearance: Black hair, eyes, mustache, and goatee; cutting edge blue camouflage color scheme fatigues with Argentinian flag on left arm, black boots, yellow trim, black beret
Accessories: Blaster, JUMP jet pack, knife, pistol, red and yellow flames, submachine gun, web gear
Abilities: Cunning; Forest/jungle night drop specialist; Incredible aerial feats; Member of the world's most highly decorated military sky-diving team; Qualified Expert Operator: Jet pack; Skydiving world champion; Tactical skills
Conditions: Always up for a challenge; Incredible ego; Likes dangerous missions; Reputation: Part of the mythical "Argen Seven"; Waits until the last moment to pull the ripcord
Quote/Motto: "Look up and the only thing you will see is my boot slamming into your face!"

Mariner

Real Name: David Adcox
Gender: Male
Grade/Rank: Chief petty officer
Service Branch: Navy
Faction(s): G.I. Joe, Greenshirts
Notably Served At: Cobra Island
Primary MOS: Amphibious Warfare Specialist
Appearance: Brown hair, blue eyes, highly muscular, 6', 195 pounds, single; a large portion of Mariner's field uniform consists of hardened armor plates. This gear collectively combines to offer the man Type 6 protection from physical attack, whether shooting, stabbing, smashing, or other similar assaults are aimed at his person; carries a marine knife, gun, and Joe Communicator. His field uniform consists of a black stretch fabric T-shirt beneath a steel armored vest, blue trousers with black tiger stripes dyed on, armored metal boots, wrist guards and knee pads, a dark blue belt, and dark blue holsters for his twin firearms.
Abilities: Amphibious warfare specialist; Contacts: Greenshirts; Knowledge Skill: Boats of all kinds; Hand-to-hand combat; Navy veteran; Qualified Weapons Expert: Modern firearms; Uses two guns at once
Conditions: Cocksure; Distinctive Feature: Eye black grease when on the job; Has a big mouth; Headstrong; Somewhat "salty"; Veteran of the United States Navy

Marissa Faireborn

Alias/Variations: Marissa Bishop; Marissa Fairborne
Real Name: Marissa Faireborn
Place of Birth: New York City, New York
Gender: Female
Grade/Rank: O-3 captain in the Earth Defense Command (EDC)
Service Branch: Air Force
Faction(s): G.I. Joe, Earth Defense Command (EDC)
Stationed: EDC's base on Mars; EDC's space station in orbit above Earth
Appearance: Wavy brown hair, shapely athletic build; typically wears clothing with light blue trim, whatever the occasion
Abilities: Bold; Calm in a crisis; Communications; Contact: Smuggler "free trader" Dirk Manus and his ship *Lazy Sue*; EDC Cybertronian Liaison; Good shot; Hobby Skill: Surfboarding; Martial arts; Nimble; Performs duties with strict professionalism; Respected by Autobots and Decepticons; Shuttle pilot; Starship pilot; Starship repair; Strength of heart!; Take-charge personality; Take stock of a situation; Tough; Weapon familiarity
Conditions: Comes from a military family; Feels the burden of leadership; Headstrong; Independent; Job comes first; Likes men who are scoundrels; Loves her father; Militaristic; Reputation: Genuine adversary to the Decepticons; Reputation: Trusted ally and friend to the Autobots; Small; Unlikely love interest for Autobots Jazz and Optimus Prime (G.I. Joe / Transformers Verse)
Notes: She is the daughter of Flint (father) and Lady Jaye (mother). She is a character in the IDW Universe.

M.A.S.K.

Alias/Variations: Mobile Armored Strike Kommand
Purpose: Uses machines that transformed from everyday civilian vehicles into combat machines to confront and combat criminal and malicious organizations
Leader: Specialist Matt Trakker
Members: Numerous and unnamed
Notes: Originally produced by the Kenner toy company; eventually purchased by Hasbro bringing their characters and creations under the same holdings as G.I. Joe

Maverick

Series: Six (1987)
Alias/Variations: Biomassa (Brazil)
Real Name: Thomas P. Kiley
Place of Birth: Ida Grove, Iowa
Gender: Male
Grade/Rank: O-3 (Air Force captain)
SN: 519-46-7007
Service Branch: Air Force
Faction(s): G.I. Joe, Battleforce 2000
Stationed: Frusenland
Notably Served At: The Battle of Benzheen; Sierra Gordo
Primary MOS: Pilot
Appearance: Brown hair; white shirt with silver armor vest (olive chest panel); blue gloves; white pants with a silver belt, blue pockets, and olive-green boots
Accessories: Helmet with ribbed collar and open space for eyes; laser pistol with rounded energy chamber
Background Information: Air Force Academy

Abilities: Fighter pilot; Heightened perception; Heightened reflexes; Natural pilot; Physical strength to withstand massive g-forces; Qualified Expert Operator: VTOL jet fighter Vector

Conditions: Volunteers for every experimental flight program

Quote/Motto: "He's a natural flyer. He can't remember a time when he wasn't flying. Honest. You see, his mom flew a crop duster all across the Corn Belt. An old Stearman biplane. This was back before day-care, right? She'd just strap him in, hand him a water gun and a jelly sandwich, and take off for a day of dusting bollworms!"

Notes: KIA during the Battle of Benzheen when it was bombed by Cobra Commander. He is buried in Arlington National Cemetery. Maverick is not to be confused with the energy specialist named Biomassa.

Mayday

Real Name: Paige Adams
Gender: Female
Grade/Rank: 7/O-4: Major or 0/E-4: Specialist
Service Branch: Army
Faction(s): G.I. Joe, Greenshirts, and Team Extreme
Notably Served At: Cobra Island
Primary MOS: Urban warfare
Secondary MOS: Marksmanship
Appearance: Shoulder-length red-brown hair
Accessories: Convertible all-terrain ski backpack; large gun
Abilities: Determined; Firearms expert; Sharpshooter; Skilled fighter; Skilled pilot; Undercover operative
Conditions: Aggressive

Mayday 2

Real Name: Ayana Jones
Place of Birth: Brighton Beach, New York
Gender: Female
Grade/Rank: Earth Defense Command, second-in-command; warrant officer
Service Branch: Earth Defense Command (EDC)
Faction(s): G.I. Joe, Earth Defense Command, and Skywatch
Stationed: Berlin, Eastern Europe; Marshall Islands
Notably Served At: The Nanzhao conflict; Portland; Governor's Island; Monument Valley; Verenya, Schleteva

Appearance: Attractive African American woman; short military buzz haircut
Background Information: Attended the University of California, Berkeley
Abilities: Emissary to weapons supplier Garrison Blackrock; Veteran member of G.I. Joe
Conditions: Dislike of spacesuits; No-nonsense; Prefers being in the thick of the action; Sticks up for her commander; Wry sense of humor
Notes: Recruited into G.I. Joe by Duke; worked with Big Ben; joined the EDC under Marissa Faireborn

Med Alert

Series: Twenty-two (2006)
Real Name: Kirk Bacus
Place of Birth: Nashville, Tennessee
Gender: Male
Grade/Rank: E-4 (Corporal)
SN: 892-75-MA73; 519-46-7007, sources conflict
Service Branch: Army
Faction(s): G.I. Joe
Stationed: Walter Reed Army Medical Center
Primary MOS: Medic
Secondary MOS: Tai Chi Chuan instructor
Accessories: Helmet with microphone (attached belt), pistol, rifle
Abilities: Cool under fire; Dodges gunfire and explosions; Hand-to-hand combat expert; Knowledge Skill: Inner cities; Seasoned ER; Tai Chi
Conditions: Doesn't hesitate in battle
Quote/Motto: "Success does not always go to the swift, nor does victory always belong to the strong."
Notes: Currently, he is a reserve member of the current Joe team assigned to domestic operations in the United States. *All reservists can be called back into action if a mission calls for it.

Mega-Marines

Alias/Variations: Mega Marines
Purpose: Joes from the U.S. Marine Corps, specially equipped to combat Cobra's mutated and allied monster force, the Mega-Monsters. "This specialized team was formed for one specific mission: to repel and destroy Cobra's Mega-Monsters! These bio-tech fighters also battle new Cobra Vipers, and feature moldable Bio-Armor, a breakthrough in bio-mechanical armament! The 'bug-hunt' is on!"
Leader: Gung Ho

Members: Blast-Off, Clutch, and Mirage
Vehicles: Monster Blaster APC
Notes: Mega-Monsters, a recently emerging threat, are vulnerable to fire.

Mercer

Series: Six (1987)
Alias/Variations: Richard Cecil, Richard S. Cecil (1991); mercenary
Real Name: Felix P. Stratton
Place of Birth: Spencer, West Virginia (Richmond, Virginia, with alias)
Gender: Male
Grade/Rank: E-5 (equivalent, Renegades have no official status)
SN: 010-5639-JE09; 933-41-5632
Service Branch: Army
Faction(s): G.I. Joe, Slaughter's Renegades
Stationed: Western Asia, Cobra Unity, Qabdat Khafia base
Notably Served At: Cobra Island; Iran
Primary MOS: Small arms armorer (mercenary with alias)
Secondary MOS: Explosives expert
Appearance: Brown hair and beard; red and black vest with silver piping; silver sleeve on right arm; black gloves; blue pants with red belt and holsters; black boots
Accessories: Cylindrical spring-loaded missile launcher, laser rifle with two grips and large rear-mounted power pack, missile, small backpack with a slot for launcher, submachine gun with four grips joined at the bottom
Abilities: Cool under fire; Explosives expert; Hot-wire vehicles; Mercenary; Physically strong; Qualified Weapons Proficient: All Cobra Explosive Devices; Qualified Weapons Proficient: All Cobra small arms; Small arms armorer; Source of inside information on Cobra tactics and battle doctrine; Tough fighter
Conditions: Disavowed: Gets no credit when successful; Disenchanted with Cobra's philosophy; Does not like G.I. Joe; Joined Cobra for the adventure and promise of material gain; No-nonsense; Not liked by the Joes; Operates without support; Operates outside the military command structure
Quote/Motto: "Although the rest of the G.I. Joes weren't too thrilled about having a defector in the ranks, especially one from Cobra, we soon developed a grudging respect for his no-nonsense attitude and coolness under fire. We also didn't mind the fact that Mercer is strong enough to carry an 88 mm Stanford Rocket Launcher with an ample supply of anti-tank armaments. None of this means that we like him very much, but then again, he doesn't like us very much either.... Mercer found his true home with the Renegades. He gets three meals a day, a warm place to sleep, and a chance to shoot at Cobras!" Quote by an unnamed G.I. Joe team member.
Notes: He is the only Cobra Viper to defect to G.I. Joe and survive.

Metalhead

Series: Nine (1990)
Alias/Variations: Stuart A. Finley
Real Name: Matthew Hurley
Gender: Male
Grade/Rank: None given
SN: 0045H8I8
Service Branch: Army
Faction(s): G.I. Joe, Team Extreme
Notably Served At: Any unstable, war-torn area
Primary MOS: Computer communications
Secondary MOS: Electronic warfare
Appearance: Muscular, mane of wild blond hair, ripped jeans, combat boots, black leather vest, large peace medallion
Accessories: Missile launcher and two missiles. Version 2: Air-powered missile launcher, armor, foam missile, gun, speakers
Abilities: Computer communications genius; Computer expert; Electronic warfare expert; Gets the job done!; Hacker; Urban assault expert
Conditions: Blasts rock 'n' roll music in the heat of battle; In-your-face attitude
Quote/Motto: "The Louder the Better!"
Notes: He is unrelated to the Iron Grenadier. There is also a female Joe by the name of Metal-Head.

Mirage

Series: Twelve (1993)
Alias/Variations: Joseph Balkun, Joseph R. Balkun (1993)
Real Name: Joseph R. Baikun
Place of Birth: Molson, Washington
Gender: Male
Grade/Rank: 2/E-6: Staff sergeant
SN: 5060-JB-824; Version 2: 606-JB-824
Service Branch: Marines
Faction(s): G.I. Joe, Mega-Marines, Winter Operations

Stationed: Fort Riley, Kansas
Notably Served At: New Moon, Colorado
Primary MOS: Rocket-fire assaults
Secondary MOS: Heavy artillery
Appearance: Yellow hair; blue visor (glued on); olive-green shirt with orange diagonal strap; blue armbands and gloves; olive green and black pants with a blue belt, leg straps, and boots
Accessories: Bio-armor mold (moldable bio-armor), knife, laser rifle, missile launcher with a trigger, submachine gun, two missiles. Version 3: Goggles, knife, two rifles
Abilities: Bio-Artillery Expert; Instruction: Weapon fire assault; Qualified Weapons Expert: Heavy weapons armaments (bazookas, AK-47 assault rifles, MAC-10 submachine guns, and "ripple-fire" rocket launchers); Qualified Weapons Expert: Various weapons; Skilled soldier
Conditions: Cool under fire; Distinctive Feature: Lays down heavy cover fire and launches shoulder-mounted rockets; Does not hold back with telling the truth; Finish the mission!
Quote/Motto: "Bazookas are OK, but I'll take a shoulder-mounted rocket launcher any day!" Version 2: "It's not just knowing how to use your weapons; it's knowing when to use them."
Notes: Mirage was trained by Roadblock. He ran the mission where Greenshirts, Curtis Letson, and Julie Haun are killed by the direct actions of Thomas Stall, a.k.a. Blackout.

Misha

Series: Twenty-two (2006)
Alias/Variations: Sgt. Misha Zubenkov
Real Name: Misha L. Zubenkov
Place of Birth: Smolensk, Russia
Gender: Male
Grade/Rank: E-5 (Sergeant, equivalent)
Service Branch: Army (Soviet/Russian) 2006
Faction(s): Oktober Guard
Notably Served At: Sierra Gordo
Primary MOS: Artillery expert
Secondary MOS: Special ops
Appearance: Average height (5'5"), black hair, brown eyes, 150 pounds; long, eastern-style mustache, thick, round-rimmed glasses. Wears black leather boots, brown bandolier, belt, webbing, and holsters; green camouflaged long-sleeved shirt and trousers, and his signature green pith helmet

Accessories: Hat, knife, rifle, strap
Background Information: From the ranks of the Soviet Union's elite Spetsnaz units; came from the "old" brand of Spetsnaz
Abilities: Contacts: Russian military; Contacts: Spetsnaz units; Determined; Digs up information; Dirty Tricks; Expert marksman; Fights hard; Hand-to-hand combat; Highly skilled with conventional firearms; Knowledge Skill: Ins and outs of military command structure; Knowledge Skill: Line of sight weaponry; Language Skill: English; People owe him favors; Sees beyond borders and rivalries; Soldier; Tough; Well-read; Well-off: Generational family owned glass factory
Conditions: All business on the job; Always carries a blade; Always carries at least one grenade; Belief: Work with other nations against Cobra; Loves Russia; Patriot; Proud; Seeks to prove himself to superiors; Waxes philosophical on the battlefield
Quote/Motto: "Sometimes a persuasive discussion can help Cobra see the error of their ways. If that doesn't work, a well-aimed rocket launcher will definitely get them to change their minds."

Mr. Clancy

Real Name: Unknown
Gender: Male
Grade/Rank: Team leader of G.I. Joe Team Extreme
Faction(s): G.I. Joe, Team Extreme
Primary MOS: Joe Team's Presidential Liaison
Abilities: Command; Knowledge skill: Knows his people; Leadership; Presidential Liaison; Team leader
Conditions: Distinctive Feature: Always wears sunglasses; Distinctive Feature: Dresses in a black suit; Feels the burden of leadership; Mysterious; True team leader

Moondancer

Series: Three (1984)
Alias/Variations: Captain Tariq
Real Name: Tariq el Shafei
Place of Birth: Kuwait
Gender: Male
Grade/Rank: Captain
SN: AF 934818
Service Branch: Air Force
Faction(s): Action Force, Space Force
Stationed: Space Station "Mothership"
Primary MOS: Astral assault tactics

Secondary MOS: Rapid deployment
Appearance: Blond hair, dark eyes, gray bodysuit with white trim, black boots
Accessories: Backpack, helmet, mortar, mortar stand, visor
Background Information: Trained in the Air Force
Abilities: Air Force training; Cosmic security; Jetfighter pilot; Strategic training; Tactician: Space combat
Quote/Motto: "Moondancer's thoughtful tactics have saved many a lost engagement." Quote by an unnamed G.I. Joe team member.

Mouse

Series: Twenty-nine (2013)
Alias/Variations: Agent Mouse
Real Name: (First Name Unknown) Gaines
Gender: Male
Grade/Rank: Private
Service Branch: Army
Faction(s): G.I. Joe
Primary MOS: Marksman
Accessories: Clamp connected to a harness, flak vest, helmet, knife, two rifles
Abilities: Marksman; Remote-Guided bullets
Conditions: Distinctive Feature: Looks like a basic military man
Notes: Relatively new member of the Joe team; Airborne and Mouse work well together

Mouse 2

Real Name: Morris L. Sanderson
Place of Birth: Dubach, Louisiana, 1918
Gender: Male
Grade/Rank: E-5 Sergeant
Service Branch: Army
Faction(s): G.I. Joe, Screaming Eagles
Notably Served At: Artic; Uganda
Primary MOS: Computer technology
Appearance: Gigantic hulking brute, green camos
Abilities: Highly trained; Mountain of a man
Conditions: Clumsy; Undisciplined
Notes: Not much is known of his life before he joined the Screaming Eagles. He is a reserve member of the current Joe team assigned to domestic operations. *All reservists can be called back into action if a mission calls for it.

Muskrat

Series: Seven (1988)
Alias/Variations: Bad-Bayou, Bayou, Gumbo, Mossback, Swamp Dawg, Swamp-Runner, Wet Willy
Real Name: Ross A. Williams
Place of Birth: Thibodaux, Louisiana
Gender: Male
Grade/Rank: 1/E-5 Sergeant
SN: 564-68-2954
Service Branch: Army
Faction(s): G.I. Joe, Battle Corps, Drug Elimination Force (D.E.F.), and Night Force
Notably Served At: Eastern Asia; Sao Cristobel
Primary MOS: Infantry
Secondary MOS: Social services
Appearance: Dark green hat with black hatband; red hair; green vest with black knife and holster; black gloves; green pants with black belt and holster; green and brown boots
Accessories: Backpack with red stripe, helmet, knife, machete with groove on side of the blade, pistol, shotgun with trigger guard and triangular stock, spring-loaded missile launcher with trigger, two missiles, XM-15
Background Information: Ranger school, Jungle Warfare Training Center
Abilities: Camouflage; Counter tracking; Hunter (boar, possum, raccoon); Instruction: Nighttime swamp fighting; Knowledge Skill: Swamp flora and fauna; Knowledge Skill: Swamps; Setting primitive traps; Heavy fire specialist (Battle Corps); Swamp fighter; Tracking; Wilderness Survival: Swamp
Conditions: Confronts poachers; Particular mutual hate for Voltar
Quote/Motto: "No one can outrun me in the swamps!" "If I had to go chase down Muskrat in the swamp, I'd give up before I started. He'd be sprinkling cayenne pepper in his tracks to throw the dogs off, laying false trails into water moccasin lairs, rigging deadfalls, setting snares, and having himself a good ol' time, never even workin' up a sweat. I'd just as soon go home and watch TV." Quote by an unnamed G.I. Joe team member.
Notes: In Battle Corps, his function is redesignated as Specialist: Heavy Fire. The Swamp Skimmer board is a tactical floatation device strong enough to dissuade snakes and alligators. It can also be wielded as a ballistic shield to deflect gunfire. Offensively, it can be used to silently knock an enemy combatant unconscious.

Mutt and Junkyard

Series: Three (1984)

Alias/Variations: Dog-Face and George; Mutt and Dawg; Sgt. Mutt; Cao Bravio; Mastim (Brazil). Junkyard was *Fiero* in Spain and *Lupus* in Italy.
Real Name: Stanley R. Perlmutter
Place of Birth: Iselin, New Jersey (Madrid, Spain in Europe)
Gender: Male
Grade/Rank: 1/E-5: Sergeant (specialist); (staff sergeant) E-6
Abilities (Junkyard): Joes like him; Loyal; Provides perimeter security for the current Joe base; Smart; Well-Trained
SN: RA757793443
Service Branch: Army
Faction(s): G.I. Joe, Anti-Venom Task Force, Battle Corps, Drug Elimination Force, Slaughter's Marauders, and Tiger Force
Primary MOS: Dog handler (K-9)
Secondary MOS: Infantry
Appearance: Black hair and mustache; a green short-sleeved shirt with open collar; green pants; brown vest with red straps; brown kneepads, holster, and boots; black glove on the left hand. In Slaughter's Marauders he wears an open-collared, short-sleeved shirt striped brown and yellow-green; a blue vest; pants striped dark green, yellow-green, dark green, and brown; a black belt, boots, and a glove on the left hand. Drug Elimination Force: black helmet; a green shirt with a blue vest and light brown wristbands; black gloves; yellow-green pants with black belt and boots and light brown shin guards. Battle Corps: black hair and mustache; black helmet; a green shirt with a neon orange vest and light brown wristbands; black gloves; blue pants with black belt and boots and light brown shin guards.
Accessories: 1984: Dog named "Junkyard," face mask helmet (reminiscent of a dog's snout and muzzle), Ingram Mac-11 submachine gun with silencer, leash, nightstick. Drug Elimination Force: auto pistol, net attached to two missiles, transparent spring-loaded net launcher, two round counterweights
Background Information: Jungle Warfare Training School, Special Ops School, Security, and Enforcement Committee
Abilities: Animal control and utilization; Covert operations; Dog handler; Infantry; Knowledge Skill: Security force operations; Natural with animals; Qualified Weapons Expert: M-16, M-14, M1911A1, auto pistol, MAC-11

Conditions: Distinctive Feature: Junkyard and Junkyard II are each more popular than Mutt; Gets along better with dogs than humans; Reputation: Dog trainer; Parents neglected him during the holiday season
Quote/Motto: "If you're sitting next to Mutt in the mess hall, don't try filching anything from his tray—he'll bite your leg off!" "Simply a natural with animals. He likes them and they like him. The problem is that he gets along better with dogs than he does with people." Quotes given by an unnamed G.I. Joe team member.
Notes: Mutt has family in Millville. Junkyard, the dog who joined the military with him, retired; he died during the seven years G.I. Joe was disbanded. Junkyard II now serves with Mutt.

Natalie Poole

Series: Twenty-six (2010)
Alias/Variations: Agent Natalie Poole; Natalie
Real Name: Natalie Poole
Place of Birth: London, England
Gender: Female
Grade/Rank: 9/O-7 Brigadier General; E-7/OR-7 (equivalent)
SN: AF 362434
Service Branch: Army (S.A.S.)
Faction(s): G.I. Joe, Q-Force, and Special Action Force
Primary MOS: Espionage
Secondary MOS: Martial arts
Appearance: Blonde hair, blue eyes, a red headband with red polka-dots, blue tank top, green camo pants, black boots; busty
Accessories: Kayak counterweight, kayak, machine gun mount for the kayak, paddle, rifle
Background Information: Trained by the British Secret Intelligence Service
Abilities: Adventurer; Athletic; Covert Operations specialist; Liaison to Action Man; Highly intelligent; Martial Artist; Master of Extreme Sports; MI6 Special Action Force; Well-traveled
Conditions: Competes against male counterparts; Danger hound; Distinctive Feature: British accent; Does not consider herself a feminist; Exceedingly cool head; Flirtatious relationship with Action Man; Guardian angel to Action Man; Jealous of Ursula; Lets friends call her Natalie
Quote/Motto: "Weapons have their place, but if you're disarmed, you better be able to kick your way out of trouble!"

Notes: Upon hearing of the prowess of G.I. Joe Warrant Officer Flint, she issued an invitation and challenge for him to compete in some outdoor athletics across the pond (Action Force alternate continuity).

Night Force

Series: Seven (1988)
Purpose: The largest of the covert sub-teams, they are outfitted and equipped for nighttime surveillance and defensive operations. They have advanced technology, skills, and sophisticated hardware, utilizing the element of surprise to strike under cover of darkness to accomplish their mission. "When the sun goes down, the G.I. Joe Night Force squad is ready for action! Night Force is a covert team specializing in nighttime surveillance and defensive operations. Missions conducted in the darkness have special problems, which the Night Force squad has overcome with enhanced skills, sophisticated hardware, and advanced technology. They use the element of surprise to vanquish the enemy, striking under cover of darkness and disappearing into the night, mission accomplished!"
Leader: None stated, defer to rank
Members: 1988: Crazylegs, Falcon, Outback, Psyche-Out, Sneak Peek, Tunnel Rat. 1989: Charbroil, Lightfoot, Muskrat, Repeater, Shockwave, Spearhead. 2003: Cross Hair, Duke, Nunchuk. 2004: Action Man, Beach Head, Flint, Grunt, Gung Ho, Roadblock, Short Fuze, Tunnel Rat. 2009: Outback, Shockblast, Tunnel Rat. 2013: Charbroil, Chuckles, Freestyle, Hit and Run, Lady Jaye, Muskrat, Psyche-Out, Repeater, Spearhead, Steeler. 2014: Crazylegs, Falcon.
Vehicles: 1988: Night Blaster, Night Raider, Night Shade, Night Storm, Night Striker. 1989: Night Boomer, Night Ray, Night Scrambler. 2004: Night Force, Grizzly. 2013: Covert Ops A.T.V., Night Boomer, Night F.L.A.K.

Night Fox

Series: Twenty-six (2010)
Real Name: Armando M. Ortiz
Gender: Male
Grade/Rank: 1/E-5: Petty officer first class (PO2)
SN: 412-37-A089
Service Branch: Navy
Faction(s): G.I. Joe
Stationed: Naval Amphibious Base Coronado, California
Primary MOS: Special combat and operations expert
Appearance: Brown eyes
Accessories: Ammunition backpack, ammunition belt, H.A.S.T.E. (Hypersonic Air-Surface Trajectory Electromagnetic) Cannon, hat, helmet with night vision goggles, machine gun with tripod, neckerchief, shotgun, two pistols; web gear
Abilities: Combat diver; Explosives expert; Marksman; Ninja commando; Ninja-trained; Professional Skill: Navy SEAL (Retired); Special combat and operations expert; Strategic impact; Tactical force; Wilderness Survival: Desert
Notes: SECURITY CLEARANCE: TOP SECRET

Nightingale

Real Name: Michelle Miller
Gender: Female
Grade/Rank: 6/O-3: Captain
Service Branch: Army
Faction(s): G.I. Joe
Primary MOS: Doctor
Secondary MOS: Counselor
Background Information: Child of immigrants
Abilities: Combat medic; Commitment to duty; Counselor; Excellent bedside manner; Surgeon; Tunes out distractions
Conditions: Battle shy; Bitter divorcée; Blames the Baroness, Cobra Commander, and Major Bludd for her son's death; Ex-husband Damien; "Isn't naive, but…"; Keeps relationship with Lifeline a secret; Nothing gets in the way of medical duties; Overly compassionate; Protective of "her soldiers"; Rescues the wounded of either side; Romantically pursued by Lifeline; Seeks to fill void created by son's death; Touched by tragedy (son, William, was killed in combat); Unending compassion; Unkind to her ex-husband; Views Cobra soldiers as misguided and in need of help
Quote/Motto: "It isn't enough to mend the body; you must treat the soul as well."
Notes: She is a character in the Transformers Universe MUX. Her daughter, Rachel, is happily married to an intelligent and hardworking man named Bradley; they live outside of Toronto.

Nightstalker

Alias/Variations: Tem
Real Name: Temera White Eagle

Place of Birth: New York laboratory owned by a dummy corporation of Extensive Enterprises and Cobra
Gender: Female
Grade/Rank: 0/E-4: Advisor/Probationary Member/Specialist
Service Branch: Army
Faction(s): G.I. Joe
Appearance: Black fingernails, long thin black tongue, diamond pattern down her spine
Abilities: Armored skin*; Burglary skills; Can sense heat even with her eyes closed*; Highly enhanced sense of smell*; Fast*; Flexible*; Tough*; Pickpocket; Professional Skill: Prostitution; Razor-sharp claws*; Self-sufficient; Spits venom*; Unhinging jaw*; Venomous bite*; Wilderness Survival: Urban
Conditions: A nice girl; Cold-blooded physiology; Conflicted personality; Dislikes her code name; Distinguishing Feature: Reptilian eyes; Distinguishing Feature: Extremely long, thin, black forked tongue; Does bad things sometimes; Does what she must to survive; Feels guilt when she hurts someone; Functional rattle on her tailbone; Mating cycle runs every three months; Not-quite-normal appearance; Prefers to eat live prey
Quote/Motto: "Where are my sunglasses?"
Notes: This character is in the Transformers Universe MUX. *She is a Cobra experiment in recombinant genetics; her genes are infused with DNA fragments from various reptiles and snakes. Her human genetic material was from Lori Ann White Eagle, one of the junior lab staffers needing the money.

Ninja Force

Series: Eleven (1992)
Purpose: An elite martial arts and silent weapons G.I. Joe sub-team. "These swift and silent commandos are the true elite forces for G.I. Joe and Cobra! Each Ninja warrior is fully capable of neutralizing an adversary in milliseconds with his spring-action, martial arts moves, and lethal weapons!"
Leader: Storm Shadow
Members: Banzai, Bushido, Dojo, Nunchuk, Scarlett, Snake-Eyes, T'gin-Zu (with Pile Driver), T'jbang
Vehicles: Ninja Lightning motorcycle (1993); Pile Driver (1993), Ninja Raiders

Nunchuk

Series: Eleven (1992)
Real Name: Ralph Balducci
Place of Birth: Brooklyn, New York
Gender: Male
Grade/Rank: E-5 Sergeant
SN: 980-4290-KB22
Service Branch: Army
Faction(s): G.I. Joe, Ninja Force
Stationed: Denver School of the Blind Master; Army Language Center in San Francisco
Primary MOS: Self-defense instructor
Secondary MOS: Ordnance
Appearance: Black helmet and face mask with cloth hood; green shirt and pants with black stripes; black straps, gloves, belt, and boots
Accessories: Long nunchuks and a sword with a long hilt and thick, curving blade
Abilities: Commands the Battle Wagon; Fights hand-to-hand against large numbers; Knowledge Skill: Mystic fighting forms; Ninja; Ordnance; Qualified Expert Combatant: Hand-to-hand combat; Self-defense instruction; Nunchaku specialist; Utilizes the terrifying form "Samurai Smash"
Preferred Weapon: Nunchaku
Conditions: Belief: Firefly uses martial arts for evil purposes; Distinctive Feature: Distinctive fighting style; Driven to perfect his form; Enjoys taking on Cobra; Grudge against Cobra operative Firefly; Supervised by Storm Shadow; Student of Blind Master
Quote/Motto: "You take the two on the left, I'll deal with the other seventeen!"
Notes: Personally recruited and trained by Storm Shadow

Oktober Guard

Alias/Variations: October Guard; Pravda Patrol
Purpose: This Soviet special operations unit often operates internationally, protecting and promoting Soviet and Warsaw Pact interests. Thought of as the Soviet/Russian equivalent of G.I. Joe, they are composed of members from several Warsaw Pact countries. They are never portrayed as evil, but as military professionals serving their country. Their missions often put them at odds with G.I. Joe, but when the situation arises, they will temporarily ally with them against a common foe. Unlike G.I. Joe, they are a small squad, and most members do not have code names.
Leader: Colonel Brekhov (the original commander of the Oktober Guard); General Vaskovia, General Iron Bear/General Mayhem

Members: Colonel Brekhov, Diana, Dragonsky, Horror Show, Shrage, Stormavik. Additional Members: Big Bear, Gorky, Misha, Red Star, Ruslan, Wong

Operations Support Squadron

Purpose: The Operations Support Squadron has an Intelligence Support Troop (Company) and a Combat Support Troop (Company). They each supply individual teams to the Sabre Squadrons. For instance, the Combat Support Troop would have: HQ Detachment EOD Platoon—HQ (Platoon Commander, Platoon NCO, Ops NCO)—Team 1 (Supports A Squadron)—Team 2 (Supports B Squadron)—Team 3 (Supports C Squadron)—Team 4 and Team 5 (Supports Base/Training) The Support Squadron would have: Squadron HQ Supply Platoon Maintenance Platoon Distribution Platoon Medical Platoon Logistic Support Troop—Troop HQ—Logistic Support Team 1 (Supports A Squadron)—Logistic Support Team 2 (Supports B Squadron)—Logistic Support Team 3 (Supports C Squadron)—Logistic Support Team 4 (Supports Operations Support Squadron if needed)—Logistic Support Team 5 (Reserve/Campaign Support). In the event of large-scale operations, they can deploy with a small C2 element.

Ophelia Gabriel

Real Name: Ophelia Gabriel
Gender: Female
Faction(s): Arashikage clan
Primary MOS: Ninja
Appearance: Short red hair
Abilities: Trained by Nunchuk; Trained by Snake-Eyes; Trained by T'Jbang
Notes: A mission concerning Firefly, a former Cobra agent and Arashikage enemy, was to be Ophelia's final test as she passed all the others. If successful, she would become a ninja and a full member of the clan. During the operation, Firefly discovered the trap laid for him and killed everyone. He shot Ophelia.

Outback

Series: Six (1987)
Alias/Variations: Forasteiro (Brazil); Action Force (alternate continuity): Stuart Selkirk
Real Name: Stuart R. Selkirk
Place of Birth: Big Piney, Wyoming (Stirling, Scotland for European distribution)
Gender: Male
Grade/Rank: E-5 (Army sergeant)
SN: 688-27-4213
Service Branch: Army
Faction(s): G.I. Joe, Battle Corps, Night Force, and Tiger Force
Stationed: Instructor at Survival School and the Jungle Warfare Training Center; The Pit, Utah, located beneath Fort Wadsworth; Action Force (alternate continuity): the Australian desert
Notably Served At: Central America; Cobra Island; Mideast; the Rocky Mountains; the Soviet republic of Borovia; Jordan
Primary MOS: Infantry/survivalist
Secondary MOS: Survival training instructor
Appearance: Red hair and beard; green headband; white T-shirt with "SURVIVAL" on front; dark gray gloves; green and gray camouflage pants; beige belt; black boots. In Action Force (alternate continuity): white hair and beard; blue headband; orange T-shirt with a picture of a tiger on front; dark gray gloves; green and brown camouflage pants; brown belt; gray boots. Battle Corps: yellow hat; red hair and beard; a light blue short-sleeved shirt with orange straps and wristbands; black gloves; light blue and yellow splotched pants with an orange belt and black boots. Battle Corps v2: black hat; red hair and beard; a green short-sleeved shirt with orange straps and wristbands; blue gloves; beige pants with a blue belt and black boots
Accessories: Flashlight, Heckler & Koch 3G rifle, survival backpack, web belt Action Force (alternate continuity): Heckler & Koch rifle; web belt; flashlight; survival backpack. Battle Corps: submachine gun; submachine gun; sniper's rifle; spring-loaded missile launcher with a red trigger; two red missiles. Battle Corps v2: submachine gun; submachine gun; sniper's rifle; spring-loaded missile launcher with a trigger; two missiles
Background Information: Action Force (alternate continuity): Grew up with few friends and enjoys being on his own
Abilities: Access to the latest gear and military technology; Buddies with Leatherneck; Determination; False identity of the emissary of an Arab oil sheikh; Infantry; Instructor; Improvises solutions; Lore Skill: Animal behaviors and habitats; Navigation; Survival Skill: Extreme climates; Survival Skill: Extreme environments; Survival training instructor;

Survivalist; Tests new survival gear in the field

Conditions: Belief: Be part of the environment; Loner; Needs to prove his ability to do without modern technology; Reputation: Crazy hermit; Reputation: Master of extreme climates and environments; Sees modern world and technology as distractions to surviving. Action Force (alternate continuity): His psychological evaluation claimed he was driven mad by isolation and obsessiveness but was still given a positive evaluation.

Ozone

Series: Ten (1991)
Alias/Variations: Fresh Air
Real Name: David F. Kunitz
Place of Birth: Three Mile Island, Pennsylvania
Gender: Male
Grade/Rank: E-4 Corporal
SN: 245-7001-DK27
Service Branch: Army
Faction(s): G.I. Joe, Eco-Warriors, and Star Brigade
Primary MOS: Environmental health specialist
Secondary MOS: Chemical laboratory specialist
Appearance: Brown hair and beard; a light blue shirt with dark blue chest panel, neon green grenades, and yellow straps and gloves; light blue pants with dark blue leggings, yellow shin guards, and black boots. Star Brigade: brown hair and beard; a light brown shirt with silver chest panel, red grenades, and blue straps and gloves; light brown pants with blue leggings, silver shin guards, and blue boots. Star Brigade 93: brown hair and beard; a gray shirt with silver chest panel, red grenades, and blue straps and gloves; gray pants with blue leggings, silver shin guards, and blue boots
Accessories: Frame backpack and water tank; soft helmet with goggles and air tube; vacuum gun; water cannon with a hose. Version 3: Helmet, knife, missile launcher (spring-loaded, actually fires), three guns, two missiles. Star Brigade: Helmet with visor, machete, machine gun, missile launcher, shotgun; submachine gun; two missiles
Abilities: Airborne sludge specialist; Atmospheric-dispersal toxins specialist; Chemical science; Environmental health specialist; Knowledge Skill: Atmospheric poisons; Knowledge Skill: Harmful chemicals; Replenisher Trooper

Conditions: Environmentalist
Quote/Motto: "Fighting Cobra is tough enough but having to duke it out with the bad guys while encumbered by a bulky, airtight suit, and heavy breathing gear is next to impossible. But with Ozone on the job, neutralizing the atmospheric sludge, the G.I. Joes can shed their protective suits and bring the fight to Cobra in top form."
Notes: His backpack has built-in sensors, an analysis suite, and an advanced chemical countermeasure computer, all accessible by voice command through Ozone's wide-angle, holographic head-up display helmet faceplate.

Paquette

Series: Eighteen (2002)
Alias/Variations: Specialist Dusty; Specialist Paquette
Real Name: Jeffrey Paquette
Place of Birth: North Kingstown, Rhode Island
Gender: Male
Grade/Rank: E-4 Specialist
SN: 371-11RT05
Service Branch: Army
Faction(s): G.I. Joe, Specialist
Stationed: Fort Bliss, Texas
Notably Served At: Syria
Primary MOS: Desert trooper; infantry
Secondary MOS: Refrigeration and air-conditioning maintenance
Appearance: Pencil-thin black mustache, black hair, and eyes. Practical G.I. Joe field uniform includes brown camouflage trousers, a brown camouflage jacket, a collared shirt over a black T-shirt, black leather boots, a black leather belt, and a tan helmet with a cooling shroud mounted on the back; 5'11" and 170 pounds. Tiger Force: Brown trousers, a green collared shirt with orange tiger stripes over a red T-shirt, dark brown leather boots, a brown leather belt, and a green helmet with a cooling shroud mounted on the back
Accessories: Knife, submachine gun, semi-automatic pistol
Abilities: Contacts: Military personnel; Contacts: Undocumented military personnel; Desert trooper; Hand-to-hand combat; Infantry; Knowledge Skill: Military protocols and procedures, Language Skill: All languages spoken in desert regions; Lore Skill: Desert fauna; Lore Skill: Desert weather; Lore Skill: Desert flora; Natural prowess in

the desert; Paratrooper; Qualified Expert: Night desert operations; Qualified Operator: Amphibious fighting vehicles, Night Rhino; Refrigeration and air-conditioning maintenance; Sneaking; Stealth; Tracking; Toughness; Wilderness Survival: Desert

Conditions: Cheerful; Distinctive Feature: Always has desert survival gear with him; Easy-going; Loved basic training; Loves the desert; Occasionally rankles his fellow Joes (with upbeat attitude); Respected by fellow Joes; Sees the best in any situation; Truly loves his job

Quote/Motto: "If the enemy thinks they can hide in the desert, are they wrong! I can track them silently, then sneak up on them at the right time and pop a can of firefight!"

Notes: He uses the code name Dusty on missions that don't include the original Dusty, Ronald Tadur. He is a reserve member of the current Joe team assigned to domestic operations. *All reservists can be called back into action if a mission calls for it.

Pathfinder

Series: Nine (1990)
Alias/Variations: Brushfire, Bushmaster, Path Finder, Whacker, Wildfire, Wildwood
Real Name: William V. Iannotti
Place of Birth: Key West, Florida
Gender: Male
Grade/Rank: 2/E-6: Staff sergeant
SN: 040-9812-JA41*
Service Branch: Army
Faction(s): G.I. Joe
Notably Served At: Cobra Island
Primary MOS: Jungle assault specialist
Secondary MOS: Forward observer/recon
Appearance: Dark green hat with black brim; black hair; light green sunglasses; a black short-sleeved shirt with an open orange vest; black pants with orange and light green camouflage; dark and light green belt with cannon posts; black boots
Accessories: Belts, fuel-tank backpack, hose, two cannons with handles on sides and holes for waist pegs, two short ammo belts, weed trimmer with detachable silver blade
Background Information: Grew up in the alligator-infested swamplands of southern Florida and was taught by his father, a decorated reconnaissance grunt from the Korean War
Abilities: Ain't Got No Quit!; Ambush; Blaze a trail; Detect unnatural jungle sounds; Forward observer/recon; Friends with Ambush, Bullhorn, Captain Grid-Iron, Salvo, and Topside; Knowledge Skill: Jungle flora and fauna; Jungle assault specialist; Jungle recon specialist; Navigation; Qualified Expert Operator: A.W.E. Striker; Qualified Operator: VAMP; Stealth; Teaches the instructors who teach jungle survival; Wilderness Survival: Jungle

Conditions: Intends to be the governor of Florida one day; Loves Big Cypress Swamp; Never surrenders; Responsible for all covert operations involving attacks on Cobra Island; Won't stop until the job is completed; Won't stop until all objectives are accomplished

Quote/Motto: "I don't stop until all objectives have been accomplished. And I mean ALL objectives." Said about him: "We could be chest-deep in a midnight swamp, with mosquitoes in our ears, leeches in our boots, and Cobra Night-Vipers firing up our tails with tracers, but as long as Pathfinder has the point, we'll come out smelling like roses. He learned everything from his father, a decorated reconnaissance grunt from the Korean War. Like his father, he doesn't know the meaning of the word surrender. When Pathfinder leads a jungle patrol, he doesn't stop until the job is successfully completed and all objectives have been accomplished. And I mean ALL objectives!"

Notes: *He has the same serial number as fellow 1990 release Stretcher.

Patrulha Do Ar

Alias/Variations: ("Sky Patrol")
Purpose: Assumed to be the same as Sky Patrol
Members: This set consisted of four exclusive figures: two G.I. Joes (Albatroz and Aguia Commando) and two Cobras (Abutre Negro and Escorpiao Voador).

Payload

Series: Six (1987)
Alias/Variations: Nile S. Weatherby*
Real Name: Mark Morgan, Jr.
Place of Birth: Cape Canaveral, Florida
Gender: Male
Grade/Rank: 8/O-6: Colonel—Space Cos (Space CO); Pilot O-6
SN: 2579-7507
Service Branch: Air Force
Faction(s): G.I. Joe, Star Brigade, Strike Team: Charlie

Notably Served At: Southeast Asia, Earth's orbit; Trucial Abysmia; Sierra Gordo
Primary MOS: Astronaut
Secondary MOS: Fixed-wing pilot
Appearance: Red hair and mustache; white spacesuit with silver structural supports and red padding on arms and legs
Accessories: Astronaut's helmet with transparent face shield; manned maneuvering unit backpack and two detachable control arms. Version 3: Knife, missile launcher (spring-loaded, actually fired), three guns, two missiles
Abilities: Astronaut; Certified Expert Operator: *Crusader* space shuttle; Certified Expert Operator: *Defiant* space vehicle complex; Frequently works with Hardtop; Pilot for Strike Team: Charlie; Qualified Expert Operator: F-4 Phantoms; Works well with Oktober Guard
Conditions: Belief: People need to "pay their dues"; Chants "Vrooom! Vrooom!" when piloting
Quote/Motto: "Space is the place to bust Destro in the face!" "Here's a guy who has spent most of his waking hours for his entire life working on getting himself into space. Sometimes, as he's executing a complicated maneuver in free fall or when he's cutting in his boosters, he seems to be chanting softly under his breath. If you turn up the volume on the ship-to-ship channel and listen very carefully, you can hear him quite clearly: 'Vrooom! Vrooom!'" Quote by an unnamed G.I. Joe team member.
Notes: *Certificate of Commendation for Hasbro's official "Live the Adventure Assignment II" contest (1987) identifies Payload as Nile S. Weatherby.

Phones

Real Name: Patrick Liam O'Flaherty
Place of Birth: Dublin, Ireland
Gender: Male
SN: AF 934037
Service Branch: Navy
Faction(s): Action Force, Q Force
Primary MOS: Communications
Secondary MOS: Survivalist
Appearance: Orange, tan, yellow uniform, sidearm
Background Information: Ex-leader of Specialist Survival School
Abilities: Communication systems; Communication technology; Hand-to-hand unarmed combat expert; Leadership; Qualified Expert Operator: Swordfish; Radio Operator; Sonar officer; Survival specialist
Conditions: Hates anything to go wrong with his equipment; Perfectionist; Rivalry (friendly) with Breaker of Z Force
Quote/Motto: "Phones is an expert and hates for anything to go wrong with his equipment." Quote by an unnamed G.I. Joe team member.

Psyche-Out

Series: Six (1987)
Real Name: Kenneth D. Rich
Place of Birth: San Francisco, California (Birmingham, Somerset, England, for European distribution)
Gender: Male
Grade/Rank: O-2 (First Lieutenant) (1987); O-3 (Captain) (1991)
SN: 091-87-6274
Service Branch: Army
Faction(s): G.I. Joe, Night Force, Sonic Fighter, and Tiger Force
Stationed: Deceptive Warfare Center at Fort Bragg; Joe's "Americana Museum" sub-base
Notably Served At: Afghanistan; Cobra Island; Jordan; Sierra Gordo
Primary MOS: Psy-Ops
Secondary MOS: Social services counselor
Appearance: Yellow hair; silver headset; a bright green shirt with black and silver vest; light gray sleeves; black gloves, belt, and boots; dark gray pants
Other Known Appearances: When he joined Tiger Force, his blond hair was too bright, so he dyed it brown.
Accessories: Antenna attaching to hole in the scalp; tech backpack with two antennas; pistol with ribbed grip and no trigger guard; two arm clips with detachable radar dishes; triangular transmitter with handle and detachable radar dish
Background Information: Degree in psychology from Berkeley; worked on various research projects involving the inducement of paranoia using low-frequency radio waves. Continues pioneering work in the field of wave-induced behavior modification out of the Deceptive Warfare Center at Fort Bragg
Abilities: Deceptive Warfare Expert; Degree in psychology; Evaluating the young child clones of Serpentor; Interrogation; Knowledge Skill: Low-frequency radio waves; Knowledge Skill: Paranoia; Provides advice

based on overheard communications; Provides analysis of the Joe team; Someone you can talk to about your problems; Team's resident shrink

Conditions: Devises elaborate plans; Has creepy secrets; Manipulates people; Overeager in analyzing teammates

Quote/Motto: "The point at which you win a battle is when you've convinced the enemy that he has lost. This can be accomplished through something as simple as constant repetition. For example, you see a commercial on TV ten times a day for a particular brand of cookies. Confronted by an array of unknown brands, you choose the one that you saw advertised. They've won.... And you've lost."

Notes: In a separate continuity, he is killed in a battle with Cobra BATs in a Cobra underwater facility after being captured by the Baroness and Interrogator. His small radar accessories and high-tech backpack are most likely a device that can send low-level radio waves to generate paranoia in humans.

Q-Force

Purpose: The Q-Force was the ocean-themed wing of the Action Force.
Leader: None stated, defer to rank
Members: Aqua Trooper, Deep Sea Defender, Deep Sea Diver, Sea Skimmer, Sonar Officer, Sting Ray (with S.H.A.R.K., a type of aqua-sled), Swordfish
Notes: Members listed are generic designations, not specific individuals.

Quarrel

Series: Twenty-nine (2013)
Real Name: Hedda L. Pulver
Place of Birth: Interlaken, Switzerland
Gender: Female
Grade/Rank: 1/E-5: Sergeant (SGT)
SN: AF 396942
Service Branch: Army (Switzerland)
Faction(s): G.I. Joe, S.A.F. (Special Action Force), and Z Force
Notably Served At: Verenya; Buenos Aires
Primary MOS: Undercover operations
Secondary MOS: Commando
Appearance: Short blonde hair, shaved on the sides of her head; blue eyes
Accessories: Backpack, helmet, pistol, rifle, two-part crossbow

Background Information: Graduated at the top of her class in Undercover Ops school and Advanced Unarmed Combat school
Abilities: Celebrity: Top ranking competitor in the annual British Grand Prix Motorcycle Championships; Daughter of a Swiss diplomat; Hand-to-hand unarmed combat expert; Heightened reflexes; Infantry, armor, and artillery unit; Martial arts expert; Qualified Expert Operator: Motorcycles, Tomahawk; Qualified Operator: Anything that moves!; Qualified Weapon Expert: Cantonese butterfly knives, Swiss Army knife; Undercover Operations; Unlimited access to high-speed vehicles
Conditions: Distinctive Feature: Uses Chinese butterfly knives (dao); Distinctive Feature: Uses modified crossbow; Distinctive Feature: Uses throwing stars (shurikens); Motorcycle daredevil; Normally passive; Reputation: All-around sportswoman; Seeking daddy's attention
Quote/Motto: "I'll drive anything that moves but I'll outride anyone on a motorcycle."
Notes: Action Force (alternate continuity)

Quick Kick

Series: Four (1985)
Alias/Variations: Flits ("Flash," Holland), Pied Blinde ("Armored Foot," Belgium), Quick Kick, Quickkick, Sigilo (Argentina)
Real Name: Ito S. MacArthur
Place of Birth: Watts, Los Angeles, California (Canton, China for European distribution)
Gender: Male
Grade/Rank: E-4 Army corporal
SN: 631-42-7104
Service Branch: Army
Faction(s): G.I. Joe, Action Force (alternate continuity)
Notably Served At: Borovia, Cobra Island, Trucial Abysmia
Primary MOS: Infantry/silent weapons
Secondary MOS: Intelligence
Appearance: Black hair; white "Japanese flag" headband; no shirt; red sash with throwing stars; black wristbands, belt, and pants; no shoes; blue pockets on belt and boots
Other Known Appearances (Cartoon): Usually no red circle on headband; brown vertical straps when wearing a backpack; wristbands were larger than the figure's. The 1991 mail-in exclusive action figure was made of inferior plastics and quickly yellowed. The weapons

included a sword and nunchakus also made of inferior materials.
Accessories: Small backpack (round on bottom); unique Samurai sword with round hilt; rounded nunchakus
Background Information: Japanese father and Korean mother owned a grocery store in the Watts neighborhood of Los Angeles
Abilities: Knowledge Skill: Movie quotes; Professional Skill: Hollywood stunt man; Professional Skill: Karate movie actor; Qualified Operator: Dragonfly, H.A.V.O.C., JUMP, LCV Recon Sled, Silver Mirage, Tomahawk, Trubble Bubble; Qualified Weapons Expert: All NATO and Warsaw Pact small arms; Ranking black belt in Tae Kwan Do, Go Ju Ryu, Southern Praying Mantis Kung-Fu, Tai-Chi Sword, Zen Sword, Wing-Chun; Voice impersonations
Conditions: Not accepted by neighborhood because of his mixed ancestry; Quotes movie lines; Reputation: Fought and defeated Storm Shadow; Short
Quote/Motto: "Here's the situation. You want to gain access to a fortified villa. Twelve-foot-tall continuous wall topped with razor spiral and only one gate through it. Two-inch steel plate on the gate, two sand-bagged guard houses with a direct telephone link to the main house, four guards with submachine guns, two Dobermans, and a silent alarm hooked to a dead man's switch that one of the guards is leaning on at all times. How to do it? Have Quick Kick hit it, that's how!" Quote by an unnamed G.I. Joe team member.
Notes: Crazylegs, Quick Kick, and Breaker died in a vehicle explosion while escaping in a stolen Cobra Rage tank in Trucial Abysmia. Cross Country, Duke, and Falcon managed to escape. Even though it is never shown, it is implied Quick Kick's name is part of the memorial to deceased Joes located at Arlington National Cemetery.

Quick Stryke

Real Name: Rando Bama
Place of Birth: Black River, Jamaica
Gender: Male
SN: SDK30HN5
Service Branch: Army
Faction(s): G.I. Joe, former S.K.A.R. operative, and Team Extreme
Primary MOS: Recon
Appearance: African American, dreadlocks, powerfully built; green shirt, blue pants, twin brown bandoliers, knife, grenades, black knee-high boots, black gloves, green headband, leg pouches
Accessories: Mountain Rescue Grappling Claw
Background Information: Former mercenary
Abilities: Former mercenary; Former S.K.A.R. operative; Mountaineer; One Man Army!; Recon; Trusted by the G.I. Joe team; Wilderness Survival: Mountains
Conditions: Blames Iron Klaw for Jonathan's death; Deceased brother Jonathan; Dedicated to bringing down Iron Klaw and S.K.A.R.; Defected to G.I. Joe from S.K.A.R; Hates Iron Klaw; Lone wolf; Motivated by the death of his brother; Mysterious (keeps background a secret); Prefers solo recon missions; Reputation: Former bad guy

Rampage

Series: Eight (1989)
Alias/Variations: Comando Avancado (Brazil)
Real Name: Walter A. McDaniel
Place of Birth: Brooklyn, New York
Gender: Male
Grade/Rank: E-4
SN: 632-45-6200
Service Branch: Army
Faction(s): G.I. Joe
Stationed: Fort Belvoir
Primary MOS: Armor
Secondary MOS: Finance
Appearance: Five o'clock shadow; handlebar mustache; green camos
Accessories: Pistol, rifle with two removable ammunition clips, submachine gun, two-piece cardboard briefcase, vest
Abilities: Qualified Operator: Tanks; Qualified Weapons Expert: M-16, M-1911A1, M2 50 Cal, MG, M60 MG
Conditions: Aspires to be middle-class; Dreams of being a CPA
Quote/Motto: "Many people find comfort and order in the discipline. Mathematics reduces the complexities of the world to manageable sums. Rampage liked tanks. They are immutable statements in iron."
Notes: See Heavy Metal

Rampart

Series: Nine (1990)
Alias/Variations: Airburst, Checkmate, Counterfire, Deadline, Groundfire

Real Name: Dwayne A. Felix
Place of Birth: New York City, New York
Gender: Male
Grade/Rank: E-4 (Navy petty officer, 3rd class)
SN: SN: 313-6094-SP19
Service Branch: Navy
Faction(s): G.I. Joe
Stationed: Naval Amphibious Base Coronado, California
Notably Served At: Battle of Benzheen
Primary MOS: Shoreline defender
Secondary MOS: ADA missile specialist (Air Defense Artillery); tuba player
Appearance: Beige cap with blue goggles and black microphone; beige shirt; black jacket and gloves; beige pants; green and black camouflage boots; cannon post on waist and missile slot on the left leg
Accessories: Cannon with a handle on the side and notch for waist peg; short missile launcher with detachable sling/handle; two detachable cannon support legs; two missiles with pins on tips
Abilities: College degree; Expert tuba player; Heightened hand-eye co-ordination; Heightened reflexes; Logical and accurate decision maker; Quickly analyze shifts in the spatial movement of images; Video game expert
Conditions: Enjoys football with teammates; Gets his jollies shooting down Cobra heat-seeker missiles; Reputation: Highest combat success ratio in the 7th Fleet for "splashing" enemy aircraft
Quote/Motto: "Proficiency in most video games depends upon one's ability to quickly analyze shifts in the spatial movement of images, and to react to such changes faster than anybody else. The same is true in destroying incoming enemy missiles. Rampart gets his jollies seeing a Cobra heat-seeker explode just before it hits the target. It beats the heck out of logging initials into a video game's 'Top Ten' listing." Quote by an unnamed G.I. Joe team member.
Notes: While on assignment in South America, Rampart, along with Glenda and Hardball, is killed by the Red Shadows.

Rapid Deployment Force

Series: Twelve (1993)
Alias/Variations: RDF; R.D.F.
Purpose: This is a Special Unit assignment.
Leader: None designated; defer to rank
Members: Fast Draw, Repeater, and Shockwave
Quote/Motto: "Cobra intelligence orders issued over a cellular communications transmitter have recently been intercepted by G.I. Joe surveillance operatives. A team of Austrian physicists is being held captive in a fortress and forced to develop Cobra's latest nuclear threat, a bomb referred to by its Top-Secret Code Name: 'XTERMIN8.' G.I. Joe has engaged RDF (Rapid Deployment Force) commandos to get to the fortress and stop the bomb's completion before it's too late! Three RDF members have been chosen for the risky mission: Fast Draw, a mobile missile specialist, will launch a surprise missile attack and blast an entry hole into the fortress; Repeater, the Steadicam machine gunner, will provide initial cover fire to take on any Cobra resistance; and Shockwave, the SWAT specialist, will penetrate the fortress, destroy the bomb, and bring the scientists to safety. Time is of the essence ... can the RDF pull it off?"

Rapid-Fire

Series: Nine (1990)
Real Name: Robbie London
Place of Birth: Seattle, Washington
Gender: Male
Grade/Rank: 6/O-3: Captain
SN: 903-9432-TY32
Service Branch: Army
Faction(s): G.I. Joe
Stationed: West Point Cadet Summer Orientation, United States Military Academy
Primary MOS: Fast attack expert
Secondary MOS: Sabotage
Appearance: Brown hair; black sleeveless shirt under neon green armor vest; orange armbands and blue pants; silver belt; black boots; orange kneepads
Accessories: Helmet; submachine gun
Background Information: West Point graduate; recipient of the Congressional Medal of Honor
Abilities: Airborne qualified; Contacts: West Point graduate; Highly motivated; Language Skill: Fluent in three (unspecified) languages; Light ordnance assault operations expert; Sabotage tactics
Conditions: Constantly on the go; Driven to succeed; Highly motivated; Never takes the easy way out; Trying to be the best Joe
Quote/Motto: "Rapid-Fire never takes the easy way out when it comes to doing things—but completed the Point's grueling 10-week Cadet Summer Orientation in only five weeks. He

went to West Point the hard way—by enlisting in the Army straight out of high school. This guy is constantly on the go, trying to be the best G.I. Joe at everything! If he keeps it up, he'll be calling the shots at the Pentagon soon enough!" Quote by an unnamed G.I. Joe team member.

Raven

Real Name: Unknown
Place of Birth: Unknown
Gender: Female
Service Branch: Cobra Air Force
Faction(s): G.I. Joe, Cobra, The Plague, and Strato-Viper
Notably Served At: Doctor Mindbender's secret island
Primary MOS: Pilot
Secondary MOS: Unknown
Appearance: African American; Well-built
Abilities: Contact: Slipstream; Qualified Expert Operator: Night Raven; Strato-Viper; Vehicle gunner
Conditions: Defected to the Joes; Newly defected from Cobra

Rawhides

Purpose: This is a Special Unit assignment, a program which allows individuals the flexibility to only report for missions needing their specialized expertise. They are under the supervision and training of Beach Head.
Leader: Beach Head
Members: Big Lob (Grenadier), Chuckles (Undercover Ops), Falcon (Special Forces soldier), Jinx (Martial Arts), Law and Order (Military Law), Tunnel Rat (E.O.D.)

Recoil

Series: Eight (1989)
Alias/Variations: Tigor (Brazil)
Real Name: Joseph Felton
Place of Birth: Vashon Island, Washington (Clifton, Derbyshire, England, for European distribution)
Gender: Male
Grade/Rank: 1/E-5: Sergeant
SN: 007-3461-0077; 007-8866-DD66, 007-34-0277**
Service Branch: Army
Faction(s): G.I. Joe
Notably Served At: Benzheen; Cobra Island; Sao Cristobel
Primary MOS: Infantry
Secondary MOS: RTO (Radio Telephone Operator)
Appearance: Dark green hat; yellow hair; bright green sunglasses; greenish beige shirt and pants with dark green urban camo; dark green backpack straps, belt, and leg holster; brown gloves and boots
Accessories: Explosives case with a short handle, machine gun with scope and bayonet, machine pistol with a grenade launcher under grip, small pouch backpack with attached bent antenna
Background Information: Ranger school
Abilities: Excellent physical shape; Infantry; "Lurp"*; LRRP (Long-range recon patrol); Marathon runner; Professional Skill: Bodybuilder; RTO (Radio Telephone Operator); Reconnaissance specialist
Conditions: Disquieting presence; Makes no apologies; Practices all the time; Reputation: Most qualified personnel to infiltrate enemy territory and gather intelligence; Sneaks up on people then just stands there
Quote/Motto: "Recoil would be a lot more popular if he wasn't practicing all the time. Oh, he puts in regular time at the survival ranges, but that's not what I mean ... he practices SNEAKING UP ON PEOPLE. You think you're all alone, lost in your thoughts, then all of a sudden, he's standing right next to you! When people ask him what his job in the Army is, he tells them, 'Being quiet.'" Quote by an unnamed G.I. Joe team member.
Notes: *A Lurp sneaks out into the bush carrying 100 pounds of gear, including rations, radio, weapons, ammo, and climbing rope. He is expected to penetrate deep within enemy territory, gather intelligence, and extricate himself without being detected. A Lurp who must use weapons is not a true Lurp! **All three of his security numbers are correct.

Recondo

Series: Three (1984)
Alias/Variations: Boonie-Rat (original character name); Leopardo ("Leopard" Brazil)
Real Name: Daniel M. LeClaire
Place of Birth: Wheaton, Wisconsin (Snowy River, Australia for European distribution)
Gender: Male
Grade/Rank: E-4 (Corporal); 3/E-7: Sergeant first class in *Devil's Due* comics

SN: 158-23-0074
Service Branch: Army
Faction(s): G.I. Joe, Patrulheiro da Selva ("Jungle Patrol" Brazil), and Tiger Force
Notably Served At: Battle of Springfield; Cobra Island; Sierra Gordo
Primary MOS: Jungle trooper/infantry
Secondary MOS: Intelligence
Appearance: Large, thick brown, handlebar mustache. Figure came in three different camo variations: bright green, wide markings, and tan. Bright green pants are the rarest.
Accessories: Cross country backpack, M-14E2X rifle
Background Information: Cadre member at the Jungle Warfare Training Center. His prototype file card says he "plain and simple, hates the cold...[for] there's nothing he likes better than to be hauling a rucksack through the brush and sweating through his cammies. When he's in the jungle, he owns it. Anybody else is trespassing."
Abilities: Contacts: Jungle native allies; Excellent soldier; Extensive experience with helicopters; Infantry; Intelligence; Jungle trooper; Knowledge Skill: Jungle flora and fauna; Member of the Jungle Warfare Training Center; Qualified Expert Operator: "Tiger Fly" attack helicopter; Qualified Operator: Helicopters; Qualified Weapons Expert: M-16, Swedish K, grease gun, M-1911A1 Auto Pistol, M-79 grenade launcher; Wilderness Survival: Jungle
Conditions: Hates the cold; Loves being in the jungle; Reputation: Killed by Major Bludd; Respects local beliefs and religions
Quote/Motto: "A jungle is like some single, gigantic, hostile organism. It can sense when you fear or hate it—and it is wholly without mercy. When Recondo steps into a jungle, it sings to him like a mother soothing a troubled child." Quote by an unnamed G.I. Joe team member.

Red Dog

Series: Six (1987)
Real Name: David Taputapu
Place of Birth: Pago Pago, Samoa
Gender: Male
Grade/Rank: E-5 (Army sergeant equivalent, Renegades have no official status)
SN: 425-80-2173
Service Branch: Army
Faction(s): G.I. Joe, Slaughter's Renegades
Primary MOS: Infantry
Appearance: Samoan; black curly hair; gold headband, tooth necklace, and wristbands; red sports shirt with "1" on front; white short sleeves; blue pants with brown belt and holster; black boots
Other Known Appearances (Cartoon): Brown vertical chest straps; horizontal strap gray with brown detail
Accessories: Backpack; pistol with a long hammer and trigger some distance from the grip
Abilities: Fights with a cricket bat in one hand and a gun in the other; Professional Skill: B-movie stuntman
Conditions: Disavowed: Gets no credit when he succeeds; Distinctive Feature: Samoan accent; Operates without support and outside the military command structure; Pre-professional football barefoot place-kicker; Reputation: Excessive roughness
Quote/Motto: "The other Renegades think that Red Dog is a handy gun to have along on missions. If they encounter an obstacle of any kind: barricade, tank-trap, or a phalanx of armed guards, they simply point Red Dog in the appropriate direction, let him go, and wait for the dust to settle." Quote by an unnamed G.I. Joe team member.

Red McKnox

Series: Fourteen (1995)
Gender: Male
Faction(s): G.I. Joe, Team Extreme
Background Information: Designed most of the equipment used by the Joe Team. Lab Assistant: Julia
Abilities: Scientist, Weapon designer
Conditions: Scottish

Red Spot

Series: Nineteen (2003)
Real Name: Michael P. Ritchie
Place of Birth: Cincinnati, Ohio
Gender: Male
Grade/Rank: E-4
SN: 407-27-PM94
Service Branch: Army
Faction(s): G.I. Joe
Primary MOS: Laser weapons systems operator
Appearance: Brown hair and eyes, brown and tan camos
Accessories: Ghillie suit, helmet, two rifles
Abilities: Designs lasers; Knowledge Skill:

Electronics; Knowledge Skill: Rated chess masters; Laser trooper; Laser weapons systems operator; Non-traditional classical Greek expert; Plays centerfield for Joe softball team; Second-degree black belt in Aikido; World-class rated master in chess

Conditions: Frequently dates; Sci-Fi fan

Quote/Motto: "The theoretical stuff and the practical application to hardware are all the fun stuff, but the real challenge is out in the field, crawling through the mud with tracers zipping by overhead. That's where you find out whether you're a soldier or not."

Red Star

Series: Ten (1991)
Alias/Variations: Colonel Krimov; Krasnaya Zvezda
Real Name: Anatoly Fydorovich Krimov
Place of Birth: Odesa, Ukraine, Russia
Gender: Male
Grade/Rank: O-3 (Army Captain equivalent)
Service Branch: Soviet Navy
Faction(s): Oktober Guard, leader
Notably Served At: Afghanistan
Primary MOS: Oktober Guard commander
Secondary MOS: Commando operations (Naval infantry)
Appearance: Brown hair; tan and brown camouflage jacket with rolled-up sleeves; green straps; tan pants with red stripes on the side; gray boots
Accessories: AK-103 assault rifle; backpack with large roll, clips on the side for the knife, and detachable antenna; officer's cap with a star on front; short, textured ammo belt; smooth knife, slightly curved at the tip; wrist machine gun with two detachable barrels
Background Information: Black Sea Regiment of the Soviet Naval Infantry (the equivalent of our Marine Corps)
Abilities: Base of Operations: The General Mobile Command; Chess master; Coaches the pistol team at the Dynamo Sports Club in Moscow; Experience fighting the undead (mummies); Experienced field commander; Highly intelligent; Hobby Skill: American pop culture; Instruction; Oktober Guard Officer; Published Pushkin scholar; Russian naval infantry captain; Student of the studies of Carl von Clausewitz; Zero-g experience
Conditions: Appreciation for cigars; Belief: Oktober Guard represents the best Russia has to offer; Distinctive Feature: Scar running from right cheek to his mouth; Distinctive Feature: Red star on his right hand; Grizzled veteran; Reputation: Youngest chess master in Odesa (age of 11); Wants revenge for what the Cisarovna family did to his people; Uncanny resemblance to Colonel Brekhov

Quote/Motto: "Red Star came home from that mess in Afghanistan with a bad attitude and a funny look in the eye, but when they needed an experienced field commander to lead the Oktober Guard, he leaped at the chance. He wasn't about to let the top volunteers from all the best units be led by some party toad with relatives in the high command and a yen to become a hero of the Soviet Union." Quote by an unnamed G.I. Joe team member.

Notes: He is the successor to Colonel Brekhov, the previous leader who died in action.

Red Zone

Series: Twenty-two (2006)
Real Name: Luke Ellison
Place of Birth: Stockton, California
Gender: Male
Grade/Rank: 0/E-4: Advisor/Probationary Member/Specialist
SN: 815-82-EL45
Service Branch: Army
Faction(s): G.I. Joe, Steel Brigade
Primary MOS: Urban warfare
Secondary MOS: Rotary wing pilot
Appearance: Dark brown hair, black eyes. His khaki pants are not tucked into his boots, his shirt is sleeveless, and his gloves reach nearly to his elbows.
Accessories: Helmet, revolver, pistol, shotgun
Background Information: Trained by the Federal Bureau of Investigation
Abilities: Can fight his way through a legion; Distinctive Feature: Rocket launcher in one hand and machine gun in the other; Keeps situations from escalating; Strong; Urban assault trooper
Conditions: Disabling the enemy isn't enough; Quick to help teammates; Reputation: Beats the crap out of bad guys; Reputation: Trigger happy; Reputation: Leaves large holes in enemy installations; Too much of a man for sleeves; Uses more force than necessary
Quote/Motto: "Red Zone and his teammate Rook are a perfect match; Rook sets them up and Red Zone knocks them down." Quote by an unnamed G.I. Joe team member.
Notes: It's ambiguous whether Red Zone was

once a human who was absorbed and replaced by a Wraith or whether he was always a Wraith who constructed a false identity. This is not to be confused with the Cobra operative Wraith who wears the Wraith stealth armor.

Redmack

Series: Twenty-five (2009)
Real Name: Reginald Cob
Place of Birth: Devil's Thumb, Colorado
Gender: Male
Grade/Rank: E-5 Sergeant
SN: 657-94-7655
Service Branch: Army
Faction(s): G.I. Joe, Comandos Heroicos, the Argentine branch of G.I. Joe
Stationed: He is on permanent transfer to Comandos Heroicos, the Argentine branch of G.I. Joe
Notably Served At: Andes Mountains; Rocky Mountains
Primary MOS: Counterintelligence
Secondary MOS: Cavalry scout (19D)
Appearance: Light red-brown hair, light brown eyes, basic brown camo
Accessories: Backpack, clear visor, helmet, knife, pistol, rifle, submachine gun, web gear
Background Information: Sergeant Shimik, Sergeant Redmack, and Sergeant Topson makes up the Argentina branch of G.I. Joe. He grew up on an Arapaho reservation.
Abilities: Counterintelligence; Cavalry Scout; Exceptional soldier; Knowledge Skill: Knows every inch of the Rocky Mountains; Knowledge Skill: Flora and fauna of the Rocky Mountains
Conditions: Always suspicious; Concerned about the potential loss of life of a mission; Environmentalist; Man of few words; Vowed to rid the world of Cobra; Worries about the financial ramifications of a mission
Quote/Motto: "Make no sound, leave no trace."

Repeater

Series: Seven (1988)
Alias/Variations: Retaguarda, Urzor (Brazil)
Real Name: Jeffrey R. Therien
Place of Birth: Cumberland, Rhode Island (Penrith, Cumberland, England, for European distribution)
Gender: Male
Grade/Rank: 2/E-6: Staff sergeant
SN: 343-26-7890
Service Branch: Army
Faction(s): G.I. Joe, Night Force, and Rapid Deployment Force
Stationed: The Pit, Utah, located beneath Fort Wadsworth
Notably Served At: Atlantic City Freeway Battle; The Pit, Utah
Primary MOS: Infantry
Secondary MOS: Heavy weapons
Appearance: Beige cap; black hair; beige short-sleeved shirt with black urban camouflage; green vest; beige, urban-camo pants with a green belt; black left half-glove
Accessories: Base attached to gun and the figure's belt, flat machine gun with a handle on the rear and hole for the base, large pouch backpack with a roll-on top
Abilities: Army veteran; Can fire from the shoulder, hip, or underarm; Machine gunner; Steadicam machine gunner; Strong; Versatile
Conditions: Bring the grunts back in one piece!; Cannot hack it in garrison; Draws enemy fire; Not a barracks soldier, Stand-up type of guy
Quote/Motto: "I make them eat lead or eat the dirt!" "Being the machine gunner is probably the toughest job in an infantry squad. Number one, he's got the heaviest load to carry. Number two, as soon as he starts firing, the enemy knows where he is and [he] becomes their primary target. Number three, the squad depends on him to keep firing through all this to provide maneuvering cover. Your machine-gunner should always be the strongest, most stand-up troop you have...." Quote by an unnamed G.I. Joe team member.

Reservist

Series: Eighteen (2002)
Gender: Male
Service Branch: Army
Faction(s): G.I. Joe
Appearance: Feature-covering helmet and goggles, dark green padded body armor, black gloves, and boots
Accessories: Submachine gun
Background Information: Graduates of G.I. Joe Reservist Training
Abilities: Ideal guardians of birthplaces; Stand ready to defend freedom at a moment's notice; True respect for freedom
Conditions: Aren't even a footnote in Joe history; As devoted to the cause as a full-service G.I. Joe team member; Defending

their home soil is their first duty; True respect for freedom

Quote/Motto: "We'd like to have him on as a full-time G.I. Joe, but we need [Code Name] in [Birthplace] where he can protect his family and community. When needed, [Code Name] will travel with the G.I. Joe team to fight Cobra but defending the home soil is his first duty." Quote given by Duke.

Rip Cord

Series: Three (1984)
Alias/Variations: Halo Jumper; Ripcord; both Fuego and Sokerk (Argentina); Relampago (Brazil)
Real Name: Wallace A. Weems
Place of Birth: Columbus, Ohio (Manchester, England, for European distribution)
Gender: Male
Grade/Rank: 1/E-5: Sergeant
SN: RA148231056
Service Branch: Army
Faction(s): G.I. Joe, Action Force, Former member of the Action Force Parachute Regiment freefall team, the Red Devils, Python Patrol
Stationed: The Pit, Utah, located beneath Fort Wadsworth
Notably Served At: The Battle for Springfield; Cobra Island; Cobra Civil War; Sierra Gordo
Primary MOS: Airborne infantry
Secondary MOS: Demolitions
Appearance: Red hair; olive green and darker green camouflage shirt and pants; light green belt; black gloves and boots
Other Known Appearances (Cartoon): Black belt and vertical chest straps; parachute and webbing usually white. Often no gloves, and usually no goggles when wearing a mask. In the IDW comics, Rip Cord is a young African American who hates his code name and wishes to stop jumping out of planes and become a pilot one day. Rip Cord is an African American recruit in the *Renegade* comics as well.
Accessories: Face mask with hose, parachute harness, slightly flared helmet (with or without holes), SLR-W1L1 rifle with sight and a handle on top
Abilities: HALO (High Altitude Low Opening) jumper; Qualified Weapons Proficient: FN FAL rifle; Qualified Weapons Expert: M-16, M-1911A1 Auto Pistol, Carl Gustav 9-mm Parabellum, Browning high-power; Skydiving; Veteran G.I. Joe

Conditions: Belief: Best to confront a problem head-on; Cannot tell Candy his real name or explain why they draw the attention of Cobra forces; Civilian girlfriend: Candy Appel; Dislikes Adele Burkhardt

Quote/Motto: "Let's say you got a trouble spot—you can't sail, walk, or ride in. So you send a plane in so high that it can't be seen or heard. Rip Cord jumps and drops like a rock for thousands of feet then opens his chute at the last possible moment to avoid visual and electronic detection. What he does once he hits the ground you don't want to hear about." "Let's say you got what you call a trouble spot in some remote hostile out-back. You can't sail in or walk in, or ride in. What you do is send in a plane so high that it can't be seen or heard and this guy Rip Cord jumps out and drops like a rock for thousands of feet and opens his 'chute at the last possible moment to avoid visual and electronic detection. What he does once he hits the ground you don't want to hear about." Quote by an unnamed G.I. Joe team member.

Notes: Rip Cord was responsible for giving Scarlett, Tunnel Rat, and Roadblock their code names.

Rip Cord 2

Series: Twenty-five (2009)
Real Name: Wallace A. Weems
Gender: Male
Grade/Rank: Master Sergeant (E-8)
SN: 845-99-WA76
Service Branch: Army
Faction(s): G.I. Joe
Primary MOS: Pilot
Appearance: African American
Abilities: Marksmanship comparable to Scarlett; Openly attracted to Scarlett; Pilot; Test scores comparable to Duke's
Conditions: Attempts comic relief; Duke's best friend; Duke's partner; Loves flying planes; New to the Joes

Roadblock

Series: Three (1984), Five (1986)
Alias/Variations: Barricade; Bubba, Hardball, Steamroller
Real Name: Marvin F. Hinton
Place of Birth: Biloxi, Mississippi (Brixton, London, England, for European distribution)
Gender: Male

Grade/Rank: E-4 (Corporal) (1984–1985); E-5 (Sergeant) (1988); E-6 (Staff sergeant) (1992) E-7 (Sergeant first class) (comic book series)
SN: RA538203485 (original); 434-2390-WT27 (1992); 825-38-MF48 (2003)
Service Branch: Army
Faction(s): G.I. Joe, Anti-Venom Task Force, Battle Corps, Heavy Assault Squad, Sound Attack, Star Brigade, Strike Team: Alpha (crew chief), and Tiger Force
Primary MOS: Infantry heavy weapons
Secondary MOS: Cook
Appearance: African American; bald with black mustache and goatee; off-white short-sleeved shirt; light green vest with beige strap and red pads; black gloves and boots; light gray pants with beige belt and boots
Other Known Appearances (Cartoon): Same but with a darker green vest, a brown belt, and right chest strap. In the Sunbow cartoons, the character spoke in catchy, quick rhymes.
Accessories: 1984: Ammo box, helmet, M-2X machine gun with tripod. 1986: L7A21 GPMG (general purpose machine gun) heavy machine gun with tripod
Vehicles: Qualified Operator: APC, Armadillo, A.W.E. Striker, Conquest, H.A.V.O.C., JUMP, Killer W.H.A.L.E., Mauler, RAM, SHARC, SkyStriker, Snow Cat, VAMP, Cobra ASP, ordinary jeep (probably personal vehicle)
Background Information: From his prototype dossier: "[Roadblock's] lifelong dream was to be a gourmet chef. He was working as a bouncer in the Biloxi [Mississippi] area to earn enough money to attend the Escoffier school in France when an Army recruiter convinced him that the Army could train him in the basics and that later he could use the GI Bill to further his gastronomic education. Upon enlistment, he discovered army menus and preparation techniques too appalling for his cultured tastes and promptly transferred to the infantry."
Abilities: Boy Scout; Celebrity: Chef (several bestselling cookbooks; hosted a cooking show; a product line of kitchen pots, pans, utensils); Chief mechanic and technical support person (*G.I. Joe: Renegades* Universe); Cousin is Heavy Duty; Heavy machine gunner; Leadership; Infantry heavy weapons; Mech pilot (Transformers Universe); Partners with Tunnel Rat; Physically strong; Professional Skill: Bouncer; Qualified Weapons Expert: M-2X Browning .50-caliber, Heavy machine gun, all Warsaw Pact Heavy MGs, M-16, M-1911A1 Auto Pistol; Sings in church choir
Conditions: Affinity for the team's van nicknamed "Coyote"; Close with his cousin, Hershel (alternate continuity); Close to uncle and aunt, Caleb and Sarah Bronson; Distinctive Feature: Large sideburns (alternate continuity); Dreams of attending Escoffier School in France; Enjoys heavy metal music (alternate continuity); Fierce temper that "is a long time building, and a long time going" (comics); Hates Army food; Large extended family; Particularly good friends with Flint and Lady Jaye; Passion for good food; Reputation: Biggest and strongest member of G.I. Joe; Reputation: Most good-natured of the Joes; Shy
Quote/Motto: "Flush 'em out with a burst of fifty cal." "Desist in your actions or I will be obliged to reduce your head to a fine red mist." "A .50 cal. Browning weighs 84 pounds. Add 50 pounds for the ammo—that's about 134 pounds of steel generating 2930 fps in muzzle velocity at a cyclic rate of 550 rpm. Anybody who can handle that doesn't need a machine gun to keep me away!" Quote by an unnamed G.I. Joe team member.
Notes: Roadblock is sometimes called Barricade but is not to be confused with fellow Joe, Barricade. The character Double Blast was renamed Roadblock in 2002 but is not the same individual. His cousin is fellow Joe Heavy Duty.

Robo-J.O.E.

Series: Twelve (1993)
Real Name: Greg D. Scott
Place of Birth: Casper, Wyoming
Gender: Male
Grade/Rank: E-3 (Army private first class)
SN: 23H-1436-59
Service Branch: Army
Faction(s): G.I. Joe, Star Brigade
Primary MOS: Jet power technology
Secondary MOS: Outlaw incarceration
Appearance: Cyborg; black hair; gold plating on the left side of face; orange armor suit with black armor on lower arms, upper legs, and feet
Accessories: Machete, opaque full-head crested space helmet, shotgun, spring-loaded missile launcher with a trigger, submachine gun, two missiles
Abilities: Army R&D; Cyborg; Inventor; Jet-tech operations; Scientific engineering genius

Conditions: Cyborg-permanently integrated bio-armor space suit linked with silicon wires, computer chips, and muscle tissue; Ill-fated; Seeking justice and revenge on Destro

Quote/Motto: "I am stronger. I am faster. I am ROBO-J.O.E.!"

Notes: If the acronym J.O.E. stands for anything, it is yet to be revealed.

Rock 'N Roll

Series: One (1982)

Alias/Variations: Bench Press (2009); Craig "Rock 'n Roll" McConnel; Rock & Roll

Real Name: Craig S. McConnel

Place of Birth: Malibu, California (Truro, Cornwall, England, for European distribution)

Gender: Male

Grade/Rank: E-5 (Sergeant) (1982); E-6 (Staff sergeant) (1989); E-9 (Sergeant major) (1991); E-4 (Corporal) (1993); E-7 (Sergeant first class) (1997)

SN: RA989091452; 989-1314-MC53 and 989-1302-NO53

Service Branch: Army

Faction(s): G.I. Joe, Sonic Fighters, Star Brigade, and Stars and Stripes Forever

Notably Served At: Broca Beach; Canada; Chicago; Israeli "Wailing Wall"; Japan; Middle East; Millville; Sierra Gordo; Turkey

Primary MOS: Infantry, machine gunner

Secondary MOS: PT instructor

Appearance: Yellow hair and beard, dark green short-sleeved shirt with two gold ammo belts across chest; dark green pants with gold pockets; brown boots

Other Known Appearances (Cartoon): Ammo belts on the chest were brown with gray bullets. The outfit was slightly lighter than that of the figure. In the Marvel Comics Universe, he had a beard and long hair.

Accessories: 1982–83: Dark green helmet; M-60 machine gun with bipod

Background Information: Advanced infantry training (top of class); Specialized Education: Covert Ops school; The 1982 Rock 'n Roll figure was produced straight-armed.

Abilities: Accustomed to loud, amplified noises; Disguise; Consistently updating his equipment and his skills; Covert Ops; Cunning; Familiar with all NATO and Warsaw Pact light and heavy machine guns; Forceful; Hobby Skill: Bass guitar; Hobby Skill: Electric guitar; Hobby Skill: Surfer; Hobby Skill: Weight lifter; Holds the line!; Infantry; Machine Gunner; PT Instructor

Preferred Weapon: Favorite Weapon: General Monopolies 5.56-mm, six-barreled, electronically driven, mini–Gatling machine gun! It's fitted with inert-gas recoil absorbers and scoped with third-generation laser optics. This weapon, including a power pack and factory-loaded 1000-round ammo drum weighs in at 85 pounds and delivers 4000 rounds per minute at a muzzle velocity of 3300 feet per second.

Conditions: Forceful; Honorable; Inherent decency; Loves his classic 1956 Bel Air Nomad; Naïve; Obstinate; Proud; Reputation: Man of contradictions; Reputation: Man of honor and integrity; Reputation: Plays bass in a local band; Self-deprecating; Shy; Sincerely concerned about teammates' well-being; Strong sense of loyalty to teammates; Will hold the line

Quote/Motto: "Rock 'n Roll is cunning but naïve, forceful but shy. Possesses a strong sense of loyalty to his teammates and is sincerely concerned about their well-being. A man of honor and integrity who can be counted on to hold the line." "When Rock 'n Roll was a surfer and weightlifter back home in Malibu, he used to play electric guitar in local bands. During that time, his ears became accustomed to loud, amplified noises. So today, whenever he hears the roar of his mini–Gatling gun laying down maximum suppressive firepower, the sound of it is simply music to his ears!" Both quotes were taken from a transcript of a taped Peer Personality Profile review, given by a fellow G.I. Joe team member.

Rocky

Series: Never produced; intended to be a mail-away exclusive in 1987

Real Name: Rocky Balboa

Place of Birth: Philadelphia, Pennsylvania

Gender: Male

Grade/Rank: E-5 (Enlisted reserve)

Faction(s): G.I. Joe

Primary MOS: Personal combat instructor

Appearance: Prototype drawing shows him bare-chested with blue-gray sweatpants and red, white, and blue stripes diagonally on the shins; white boxing boots, white boxing gloves, and blue headband holding back long black hair

Other Known Appearances (Cartoon/Comic/Movie): White prototype art shows him the same, but with a blue muscle shirt and sporting a pugil stick with red boxing gloves on the ends.

Conditions: Intended Cobra counterpart was to be Big Boa. Per Larry Hama, his hands were to be considered a deadly weapon.

Quote/Motto: "How does a well-known boxing champion serve out his Reserve time? He can take the easy route—be a showpiece for Special Service exhibitions bouts and racking up brownie points for officers with no combat ribbons and shiny trouser bottoms—or he can take a secret posting to train the G.I. Joe Team in the finer points of the sweet science of pugilism. The assignment to the Joe Team would be strictly under the counter. No special pay, no extra privileges, and no publicity. All he would get would be the satisfaction of doing something for his country…." Quote by an unnamed G.I. Joe member. "He's one of the best there is with his fists and nobody can touch him with pugil-sticks, but that's not the reason I want him training the Joes. Anybody can teach technique. I want the Joes to see what it is to take a beating and come back fighting: To stand up and take everything the other guy's got to give—and give back a full measure. That's worth more than a tip on how to protect your right hook." Excerpt taken from a memo from Brigadier General Abernathy (Hawk)

Notes: The G.I. Joe figure was dropped as Coleco was introducing a line of Rambo toys, *Rambo: The Force of Freedom*, with an accompanying cartoon of the same name they hoped would directly compete against the G.I. Joe line.

Rollbar

Series: Twenty (2004)
Alias/Variations: Reed D. Wilson (version 3), Reed D. Williston
Real Name: Robert D. Dube
Place of Birth: East Greenwich, Rhode Island
Gender: Male
Grade/Rank: 0/E-4: Specialist
SN: 345-68-RD89
Service Branch: Army
Faction(s): G.I. Joe
Primary MOS: Assault vehicle driver
Secondary MOS: Mechanic
Appearance: Short blond hair; long, dark gray jacket with a light green belt; dark gray baggy pants; dark gray boots
Accessories: Helmet with strap and removable chinstrap. Version 3: Backpack, helmet, pistol, rifle, vest
Abilities: Close-quarters battle expert; Cool-headed self-confidence; Highly trained; Qualified Expert Operator: Humvee driver; Specialist: Mobile weapon; Tuner (master of radical performance upgrades on small import cars); Urban combat expert
Preferred Weapon: 820 selective fire long-range fully automatic assault rifle
Conditions: Distinctive Feature: Swaggers when he walks; Fast and furious approach to driving; Never doubts he'll make it back to HQ
Quote/Motto: "I can take an engine and some wheels and turn them into a road-chewing, Cobra-thumping, mobile motorcade of justice."

Rook

Series: Twenty-two (2006)
Real Name: Andy Lombardi
Place of Birth: La Crosse, Wisconsin
Gender: Male
Grade/Rank: E-4 Specialists
SN: 264-91-LA42
Service Branch: Army
Faction(s): G.I. Joe, Steel Brigade
Stationed: The Coffin, the Joes' Arctic prison
Primary MOS: Lie detector
Secondary MOS: Interpreter
Appearance: Short military cut light brown hair, soldier's physique, light blue T-shirt, tan cargo pants, black boots, brown suspenders
Accessories: Flak vest, helmet, rifle, shotgun
Abilities: Body language expert; Interpreter; Interrogation; Language Skill: Fluent in 14 different (unspecified) languages; Lie detection; Lore Skill: Urban settings; Survival: Urban areas
Quote/Motto: "His fellow Steel Brigade members know not to play No-Limit Texas Hold 'em against Rook; it's pointless. Why? Because he knows you are bluffing before you do."
Notes: He is a reserve member of the current Joe team assigned to domestic operations. *All reservists can be called back into action if a mission calls for it.

Rumbler

Series: Six (1987)
Alias/Variations: Motor-Face, Down-Shift, Overdrive, Long-Gone, Scrambler

Real Name: Earl-Bob Swilley
Place of Birth: Raeford, North Carolina
Gender: Male
Grade/Rank: 3/E-7: Sergeant first class
SN: 654-56-8723
Service Branch: Army
Faction(s): G.I. Joe
Primary MOS: Fast attack vehicle driver
Secondary MOS: Armorer, small arms
Appearance: Brown hair and mustache; dark gray open-collar shirt; brown open jacket; green gloves; yellow pants and belt; green boots
Accessories: Helmet; machine gun
Abilities: Professional Skill: Revenue agent; Qualified Expert Operator: R/C Crossfire
Conditions: Dedicated to the pursuit of individuals or organizations against the government; Propensity toward high-speed car chases
Quote/Motto: "What you do is sling Rumbler and his crossfire under a heavy-lift chopper and drop them on the run from 20 feet up, 50 miles behind enemy lines. Sort of like dropping a weasel in a henhouse. You know you're going to see some feathers fly." Quote by an unnamed G.I. Joe team member.
Notes: In the comics, the character Armadillo was given the code name "Rumbler." His figure is frequently mislabeled as Footloose.

Ruslan

Alias/Variations: Young Ruslan
Real Name: Ivan Koskov
Place of Birth: Kaliningrad, Russia
Service Branch: Army (Russian)
Faction(s): Oktober Guard
Notably Served At: Africa, Asia, Central America, Eastern Europe
Primary MOS: Demolitions
Secondary MOS: Ordnance disposal
Appearance: 5'9" tall, brown hair and eyes, 165 pounds; field uniform consists of a gray jacket with brown camouflage printed on atop a white T-shirt, similarly shaded trousers, black leather boots, brown leather belts, webbing, and holsters to secure his gear, brown gloves, and a black cap to fend off the brisk Russian winter air
Background Information: Went to Oktober Guard from the Russian VDV Airborne Forces
Abilities: Demolitions expert; Endeared himself to Big Bear; Heightened perception; Knowledge Skill: Demolitions; Knowledge Skill: Firearms; Knowledge Skill: The ins and outs of the military command structure; Ordnance Disposal; Qualified Weapons Expert: AK-47; Qualified Weapons Expert: Warsaw Pact Firearms
Conditions: Always carries at least one grenade; Braggart; Carries a blade at all times; Cryptic; Has no hobbies; In awe of his Oktober Guard superiors; Never wastes materials to blow something up; Only speaks Russian; Only reads technical journals; Proud; Quiet; Reputation: Never discusses his childhood

Salvo

Series: Nine (1990)
Real Name: David K. Hasle
Place of Birth: Arlington, Virginia
Gender: Male
Grade/Rank: 3/E-7: Sergeant first class
SN: 524-7110-AR42
Service Branch: Army
Faction(s): G.I. Joe
Stationed: G.I. Joe headquarters in Utah
Notably Served At: Benzheen; Island Club Joe; Pyramid City
Primary MOS: Anti-armor trooper
Secondary MOS: TOW/dragon repair technician
Appearance: Bald; brown T-shirt with white "THE RIGHT OF MIGHT" on chest; black half-gloves, belt, and boots; green pants with gold ammo belts
Accessories: Briefcase, five land mines with clips for a rifle, five missiles with long pins, goggles, helmet with chinstrap, mine-layer rifle, missile launcher/backpack with a long handle
Abilities: Anti-armor trooper
Conditions: Aggravated if they don't find Cobra on patrol; Belief: No need to practice at the firing range; Distinctive Feature: Carries great quantities of conventional weaponry and ammunition; Profound distrust of advanced electronic weaponry
Quote/Motto: "Salvo doesn't believe in wasting perfectly good ammunition on wooden targets on firing ranges. He'd rather test his anti-armor projectiles on actual enemy tanks and armored personnel carriers, such as the Cobra H.I.S.S. II. Nothing aggravates him more than to go out on patrol and not find any Cobra targets to blow away. That means he'd have to lug all his unused ordnance back to G.I. Joe headquarters, and he doesn't enjoy that at all!" Quote by an unnamed G.I. Joe team member.

Notes: Salvo maintains a good friendship with Ambush, Bullhorn, Grid-Iron, General Hawk, Lady Jaye, Pathfinder, and Sergeant Slaughter.

Sandstorm

Series: Twenty-six (2010)
Alias/Variations: Sand Storm, SPC Benjamin, SPC Sandstorm, Specialist Sandstorm
Real Name: Joseph M. Benjamin
Gender: Male
Grade/Rank: E-4 (Specialist)
SN: 888-92-JB96
Service Branch: Army
Faction(s): G.I. Joe
Stationed: The Pit, Utah, located beneath Fort Wadsworth
Primary MOS: Military police
Secondary MOS: Advanced driver
Accessories: Belt, helmet, rifle
Abilities: Counter-sabotage; Military police officer; Qualified Operator: RAM Cycle; Law enforcement specialist
Preferred Weapon: 820 selective-fire long-range fully automatic assault rifle
Conditions: Does what's necessary to secure his charge
Notes: Fellow Joe member Dusty has an animal companion named Sandstorm.

Satin

Real Name: CLASSIFIED
Place of Birth: CLASSIFIED
Gender: Female
Service Branch: Civilian
Appearance: While she was blonde during her appearance in "The Pyramid of Darkness" arc, she was shown with orange hair in "Glamour Girls." The music video visible in the club in "Joe's Night Out" showed her as blonde once again, though with longer hair, a red dress, and matching heels.
Abilities: Band: "Her Dolls!"; Beautiful; Celebrity: Hit Song "The Cobra Who Got Away"; Contact: Dial Tone; Contact: Leatherneck; Contact: Shipwreck; Contact: Snake Eyes; Contact: Wet Suit; Friend and Roommate of Una (Low Light's sister); Hidden Room in her dressing room; Professional Skill: Cabaret singer; Vehicle: Armor-plated van
Conditions: Brave; Flirt; Reckless

Savage

Series: Fourteen (1995)
Alias/Variations: Robert Steven Savage Jr.; Robert S. Savage, Michael K. Savage
Real Name: Robert S. Savage Jr.
Place of Birth: Albany, New York
Gender: Male
Grade/Rank: E-8 Master sergeant
SN: SVGA586566
Service Branch: U.S. Army Air Forces
Faction(s): G.I. Joe, Sergeant Savage and his Screaming Eagles, Team Extreme, and Special Counter-Terrorism Unit Delta
Notably Served At: Omaha Beach; numerous undisclosed European locations; the Arctic; the Sahara Desert; Algeria; flew as part of the 23rd Fighter Group in China; served in Operation Shingle
Primary MOS: Combat mission squad leader/heavy weapons
Secondary MOS: Fighter pilot
Appearance: Bandage on his left temple, basic green camos
Accessories: Ammo box, catapult, gun, helmet, knife, missile launcher, missile, rocket, Team Extreme: Detonator combat cannon, two different rifles, two pistols
Background Information: During his years of service, he earned multiple medals of valor; Congressional Medal of Honor recipient
Abilities: Acclimated to the times; Ace pilot; Combat mission squad leader; Cyborg combatant; Enhanced reflexes; Fighter pilot; Hard charger from the greatest generation!; Heavy weapons expert; Increased reflexes; Incredible physical strength; Infantry commander; Lore Skill: Traitors to America; Lore Skill: War criminals; Qualified Expert Operator: P-40 Warhawks; Ready to fight the good fight!; Robot combatant; Urban assault expert; Wilderness Survival: the Artic
Conditions: Anachronist; Cryogenically preserved; Devoted to destroying I.R.O.N. Army; Favorite foods: hamburgers, French fries, cola, and ice cream; Hobby Skill: Baseball, basketball, and catching up on the past 50 years of military history; The oldest member of Team Extreme; Once had a wife and child; Remanded to the custody of G.I. Joe; Reputation: helped destroy the "guns at Navarro"; Reputation: Renowned for his skill; Reputation: Survivor of Omaha Beach; Reputation: Toughest commander on the battlefield; World War II hero
Quote/Motto: "This 'blast from the past' is about to show the world what being a hero is all about!"

Notes: He operated as second-in-command of Special Counter-Terrorism Unit Delta.

Scanner

Real Name: Scott E. Sturgis
Place of Birth: Fort Huachuca, Arizona
Gender: Male
Grade/Rank: E-4
Service Branch: Army
Faction(s): G.I. Joe
Stationed: Reykjavík, Iceland, a listening post
Notably Served At: The Pit
Primary MOS: Information technology
Appearance: Bald; black-frame eyeglasses with blue-tinted glass
Abilities: Amateur Journalist; Communications Monitoring; Photographer; Professional Skill: Conspiracy Theorist; Professional Skill: Investigator; Satellite surveillance
Conditions: Reasonable man
Notes: Recruited by Duke and Shockwave. He died saving Snake Eyes, Scarlett, and Duke, and subsequently killing Overlord.

Scarlett

Series: One (1982)
Alias/Variations: Glenda (Argentina); Quarrel (Europe); Agent Scarlett; Shana "Scarlett" O'Hara
Real Name: Shana M. O'Hara
Place of Birth: Atlanta, Georgia; (Bruges, Belgium for European distribution)
Gender: Female
Grade/Rank: E-5 (Sergeant) (1982); E-6 (Staff Sergeant) (1997); E-8 (Master Sergeant) (*Devil's Due* Image Comics Universe 2001-2005); O-1 (Second Lieutenant) (Renegades); O-6 (Colonel) (IDW Verse)
SN: RA242967434 (1982); RA24-29-7634 (1993); 624-29-SC34 (2002)
Service Branch: Army
Faction(s): G.I. Joe, Desert Patrol Squad, Ninja Force, Stars and Stripes Forever, Strike Team: Bravo Leader
Notably Served At: Antarctica; Appalachian Mountains; Battle of Springfield; Borovia; the Cobra Consulate in New York; Colorado; Hawaii; Japan; the Middle East; New Moon, Oregon; Priest Lake, Idaho; Puerto Rico; Sierra Gordo; Trans-Carpathia
Primary MOS: Counter intelligence
Secondary MOS: CLASSIFIED (Pilot, 2008)
Appearance: Red hair, dark gray shirt with yellow vest and waist piece (red pad on shoulder); yellow gloves and boots; gray leggings; also in a black uniform, camouflage uniform, blue and silver uniform; dark green and black uniform, green and black uniform, and blue and white uniform
Other Known Appearances (Cartoon): Same, but with a wide, white belt and long hair usually in a ponytail
Accessories: 1982–83: XK-1 power crossbow
Background Information: Graduated summa cum laude from law school; CIA operative; Advanced Infantry Training and Ranger School; Special Education: Covert Ops School; Marine Sniper School; Specialized Air Service School; Marine Tae Kwan Do Symposium
Abilities: Acrobatics; Adept with standard weapons; Advanced Infantry; Counterintelligence; Covert operative; Highly intelligent; Helicopter pilot; Instructor: Hand-to-hand combat; Intelligence officer; Martial arts expert; Ninjutsu; Operates a mecha robot (alternate universe); Professional Skill: CIA agent; Professional Skill: Information processing analyst; Professional Skill: Lawyer; Qualified Operator: Armadillo, Conquest, Dragonfly, JUMP, LCV Recon Sled, Polar Battle Bear, RAM, Silver Mirage, Sky Hawk, Sky-Striker (in 12 episodes), VAMP, Wolverine, SHARC prototype; Qualified Weapons Expert: M-14, M-16, M1911A1 Auto Pistol, M79 grenade launcher, M-3A1, M-700 Remington sniper rifle, MAC-10, throwing stars, garrote, and KA-BAR (Combat Knife); Ranger; Resilient; Sense of humor; Sniper; Weapon Mastery: Garrote
Preferred Weapon: XK-1 power crossbow, which fires various bolts with specialized functions. In the movie, her preferred weapon is a 15P laser-guided, solid alloy compound crossbow with a scope.
Conditions: Belief: Ghosts are real; Confident; Distinctive Feature: Long red hair in a ponytail; In love with Duke (cartoon); In love with Snake Eyes (comics); Never treated differently from any of the guys; Occasional affected Southern accent; Past romantic relationships with Duke and Snake Eyes (recent comics); Rough around the edges; Sister: Siobhan; Strong-willed; Talks to her father's ghost
Quote/Motto: "Beauty may only be skin deep, but lethal is to the bone" "Scarlett is confident and resilient … it's remarkable that a person so deadly can still retain a sense of humor." Both of the above quotes are taken

from a transcript of a taped Peer Personality Profile review, given by fellow unnamed G.I. Joe team members. "I gotta admit that I was leery as the other guys about having a woman on the team...'specially one as foxy as her, but after her first mission with us everything was just copacetic. Fifteen feet above the LZ, she was out of the Huey on the jump and off the skid WHAM into the bush pumping cover fire at the bad guys before the team leader hit the tiger grass. She made her bones the first time out. Confirmed." Quote taken from a transcript of a taped Peer Personality Profile review, given by fellow G.I. Joe team member Grunt.

Notes: She graduated from college at the age of 12 and does not understand why men are attracted to her. The 1982 Scarlett figure was produced straight-armed; she was the first female member of G.I. Joe.

Sci-Fi

Series: Five (1986)
Alias/Variations: Hot Line, Seymour "Sci-Fi" Fine; prototype names were Hot-Spot and Red Light
Real Name: Seymour P. Fine
Place of Birth: Geraldine, Montana (Strasbourg, France for European distribution)
Gender: Male
Grade/Rank: 6/O-3: Captain, specialist
SN: RA 793-29-1929
Service Branch: Army
Faction(s): G.I. Joe, Action Force, and Star Brigade
Stationed: Action Force's London base
Notably Served At: Germany; London; Persian Gulf
Primary MOS: Infantry/laser trooper
Secondary MOS: Electronics
Appearance: Bright neon green and silver helmet; black visor; bright neon green shirt and pants; silver vest with bright neon green padding; black gloves; silver boots
Other Known Appearances (Cartoon): Regular (not bright) green uniform; black padding on the vest; hair was brown in some episodes and black in others.
Accessories: Version 1: Bright green backpack with clips on the side for a rifle; large black XH 86 LLOM beam laser rifle with a peg for a hose; long, black hose.
Abilities: Can hold his position for an extended time; Elite combat trooper; Experienced marksman; Intense concentration; Laser trooper; Master of precision and patience; Qualified Expert Operator: Starfighter jet; Qualified Operator: A.W.E. Striker, Conquest, Falcon Glider, LCV Recon Sled, Mauler, Silver Mirage, Tomahawk; Transcends mere stillness to another plane of immobility; Willpower
Conditions: Attends science fiction conventions; Easy to make friends with; Never in a hurry; No sense of humor; Obsession over his electronics; Reputation: Better shot than Leatherneck and Wet Suit; Takes everything in stride; Teammates trust him to hit his mark; Would rather talk about the latest technology in integrated circuits and complex optics
Quote/Motto: "When Sci-Fi braces his weapon and sights in on a target, he becomes a rock—no discernible movement of any kind. Birds perch on top of his helmet. He transcends mere stillness to another plane of immobility. You don't even see the trigger finger move. It's like he wills that beam of light to stab the darkness...." Quote by an unnamed G.I. Joe team member.
Notes: His primary weapon is the L-LAT laser assault targeting weapon

Scoop

Series: Eight (1989)
Real Name: Leonard Michaels
Place of Birth: Chicago, Illinois (Dublin, Ireland for European distribution)
Gender: Male
Grade/Rank: E-4 (Army corporal) Specialist
SN: 887-1199-XE86; 887-1199-ML86 [unconfirmed]
Service Branch: Army
Faction(s): G.I. Joe
Notably Served At: Himalayas; Sierra Gordo
Primary MOS: Journalist
Secondary MOS: Microwave transmission specialist
Appearance: Brown hair; yellow shirt and pants; green vest with black binoculars and camera; black belt, holster, and boots
Accessories: Large news camera; large pistol with trigger guard; mic attaching to the helmet; soft helmet with goggles; standard short hose; tech backpack with radar dish
Background Information: Chosen by Congress to observe and document G.I. Joes' actions for evaluation on behalf of the congressional committee

Abilities: Advanced degree in journalism; Contact: Close friends with a Crimson Guardsman; Earned the respect of the Joes; Endurance; Has the trust of Stalker; Master's degree in electrical engineering; Professional skill: Journalist; Rugged; Soldier; Specialist: Combat Information; Specialist: Microwave Transmission; Spycraft

Conditions: Barely meets G.I. Joe standards; Courageous; Defected member of the Crimson Guard; Interacts badly with Hit and Run, Leatherneck, Muskrat, Stalker, and Tunnel Rat; Steps out from cover to get footage; Wants to be where the news is happening

Quote/Motto: "The other G.I. Joes were a bit put off by Scoop at first. They resented having a 'third wheel' tagging along lugging 60 pounds of video equipment and not much firepower! They changed their minds after he carried a wounded comrade two clicks to an extremely hairy evacuation site for a medivac. All the while his camera captured the whole thing on tape! Now that's called doing your job and then some!"

Notes: Scoop was recruited by Sergeant Slaughter for his Marauders sub-team after saving him from a burning building.

Scout

Series: Twenty-six (2010)
Real Name: Wolfgang Dremmler
Place of Birth: Leipzig, East Germany
Gender: Male
SN: AF 396954
Faction(s): G.I. Joe, Z Force
Notably Served At: Mid–African states
Primary MOS: Mine warfare
Secondary MOS: Bomb disposal
Accessories: Mine detector, specialist backpack, three landmines
Abilities: Almost psychic understanding with Steeler; Bomb disposal; Defusing car bomb expert; Minesweeper; Mine warfare; Sixth sense of danger; Wilderness Survival: Desert; Z Force Battle-Tank driver
Conditions: Formerly of the Soviet tank command; Water divining
Quote/Motto: "You don't have to see the danger to know it's there."

Screaming Eagles

Series: Fourteen (1995)
Purpose: A team of six well-seasoned sergeants and specialists in every technology and military field led by Sergeant Savage. "Deep behind enemy lines, World War II's greatest military hero leads a small platoon of soldiers on a top-secret mission. The year is 1944, and Master Sergeant Robert Steven Savage is about to be ambushed by a traitor in his ranks! Fifty years after that fateful ambush, Savage's cryogenically frozen body is discovered among the ruins of a mysterious laboratory dating back to the 1940s. Incredibly, Savage is revived by the G.I. Joe team and given a special DNA formula to maintain his youth and super-enhanced strength. Hawk gives him command of the Screaming Eagles, and the chance to avenge his fallen platoon. Once again, this 'blast from the past' is about to show the world what being a hero is all about!" Text from package.
Leader: Sergeant Savage
Members: D-Day, Dynamite, Grill, Head Banger, Hep Cat, Mouse 2, Tank

Selina

Real Name: Selina (surname, if any, unknown)
Gender: Female
Service Branch: Civilian
Faction(s): G.I. Joe
Appearance: Long straight black hair, tanned skin, naturally red lips
Abilities: Favor: Duke; Immune to mind control headband; Knowledge Skill: Secret passageways in Cobra Castle; Leadership; Leader of a (short-lived) slave rebellion; Laborer: Water bearer at a dig site
Conditions: Brave; Slave

Senator Barbara Larkin

Real Name: Barbara Larkin
Gender: Female
Grade/Rank: United States senator
Faction(s): G.I. Joe, Cobra
Stationed: Washington, D.C.
Notably Served At: Fort Lewis
Appearance: Cute; short blonde hair and blue eyes
Abilities: Beloved United States senator; Cute; Influential; Liaison with Cobra: the Baroness; Political maneuvering
Conditions: Ambitious; Hopes to usher in a new age of energy independence; Periodically accosted by the press; Personal Pet Project: Power station Alpha; Romantically linked with Hawk
Quote/Motto: "Please, call me Barbara!"

Notes: She made a deal with Cobra about the power station. She would promote it as a way to get money to her home state and generate a good number of jobs. Then Cobra would steal and destroy the power station for reasons of their own. When the Dreadnoks fail, she managed to manipulate G.I. Joe into destroying the power station by insisting it would be a better option than letting it fall into the wrong hands. She was assassinated by a Cobra gunman for being a "loose end"; she was only 37 years old. Hawk later mourned her death and left a rose on her grave.

Sgt. Slaughter

Series: Four (1985), five (1986)
Alias/Variations: Sgt. Slaughter, "Alan Heavy" (Argentina); Sgt. Slammer (India); Super Cop (India)
Real Name: CLASSIFIED: TOP SECRET (Robert Rudolph Remus)
Place of Birth: Parris Island, South Carolina
Gender: Male
Grade/Rank: 3/E-7: Gunnery Sergeant
SN: 817-76-981
Service Branch: Marine Corps
Faction(s): G.I. Joe, the Renegades, and Sgt. Slaughter's Renegades
Stationed: Pendleton
Primary MOS: Infantry/drill instructor
Secondary MOS: Survival trainer
Appearance: Brown military hat; brown hair and mustache; silver sunglasses; whistle around his neck; green tank top with "USA" on front; red wristbands and black gloves; black pants with a white belt and green and black boots (1985). Green military hat; brown hair and mustache; silver sunglasses; whistle around his neck; black tank top; black wristbands; light and dark green camouflage pants with dark green belt and green and black boots. There are two different versions of the pattern on his camo pants (1986).
Other Known Appearances (Toy): Slight variation in the font of "USA," and red or orange backgrounds on boot chevrons; *(Cartoon):* Brown hat, black shirt, green and light brown camo pants, white belt, and brown boots
Accessories: Baton (1985); Included with the Triple T-Tank, baton (1986)
Abilities: Can drill for 72 hours before breaking a sweat; Can fend for up to 12 people in the roughest terrain; Can smell and taste evil in the air; Drill Instructor; Everything and everywhere is a battlefield!; Hand-to-hand combat, Heavy-duty honcho; Incredible endurance; Incredible strength; Knocks out targets with one punch; Language Skill: Latin; Lucky; Physically strong; Qualified Expert: M60 Patton tank; Qualified Operator: Warthog A.I.F.V; Devilfish, H.A.V.O.C., Triple "T," Cobra Trubble Bubble; Remarkable fighting ability; "The man be rough and he takes no guff!"; Understands Ancient Greek; Wrestling
Conditions: Belief: Luck; Belief: His mission is to kick the butt of every boot in Pendleton; Extremely mean; Garnered tales to the point where he is credited with superhuman feats; Personal mission: to beat all trainees into examples of military perfection; Reputation: Chews nails and spits bullets; Reputation: Drives his tank through enemy fortresses because it's fun; Reputation: Toughest of all the Joes; Severe impatience; Spends time visiting his adult sister; Spews out brutal verbiage
Quote/Motto: "No one is going to give you a break on the battlefield." "There are two ways out of my command. On your feet like a man or in a ditty bag. An itty ... bitty ... ditty bag." When in combat: "Either we all go home, or nobody goes home." "They say he cut his teeth on a bogey wheel from a Patton tank and that his first words were 'Semper Fi.' They say that when the Sarge dresses down a boot in Camp LeJeune, the trainees cringe all the way to 'Pendleton.' Most boots would rather dive for apples in the grease trap than cross the Sarge. They say he can blow a month's pay in one night in Thule, Greenland. Of course, 'jarheads' are prone to exaggeration. We all know it's impossible to blow a month's pay in Thule, Greenland." Quote by an unnamed G.I. Joe team member. "They say his favorite pastime is marching over the boys' backs while they do finger pushups in the mud while spewing out brutal verbalities. He has been known to ride his tank through enemy fortresses rather than blow them up because its more fun. They say he eats nails and spits out dum-dum bullets. They say he cleans his teeth with barbed wire, brushes his hair with a rat-tail file, and shaves with a blowtorch. Everything and everywhere is a battlefield to Sgt. Slaughter." Quote by an unnamed G.I. Joe team member.
Notes: Sgt. Slaughter is fifth in command of the G.I. Joe team as a Special Drill Instructor (behind General Hawk, Duke, Flint, and Beach

Head). The 1985 Sgt. Slaughter's action figure was a mail-in exclusive and he was the very first celebrity spokesperson for the Sunbow cartoon, even voicing his own character.

Sgt. Slaughter's Renegades

Alias/Variations: The Renegades
Purpose: Officially, this sub-team does not exist; they are not on the rosters of any existing military unit, and there is no computer access to their dossiers. They were selected for combat training and discipline by Sgt. Slaughter. They receive their pay through a special fund earmarked "Pentagon Pest Control." Answering only to themselves, these rough-edged mercenary-type fighters partake in highly sensitive, bottom drawer–CLASSIFIED missions for the United States. This gives them a freedom of operation that the Joes can't match, allowing them to function with little restraint. It also means the government can disavow them if they're caught.
Leader: Sgt. Slaughter (not himself a member)
Members: Mercer, Red Dog, Taurus. Falcon was unofficially a member.

Shark

Real Name: Jean-Paul Rives
Place of Birth: Toulouse, France
Gender: Male
SN: 934038
Service Branch: Navy (French)
Faction(s): Action Force, Q Force
Primary MOS: Torpedo technology
Secondary MOS: Underwater demolitions
Appearance: Yellow wetsuit with blue and red markings
Background Information: Basic military training at French Naval School, Brest, France
Abilities: Aquatrooper; Combat expert; Knowledge Skill: City of Martinique; Professional Skill: Underwater treasure hunter; Qualified Expert Operator: Stingray; Strong Swimmer; Torpedo training (top of class); Torpedo Officer; Underwater demolitions
Conditions: Acts on his own; Dislikes obeying orders
Quote/Motto: "Shark is a high-quality fighter. Does act on his own. Dislikes obeying orders." Quote by an unnamed G.I. Joe team member.
Notes: Recipient of the Sword of Honor

Sharp

Alias/Variations: Colonel Sharp
Real Name: Dexter Sharpe; Warwick J. Sharp (sources conflict)
Gender: Male
Grade/Rank: 8/O-6: Colonel
Service Branch: Army
Faction(s): G.I. Joe
Primary MOS: Command officer
Secondary MOS: Strategist
Appearance: Gray hair and glasses and a beige officer's uniform
Other Known Appearances: Highly decorated, mustard yellow officer's uniform
Background Information: West Point graduate
Abilities: Adequate combat expert; Administrator; Cool under fire; Contacts; Gives deliberate, concise orders; Intelligence/MAC-V SOG agent (in 'Nam); Knowledge Skill: Administrative skills; Leadership; Mission planner; Personal acquaintance of General Flagg; Strategist
Conditions: Brave; Comes off as stiff; Distinctive Feature: Gravelly voiced; Gives Flint and Duke leeway to get the job done; Pessimistic in crises
Notes: He is one of the overall commanders of G.I. Joe before the appearance of General Hawk, along with General Flagg. He is not officially a member of the G.I. Joe Team; he relays orders from the Pentagon and gives the Joes their briefings and assignments before General Hawk joins.

Shaz

Series: Twenty-five (2009)
Alias/Variations: Abel "Breaker" Shaz; Cpl. Breaker
Real Name: Abel Shaz
Gender: Male
Grade/Rank: E-4 (Corporal)
SN: 757-79-AR35
Service Branch: Army
Faction(s): G.I. Joe
Primary MOS: Communications specialist
Appearance: Black parted pencil mustache
Accessories: Belt, cable, laptop, missile, pistol, spring-loaded missile launcher with stand, submachine gun, vest
Abilities: Former Moroccan military; Innovative thinking; Hacking expert; Technical surveillance
Preferred Weapon: Dair-1 Directed Artificial Intelligence Robotic Weapon

Conditions: Distinctive Feature: Chews gum and blows bubbles
Notes: Shaz is the movie version of the Marvel Comics version of Breaker

Shimik

Series: Twenty-five (2009)
Alias/Variations: Cat Eyes
Real Name: Jerome Ford
Place of Birth: San Luis, Argentina
Gender: Male
Grade/Rank: E-8 (Equivalent) Sargento Ayudante
SN: RA693648965
Service Branch: Army (Argentine)
Faction(s): G.I. Joe, Comandos Heroicos, the Argentine branch of G.I. Joe
Stationed: Argentina
Notably Served At: Argentina
Primary MOS: Infantry squad leader
Secondary MOS: Heavy machine gunner
Appearance: Painter's brush mustache; dark-skinned
Accessories: Ammunition belt, belt, helmet, knife, machine gun with removable bipod, rifle, two bandoliers
Background Information: Sergeant Shimik, Sergeant Redmack, and Sergeant Topson make up the Argentina branch of G.I. Joe.
Abilities: Brilliant strategist; Heightened perception; Infantry squad leader; Heightened perception in total darkness
Conditions: Brave; Fights corrupt political regimes; Infuriated Cobra invaded his homeland; Patriotic; Protective of his country's resources; Vowed to bring evil men to justice
Quote/Motto: "If you prey on my people, I will leap at you from the shadows and tear you apart!"
Notes: Shimik is an old family name; he uses it to hide his identity from his enemies.

Shipwreck

Series: Four (1985)
Alias/Variations: Marujo (Brazil); Carlos Alazraqui
Real Name: Hector X. Delgado
Place of Birth: Chula Vista, California
Gender: Male
Grade/Rank: E-7 (Navy chief petty officer)
SN: 924-92-5456
Service Branch: Navy
Faction(s): G.I. Joe, Battle Corps
Stationed: The Pit II
Notably Served At: "Gitmo," Cobra Island; Greenland; Mekong Delta; Middle East; Springfield; Thule, Venice, Italy; White House lawn; Yokosuka
Primary MOS: Gunners mate
Secondary MOS: Machinist
Appearance: Unkempt red-brown hair and beard with a slender build; white sailor's hat; an open-collared, short-sleeved blue shirt with red stripes on right arm; blue bell-bottom pants with black gloves, belt, holster, and shoes; hook on waist; a tattoo of an anchor on left forearm.
Other Known Appearances (Cartoon/Comic): Black hair and beard; shirt usually open to just below the sternum; tattoo on the right arm was black and pants a darker blue with a brown or beige belt. Polly had yellow on her wingtips and around her eyes. In the Sunbow cartoon, his voice rasped slightly; he and his parrot Polly added comic relief.
Accessories: Boarding hooks with string; old-fashioned percussion revolver with short strap; Polly the parrot
Background Information: Graduated Naval Gunnery School, Great Lakes; Lied about being the minimum age of 17 to join the Navy; Adopted
Abilities: Animal Companion: Polly*; Hand-to-hand combat expert; Knowledge Skill: Cooking; Knowledge Skill: Insurgents; Knowledge Skill: Knots; Knowledge Skill: River pirates; Knowledge Skill: Ropework; Knowledge Skill: Smugglers; Knows how to party!; Lore Skill: Stories; Professional Skill: Tour guide operations; Qualified Operator: A.W.E. Striker, Devilfish, Dragonfly, H.A.V.O.C., Killer W.H.A.L.E., Mauler, SHARC, Silver Mirage, and Sky Striker, Trubble Bubbles, jeeps, desert skiffs, handcars, Cobra sub; Qualified Weapon Expert: M-16, M-14, Browning .50-caliber, 20-mm Oerlikon AA gun, M1911A1; Quintessential sailor; Trained Navy SEAL
Conditions: Arrogant; Brash; Dislikes the use of "gadgets" in war; In love with escaped Cobra agent Mara; Often in trouble with superiors; Philosophy: "See the target, shoot the target"; Poor culinary skills; Prefers to take his own orders; Pretends to despise Polly; Reputation: Rambunctious; Reputation: Tells tall tales; Stereotypical sailor
Quote/Motto: "Shipwreck is your quintessential sailor. He can splice a line, fry powdered eggs

in the tooth of a gale and eat them, tell taller tales than a Senate Appropriations committee and take three-day liberty in Thule, Greenland and come back smiling." Quote by an unnamed G.I. Joe team member.

Notes: *Polly is Shipwreck's parrot. Polly will often repeat commands or bark out nautical terms. On rare occasions, she proved capable of holding brief but meaningful conversations with human beings. Polly shows far greater intelligence than a typical parrot. Polly knows sailing songs and is prone to including Shipwreck's name in them. Polly addresses Shipwreck as "Sailor." Because of Polly's irritating behavior, Shipwreck sometimes leaves him home while on missions. Polly dreams about being the leader of the P.E.T.S. (Primal Emergency Tactical Squad), which is a sub-team of G.I. Joe composed of all Joe's pets and companions.

Shockwave

Series: Seven (1988)
Alias/Variations: Night Force Shockwave; Shockblast
Real Name: Jason A. Faria
Place of Birth: Dearborn, Michigan (Manchester, London, England, for European distribution)
Gender: Male
Grade/Rank: E-4 (Corporal) (1988); E-7 (Sergeant first class) (1992)
SN: 369-0965-SW34
Service Branch: Army
Faction(s): G.I. Joe, Drug Elimination Force, and Night Force
Notably Served At: Chrysler Building; Cobra Island; Colombia; Sao Cristobel; Destro's Scotland castle; Sierra Gordo
Primary MOS: Special weapons and tactics
Secondary MOS: Choir
Appearance: Light blue cap with dark blue urban camo; dark blue face mask and vest; light blue shirt and pants with dark blue urban camo; dark blue gloves, belt, holster
Accessories: Square pouch backpack with clips on the side for a knife; pistol with small pin forward of textured grip; submachine gun with thin, curved stock and holes in muzzle; thick knife with a partially serrated blade
Background Information: Two citations for bravery from the Detroit Police Department
Abilities: Knowledge Skill: Detroit Police Department; Professional Skill: Policeman; Professional Skill: Military police officer; SWAT specialist; Tenor
Conditions: Brave; Does not care about money; Singing voice is not always at its best
Quote/Motto: "What, you think I do this for the money?" "Everybody on a S.W.A.T. team has a specific job, like in a choir. Choirs have tenors, baritones, altos, etc. S.W.A.T. teams have sharpshooters, climbers, and 'inside men.' Shockwave is the door kicker. He's the first inside and the first to find out how bad it really is. He's also a half-decent tenor when his voice is in shape...." Quote given by an unnamed G.I. Joe member.
Notes: With Duke, they recruited Scanner.

Shooter

Series: Thirty-two (2016)
Real Name: Jodie Craig
Place of Birth: Montclair, New Jersey
Gender: Female
Grade/Rank: E-5 Sergeant; E-7 Sergeant first class
SN: RAO12070700; 012-07-JF70
Service Branch: Army
Faction(s): G.I. Joe
Stationed: As a cadre non-commissioned officer at the chaplain's assistant school
Notably Served At: Sierra Gordo
Primary MOS: Infantry
Secondary MOS: Chaplain's assistant
Appearance: Short windswept dark brown hair, dark eyes, dark skin
Abilities: Being still; Escape routes; Esoteric knowledge; Expert marksman; Patience; Precise breathing control; Running; Sharpshooter; Stealth; Willpower
Notes: A member of the G.I. Joe team so secret that not even the other members of G.I. Joe knew about her (exceptions being General Flagg and Sparks); She was killed during the first meeting between G.I. Joe and Cobra, code named "Operation: Lady Doomsday"; she was forced to attack a group of Cobra troops with only her knife.

Short Fuze

Series: One (1982)
Alias/Variations: Mark W. Brenstan (1986 mail-in); Mark W. Freistadt (mail-in after 1986); Short-Fuze, Short Fuse
Real Name: Eric W. Freistadt

Place of Birth: Chicago, Illinois
Gender: Male
Grade/Rank: E-4 (Corporal) (1982), E-5 (Sergeant) (1997), E-6 (Staff sergeant)
SN: RA380225432; 380-22-EW32
Service Branch: Army
Faction(s): G.I. Joe, Strike Team: Bravo, Team Extreme, and Winter Operations
Notably Served At: Alcatraz; The battle at the Statue of Liberty; Blackwater Prison, Cobra Island; Fort Knox; Midtown Manhattan, New York; Springfield; Washington, D.C.
Primary MOS: Artillery, mortar soldier
Secondary MOS: Infantry engineer
Appearance: Blond-brown hair; yellow hair; a dark green shirt with black straps (one horizontal) and silver pockets; dark green belt and pants with brown pockets and boots
Accessories: 1982–83: Ammo pack, helmet, M-1 (81-mm medium mortar) with stand, visor; backpack (with engraved mortar shells), clear visor (the prototype visor was black), helmet, knife mortar with a removable bipod, small mortar and mortar stand, two pistols, webgear
Background Information: Comes from a military family (father and grandfather both career sergeants); Artillery School; Engineer School; Advanced infantry training
Abilities: Abstract mathematics; Career military; Demolitions experts; Highly self-disciplined; Infantry engineer; Mortar Soldier; Plots artillery azimuths and tribulations in his head; Professional Skill: Administrative duties; Qualified Weapons Expert: M-14, M-16, M-1911A1, M-79 (grenade launcher), M-2 (60-mm light mortar), M-1 (81-mm medium mortar)
Conditions: Enjoys abstract mathematics; Explodes in offensive verbal abuse; Fastidious dresser; Logical; Noticeable temper; Poor equestrian skills; Poor inter-personal skills; Reputation: Hothead; Sensitive; Vulnerable ego
Quote/Motto: "I can pinpoint targets with 95 percent accuracy so that we give Cobra forces a real incentive to turn tail and run if they know what is good for them." "Short Fuze is logical and sensitive. Tends to blow his stack—hence the nickname…." "He's OK for an army-brat lifer, catch my drift? Can you imagine what it must've been like to have top sergeants for a father and grandfather? Hardcore. Yeah, he blows his stack a lot but he don't mean anything by it … the whole team knows that and they play along with him and everybody's happy. Entertained too." The above quotes were taken from a transcript of a taped Peer Personality Profile review, given by unnamed G.I. Joe team members.
Notes: Often works with Steeler. A "restricted-level psychological profile" said he "tends to explode into verbal abuse involving very imaginative vitriolic [caustic, scathing] content … however, vituperative [harshly abusive] outbursts are merely a smokescreen masking a vulnerable ego." The 1982 Short Fuze figure was produced straight-armed. He came with one of three different types of mortars. Type one had a thin, closed handle; type two had an open, thin handle; and type three had an open, thick handle.

Shrage

Alias/Variations: Schrage
Real Name: CLASSIFIED
Place of Birth: CLASSIFIED; East German
Gender: Male
Service Branch: East German Army
Faction(s): Oktober Guard
Primary MOS: Infantry
Secondary MOS: Battle technician
Appearance: Platinum blond hair, blue eyes, 6'1", 155 pounds; brown-gray officer's cap; brown-gray jacket with collar and gold ammo belts across chest; brown-gray pants; black boots. Uniform is simple and utilitarian. It consists of a long-sleeved, collared tan shirt over a black T-shirt, tan trousers, black leather boots, a black leather belt, gray leather gloves, a tan infantryman's cap, and brown webbing and ammunition belts to hold his supplies.
Accessories: AK-47; machine gun
Background Information: Former East German infantryman
Abilities: Battle Technician; Determined; Expert Marksman; Hand-to-hand unarmed combat; Highly skilled combatant; Knowledge Skill: Firearms; Knowledge Skill: Warsaw Pact nation command structures and procedures; Language Skill: English and Russian; Man of action!; Natural tactician; Spotless record
Conditions: Always carries at least one grenade; Carries a blade on him at all times; Compulsive chain-smoker; Courageous; Distinctive Feature: Monosyllabic comments and protracted silences; Goes above and beyond; Known for his courage; Known for his determination; Loyal to a fault; More comfortable on the battlefield than anywhere else;

Reputation: Best infantryman East Germany has ever produced; Reputation: Reliable; Takes great pride in his work
Quote/Motto: "Words are easy. How you fight, that's everything."
Notes: He met his end in Sierra Gordo, sacrificing himself to save (what he thought) was a train full of revolutionaries—along with most of the original Oktober Guard.

Side Track

Series: Sixteen (2000)
Alias/Variations: Sidetrack
Real Name: Sean C. McLaughlin
Place of Birth: Hingham, Massachusetts
Gender: Male
Grade/Rank: 2/E-6: Staff Sergeant (SSG), 3/E-7: Sergeant first class (SFC)
SN: Unknown
Service Branch: Army
Faction(s): G.I. Joe
Primary MOS: Wilderness survival specialist
Secondary MOS: Demolitions expert
Appearance: Brown hair and bush handlebar mustache; brown short-sleeved shirt with dark brown diagonal strap and sleeves; light and dark green camouflage pants; black belt and boots. Plain military uniform, highlighted by black bandolier and black sleeves
Accessories: Backpack, four tent poles, helmet; pistol, submachine gun, two nets
Abilities: Breathing regimen; Professional Skill: Professional wrestler; Stealth; Specialist: Wilderness survival, Australian Outback
Conditions: Fascinated with the survival techniques of frogs; Favorite vacation spot: Australian Outback
Notes: Ranger John Boyce began using the code name Side Track in 2002.

Side Track 2

Series: Eighteen (2002)
Real Name: John Boyce
Place of Birth: New Manchester, West Virginia
Gender: Male
Grade/Rank: E-7
Service Branch: Ranger
Faction(s): G.I. Joe
Primary MOS: Infantry
Secondary MOS: Medic/interpreter
Appearance: Sandy brown hair
Accessories: Handgun, knife, submachine gun, rifle
Abilities: Uses wrestling persona to strike fear into his enemies
Conditions: Explosive personality; Patriot, Propensity for physical violence
Quote/Motto: "I don't want to talk them to death, I want to get my fist in their faces—now!"
Notes: He was killed by a trap laid by Shadow Tracker.

Sideswipe

Series: Eighteen (2002)
Real Name: Andrew Frankel
Place of Birth: Philadelphia, Pennsylvania
Gender: Male
Grade/Rank: E-5 Sergeant
SN: Unknown
Service Branch: Army
Faction(s): G.I. Joe
Stationed: Walter Reed Medical Center
Primary MOS: Medical specialist
Secondary MOS: Troop transportation
Appearance: Brown hair; white shirt with rolled-up sleeves and red collar; black backpack straps and gloves; gray holster; dark gray pants with black belt and white panel on left leg; brown boots with black pads
Accessories: Antenna, backpack, flare pistol, flashlight, hover sled with control stick and clear shield
Abilities: Ferrets out new medical techniques and equipment; Hobby Skill: Weightlifting; Maintains an arsenal of life-saving equipment; Medical specialist
Conditions: Brave; Offices and clinics don't appeal to him
Quote/Motto: "A plaque on the wall and golf on Wednesdays.... Nah! Where the battle is thickest is where you'll find me!"

Sightline

Series: Thirty-one (2015)
Real Name: Gary Goggles
Place of Birth: Chicago, Illinois
Gender: Male
Grade/Rank: 2/E-6: Staff Sergeant
SN: 044-77GM31
Service Branch: Army
Faction(s): G.I. Joe
Stationed: The Pit, Utah, located beneath Fort Wadsworth
Primary MOS: Anti-aircraft weapons
Secondary MOS: Infantry
Appearance: Black and gray camo body armor; red goggles

Accessories: Knife, laptop, pistol, rifle, shovel, vest, walkie-talkie
Abilities: Anti-Aircraft Support expert; Professional Skill: Trash hauling business; Professional Skill: Military air defense
Conditions: Plays "pretend"; Vivid imagination

Sigma 6

Alias/Variations: Sig 6
Purpose: A new group of G.I. Joes with highly specialized capabilities, which they use to protect the world from the Cobra Commander and his evil forces. The premise is that it is now the twenyt-first century, and G.I. Joe is still fighting to prevent Cobra from taking over the world. The Joes are equipped with Sigma suits. Designed by Hi-Tech, these special bodysuits protect the Joes from Cobra's laser blasts and, in addition, enhance their abilities. The Joes are code-named Sigma 6.
Leader: Duke, with Scarlett second in command
Members: Original: Duke, Heavy Duty, Long Range, Scarlett, Snake Eyes, Tunnel Rat. Other members include Boulder, Desert Wolf, Flint, Grand Slam, Gung Ho, Hi-Tech, Inferno, Kamakura, Leatherneck, Lockdown, Recondo, Shipwreck, Shockwave, Stone, Spirit Iron-Knife, Torpedo, and Wet Suit.
Vehicles: R.O.C.C. (Rolling Operations Command Center), a small, mobile, maneuverable, and armed base. It features cutting-edge holographic technology, which can disguise the ROCC as a trailer truck or large camper, allowing for surprise attacks. It has a hidden launcher for eight missiles on the six-seating cab that can separate from the trailer section. A command station is in the trailer section; a mini jet can launch and land on the roof near the movable claw. The Dragonhawk attack copter and the Sea Titan ship, a self-sustained base for operations, were gifted to Sigma 6 by British Joe operative Lt. Stone.
Notes: Sig 6 has a recurring man-versus-machine theme.

Skidmark

Series: Seven (1988)
Real Name: Cyril Colombani
Place of Birth: Los Angeles, California
Gender: Male
Grade/Rank: E-4 (Army corporal); 1/E-5: Sergeant
SN: 470-38-8412
Service Branch: Army
Faction(s): G.I. Joe
Notably Served At: Cobra Island
Primary MOS: Fast attack vehicle driver
Secondary MOS: Infantry
Appearance: Orange helmet with black goggles; a dark green shirt with an orange vest; light green pants with an orange holster
Accessories: None
Abilities: Does the job!; Fast attack vehicle driver; Infantry; Keen sense for detail; Qualified Expert Operator: Desert Fox 6WD; Operates vehicles under extreme conditions; Recon soldier
Conditions: Annoyingly polite; OCD behaviors; Hellion on the road; Love of speed; Numerous speeding violations; Reliable; Reputation: Fastest and most reliable recon driver around; Shining example of everything you are not!; Well-groomed
Quote/Motto: "He keeps his locker and bay area squared and spotless; it makes everyone else look bad by comparison. This could have been cause for resentment if he wasn't the fastest and most reliable recon driver around. The worst thing that his teammates can say about him is the best thing that a soldier can say about another soldier: He does his job."
Notes: Possibly killed in action during the second invasion of Cobra Island; he was crushed by a falling helicopter while aiding General Hawk, who was attempting to arrest Overlord. However, Skidmark is currently listed as a reserve member of the Joe team assigned to domestic operations in the United States. In the alternate universe, during a banquet held by Cobra and the Decepticons celebrating the destruction of Earth, a captured Skidmark was served to Megatron as "Earth food" and eaten alive.

Sky Patrol

Series: Nine (1990)
Purpose: This highly trained airborne unit specializes in advanced stealth technology and laser weaponry. They used this equipment to neutralize Cobra's aerial assaults. "Coated with a scientifically advanced, radar reflective protectant, these seasoned combat crafts have been refurbished and re-equipped with the latest in high-impact armaments, giving G.I. Joe total air-superiority over Cobra!"
Leader: Skydive

Members: Airborne, Airwave, Air Raid, Albatroz, Altitude, Aquia Commando, Drop Zone, Sky Dive, Static Line
Vehicles: Sky H.A.V.O.C., Sky Hawk, Sky Raven, Sky SHARC
Notes: In Brazil, Sky Patrol was called Patrulha Do Ar.

Skydive

Series: Nine (1990)
Alias/Variations: Jump Master
Real Name: Lynton N. Felix
Place of Birth: Pensacola, Florida
Gender: Male
Grade/Rank: 4/E-8: Master sergeant
SN: 131-4569-FX90
Service Branch: Army
Faction(s): G.I. Joe, Sky Patrol, leader (Skydive is the leader, but, Altitude carries the highest rank)
Stationed: Staff at the Ranger School in Fort Benning; el-Hassim military base in Iraq
Notably Served At: Bangkok
Primary MOS: Sky patrol leader
Secondary MOS: Personnel administration
Appearance: Brown hair and mustache; blue flight suit with silver straps on torso; white piping on forearms and legs; dark gray gloves; white holster, boots; and panel on the right leg
Accessories: Helmet with goggles; M-16 machine gun with a sling and handle on top; parachute in a parachute pack; pistol with a dotted muzzle
Abilities: Battle-hardened; Leadership; Professional Skill: Instructor
Conditions: Philosophy: Train hard and fight easy; Reputation: The toughest NCO at the Ranger School, Fort Benning
Quote/Motto: "Sky Patrol operates deep within enemy territory, cut off from supply and support. There can be no margin for error when you're that far behind the lines. One mistake and you're history! Only a battle-hardened veteran can pull off a mission without a hitch. That's just the type of leader you'll get with Skydive—the most successful head-knocker in the patrol!" Quote by an unnamed G.I. Joe team member.
Notes: He maintains a good friendship with Grid-Iron, Lady Jaye, Pathfinder, and his fellow Sky Patrol members. Although the leader of Sky Patrol, he acts as commander and field leader in the absence of General Hawk, Sgt. Slaughter, Duke, and Grid-Iron.

Skymate

Series: Ten (1991)
Alias/Variations: Digger, Dingo, Jackaroo, Luchtmakker (Holland), Planeur ("Glider") France)
Real Name: Daniel T. Toner
Place of Birth: Queenstown, Australia
Gender: Male
Grade/Rank: E-4; E-5 (Sergeant equivalent)
SN: 026-3425-RG90
Service Branch: Army (Australian)
Faction(s): G.I. Joe, Air Commandos, and Special Air Service
Notably Served At: Europe
Primary MOS: Air commandos
Appearance: Pink helmet; brown hair and mustache; a dark green short-sleeved shirt with yellow straps; green gloves; black pants with a yellow belt and green boots
Accessories: Bow, hang glider, small boomerang, transparent visor for the helmet
Abilities: Air commando; Fast; Glider trooper; Exotic weapons training; Knowledge Skill: Exotic weapons; Qualified weapons expert: Boomerangs, compound bow, knives, woomeras; Specialist: Glider; Stealth; Tough
Preferred Weapon: Bow and arrow
Quote/Motto: "S.A.S. troopers are a tough lot. They think wrestling crocodiles is a sport for sissies and shouldn't be engaged in by real men with important things to do. Now, Skymate, he's one of the toughest of the lot and he's twice as dangerous because, on top of being tough, he's quiet and fast. Not the bloke you'd want soaring down on you on a dark night with a compound bow in his hand...."
Notes: He is attached to G.I. Joe on second assignment from 3 Saber Sgn., Australian SAS. Skymate is not to be confused with G.I. Joe member Digger.

Skyraider

Alias/Variations: Chuck
Real Name: Charles Theodore Connors
Place of Birth: Cincinnati, Ohio
Gender: Male
SN: AF 93410
Service Branch: Air Force
Faction(s): Action Force, Space Force
Primary MOS: Space battle tactics
Secondary MOS: Space command
Appearance: Dark hair and eyes
Background Information: NASA trained astronaut; Space Agency instructor in Advanced Space Technology

Abilities: Astronaut; Energetic; Instruction; Knowledge Skill: Advanced space technology; Leadership; Quick decisions
Conditions: Not a man to be trifled with!; Reputation: Makes a plan and makes it happen
Quote/Motto: "Skyraider is not a man to be trifled with. Quick decisions and the energy to carry them through are his hallmarks." Quote by an unnamed G.I. Joe team member.

Skystriker

Series: Seven (1988)
Real Name: Alexander P. Russo
Place of Birth: Providence, Rhode Island
Gender: Male
Grade/Rank: 8/O-5: Lieutenant colonel
SN: 780-45-9887
Service Branch: Air Force
Faction(s): G.I. Joe, Tiger Force
Stationed: USS *Flagg*
Notably Served At: Cobra Island
Primary MOS: Tiger Rat pilot
Secondary MOS: Combat technician
Appearance: Brown hair; yellow jacket with black stripes; orange shirt and pockets on jacket; dark gray pants with white panels on thighs; black straps; brown belt, gloves, and shoes
Accessories: Clear visor, headset, helmet
Background Information: United States Air Force Academy; Officer's Flight Training School
Abilities: Combat acrobatics; Daredevil pilot; Jetfighter pilot; Qualified Expert Operator: "Tiger Rat" fighter plane
Conditions: Fascinated with fighter jets; Fearless; Reputation: Destroyed more than 15 Cobra planes during attacks on Cobra Island.
Quote/Motto: "The man was born to fly! I saw Skystriker pull off a double-looped nosedive in front of two enemy fighters, then shoot them down before they could pick him up on their radar scopes! It was unbelievable! When it comes to combat acrobatics, this 'fly-boy' takes the cake!" Quote by an unnamed G.I. Joe team member.
Notes: There is also a vehicle with this name, but it is written as SkyStriker.

Slaughter's Marauders

Series: Eight (1989)
Purpose: This unit specializes in camouflage, heavy artillery, and rapid offensive attacks. They were chosen to spearhead the global land offensive against Cobra. They were so secret, the Pentagon never acknowledged their existence. "They're a highly specialized, fast attack, ground assault unit that strikes the first blow for G.I. Joe against Cobra's forces of evil! Heavily armored tanks serve as the spearhead in G.I. Joe's frontal assault against Cobra and the Iron Grenadiers! Each ground-rumbling vehicle specializes in infiltrating and annihilating fortified garrisons and strongholds! Three-color camouflage design enables them to successfully blend into a woodland or jungle environment when conducting offensive maneuvers behind enemy lines!" Text from catalog.
Leader: Sergeant Slaughter
Members: Barbecue (firefighter), Footloose (ground pounder), Low Light (night operations sniper), Mutt & Junkyard (K-9 handler), and Spirit and Freedom (the tracker)
Vehicles: Armadillo, Equalizer, and the Lynx
Notes: Uniforms are a green, brown, and blue camouflage version of their original outfits.

Slipstream

Series: Five (1986)
Alias/Variations: Slip-Stream, Slip Stream
Real Name: Gregory B. Boyajian
Place of Birth: Provo, Utah
Gender: Male
Grade/Rank: O-2 (Air Force first lieutenant)
SN: RA 463-42-4892
Service Branch: Air Force
Faction(s): G.I. Joe
Notably Served At: Afghanistan, Benzheen; Cobra Island
Primary MOS: Fighter pilot
Secondary MOS: Computer technology
Appearance: Brown helmet with silver goggles; brown mustache; white shirt with dark gray half-vest, brown shoulder guards, and black gloves; white pants with dark gray belt and leg coverings; black shoes and holsters
Other Known Appearances (Cartoon): White portions of the figure's uniform were light brown. A prototype with a white helmet is pictured in the 1986 catalog. The mouth shows individual teeth on some figures, simply white on others.
Accessories: Included with the Conquest X-30
Background Information: The Jr. Civil Air Patrol
Abilities: Computer hacker; Fast Thinking; Guts; Hand-to-hand combat; Hobby Skill: Table tennis; Intelligent; Language Skill: Armenian, French, and Greek; Perception;

Perfect hand-eye coordination; Professional Skill: Conquest X-30 Pilot; Qualified Operator: Conquest X-30; Reflexes, Reputation: Unrepentant joker and mimic; Video-game whiz
Conditions: Competitive edge; Loves flying
Quote/Motto: "An aircraft with computer-assisted control surfaces can do things that are impossible for a conventional plane. (Flat turns without banking, flight axis shift, and horizontal rolls.) The controls are incredibly sensitive, the slightest tremor being translated into drastic movement. It takes a light touch to fly a ship like that and Slipstream has the touch, the eye, the brain, and the guts to make that aircraft do exactly what he wants." Quote by an unnamed G.I. Joe team member.
Notes: He also goes on ground missions.

Snake-Eater

Real Name: Jason B. Lee (alias)
Place of Birth: CLASSIFIED
Gender: Male
SN: CLASSIFIED
Service Branch: Army
Faction(s): G.I. Joe, Phoenix Guard
Stationed: Fort Benning
Primary MOS: Saboteur
Secondary MOS: Sabotage, demolitions, and terror
Background Information: Basic training, advanced infantry training, Airborne School and Ranger School at Fort Benning; Special Forces Qualification Course at Fort Bragg
Abilities: Cartography; Counterintelligence; Demolitions; Expert in all NATO and Warsaw Pact detonators and explosives; Ninja master; Ranger; Sabotage; Terror
Conditions: Brutal, Impulsive; Unpleasant to be around
Notes: Snake-Eater is the code name given to the alias Jason B. Lee, which was being used by Cobra operative Firefly.

Snake Eyes

Series: One (1982); four (1985)
Alias/Variations: Chatterbox; Cobra De Aco (Brazil); "Hebi no me" ("Snake Eyes"); Spook (original code name); Werewolf (see Timber)
Real Name: CLASSIFIED
Place of Birth: CLASSIFIED
Gender: Male
Grade/Rank: E-5 (Sergeant); E-7 (Sergeant first class) (1989–2008); E-8 (Master sergeant); CLASSIFIED (2009–)
SN: CLASSIFIED
Service Branch: Army
Faction(s): G.I. Joe, Desert Patrol Squad, Heavy Assault Squad, Ninja Force, Shadow Ninjas, Sound Attack, Stars and Stripes Forever, and Winter Operations
Stationed: High Sierras; a base in Yellowstone National Park code-named "The Rock"
Notably Served At: The Amazon; the Appalachian Mountains; Chicago; the Florida Everglades; London; Middle East; New York City; Southeast Asia; Spanish Harlem; Trans-Carpathia; the USS *Flagg*; Vietnam
Primary MOS: Infantry, commando
Secondary MOS: Hand-to-hand combat instructor
Appearance: Usually wears a black bodysuit, along with a balaclava and visor to cover his face. Out of his uniform, he is shown to be Caucasian with an athletic build, blond hair, and blue eyes. Arctic Appearance: white winter parka, with a traditional black mask. The Series 4 action figure had a plated armor visor.
Accessories: 1982–83: Explosives pack, Uzi gun. 1985: Backpack, sword, Uzi gun, wolf named Timber
Background Information: Trained at the MACV Recondo School (Nha Trang); served in LRRPs in Southeast Asia with Stalker and Storm Shadow; studied martial arts with Storm Shadow's Arashikage ninja clan. For his Series 5 figure, Marvel Comics expanded on his background. After the death of Storm Shadow's uncle, Hard Master, Snake Eyes went and traveled the High Sierra mountains and befriended a wolf he named Timber. Stalker made the recommendation to Hawk to recruit Snake Eyes. In one of their earliest missions in the Middle East, Snake Eyes was rescuing Scarlett, who was trapped in a crashed helicopter. Although the rescue was successful, there was an explosion and the heat from the blast scarred his face and damaged his vocal cords.
Abilities: Animal Companion: wolf, Timber; Commando; Concentration; Contact: Former apprentice Jinx; Contact: Former apprentice Kamakura; Contact: Former apprentice Ophelia; Contact: Former apprentice Tiger Claw; Disguise; Edged weapons expert; Hobby Skill: Break dancing; Holistic medicine; Language Skill: Coded language between himself and Scarlett; Mountaineering; Ninja Commando; Professional Skill: Drill

sergeant; Professional Skill: Hand-to-hand combat instructor; Proficient in 12 different (unspecified) unarmed fighting styles; Qualified Weapons Expert: All NATO and Warsaw Pact weapons; Qualified Weapons: Explosives; Qualified Weapons: Firearms; Sense of humor; Specialist: Commando Covert Missions; Stealth; U.S. Army Special Forces; Underwater demolitions; Wilderness Survival: Arctic; Wilderness Survival: Desert; Wilderness Survival: Jungle

Conditions: Distinctive Feature: Face severely disfigured (but since repaired); Distinctive Feature: Scar on the right check; Distinctive Feature: Scar over left eye; Distinctive Feature: the "steely gaze of a serpent"; Honorable; Lives a life of strict self-denial and seclusion; Love Triangle: Snake Eyes, Scarlett, and Duke; Mute; Mysterious; Not used to teamwork; Professional Rival: Storm Shadow; Rarely relies on one set of weapons to the exclusion of others; Reputation: Former Delta Force operator; Rigorous life of training; Tragic Past: Family killed in a car accident; Trusted and loyal teammate; Valiant

Quote/Motto: "Move with the wind, and you will never be heard." "The man is a total mystery, but he's real good at his job, heck, he's the best." Quote by an unnamed G.I. Joe team member.

Notes: He and Scarlett had implanted tracking devices in one another; only they know the frequencies. Scarlett can "translate" what he is thinking. Snake Eyes knew Scarlett's father and promised he would look after her, but after meeting her he fell in love. The 1982 Snake Eyes figure was produced straight-armed. The figure was also left remaining a bland black, completely unpainted; this was done to reduce production costs.

Snapdragon

Alias/Variations: Specialist Snapdragon
Gender: Female
Grade/Rank: E-4, Specialist
Service Branch: Army
Faction(s): G.I. Joe
Primary MOS: Intelligence
Appearance: Asian; "Dream Girl" brown/red hair, a well-toned body, and innocent demeanor. She emulates money and "party."
Abilities: As beautiful as she is dangerous; Beautiful; Humanitarian; Intelligent; President and CEO of Arkoma Technology; Translator; Wealthy socialite
Conditions: Dark side; Innocent demeanor; Looking to gain more power; Only wears custom-tailored clothes; Spoiled
Quote/Motto: "The mind is a terrible thing to waste ... and so is this body."

Sneak Peek

Series: Six (1987)
Alias/Variations: Biosfera (Brazil)
Real Name: Owen S. King
Place of Birth: Bangor, Maine (High Wycombe, Buckinghamshire, England, for European distribution)
Gender: Male
Grade/Rank: E-5 Army sergeant
SN: 150-77-4411
Service Branch: Army
Faction(s): G.I. Joe, Night Force, and Tiger Force (Europe)
Notably Served At: Battle of Benzheen; Cobra Island; Darklonia
Primary MOS: Infantry
Secondary MOS: Radio telecommunications
Appearance: Gray helmet with black goggles; a gray shirt with red collar and pads on chest and arms; gray gloves and pants; black boots; hook on green belt to hold binoculars
Accessories: Binoculars with strap, communicator attaching to periscope, long mic attaching to hole in helmet, M-16, periscope with a detachable handle and side clip
Abilities: Advanced recon; Best Friend: Dusty; Cartography; Endurance; Guts!; Meticulous; Note Taking; Observation; Patience; Proficient with all NATO night-vision devices; Ranger qualified; Wilderness Survival
Conditions: Careful; Patient; Reputation: Legend in the Ranger recon battalions
Quote/Motto: "Patience, endurance, and guts are what Sneak Peek has plenty of. He's got the patience to creep inch by inch into enemy territory, carefully bending back every branch and twig in his way and just as carefully replacing them. He's got the endurance to sit motionless in cramped cover for days on end, waiting for the bad guys to show up, and when they do, he's got the guts to stick around and watch!" Quote by an unnamed G.I. Joe team member.
Notes: He was believed killed during the battle of Benzheen when shot in the head, but he survived and was swept deep undercover; his survival has been kept from family and friends alike. He is not to be confused with the environmental engineer named Biosfera.

Sneak Peek 2

Alias/Variations: Tony Beuke
Real Name: Anthony Beuke
Gender: Male
Service Branch: Army
Faction(s): G.I. Joe, Greenshirts
Appearance: Short, green mohawk
Abilities: FBI agent; Infiltration; Infantry Trooper; Professional Skill: F.B.I Agent; Reconnaissance; Undercover work
Conditions: Distinctive Feature: Green Hair
Notes: The code name Sneak Peek was previously used by a late member of the original team. Sneak Peek 2 was killed when Doctor Mindbender's experimental upgraded B.A.T. shot him through the head while he was spying on the new, advanced Cobra B.A.T.

Snow Job

Series: Two (1983)
Alias/Variations: Redbeard
Real Name: Harlan W. Moore
Place of Birth: Rutland, Vermont (a small unnamed village north of the Arctic Circle in Norway for European distribution)
Gender: Male
Grade/Rank: E-6 (Staff Sergeant) (1983); E-7 (Sergeant First Class) (1997)
SN: RA773658456
Service Branch: Army
Faction(s): G.I. Joe
Notably Served At: The Bering Strait; Cobra Island
Primary MOS: Arctic ski patrol
Secondary MOS: Rifle instructor
Appearance: Red hair and beard; large black goggles; white hooded snowsuit with gloves and boots; brown backpack straps and belt; black pockets on legs
Other Known Appearances (Cartoon): Similar but with blue-tinted goggles, beige straps, and gloves, and a beige or white belt
Accessories: Polar pack backpack with handle, two skis, two ski poles, XMLR-3A laser rifle
Background Information: "…a major Biathlon contender who enlisted initially [for] the training and support the army would give him for the privilege of having a biathlon contender in the ranks. Somewhere along the line, priorities were rearranged and to the consternation of the Army PR flacks [Snow Job] volunteered for the G.I. Joe team and was accepted!" Taken from his prototype dossier.
Abilities: Arctic ski patrol; Arctic trooper; Cold weather operations expert; Con artist; Olympic biathlon contender (cross-country skiing and rifle shooting); Qualified Operator: Devilfish, H.A.V.O.C., LCV Recon Sled, Polar Battle Bear, Snow Cat; Qualified Weapons Expert: All NATO long-range sniper rifles, XMLR-3A laser rifle; Rifle instructor
Conditions: No love for the cold; Practical joker; Reputation: Con artist; Reputation: Considered one of the best marksmen; Reputation: Setting up practical jokes, especially on recruits
Quote/Motto: "You think we call him Snow Job because he does his job on skis? Negative. He's a con artist, pure and simple. He conned his family, he conned the Olympics, and he conned the US Army! He's always got some sort of deal cooking and whenever you think you got him pegged—he pulls the double whammy on you! One thing about him that ain't a con. When he picks up that rifle, sure as spit, something is going to fall down." Quote taken from G.I. Joe team member Rock 'n Roll.
Notes: He enlisted in the military for the special training and support privileges the Army gives to Olympic champions. It has been suggested he got his nickname more from being a con artist than from his primary military specialty on the Arctic ski patrol. The rifle Snow Job prefers to use, the XMLR-3A Laser rifle, is the most commonly used weapon in the G.I. Joe Sunbow animation *G.I. Joe: A Real American Hero*. It does not require a power pack to function. The XM stands for eXperimental Model. In 1986 Snow Job, one of the original G.I. Joes, was replaced by Iceberg.

Snow Storm

Series: Twelve (1993)
Real Name: Guillermo "Willie" Suarez
Place of Birth: Havana, Cuba
Gender: Male
Grade/Rank: 2/E-6: Staff sergeant (Army staff sergeant)
SN: 042-69-DR
Service Branch: Army
Faction(s): G.I. Joe, Battle Corps (#12 of 36 members)
Primary MOS: Cold weather operations
Secondary MOS: Cold weather survival instructor
Appearance: Brown hair; white helmet with clear face shield; white shirt with orange

chest armor and gloves; white pants with an orange belt and thick boots
Accessories: Knife; machine gun; pistol; submachine gun; spring-loaded missile launcher with a trigger; two missiles
Abilities: Cold weather operations; Cold weather survival instructor; High-tech snow trooper
Conditions: Hates the cold
Quote/Motto: "If only I wasn't so good at my job, maybe I'd get assigned somewhere south of the equator!"
Notes: Recruited by Colonel Courage, who saw him defeat an entire band of hostile revolutionaries who were trying to infiltrate a peaceful Caribbean village. He wears a customized, high-tech thermal suit.

Soft Master

Real Name: Unknown
Place of Birth: Japan
Gender: Male
Faction(s): Arashikage clan
Notably Served At: Britain; New York; Paris; Rangoon; Springfield, Illinois; Tibet; Tierra Del Fuego
Appearance: Asian
Abilities: Arashikage Martial Arts; Can block Destro's wrist-rockets with a pickaxe; Computer hacking; Instruction; Knowledge Skill: Arashikage martial arts; Ninja master; Professional Skill: Restaurant management (owns a Cuban-Chinese restaurant); Proficient in many martial arts; Seems harmless; Well-traveled
Conditions: A few screws loose!; Belief: In a balance between warfare and discipline; Belief: Be kind on the battlefield when the situation calls for it; Convinced Storm Shadow killed his brother; Helpful; Kind; Poses as a street prophet; Reputation: Taught Snake Eyes; Reputation: Taught Storm Shadow; Seeking the truth about his brother's death; Soft-spoken
Quote/Motto: "He who dons the ninja's mask is forever apart. He leads a life of rigorous training, intense concentration ... and danger."
Notes: His brother is the Hard Master. Scrap-Iron shot at a station wagon containing Billy Arboc and Candy Appel, but Soft Master intercepted the missile and was killed by the shot.

Sonic Fighters

Purpose: A new unit trained set to operate the latest in high-tech portable sonic weapons and equipment against Cobra. "These specially trained front-line fighters blast into action, equipped with a devastating arsenal of battle-ready weapons! Take command of these front-line commandos and put the sounds of battle at your fingertips!" From the package.
Leader: Falcon
Members: Dial Tone, Dodger, Law, Psyche-Out, Rock 'n Roll, Tunnel Rat, and Zap
Vehicles: AH-74 Desert Apache, Battle Wagon, and Fort America

Space Shot

Series: Thirteen (1994)
Real Name: George A. Roberts
Place of Birth: Everett, Massachusetts
Gender: Male
Grade/Rank: E-4 (Army corporal); 6/O-3: Captain
Service Branch: Air Force
Faction(s): G.I. Joe, Star Brigade
Primary MOS: Interstellar pilot
Secondary MOS: Combat operations engineer
Appearance: Black hair and mustache; white shirt with blue shoulder armor and red braid; white gloves; white pants with a red belt; white and blue boots
Accessories: Armored helmet with chinstrap; octagonal backpack with attachments; pistol
Abilities: Blind piloting; Combat freighter pilot; Military discipline; Skilled pilot
Conditions: Heroic; Rebellious; Reputation: Fly-by-night freighter pilot
Notes: Recruited by Duke. Star Brigade was numbered 20 through 27; Space Shot was number 23.

Sparks

Series: Twenty-three (2007)
Alias/Variations: Alex to his friends
Real Name: Alessandro D. Verdi
Place of Birth: Carcare, Italy
Gender: Male
Grade/Rank: 1/E-5: Sergeant
SN: None listed on file card
Service Branch: Army
Faction(s): G.I. Joe
Stationed: The Pentagon; The Rock
Notably Served At: Sierra Gordo
Primary MOS: Telecommunications operator
Secondary MOS: Electronic warfare/cryptologic operations specialist [98X]

Appearance: Dark hair and eyes
Accessories: Backpack, helmet, hose, pistol, thin antenna, microphone
Background Information: Born the son of a former U.S. ambassador; graduated from Harvard
Abilities: Archivist; Authored more than 15 bestselling books; Bureaucracy; Coordinates with reserve members; Communications expert; Computer expert; Cryptologic operations; Cryptology; Diplomacy; Interpreter; Information technology; Liaison to the Pentagon for G.I. Joe; Maintains G.I. Joe's database; Language Skill: Fluent in 13 (unspecified) languages; Personal advisor to General Colton; Radio Operator; Telecommunications; Well-read
Conditions: Avowed pacifist; Celebrity: Famous author; Dedication without limits; Enjoys discussing and debating great literary works; Love of language; Good friend of Recondo; Poor combat skills; Strong loyalty
Quote/Motto: "Cracking Cobra defenses is just like cracking a computer code—it requires patience and persistence!"
Notes: He recommended Steeler become a member of the G.I. Joe team. He knew of the existence of the team's top-secret fourteenth member, Shooter. He is the only person who knows that Recondo is still alive.

Sparrow Hawk

Series: Two (1983)
Real Name: Pieter Van der Burgh
Place of Birth: Brussels, Belgium
Gender: Male
SN: 342101
Service Branch: Air Force
Faction(s): G.I. Joe, Action Force, SAS Force
Primary MOS: Shock paratrooper
Secondary MOS: Automatic weapons
Appearance: Dark Paratrooper outfit
Accessories: Air mask, automatic rifle, parachute
Abilities: Calm; Highly experienced combatant; Hobby: Hang gliding; Paratrooper; Qualified Weapons Expert: All NATO and Warsaw Pact Automatic Weapons
Conditions: Compassionate; Reputation: Calmest member of the SAS Force
Quote/Motto: "The calmest member of the SAS Force. A highly experienced fighter, a good man to have on your side." Quote by an unnamed G.I. Joe team member.

Sparta

Series: Twenty-seven (2011)
Alias/Variations: Agente Secreta (Brazil); Jean Cornington
Real Name: Brigid Cortez
Place of Birth: Sao Paulo, Brazil (Albuquerque, New Mexico)
Gender: Female
Grade/Rank: E-7
SN: 318-97222
Service Branch: Army
Faction(s): G.I. Joe
Notably Served At: Brazilian Amazon
Primary MOS: Undercover operations
Secondary MOS: Munitions expert
Appearance: Long, flowing red hair
Accessories: Pistol, rifle
Abilities: Devilishly sharp wit; Intelligence; Instruction; Infiltration expert; Professional Skill: Actress; Uncanny ability to extract information
Conditions: Cold-blooded attitude (which may be an act)

Spearhead

Series: Seven (1988)
Alias/Variations: Baioneta (Brazil); Frontline; First-Wave; Walter C. Hallgren
Real Name: Peter R. Millman
Place of Birth: St. Louis, Missouri
Gender: Male
Grade/Rank: E-4 (Army corporal); 1/E-5: Sergeant
SN: 075-0948-MP76
Service Branch: Army
Faction(s): G.I. Joe, Night Force
Notably Served At: New York
Primary MOS: Infantry
Secondary MOS: Finance
Appearance: Brown hair; light and dark orange camouflage shirt and pants; beige vest with gold ammo belt; brown boots
Accessories: Bobcat Max, camouflage helmet with long brim; pouch backpack with roll, machine gun with bayonet and sling, machete with decorative markings on the blade
Abilities: Animal Companion: Max, bobcat; Incredible charisma; Inspiring; Leadership; Point man; Professional Skill: Insurance salesman; Well-liked; Trusted
Conditions: Feels the responsibility of the people who follow him
Quote/Motto: "Some guys, they're gonna lead a combat assault, right? They jump up and

holler, 'Follow me!' and charge full tilt at a bunker—halfway there, they look back, and no one's behind them! Of course not. The guy was a jerk. Spearhead could jump face-first into a vat of rabid hyenas and 15 guys would follow him. No hesitation. They'd jump SMILING. And of course, Spearhead's mad cat, Max, is always a source of inspiration." Quote by an unnamed G.I. Joe team member.

Special Action Force

Alias/Variations: Action Force, S.A.F.
Purpose: This is essentially Action Force but in an alternate continuity.

Special Mission: Brazil (boxed set with cassette)

Series: Five (1986)
Purpose: "The Covert Operations Officer and his selected specialists set out to infiltrate the Cobra infested jungles of Brazil. Their mission was to retrieve an important military satellite concealed deep within Cobra territory. The Joes chosen for this critical mission are the perfect representatives of the mobile strike force—the masters of the game! When united, they create the absolute standard of military excellence."
Leader: None specified
Members: "…Mission Specialists: Wet Suit, Leatherneck, Dial Tone, Mainframe, and the new Covert Operation Officer [Claymore]"
Notes: This was a Toys "R" Us exclusive.

Spirit

Series: Three (1984), twenty-one (2005)
Alias/Variations: Spirit Iron-Knife; Shaman (Canada); Olhos de Fenix (Brazil)
Real Name: Charlie Iron-Knife; Flecha Veloz (Brazil)
Place of Birth: Taos Pueblo Reservation, Taos, New Mexico; in error it was once listed as Grand Canyon, Arizona
Gender: Male
Grade/Rank: E-4 (Specialist); E-7 (Sergeant first class)
SN: RA146231009
Service Branch: Army
Faction(s): G.I. Joe, Air Commandos (Leader), International Action Force, Slaughter's Marauders, and Strike Team: Charlie
Stationed: The Pit, Utah, located beneath Fort Wadsworth
Notably Served At: Battle of the Statue of Liberty; Cobra Island; Invasion of Springfield; Millville; Moscow; Sao Cristobel; Southeast Asia
Primary MOS: Infantry
Secondary MOS: Social services
Appearance: Black hair braided on sides and red headband; a light blue short-sleeved shirt with red undershirt and stripes on sleeves; beige holster and pants; brown boots, a brown and red belt, a light green arrow cassette pack, a light green auto-arrow launcher, and a brown and white eagle named "Freedom."
Accessories: Arrow cassette pack, auto-arrow rifle, belt with a loincloth, bald eagle
Background Information: "[Came] from a family so far below the poverty line they never realized they were poor. Charlie put himself through high school working as a hunting guide, but he wanted a doctorate in psychology. He opted for the army and the G.I. Bill, doing his initial service time during the late sixties in various parts of Southeast Asia."
Abilities: Animal Companion: eagle, Freedom; Animal Companion: falcon, Billy; Attuned to nature and his surroundings; Cartography; Degree in psychology; Healer; Hunter; Infantry; Long range recon patrol soldier; Mystic warrior; Professional Skill: Hunting guide; Professional Skill: Native American medicine man and shaman; Proficient: Compound bow and throwing knife; Psychiatric healer; Qualified Weapons Expert: M-16, M1911A1 Auto Pistol, the Remington sniper rifle; Tracker
Conditions: Cobra POW; Foil to Storm Shadow; Lived childhood below the poverty line; Mysterious; Not a doctor; Performs rituals; Respects nature and his ancestors; Storm Shadow has a rivalry with Spirit.
Quote/Motto: "Charlie is a Shaman, a medicine man. He's not a healer or a priest or a witch doctor. There isn't any equivalent in our culture for what he is unless we had shrinks that could actually help people. Spirit's mysterious powers of the mind extend the limits of the most advanced psychiatric procedures known in our culture." Quote by an unnamed G.I. Joe team member.
Notes: Spirit once healed Quick Kick's broken leg in moments.

Spitfire

Series: One (1995)

Alias/Variations: Farooq Bin Nasir, a.k.a. "Big Bin"
Real Name: Farooq Shah
Place of Birth: Not given
Gender: Male
Grade/Rank: Not given
SN: None
Service Branch: Air Force
Faction(s): G.I. Joe, International G.I. Joe team
Notably Served At: Royal Air Force (veteran)
Background Information: Served in the Royal Air Force
Abilities: Heroic instincts; Professional Skill: Football (soccer) player; Qualified Operator: Jetpack; RAF training; Specialist: Aerial Combat; Talented aerial combatant
Conditions: Always friendly to his fans; Kind; Heroic; Humble; Rushes into action; Superstar football (soccer) player
Quote/Motto: "You don't look much like a battering platform, mate."
Notes: Recruited by Scarlett. His ethnic heritage is Pakistani-British.

Stalker

Series: One (1982)
Alias/Variations: Manleh (Argentina), Jammer (Europe); Sergeant Stalker; Stalker One
Real Name: Lonzo R. Wilkinson
Place of Birth: Detroit, Michigan (Reykjavík, Iceland for European distribution)
Gender: Male
Grade/Rank: E-5 (Sergeant) (1982); E-6 (Staff Sergeant, Marvel Universe); E-7 (Sergeant first class) (1989); E-8 (First Sergeant) (1997); E-9 (Sergeant Major)
SN: RA725054399
Service Branch: Army
Faction(s): G.I. Joe, Arctic Attack Force, Battle Corps, Desert Patrol Squad, Stars and Stripes Forever, Strike Team: Bravo, Tiger Force, and Winter Operations
Notably Served At: Cobra Island; Sierra Gordo; Vietnam War; Wolkekuck-Uckland
Primary MOS: Infantry, Ranger qualified
Secondary MOS: Medic; interpreter
Appearance: African American; black mustache; dark green beret; green camouflage outfit with black straps. African American; black beret; black hair and mustache; black shirt with blue straps and gloves; orange pants with tiger stripes and black boots
Other Known Appearances (Cartoon): Same, but with more contrast in camo colors, and with belt and chest straps matching the light green of the uniform
Accessories: 1982–83: M-32 "Pulverisor" submachine gun
Background Information: Basic combat training (top of class); Advanced infantry training (top of class); Special Training: U.S. Army Language School in Monterey; Intelligence School at Fort Holabird; Ranger School at Fort Benning; EOD Training Facility
Abilities: Blocks out distractions; Command; Elite light infantry Special Ops trooper; Friendship with Snake Eyes; Explosive ordnance disposal technician; Language Skill: Arabic, French, Spanish, and Swahili; Perceptive; Professional Skill: Recruiter; Leadership; Qualified Jump Instructor; Qualified Operator: Dragonfly, JUMP, LCV Recon Sled, RAM, and VAMP, SHARC prototype; Qualified Weapons Expert: M-14; M-16; M-1911A1 (auto-pistol); M-3A1 Grease Gun; M-32 Pulverizer Sub-Machine Gun; Qualified Weapons: Expert in all NATO and Warsaw Pact Small Arms; Ranger Qualified; Stealth; Strong; Steady hand
Conditions: Former POW in Borovian prison camp; Patience; Reputation: Former warlord of a large street gang in Detroit; Suffers from night terrors; Suffers from the death of his two brothers (gang-related violence)
Quote/Motto: "You have to be thorough and patient because one mistake can be deadly." "Functions well under high-stress situations. Intelligent. Perceptive. Moves like some sort of jungle cat—silent—fast … strong." Quote by an unnamed G.I. Joe team member.
Notes: In the Marvel Comics Universe, he served on the same LRRP team as Snake Eyes and Storm Shadow during their tour in the Vietnam War. Has a friendship with Snake Eyes. The 1982 Stalker figure was produced straight-armed. In 1986 Stalker, one of the original G.I. Joes, was replaced by Beach Head.

Stanley

Gender: Female
Faction(s): G.I. Joe, Greenshirt
Stationed: Los Angeles bureau
Appearance: Green eyes

Star Brigade

Series: Twelve (1993)

Purpose: An elite fighting force assigned to defend orbital satellites, intercept, and prevent orbital assaults, and protect space travel from Cobra. "High-tech astronauts race to space to protect the universe from Cobra and the Lunartix Empire! With specialized spacesuits and accessories, this cosmic clash is hotter than the sun!"
Leader: Duke
Members: Countdown, Effects, Gears (with Power Fighter), Hawk (with Armor-Bot), Heavy Duty, Ozone, Payload, Roadblock, Robo-J.O.E., Rock 'n Roll, Sci-Fi (with Starfighter), and Space Shot
Vehicles: The Armor-Bot, Starfighter Space Jet, and the Power Fighter

Starduster

Series: Six (1987)
Alias/Variations: Skyduster, Star Duster, Star-Duster
Real Name: Edward J. Skylar
Place of Birth: Burlingame, California
Gender: Male
Grade/Rank: E-6 (Army staff sergeant)
SN: RA 989-31-5248
Service Branch: Airborne Ranger
Faction(s): G.I. Joe, Comandos Heroicos (Leader)
Primary MOS: Infantry transportable air recon
Secondary MOS: Helicopter assault
Appearance: Black hair; short-sleeved, open-collared light blue shirt with beige strap or holster; gray gloves and boots; light blue pants with green camouflage; black belt and boots
Accessories: Grenade launcher, helmet with a star on front; JUMP jet pack, visor
Abilities: Boundless energy; Infantry transportable air recon; Helicopter assault; Jet pack trooper; Professional Skill: Circus trapeze artist
Conditions: Distinctive Feature: Grin like a Cheshire cat; The show must go on!
Quote/Motto: "We could be pinned down by artillery, rockets, and flanking small-arms fire—every inch of the sky lit by tracers, the lead so thick in the air even the mosquitoes would take cover—but Starduster would be out there in a flash to spot the bad guys. No questions. Straight up into the flack with his characteristic 'show must go on' attitude, grinning like a Cheshire cat as he calls in enemy positions for our own artillery to hit. The guy never fails to keep the act interesting." Quote by an unnamed G.I. Joe team member.
Notes: Recruited by Duke. Starduster became commander of this Argentine branch of the G.I. Joe team. Originally this action figure was a promotional mail-in offered through G.I. Joe Stars cereal. There were three versions of this figure, the mail-in and two distributed by Hasbro.

Stars and Stripes Forever

Series: Fourteen (1997)
Purpose: An assembly of the nine original Joes
Leader: None stated, defer to rank
Members: Breaker, Flash, Grunt, Rock 'n Roll, Scarlett, Short Fuze, Snake Eyes, Stalker, Zap
Notes: The American flag is sculpted with 56 stars.

Static Line

Series: Nine (1990)
Real Name: Wallace J. Badducci
Place of Birth: Chicago, Illinois
Gender: Male
Grade/Rank: E-7 (Army sergeant first class)
SN: 782-6001-XR52
Service Branch: Army
Faction(s): G.I. Joe, Sky Patrol
Primary MOS: Sky Patrol demolitions expert
Secondary MOS: Aircraft maintenance
Appearance: African American; black hair; blue shirt with silver chest and shoulder armor; gray gloves; white pants with black belt and holsters; blue and black boots
Accessories: Crescent-shaped twin laser with two handles, helmet with a visor (painted on), laser pistol with a sound suppressor, parachute in a parachute pack
Abilities: Demolitions expert; Eye for detail; Knowledge Skill: Laser weaponry; Knowledge Skill: Stealth technology; Nose for finding hard-to-find things
Conditions: Constantly scanning the ground
Quote/Motto: "Static Line has a nose for finding hard-to-find things, such as money. He picks up five-dollar bills off sidewalks in front of movie theaters, twenties from the supermarket check-out line, or even loose change that people carelessly pull out of their pockets. Is he lucky? No. He is just the type of person who constantly examines every square inch of ground before he steps on it!" Quote by an unnamed G.I. Joe team member.

Steam-Roller

Series: Six (1987)
Real Name: Averill B. Whitcomb
Place of Birth: Duluth, Minnesota
Gender: Male
Grade/Rank: E-5 (Army sergeant)
SN: 500-54-7793
Service Branch: Army
Faction(s): G.I. Joe
Notably Served At: The Utah desert
Primary MOS: Heavy equipment operator
Secondary MOS: Armor
Appearance: Black hat with "DOG" on front; red hair; no shirt; open black vest with green grenades; red heart tattoo on left shoulder; brown gloves; light brown pants with brown belt and boots
Accessories: Stubby dagger with ribbed handle
Abilities: Gut instincts; Hobby Skill: Bowling; Mobile command center operator; Professional Skill: Earth mover; Professional Skill: Heavy crane operator; Professional Skill: Strip miner; Qualified Weapons Expert: All NATO small-arms and explosives; Qualified Operator: M-15A2, 50-ton transporter
Conditions: Bad-humored; Barred from bowling alleys for damaging the pins; Mean-tempered; Ornery; Stubborn; Uncouth
Quote/Motto: "He's a moose. He considers a Peterbilt 10-wheel tractor a personal vehicle and a .44 Magnum a pocket pistol. He gets barred from bowling alleys for damaging the pins. He's stubborn, ornery, mean-tempered, bad-humored, and uncouth. Has he got any good points? Well, he's on our side...." Quote by an unnamed G.I. Joe team member.

Steel Brigade

Series: Six (1987)
Faction(s): G.I. Joe
Appearance: Beige pants with green kneepads and black or silver belt; black boots; green and silver helmet with black visor and underside; green vest with black strap and gloves; light blue shirt
Accessories: Backpack, rifle
Notes: The Steel Brigade file card was fully personalized. Buyers for this mail-in figure selected a code name, characterization (leader, corpsman, or loner), best situation, personality, service branch, military specialties, weapons expertise, martial arts expertise, and training. The character wore a full, head-covering helmet and gloves so the buyer could pretend they were the one in the suit. There were five versions of the figure, each came with a backpack, one of two different types of assault rifles, and a Steel Brigade patch.

Steeler

Series: One (1982)
Real Name: Ralph W. Pulaski
Place of Birth: Pittsburgh, Pennsylvania (Salonika, Greece for European distribution)
Gender: Male
Grade/Rank: O-1 (Second lieutenant) (1982); O-2 (First lieutenant) (2007); on his prototype card he was listed as an E-5 (Sergeant)
SN: RA035386098
Service Branch: Army
Faction(s): G.I. Joe, Strike Team: Bravo; Z Force
Notably Served At: Cobra Island; the Everglades; the invasion of Springfield; New York City
Primary MOS: Armor; tank commander
Secondary MOS: Artillery and transportation officer (88A)
Appearance: Brown hair; black pockets and boots; light-green fatigues with an open collar and black holster and gloves; light green pants; gold undershirt
Other Known Appearances (Cartoon): Heavily simplified; blond hair with dark green pants and short gold visor; no gloves, and no straps or holster on chest
Accessories: 1982: Headset, helmet; telescopic black visor Uzi-gun. 1983: Binocular headset, helmet, Uzi gun. Mail-in: swivel-armed Steeler. 1991: Black binoculars and an Uzi pistol. Convention versions also came with binoculars.
Background Information: Attended college on an ROTC scholarship; graduated from Armor School at Fort Knox, top of his class. Special Training: Cadre-X AFV Project at the Aberdeen Proving Ground; Artillery School at Fort Sill; AFV Desert Exercise at Fort Hood; Covert Ops School at Langley
Abilities: Professional Skill: Familiar and proficient with all NATO and Warsaw Pact AFVs; Heavy equipment operator; Qualified Operator: JUMP, Mauler, MOBAT (MOtorized Battle Assault Tank), motorcycle, TROC 5; Qualified Weapons Expert: M-16, M-1911A1, MAC-10, Uzi; Tank commander; Tough
Conditions: Blue-collar background; Clashes with superior officers; Challenges teammates to physical endurance tests; Reckless;

Respects people after they beat him in a physical contest; Romantically linked with the Baroness (in a parallel universe); Trouble taking orders; Young

Quote/Motto: "Young, reckless, often clashes with authority (superior officers), but he's one tough soldier!" Quote by an unnamed G.I. Joe team member. "And in spite of our differences in upbringing and education, I must admit that I could almost like the fellow … you know his manners are appalling—stirs his coffee with a soup spoon … appalling." Quote given by fellow G.I. Joe team member Hawk. "Steeler is either the most normal, well-adjusted man in the world or the best disguised psychotic. There's something seething beneath the surface … he lies to me all the time, fabricating the most outlandish—say … you don't really want to know about Pulaski … this is about that time at Fort Leonard Wood. Why can't you leave me alone!" This quote was taken from a transcript of a taped psychological profile, provided by Major A. Milgrom, USAMC (United States Army Material Command). The quote was from the original, unpublished prototype card for the character.

Notes: In an alternate storyline, Steeler is a deep-cover Cobra agent feeding information to Major Bludd. He kills two Joes to protect his identity and severely injures three more. To protect Cobra's interests, Steeler is then slain by Cobra agent Blacklight. The 1982 Steeler figure was produced straight-armed. According to the 1982 file card, the visor has an "infra-red lens, zoom control knob, shutter release button, and a motor drive."

Stiletto

Series: Thirty-two (2016)
Real Name: Paithoon Kwaigno
Place of Birth: Hua Hin, Thailand
Gender: Female
Grade/Rank: E-5; Cobra Commander's agent
SN: 414-33-PK72
Service Branch: Thailand military
Faction(s): Cobra, but defected to G.I. Joe with Mercer, Felix P. Stratton
Notably Served At: Alejandro Selkirk Island, Chile; Casamance, Senegal; Flores, Indonesia; Gotland, Sweden; Kersab, Trucial Abysmia; Laos; The Pit, Utah
Primary MOS: Covert operations
Secondary MOS: Infantry
Appearance: Asian woman, in her late twenties or early thirties with streaks of white in her hair; she keeps it in a long braid that hangs down her back. Walks with confidence; wears a tight-fitting black outfit accentuated with a bandolier. Several knives are sheathed on both the bandolier and her belt. There is a grotesque scar that runs the length of her face, straight through her left milky dead eye, continuing down her face to the left of her bottom lip, ending on her chin.
Accessories: Customized MP5 and an M&P backup pistol, Dragunov sniper rifle with woodgrain painted in a darker shade of brown, neckerchief, sheath backpack, submachine gun, two knives, two swords
Abilities: Cobra affiliation; Covert training; Extensive military training; Highly skilled in the use of bladed weapons; Knife-edged battle skills; One of Cobra Commander's most loyal and trusted agents; Proficient in demolition; Proficient in infiltration; Qualified Weapons: With most NATO and Warsaw Pact small arms; Special forces training
Conditions: Ambitious; Blind in left eye; Cobra Commander personal agent; Covets the Baroness's position; Defected to G.I. Joe with Mercer; Distinctive Feature: Facial scar; Distinctive Feature: Dead eyes; Distinctive Feature: Looks like she is scowling; Distinctive Feature: Streaks of white hair; Mysterious past; Pledged service to Cobra Commander; Makes the G.I. Joe team nervous; Responsible for training Whisper; Responsible for training William (Billy) Kessler; Tortured and permanently disfigured
Notes: Her unique fighting style was developed for her by Storm Shadow; it allows her to capitalize upon an enemy's attempts to exploit her blind spot. ***This character was the winner of the G.I. Joe Kindle Worlds Fan Vote. Through Amazon's Kindle Worlds program, fans could create and sell their own G.I. Joe stories with Hasbro's authorization.

Stone

Real Name: Daniel Will Stone
Place of Birth: Unknown
Gender: Male
Grade/Rank: O-1 Lieutenant
SN: 4YH881UN
Service Branch: Marine

Faction(s): G.I. Joe, Team Extreme (Field commander)
Notably Served At: Hong Kong
Primary MOS: Tactical warfare
Appearance: Brown hair, black eyes
Abilities: Counterterrorism; Leadership; Marine field commander; Old friends with Mr. Clancy; Specialist: Covert ops
Conditions: Archenemy of Iron Klaw
Notes: Recruited by Mr. Clancy

Stone 2

Real Name: Geoffrey Stone IV
Gender: Male
Grade/Rank: E-5 (Sergeant)
SN: 501-13-LS47
Faction(s): G.I. Joe, member of an unsaid division of the Joes within The Pit
Stationed: The Pit
Primary MOS: Special operations instructor
Appearance: Short brown hair, green eyes. Gray and black military fatigues, a black beret and combat vest; black short-sleeved shirt; black gloves; blue camouflage pants; black boots
Accessories: Cable, knife, missile, pistol, rifle, spring-loaded missile launcher, vest
Abilities: Combat tactics; Commando skills; Highly regarded by all members of G.I. Joe; Marksmanship; Qualified Operator: Military-grade Can-Am Spyder Roadster; Qualified Weapons Expert: 820 Selective-Fire, Long-range fully automatic rifle; Special operations instructor; Trainer; Survival techniques
Conditions: Constantly optimistic; Quite cheerful
Quote/Motto: "Are they Joes?" "Hell, no. They're jokes." Sergeant Stone and Heavy Duty, unimpressed.
Notes: He was portrayed by Brendan Fraser in the live-action film.

Stone 3

Real Name: Daniel Will Stone
Place of Birth: Avonmouth, Bristol, England
Gender: Male
Grade/Rank: O-2
SN: S6PF7773
Faction(s): G.I. Joe, MI6, and Sigma 6
Stationed: The Sea Titan
Primary MOS: Lieutenant (Commando)
Secondary MOS: Rotatory wing aircraft pilot
Appearance: Light brown/blond hair, brown eyes

Abilities: Bionic left arm; Codebreaker; Elite member of MI6; Exceptional pilot; Experienced pilot; Disguise expert; Leadership; Old friend of Hawk and Duke; Qualified Expert: Pilot; Reads ancient languages; Specialist: Covert ops
Conditions: Betrayed by Firefly; Collects spy-gadgets; Daring; Devious; Distinctive Feature: British; Distinctive Feature: Eyepatch; Enjoys solving mysteries; Eccentric plans; Interest in strange devices; Prefers to be called a spy, not covert operative; Reserved (after Firefly's betrayal); Show-off; Underconfident (after Firefly's betrayal)
Quote/Motto: "He's the best spy I've ever known."—Firefly
Notes: The *Sea Titan* functions as a self-sustained base, has advanced weaponry, and is capable of underwater transport. It also comes with the Dragonhawk, a heavy armor dropship. His bionic left arm is made of ultra-hard dimantium metal. His eyepatch conceals a special eyepiece that can scan and duplicate the clothing of anyone.

Storm Shadow

Series: Three (1984)
Alias/Variations: Cobra do Gelo (Brazil); Cobra de Hielo (Argentina); Ghost Shadow (prototype name); Ninja-Ku (Argentina); Phoenix Master; Satan (Argentina); Sombra (Spain); Sombra Blanca (Mexico); Thomas M. Arashikage (2004); Tomisaburo Arashikage; Tommy Yureikage; Young Master
Real Name: Thomas "Tommy" S. Arashikage (1997)
Place of Birth: Fresno, California; San Francisco, California; St. Louis, Missouri (sources conflict) (Osaka, Japan for European distribution)
Gender: Male
Grade/Rank: CLASSIFIED (E-8 Master sergeant; only listed with a rank while a member of the Joe team)
SN: CLASSIFIED
Service Branch: Army; Ninja Force (G.I. Joe) Cobra Urban Strike; Cobra Ninja Strike Force
Faction(s): Cobra, G.I. Joe 1988, Ninja Force 1992 (Leader), Shadow Ninjas 1994, and Sound Attack (Leader)
Notably Served At: Battle of Benzheen; Borovia; Cobra's Arctic base; Cobra Island; the High Sierras; Hong Kong; Manhattan; Millville;

New Moon, Colorado; Southeast Asia; Tibet; Trans-Carpathia; Vietnam

Primary MOS: Assassin, covert operations (sources conflict), Sabotage

Secondary MOS: Intelligence; martial arts instructor (sources conflict)

Appearance: Japanese American with black hair and dark eyes. 1984: White face mask, short-sleeved tunic, wrist wraps, pants, and boots; black diagonal strap; red Cobra insignia on left chest. 1988: White ninja suit with hood and face mask, all with dark gray urban camo; dark gray rope across chest; red tattoo on right forearm; white boots. 1992 Ninja Force: Black helmet and face mask with cloth hood; green shirt and pants with black stripes; black straps, gloves, belt, and boots. There were 50 different versions of Storm Shadow created for retail.

Other Known Appearances (Cartoon/Comic/Movie): White uniform with a long jacket (*G.I. Joe: Reloaded* Universe)

Accessories: 1984: Quiver-backpack with engraved arrows; wakizashi knife; katana sword; longbow; small nunchuks. 1988: Large square backpack with clips on the side for sword; high-tension Yumi bow with telescopic sights and sculpted arrows; sword with ribbed hilt; three-tined claw attaching to the wrist. Ninja Force 1992: A sword with a long hilt and thick, curving blade; nunchuks

Background Information: Began his career in mainstream U.S. intelligence groups (*G.I. Joe: Sigma 6*); Ranger School; Served on Long Range Recon Patrol (LRRP); Served in U.S. Army special operations. He can trace his family history through 30 generations of assassins. His lengthy prototype dossier reads: "[Storm Shadow] can trace his family history back through thirty generations of assassins. His forefather worked for feudal lords developing espionage and martial arts secrets that were handed down only to family members. He can scale sheer walls with bare hands and feet, remain immobile and silent for long periods, move with blinding speed and endure unspeakable hardships of pain."

Abilities: Apprentice: Junko Akita; Arashikage martial arts; Climb sheer surfaces with bare hands and feet; Covert operations; Covert ops counterintelligence expert; Covert ops specialists; Eighth-degree black belt in several martial arts; Followers: Highly trained support troopers (*G.I. Joe: A Real American Hero*); Followers: Ninja B.A.T.s as support troopers (*G.I. Joe: Sigma 6*); Instruction: Intelligence; Instruction: Martial arts; Knowledge Skill: Billy Arboc; Knowledge Skill: Cobra's operations; Language Skill: Korean; Martial arts specialist; Ninja; Professional Skill: Assassin; Professional Skill: Bodyguard; Qualified Weapons Expert: Katana, longbow, nunchaku, shuriken; Quick; Ranger; Resist interrogation; Resist pain; Sabotage; Stealth; Training; Undercover sabotage operations

Conditions: Belief: He cannot be redeemed (*G.I. Joe: Renegades* Universe); Belief: Somehow, he'll make things right; Belief: Snake Eyes caused the downfall of the Arashikage Ninja Clan (*G.I. Joe: Sigma 6*); Bloodlust (*G.I. Joe: Resolute* Universe); Cousin of Kimi Arashikage, Jinx (*G.I. Joe: Renegades* Universe); Distinctive Feature: Paired Snake Eyes; Distinctive Feature: Tattoo of the *I Ching jì jì* ("Already Fording"); Distinctive Feature: White uniform and mask; Family in Japan; Hunted by Red Ninjas; In love with Junko Akita; Long history with Snake Eyes; Loyal to Cobra (Sunbow Universe); Natural enemy of Quick Kick (Sunbow Universe); Natural enemy of Spirit (Sunbow Universe); Reputation: Bodyguard and mentor to the Baroness (*G.I. Joe: Retaliation*); Reputation: Cobra Commander's ninja bodyguard; Respects Snake Eyes's ninja abilities; Rivalry with Snake Eyes (*G.I. Joe: Resolute* Universe); Watched by Shipwreck

Quote/Motto: "The great Ninja assassin clans disappeared a hundred years ago. If they were wiped out, nobody took the credit for it and if they're still around—who are they working for?" "Will my past ever stop catching up to me?" "Tommy's unpronounceable name? It translates directly into English as 'Storm Shadow.'" Quote by G.I. Joe team member Stalker.

Notes: The character's surname is pronounced Ara-shi ("storm")-ka-ge ("shadow"). He had been captured by Cobra and brainwashed into thinking the Joes and Snake Eyes were his enemies; after breaking control of the device, he would occasionally hallucinate devils. Periodically he falls under its control. (*G.I. Joe: Sigma 6*) In the DiC Universe, Storm Shadow claims he only joined Cobra to find out who had dishonored his ninja clan. Currently, Storm Shadow is on reserve status. Storm Shadow has changed sides several times; conflicted in loyalties between Cobra,

G.I. Joe, and his blood brother, Snake Eyes. The duo has been everything to one another from the bitterest of enemies to the most loyal of friends. He was trained by his estranged uncle, the Hard Master.

Stormavik

Series: Twenty-one (2005)
Real Name: CLASSIFIED, Unrevealed
Place of Birth: Moscow, Russia
Gender: Male
Grade/Rank: Unknown
Service Branch: Army (Soviet/Russian)
Faction(s): Oktober Guard
Notably Served At: Afghanistan; Pakistan; Sierra Gordo
Primary MOS: Para-trooper airborne soldier
Secondary MOS: Infantry
Appearance: Gray (sometimes tan) long-sleeved shirt over a blue and white T-shirt with brown elbow pads, gray (sometimes tan) trousers with knee pads, brown leather boots, green webbing, and a gray (sometimes tan) beret
Appearance: Strawberry blond hair, blue eyes, 6', 180 pounds
Accessories: Handgun, rifle
Abilities: Airborne soldier; Expert marksman; Gives his all!; Hand-to-hand unarmed combat; Knowledge Skill: Firearms; Knowledge Skill: Military Command Structure; Language Skill: English; Motivated; Contacts: the Soviet military; Paratrooper; Soldier; Strong; Tough
Conditions: Acts with honor and dignity at all times; Always carries at least one grenade; Carries a blade on him at all times; Believes in his country; Believes in Colonel Brekhov; Distinctive Feature: Pronounced lantern jaw; Patriot; Serves with pride
Quote/Motto: "Fight with everything you are, everything you have. That is the way to victory."
Notes: He met his demise in a seedy South American country called Sierra Gordo, attempting to rescue what he thought was a train full of revolutionaries out to topple decadent capitalist mercenaries. He singlehandedly fought off 10 Iron Grenadiers and lived only just long enough to pull the switch for the train to safely pass.

Strawhacker

Real Name: George Strawhacker
Gender: Male
Faction(s): G.I. Joe
Primary MOS: Spy
Abilities: Contact: Soviet information brokers; U.S. spy
Conditions: Deceased fiancée; Formerly engaged to Snake Eyes's twin sister; Left to rot in a Borovian prison for years by the U.S. government
Notes: After he was rescued from the prison by Snake Eyes, Strawhacker was killed by Borovian rebel leader Metz.

Stretcher

Series: Nine (1990)
Alias/Variations: Housecall
Real Name: Thomas J. Larivee
Place of Birth: Hartford, Connecticut
Gender: Male
Grade/Rank: E-5 (Army sergeant)
SN: 040-9812-JA41
Service Branch: Army
Faction(s): G.I. Joe
Notably Served At: Benzheen; Cobra Island; Sierra Gordo
Primary MOS: Medical specialist
Secondary MOS: Troop transportation
Appearance: African American; gray cap with black chinstrap; black hair; a light gray shirt with rolled-up sleeves and a blue-collar; green backpack straps and gray holster and gloves; gray pants with green belt and yellow panel on left leg; gray boots with green pads
Accessories: Antenna, control stick, hover sled, small flashlight, tech backpack, top-loading flare pistol, triangular shield
Abilities: Medical specialist; Professional Skill: front-line medic; Professional Skill: Olympic weight lifter; Proficient in all the latest first-aid techniques; Strong; Troop transportation
Conditions: No matter what, will carry the wounded from danger
Quote/Motto: "Doc may have a medical degree from a top medical school and Lifeline may be the next best thing to a real doctor, but if I'm wounded and Cobra tracers are buzzin' above my head, I'll breathe a lot easier knowing that Stretcher is coming to get me. The other two guys can patch you up fine and dandy, but he will definitely deliver you from danger, pronto!" Quote by an unnamed G.I. Joe team member.
Notes: Stretcher confirmed the death of Sneak Peek, who had died saving a child. He also

has the same serial number as fellow 1990 release Pathfinder.

Strike Team: Alpha

Leader: Duke
Members: Beach Head, Chance, Cookie, Gung Ho, Torpedo
Pilots: Wild Bill, Lift-Ticket
Crew Chief: Roadblock
Notes: Overseeing this team is Hawk, the Commanding Officer of the Joes. Equal to Duke is Wet Down as Navy Field Commander. Joe rank is fluid, as Stalker could give Falcon an order, expecting it to be followed; experience and expertise matters more than rank and pay grade.

Strike Team: Bravo

Leader: Scarlett
Members: Chi, Evac, Flash, Kamakura, Low Light, Short Fuze
Drivers: Clutch, Steeler
Crew Chief: Stalker
Notes: Overseeing this team is Hawk, the Commanding Officer of the Joes. Equal to Duke is Wet Down as Navy Field Commander. Joe rank is fluid, as Stalker could give Falcon an order, expecting it to be followed; experience and expertise matters more than rank and pay grade.

Strike Team: Charlie

Leader: Altitude
Members: Cross Country, Lightfoot, Alpine, Spirit, Charbroil, Wildcard
Pilots: Ace, Payload
Crew Chief: Lowdown
Notes: Overseeing this team is Hawk, the Commanding Officer of the Joes. Equal to Duke is Wet Down as Navy Field Commander. Joe rank is fluid, as Stalker could give Falcon an order, expecting it to be followed; experience and expertise matters more than rank and pay grade.

Sub-Zero

Series: Nine (1990)
Real Name: Mark Habershaw
Place of Birth: Smithfield, Rhode Island
Gender: Male
Grade/Rank: O-2 First Lieutenant
SN: 000-0617-AT89
Service Branch: Army
Faction(s): G.I. Joe, Arctic Attack Force
Stationed: Army Northern Warfare Training Center in Fort Greely, Alaska
Primary MOS: Winter operations specialist
Secondary MOS: Field artillery
Appearance: White snowsuit with hood; blue fur on the hood over a gray cap; blue straps, buttons, and belt; black knife, gloves, and boots
Accessories: Curved ammo belt, machine gun with top handle and slots for ammo belt, mortar launcher with round stand, rectangular tech backpack with roll, two disc-like snowshoes, two finned mortar shells
Abilities: Cold weather combat tactics; Cold weather endurance; Cold weather operations expert; Consultant; Instructor; Winter operations specialist
Conditions: Enjoys being mean; Hates the cold; Reputation: Mean!; Willpower
Quote/Motto: "All the other G.I. Joe Arctic specialists like the cold. Not Sub-Zero! He hates it to the MAX! It drives him so far up the wall that it brings out a special kind of meanness unheard of in the western world. We're talking MAXIMUM MEANNESS! So why does he keep volunteering for cold weather assignments? Because he enjoys being MEAN!"

Super Trooper

Series: Seven (1988)
Alias/Variations: Joe De Niro (in Action Force comics); Virgil M. Carmody ("Hard Corps")
Real Name: Paul Latimer
Place of Birth: Dayton, Ohio
Gender: Male
Grade/Rank: O-2 (Army first lieutenant)
SN: 981-88-3819
Service Branch: Army
Faction(s): G.I. Joe
Stationed: Pentagon, Washington, D.C.
Primary MOS: Infantry
Secondary MOS: Public relations
Appearance: Black hair; light green sleeveless shirt under silver "metalized" armor vest; dark green armbands and pants; dark gray belt; black boots; silver kneepads
Accessories: Helmet; submachine gun; shield with handle
Background Information: West Point graduate; Recipient of the Expert Infantryman's Badge. The man who was Lt. Latimer disappeared

into a highly CLASSIFIED training program. The exact nature of the training is never found out.

Abilities: Airborne qualified; Assault operations expert; Deep penetration operations; Expert infantryman; Language Skill: Fluent in three (unspecified) languages; Marksmen; Motivated; Resourceful

Conditions: Adventure seeker; Honorable; Keeps a low profile; Loyal; Reputation: Thrillseeker; Super patriot; Unyielding Integrity

Quote/Motto: "He went to West Point the hard way, by enlisting in the Army straight out of high school. He then took the test for admission to West Point Prep School, a grueling ten-week program with a 60% attrition rate and no guarantee of an appointment to the Academy at the end of it! He could have been staff material. The Joint Chiefs had their eyes on him. So why did he sign up for a secret program with an extremely low profile and little chance for personal advancement? Was it because he preferred an assignment where honor, integrity, and loyalty were considered assets instead of liabilities? Or was he simply seeking adventure?" Quote by an unnamed G.I. Joe team member.

Notes: He was the first Joe not to have a "function" name, such as "Infantry Trooper" for Grunt or "Green Beret" for Falcon.

Sure Fire

Series: Seventeen (2001)
Real Name: David S. Lane
Place of Birth: Los Angeles, California
Gender: Male
Grade/Rank: O-5 Lt. Colonel
SN: 442-94J-DS48
Service Branch: Army
Faction(s): G.I. Joe
Stationed: The Pit
Primary MOS: CID (Criminal Investigation Division) Special Agent
Secondary MOS: Telecommunications
Appearance: Black hair; blue shirt with black vest and gloves; blue pants with black belt, holster, kneepads
Accessories: Helmet; pistol; Uzi
Background Information: Los Angeles Police Academy graduate
Abilities: Black belt in Shoto-Kan Karate-Do; Highly perceptive; Leadership; Martial arts; Professional Skill: Former chief of Pit Security Chief of Communications and Security; Professional Skill: Commander of the Army's Criminal Investigation Division; Professional Skill: Military police; Professional Skill: Special Investigation Unit of the FBI

Conditions: By the book!; Dedicated to fighting crime; Grew up in a poor, rough neighborhood; Long list of enemies; Target practice daily; Vowed to defend the rights of others at all costs

Quote/Motto: "If evil is being done anywhere in the world, I'll find out about it—and stop it." "To overcome your enemies, you have to have knowledge and leverage over them."

Surfer

Real Name: Hoxworth Whipple
Place of Birth: Hawaii, America
Gender: Male
SN: AF 934119
Service Branch: Navy
Faction(s): Action Force, Q Force
Primary MOS: Seaborne rescue
Secondary MOS: Rocket assault
Abilities: Arrives in the nick of time!; Champion surfer; Equipment designer and developer; Intuitive to moods and weather changes on the ocean; Qualified Expert Operator: Sea Skimmer; Rocket assault; Seaborne rescue
Conditions: Courageous, Fearless; Happy at sea; Reputation: Holds the record for most successful rescue and recovery missions
Quote/Motto: "A courageous and fearless team member of Q Force. Always arrives in the nick of time." Quote by an unnamed team member.
Notes: He designed and developed the Sea Skimmer, a seaboard capable of hitting 50 knots.

Susan Hoffman

Alias/Variations: Doctor Hoffman
Real Name: Doctor Susan Hoffman
Place of Birth: Unknown
Gender: Female
Service Branch: Civilian
Faction(s): G.I. Joe
Primary MOS: Archaeologist
Secondary MOS: Explorer
Appearance: Curly, long black hair
Abilities: Archaeologist; Assistants*; Beautiful; Feisty; Fights like a mean girl; Fortitude; Intelligent; Investigation; Knowledge Skill: Ancient artifacts; Leadership; Motorcycle

driving; Mountain climbing; Navigation; Physically fit; Spelunking
Conditions: Brave; Dislikes interruptions; Dislikes delays; Gets directly to the point; Seeks ancient artifacts; Takes matters into her own hands; Tolerates Autobots
Notes: She is a character in the Action Force/Transformers Universe. *Dr. Hoffman's assistants include three scientists and an unnamed woman; all have a tendency to become involved with paranormal activity. The three male assistants bear more than a slight resemblance to the animated appearances of Dr. Egon Spengler, Dr. Peter Venkman, and Dr. Ray Stantz from the DiC animation "Ghostbusters." The unnamed female resembles Janine Melnitz. Winston Zeddemore was not represented.

Switch Gears

Series: Nineteen (2003)
Real Name: Jerome T. Jivoin
Place of Birth: Bogota, Colombia
Gender: Male
Grade/Rank: 1/E-5: Sergeant
SN: 856-44-JT23
Service Branch: Army
Faction(s): G.I. Joe, Desert Patrol Squad
Primary MOS: Armored vehicle driver
Secondary MOS: Intelligence field operative
Appearance: Brown hair, white shirt with three-quarter-length sleeves, blue-green vest, dog tags, black belt, tan pants; silver knee pads, black gloves
Accessories: Chest plate to disguise himself as Overkill, gun attachment, helmet, rifle
Abilities: Ain't got no quit!; Can drive anything with tracks and bogie wheels; Disguise; Forgery; Prefers barehand combat to weapons; Qualified Weapons Expert: Assault rifles, Heavy machine guns; Resists pain; Solidly built; Strong; Tank driver
Conditions: Doesn't know when to quit; Risk-taker
Quote/Motto: "That karate stuff is too complicated for me. I just keep punching with one hand until it gets tired. Then I switch to the other."
Notes: He likes to show up at fortified Cobra positions disguised as a Cobra courier with fake retreat orders.

Taeko

Alias/Variations: Teiko
Real Name: Teiko Sasaki
Gender: Female
Service Branch: Army; currently a reserve member*
Faction(s): G.I. Joe
Stationed: The Philippines
Appearance: Japanese, white gee
Abilities: Martial arts expert
Preferred Weapon: Throwing Stars
Conditions: Trainee
Quote/Motto: "Hamburgers? Yuck."
Notes: All reservists can be called back into action if a mission calls for it.

Tall Sally

Real Name: Salindra (surname unknown)
Gender: Female
Service Branch: Army
Faction(s): G.I. Joe, Team Extreme
Appearance: Tall, brunette; uniform is mostly red
Conditions: Comes from a loving home; Romantically linked to Metalhead (Team Extreme version); Rookie; Writes letters in longhand
Notes: She and Short Fuze (Team Extreme version) sacrificed their lives in blowing up the Big Bad Superweapon to keep it out of enemy hands.

Tank

Real Name: Dwight M. Prudence
Gender: Male
Grade/Rank: E-5
Service Branch: U.S. Army
Faction(s): G.I. Joe, Savage Eagles
Primary MOS: Vehicles master operator
Abilities: Highly trained; Vehicles master operator
Conditions: Undisciplined

Taurus

Series: Six (1987)
Real Name: Varujan Ayvazyan
Place of Birth: Istanbul, Turkey
Gender: Male
Grade/Rank: E-5 (Army sergeant equivalent)
SN: 401-19-8426
Service Branch: Army
Faction(s): G.I. Joe, Sgt. Slaughter's Renegades
Primary MOS: Demolitions
Secondary MOS: Assistant drill sergeant
Appearance: Bald with a red beard; yellow

short-sleeved shirt with black shoulder guards and holster; silver left-hand armor; green pants with black kneepads and boots; brown belt and boots

Accessories: Backpack; short laser rifle

Abilities: Assistant drill sergeant; Freedom of operation; Investigative Nature; Language Skill: Fluent in a dozen (unspecified) languages; Professional Skill: Circus acrobat; Professional Skill: Circus strongman; Professional Skill: Occasional undercover work for INTERPOL; Qualified Operator: Devilfish, Motorcycles; Mountaineer; Weapon Familiarity: Explosives

Conditions: Disavowed: Gets no credit when they succeed; No official status; Penchant for exotic edged weapons; Receives no support if captured; Reputation: Breaks 2x4s with his face; Rough-edged; Operates without support and outside the military command structure; Stereotypical circus strongman; Wildcard nature

Quote/Motto: "He's an animal. He stops hockey pucks with his forehead and opens bottles with his nostrils. Luckily for us, he does everything G.I. Joe HQ tells him!" Quote by an unnamed G.I. Joe team member.

Team Extreme

Alias/Variations: G.I. Joe Extreme, G.I. Joe Team Extreme, Joe Team Extreme

Purpose: In a "near-future" (2006) continuity, a "former super-power" has collapsed, and a new G.I. Joe Team assembles to stop a rising new global terrorist organization called S.K.A.R. (Soldiers of Kaos, Anarchy, and Ruin). Their leader is a mysterious, shrewd, and incredibly powerful military leader only known as Iron Klaw, the former count of an Eastern European country. His goal is nothing less than total world domination. The new Joe team operates in a post–Cold War world wracked by chaos and carnage and battling against both SKAR and independent mercenaries, who seek to further destabilize an already unstable world.

Leader: Lt. Stone (Commander)

Members: Ballistic (Sharpshooter), Black Dragon (Ninja and Martial Artist), Clancy (Presidential Liaison), Freight (Demolitions Expert), Harpoon (Nautical Expert), Mayday (Skilled Fighter and Pilot), Metalhead (Communications and Computer Expert), Quick Stryke (Former SKAR Operative), Red McKnox (Scientist and Weapons Designer), Sgt. Savage (Soldier Frozen During World War), Short Fuze (Expert in Demolitions), Tall Sally (none stated), Tracker (Expert Tracker), and his animal companion, a wolf name Dakota.

Quote/Motto: "Extreme times call for extreme heroes!"

T'gin-Zu

Series: Twelve (1993)
Real Name: Joseph R. Rainone
Place of Birth: Somers, New York
Gender: Male
Grade/Rank: E-4 (Army corporal)
SN: 272-3712-PD
Service Branch: Army
Faction(s): G.I. Joe, Ninja Force
Primary MOS: Pile Driver vehicle operator
Secondary MOS: Ninja sword master

Appearance: Red face mask and white hood; white shirt with blue shoulder armor; red belt and sash; white pants with white boots. Loose-fitting white shirt and trousers, both with neon orange "camouflage" painted on, a white hood over a neon orange mask, neon orange foot and hand wraps, neon orange boots and gloves, a neon orange sash, and blue shoulder pads

Other Known Appearances: Character art shows orange shoulder pads and boots with a black face mask

Accessories: Sword

Abilities: Contacts: Numerous in martial arts circles; Covert operations; Endurance; Knowledge Skill: Military policies and procedures; Knowledge Skill: Secrets of the Arashikage ninja clan; Knowledge Skill: Arcane arts of the Arashikage ninja clan; Modern firearms expert; Ninja master; Qualified Operator: Pile Driver (dune buggy); Self-discipline

Conditions: Dedicated his life to the study of martial arts; Does not use guns in the field; One-man war against the Red Ninjas; Personal quest to sanitize the Arashikage clan's good name; Reputation: Best martial arts student Storm Shadow ever taught; Strives to clean up all of Arashikage messes

Quote/Motto: "Driving a Ninja Raider is like being strapped to a lightning bolt!"

Notes: He was recruited by Storm Shadow. The "T" is silent; his name is pronounced just like the famous direct-market knives sold by the Scott Fetzer company. He carries a fast-grab battle sickle with a dagger end; quick-flick, steel-spiked throwing stars; a razor-sharp steel katana sword; and two delayed fuse concussion grenades. He wears soft-tread foot wraps, a specialized camouflage battle uniform, and a steel-threaded concealment mask.

Thomas Stall

Real Name: Thomas C. Stall
Place of Birth: Cincinnati, Ohio
Gender: Male
Service Branch: Army
Faction(s): G.I. Joe, Greenshirt
Stationed: Fort Huachuca, Arizona
Notably Served At: New Moon, Colorado
Appearance: Blond hair, blue eyes, tall
Background Information: Faced a general court-martial for his admitted negligence and possible treasonous acts. He left the Joes and joined Cobra as code name Blackout.
Conditions: Can't keep his head in the game; Childish; Difficulty following orders; Fearful; Hot-mess of a soldier!; Inattentive; Panics; Thinks of self and not the team; Whiner
Quote/Motto: As described by Mirage, he is "a childish inattentive mess of a soldier, an arrogant blemish on a family of career military men and the last person in the world I'd trust my life to."
Notes: His brothers are Barrel Roll (sniper) and Bombstrike (forward air controller).

Thunder

Series: Three (1984)
Alias/Variations: Sgt. Thunderblast
Real Name: Matthew Harris Breckinridge
Place of Birth: Louisville, Kentucky
Gender: Male
Grade/Rank: E-5
SN: RA135306694
Service Branch: Army
Faction(s): G.I. Joe
Notably Served At: Arabia; Trucial Abysmia
Primary MOS: Artillery
Secondary MOS: Bandsman (drummer)
Appearance: Red hair; brown jacket and boots; green vest and belt; black gloves and pants
Other Known Appearances (Cartoon): White headset, eyepiece, and goggles with white or blue-tinted lenses
Accessories: Included with the Slugger, self-propelled cannon. Helmet, radio headset, smooth monocular, visor with nose-notch
Abilities: Distinctive Feature: Southern accent; Lucky; Qualified Expert Operator: The Slugger; Qualified Operator: Mauler, motorcycle (personal vehicle), Silver Mirage, Wolverine; Self-propelled gun artilleryman; Trigonometry
Conditions: Fondness for loud noises; Drawn to loud noises; Passion for heavy metal, peanut brittle, and cars with bad mufflers; Romantic relationship with Cover Girl
Quote/Motto: "I like to hear things go BANG!" "If you know where you are and you know where the enemy is, then artillery can be an exact science. But in the real world, artillery is half trigonometry and half blind luck. In other words, if you hit something, take the credit. If you miss, write it off as margin of error." Taken from Joe personnel files.
Notes: Thunder died along with Crankcase, Doc, and Heavy Metal while being held captive; it was due to an unfortunate misunderstanding of Cobra Commander's orders, by bloodthirsty S.A.W. Viper Robert "Overkill" Skelton. Doc is shot first; Crankcase, Thunder, and Heavy Metal are killed next.

Thunderwing

Series: Fifteen (1998)
Real Name: Spencer D. Crecelius
Place of Birth: Las Vegas, Nevada
Gender: Male
Grade/Rank: O-1 (Army second lieutenant)
SN: 549-08-1969
Service Branch: Army
Faction(s): G.I. Joe, Stars and Stripes Forever
Stationed: Basic tank training: Western Asia, Cobra Unity, Qabdat Khafia base; Lt. Thunderwing is a senior officer at the base.
Primary MOS: Armor
Secondary MOS: Heavy equipment operator
Appearance: Black hair; green jacket and pants; gray vest; black gloves, belt, and boots
Accessories: AK-S74U assault rifle, antennas, backpack, helmet, visor
Abilities: Deployment; Leadership; Logistics; Tank Commander; Tough
Conditions: Distinctive Feature: Frontman for the G.I. Joe armored tank division; Distinctive Feature: tattoos counting off the tanks he has destroyed; Professional skill: Construction; Professional Skill: Nightclub bouncer; Proud of his tank's capabilities; Ready to protect the frontlines!; Seeks excitement

Quote/Motto: "Cobra tanks are just smoking craters waiting to happen." "Thunderwing is proud of his tank's capabilities and is always ready to protect the frontlines. To just say this guy is tough is quite an understatement. Ask him to show you his arm of tattoos counting off all the tanks he's destroyed—then you'll know and knowing is half the battle." Quote by an unnamed G.I. Joe team member.

Notes: His MOBAT (Motorized Offensive Battle Attack Tank) upgrades include additional armor protection, advanced thermal imaging systems, digital fire control computers, laser range finders, night vision, and smokescreens. He uses the smokescreen system to gain the element of surprise.

Tiger Claw

Series: Twenty-one (2005)
Real Name: Chad M. Johnson
Place of Birth: Douglas, Massachusetts
Gender: Male
Grade/Rank: E-4 (Army corporal)
SN: 889-34-CM27
Service Branch: Army
Faction(s): G.I. Joe
Primary MOS: Infantry
Secondary MOS: Weapons instructor
Appearance: Orange face mask; gray ninja tunic with orange collar; gray pants; black pads on wrists and legs; gray belt with yellow tip
Accessories: Sheath with carrying handle, sword with handle
Abilities: Determined; Graceful; Knowledge Skill: Art of the Shadow; Knowledge Skill: Indirect fire systems; Knowledge Skill: Individual, crew-served, and anti-armor weapons; Knowledge Skill: Snake Eyes; Knowledge Skill: Storm Shadow; Knowledge Skill: Ways of the warrior; Lore Skill: Arcane lore; Ninja apprentice; Qualified Weapons Expert: Indirect fire systems, individual, crew-served, and anti-armor weapons; Stealth; Strong; Weapons instructor
Conditions: Distinctive Feature: Arashikage tattoo on right arm; Fan of martial arts movies; Ninja apprentice of Snake Eyes
Quote/Motto: "I dedicate my strength, my skill, and my sword to the fight for good."

Tiger Force

Series: Seven (1988)
Purpose: These experienced and skilled soldiers were selected for a global jungle and desert campaign against Cobra outposts and fortifications. "Tiger Force—a special unit within the G.I. JOE team—is called up for a secret and highly dangerous mission in the remote jungle! COBRA has set up a network of power bases that will simultaneously attack key cities around the globe. It will take the combined skills of the Tiger Force team to hunt down these hidden bases and disable them. Together, Tiger Force will search relentlessly and strike deeply to save the world from the Cobra enemy!"

Leader: Duke
Members: Alpine, Bazooka, Beach Head, Big Brawler, Cross Hair, Dial Tone, Dusty, Flint, Frostbite (with Tiger Cat), Hardtop, Jinx, Lifeline, Mutt & Junkyard, Recondo (with Tiger Fly), Roadblock, Sergeant Stalker, Skystriker (with Tiger Rat), Tripwire, Wild Bill, and Wreckage. *International Members:* Ar Puro, Blizzard, Duque (Duke), Felino, Flint, Forasteiro, Hit and Run, Lifeline, Marujo, Outback, Psyche-Out, Sneak Peek, Tunnel Rat
Vehicles: Tiger Cat, Tiger Fish, Tiger Fly, Tiger Paw, Tiger Rat, Tiger Shark, Tiger Sting, and the Tiger Ray

Timber

Place of Birth: The High Sierras, California
Gender: Male
Service Branch: Canine companion of Snake Eyes
Faction(s): G.I. Joe
Appearance: Large gray wolf
Abilities: Creates distractions; Distinctive Feature: Goes for the crotch of Cobra operatives; Human Companion: Snake Eyes; Paranormal bond to Snake Eyes; Reliable; Uncanny communication with Snake Eyes
Conditions: Trusts Snake Eyes; Unknown past; Untamed
Notes: Timber lived to a very old age, dying of natural causes at the High Sierras cabin; he is buried near it. Before passing, Timber fathered a litter of wolf pups, many still live near the cabin today. Some people in the tiny town at the foot of the mountains where Snake Eyes lived referred to him as a werewolf because Timber was never far from him.

T'jbang

Series: Eleven (1992)
Real Name: Sam LaQuale

Place of Birth: East Greenwich, Rhode Island
Gender: Male
Grade/Rank: 3/E-7: Sergeant first class
SN: 090-6721-HA77
Service Branch: Army
Faction(s): G.I. Joe, Ninja Force
Primary MOS: Martial arts swordsman
Secondary MOS: Infantry
Appearance: Tanned skin; yellow helmet with eyeholes, black stripes, and yellow sash; sleeveless yellow vest with black straps; yellow half-gloves; blue pants with a black belt; yellow and black boots
Accessories: Backpack, chest armor, crossbow, double-edge battle-ax; gauntlets, kusarigama, sword, two hook swords
Abilities: Expert sword skills; Former disciple of Onihashi (master swordsman of the Arashikage Ninja clan); Meditation; Night fighting; Ninja swordsman; Professional Skill: Weaponsmith: hook swords; Qualified Operator: Helicopters; Qualified Weapons Expert: Ranged weapons; Secret combat technique: "Silent Backslash"; Zombie hunter
Conditions: Sworn an oath of silence for reasons known only to Storm Shadow; Sworn to confront and defeat zombies
Quote/Motto: "I put my fear behind me and my skill before me. Thus, I am unassailable!"
Notes: Storm Shadow is his second cousin.

TNT

Series: Twenty-nine (2013)
Alias/Variations: Ted Nicolas Thomas
Real Name: Theodore M. Thomas
Place of Birth: Buenos Aires, Argentina
Gender: Male
Grade/Rank: E-6 (equivalent) (Sargento Primero)
SN: RA 332284828
Service Branch: Army (Argentine); Fuerzas Armadas de la República Argentina (armed forces of the Argentine Republic)
Faction(s): G.I. Joe, Comandos Heroicos (South American branch of G.I. Joe)
Primary MOS: Explosives deactivator
Secondary MOS: Artillery engineer
Appearance: Black gloves, blue helmet, electric blue pants, silver knee pads, yellow shirt
Accessories: Backpack case with two doors and a handle, chest plate, flashlight, gas tank, helmet, multi-tool, shovel, submachine gun
Abilities: Bomb disposal technician; Memorized more than 120 additives, explosive chemical formulas, fuels, and oxidizing agents; Quick thinking; Nerves of steel; Steady hands
Conditions: Brave; Dedicated soldier; Never hesitates; Reputation: Pristine record; Vowed to protect his mother and his homeland; Selfless
Quote/Motto: "My work is either an immediate success or permanent failure."
Notes: The Figure Subscription Service figures were given a number: Theodore N. Thomas was number 1-12.

Tollbooth

Series: Four (1985)
Real Name: Chuck X. Goren
Place of Birth: Boise, Idaho
Gender: Male
Grade/Rank: Spc-5 (Army specialist 5); 5/W-1: Warrant officer 1
SN: 373190360
Service Branch: Army
Faction(s): G.I. Joe
Stationed: The Pit, Utah, located beneath Fort Wadsworth
Notably Served At: Cobra Island
Primary MOS: Combat engineer/bridge layer driver
Secondary MOS: Transportation
Appearance: Orange hard hat sculpted cocked to the side; brown hair; an open-collared, short-sleeved, olive green shirt with silver dog tag, brown vest, and black gloves; orange-brown pants with brown belt and boots and black holster
Other Known Appearances (Cartoon/Movie): Dark green vest and sleeves; light green gloves, hardhat, and high-collared shirt; wore a white hardhat and red vest in the movie
Accessories: Included with the Toss 'n' Cross; Sledgehammer
Background Information: Master's in engineering from MIT
Abilities: Airfield fabrication and repair; Clears minefields; Combat engineer; Demolitions; Engineering prodigy; Field defenses operations; General construction; Qualified Operator: Toss 'n' Cross, a bridge-laying vehicle; Road fabrication and repair
Conditions: Love for construction; Reputation: Can make a bridge out of anything; Reputation: Finds solutions to problems on the drawing board; Seeking a bigger challenge
Quote/Motto: "River, crevasse, mountain, whatever.... I've got a way to cross it!" "We're on

our way to an objective and come to an obstacle we can't cross. River, crevasse, mountain, whatever.... Tollbooth gets us across. He may build a bridge out of whatever's there. Blast a pass through solid rock or lay down a four-lane blacktop.... The man's got magic." Quote by fellow G.I. Joe team member Stalker.

Notes: The Tollbooth figure does not have a ball-jointed head; he may have been designed in 1984 as he was released with the Toss 'n' Cross vehicle in the *Sears Wish Book* as an exclusive.

Tomahawk

Series: Twenty-six (2010)
Real Name: William P. Folger
Gender: Male
Grade/Rank: 5/O-2: 1st Lieutenant
Service Branch: Air Force
Faction(s): G.I. Joe
Abilities: Can fly every type of fixed-wing aircraft; Professional Skill: Air Force pilot; Tested numerous advanced-design prototypes

Ton Up

Series: Four (1985)
Real Name: Not Listed
Place of Birth: Malmö, Sweden
Gender: Male
Faction(s): Action Force
Abilities: Contact: Criminals; Getaway driver; Driver of tracked vehicles
Conditions: Always appears to be in control; Brother murdered by Cobra Commander; Lives life at high speed; Qualified Expert Operator: Wolverine; Reputation: Most proficient driver of tracked vehicles; Self-reformed

Topside

Series: Nine (1990)
Alias/Variations: Barracuda, Gaff, Marlinspike, Salty Dog, Snipe, Swabbie
Real Name: John Blanchet
Place of Birth: Fort Wayne, Indiana
Gender: Male
Grade/Rank: E-6 First class petty officer
SN: 692-8812-HO89
Service Branch: Navy
Faction(s): G.I. Joe
Notably Served At: Cobra Island
Primary MOS: Navy assault seaman/Navy security
Secondary MOS: Telecommunications specialist
Appearance: Yellow hair and beard; blue short-sleeved shirt with an orange life jacket ("NAVY" on chest); gray pants with a yellow rope belt and black boots
Accessories: Helmet; missile launcher backpack with detachable U-shaped stand; short submachine gun with a long magazine and extra pole-like grip in front; two missiles
Abilities: Brawler; Gunner's mate; Iron stomach; Navy assault trooper; Master-at-arms; Military law enforcement; Navy security; Pipefitter; Hobby Skill: Raises prize-winning pigs; Rolls with blows; Tough
Conditions: Bold; Fearless; Reputation: Fort Wayne's hog master; Seeks excitement
Quote/Motto: "I train for the impossible so the impossible never happens." "A really intense training program can produce a fairly tough individual, but Topside was born tough. He can down a plate of greasy scrambled eggs and weiners [sic] while sailing through seas rough enough to send salty chief petty officers to the rail! I saw him take a full wind-up, upper-cut punch from another seaman and not even budge. Needless to say, that other seaman didn't stay around to get Topside's response." Quote by an unnamed G.I. Joe team member.

Topson

Series: Twenty-five (2009)
Alias/Variations: Sgt. Topson
Real Name: Frank Barbieri
Gender: Male
Grade/Rank: E-6 (Equivalent)
SN: RA367894536
Service Branch: Army (Argentine)
Faction(s): G.I. Joe, Comandos Heroicos, the Argentine branch of G.I. Joe
Notably Served At: Andes Mountains
Appearance: Red-brown hair and Hollywoodian beard; gray and black camo shirt and pants, black boots
Accessories: Backpack, helmet, knife, pistol, rifle, walkie-talkie, web gear
Background Information: Sergeant Shimik, Sergeant Redmack, and Sergeant Topson makes up the Argentine branch of G.I. Joe.
Abilities: Best of the best!; Hacker; Inventor of his own telecommunication equipment; Member of a well-armed civilian militia group; Underground radio operator
Conditions: Mysterious; Puts life, liberty, and pursuit of happiness above all else; Quick to act

Quote/Motto: "Maintain radio silence, or you'll give up more than your position."
Notes: When asked, he will not reveal the significance of his code name.

Torpedo

Series: Two (1983)
Alias/Variations: Chief Torpedo (2003)
Real Name: Edward W. Leialoha
Place of Birth: Aiea, Oahu, Hawaii (Goa, India for European distribution; also listed Rotterdam, the Netherlands in other editions)
Gender: Male
Grade/Rank: 5/W-4: Chief warrant officer
SN: RN946775409
Service Branch: Navy SEAL
Faction(s): G.I. Joe, Strike Team: Alpha
Stationed: Naval Amphibious Base Coronado, California
Notably Served At: Baltic Sea; Cobra Island; Florida Everglades; the Pit, Utah; Sierra Gordo; Springfield; Washington, D.C.
Primary MOS: Navy SEAL
Secondary MOS: Demolitions
Appearance: Black diving mask with eyes exposed; black and gray diving suit with a gray belt, gloves, and boots
Other Known Appearances (Cartoon): Skin-tight blue-black wet suit without the gray trim of the figure; face usually exposed, with white-rimmed, blue-tinted goggles on the forehead, and a white vertical stripe on top of the hood. When underwater, had a light gray air mask with a tube connecting to the backpack, no gloves. Wears jeans and a T-shirt when on land
Accessories: SCUBA backpack tank; thin, harpoon rifle; swim fins
Background Information: Training records after SEAL school: CLASSIFIED. The prototype dossier reads: "Subject was [a] SCUBA instructor prior to enlistment and attained black belts in three martial arts by age 19 (Wushu, Kenpo, and Go-Ju-Ryu). Also proficient with [the] Filipino butterfly knife (Bali-Song)."
Abilities: Black belt in Go-Ju-Ryu; Black belt in Kenpo; Black belt in Wushu; Command; Consummate professional; Discipline; Endurance; Hobby Skill: Subsistence farming; Marine environment specialist; Qualified Operator: SHARC; Qualified Weapon: Filipino butterfly knife (Bali-Song); Qualified Weapons Expert: Most NATO small arms, NATO, and Warsaw Pact explosive devices; SCUBA Instructor; Skilled diver; Swimming; Stealth; Surfer
Conditions: Aloof; By the book; Committed to the task at hand; Eats alone; Extroverted (cartoon only); Gregarious (cartoon only); Hates pollution; Jocular (cartoon only); Knows he's "that good"; No-nonsense; Personality of a cold fish; Prefers the company of the ocean over people; Spends off-duty hours perfecting his fighting skills and marksmanship; Strict vegetarian
Quote/Motto: "Challenge me and you'll wash up on shore." "Discipline is the key on land or under the sea." "If discipline is the key, Torpedo is the lock. Torpedo's talent in underwater demolitions is extraordinary. When he sets his mind to something, nothing stands in his way. I've never seen anybody hold their breath as long as this guy either. I value his judgment and his skill." Quote by General Hawk. A quote taken from a transcript of a taped Peer Personality Profile review (from his prototype dossier) given by an anonymous G.I. Joe team member reads: "Subject has absolutely no sense of humor. Period. Spends off-duty hours perfecting fighting skills and marksmanship. Competes in combat pistol matches and various swim meets. Strict vegetarian. Regarded by his team-mates has a highly competent professional albeit Psycho-Chicken to the max."
Notes: He was the first Navy man on the G.I. Joe team. Larry Hama once said he intended the martial art to be *Kempo*, a style based on the Shaolin Temple Boxing; it is a non-competitive Zen form. In 1986 Torpedo, one of the original G.I. Joes, was replaced by Wet Suit.

Tracker

Series: Ten (1991)
Alias/Variations: Bloodhound; Trakker
Real Name: Christopher R. Groen
Place of Birth: Helena, Arkansas (Madrid, Spain for European distribution)
Gender: Male
Grade/Rank: E-7 (Navy chief petty officer); 6/O-1: 2nd Lieutenant
SN: 672-4792-XM42
Service Branch: Navy SEAL
Faction(s): G.I. Joe, Z Force
Primary MOS: Navy SEAL
Secondary MOS: Underwater arms developer

Appearance: Brown hair; a red sleeveless shirt with "Joe 34" on the chest and "Groen 34" on the back; black holster and gloves; yellow pants with black holster and white leg bands; yellow and purple boots

Accessories: Soft, round visor; submachine gun with round forward grip and very long, angled magazine; inflatable raft with black seat; two one-sided orange oars

Abilities: Escaping; Evading; Extra-sensory perception; Tracking expert

Quote/Motto: "Sometimes the bad guys get smart and think they can throw us off the scent by cutting across a swamp or going up a stream. Whenever the trail seems to stop at a body of water, we just call Tracker to take it from that point. He just pumps up his covert insertion raft and paddles away until the track shows up on dry land again. It's almost as if he can see footprints on the surface of the water!" Quote by an unnamed G.I. Joe team member.

Notes: He was recruited by Stone because he ran Snake Eyes and Spirit to ground in less than 12 hours. While on vacation in Suva, Fiji, he was shot and killed by an agent of the mysterious terrorist organization Red Shadows.

Trakker

Series: Twenty-four (2008)
Real Name: Matt Trakker
Place of Birth: CLASSIFIED
Gender: Male
Grade/Rank: Specialist
SN: CLASSIFIED
Faction(s): G.I. Joe, M.A.S.K. (Mobile Armored Strike Kommand), and a secret unit
Primary MOS: Vehicle designer
Secondary MOS: Advanced technology
Appearance: Blond hair; gray jumpsuit with red kneepads and stripes on the arms; brown harness; red gloves; gray boots with red straps
Accessories: Blade; control stick; helicopter backpack; mask with visor and neck ring; mounted machine gun; spindle; submachine gun
Abilities: Advanced vehicles specialist; Command; Highly intelligent; Knowledge Skill: Next-gen technology; Leadership; Leader of M.A.S.K.; Vehicle designer
Conditions: Deep sense of responsibility
Quote/Motto: "We have a responsibility to use our ingenuity and advancements to help the world—and stop the power-hungry despots and criminals who hunger for their own glory."

Notes: He creates seemingly normal-looking vehicles that transform by use of his next-gen technology into combat vehicles. Tracker sometimes uses the alias Trakker.

Tripwire

Series: Two (1983); four (1985)
Alias/Variations: Blades (Europe); Cable; Private Skoog; "Listen 'n' Fun Tripwire" (1985)
Real Name: Tormod S. Skoog
Place of Birth: Hibbing, Minnesota (Swansea, Wales for European distribution)
Gender: Male
Grade/Rank: E-4 Specialist; 2/E-6: Staff Sergeant (SSG) EOD
SN: RA892399255 (1983); 089-32-9227 (1988); 892-39-TS92 (2008)
Service Branch: Army
Faction(s): G.I. Joe, Tiger Force
Notably Served At: The Arctic; Cobra Island; Cobra-La; the Florida Everglades; Invasion of Springfield; Jordan; the U.S. Treasury
Primary MOS: Explosive ordnance disposal
Secondary MOS: Demolitions (1983); Tiger Fly co-pilot (1988 Only)
Appearance: Olive green helmet with large black goggles; an olive-green shirt with red stripes on right shoulder; gray gloves and dark gray padded vest; olive green belt and pants with gray boots and dark gray pockets
Other Known Appearances (Cartoon): Same but with blue-tinted goggles; vest was occasionally light gray. Listen 'n' Fun Series 4 Tripwire wore a red bodysuit with maroon chest plate, red helmet with silver goggles, and black boots.
Accessories: Backpack with space for mines; mine detector with cord; three green mines. Listen 'n' Fun Series 4 Tripwire came with gray-white mine swiper, mine detector backpack, three land mines, and "The Cobra's Revenge" cassette.
Background Information: High school at a naval base in Yokosuka, Japan; Spent two years in a Zen monastery pondering the meaning of life; Received his training at Fort Bragg, North Carolina. His original prototype dossier reads: "Subject dropped out of high school at Naval base in Yokosuka Japan (father is career Navy). Spent two years in a Zen monastery pondering the meaning of existence until he was expelled for breaking

too many dishes and spilling every conceivable liquid. Joined the Army at age 19 and received spiritual awakening on the grenade range. Immediately applied for Demolitions School."

Abilities: Bomb disposal expert; Conceals explosives; Cool under fire; Detects mines; Meditation; Precise; Qualified Operator: Dragonfly, Polar Battle Bear, SHARC prototype; Qualified Weapons Expert: M-1911A auto pistol; Qualified Weapons: All NATO and Warsaw Pact explosives, detonators, ignition initiators, and blasting machines; Sets tripwires

Conditions: Clumsy; Comic relief; Drops things; Explosives calm him down; Father is career navy; High school dropout; Jittery; Nervous; Reputation: One of the best bomb disposal experts; Unneeded heroism

Quote/Motto: "You need to know everything there is about explosives before you ever go near them. I make sure anything that goes boom only does so when we want it to." "I know I freak people out, being clumsy and jittery and all that and dropping things, you know. But when I sit down with an explosive device, the world in my oyster. Anyway, working with high explosives is the only thing that calms me down." Quote from his G.I. Joe application. "Tripwire freaks people out. He's always clumsy, jittery, and dropping things except when he's working with high explosives. Explosives are the only things that calm him down." Quote by an unnamed G.I. Joe team member.

Trooper

Series: Twenty-four (2008)
Gender: Male
Service Branch: Army
Faction(s): G.I. Joe
Primary MOS: Infantry
Secondary MOS: Reconnaissance, infiltration
Appearance: Trooper was available with four different heads: one with brown hair, one with red hair, one with blond hair, and one with black hair.
Other Known Appearances (Other): Figure also came with a blue collar, gas mask, and cloak, or a tan collar, gas mask, and cloak.
Accessories: Alternate head, backpack, cloak, four pistols, gas mask, grenade launcher, sheaths, shovel, two knives, two rifles, web gear
Abilities: Armed for action!; Knowledge Skill: Cobra fighting tactics; Overwhelming firepower; Muscular; Highly skilled; Willpower; Wilderness Survival: Brutal battle conditions
Conditions: Ferocious determination; Heightened willpower
Quote/Motto: "We don't know the meaning of the word 'quit' and we never will. If you want to be one of us, then burn this word into your brain: Victory."

Tunnel Rat

Series: Six (1987)
Real Name: Nicky Lee
Place of Birth: Brooklyn, New York
Gender: Male
Grade/Rank: E-5
SN: 367-84-9090
Service Branch: Army
Faction(s): G.I. Joe, Assault Team Beta, Desert Patrol Squad, Night Force, and Sonic Fighters
Stationed: Brooklyn, New York
Notably Served At: The Appalachian Mountains; Battle of Benzheen; Cobra Island; Grenada; Millville; New York City; the Pit; Sierra Gordo; South America; Southeast Asia; Utah desert; Vietnam
Primary MOS: Explosive ordnance disposal specialist
Secondary MOS: Combat engineer
Appearance: A small, wiry build
Accessories: Backpack, bag, controller, phone, rifle, robotic bomb diffusion device, shovel, survival gear, survival pack, two flashlights
Background Information: Fort Benning's Ranger Course
Abilities: At home in dark places; Combat engineer; Demolitions expert (*Sigma 6*); Explosive ordnance disposal (EOD) expert; Hand-to-hand combat expert; Infiltration expert; Knowledge Skill: Natural healing remedies; Point walker; Reconnaissance; Streetwise; Tough scrapper; Unorthodox infiltration (*Sigma 6*)
Conditions: Belief: "Anything that does not kill you makes you stronger"; Bug-eater (*Sigma 6*). Easy-going off duty; Fearless; Ready for a fight; Sense of humor. In the Cartoon: Brooklyn accent; Cavalier; Cocky; Good-natured; Macho attitude; Wisecracking
Quote/Motto: "Tunnel Rat believes that anything that doesn't kill you makes you stronger. His feeling about crawling into an enemy tunnel with a knife in one hand, a pistol in

the other, and a flashlight in his mouth is simple—he can shoot straighter, bite harder, and run faster than anything he's ever encountered in a tunnel, so why worry." Quote by an unnamed G.I. Joe team member.

Notes: Diverse family tree is Trinidadian Chinese with Irish, Spanish, and Indian. Currently he is a reserve member of the Joe team assigned to domestic operations in the United States. *All reservists can be called back into action if a mission calls for it.

Una MacBride

Real Name: Una MacBride
Gender: Female
Primary MOS: Model
Appearance: Beautiful and young
Abilities: Knowledge Skill: Modeling; Professional Skill: Model
Notes: The younger sister of the G.I. Joe member Low Light. She was victimized by Madame Veil, who wished to regain her own youth by stealing the faces of younger women using a device created by Doctor Mindbender.

Updraft

Series: Nine (1990)
Alias/Variations: Eggbeater
Real Name: Matthew W. Smithers
Place of Birth: Bismarck, North Dakota
Gender: Male
Grade/Rank: Pilot O-3 (Army captain)
SN: 223-2088-NQ43
Service Branch: Army
Faction(s): G.I. Joe
Notably Served At: Cobra Island
Primary MOS: Retaliator pilot
Secondary MOS: Weapons systems officer
Appearance: Brown hair; a dark gray shirt with brown shoulder pads and half-gloves; off-white pants with a brown belt, holster
Accessories: Helmet with raised double-visor; large pistol with a ribbed muzzle and large scope
Background Information: Special instructor at the Flight Warrant Officers School at Fort Rucker
Abilities: Beats the odds; Gets what he wants; Helicopter designer; Special instructor; Leadership; Qualified Operator: Helicopter
Conditions: Pushy; Not well-liked; Reputation: World helicopter champion two years in a row
Quote/Motto: "Updraft molds the Retaliator to him the way he would a new suit. The machine becomes a part of him and even takes on his body language. If the G.I. Joes are in a hot situation, they'd like to see Updraft fly in to lay down cover fire and get them out of there!" Quote by unnamed G.I. Joe team member.

Wet Down

Series: Seventeen (2001)
Alias/Variations: Skimmer
Real Name: Daniel R. Alexander
Place of Birth: Norfolk, Virginia
Gender: Male
Grade/Rank: E-5 (Petty Officer 2nd Class); E-6 (Petty Officer 1st class) (1992–present)
SN: RA701548793
Service Branch: Navy
Faction(s): G.I. Joe, Battle Corps
Stationed: Naval Amphibious Base Coronado, California
Notably Served At: Cobra Island; Cobra-La
Primary MOS: Covert naval operations; SEAL
Secondary MOS: Martial arts instructor; UDT
Appearance: Black diving mask with eyes exposed; black and gray diving suit with a gray belt, gloves, and boots. A U.S. flag appeared on Wet Down's left or right arm.
Accessories: Backpack; harpoon gun; two flippers
Background Information: Naval Amphibious Base Coronado, California; BUD/S (Basic Underwater Demolition/SEAL program)
Abilities: Amphibious assault operations expert; Covert naval operations; Excels at everything!; Intelligent; Knowledge Skill: Seaborne attack procedures; Martial arts instructor; Quick; Well-read
Conditions: Abrasive personality; Adventurous; Crass; Fierce demeanor; Flippant; Happiest in battle; Impatient; Married and expecting a child; Mean natured; Reputation: Tough and mean; Rivalry with Leatherneck; Sarcastic; Tender home life

Wet Suit

Series: Five (1986)
Alias/Variations: Prototype names: Gator, Hammerhead, and Soggy
Real Name: Brian M. Forrest (–1998); Brian C. Forrest (2001–)
Place of Birth: Myrtle Beach, South Carolina (Toronto, Canada for European distribution; later changed to Torquay, England)

Gender: Male
Grade/Rank: E-5 (Navy petty officer)
SN: RA 701-54-8793
Service Branch: Navy
Faction(s): G.I. Joe, Battle Corps, Sound Attack, Special Mission: Brazil (1986)
Notably Served At: Persian Gulf
Primary MOS: SEAL
Secondary MOS: Navy SEAL/UDT (Underwater demolitions)
Appearance: Blue diving suit with white chest panel and gray straps; black wristbands; orange helmet with black underside
Other Known Appearances (Cartoon): Always without helmet unless underwater; curly red-brown hair; propellers on the backpack. In several shots, he was erroneously given one of the generic yellow frogman outfits. Special Mission: Brazil (1986) wears short short-sleeved-gray diving suit with helmet, black rebreather, blue chest pad, black belt, black diving watch on left hand, silver band on right hand. The set also included Claymore, Dial Tone, Leatherneck, and Mainframe.
Accessories: Air tube with long hoses; scuba backpack with holes for air tube; searchlight with small strap; sea sled with handle; two flippers. Special Mission: Brazil 1986: Black mouthpiece with hose, black swim fins, yellow-gold SCUBA tanks, yellow-gold underwater sea sled, and yellow-gold underwater searchlight
Abilities: Best at what he does!; Hand-to-hand combat; Hobby Skill: Partakes in fighting competitions; Intelligent; Knowledge Skill: Clausewitz's *Vom Kriege* (*On War*); Knowledge Skill: Machiavelli's *The Prince*; Knowledge Skill: Musashi's *The Five Rings*; Knowledge Skill: Sun Tsu's *Art of War*; Navy SEAL; Qualified Operator: Devilfish, Killer W.H.A.L.E., LCV Recon Sled, Mauler, SHARC; Tough; Underwater demolitions; Well-read; Works well with Leatherneck
Conditions: Mean to the bone; Ornery; Reputation: Mean to the bone; Reputation: Tough and mean; Trades insults with Leatherneck; Wild; Unruly; Vulgar
Quote/Motto: "Wet Suit may be mean to the bone, but he's also quite bright, being well-read in both the classics and the standard texts of military tactics. Pretty amazing considering that the level to which he has developed his toughness would seem to indicate full-time occupation...." Quote by unnamed G.I. Joe team member.

Wheels

Series: Twenty-six (2010)
Real Name: Frits Van Eyck
Place of Birth: Eindhoven, Netherlands
Gender: Male
SN: AF 396900
Faction(s): G.I. Joe, Z Force
Primary MOS: Transportation
Secondary MOS: Infantry
Accessories: Z Force jeep
Background Information: Completed basic infantry training with distinction
Abilities: Advanced convoy driving expert; Infantry; Mechanic; Qualified Operator: Jeep; Qualified Weapon Expert: M14, M16 rifle; Transportation
Conditions: Calls all vehicles "she"; Distinctive Feature: Always covered in motor oil

The White Clown

Real Name: Unknown
Place of Birth: Unknown
Gender: Male
SN: 317-43-8977
Primary MOS: Circus owner
Appearance: Ringmaster outfit; whiteface makeup
Abilities: Professional Skill: Owner operator of a circus; Ringmaster of a European circus
Conditions: In love with Magda
Quote/Motto: "We'll miss him." Quote given by Hawk.
Notes: In the ghettoes of Borovia, the White Clown was gunned down by Cobra Commander in cold blood.

Whiteout

Series: Sixteen (2000)
Real Name: Leonard J. Lee III
Place of Birth: Bridgeport, Connecticut
Gender: Male
Grade/Rank: E-6 (Army staff sergeant)
SN: 999-46-LL27
Service Branch: Army
Faction(s): G.I. Joe
Stationed: Arctic prison, The Coffin
Primary MOS: Arctic ski patrol
Secondary MOS: Communications
Appearance: Brown hair and beard; large black goggles; off-white hooded snowsuit with gloves and boots; gray backpack straps and belt; black boots
Accessories: Backpack; C-102 impact-resistant insulated helmet with anti-glare protective

goggles; two skis; two ski poles; XMLR-3A laser rifle
Abilities: Arctic ski patrol; Arctic trooper; Cold weather strategist; Mountain climbing; Mountain rescue patrol; Polar combat mobility expert; Professional Skill: Publishing; Professional Skill: Owns and operates political magazine with a Libertarian bent titled *Live Free or Else!*; Skiing; Top secret security clearance; Hobby Skill: Collects baseball cards; Wilderness Survival: Cold weather
Conditions: Highly valuable baseball card collection; Loves cold weather; Loves to ski

Wide Scope

Series: Nineteen (2003)
Real Name: Larry M. Kranseler
Place of Birth: Newton, Massachusetts
Gender: Male
Grade/Rank: E-5 (Army sergeant)
SN: 192-29-KL01
Service Branch: Army
Faction(s): G.I. Joe
Primary MOS: Infantry
Secondary MOS: Negotiations
Appearance: "SWAT" hat and face mask; light blue shirt with dark blue vest; black gloves and belt; light blue pants with white camo spots; dark blue shin pads; black boots
Accessories: Gas mask, German shepherd (Lamont) with harness, hat, leash; radio, rifle with gray bipod, riot shield and handle, shield, tactical vest
Abilities: Animal Companion: Lamont; Assess the situation; Kick in the door!; Special weapons and tactics specialist; Urban combat specialist; Split-second decision making
Conditions: Bonded with Lamont; Calm; Easy-going; Mellow; Never gets excited about anything; Sensitive about Lamont
Quote/Motto: "Are you saying my dog has a sissy name? What's so sissy about Lamont? Well? I'm waiting." "Anybody that says my dog has a sissy name can expect to be bitten on their backside."
Notes: In addition to his SWAT duties, Wide Scope sees to the security of the new Joe headquarters along with fellow SWAT specialist Shockwave.

Wild Bill

Series: Two (1983)
Real Name: William S. Hardy
Place of Birth: Brady, Texas (Hull, East Riding of Yorkshire, England, for European distribution)
Gender: Male
Grade/Rank: CW-4 (Army chief warrant officer)
SN: RA056403211
Service Branch: Army
Faction(s): G.I. Joe, Battle Corps, Strike Team: Alpha, and Tiger Force
Notably Served At: The Alaskan tundra; Battle of Benzheen; Cobra Island; South East Asia; New Moon, Colorado; New York City; Sierra Gordo; Springfield; town of Millville; Tokyo; Vietnam
Primary MOS: Helicopter pilot
Secondary MOS: Fixed-wing pilot; aircraft armorer
Appearance: Red hair and mustache; dark blue cowboy hat; silver sunglasses; olive green open-collared shirt with red-brown open vest and brown holster; olive green pants over brown boots; brown holsters on legs
Other Known Appearances (Cartoon): Light tan hat; black sunglasses; blue shirt with an orange closed vest; no gloves; blue pants with a brown belt and no leg holsters
Background Information: Flight Warrant Officer School. His original prototype dossier reads: "...served as a combat infantryman and participated in LRRP (Long Range Reconnaissance Patrol) operations during [the] South East Asian debacle."
Abilities: Contact: Russian Captain Bulgakov; Combat infantryman; Crash landing expert; Experienced; Gunslinging; Helicopter pilot; Instructor; LRRP (long-range reconnaissance patrol) operations; Qualified Expert Operator: Dragonfly XH-1 helicopter; Qualified Weapons Expert: M1191A auto pistol (prefers single action .45 long Colt revolvers), XM-16 attack rifle; Qualified Operator: Cargo helicopter, Cargo plane, Dragonfly, FANG, JUMP, Silver Mirage, SkyStriker, Tomahawk; Specialized Training: CLASSIFIED; Long-range recon specialist; Tracker; Trusted and respected by all Joes; Well respected; "Work Him Over" interrogation methods
Conditions: Amiable; Distinctive Feature: Brace of single-action .45 Colt revolvers; Distinctive Feature: Slow-talking Texan accent/drawl; Distinctive Feature: Wears a blue, replica Civil War slouch hat; Fancies himself a country-western singer; Good

humor; Honest in personal dealings; Loves country-western music; Reputation: One of the most experienced and well-respected members of the G.I. Joe Team; Reputation: Gets along with everyone; Spins tall-tales for amusement; Stereotypical cowboy

Quote/Motto: "Wild Bill's had a lot of practice at crashing and burning!" Doc said, to which Wild Bill replied with his usual good humor, "Yeah. I'm a regular expert..." "Amiable and slow talking. Fancies himself a country-western singer but the less said about that, the better. Constantly bucks uniform regulations and has never been known to wear regulation headgear. Although totally honest in personal dealing, he is not beyond spinning a tall tale for the amusement of comrades...." Quote by an unnamed G.I. Joe team member.

Notes: In 1986 Wild Bill, one of the original G.I. Joes, was replaced by Lift-Ticket.

Wild Bill, Action Force

Series: Nineteen (2003)
Real Name: William S. Hardy
Place of Birth: Hull, England
Gender: Male
Service Branch: British Army; Army Air Corps
Faction(s): Action Force, Tiger Force
Notably Served At: Aden; the Amazonian jungle; the Americas; the Australian Outback; Brunei; China; Jordan; London; the Vietnam War
Appearance: Red hair and mustache; gold goggles; blue short-sleeved shirt with yellow bandana and sleeves; white gloves; brown straps, belt, and holster; black pants with brown boots; yellow stripes on legs
Accessories: Backpack (with sculpted roll, canteen, and grenades) with clips on the side for a knife; cowboy hat, missile launcher with boxlike back and trigger, missile with a flared tip, short knife with a notched tip, shotgun
Background Information: Exchange Program with a U.S. Army Aviation Squadron
Conditions: Haunted by the order to leave a man behind; Loves helicopters
Notes: After a point, the *Action Force Comic* and *G.I. Joe: A Real American Hero* match storylines; apart from these additions, the rest of the information matches Wild Bill's entry.

Wildcard

Series: Seven (1988)
Real Name: Eric U. Scott
Place of Birth: Northampton, Massachusetts
Gender: Male
Grade/Rank: E-4 (Army corporal)
SN: 102-65-0984
Service Branch: Army
Faction(s): G.I. Joe, Strike Team: Charlie
Stationed: The Pit in Utah
Notably Served At: Battle of Benzheen; Broca Beach, New Jersey; Cobra Island; Trucial Abysmia
Primary MOS: Armored vehicle operator
Secondary MOS: Chaplain's assistant
Appearance: Brown hair and mustache; torn green vest; black wristbands; dark red pants; gray boots
Accessories: Machete with blade widening near the top, "Mean Dog" 6WD heavy assault vehicle, open sheath backpack, tall helmet
Abilities: Armored vehicle driver; Chaplain's assistant; Qualified Expert Operator: Mean Dog; *Unnatural talent for breaking things
Conditions: Reputation: Destroys objects; Unnatural habit of unintentionally breaking things
Quote/Motto: "When Wildcard is driving the Mean Dog, the vehicle becomes an extension of himself; a raging engine of destruction, pulverizing all in its path. If the enemy, by sheer luck, manages to knock out the Mean Dog, they then put themselves in the position of having to deal with Wildcard directly! You could go so far as to call that a violation of the Geneva Convention!" Quote by unnamed G.I. Joe team member.
Notes: *All he has to do is touch something and it's guaranteed to break; when driving a vehicle, it becomes an extension of his destructive powers.

Windchill

Series: Eight (1989)
Alias/Variations: Jim Steel
Real Name: Jim McDonald
Place of Birth: Loch Lomond, Scotland (Cedar Rapids, Iowa, on some cards)
Gender: Male
Grade/Rank: E-6 (Army staff sergeant)
SN: 312-60-0386
Service Branch: Army
Faction(s): G.I. Joe, Battle Corps
Stationed: Exterior security for the Arctic prison, The Coffin
Primary MOS: Blockbuster driver

Secondary MOS: Cold weather survival instructor
Appearance: White cap and goggles; yellow hair and mustache; dark green jacket and gloves; white pants; dark green boots
Accessories: Machine gun with long scope, curved stock, and angled grip and magazine; rifle; two skis armed with lasers
Abilities: Cold weather survival instructor; Hobby Skill: Hunting; Quickly spots dangerous obstacles; Participates in biathlons; Perception; Qualified Expert Operator: Blockbuster; Skimobiler; Uncanny ability to "read" nature's elements
Conditions: Pre-Olympian athlete
Quote/Motto: "To be as cool as I am in a firefight, you have to have ice water in your veins."
Notes: Windchill may have qualified for a spot on the American Olympic team if Blizzard hadn't met him at the National Elimination Tournament and gave him the idea of getting paid to drive fast, heavily armed snow vehicles.

Windmill

Series: Seven (1988)
Alias/Variations: Chill; Cool-Breeze; Cyclone, X-Terminator, Xyclone
Real Name: Edward J. Roth
Place of Birth: Allentown, Pennsylvania
Gender: Male
Grade/Rank: O-3 (Army captain)
SN: 019-21-1858
Service Branch: Army
Faction(s): G.I. Joe
Stationed: Army Aviation Department Test Activity; Army Flight Warrant Officers School in Fort Rucker
Notably Served At: Cobra Island
Primary MOS: Stopped-rotor aircraft operator
Secondary MOS: Attack helicopter pilot
Appearance: Black helmet with orange crest; orange shirt with green open shirt and tubing; orange pants with black boots
Accessories: Large revolver with trigger far from the grip
Background Information: Flight instructor at the Army Flight Warrant Officers School in Fort Rucker
Abilities: Flies experimental helicopter prototypes; Flight instructor; Qualified Expert Operator: Skystorm X-Wing Chopper (a combination fighter jet and helicopter); Skilled pilot; Years of flight experience
Conditions: Dry, sarcastic sense of humor
Quote/Motto: "When the G.I. Joes are sitting on a hot LZ waiting for an extraction chopper, they want fast air support with maximum fire suppression. The X-Wing Chopper clocks at 345 mph in its stopped-rotor mode and can carry a bigger payload than a Dragonfly. Windmill can get there faster, with more thrust, and once he's there, he can make every piece of ordnance count!" Quote by unnamed G.I. Joe team member.
Notes: In the G.I. Joe versus Transformers Universe, while battling the nightmarish Monstructor, Windmill's life force was drained, causing him to lose control of his vehicle. The giant Transformer threw a Snow Cat into the tumbling helicopter, presumably killing Windmill.

Winter Operations

Series: Twenty-one (2005)
Purpose: A Joe team located in the Arctic to battle against Cobra's Venom troopers
Leader: None listed, defer to rank
Members: Backblast, Frostbite, Mirage, Short Fuze, Snake Eyes, and Stalker

Wong

Real Name: Wen-Yun Wong
Place of Birth: Ürümqi, Xinjiang, China
Gender: Male
Grade/Rank: Officer Cadet for the Oktober Guard; 6—Captain (OF-2) (Transformers Universe)
Service Branch: Chinese Army
Faction(s): Oktober Guard
Primary MOS: Reconnaissance
Secondary MOS: Infantry
Appearance: Wears a blue uniform and tan cowboy hat; wears a black cowboy outfit
Abilities: Easy to underestimate; Expert lasso usage; Observant; Pilot; Rotary wing pilot (Transformers Universe); Fixed-wing pilot (Transformers Universe)
Conditions: Bluster about the American Old West; Uses cowboy slang; Unusual mannerisms
Quote/Motto: "Holy jumpin' Jehosaphat!"

Wreckage

Series: Nineteen (2003)
Alias/Variations: Sabertooth
Real Name: Dillon L. Moreno

Place of Birth: Los Angeles, California
Gender: Male
Grade/Rank: E-4 (Army corporal)
SN: 56-34-DL77
Service Branch: Army
Faction(s): G.I. Joe, Tiger Force
Stationed: Army Jungle Warfare Training Center
Primary MOS: Demolitions specialist
Secondary MOS: Jungle warfare instructor
Appearance: Pinkish skin; light brown face mask; black shirt and pants with yellow tiger stripes; black belt and straps with green grenades; orange holsters; brown boots; Special Operations Forces Demolition Kit (SOFDK) allows him to tailor demolition charges for maximum effect with minimal carry weight
Accessories: Backpack (no cover); submachine gun; walkie-talkie
Background Information: Army Jungle Warfare Training Center as a member of the OpFor (Opposing Forces) cadre
Abilities: Defusing/disarming demolitions expert; Detects tripwires and booby traps; Heightened perception; Jungle warfare instructor; Irregular training techniques; Stealth
Conditions: Practical joker; Mean spirited
Quote/Motto: "If it goes off with a bang, I treat it with respect. Even if it's a little firecracker. Anybody who doesn't is a fool, plain and simple." "All I leave behind is enemy devastation."
Notes: The figure is an homage to the never-released Sabre Tooth. There is also a member of S.K.A.R. who uses the code name Wreckage.

Yuki

Real Name: Minami Kojima
Place of Birth: Japan
Gender: Female
Service Branch: Japan Ground Self-Defense Forces

Z Force

Series: Twenty-six (2010)
Purpose: The infantry backbone of Action Force, well supported by heavy armor and artillery. They fight alongside fellow Action Force units. They wear distinctive green and black camouflage, with a red "Z" insignia in a military-style stencil typeface.
Leader: None given, defer to rank
Members: Breaker; Captain Skip; Doc; Gaucho; Jammer; Quarrel; Scout; Steeler; Tracker; Wheels
Notes: Z Force exists in the Action Force universe (European version of the G.I. Joe).

Zap

Series: One (1982)
Alias/Variations: Falcon Piloto (Brazil); Dolphin (Europe); Sergeant Zap
Real Name: Rafael J. Melendez
Place of Birth: New York City, New York
Gender: Male
Grade/Rank: E-4 (Army Corporal, 1982); E-6 (Staff sergeant) (1997)
SN: RA633980744
Service Branch: Army
Faction(s): G.I. Joe, Sonic Fighters
Stationed: The Pit, Utah, located beneath Fort Wadsworth
Notably Served At: Uncountable missions, many CLASSIFIED; Kennedy Space Center, Cape Canaveral, Florida; Cobra Island; Madrid, Spain; Sierra Gordo; Springfield
Primary MOS: Engineer, missile specialist
Secondary MOS: Infantry; artillery
Appearance: Hispanic with black hair; belt, light green fatigues, with bright green pockets and brown straps and boots (one horizontal)
Other Known Appearances (Cartoon): Light green outfit with dark brown straps, yellow collar and cuffs, and a thin mustache; the distinctive horizontal chest strap was usually missing
Accessories: 1982–83: Ammo pack (with engraved bazooka shells), bazooka, helmet
Background Information: Specialized Education: Engineer School; Ordnance School; Advanced Infantry Training
Abilities: Assesses and judges recruits; Bazooka soldier; Cool under fire; Demolitions expert; Disarm nuclear bombs; Instruction; Qualified Operator: Helicopter, JUMP, Silver Mirage; Qualified Weapons Expert: M-14, M-16, M-1911A1, M-79 (Grenade Launcher), M-72 (LAW Rocket), XM-71A (TOW Missile), XM-47 (Dragon Missile); Recruiting; Armor-piercing and anti-tank weapons specialist; Missile (bazooka) specialist
Conditions: Belief: His life is blessed; Extreme self-criticism; Extremely pragmatic outlook of life; Fun-loving; Gregarious; Laid-back; Reputation: Strange and dark sense of humor; Wants to give back to society

Quote/Motto: "Zap is the fun-loving type ... he's cool under fire. The stuff he works on could blow up at any time." "He's square—I mean that in the old-fashioned good sense ... like he can look you in the eyes and not flinch 'cause he's got pullin' any fast ones on you." Quote by fellow G.I. Joe team member Eric W. Freistadt, a.k.a. Short Fuze.

Notes: Zap was one of the original 13 members of the G.I. Joe team; he was one of about fifteen Joes to answer an illegal call for action by Roadblock. Zap was promoted to the head of the New York G.I. Joe branch. He is not to be confused with fellow Joe member, Dolphin. The 1982 Zap figure was produced straight-armed. He was distributed with one of three different style bazookas: a two handled bazooka (the rarest) a single thin handled bazooka, and a single thick handled (most common).

Section Two

Cobra

Cobra Command

Cobra Command, or as it is commonly known, The Cobra Organization—or even just Cobra—is a global terrorist organization. The original action figure for the leader of this organization was a mail-in exclusive in 1982; he cost five Flag points (proofs of purchase) plus 50 cents to cover shipping. The name of this figure was Enemy Leader; Cobra Commander was his MOS (Military Occupational Specialty), but for the sake of continuity, he will be referenced as Cobra Commander throughout the book as this is the name he is known by.

In the cartoon, Cobra Command is often portrayed as an ineffectual cadre of self-defeating buffoons but the comic portrays the group more realistically, as a military and political machine.

Each incarnation of the franchise has its own continuity, and the origin and portrayal of the organization and the individuals therefore vary.

Four variations of Cobra Soldier.

Cobra Commander variants.

Marvel Comics Universe

Here, Cobra Command was portrayed in a fairly realistic way, as a highly successful fascist terrorist organization. There was a great use of strong symbolic imagery fronting a highly charismatic and ruthless leader atop a fanatical hierarchy.

When the man who would become Cobra Commander and establish Cobra Command settled in the town of Springfield, he took his hate of the United States government with him. He blamed every problem in his life on the government and began recruiting people who felt the same in this run-down and neglected town. Ranks swelled, and word spread nationwide. The movement was financed by a pyramid scheme company called Arboc. When the government ruled Arboc to be an illegal undertaking and had court orders to close it down, the man who would be Cobra Commander declared: "I'm not going to be ground under the wheels of big government! … I'm going to create an underground organization that will bypass government restrictions and garners power through terrorism and extortion! … I won't stop until my organization coils around the whole world like a giant cobra!"

Operating in secret, now calling itself Cobra Command, the organization began to grow in size and spread across the country, becoming a military organization. It attracted members with the promise of fast financial rewards and power to those

Cobra Commander with voice pack.

willing to be ruthless. By the time the U.S. government realized Cobra Command was a threat, it had spread nationally and had a foothold worldwide.

This highly powerful and wealthy private army had members who lead normal lives in the eyes of outsiders. Cobra Command achieved temporary legitimacy with the creation of the artificial island, Cobra Island, as it was recognized by the international community. This allowed it to have diplomatic facilities in the United States.

During Serpentor's rule, Cobra Command made most of its income selling arms to Third World nations; this put them in direct competition against Destro's M.A.R.S (Military Armaments Research System). The Terrordrome was Cobra's most popular product, especially for poor dictators.

Cobra Command troops were motivated by money, power, and a sense of brotherhood but were not fanatical to the point of holding at all costs or using suicidal tactics. The brutal training these troops underwent shared many characteristics of ritualistic hazing.

The Animated Series

The Sunbow animations never explored how Cobra came into existence. The animated film *G.I. Joe: The Movie* revealed Cobra Command as part of a 40,000-year-old underground civilization called Cobra-La that had snake-like inhabitants, one of which was Cobra Commander. This contradicts facts presented in the original series. The movie also claims that the creation of Serpentor was an idea they implanted into the mind of Doctor Mindbender as a means to discipline Cobra Commander. The Cobra-La story arc, not well received, was abandoned in future plotlines.

The story editor said that the idea for the origin of Cobra Command was meant to be an extremist organization founded by a Karl Marx/Friedrich Nietzsche type of person but with a strong set of ideals. This person would then be usurped by Cobra Commander, who would lock him up in a secret prison.

Action Force

In the UK, G.I. Joe was known as Action Force and their original antagonists were named Red Shadows—a terrorist organization run by Baron Ironblood and his lieutenant the Black Major. Eventually, the storyline was written to match the American counterpart more closely; in doing so, Ironblood destroyed the Red Shadows before reimagining the organization, changing its name to Cobra Command and his own name to Cobra Commander. After defeating Jackal, he decided not to kill him but rather change his name to Destro and force him into servitude.

Sigma 6

This is a more modern take on the series utilizing next-gen technology and the staple characters; cybernetics and cybernetic enhancements are not uncommon. B.A.T.s make up the primary bulk of Cobra's army; human personnel are mostly their technicians.

Cobra High Command

The Cobra High Command, typically led by Cobra Commander, is unstable and fluid; its members are constantly falling in and out of favor both with one another and the organization itself. Assassination attempts are not unheard of.

Major Reoccurring Cobra Characters

Baroness Anastasia DeCobray—The daughter of a European aristocrat, the Baroness (as she is commonly known) is Cobra Command's director of intelligence. She is romantically entangled with Destro.

Rare Destro signed by voice actor.

Cobra Commander—The horribly disfigured face (by some accounts) of this leader and founder of the Cobra Command organization is hidden either by a hood or high-tech battle helmet wired to explode if it were ever to be removed against his will. Only the Baroness and Destro have seen his face. He was temporarily deposed by Serpentor and, depending on the universe, is not the original founding Cobra Commander but rather one of the many Freds.

Destro—A Scotsman, Laird James McCullen Destro XXIV is an arms dealer with a long history. He wears a full metal face covering and has frequently attempted to take over and control Cobra Command with varying levels of success. The hereditary leader of M.A.R.S. (Military Armaments Research Syndicate), he also has his own private army, the Iron Grenadiers, which he uses to stir up conflicts worldwide to sell weapons to engaging parties.

Dr. Mindbender—An insane scientist and inventor with a startling intellect, he is the progenitor of Cobra Command's most dangerous creations and devious devices. Although powerfully built and physically capable, he is a coward.

The Dreadnoks—A small-time regional biker gang that grows into a recognized global chapter, Zartan built the club into a force able to hire out its underworld services to the likes of Cobra Command and Destro.

Serpentor—Created by Doctor Mindbender, Serpentor is a clone created from the DNA of history's greatest, most ruthless, and most effective military leaders—including members of G.I. Joe. During the Cobra Civil War, he was seemingly killed by Zartan but was revived by a cabal of scientists calling themselves The Coil.

Dreadnoks.

Storm Shadow—A ninja from the Arashikage clan who began his career with Snake Eyes and Stalker, Storm Shadow has been brainwashed to varying degrees of success and has worked for and with both sides.

Tomax—He leads the Crimson Guard with his mirror twin, Xamot. They are the respectable corporate face of Cobra Command. When not in combat gear in the field, he is in a suit managing operational business affairs. He and his brother share an empathic link allowing speechless communication between them.

Xamot—He leads the Crimson Guard with his mirror twin, Tomax, and has a red scar on the right side of his face. Their corporation is called Extensive Enterprises.

Zartan—A master of disguise, an assassin, and a spy, he leads the Dreadnoks, a biker gang of such strength, power, and influence that they sell their services to the likes of Cobra Command and Destro. He can alter the color of his skin due to a genetic procedure he underwent while working for an undisclosed government agency.

Rank and File

Faceless, nameless legions of soldiers sent in waves against G.I. Joe constitute the bulk of the Cobra Command organization. There are diversified subsets according to specializations.

B.A.T.s—Battle Android Troopers are inexpensive to mass produce and allow the heroes to gun them down *en masse*. Unfortunately, they can be a deadly threat to friends and foes alike.

Cobra Soldiers and Officers—Also known as "Blue Shirts," these soldiers and officers were the original ground troops of the Cobra Command army.

Cobra Vipers—These infantry soldiers who complimented the Blue Shirts are the "backbone of the Cobra Legion." If you want to get anywhere in Cobra Command, you have to start out as a Viper. Also, "Viper" becomes a suffix added to many Cobra Command Divisions, regardless of ability level or rank.

The Crimson Guard—Led by mirror twins Tomax and Xamot, these are elite soldiers. In addition to a higher level of intense military training, all members must have a degree in either accounting or law (later this is relaxed to a master's in any field). Doing as much damage in the courtroom as they can on the battlefield, they frequently go into deep-cover operations as civilians and politicians.

Night Creepers—These are ninjas-for-hire with a specialty in business and technology. Their leader is Aleph (Incision), but in other universes he is called Night Creeper Leader.

Bases and Holdings

Cobra Command—This global organization that has been recognized as a legitimate nation on the world stage. It has many holdings, but some are more significant than others.

Cobra Viper Python Patrol.

Borovia—Borovia is a fictionalized Eastern European Communist country in the Marvel Comics Universe.

Broca Beach—This abandoned seaside town was recreated and transformed by Cobra Command to be a secret base of operations in America. After the Battle of Springfield, many of its residents were relocated there.

Castle Destro—The ancestral home of Laird Destro, it is also the training grounds for his Iron Grenadiers.

Cobra Citadel—Also known as the Silent Castle, this is Cobra Command's base of operations in Eastern Europe. Located in Trans-Carpathia and designed by Destro, it became his second castle.

Cobra Consulate—A high-rise located in New York City, this is the Cobra embassy in America and the base of operations after Cobra Island was declared a sovereign nation.

Cobra Island—Created by a massive earthquake G.I. Joe was tricked into causing, Cobra claimed Cobra Island as its own territory. The location of the Cobra Civil War, it was eventually seized by the United Nations. The Coil next came to power on the island, but it was ultimately destroyed by a nuclear strike killing all members of Coil.

Millville—Cobra Command took control of this steel town using Doctor Mindbender's brainwashing device.

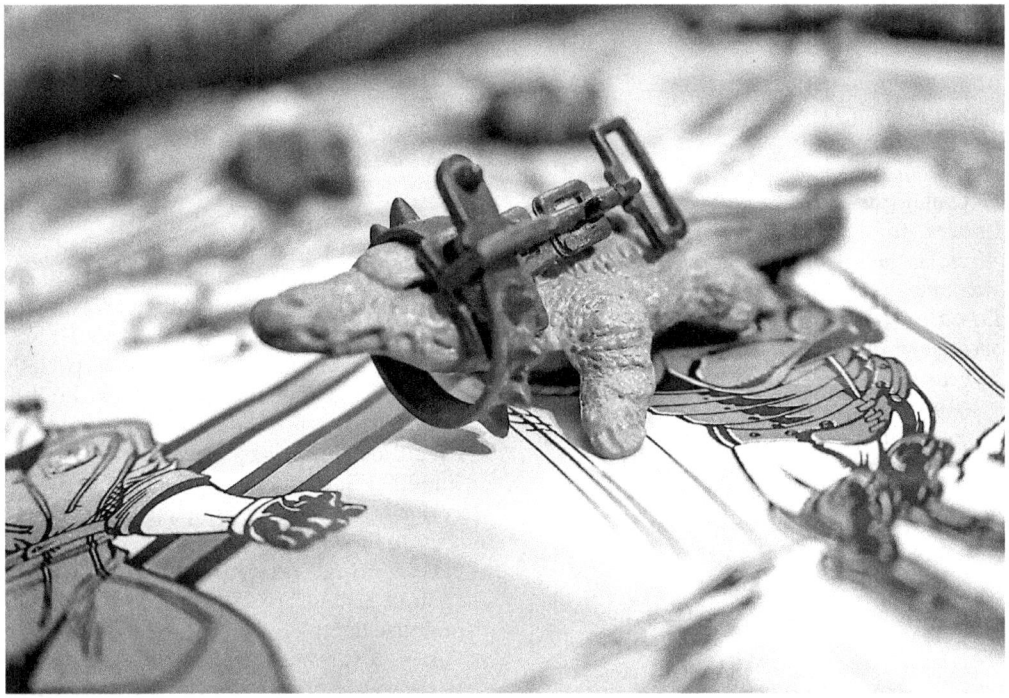

Croc Master's croc.

Monolith Base—Located in Badhikistan, this massive mountain complex served as Cobra's main base but was taken by G.I. Joe.

Springfield—Somewhere in middle America, this small, anonymous town was a Cobra Command base of operations—the very place in which Cobra Commander started. Many covert operations originated here, including the creation of Serpentor.

Cobra Character Field Guide

Abutre Negro ("Black Buzzer")
Series: Eleven (1994)
Gender: Male
Faction(s): Cobra, Patrulha Do Ar ("Sky Patrol")
Appearance: Padded black body armor, helmet, and boots; large red Cobra logo on the chest, silver shin guards, gloves, shoulder pads, and trim
Accessories: Backpack, handgun, parachute, rifle
Abilities: Command; Leadership; Next-generation computer hacker
Notes: The file card claims he is the leader of the Night Vultures.

Aero-B.A.T.
Series: Five (1986)
Place of Birth: Created for the Cobra Organization by Doctor Mindbender
Gender: Robot
Faction(s): Cobra
Appearance: B.A.T. with wings and machine gun on the back
Background Information: Disposable brute strength to the Cobra Army

Air Devils

Series: Eleven (1992)
Alias/Variations: Cobra A.D.D.E.R.S. (Aerial Deployment Daredevil Elite Recon Squadron) Commando
Real Name: Various
Place of Birth: Various
Gender: Any
Service Branch: Cobra Air Force
Faction(s): Cobra, Cobra A.D.D.E.R.S.
Primary MOS: Aerial assault commando
Secondary MOS: Infiltration
Appearance: Red helmet and black goggles with red lens; a red shirt with black vest and gloves; silver vest details; red pants with black belt and padding on inside legs; black boots; clear face shield and a black rifle
Accessories: Aerial assault hand rifle, clear square dark visor with peg holes, hang glider with red Cobra emblems
Abilities: Aerial assault; Air commando glider; Dirty-fighting tactics; Highly skilled in unorthodox close-quarter combat styles; Highly trained; Stealth; Unorthodox combat style; Wreak havoc
Conditions: Cursory three-day glider training course; Distinctive Feature: Target supply lines; Fights dirty; Front line aerial assault combatants; Reputation: Use devious methods; Use guerrilla warfare tactics on the ground
Quote/Motto: "Never fight in the open when you can ambush from cover; never ambush from cover when you can get a well-hidden, explosive booby trap." "There is only one way to fight, and that's dirty!"
Notes: All Air Devils are equipped with "Grabber" gloves; 100-yard radius delayed blast bomb; Air Devils sidearm with holster; air-to-surface cluster grenades; ankle support ammo-pouch; high altitude pressure-proof assault armor; infrared 360-degree vision angle anti-fog goggles; official order of the Air Devils combat belt with buckle; and a steel cutting survival knife.

Air-Vipers

Series: Nineteen (2003)
Alias/Variations: Cobra Air Force Trainee (2003); Cobra C.L.A.W. Pilot/Attack Pilot (2009); Air Viper Commando (2005)
Real Name: Various
Place of Birth: Various
Gender: Any
Grade/Rank: Consist of various military and civilian flight school dropouts
SN: 1782-AV
Service Branch: Cobra Air Force
Faction(s): Cobra
Stationed: Cobra Island
Primary MOS: Fighter pilot
Secondary MOS: Infantry
Appearance: Black robotic helmet with red eyes; black shirt with blue diagonal straps and red Cobra emblem on chest; blue gloves; black pants with blue waist piece and holster; blue boots. Each trainee is outfitted in a specially designed flight helmet that includes a built-in oxygen mask, optical display screen, and digital altimeter that alerts them exactly when to "pull the chute."
Accessories: Backpack, chest plate, parachute
Background Information: Basic Aerial Combat Training; Parachute Training Course from an A.V.A.C. (Air-Viper Advanced Class) jumpmaster
Abilities: Advanced aerial combat training with next-generation aircraft; Combat experience; Commandos; Endurance; Endured surgical procedure to become resistant to hypoxia, hyperventilation, and other decompression sicknesses; Impeccable security clearance; Incredibly well paid; Meticulous; Knowledge Skill: Extensive knowledge of aeronautical engineering; Knowledge Skill: Familiar Cobra aircraft; Qualified Operator: Night Raven jets; Rigorous parachute training; Willpower
Preferred Weapon: BVR AMM-32J (Beyond Visual Range Air-to-Air Missile)
Conditions: Detail-oriented problem solvers; Ruthless; Willing to risk danger, prison, and even death
Quote/Motto: "You earn your wings, believe me: Over 1,500 hours logged in flight time, a fixed-wing rating up to four engines, combat experience, and an impeccable security clearance." From Cobra Commander's files: "Although these pilots are taught how to bail out of a burning craft, I'm only concerned that the flight helmets are returned in one piece!"
Notes: The Night Raven was designed by M.A.R.S. Industries.

Alexander McCullen

Alias/Variations: Destro II
Real Name: Alexander McCullen

Place of Birth: Midland Valley, Scotland
Gender: Male
Faction(s): Cobra, Destro, Iron Grenadiers, and M.A.R.S.
Notably Served At: Cobra Island, Trans-Carpathia
Primary MOS: None
Secondary MOS: None
Abilities: Contacts: Criminals and gangs; Follower: Mistress Armada; Knowledge Skill: Criminals and gangs; Knowledge Skill: Destro; Personal bodyguard: Firefly; Poses as Destro; Professional Skill: Operations of M.A.R.S. Corporation
Conditions: Obsessed with gaining his father's approval; Obsessed with taking Destro's place in the family business; Raised by a single mother
Quote/Motto: "There's is nothing more to war than money and power.... He who controls the war, controls the world!!!"

Alley Viper

Series: Eight (1989)
Alias/Variations: Cobra Urban Assault Trooper; Cobra Urban Assault Weapon (1997); Cobra Trooper (2004)
Real Name: Various
Place of Birth: Various
Gender: Any
Service Branch: Cobra Army
Faction(s): Cobra
Primary MOS: Urban assault specialists
Secondary MOS: Various
Appearance: Heavy body armor, advanced night optics, covert observation gear, and an arsenal of weapons; orange helmet with blue face mask; orange shirt and pants with blue urban camo; blue right armband; black gloves and boots
Accessories: Backpack with engraved grappling hook rifle and removable grappling hook, face shield with Cobra emblem on front, knife, laser pistol, machine gun with scope, rifle, shield with Cobra emblem and handle, two Skorpion submachine guns
Abilities: Brute force; Endurance; Equivalent skills to police SWAT units or British Special Air Service commandos; Instigate chaos; Large; Strong; Specialist: SWAT tactics; Specialist: Urban combat; Uses various forms of treachery; Willpower
Conditions: Brutal; Distinctive Feature: Armored shields and fanged masks; Fearless; Ruthless; True masters of brutality
Quote/Motto: "Alley-Vipers are big and strong as well as ruthless! Their body armor alone weighs 50 pounds and they carry at least 30 pounds of weapons, ammo, grenades, and climbing gear. You definitely don't want one of these gorillas running up and kicking your door down!" "When you see us coming, you have three choices: run, fight, or surrender. If you run, we'll hunt you. If you fight, we'll crush you. If you surrender, we'll make you wish you'd never been born."
Notes: As part of their training regimen, Alley Vipers are required to survive a full burst of machine-gun fire across their frontal body armor, execute a 30-foot jump onto concrete with a full combat load, and run down a 100-meter gas-filled corridor without a mask.

Artur Kulik

Real Name: Artur M. Kulik
Place of Birth: Irkutsk, Siberia
Gender: Male
Grade/Rank: Field Agent
Faction(s): Red Scream
Primary MOS: Shock attack
Secondary MOS: Hand-to-hand unarmed combat
Appearance: Hulking man, heavy brow, large and thick Hungarian mustache
Abilities: Amazing intelligence; Hand-to-hand unarmed combat; Hobby Skill: Painting; Huge size; Right hand of Wilder Vaughn; Shock attack
Conditions: Fearsome; Fervent believer in the Russian Revolution; Loves painting; Propensity for violence; Sensitive
Quote/Motto: "Don't let that huge size, propensity for violence, and overhanging brow fool you. Beneath it all, Artur Kulik is an amazing intelligence and sensitive man. It is even said he has a love of painting. Mind you so did Adolf Hitler."

Asa Negra

Series: Twelve (1995)
Alias/Variations: Black Wing
Real Name: Unknown
Place of Birth: Unknown
Gender: Male
Grade/Rank: Agent
Faction(s): Mercenary under contract with Cobra
Stationed: Brazil

Primary MOS: Mercenary
Secondary MOS: Specialist in glider night flights
Appearance: Gray bodysuit, golden visor, red goggles
Accessories: Gun
Abilities: Flies by intuition; Mercenary; Specialist in glider night flights
Conditions: Considered a madman by peers; Evil; Irresponsible; Wanted for committing atrocities
Notes: He was killed by the Red Shadows.

AVAC (Air-Viper Advanced Class)

Series: Five (1986)
Alias/Variations: A.V.A.C., Air Viper Attack Corps; Firebat Pilot
Real Name: Various
Place of Birth: Various
Gender: Any
Service Branch: Cobra Air Force
Faction(s): Cobra
Stationed: Terror Drome
Primary MOS: Terror Drome Firebat Pilot; COBRA Air fleet pilot
Secondary MOS: Cobra air fleet pilot; ground support
Appearance: Black Cobra emblem on the chest, black gloves, belt, and boots; silver and red armor on chest, arms, and legs; silver helmet with black visor.
Other Known Appearances (Cartoon): Narrower helmet, with an extra silver band around elbows; sometimes wore large black backpacks without a visible strap. The original outfit was a black and red flight suit. Another non-standard A.V.A.C. flight suit sports an orange helmet and gloves, a blue flight suit, and a red mask with white Cobra insignia.
Accessories: Included with Cobra Terror Drome; black parachute harness with Cobra emblem on the back
Background Information: Pilots are selected from the Air Viper ranks
Abilities: Capable of getting around the limitations and controlling a mini jet at extremely high speeds; Complex mental calculations; Elite skilled pilot; Exceptional piloting skills; Exceptional navigation skills; Qualified Operator: Cobra Rattlers
Conditions: Pilots relish the challenge of the Firebat; Utter fearlessness
Quote/Motto: "The Firebat jet is an unforgiving aircraft, so you have to be the best to fly it. And of course, we ARE the best." Also said of them: "A.V.A.C. pilots are drawn from the Air Viper pool. They must be capable of complex mental calculations to make up for the lack of onboard computers and are fearless to cope with the Firebat's basic unforgiving nature. The aircraft is not what you would call user-friendly. Surprisingly, there is no lack of recruits for the program. All the best fighter-jocks want a ride on the 'Pocket Rocket.'"
Notes: Piloting a Firebat is akin to strapping yourself onto a cannonball. The cockpit is cramped and lacks amenities: no engine status display, no weather instruments, no navigation aids, and no ejection seat, just the basic flight panel, throttle, pedals, and stick. But after the initial high-g of vertical takeoff, the Firebat levels out to be the fastest, most responsive single-seat fighter in the Cobra arsenal.

Baron Ironblood

Alias/Variations: Baron Eisenblut
Real Name: Unknown (Marcus Kassels)
Place of Birth: Unknown; possible Swiss descent
Gender: Male
Grade/Rank: Leader
Faction(s): Red Shadows
Primary MOS: Organizational military strategy
Secondary MOS: Leadership
Appearance: Caucasian male with white hair and a dark goatee beard. Dressed in a white suit (jacket and trousers) with a red "V" design on the torso, together with a skull and crossbones decoration, the insignia of the Red Shadows. He also wears tall black boots, reminiscent of German military uniforms of World War II. Various editions of the figure were produced with either black or white gloves. Iron helmet with a small slot opening for vision
Accessories: Uzi submachine gun
Background Information: Studied nuclear physics at Oxford University; paratrooper officer in the British Army; lead a U.S. Army unit nicknamed "The Baron's Brigade" during the Korean War
Abilities: Author (book on the flora of South America); Born leader; Command; Expert in fine wines; Followers: Army; Hypnotic control over his men; Knowledge Skill: Flora of South America; Leader of the Red Shadows; Leadership; Mastermind; Military strategy;

Nuclear physics; Paratrooper; Scholarly tastes; South American-based warlord; Uses harsh methods to train Red Shadows

Conditions: Disgraced son of an aristocratic Swiss diplomat; Distinctive Feature: Writes *Singueno Ferris* on bombs his army drops; Dreams of world dominance; Insane; Passion for chess; Seeks to destroy all organized government in Europe; Sworn enemy of Action Force; Twisted criminal brain; Wanted for war crimes in Latin America (massacre of civilians); Wild fury when defeated

Quote/Motto: His family motto is *Singueno Ferris*, "Our blood is of iron."

Notes: Ironblood betrays the Red Shadows, leaking information about their bases and intentions to the United Nations. As the Shadows are wiped out, he goes into hiding, constructs a new identity for himself, becomes Cobra Commander, and creates Cobra Command.

Baroness

Series: Three (1984)
Alias/Variations: Anastasia DeCobray; Anna von Stromberg; Baroness DeCobray, Ana
Real Name: (CLASSIFIED) Anastasia Cissarovna
Place of Birth: (CLASSIFIED) Believed to be East Europe, possibly East Germany
Gender: Female
Grade/Rank: Second in command of Cobra
SN: 0501—AD
Service Branch: Cobra Command
Faction(s): Cobra
Stationed: Cobra headquarters, Cobra Island; Castle Destro, Scotland; the Cobra Citadel, Trans-Carpathia
Notably Served At: Alaska; the Bern Institute; Broca Beach; Cobra Island Civil War; Lucca, Italy; New York; Sierra Gordo; the town of Springfield; Switzerland; Trans-Carpathia; Vietnam; Washington, D.C.
Primary MOS: Intelligence
Secondary MOS: Fixed wing pilot
Appearance: Long black hair; glasses; black plated armor suit, gloves, and thigh-high boots; red Cobra insignia on the chest. She is a dark, sensual femme fatale whose beauty is matched only by her ruthlessness
Other Known Appearances (Cartoon): Dark gray belt and gloves reaching nearly to the elbow; segments of leg armor outlined in gray
Accessories: Angular backpack with a large, engraved Cobra emblem; high-density laser rifle
Abilities: Beautiful; Child of wealthy European aristocrats; Cobra intelligence officer; Cobra's second-in-command; Command; Contacts: the Paine Brothers; Creates holographic duplicates of herself to distract or confuse her opponents; Cybernetic fingers; Disguise; Femme fatale; Field commander; Leadership; Master of disguise; Qualified Expert: M-16, AK-47, RPG7, Uzi, H.I.S.S. tank operator; Qualified Operator: CLAW, Cobra sub, FANG, H.I.S.S., Moray, Night Raven, Rattler, the SkyStriker, Trubble Bubble, Viper Glider; Sensual; Strategic abilities; Trusted lieutenant of Cobra Commander; Wealthy
Conditions: An infamous figure; Angry; Artificial loyalty to Cobra via the Brainwave Scanner; Bitter; Causes trouble just for the fun of it; Disillusioned; Distinctive Feature: Trademark black leather outfit; Distinctive Feature: Eastern European accent (Sunbow animation); Extensive plastic surgery to repair severe burns; Humanitarian brother: Eugene (Deceased); Husband: Destro; International terrorist; Interrogated by the Joes for months; Loyalties wavering; Out-of-control spree of violence; Power-hungry; Reputation: Knows Destro's secret identity; Romantically Paired with Destro (cartoon); Ruthless; Shows contempt for other members of Cobra; Spoiled; Unable to process life-changing news; Vows vengeance on Dr. Venom; Vows vengeance on Kwinn the Eskimo; Vows vengeance on Snake-Eyes
Quote/Motto: "Her principal weakness is in the division of her loyalty between Cobra Commander and Destro. Her chief strength would seem to lie in her ability to play them against each other."
Notes: While the Baroness was imprisoned by the Joes, she delivered a child which was immediately taken from her. She escaped when rescued by the Phoenix Guard. The fate and whereabouts of the child is unknown. Throughout the storyline, the love between James and Ana can overcome any obstacle. In an alternate reality, Baroness is an American student who went to Europe and joined radical groups. In this reality, Cobra has defeated the Joes and rules the world. The Baroness is a double agent with romantic ties to Steeler and rescued the Joes trapped in her world. This Baroness does not wear glasses.

Battle Android Trooper (B.A.T.)

Series: Five (1986)
Alias/Variations: BAAT; B.A.T.S. (1986); Bionic Trooper; Robóid (Brazil). Prototype name was Bat-Bot and BATBOT.
Place of Birth: Created for the Cobra organization by Doctor Mindbender
Gender: Robot
Faction(s): Cobra
Primary MOS: Android shock trooper
Appearance: Often described as "machine guns on legs"; a black head with silver faceplate; black shirt with yellow pad; transparent chest panel covering red, yellow, and blue innards; silver arms; black pants with yellow belt and boots
Other Known Appearances (Cartoon/Comic/Movie): Red visors and grill on cheeks. Other versions exist; one has bright yellow paint highlights, and the other has orange paint highlights.
Accessories: Claw, flamethrower arm, machine gun arm, and robotic hand; trapezoidal backpack with pegs for arm attachments
Background Information: Disposable brute strength to the Cobra army
Abilities: Heightened endurance (compared to a human); Heavily armored chassis; Inexpensive to make; Easily replaceable; Never questions orders; Never shirks duty; Never surrenders; Nothing short destroying all vital core components will stop them; Heightened strength; Resilience; Unlimited stamina
Conditions: Disliked by Cobra Troops; Disposable; Distinctive Feature: Robot appearance; Does not discriminate between targets well; Does not react well to changes in field conditions; Limited intelligence (prevents them from performing more complicated strategies); Not programmed to speak; Simple automatons (only function is on the battlefield to shoot the enemy); Sometimes inadvertently shoot at their own forces; Unfortunate tendency to burst into flame when hit from behind; Will shoot anything that moves
Quote/Motto: "BATs are dangerous to everybody. They'll shoot, bayonet, or kick anything in sight; Cobra Infantrymen don't like to be on the same battlefield with BATs. When a Cobra unit is losing a battle they will dispense BATs into the midst of the firefight in order to evacuate the area easily."
Notes: There are variations of the BAT.
Aero-BAT—BAT with wings and machine gun on the back
Cobra Mantis—A BAT unit driven by Destro
Ninja BAT—A ninja type BAT
Overlord Vector—A snake torso BAT
Overlord Virus—A ninja-type BAT that was sent to Japan as backup for Storm Shadow. Under the influence of Power Stone, it is almost invincible. It later returns as a guard for an abandoned and seemingly haunted castle in Romania that Destro modified as a Cobra base.
Overlord Vortex—A BAT with a single red eye, two laser-firing arm cannons, and tank-like wheels for feet. Its metal hide is hard to penetrate.
Zeus—A megaBAT created by Destro to destroy Megalo City. Zeus's AI is run by the captured Spud.

Battle Android Trooper (B.A.T.) Generation 2

Series: Ten (1991)
Place of Birth: Created for the Cobra Organization by Dr. Knox
Gender: Android/synthroid
Faction(s): Cobra
Primary MOS: Infiltration and espionage
Secondary MOS: Independently targeted battle robot
Appearance: Various "skins" over metallic skeletal frame
Other Known Appearances (Cartoon/Comic/Movie): Squatter head, slightly thicker body and limbs
Abilities: Adaptable; Capable of self-repair; Espionage; Infiltration; Mimics human appearance and movement
Conditions: Not well suited for warfare
Notes: A more highly advanced version of the BAT Gen 2 was sent to go after Scarlett. Cobra is unable to produce more, as the only prototype was destroyed.

Bayonet

Gender: Male
Service Branch: Snow Serpent
Faction(s): Cobra, The Plague
Stationed: Cobra Headquarters
Notably Served At: The Amazon; Antarctica; the Appalachian Mountains; Lincoln, Nebraska; Malta; Manhattan, New York City; Philadelphia, Pennsylvania
Appearance: Black, cable-knit sweater and a black version of his previous division's helmet

Abilities: Best of the Snow Serpents
Conditions: Braggart; Distinctive Feature: Portable life support system; Reputation: Best of the Snow Serpents; Cocky, Self-assured; Unsure of his role with The Plague
Quote/Motto: "If we ever have to go on an Arctic mission, screw the Plague! I'm slippin' my old Snow Serpent uniform on, or I'm staying home!"
Notes: During the Scorched Earth campaign, Bayonet, Body Bags, Gallows, Guillotine, Infrared, Vanguard, and Velocity are stationed in Antarctica to guard and launch a nuclear bomb. Bayonet and the other members of The Plague were presumably captured or killed during a battle in the Appalachian Mountains.

Big Boa

Series: Six (1987)
Alias/Variations: Big Bad, Snake Charmer
Real Name: Unknown
Place of Birth: Unknown
Gender: Male
Grade/Rank: Trainer
Faction(s): Cobra
Stationed: Delhi Hills
Notably Served At: Brazil; Cobra Island
Primary MOS: Drill instructor
Secondary MOS: Physical trainer
Appearance: White helmet with red visor and silver spikes and grill over face; no shirt; red spiked straps across chest; blue pants with red belt and black and red boots
Other Known Appearances: Version 2: Off-white helmet with red visor and silver spikes and grill over face; no shirt; blue pants with black kneepads; red belt and black and red boots; blue gloves
Accessories: Punching bag reading "JOE" on pole with detachable circular stand, segmented air tube, two boxing gloves with Cobra emblems. Version 2: Dumbbell, head guard, pugil stick, sledgehammer, straps with spikes and buckle, two boxing gloves with Cobra emblems
Background Information: Military school
Abilities: Bare-knuckle fighting; Boxing; Cobra trainer; Fists the size of frozen turkeys; Hand-to-hand combat instructor; Mixed martial arts; Professional Skill: Boxer; Professional Skill: Illegal bare-knuckle toughman competitor; Voice like a bullhorn; Well-traveled
Conditions: Bully; Brutal, Unfeeling taskmaster; Distinctive Feature: Wears a unique protective helmet at all times; Disposition of a bear with a headache; Hideously ugly; Insubordinate; Loyal to Cobra Commander; Reputation: Comes from a long line of prizefighters; Reputation: He owes some debt to Cobra Commander; Rivalry with Rocky Balboa (figure never came to production); Supremely confident in his ability to subdue all opponents in physical combat
Quote/Motto: "Bring me the toughest contender G.I. Joe has to offer—I'll show them what real fighting is!" Said of him: "Big Boa kicks open the Cobra barracks door at 0500 and makes everyone do the low crawl up the mountain while pushing a bowling ball with their noses. Then, it's a 20-mile run through the bramble thickets, more push-ups than you want to know about, and a two-mile swim upstream with a flak jacket and helmet. After breakfast, he starts on the HARD stuff!"
Notes: His helmet has many cybernetic gadgets attached to it. Thermal heat sensors show him the weak spots on his opponent's body, while amplified hearing lets him know just how quickly their hearts are pumping, something that can be attributed to the fear of standing in his presence. This infamous instructor is merciless enough to weed out the weak, but his mandatory after-hours fight matches are what truly inspire only the most vicious to rise through the ranks of Cobra. Big Boa and Asa Negra were assassinated by Red Shadows operatives while in Brazil at a Cobra training facility.

Billy-Bob

Series: Twenty (2004)
Real Name: Horatio T. Wesson
Place of Birth: Auburn, Alabama
Gender: Male
Faction(s): Dreadnok Recruit
Appearance: Purple mask; light tan vest, light tan pants, brown boots; blond beard
Accessories: Rifle, shotgun
Abilities: Consummate scam artist and con man; Effortlessly smooth-talking; Knowledge Skill: Family business; Wealthy family
Conditions: Cocky attitude; Considers himself the most handsome of the cousins; Debonair; Enjoys flirting with Zarana; Hated by Road Pig; Holds a grudge against Beach Head; Suave; Watched by Road Pig

Quote/Motto: "No matter what disguise Zarana uses, she will never appear as gorgeous as I am!"

Notes: Otis, Vance, Cletus, Joe-Bob, and Roscoe are his cousins. All six cousins are identical in appearance.

Black Dragon, spy organization/warlord

Series: Nineteen (2003)
Real Name: Unknown
Gender: Male
Grade/Rank: Spy organization/warlord
Faction(s): Cobra, Black Dragon Spy Organization
Stationed: On an island headquarters in the South Atlantic, he built an impenetrable fortress beneath the ruins of their old base.
Primary MOS: Espionage
Secondary MOS: Demolitions, weapons, and tactics
Accessories: Submachine gun, two swords
Abilities: Command; Leadership; Unbending will
Conditions: Distinctive Feature: Carries nontraditional bladed or custom-designed weapons; Unbending will; Will stop at nothing to accomplish the destruction of the G.I. Joe team
Quote/Motto: "It may have cost me a fortune in weapons and armor but gaining access to a virtual army of Firefly-class field agents is invaluable."
Notes: He has joined with Cobra Commander, who has given him access to the most advanced weapons as well as tactical data that is needed for them to accomplish their mission.

Black Dragon Trooper

Series: Twenty (2004)
Real Name: Various
Place of Birth: Various
Gender: Any
Faction(s): Cobra, Black Dragon Organization
Stationed: An island headquarters in the South Atlantic
Primary MOS: Subversion and espionage
Secondary MOS: Demolition
Appearance: Gold helmet with blue face mask; black shirt with a blue vest and gold chest armor; black pants with a gold belt and gray boots
Accessories: Backpack, flamethrower, machine gun, rifle, submachine gun
Background Information: The organization has existed since the time of the Cold War, where it has since provided its services to whatever world power it deemed most important to its survival. They are recruited in secret, train endlessly, and if recruits do not measure up to the organization's exacting standards they are never heard from again.
Abilities: Cannot be brainwashed; Cannot be bribed; Cannot be broken; Counterintelligence, Demolition, Infiltration, Interrogation, Master of many martial arts disciplines; Masters of all small arms; Masters of explosives; Masters of weapons of opportunity; Personal bodyguards; Sabotage, Subterfuge, Surveillance, Unbending willpower
Conditions: Complete the mission at all costs; Coldly obedient; Dedicated to the Black Dragon Organization; Dedicated to Supreme Leader of the Black Dragons; Distinctive Feature: Carry nontraditional bladed or custom-designed weapons; Follow orders with ruthless efficiency; Willing to obey Cobra Commander's orders
Quote/Motto: "We are swift and silent, shadows in the darkest hours of the night, unseen by you until we strike." From Cobra Commander's files: "These troops are so coldly obedient, they make perfect additions to the Cobra cause—and they look so much better now that they wear Cobra uniforms!"
Notes: The organization is the foremost source of espionage around the globe. Whilst they operate for others, the true purpose of this elite body is revenge against G.I. Joe. The current Black Dragon Leader will stop at nothing to accomplish the destruction of the G.I. Joe team.

Black Out

Series: Nineteen (2003)
Alias/Variations: Blackout
Real Name: Thomas C. Stall
Place of Birth: Cincinnati, Ohio
Gender: Male
Service Branch: Cobra Army
Faction(s): Cobra
Stationed: Cobra Command
Notably Served At: The Amazon; Antarctica; the Appalachian Mountains; Badhikistan; Fort Huachuca, Arizona; Fort Riley, Kansas; Lincoln, Nebraska; New Moon, Colorado; Malta;

Manhattan, New York City; Philadelphia, Pennsylvania
Primary MOS: Sniper
Secondary MOS: Infantry
Appearance: Blond hair, blue eyes, tall
Background Information: He faced a general court-martial for his admitted negligence and possible treasonous acts. He left the Joes and joined Cobra.
Abilities: Sniper, Infantry
Conditions: Can't keep his head in the game; Childish; Difficulty following orders; Fearful; G.I. Joe Defector (former Greenshirt); Inattentive; Mess of a soldier; Prefers his black and silver costume to his Plague Trooper uniform; Prone to panic; Thinks of self and not the team; Whiner
Quote/Motto: Described by Mirage as "a childish inattentive mess of a soldier, an arrogant blemish on a family of career military men and the last person in the world I'd trust my life to."
Notes: He is the brother of the G.I. Joe members Barrel Roll and Bombstrike. In the Scorched Earth campaign, Black Out, Grim Skull, Incision (Aleph), Interrogator, Munitia, and Vector are stationed in Antarctica to guard and launch a nuclear bomb. He and Guillotine murder Sky Creeper and Rip It when they do not perform up to standards.

Blackstar

Series: Thirteen (1994)
Real Name: UNKNOWN
Gender: Male
Faction(s): Cobra, Blackstar Forces
Primary MOS: Elite space pilot
Secondary MOS: Tactical squad leader
Appearance: Black helmet with neon green visor; yellow shirt with black vest and wristbands; neon green air tube; yellow pants with black waist piece; black and neon green boots
Accessories: Backpack with a slot for launcher, laser pistol, spring-loaded missile launcher with a trigger, two missiles
Abilities: Climbing; Elite space pilot; Heightened agility; Wilderness Survival: Space
Conditions: Avoids asteroid belts; Reputation: The best pilot out of all the Blackstar ranks
Notes: The Blackstar forces are a secret legion of space pilots whose origins remain unknown. They are aligned with Cobra.
  All Blackstar forces have the following *Abilities and Conditions:* Climb planetary craters with ease; Incredible agility in zero gravity zones; Instinctively avoid asteroid belts while engaged in stellar dogfights; Behave as if space were their natural habitat; Reputation: May not be human (no one has seen a Blackstar up close)

Body Bags

Alias/Variations: Unknown
Real Name: Unknown
Place of Birth: Unknown
Gender: Male
Grade/Rank: E-4 Operative
Service Branch: Cobra Ground Forces; Range Vipers
Faction(s): Cobra, The Plague, Range Vipers, and Red Shadows
Stationed: Cobra headquarters
Notably Served At: The Amazon; Antarctica; the Appalachian Mountains; Lincoln, Nebraska; Malta; Manhattan, New York City; Philadelphia, Pennsylvania
Primary MOS: Long-range recon
Secondary MOS: Survivalist
Appearance: Black, cable-knit sweater and a black version of his previous division's helmet
Abilities: Hit-and-run raider; Iron stomach; Long-range recon; Long-term operations in enemy territory; Resistance to pain; Skirmisher; Team Player; Wilderness Survival: Forest; Wilderness Survival: Jungle
Conditions: Prefers the assault rifle
Quote/Motto: "No one enters my territory and leaves alive!"
Notes: During the Scorched Earth campaign, Bayonet, Body Bags, Gallows, Guillotine, Infrared, Vanguard, and Velocity are stationed in Antarctica to guard and launch a nuclear bomb. Body Bags and the other members of The Plague were presumably captured or killed during a battle in the Appalachian Mountains.

Brian Hassell

Real Name: Brian Hassell
Gender: Male
Faction(s): Cobra
Notably Served At: Al-Alawi; the Alps; the French Riviera
Primary MOS: U.S. ambassador
Secondary MOS: Undercover Cobra operative
Appearance: Brown hair and eyes, traditional blue suit
Abilities: Assassinate; Diplomacy; Oratory;

Professional Skill: U.S. ambassador; Professional Skill: U.S. State Department; Professional Skill: Undercover Cobra operative
Conditions: Not a convincing operative

Burn Out

Series: Nineteen (2003)
Real Name: Walter O. Jones
Place of Birth: Catskill, New York
Gender: Male
Faction(s): Dreadnok
Primary MOS: Mechanic
Secondary MOS: None
Appearance: Black hair and goatee; gray tank top with holes; black arm wraps from knuckles to bicep; black belt, leg coverings, and boots; blue pants; silver kneepads
Accessories: M.P. disguise (riot helmet with visor; shirt like chest plate; M.P. shoulder pad; waist belt; rectangular riot shield with detachable handle), shotgun with triangular stock and ribbed grip
Background Information: Dropped out of a top technical school during freshman orientation
Abilities: Hobby Skill: Builds custom motorcycles; Mechanical genius; Mimicry: body language and speech patterns; Qualified Weapon Expert: Flamethrower
Preferred Weapon: Flamethrower
Conditions: Loves working on engines; Loves riding motorcycles; Loves destroying vehicles that are not motorcycles; Proud to be a Dreadnok; Seeks revenge: Torpedo for blowing up his favorite customized motorcycle
Quote/Motto: "I love working on and riding anything that has a throttle on a handlebar. The next best thing I like is smashing anything that doesn't have a throttle on a handlebar. Hey, I am a Dreadnok, you know."

Buzzer

Series: Four (1985)
Alias/Variations: Dick Blinken
Real Name: Richard Blinken-Smythe
Place of Birth: Cambridge, England
Gender: Male
Faction(s): Dreadnoks
Notably Served At: Blackwater Prison, Cobra Island
Primary MOS: Scavenger of the Swamps
Secondary MOS: None
Appearance: Yellow hair, ponytail; silver sunglasses; beige sleeveless open-collared shirt with green strap; light blue jeans with a black belt and six thigh pads; black left wristband; snake tattoo on the shoulder; brown boots
Other Known Appearances (Cartoon): The shirt sometimes had short sleeves; gray chest grenades on a thin brown strap; brown leg padding
Accessories: Backpack with detachable fuel tank; diamond-toothed chainsaw rifle; nunchaku ax
Background Information: Cambridge dropout
Abilities: Chainsaw expert; College degree; Holds authority over newer Dreadnoks; Intellectual; Researcher; Scavenger
Conditions: Distinctive Feature: Cockney accent; Distinctive Feature: Founding member of the Dreadnoks; Extreme Indignation; Extreme left-wing Cambridge sociology don; Hates Mutt and Junkyard; Hates society's two-faced morality; Hatred for animals; High opinion of himself; Inept; Loves chainsaws; Repressed psychotic anger; Seeks to be second-in-command of the Dreadnoks; Seeks to chainsaw the expensive geegaws of technological society; Thrives on anarchy; Wanderer
Quote/Motto: "Hey mate, I let my chainsaw do the talking for me!"
Notes: Buzzer can cut through steel, wrought iron, and any metal (except armor plate) with his diamond-toothed chainsaw.

His head does not have the swivel-ball neck most of the other 1985 released figures have.

Cesspool

Series: Ten (1991)
Alias/Variations: Oil Baron; Poluicao (Brazil)
Real Name: Vincent A. D'Alleva
Place of Birth: Newton, Massachusetts
Gender: Male
Grade/Rank: Cobra Industries C.E.O.
Service Branch: Mercenary; Cobra
Faction(s): Cobra
Stationed: Plasmatox refinery in the Gulf of Mexico on an abandoned oil drilling platform; Massachusetts
Notably Served At: Cobra Island
Primary MOS: Chief executive officer
Secondary MOS: Laboratory director
Appearance: White hair; red scar on right side of face; a blue-green shirt with gold armor on shoulders and right arm; large red Cobra emblem on chest; blue gloves; blue-green pants with blue belt and kneepads; black boots. His uniform changes color when hit with warm water.

Accessories: Chainsaw rifle with a handle on top, frame backpack with water tank, hand-held water cannon with hose, soft helmet with large visor and (barely) removable mouthpiece
Abilities: Environmental operative; Knowledge Skill: High-level dirty dealings; Knowledge Skill: Corporate subterfuge; Philanthropist; Professional Skill: Chief executive officer of a multi-national corporation; Science Skill: Created plasmatox, weaponized toxic sludge
Conditions: Braggart; Despicable; Distinctive Feature: Hideously ugly; Distinctive Feature: Horribly disfigured; Ruthless; Seeks revenge on environmental groups
Quote/Motto: "I will make the world as ugly and nasty as I am!" "More ruthless and despicable than before, Cesspool is convinced that environmentalists were responsible for his accident and is determined to make the world as ugly and nasty as he is. Armed with an acid assisting chainsaw, he's taken his knowledge of high-level dirty dealings and corporate subterfuge straight to the organization that will make the best use of him—COBRA!" Quote by unnamed individual.
Notes: Plasmatox is powerful enough to dissolve and destroy everything from a person's skin to a tank's armor. It has been discovered that long-term exposure to plasmatox turned some people into uncontrollable creatures. With the help of a version of the witness protection program, Cesspool retired to a suburban home in Massachusetts where he is dying of cancer.

In an alternate universe continuity, Cesspool is captured by the Joes and transferred to the Coffin prison; later during a Cobra raid on the facility, Tomax was able to eliminate those Cobra considered loose ends.

Chop Shop
Series: Custom
Gender: Male
Faction(s): Dreadnok
Primary MOS: Car thief
Appearance: Blue vest, red headband, silver bandolier of grenades, maroon pants, black biker boots with shin guards
Abilities: Car thief
Conditions: Puts on a show that he's up for battle; Unhappy with Dreadnoks' constant warring

Notes: When Dreadnoks are on the battlefield, Chop Shop does not fight. Rather, he steals Joe vehicles and adds them to the Dreadnok ground assault fleet.

CLAWS Commander
Series: Nineteen (2003)
Real Name: CLASSIFIED
Gender: Male
Grade/Rank: Commands Unit Zeus
Service Branch: Cobra Army
Faction(s): Cobra; leads Unit Zeus
Notably Served At: Various trouble spots around the world; Cobra Island
Primary MOS: Covert light armored heavy weapons specialist
Secondary MOS: Heavy weapons
Appearance: Yellow hair and gold face mask; red dress jacket over black shirt; black armbands, gloves, belt, and boots; red dress pants
Accessories: Flared helmet with Cobra emblem and visor, complex machine pistol with L-shaped retracted stock and long magazine, knife
Abilities: Elite special operations soldier; Expert marksman with pistol and rifle; Expert with all known types of demolition materials; Knowledge Skill: Bootlegging and counterfeiting; Knowledge Skill: Criminal gangs; Language Skill: Fluent in five (unspecified) languages; Leader of the combined Cobra Choir and Glee Club; Mercenary; Qualified Weapons Proficient: Edged Weapons; Specialist: Covert light-armored heavy weapon
Conditions: Assumes responsibility for his mistakes; Belief: Lead by example; Rumor: As a teen, active in the gangs of Russia dealing in bootleg video games, counterfeit designer jeans, and pirate copies of hip-hop CDs; Seeks to be first man on the battlefield; Sings a rousing version of the Cobra marching song (in A-flat) during combat
Quote/Motto: "Cross Hair had me in his sights once, but luckily, my body armor protected me. Someday, I will have him in my sights, and he will sing a different song entirely."

Cletus
Series: Twenty (2004)
Real Name: Terrance W. Wesson
Place of Birth: Auburn, Alabama
Gender: Male
Faction(s): Dreadnok Recruit

Appearance: Purple mask; red vest, red pants, black boots
Accessories: Rifle, shotgun
Abilities: Brawler; Hand-to-hand combatant; Heightened strength; Hunter; Trapper, Wealthy: Family business; Weapon Skill: Crossbows; Weapon Skill: Automatic Rifles
Conditions: Avid hunter and trapper; Collects crossbows and rifles; Harbors ill will toward Beach Head; Likes the challenge of a fistfight; Reputation: Walking arsenal; Society annoys him; Stoic
Quote/Motto: "Come here and let me adjust your face."
Notes: Otis, Vance, Billy-Bob, Joe-Bob, and Roscoe are his cousins. All six cousins are identical in appearance.

Clyde

Alias/Variations: Old Clyde
Real Name: Clyde
Gender: Male
Occupation: Owner and operator of a bar named "Old Clyde's"
Grade/Rank: Bar owner
Service Branch: Civilian
Faction(s): Cobra
Stationed: Delhi Hills
Notes: "Clyde runs a bar, 'Old Clyde's,' in the Cobra-controlled town of Delhi Hills." There is a space in the back where members meet for meetings. The bar and many vehicles in the parking lot were destroyed when four Joes inadvertently discovered the bar's true nature.

Cobra Commander

Series: One (1982), three (1984) mail-in exclusive
Alias/Variations: Baron Ironblood, leader of the Red Shadows (UK: Battleforce: comics); Enemy Leader, Hooded Cobra Commander, Old Snake (Transformers)
Real Name: Unknown
Place of Birth: Unknown
Gender: Male
Grade/Rank: The leader of Cobra (1980s cartoon)
Service Branch: Cobra Command
Faction(s): Cobra
Notably Served At: Cobra Island; the Monolith Base in Budakistan; the town of Springfield; the Middle East; Southeast Asia; and other trouble spots
Primary MOS: Cobra Commander (1982); Cobra Leader; Intelligence
Secondary MOS: Ordnance
Appearance: Light blue uniform and his signature battle helmet were marked with the prototypical Cobra sigil known as the "Mickey Mouse" sigil as it is less sophisticated and detailed in design (1982); a darker blue uniform, a proper Cobra sigil, and the iconic hood he wore prominently in the Marvel Comics (1984); full-body Battle Armor (1987); blue and black ceremonial uniform with an ornate redesign of his original Battle Helmet (1991); blue and yellow uniform inspired by the admiral's jacket and hood worn by Cobra Commander in the comics (1992); black, with silver accents (1993); blue with yellow accents (1993); strange teal and purple spacesuit, the domed helmet was removable, revealing a masked head underneath with dark hair, and a half-mask covering his nose and mouth (1994); the iconic hood with a long flowing trench coat (2002). In the comic, it is revealed he is an average-looking American with a beatnik ponytail, beret, green-spectacled sunglasses, and a slender mustache.
Other Known Appearances (Cartoon): His face is always covered, either by a featureless chrome mask concealing his entire face or by a hood with eyehole cutouts. He wears a blue military uniform, occasionally sporting a cape and carrying a scepter, depending on the occasion. He is a brown-eyed Caucasian with a highly distinctive voice. His reason for wearing the mask was not expressly divulged, but a remark he made to Destro—"It takes a strong stomach to watch me eat, eh, Destro?"—implies some unsightly deformity. This is later confirmed in the animated movie where his face is shown to have been horribly disfigured as the result of a laboratory mishap involving "genetic altering spores."

In *The Transformers*, he wears his distinctive silver mask, has visible traces of his blue uniform underneath his trench coat, and appears to be wearing the gauntlets of Serpentor.
Accessories: 1982–83: Venom laser pistol; 1984: Venom laser pistol; 1987: Laser pistol with scope, textured grip, and energy magazine; segmented air tube; triangular backpack with four angled spines; 1991: Submachine gun (short grip, long magazine, no stock), spring catapult with trigger and bipod, two-piece glider; 1992: Short laser gun with two angled grips and large scope, talking backpack, twin missile launcher with wrist supports,

two short missiles; 1993: Incinerator flamethrower, machine gun, rifle, submachine gun, T-shaped spring-loaded missile launcher with gear at the back and a black trigger, two missiles

Abilities: Asymmetrical cluster of eyes covering his face (the movie); Followers; Former nobleman (the movie); Former scientist (the movie); Influence to corrupt; Knack for concocting creative schemes for world domination (cartoon); Leadership; Loyal personal bodyguard Storm Shadow; Professional Skill: Small businessman; Professional Skill: Used car salesman; Professional Skill: Vigilantes (alternate timeline); Rare moment of brilliance (cartoon); Well-Traveled

Conditions: Abandoned his wife; Blames all his problems on "the system"; Corrupt; Demands total loyalty; Desire for absolute power; Desires control of the world; Distinctive Feature: Raising fists skyward in exaltation with the battle cry of "Cobra!"; Embittered by the death of his older brother Dan; Fanatical; Filled with rage; Frequently promises to be a better father; Hated by his son, Billy; International fugitive; Maniacal; Master of pyramid schemes; Megalomaniac; Obsessed with vindicating his brother's death; Occasionally reflects on the folly of his ways; Paranoid; Personally executes enemies; Scrupulous; Seeks to topple big business; Seeks to topple the government; Target of the Red Shadows; Unwilling to harbor traitors (real or perceived); Uses brainwashing techniques to compel allegiance; Willing to kill

   In the cartoon: Arrogant; Coward; Distinctive Feature: Scratchy, screechy voice; Frequently hysterical; Frequently leads assaults; Greedy; Impatient; Launches into extended rants; Mistreats troops; Prone to fits of rage; Psychotic egomaniac

   In the movie: Disfigured in a laboratory accident; Distinctive Feature: Bald; Distinctive Feature: Eyes with cat-like pupils; Distinctive Feature: Pale blue skin; Distinctive Feature: Rasping voice

Quote/Motto: "Cobra Commander is hatred and evil personified. Corrupt. A man without scruples. Probably the most dangerous man alive!" "Most dictators and would-be Napoleon types are hampered by the need to pretend that they are pursuing a noble and just cause. Cobra Commander doesn't have that problem. This guy's in it for the money and the power, and if anybody else is interested in these things, he can pick up an assault rifle and get in line behind him!" These quotes were taken from transcripts of unnamed G.I. Joe members.

Notes: "Enemy Leader" was the name given by the 1982 mail-in exclusive order form, not Cobra Commander. In the comics, the hood was only for ceremonial occasions, while the helmet was worn whenever he was in the field or in danger of facing combat. In the cartoon, he wore the hood when in a Cobra base and the helmet everywhere else.

Cobra Mortal

Series: Twenty-two (2006)
Real Name: Unknown
Place of Birth: Buenos Aires, Argentina
Gender: Male
Grade/Rank: O-6 Colonel
Service Branch: Mercenary
Faction(s): Cobra, mercenary
Stationed: The Coffin (escaped)
Notably Served At: China; Derbent, Dagestan; South and Central America
Primary MOS: Assassination
Secondary MOS: Tactical sniper
Appearance: Strange looking red, silver, and black custom, reflective body armor
Accessories: Crossbow, rifle
Abilities: Cobra field operative; Conceal; Leaping; Professional Skill: Assassin; Professional Skill: Mercenary; Reconnaissance; Running; Stealth; Surveillance; Tactician
Conditions: Cold and calculating; Distinctive Feature: Custom laser crossbow; Distinctive Feature: Strange body armor; Implacable cruelty; Merciless; Reputation: Well-known in South America; Too heartless for others to stomach; Trusts his abilities, not armies
Quote/Motto: "He who wears the optimum body armor—always wins."
Notes: He was held in the maximum security prison called The Coffin, located in Greenland, and was one of several operatives who escaped during a raid led by Tomax.

Cobra Mortal 2

Real Name: Unknown/various
Place of Birth: Venezuela
Gender: Male
Faction(s): Cobra
Primary MOS: Regional crime lord
Secondary MOS: Extortionist

Appearance: All-white body armor with silver helmet and faceplate; thin slacks on legs
Accessories: Dagger, knife, pistol, satchel, submachine gun, two-part crossbow, web gear
Abilities: Contacts: Corrupt administrators within the Venezuelan government; Contacts: Political connections; Followers: Bodyguards and mercenaries who do his bidding; Foresight; Guile
Conditions: Arrogant; Belief: No military forces can supplant him; Belief: Cobra Commander will throw the world into economic turmoil; Greatly feared; Prefers to stay behind the walls of his mountain fortress
Quote/Motto: "The superstitious peasants believe I have returned from apparent demise so many times because I am a ghost. How do you know they are wrong?"
Notes: A "title" with numerous men taking the title over time. The most recent Cobra Mortal is a vicious and notorious Venezuelan crime lord.

Cobra Officer

Series: One (1982)
Alias/Variations: The enemy; Python officer
Real Name: Various
Place of Birth: Various
Gender: Male and female
Grade/Rank: O-4 Major
Service Branch: Army
Faction(s): Cobra
Stationed: Worldwide
Notably Served At: Worldwide
Primary MOS: Cobra officer; infantry; artillery; intelligence
Appearance: Cobra uniform with a silver sigil on the chest. They all had red-brown eyes and brown hair.
Other Known Appearances: All instances of the swivel arm version have black eyes and eyebrows.
Accessories: AK-47 assault rifle
Background Information: "The front-line fighters who lead Cobra attack units into battle"
Abilities: Air-traffic controller; Artillery spotting; Covert ops; Leadership; Martial arts; Sabotage; Weapons expert: AK-47; PM-63 machine pistol; M-16; M-11 Ingram
Conditions: Rise in rank through leadership or luck
Notes: According to their package description, these are "the front-line fighters who lead Cobra attack units into battle." The silver Cobra sigil on the chest rubbed easily off the action figure.

There are at least five different types of Cobra officers: Desert (tan uniform with black shoulder-harness with red shoulder pads), Night Stalker (female assault troopers using the fog of war to achieve their objectives; uniforms are black with silver trim, protective corset, black German style helmet with goggles and long ponytails), Night Watch (night-time patrol in black and blue camouflage), Python Patrol (highly skilled and experts in stealth; their python pattern uniform gives them extra stealth against electronic devices), and Regular (overseeing the basic ground infantry troops).

Cobra Soldier

Series: One (1982)
Alias/Variations: Cobra Blue-Shirts; Cobra foot soldier; Cobra Infantry Soldier; Cobra Infantry Trooper; Cobra Soldier; Cobra Trooper; Python Trooper; The Enemy
Real Name: Various
Place of Birth: Various
Gender: Male and female
Grade/Rank: E-4 equivalent
Service Branch: Army
Faction(s): Cobra
Stationed: Cobra Headquarters; Cobra Island; Cobra's base in Morocco; Cobra's rocket launch base in the Australian Outback; Cobra's supply base in the Amazonian jungle; Cobra's undersea base in the off the northwest coast of Africa; Destro's castle; Destro's oil rig; Grave Island in the Mekong Delta in Vietnam; the headquarters of Military Armaments Research Systems; the Two-Headed Serpent (splinter faction of Cobra) base in the Himalayas; and elsewhere throughout the world
Notably Served At: Worldwide
Primary MOS: Basic infantry
Secondary MOS: Sabotage
Appearance: Blue helmet, gloves, pants, and shirt; black boots, facemask, kneepads, and straps; red Cobra insignia on chest. It was also straight-armed.
Other Known Appearances: In the 1982 release, the figures had red-brown eyebrows. The 1983 release with the swivel arm had black eyebrows. There are many variations of this figure over the years including a 1984 Sears exclusive, a Hasbro direct pack, and a JCPenney two-pack.

Accessories: Black Dragunov sniper rifle

Abilities: Basic infantry; Cross-trained proficient in at least two support skills; Highly skilled in all NATO and Warsaw Pact small arms, explosives; Martial arts; Qualified Expert: Dragunov sniper rifle, M-16, Skorpion VZ0R61 machine pistol, Uzi gun; Sabotage; Terrorism

Conditions: Desires wealth and power; Reputation: Criminal, mercenary, or someone with a grudge against the world; Swore absolute loyalty to Cobra Commander

Quote/Motto: "COBRAS swear absolute loyalty to their fanatical leader…. COBRA Commander. Their goal … to conquer the world for their own evil purpose!"

Notes: Typically, we do not know the names of the individual Cobra soldiers, but Heavy Metal's childhood friend, Tony Lander, joined. Driven insane by the things he did and saw, he tried to steal lethal nerve gas to release into the upper atmosphere. Although an Action Force team was sent to stop him, Destro arrived first and shot him dead. Although there is no distinction between Vipers and Cobra soldiers, fans consider Vipers to be a step above.

The Coil

Stationed: Cobra Island

Notably Served At: Los Angeles; New York; Moscow; and the nations of Badhikistan

Notes: The Coil is an offshoot of the Cobra Terrorist Organization formed by the former "Emperor" of Cobra, Serpentor. It began as a movement by low-ranking members within the Cobra organization shortly after the Cobra Civil War ended with Serpentor's death. Members worked for three years on the abandoned Cobra Island facility to revive the fallen Emperor. Their efforts paid off, and Serpentor led Coil. He recruited former Cobra soldiers using former Hammer Team member Lt. Mikhail Derenko (Nowhere Man) and Firefly and built up the former Cobra fortress to fit The Coil's operational needs. Although The Coil had immediate success once they revealed themselves, it was short-lived. Both the G.I. Joe team and Cobra launched their own offensives at Cobra Island. Serpentor was believed to have been killed by Cobra Commander; Zandar was accidentally slain by Zartan; Firefly deserted; and General Overlord abandoned Coil and defected to the Jugglers to be their assassin. Leaderless and with most of the High Command dead or deserted, Coil's soldiers held the country of Badhikistan until Tomax and Xamot brokered a deal placing Coil forces under the control of Cobra, merging the two organizations. As the head of Cobra, Destro named Major Bludd, Mistress Armada, and Scrap-Iron as field commanders and tasked them with retraining Coil soldiers to be loyal under their strong leadership. Cobra Commander removed Destro from power and, with no room for "traitors and cowards," ordered Major Bludd and all Coil agents to Cobra Island with their arrival timed to coincide with a U.S. nuclear strike on Cobra Island. All Coil agents and the infrastructure on Cobra Island were destroyed. Overlord, Doctor Mindbender, and Serpentor were also all assassinated.

The Coil High Command Players

Clone Children—Julius, Alexander, Genghis, Ivan, Attila, Vlad, Phillip, Napoleon, and Thomas, named for one of the DNA sources used to create Serpentor, are the clones of Serpentor who, unlike Hannibal and Serpentor himself, were not given growth hormones. Each is highly intelligent and seems to share a common mind with Serpentor and Hannibal.

Doctor Mindbender—The creator of Serpentor, he and Hannibal sought out Serpentor and joined The Coil. Doctor Mindbender's tenure with the organization was brief as he was taken prisoner by Cobra following their acquisition of Cobra Island. He managed to get himself back in with the Dreadnoks and eventually Cobra before Cobra Commander shot him.

Firefly—Following Cobra's collapse in the early 1990s, he began working with Mikhail in recruiting former Cobra assets to The Coil. Although one of the longest tenured members of The Coil, he ended up deserting during the Cobra Island battle.

Hannibal—One of the first clones from the process that made Serpentor, he aided Doctor Mindbender in gathering some of the Serpentor child clones. Initially placed in a foster home with Juggler agents as parents, he killed them and then disappeared. Following the Cobra Island battle, Hannibal and the other children were all taken into custody. He demonstrated astonishing reflexes and fighting skills in his brief battle with Snake Eyes.

Overkill or Robert Skelton—A former SAW Viper, Skelton is infamous for slaughtering helpless G.I. Joe agents at Trucial Abysmia. Serpentor sent multiple Coil agents to recruit Skelton and eventually succeeded in bringing him into the fold. Skelton then took on the name Overkill and, during the Cobra Island battle, nearly killed G.I. Joe Commander General Hawk but was injured by Kamakura. In the aftermath, Skelton followed Cobra Commander to an escape sub and begged for power before passing out from blood loss. Skelton was turned over to Cobra scientists and made into a cyborg.

Overlord or Mikhail Derenko—Former Spetsnaz commander and Special Ops Hammer Team member, he spent years gathering former Cobra agents under the alias Nowhere Man on behalf of Serpentor. As the general of The Coil, had he not taken employ with the Jugglers he would likely have succeeded Serpentor as the leader. He was killed when caught in the destruction of G.I. Joe's Iceland facility.

Serpentor—Serpentor was the Supreme Leader of The Coil, and following his death/capture at Cobra Island, his position was vacated. Serpentor was kept in suspended animation and brainwashed for later use by the Jugglers but was likely killed when Red Shadow agents, led by Juggler mole Mars Harring, gained access to the secret facility they were keeping him in and broke his chamber.

Zandar—Brother of Dreadnok leader Zartan, he joined The Coil for power and respect, feeling unappreciated by the Dreadnoks. Zandar joined the newly reformed Cobra as a spy for The Coil and was able to successfully kidnap Cobra Commander. During the Cobra Island battle, Zandar attacked his brother but was nearly killed when Zartan gained the upper hand. Zartan called off his Dreadnok forces and took his brother for medical treatment. He avoided punishment by service to Cobra.

Colonel Slash

Real Name: Unknown
Gender: Male
Service Branch: Investigator
Faction(s): Cobra, freelancer
Stationed: Only in the shadiest area of Enterprise City

Appearance: Brown trench coat, gray slacks, black shoes, black fedora, dark glasses, pencil mustache; heavyset
Abilities: Investigator
Conditions: Distinctive Feature: Scar on his right cheek
Notes: Slash does Cobra's dirty work. It is never made clear if Slash is a member of Cobra or simply a hired gun.

Copperhead

Series: Three (1984)
Alias/Variations: High Tide*; Python Copperhead
Real Name: CLASSIFIED (James McCoy)
Place of Birth: Florida
Gender: Male
Service Branch: Cobra Army
Faction(s): Cobra, Python Patrol (Commander)
Stationed: The Coffin prison facility, Greenland (escaped)
Notably Served At: Amsterdam; Cobra Island; East African Coast; Gulf of Mexico; Japan; London, England; Monaco
Primary MOS: Air-Driver swamp vehicle operator
Secondary MOS: Seaborne demolitions
Appearance: Blue-green helmet, vest, and pants; light green trim on helmet and pants; light-green armbands and gloves; black holsters, belt, and boots. 1989: yellow and black helmet; yellow-green shirt and pants with a yellow crisscross pattern; black vest, gloves, holster, and boots; red vest holster; yellow waist piece. Comics revealed he had red hair.
Other Known Appearances: Early production runs of Copperhead had blue-green gloves and armbands, with no helmet trim
Accessories: Included with the Cobra Water Moccasin vehicle. 1989: Backpack, M-16/203
Abilities: Combat Skills; Fighter pilot; Gifted mechanic; Knowledge Skill: Amazon River basin; Knowledge Skill: Florida Everglades; Knowledge Skill: High-speed naval assault vehicles; Knowledge Skill: Seaborne demolitions; Professional Skill: Boat mechanic; Professional Skill: Nautical security chief for Cobra Island; Professional Skill: Speedboat racer; Professional Skill: Swamp buggy pilot; Qualified Operator: Air-Driver Swamp Vehicle, Water Moccasin, Swamp Cruiser, Swamp and Jungle Fighter; Sabotage; Wilderness Survival: Swamps
Conditions: Belief: Live hard and fast; Distinctive

Feature: Florida accent; In and out of gambling debts; Rumor: Past dealings with the Dreadnoks; Single father; Weakness for gambling

Quote/Motto: "Sure. I know the type. They're all around the Gulf Coast. Trash. Drifters. They can drive a swamp buggy like the devil himself, rebuild a V-8 with a coat hanger and spit, fight all night and raise Cain 'til the cock crows. They got a heart fulla gimme and a mouth full o' much obliged...." Quote given by Gung Ho.

Notes: *Under the direction of President Freedlowe, Copperhead joined the Phoenix Guard in the guise of a Navy SEAL code-named High Tide (real name Edward T. Johnson), born in New York City. High Tide's specialties were Navy SEAL, underwater demolition, and nautical operations. He attended U.S. Navy Boot Camp at the Naval Station in Great Lakes, Illinois. He also completed basic underwater demolition and SEAL training at the U.S. Naval Special Warfare Center in Coronado, California, and attended U.S. Army Airborne School at Fort Benning. He became known to General Rey for his cruel sense of humor.

In the IDW continuity, IDW's Copperhead was killed when a G.I. Joe team raided his home after Crimson Twin Tomax (who had defected from Cobra to work for G.I. Joe) gave up his location in hopes that by arresting him, they could then turn him informant. He was killed in front of his teenage son Scotty, who then angrily resisted Flint's attempt to get him to give up any information. Later, Scotty is recruited by Baroness; it is implied he will assume his father's alter ego within Cobra.

He was held in the maximum security prison called The Coffin, located in Greenland, and was one of several operatives who escaped during a raid led by Tomax.

Crimson Guard

Series: Four (1985)
Alias/Variations: Crimson Guard Force; Crimson Guard Immortals (armored division); Crimson Shadow Guard, Crimson Guard Force; Red Guard; Siegies (say *Cee-gees*)
Real Name: Various
Place of Birth: Various
Gender: Male
Grade/Rank: Officers
SN: Various
Service Branch: Crimson Guard is led by Tomax and Xamot
Faction(s): Cobra, Python Patrol subgroup
Primary MOS: Undercover espionage/elite shock troop
Secondary MOS: Accounting
Appearance: 1985: Red dress uniform with silver campaign ribbons and patches, and a red helmet with a black mask that covered his entire face. 1989: Yellow and gray as part of the special Python Patrol subgroup. 2005: Black and gold
Accessories: AK-48 with bayonet, dress backpack
Abilities: Contacts: Business professionals; Deep cover agent; Degree in either accounting or law; Expert fighters; Knowledge Skill: Business; Knowledge Skill: Political circles; Knowledge Skill: Politics; Political Contacts; Political Influence; Professional Skill: Business; Professional Skill: Bodyguards; Qualified Experts: Tube rocket launchers and squad automatic weapon; Rigorously trained; Sleeper agent; Top physical condition
Conditions: Loyal to Cobra Commander; Present a façade of civic responsibility and normalcy; Reputation: The elite of Cobra; Reputation: Cobra Commander's bodyguards
Notes: Crimson Guard (Cobra's version of internal affairs) is the name of the most elite soldiers of Cobra's Viper legions. It is unknown if they were supposed to be a commissioned officer-level unit of Crimson Guardsmen. Crimson Guard are under the command of Tomax and Xamot. Each member operates in secret in political arenas and the business world. Some even come with prefabricated families, giving them further legitimacy.

To prove their loyalty, many members of the "Siegies" become part of a series, the most famous being the Fred Series. These Crimson Guardsmen undergo plastic surgery to look like one another, allowing a member to completely replace another member should the need arise.

Crispo Paine

Place of Birth: Unknown
Gender: Male
Grade/Rank: Torturer
Faction(s): Cobra, the Baroness's torturer
Notably Served At: Cobra Consultant Building, New York City
Primary MOS: Interrogation expert

Secondary MOS: Torturer
Appearance: Black heather hood, black leather short shorts, black leather wrist bands, and boots; carries a gigantic fireman's ax; goggles
Abilities: Hand-to-hand combat expert with ax; Incredibly muscular physique; Interrogation expert; Strong; Torturer
Conditions: All brawn, no brains; Deranged; Distinctive Feature: Leather daddy; Distinctive Feature: Uses burning hot coals and irons to torture his victims
Notes: Crispo and his brothers, DeSade and Torquemada, were believed to have been killed by Snake Eyes as he escaped capture. When the Joe team raided what turned out to be a Cobra medical facility, one of the bedridden patients under medical care was DeSade, along with his brothers. The military is investigating each patient's status and why they were placed in that facility.

Croc Master

Series: Six (1987)
Real Name: Unknown
Gender: Male
Grade/Rank: Cobra Island security
Faction(s): Cobra
Stationed: Cobra Island
Primary MOS: Cobra Island security
Appearance: Wears a scaled vest and boots and a face mask that resembles an alligator's face; black face mask with red eyeholes and silver mouthpiece; left wristbands; belt with croc's-eye buckle; scaled holster
Accessories: Alligator; chain leash; king cobra snakes; net; oxygen tank; pistol; short, spiked leash; shotgun; snake cage; whip
Abilities: Animal Companion: alligator; Professional Skill: Burglar alarm salesman; Professional Skill: Former alligator wrestler; Professional Skill: Guard-Gators Inc.; Professional Skill: Reptile trainer; Professional Skill: Trains alligators for home security
Conditions: Amoral; Brutal; Distinctive Feature: Right upper arm has bite scar; Reluctance to submit to authority; Reluctance to take orders
Quote/Motto: "Croc Master spends his leisure hours dozing in a tub of tepid bathwater with only his nose breaking the surface. He dreams strange, green dreams while grinding his teeth and clenching his powerful jaws. He has a hunger that never leaves him...."
Notes: He referred to his fast, hostile, man-eating, and psychotic crocodiles as "his girls" and gave them female names including Chelsea, Lolita, Melissa, Tara, and Tiffany. Croc Master was buried alive in a landlocked freighter under a volcano on Cobra Island by Cobra Commander; he died of food poisoning.

Crusher

Series: Twenty (2004)
Real Name: Roberto K. Rivera
Place of Birth: Kissimmee, Florida
Gender: Male
Faction(s): Dreadnoks
Primary MOS: Wrestling
Secondary MOS: Poaching
Appearance: Spotted leopard-skin vest, animal teeth necklace, jeans, boots, black belt
Accessories: Boar, hat, knife, machete, quiver of arrows
Abilities: Knowledge Skill: Bows; Knowledge Skill: Knives; Poacher; Professional Skill: Professional alligator wrestler; Professional Skill: Professional wrestler; Wrestling
Conditions: Flaunts his animal skins and illegal trophies; Hatred of authority; Short temper; Suspected of killing Gnawgahyde; Unscrupulous behavior; Wanted by: Every environmental agency in existence
Quote/Motto: "Once the Crusher gets his hands on you, there is no escape from the pain!"

Crystal Ball

Series: Six (1987)
Alias/Variations: The Gazer; Mesmeron; Prof. Id, Trance-Master; Dr. Scott Stevens, therapist to General Philip Rey
Real Name: Unknown
Place of Birth: Unknown (native of Cobra-La)
Gender: Male
Faction(s): Cobra
Primary MOS: Cobra's Inquisitor General
Secondary MOS: Master of psychological tactics
Appearance: Black mustache and hair with white locks; red eyes; a brown short-sleeved shirt with fur collar and gold bat design on chest; brown wristbands; dark gray pants with brown belt and holster; black boots
Accessories: Hypno-shield with a multi-colored reflective surface and arm clip
Abilities: Disguise; Hypnotist; Interrogation; Knowledge Skill: European mysticism; Knowledge Skill: Human psychology; Manipulation; Mind reading; Professional Skill:

Encyclopedia salesman; Professional Skill: Theatrical hypnotist; Professional Skill: Therapist; Projects long-range illusions (in the novel *Divide and Conquer*); Telepathy (in the novel *Divide and Conquer*)
Conditions: Disquieting presence; Reputation: Seventh son of a seventh son; Insane behaviors; Son: Max; Reputation: Can read minds; Reputation: Deceased; Sadistic manipulator
Quote/Motto: "When Crystal is around, ya don't have to just watch what you're saying, you have to watch what you're thinking."
Notes: He claims his talents come from the power of the occult.

Darklon

Series: Eight (1989)
Real Name: Unknown
Place of Birth: Unknown, presumed Darklonia
Gender: Male
Faction(s): Cobra, Iron Grenadiers
Stationed: His cast-iron castle in the Alps
Notably Served At: Sao Cristobel
Primary MOS: Darklonia Ruler
Secondary MOS: Mercenary business
Appearance: Black helmet over green facemask; a green shirt with black stripes; black right glove, left wristband; dark red pants with black stripes; light brown boots with knife and braids
Accessories: Futuristic laser rifle with a hose attaching to devices under grip; pistol, two rifles, web gear
Abilities: Assault vehicle operator; Professional Skill: Investment banking; Professional Skill: Mercenary; Professional Skill: Privateering; Private armies; Professional Skill: Test drives prototype vehicles; Ruler of Darklonia
Conditions: Abrasive personality; Affinity for odd uniforms; Distinctive Feature: Wears a steel mask of his family's design; Greedy; Related to the Destro Clan; Sarcastic; Unhindered by ideology or ethics; Works for the highest bidder
Quote/Motto: "Get in my way and I'll squash you like a gnat on my windscreen!" "Completely unhindered by ideology or ethics, Darklon is motivated purely by greed. His telephone solicitors have been known to drum up business for his mercenary army by offering 'reasonable hourly rates' and cash rebates!"

Decimator

Series: Nine (1990)
Alias/Variations: Panhead
Real Name: Unknown
Place of Birth: Unknown
Gender: Male
Faction(s): Cobra
Notably Served At: Cobra Island
Primary MOS: Heavy machine operator
Appearance: Yellow face mask; dark gray double-breasted jacket, gloves with armbands, belt; dark green pants with light gray and green boots
Accessories: Flat trident-harpoon pistol, helmet with eye slot, spear gun
Abilities: Heightened peripheral vision; Heightened hand-eye coordination; Heightened reflexes; Knack for technology; Qualified Operator: Hammerhead
Conditions: Distinctive Feature: Special helmet
Quote/Motto: "The wide-angle, image-intensifier unit built into the helmet offers him a 180° view in almost complete darkness. The image he sees is compressed in the same manner used for wide-screen movie titles when they are shown on TV. In essence, he can keep the target in front of him at all times and get a clear shot at it without even turning his head. This is extremely advantageous when fighting a speeding vehicle on a flat beach!"
Notes: It is often asked if the character of Decimator is a type of Cobra trooper or a specific character. This is because of the lack of any additional fiction depicting the character. The 25th issue of *G.I. Joe: America's Elite* included a backup feature that presented a threat matrix. It seemed to indicate Decimator was meant to be a unique character.

His helmet provides heightened night vision and a 180° view that enables him to keep a target in continuous view without having to turn his head.

Dela Eden

Alias/Variations: Lilith; Mistress of Death
Real Name: Dela Eden
Place of Birth: Atebubu, Ghana
Gender: Female
Grade/Rank: Staff Sergeant E-6
Faction(s): Red Shadows
Primary MOS: Covert ops
Secondary MOS: Military intelligence
Appearance: Bald, African American woman,

large hoop earrings, white fur coat, red metal bustier

Background Information: Trained at Ghana Military Academy

Abilities: Bribery; Covert agent; Covert ops; Drug trafficking; Escape artist; Espionage; Hand-to-hand combat expert; Expert marksman; Knots; Lock picking; Master of several styles of martial arts; Military intelligence; Qualified Weapon Expert: M16 Rifle, MP5SD Submachine gun, Type 56 Rifle; Right hand of Wilder Vaughn; Small arms expert; Smuggling

Conditions: Dishonorable discharge from Ghanaian military; Follower of Wilder Vaughn; Hates Cobra; Hates G.I. Joe; Reputation: Killed Lady Jayne; Reputation: Shot Cobra Commander; Romantically linked to Wilder Vaughn; Wanted for various crimes worldwide

Quote/Motto: "She's one of the most dangerous people in the world. Wanted in at least a dozen countries for a variety of crimes—assault, battery, bribery, drug trafficking, fraud, murder, wildlife smuggling—she has little in the way of scruples or temper. You simply do not turn your back on her, ever, for a second, even if she has been knocked unconscious and hogtied and locked in a cage. She is going to stab you in the back and you will not see it coming."

Notes: Cobra Commander is the only person she shot who did not die; this haunts her.

Demolishor

Series: Twenty (2004)
Real Name: Sukko Torngark
Place of Birth: Pikangikum, Ontario, Canada
Gender: Male
Faction(s): Dreadnok
Appearance: Large, muscular, bald; green vest with large gold buttons, thick gloves, jeans. He wears a patch over his right eye.
Accessories: Rifle, shotgun
Abilities: Demolitions; Nomadic hunter; Resists pain; Wilderness Survival: Frozen north
Conditions: Frightening appearance; Easily bored; Hates the frozen north; Prone to depression; Many scars; Needs to vent frustrations; Seeks new adventures
Quote/Motto: "Tell me when it's supposed to hurt."

DeSade Paine

Place of Birth: Unknown
Gender: Male
Grade/Rank: Torturer
Faction(s): Cobra, the Baroness's torturer
Notably Served At: Cobra Consultant Building, New York City, New York
Primary MOS: Interrogation expert
Appearance: Spiky brown mullet hair; complete leather bodysuit; metal arm bracers; longsword
Abilities: Skilled torturer
Notes: DeSade and his brothers, Crispo and Torquemada, were believed to have been killed by Snake Eyes as he escaped capture. When the Joe team raided what turned out to be a Cobra medical facility, one of the bedridden patients under medical care was DeSade, along with his brothers. The military is investigating each patient's status and why they were placed in that facility.

Destro

Series: Two (1983)
Alias/Variations: Fuera de la Ley (Argentina), Red Jackal (Europe); The Specialist, Warmaster (original name of the character)
Real Name: (UNKNOWN) James McCullen Destro, James McCullen XXIV; James McCullen Destro XXIV
Place of Birth: UNKNOWN (Callander, Scotland)
Gender: Male
Faction(s): Cobra, Iron Grenadiers, M.A.R.S., and Star Brigade
Stationed: Family castle in Scotland; the Cobra Citadel in Trans-Carpathia; nuclear submarine *Cataclysm*, his mobile base of operations; oil supertanker called the *Valkyrie*
Notably Served At: The Alaskan pipeline; Borigia-Krazny/Marango; Cobra Island; the Everglades; Millville; the High Sierras; the Pit under Fort Wadsworth, Staten Island, New York; Sierra Gordo; the town of Springfield; Trans-Carpathia, Darklonia; Washington, D.C.; Wolkekuk-Uckland
Primary MOS: Weapons manufacturer
Secondary MOS: Terrorist
Appearance: Silver mask covering entire head; black jacket with open, red-rimmed collar; yellow undershirt with red Cobra pendant; silver and red wrist rockets; black gloves, boots, and pants with red holster. 1988: Gold mask; black shirt and gloves with a red undershirt and cloth cape; black pants with a gold belt; black hook on the waist for a sword.

1992: Silver mask; a yellow shirt with red medallion; black jacket with a large red hood, shoulder armor, and gloves; black pants with a red belt; black boots. 1993 Star Brigade: silver helmet; dark red armor suit with gray on the right upper arm and lower legs; black armor on shoulders; black left missile launcher arm

Other Known Appearances (Cartoon): Same but with a more pronounced red collar; gloves were entirely silver with (usually) no wrist rockets

Accessories: 1983: Armed attaché case (with molded tools and weapons on the interior); high-density laser gun; 1988: Saber with a short chain and decorative tip; 1992: Machine gun (new, laser-powered XL-14), disc launcher, two discs; 1993 Star Brigade: Clear, tinted dome helmet; laser pistol; submachine gun; laser rifle; knife; two missiles

Background Information: Prototype file card claims he believes in two things: "War and family tradition.... For nearly a thousand years, his family has been warriors and arms makers.... [Destro] is able to maintain apartments and office buildings in most major cities of the world. His luxurious lifestyle more than matches that of the most famous oil sheiks or flamboyant shipping magnates ... He is one of the very few holders of the American Express Platinum Card.... He believes in the spoils of war and the vast wealth M.A.R.S. provides is just that to him. War is his business and passion. Where war exists, M.A.R.S will provide high-tech arms to any side able to meet the price. Where war does not exist [Destro] will strike to start one."

Abilities: Blackmail; Cool under pressure; Field commander; Friendship: Billy; Friendship: Flint; Friendship: Lady Jaye; Friendship: Zartan; Has a spy in Cobra (Metal-Head); Intelligent; Laird of Castle Destro, the Scottish Highlands; Luxurious lifestyle; Military advisor; Multi-billionaire; Possesses bionic enhancements (direct to video movie); Private army: The Iron Grenadiers; Professional Skill: Businessman; Qualified Operator: CLAW, FANG, Firebat, H.I.S.S., Rattler, Stinger, Trubble Bubble, Viper Glider, the A.W.E. Striker, Dragonfly, SkyStriker, VTOL transport plane, plasma cannon tank; Tactics; Torture; Vast resources; Weapons supplier; Well-read in military strategy

Conditions: Abhors G.I. Joe for wasting their skills to maintain peace; Contacts: The worst elements of society; Dedicated to seeing G.I. Joe undermined, subverted, or destroyed; Disdain for Cobra Commander (cartoon); Distinctive Feature: Silver battle mask forged from beryllium steel (a family tradition); Illegitimate son, Alexander; Intolerance for incompetence and inefficiency; Philosophy: The fittest survive and the greatest technological advances are made; Philosophy: War is man's most natural state; Romantically paired with the Baroness; Sense of honor; Speaks his mind (cartoon); Undying love for the Baroness; Unyielding; Wavering loyalties; Will incite war where it does not exist; Will not condone patricide

Notes: The head and current incarnation of M.A.R.S. (Military Armaments Research System), the largest manufacturer of state-of-the-art weaponry

Dice

Series: Eleven (1992)
Alias/Variations: Cobra Dice
Real Name: Unknown
Place of Birth: Unknown
Gender: Male
Faction(s): Cobra
Notably Served At: Cobra Island; Destro's castle in Trans-Carpathia; Millville
Primary MOS: Ninja commando
Secondary MOS: Protective services
Appearance: 1992: Purple and black mask; purple vest with black straps; black right armband; black and purple wristbands; purple pants with black boots and kneepads; padded, combat knee protectors; traditional Dice clan face mask; arm brace
Accessories: Ax, bo staff
Abilities: Battleax expert; Bo staff expert; Close-quarters combat expert; Contact: Dr. Biggles-Jones; Dirty fighting: Eye-gouging, pressure points, and chokeholds; Delayed blast smoke bomb expert; Fast fling throwing star expert; Heightened speed; Heightened strength; Professional Skill: Bodyguard; Qualified Weapons Expert: Blunt instruments; Physically large; Snares and traps
Conditions: Former brainwashed slave of Red Ninja Master (Firefly); Loyal bodyguard to the Cobra hierarchy; Rumor: Kicked out of the Night Creepers for being *too* evil; Sadistic; Unpredictable when cornered; Will do anything for self-preservation

Quote/Motto: "I'm a back-breaker, face-stomper, and bone-breaker! Don't mess with me, or I'll mess you up!" "Man or woman, Ninja or neophyte, my 'Flying Dragon' will be your demise!"
Notes: His most dreaded technique is an attack he calls the "Flying Dragon."

Doctor Biggles-Jones

Series: Thirty-three (2017)
Alias/Variations: Dr. Sid, Doc Sid
Real Name: Dr. Sidney Biggles-Jones
Place of Birth: Ridgewood, New Jersey
Gender: Female
Service Branch: Double agent sent by some unknown force to infiltrate and undermine Cobra (likely the United States Department of Defense)
Faction(s): Cobra
Notably Served At: Amalgamated Super-Conductor Corporation in New Jersey
Primary MOS: Physics
Secondary MOS: Hypervelocity weapons research
Appearance: Nearly floor-length brown hair she keeps in a ponytail, knee-high boots, tights, and a stunning, contour-hugging one-piece under her open, flowing lab coat
Accessories: White lab coat, rifle
Background Information: PhD in Physics from MIT, a second PhD in Electrical Engineering from CalTech; she published multiple breakthrough articles in hypervelocity propulsion technology
Abilities: Hand-to-hand armed combat; Gifted scientist; Head of the "Rail Gun Project"; Peak physical condition; Physics; Scientist; Trash talk
Conditions: Brave; Confident; Belief: Science can level all playing fields; Cares about the welfare of others; Dedication to technology; Follows an agenda set in place by her employers; Reputation: Leading scientist in her field; Self-sacrificing; Young
Quote/Motto: "Okay, I'll join Cobra, and I'll trade in my skirt for a leotard, but I get to keep my lab coat, all right?" "Wait until you see my new and improved weapon!"
Notes: She designed the Generation 2 Megatron's shoulder-mounted electromagnetic railgun. In the alternate Transformer Joe universe continuity, Dr. Biggles-Jones is a prisoner in the Coffin prison. Later during a Cobra raid on the facility, Tomax was able to eliminate those Cobras considered loose ends. Her name appeared on the list of those terminated.

Doctor Cassandra Knox

Real Name: Cassandra Knox
Place of Birth: Unknown (Boston, Massachusetts)
Gender: Female
Service Branch: Civilian
Faction(s): Cobra, M.A.R.S.
Notably Served At: Salt Lake City; Siberia
Primary MOS: Robotics
Appearance: Beautiful and curvaceous; blonde hair, blue eyes
Background Information: Attended MIT at the age of 16
Abilities: Heightened intelligence; Professional Skill: Head of M.A.R.S. Research & Development division; Develops artificial intelligence (AI) programs; Robotics engineer; Scientist; Works with AI-organic combinations
Conditions: Belief: People are jealous of her; Belief: She deserves opportunities; Enraged when frustrated; Desires wealth; Extremely ambitious; Reputation: Child prodigy; Seldom taken seriously: Beautiful and young; When furious will attack with her bare hands
Notes: She developed a highly advanced prototype of Battle Android Trooper that could target specific individuals using their brain-wave patterns.

Doctor Mindbender

Series: Five (1986)
Alias/Variations: Dr. Mindbender; The Interrogator, Dr. Brainwave, Dr. Brain-Wave, Professor Paine, Count Vlad the Cruel; prototype name was Dr. ?
Real Name: Brian Binder
Place of Birth: Eastern Europe
Gender: Male
SN: 4712—MB
Faction(s): Cobra
Primary MOS: Mind control
Secondary MOS: Experimental systems
Appearance: Bald, black belt, black gloves, black mustache, black thigh holster, purple pants, purple wristbands, shirtless, silver codpiece, silver leather metal-studded suspenders, silver monocle; 1993: Bald, black belt and boots, black headset, black mustache, purple short-sleeved shirt with yellow straps and

wristbands, yellow pants with purple stripes on legs

Other Known Appearances (Cartoon): Dark purplish-gray cape attached to chest straps with red Cobra insignia

Accessories: Black cloth cape with silver Cobra emblem, black generator, black hose, gray electric prod, light gray .45-caliber pistol; 1993: Knife, laser pistol, laser rifle, spring-loaded missile launcher, submachine gun

Abilities: Cloning expert; Cybernetic expert; Genetics expert; Heightened intelligence; Interrogator; Methodical; Persistent; Professional Skill: Bill collector for a mail-order record club; Professional Skill: IRS investigator; Professional Skill: Orthodontist; Professional Skill: Professional wrestler; Qualified Operator: Night Raven, Stun, and Trubble Bubble; Scientist

Conditions: Arrogant; Distinctive Feature: German accent; Easily shocked; Loyal member of Cobra's High Command; Medical quack; Merciless; Prone to comical calamities; Rumors: Once kind and honest

Quote/Motto: "Doctor Mindbender doesn't think he's deluded—he feels he used to be. Now that he has seen the light, or the dark if you will, he feels it is his mission to bring the miracle of thought control to each and every one of you!" "Hrmph! This Doctor Mindbender thinks more highly of himself than Major Bludd does!" Quote given by Cobra Commander.

Notes: Doctor Mindbender was buried alive in a landlocked freighter under a volcano on Cobra Island by Cobra Commander; he died of food poisoning. Later, Cobra Commander re-created him as a clone with most, if not all, of the memories of the original. Eventually, Cobra Commander shot and murdered the clone. Doctor Mindbender was the inventor of the Battle Android Troopers (BATs) and perfected the Brainwave Scanner. He created the composite-clone Serpentor, germinated "creeper bombs" (incredibly fast-growing vines that grew pods that could burst open and release sleeping gas), the surgically enhanced Cobra pilot known as the Star-Viper, and a weapon of mass destruction called the Tempest.

Doctor Venom

Series: Twenty-six (2010)
Real Name: Dr. Archibald Monev
Place of Birth: Brooklyn, New York
Gender: Male
Service Branch: Cobra Scientist
Faction(s): Cobra
Notably Served At: Sierra Gordo; the town of Springfield
Primary MOS: Mind control research
Secondary MOS: Botany
Appearance: Brown hair with spit curl falling onto forehead; white lab coat; pale blue dress shirt with a black necktie; blue pants; black shoes
Accessories: Man-eating plant, two large handguns, two test tubes
Abilities: Accomplished pilot; Brilliant scientist; Biological manipulation; Mind control; Private lab on Brooklyn's waterfront; Private lab in a remote jungle area
Conditions: Belief: His devices are unbeatable; Blacklisted as a scientist by the U.S. government; Dishonorable coward; Evil tendencies; Heightened ego; Overestimates himself; Rumor: Once a brilliant scientist; Shunned by the scientific community; Underestimates his opponent; Will not have his genius stifled!
Quote/Motto: "Cross my path and I'll poison your body and mind!"
Notes: He created the Brain-wave Scanner, a device that, through a painful process, allowed Venom to peer into the mind of his subjects and pull out images and information. After Doctor Venom shot the mercenary Kwinn the Eskimo in the back, killing him, the lifeless Kwinn let go of a grenade he was holding; the explosion killed Venom. He was eventually buried in a potter's field, his body claimed by no one.

Dreadnoks

Purpose: They began as a violent biker gang; terrorizing innocent people, destroying property, and committing the occasional felony seemed to be their only goal. A reprehensible group of mercenaries, vandals, and thieves who worked for Cobra over the years, the Dreadnoks specialize in violence and destruction and have no regard for anyone or anything but themselves and fast money. Their diet consists of little more than chocolate-covered donuts and grape soda.
Leader: Zartan
Members: Billy-Bob, Burn Out, Buzzer, Chop Shop, Cletus, Crusher, Demolishor, Gnawgahyde, Heart-Wrencher, Joe-Bob, Machete,

Monkeywrench, Otis, Ripper, Road Pig, Roscoe, Rugrat, Thrasher, Torch, Vance, Zandar, Zanya, Zanzibar, Zarana, plus nameless others to fill out a global Motorcycle Club

Eels

Series: Four (1985)
Alias/Variations: Cobra D'Agua (Brazil 1987); Cobra Hombre-Rana (Argentina)
Real Name: CLASSIFIED (various)
Place of Birth: Various Countries
Gender: Male
Grade/Rank: E-4
Service Branch: Cobra Navy
Faction(s): Cobra, Battle Corps
Stationed: Marine outposts worldwide
Primary MOS: Frogman/underwater demolitions expert
Secondary MOS: Marine engineering
Appearance: 1985: Black and gray diving shirt with red chest and silver Cobra insignia; black gloves, belt, and knife; gray diving pants, gray helmet. Sometimes the knife was painted on the figure. 1992: Neon yellow helmet with red visor; blue shirt with neon yellow chest armor and arm fins; blue pants with yellow belt and leg fins; blue boots. 1993: Neon yellow helmet with red visor; purple shirt with neon yellow chest armor and arm fins; purple pants with yellow belt and leg fins; purple boots.
Accessories: 1985: Air hose, air tank, flippers, jetpack, JLS double harpoon with stunner. 1992: Black figure stand; bright yellow missile and trident gun; silver shark-shaped missile launcher with removable fin, tail, and jaw; two silver flippers. 1993: Neon spring-loaded missile launcher with red trigger, neon yellow flippers, red flamethrower, red machine gun, red rifle, red submachine gun, red-figure stand, two red missiles
Abilities: Disguise; Knowledge Skill: Cobra navy vessels; Knowledge Skill: Offshore drilling rigs; Knowledge Skill: Waters of the Caribbean; Knowledge Skill: Waters of the Cayman Islands; Knowledge Skill: Waters of the North Atlantic; Operate Cobra marine outposts; Professional Skill: Diver; Professional Skill: Marine geology; Professional Skill: Marine structural engineering; Professional Skill: Underwater demolitions; Underwater combat

Escorpiao Voador

Series: Eleven (1994)
Alias/Variations: ("Flying Scorpion")
Place of Birth: Brazil
Gender: Male
Faction(s): Cobra, Patrulha Do Ar ("Sky Patrol")
Appearance: Dark skin, orange shirt, gray pants, black boots, silver harness
Accessories: Backpack, handgun, helmet, parachute, rifle

Extensive Enterprises

Purpose: Cobra's public international corporate front involved in commerce and finance, Extensive Enterprises is involved in legitimate businesses, such as manufacturing Garbage O's breakfast cereal. Run by Tomax and Xamot, it also provides a cover for their many illegal operations. Extensive Enterprises corporate headquarters is located in Enterprise City.
Leader: Tomax and Xamot
Members: Presumably, The Crimson Guard in their civilian identities

Firefly

Series: Three (1984)
Alias/Variations: Faceless Master; Snake-Eater; Michel LeClerc; George Winston; Helmut Knopf; Jason B. Lee; Monkey-Wrench; Sapper; The Firefly
Real Name: Unknown
Place of Birth: France
Gender: Male
Grade/Rank: Cobra: Phoenix Guard
Faction(s): Cobra, G.I. Joe, and Sound Attack
Stationed: The Coffin, maximum security prison in Greenland
Notably Served At: Afghanistan; Antarctica; Appalachian Mountains; Baltic Sea; Chicago; Cobra Island; Florida Everglades; Golden Gate Bridge; Japan; the Rock; town of Green Ridge; town of Springfield; Tokyo
Primary MOS: Sabotage, demolitions, and terror
Secondary MOS: Ninja
Appearance: African American; ski mask and BDU fatigues, urban or gray camouflage. 1984: Light and dark gray camouflage face mask, shirt, pants, and belt; dark gray gloves and boots; black or brown eyes and eyebrows
Accessories: Demolition backpack, submachine gun, walkie-talkie
Background Information: From childhood, trained by the Koga Ninja Clan, who owed his father a favor. His prototype dossier reads:

"The Firefly served in the French Foreign Legion Paras as Michel LeClerc; in Biafra [the briefly existing secessionist state in southeastern Nigeria] as Helmut Knopf; in Nicaragua as George Winston."
Abilities: Cartography; Contacts: High-profile underworld individuals; Counterintelligence; Escape; Fire-based weapons; Highly skilled combatant; Infiltration skills; Mercenary; Ninja master; Qualified Operator: Motorcycles; Qualified Weapons Expert: All NATO and Warsaw Pact explosives and detonators; Ranger, Saboteur
Conditions: Disfiguring burns all across his body (re-imagination); Mildly enraged when referred to by his code name; Native Frenchman; Paranoid about concealing his identity; Pyromaniacal arsonist (re-imagination); Reputation: globally renowned for infiltration skills; Sister (unnamed); Tag: Always places explosive charges for maximum damage
Quote/Motto: "I came, I saw, I blew it up!" "Even Cobra Commander doesn't know much about Firefly. His fees are paid into a numbered Swiss bank account and are always payable in advance. He makes no guarantees and gives no refunds."
Notes: As a merc, his fees are paid into a numbered Swiss bank account and are always paid in advance. He makes no guarantees and gives no refunds. In Cobra, he worked well with Black Out and Munitia as H.I.S.S. (Hierarchy of Infiltration, Stealth, and Sabotage). He was held in the maximum security prison called The Coffin, located in Greenland, and was one of several operatives who escaped during a raid led by Tomax.

Flak-Viper

Series: Eleven (1992)
Real Name: Various
Place of Birth: Various
Gender: Various
Service Branch: Cobra Army
Faction(s): Cobra
Primary MOS: Cobra anti-aircraft trooper
Secondary MOS: Infantry
Appearance: Neon blue helmet with black visor; green shirt with neon blue sleeves and green gloves; gray half-vest with neon blue shoulder anchor; neon blue pants with gray leggings and black boots
Accessories: Backpack/missile launcher (spring-loaded, actually fired), laser rifle with a bayonet, two missiles with squared-off fins
Abilities: Ability to concentrate simultaneously on two or more targets in their range of sight; Cobra anti-aircraft trooper; Exceptional natural hand-eye coordination; Infantry; Knowledge Skill: Portable artillery weapons
Conditions: Dedicated; Motivated; Practice every day; They get a kick roaming the battlefield in the Cobra parasite while "picking off" incoming enemy aircraft
Quote/Motto: "We could positively max-out our high score if only we had Turbo-Joystick Controllers!"
Notes: They have a passive, infrared targeting and sighting system built into their helmets that allows them to be extremely accurate aiming their Tail-Biter missiles at G.I. Joe aircraft.

Shane R. Nostaw is the only named individual in the Flak-Vipers; he hails from the United Kingdom.

Flak-Viper Nostaw

Series: Twenty-two (2006)
Real Name: Shane R. Nostaw
Place of Birth: United Kingdom
Gender: Male
Service Branch: Cobra Army
Faction(s): Cobra
Primary MOS: Cobra anti-aircraft trooper
Secondary MOS: Artillery coordinator
Appearance: Black helmet with visor; brown shirt, black gloves; brown pants, black boots
Accessories: Backpack, rifle, two missiles
Abilities: Ability to concentrate simultaneously on two or more targets in their range of sight; Cobra anti-aircraft trooper; Exceptional natural hand-eye coordination; Family owns a bus company; Infantry; Knowledge Skill: Portable artillery weapons; Unparalleled hit ratio
Conditions: Dedicated; Hates being helpless; Motivated; Practice every day; Gets a kick roaming the battlefield in the Cobra Parasite while "picking off" incoming enemy aircraft
Quote/Motto: "My thumbs never get tired—show up in my sights and it's GAME OVER!"

Fred I

Alias/Variations: Fred 1, Smith
Real Name: Fred Broca
Place of Birth: Unknown
Gender: Male

Grade/Rank: General of the Guard
Service Branch: Crimson Guardsman
Faction(s): Cobra
Stationed: Staten Island, New York, just outside the gates of Fort Wadsworth, army base (The Pit)
Notably Served At: High Sierras
Primary MOS: Elite trooper; espionage
Secondary MOS: Accounting
Appearance: Blond hair, brown eyes
Abilities: Accounting; Degree in international business; Degree in law; Elite trooper; Espionage; Infiltrates a society; Professional Skill: Vice president of Extensive Enterprises; Small arms; Special forces training; Well-connected politically; Willpower
Conditions: Rumor: Likely the original Fred; Rumor: Plastic surgery made Fred look like Cobra Commander in his youth; U.S. military training; Vengeful
Notes: Virtually nothing is known of Fred I's past. It is unknown if the other Freds were patterned after him, or if he, too, underwent plastic surgery to have a new face. Fred, his wife, and two children—Shaun (a.k.a. Sean) and Heather—were the first undercover Crimson Guard family, living like average suburban Americans. Fred I was shot while on a mission in the High Sierras where he eventually bled out. He was buried beneath a waterfall with a headstone reading, "Here lies Fred. Whatever he did in life, he died well." Not long thereafter, Fred II (a Vietnam veteran named Wade Collins and an old friend of Snake Eyes, Stalker, and Storm Shadow) returned "home" to the Broca family.

Fred II

Alias/Variations: Fred Broca; Fred 2
Real Name: Wade Collins
Gender: Male
Service Branch: U.S. Army; Cobra Army; Crimson Guard
Faction(s): Cobra, Crimson Guard
Notably Served At: Springfield; Vietnam
Background Information: Graduated from Ranger school
Abilities: Contact: Stalker; Contact: Storm Shadow; Espionage; Fred Clone; Infantry; Long-range recon patrol (LRRP); Master's degree in law; Sabotage; Wilderness Survival: Jungle
Conditions: Bitter; Disillusioned; Divorced (first wife); Defected from Cobra; Devastated by second wife's death; Double agent for G.I. Joe; Easily swayed by Cobra's propaganda; Loves his Cobra family: wife (deceased) and three children Sean (Kamakura), Heather, and Marina; Nightmares; Reputation: One of the first Crimson Guard; Spent three years as a Vietnam prisoner of war
Notes: He died in his "son's" arms after a firefight.

Fred VII

Alias/Variations: Cobra Commander, Fred 7
Real Name: Unknown
Place of Birth: Unknown
Gender: Male
Grade/Rank: Commander in Chief
Faction(s): Cobra
Stationed: Denver, Colorado
Notably Served At: Gulf of Mexico, Cobra Island
Primary MOS: Intelligence
Secondary MOS: Ordnance (experiential weaponry)
Appearance: Blond hair, brown eyes; Impersonated Cobra Commander in a battle armor suit
Accessories: Backpack, belt with thigh holster, breather hose for the helmet, helmet, pistol
Abilities: Command; Contact: Raptor; Elite trooper; Espionage; Followers: Cobra supporters; Impersonation; Inspire; Inventor: High-tech battle armor; Inventor: Pogo assault pod; Knowledge Skill: Cobra Commander; Knowledge Skill: Cobra; Mechanical engineering genius; Professional Skill: Auto mechanic (his cover occupation); Resist interrogation; Robotics genius; Secret laboratory in the back of his business, Fred's Garage, in Denver, Colorado
Conditions: Ambitious; Baroness knows his secret; Devoted to Cobra; Emotionless relationship with Baroness; Inability to make a decision; Inept leader; Lacks knowledge of Cobra operations; Occasionally paralyzed with fear; Overestimates himself; Pawn of the Baroness; Tactician: Bold but ill-conceived plans; Watched by Serpentor
Quote/Motto: "Funny thing about this helmet…. Could be anybody inside…." "If Cobra Commander taught me anything, it's to seize an opportunity when it presents."
Notes: Fred was asked by Cobra Commander to construct a new prosthetic leg for his comatose son, Billy. Fred VII was buried alive in a landlocked freighter under a volcano on

Cobra Island by Cobra Commander; he died of food poisoning.

Fred LXV

Alias/Variations: Fred 65
Gender: Male
Service Branch: Crimson Guard
Faction(s): Cobra
Notably Served At: Broca Beach
Appearance: The same face as every other Fred
Conditions: Son addicted to drugs
Notes: Fred LXV was shot and killed by the Headman's Headhunters when confronting them for selling his son drugs. His wife was killed when she tried to avenge her husband's death; their son, Fred Junior (Sean), moved to the next town over and tried to trade his mother's rifle for more drugs.

Fred Series

Alias/Variations: Fred Broca
Real Name: Various
Place of Birth: Various
Gender: Male
Faction(s): Cobra
Primary MOS: Undercover espionage
Secondary MOS: Accounting
Abilities: Crimson Guard abilities; Rigorously trained
Conditions: In addition to Crimson Guard conditions: Behavior modification; Inducted in a secret ceremony; Looks and acts like every other Fred; Swore absolute loyalty to Cobra and Cobra Commander; Underwent plastic surgery
Notes: Each Fred is assigned a wife, a son (Sean), and a daughter (Heather).

Gallows

Series: Twenty-two (2006)
Alias/Variations: Guillotine
Real Name: Unknown
Place of Birth: Unknown
Gender: Male
Service Branch: Cobra Army
Faction(s): Cobra, Cobra Saw Viper, and The Plague
Stationed: Cobra headquarters
Notably Served At: The Amazon; Antarctica; the Appalachian Mountains; Lincoln, Nebraska; Malta; Manhattan, New York City; Philadelphia, Pennsylvania
Primary MOS: Machine gunner

Appearance: Black, cable-knit sweater and a black version of his previous division's helmet
Accessories: Knife, mini-gun, mini-gun strap
Abilities: Machine gunner; Marksman's accuracy; Plague trooper; Rapid reload
Quote/Motto: "Gallows sees himself as the judge, jury, and hangman. If he comes to a battlefield near you, expect heavy fire with a marksman's accuracy combined with remarkable speed and ability."
Notes: During the Scorched Earth campaign, Bayonet, Body Bags, Gallows, Guillotine, Infrared, Vanguard, and Velocity are stationed in Antarctica to guard and launch a nuclear bomb. Bayonet and the other members of The Plague were presumably captured or killed during a battle in the Appalachian Mountains.

General Mayhem

Series: Twenty-one (2005)
Real Name: Vladimir P. Mayhemovski
Place of Birth: Kirovograd, Ukraine
Gender: Male
Grade/Rank: General
Faction(s): Cobra, Iron Grenadiers
Primary MOS: Infantry commander
Secondary MOS: Counter intelligence
Appearance: Gray hair, mustache, mutton chops, military uniform
Accessories: Pistol, rocket launcher
Abilities: Contact: Destro; Deep reconnaissance; Followers: Devoted cadre of soldiers and officers; Contacts: Personnel in Russian Army; Former Spetsnaz general; General of the Iron Grenadiers; Heightened efficiency; Interrogation; Military brilliance
Conditions: Arrogant; Assumes the blame or the credit; Belief: Utter destruction of the weak; Cruel; Distinctive Feature: Blitzkrieg-style attacks; Eliminates alleged enemies; Mad Genius; Unafraid of making unpopular decisions; Relentlessly pursued by the Oktober Guard; Rumor: General Iron Bear and General Mayhem are the same (untrue); Ruthless; Vicious; Wanted for war crimes
Quote/Motto: "Friend, foe, or innocent bystander, anyone foolish enough to get in our way will be crushed beneath my boot heels!"
Notes: His arrogance inevitably leads to his downfall.

Ghost Bear

Series: Twenty (2004)

Real Name: Jesse Kwinn Jr.
Place of Birth: Chukchi Peninsula, Eastern Siberia; an Inuit village on the Russian side of the Bering Strait
Gender: Male
Faction(s): Cobra
Primary MOS: Mercenary
Secondary MOS: All-terrain vehicle operator
Appearance: Orange hair sprouting from gray ski mask and red-tinted goggles; gray shirt and pants with black gloves, chest strap, belt, and boots; red pads on gloves and boots, and red Cobra emblem on the right side
Accessories: Knife with smooth hilt and blade; round belt
Abilities: Expert long-range rifleman; Hunting; Qualified Operator: Pulverizer; Qualified Weapon Expert: Pistola knives; Tracking; Wilderness Survival: Artic
Conditions: Grudge against G.I. Joe; Grudge against Snake Eyes; Never learned his father switched sides and became a Joe; Son of tracker Kwinn
Quote/Motto: "When I'm driving a Pulverizer, I become the Pulverizer, and can make it do anything I want."
Notes: He was the son of late Cobra mercenary.

Gnawgahyde

Series: Twenty-seven (2011)
Alias/Variations: "Gnaw" Hyde
Real Name: Clyde Hyde
Place of Birth: Unknown
Gender: Male
Faction(s): Dreadnoks
Notably Served At: Cobra Island
Primary MOS: Poacher
Appearance: Bald with brown mustache; yellow open vest with black spots; black half-glove on the left hand; black right wristband; blue pants with a green belt; black boots with green knife sheath
Accessories: Clyde the boar; jacket; knife serrated on one side with razor edge on other; machete with a notch in tip and clip for wrist; quiver backpack; rifle; safari hat; sniper rifle with scope and a tall, detachable bipod
Abilities: Ambush; Animal Companion: Warthog Clyde; Cardsharp; Knife fighting; Knowledge Skill: Hunting rifles; Knowledge Skill: Survival knives; Knowledge Skill: Traps and snares; Murderous presence; Shooting; Trapping; Wilderness Survival: Forests; Wilderness Survival: Jungles
Conditions: Belligerent; Belief: Clyde is the only animal deserving of life; Belief: The artifice of civilization is a sign of weakness; Belief: Live off the land; Cheats at cards; "Goes native" when hunting; Hates cosmetics; Hates deodorants; Obnoxious; Other poachers can't stand him; Refuses to eat processed food; Smells bad; Will not wear synthetic fibers

Golobulus

Series: Six (1987)
Place of Birth: Cobra-La, Himalayas
Gender: Male
Grade/Rank: The original founder of the Cobra Organization and the ruler of Cobra-La, he is the "last of the Serpent Kings"
Faction(s): Cobra, Cobra-La
Primary MOS: Cobra-La supreme ruler
Secondary MOS: Biotechnology
Appearance: A human-snake hybrid, he has replaced just about every part of his body many times except for his nervous system and brain.
Other Known Appearances (Cartoon): Large, humanoid being with a bald head and a strange Cobra-La organism covering his right eye. His upper body is covered with scaly skin, much like the chitinous shell covering insects. His lower body is that of a large snake.
Accessories: Bio-gun
Abilities: Knowledge Skill: Sacrifice ceremonies; Knowledge Skill: Magic; Immortal (centuries or millions of years old); Spell Caster: Summoned the dark god Unicron
Conditions: Belief: Survive at all costs; Hatred of technology; Hatred of humanity; Rants and rages; Utterly despises *Homo sapiens*; Will let nothing get in the way of his goals
Notes: He created the Cobra Emperor, Serpentor. Golobulus perished in an avalanche in the Arctic in the animation; in the comics, he was crushed beneath the fist of Optimus Prime.

Gregor

Real Name: Unknown
Gender: Male
Faction(s): Cobra
Appearance: Brown hair; posed as a camera crewman for an unnamed man in a blue suit (presumably a fellow Cobra operative) posing

as a news reporter during a press conference
Accessories: Machine gun disguised as camera equipment
Abilities: Disguise; Small arms expert
Conditions: Enemy of G.I. Joe
Quote/Motto: "Yes, Baroness."
Notes: The Baroness ordered Gregor to cover her escape with Dr. Adele Burkhart; they left out a window and climbed into a hot air balloon.

Grim Skull

Series: Twenty-two (2006)
Real Name: Unknown
Place of Birth: Unknown, possibly Egypt
Gender: Male
Grade/Rank: E-4, special operative
Service Branch: Sand Viper; Cobra special operations
Faction(s): Cobra, The Plague
Stationed: Cobra headquarters
Notably Served At: The Amazon; Antarctica; the Appalachian Mountains; Lincoln, Nebraska; Malta; Manhattan, New York City; Philadelphia, Pennsylvania
Primary MOS: Desert operations
Secondary MOS: Retrieval
Appearance: Black, cable-knit sweater and a black version of his previous division's helmet
Accessories: Desert-equipped rifle, Uzi
Abilities: Elite Sand Viper
Conditions: Will sacrifice his men to get a promotion
Notes: During the Scorched Earth campaign, Black Out, Grim Skull, Incision (Aleph), Interrogator, Munitia, and Vector are stationed in Antarctica to guard and launch a nuclear bomb. Grim Skull and the other members of The Plague were presumably captured or killed during a battle in the Appalachian Mountains.

Gristle

Series: Twelve (1993)
Alias/Variations: Brutus Vandalo; Vandalo (Brazil)
Real Name: Danimal J. Rogers
Place of Birth: Montego Bay, Jamaica
Gender: Male
Faction(s): Cobra
Primary MOS: Urban crime commander
Secondary MOS: Logistics
Appearance: Long brown hair with loose locks; black sunglasses; a dark red shirt with a black vest and neon yellow collar and zipper; dark red knives on chest; black gloves with neon yellow wristbands; neon yellow and black pants with dark red holster and boots
Other Known Appearances (Cartoon): Headhunter's outfit without the helmet; his jacket is sleeveless, but he wears a long-sleeved red shirt underneath. He had yellow hair and did not wear sunglasses.
Accessories: Knife; machine gun; spring-loaded rectangular missile launcher with inside bar handle and trigger; two missiles with squared-off fins and notched cylindrical tips; XL-14 submachine gun
Abilities: Big and bad!; Followers: private army of vicious, highly trained guards; Gritty street thug; Instruction; Professional Skill: Operates illegal warehouses disguised as legitimate comedy clubs; Professional Skill: Corrupt crime boss; Professional Skill: Right-hand man to some major crime lords; Street fighting; Resilient; Respected and feared in the underworld
Conditions: Bad hair; Confessed to feeling "crazy" when pursued by G.I. Joe; Corrupt; Distinctive Feature: Bloodshot eyes; Distinctive Feature: Sunglasses; Distinctive Feature: Exceedingly large head; Eyes highly sensitive to light; Personal hygiene is disgusting; Professional Skill: Crime boss; Rumor: Relocated to South America
Quote/Motto: "I go crazy when those G.I. Joes come after me, they just keep chasing, and chasing, and chasing...." "Don't waste your time ... you'll never get your hands on me!"
Notes: Somehow he masterminded the exponential growth of the newly motivated Headhunters into a powerful worldwide crime organization by working as international smugglers for Cobra. They specialized in goods deemed dangerous or questionable.

Guillotine

Series: Twenty-two (2006)
Gender: Male
Grade/Rank: Plague Trooper Commander
Service Branch: Cobra Eel
Faction(s): Cobra, The Plague (Leader)
Stationed: Cobra Headquarters
Notably Served At: The Amazon; Antarctica; the Appalachian Mountains; Lincoln, Nebraska; Malta; Manhattan, New York City; Philadelphia, Pennsylvania
Appearance: Bald, light brown mustache and

soul patch; a black, cable-knit sweater and a black version of his previous division's helmet
Accessories: Backpack, helmet (with permanent hoses attached to the bottom), rifle, sword
Abilities: Aquatic training; Breaks the will of others; Designed The Plague's training program; Former Navy SEAL; Jungle training; Leadership
Conditions: Belief: U.S. Navy SEALs are not ruthless enough; Defected to Cobra; Ruthless; Truly sinister
Quote/Motto: "I don't give quotes, I break bones."
Notes: Guillotine was personally selected by Cobra Commander to lead the elite Plague Troopers; he then selected the unit's members. During the Scorched Earth campaign, Bayonet, Body Bags, Gallows, Guillotine, Infrared, Vanguard, and Velocity are stationed in Antarctica to guard and launch a nuclear bomb. Bayonet and the other members of The Plague were presumably captured or killed during a battle in the Appalachian Mountains.

Hannibal

Series: Twenty-two (2006)
Alias/Variations: Hannibal Reborn; named after Hannibal Barca
Place of Birth: Secret lab of Doctor Mindbender
Gender: Male
Grade/Rank: General
Faction(s): Cobra
Stationed: Cobra Island
Primary MOS: Warrior
Secondary MOS: Conqueror
Appearance: Long black hair, black eyes, black T-shirt with a skull on it; long black leather trench, dark gray pants, black boots
Accessories: Base, helmet with clear dome, jacket, stand, sword
Abilities: Brilliant tactician; Professional Skill: General; Psychic connection to his clone brothers
Conditions: Aged to be a teenager; Belief: The end always justifies the means; Killed his foster parents; Raised by agents pretending to be his parents; Willing to sacrifice his men to win a battle; Wants to achieve the goal he set centuries ago: Liberate and Conquer; Watched by the Jugglers
Quote/Motto: "With my help, Cobra Commander will rule the world—and I will rule it beside him."
Notes: He was one of 10 clones created by Doctor Mindbender alongside Serpentor; he is a clone of—or was named after (sources conflict)—Hannibal, the Carthaginian general who fought Rome in the Second Punic War. He was aged at a faster rate than the others, so he was a teen while they were younger as he was intended to be an emergency backup clone of Serpentor.

Headhunters

Series: Twelve (1993)
Alias/Variations: Brutus (Brazil)
Purpose: To deal drugs and steal weapon designs. Cobra recruited these highly trained guards from the greediest, most ruthless criminal organizations in the world! They offered them a big-money stake in Cobra's global operation and a chance to live out their meanest fantasies in return for absolute loyalty and obedience. Headhunters are driven workaholics with evil ambitions. They are willing to undergo constant and rigorous training in advanced weapon systems and fighting styles to further their careers in the Cobra's highly illegal—and ruthless—business ventures.
Leader: The Headman
Members: Highly trained, greedy, ruthless guards recruited from the most ruthless criminal organizations. In addition to utilizing Headhunter B.A.T.s (Headhunter Battle Android Troopers) Headman also employs Headhunter Elite Urban Crime Guards, Headhunter Guardians, Headhunter Vehicle Operators, and Headman's Narcotic Guard.
Accessories: Backpack; shotgun; spring-loaded missile launcher and missile
Quote/Motto: "If anyone so much as looks at us the wrong way, we'll just have to adjust that person's vision by knocking his lights out … literally!"
Notes: They wore black helmets with gold faceplates; a light blue shirt; a black jacket with neon green spiked shoulder pads and gloves; black pants with neon green holsters and boots. There is strict discipline and a respected chain of command. Headman recruits the greediest and most ruthless drug dealers. He pays big money but demands absolute loyalty and obedience. Headhunters are driven workaholics with evil ambitions. They must maintain the constant rigors of training and keep up with weapon developments. Headhunters also earn a financial stake in Headman's global drug empire.

Headman

Series: Eleven (1992)
Real Name: Unknown
Place of Birth: Unknown
Gender: Male
Grade/Rank: Leader of Headhunters
Faction(s): Headhunters
Primary MOS: Drug kingpin
Secondary MOS: Illegal narcotics
Appearance: Wide-brimmed fedora, wrap-around purple sunglasses, trench coat; pencil mustache, goatee; black hat and mask; yellow hair with a ponytail and black goatee; white shirt; black jacket with gold stripes; black pants and shoes; wears outrageously tacky but insanely expensive suits made of the finest materials by top fashion personalities and labels
Accessories: Backpack; electronic battle-flash rocket launcher (spring-loaded, actually fired); missile with fins near the tip; short, rectangular rifle with small stock, grip, and trigger guard; shotgun; transparent spring-loaded missile launcher with an attached bipod
Abilities: Leadership; Former right-hand man to Major Bludd; Intimidation; Knowledge Skill: Operating a global drug empire; Manufacturing plant; Professional Skill: Operating a global drug empire; Professional Skill: Drug kingpin; Secret base in the desert; Wealthy
Conditions: Feared; Demands absolute loyalty and obedience; Paramilitary mindset; Reputation: Steals weapon plans; Reputation: Collects priceless art treasures; Reputation: Decapitates his foes
Quote/Motto: "If anyone so much as looks at Head Man 'the wrong way,' we'll just have to adjust that person's vision by knocking his lights out ... literally."
Notes: He was executed by Tomax during a raid on G.I. Joe prison facility the Coffin, a high-security G.I. Joe operated prison in the country of Greenland.

Heart-Wrencher

Real Name: Unknown
Gender: Female
Faction(s): Dreadnoks
Notably Served At: Cobra Island; Los Angeles, California
Primary MOS: Mechanic
Appearance: Blue-black pixie-cut hair
Abilities: Mechanic
Preferred Weapon: Wrench
Conditions: Mysterious past
Notes: Heart-Wrencher is the first female Dreadnok who is not a relative of Zartan.

Heat Viper (High Explosive Anti-Tank) Viper

Series: Eight (1989)
Real Name: Various
Service Branch: Cobra Army
Faction(s): Cobra
Primary MOS: Anti-tank trooper
Secondary MOS: Earthquake operator
Appearance: Black helmet with face half-shield; black shirt with gold stripes on chest; black backpack straps and belt; gold gloves; black pants and sleeves with a red crisscross pattern, silver kneepads; black and gold boots; blades on ankles to hold missiles. Version 2: Helmet; a neon green shirt with black diagonal strap and gloves; neon green pants with black waist piece, holster, and boots
Accessories: Bazooka, backpack, hose, six bazooka shells; Version 2: Three guns, missile launcher (spring-loaded, actually fired), two missiles
Abilities: Knowledge Skill: Hyper-kinetic, high-speed, wire-guided, armor-piercing technology; Nerves of steel; Qualified Operator: Earthquake; Specialist: Anti-tank
Conditions: Distinctive Feature: Firing stance is left foot forward; Not the most skilled soldiers
Quote/Motto: "We don't just fire at anything; we fire at everything!" "You gotta hand it to these guys. It takes a lot of nerve to squeeze off a hand-held rocket at 60 tons of rolling G.I. Joe armor and sit still while holding the tracker sights on target to guide in the projectile. If he misses with the first shot, there isn't a G.I. Joe worth his salt who'll let that poor fool try for seconds! A proverbial world of hurt is gonna hit Cobra like a ton of bricks."
Notes: Cobra soldiers may not share the skill of one G.I. Joe specialist, but they compensate by incorporating stealth technology to supplement their function on the battlefield. Their harness-supported launch tube has active heat vents and an infrared suppressor to cut down detection hazards. The sighting system is fiber-optically linked to the operator's helmet, which contains range-finders, trajectory computers, and image intensifiers. This

allows the Cobra H.E.A.T. Viper troops to fire their weapons from behind cover under adverse visibility conditions. The rocket launcher has heat suppression technology allowing them to escape infrared detection.

Heavy Water Trooper

Series: Nineteen (2003), G.I. Joe Collector's Club Exclusive
Alias/Variations: The "leaky suit brigade"
Real Name: Various
Place of Birth: Various
Service Branch: Army
Faction(s): Cobra
Primary MOS: Radiological weapons specialists
Secondary MOS: Toxic trooper
Appearance: Blue full-head helmet; orange goggles; blue belt and boots; black bodysuit with light green chest, shoulders, wrists, thighs, and shins
Other Known Appearances: Version 2 glowed in the dark; it had a red visor and a gray belt. Chest, shoulders, wrists, thighs, and shins glowed in the dark.
Accessories: Belt with a clear hose, black backpack with green hoses, black SCUBA tank, black speargun, glow-in-the-dark stand; The hoses plugged into the figure.
Background Information: Their "suits are composed of lead foil and ultra-dense composites in multiple laminations, with self-contained cooling systems that also serve to theoretically wash away dangerous accumulations of radioactive materials."
Abilities: Infiltration Experts: Government facilities; Knowledge Skill: Leaking reactors; Knowledge Skill: Unstable munitions stockpiles; Knowledge Skill: Renegade and outlaw states; Power plant repair technician; Secret weapon lab repair technician; Specialists: Radiological weapons
Conditions: Cobra troopers avoid them; Distinctive Feature: They slosh when they walk; Distinctive Feature: They sound like they are gargling when they speak; Distinctive Feature: Unique radioactive glow; Reputation: Most feared division of the Toxo-Viper troopers
Quote/Motto: "By the time you see us, it's already too late…." "Radiation is our friend. Carelessness with shielding is our enemy." The sign over their locker room.
Notes: Version 2 glows in the dark; there was a limited production run of 3,500.

H.I.S.S.

Alias/Variations: Hierarchy of Infiltration, Stealth, and Sabotage
Purpose: Three highly skilled individuals found each other and work in perfect synchronicity together due to their single-minded passion for devastation and darkness.
Members: Black Out, Firefly, and Munitia

Hotwire

Series: Twenty-four (2008)
Real Name: Unknown
Place of Birth: Lauingen, Bavaria, Germany
Gender: Male
Service Branch: Cobra scientist
Faction(s): Cobra
Stationed: Lab in Southeast Asia
Primary MOS: Battler android maintenance and repair
Secondary MOS: Biomechanical engineer
Appearance: Slicked back brown hair; white lab coat with red Cobra logos; blue pants; black belt, gloves, and boots
Accessories: Blowtorch, grenade launcher, white coat
Background Information: Expelled from M.I.T. for biomechanical experiments on non-consenting humans
Abilities: B.A.T. Mechanic; B.A.T. Maintenance and repair; Biomechanical engineer; Brilliant; Scientist; Conducts experiments on poorly performing Cobra troops; Helps develop next-gen Cobra weapons; Secret lab in Southeast Asia
Conditions: Deranged mind; Doctor Mindbender's lackey; Eccentric; Family tradition of mad scientists; Oblivious to his insanity; Paranoid; Maniacal smile; Works without the hindrance of morality
Quote/Motto: "Doctor Mindbender wants to make B.A.T.S. finally recognize friend from foe—but what's the fun in that?"
Notes: He is a descendant of Dr. Victor Frankenstein.

Incision

Alias/Variations: Aleph
Real Name: Unknown
Place of Birth: Unknown
Gender: Male
Faction(s): Cobra, The Plague
Stationed: Cobra headquarters
Notably Served At: The Amazon; Antarctica; the

Appalachian Mountains; Lincoln, Nebraska; Malta; Manhattan, New York City; Philadelphia, Pennsylvania
Primary MOS: Assassin
Secondary MOS: Leadership
Appearance: Black, cable-knit sweater and a black version of his previous division's helmet
Abilities: Former leader of the Night Creepers; Highly skilled assassin; Highly skilled hand-to-hand combatant; Silent weapons expert; Skilled with a crossbow
Preferred Weapon: Crossbow
Conditions: Arrogant; Greedy; Ongoing rivalry with Blackout
Notes: During the Scorched Earth campaign, Black Out, Grim Skull, Incision, Interrogator, Munitia, and Vector are stationed in Antarctica to guard and launch a nuclear bomb. Storm Shadow kills Incision in battle in the Amazon.

Inferno, S.K.A.R.

Series: Fourteen (1995)
Real Name: Kidwell Pyre
Gender: Male
SN: 19L23LKJ
Service Branch: S.K.A.R.
Faction(s): S.K.A.R.
Primary MOS: Sky Stalker squadron leader
Appearance: Bald, tight red shirt, black pants with silver stripes, red gloves, black boots, square monocle or aiming device
Accessories: Backpack attached to a flamethrower
Abilities: Access to newly invented vehicles and gadgets; Qualified Weapons Expert: Flamethrower
Conditions: Bullied by his brothers Fredwick and Miles; Desires love and attention from others; Dimwitted; Distinctive Feature: Talks with a hissing voice; Grew up the adopted son of a poor single mother (maid for the Grunbach family); Notorious joker who is not funny; Refers to flamethrowers as his "toys"
Notes: At one time, Inferno had a mind-altering device allowing him to control people while within proximity. He used this power to make people love (or, in the case of Iron Klaw, fear) him.

Infrared

Real Name: Unknown
Place of Birth: Unknown
Gender: Male
Service Branch: Cobra Army
Faction(s): Cobra, Cobra Crimson Guard Immortal, and The Plague
Stationed: Cobra headquarters
Notably Served At: the Amazon; Antarctica; the Appalachian Mountains; Lincoln, Nebraska; Malta; Manhattan, New York City; Philadelphia, Pennsylvania
Primary MOS: Intelligence
Secondary MOS: Infantry
Appearance: Black, cable-knit sweater, a black version of his previous division's helmet, and all black gear and armor trimmed in silver
Accessories: Backpack, bayonet, holster, pistol, rifle, saber, sheath, submachine gun
Abilities: Accounting; Battle ready; Bodyguard; Computer hacking; Dapper; Hitman; Heightened intelligence; Stealth; Undercover espionage
Conditions: Considers himself elegant and handsome; Likes to be well dressed (even in battle)
Quote/Motto: "The infrared wavelength isn't visible to the human eye, but it is there. Infrared is the same; you won't know he's around you until it is too late."
Notes: During the Scorched Earth campaign, Bayonet, Body Bags, Gallows, Guillotine, Infrared, Vanguard, and Velocity are stationed in Antarctica to guard and launch a nuclear bomb. Infrared and the other members of The Plague were presumably captured or killed during a battle in the Appalachian Mountains.

Interrogator

Series: Ten (1991)
Alias/Variations: Major Peters; Inquisitor, Probe, Third-Degree
Real Name: Unknown
Place of Birth: Unknown
Gender: Male
Grade/Rank: CLASSIFIED
Service Branch: Cobra Army
Faction(s): Cobra, The Plague
Stationed: Cobra Headquarters
Notably Served At: The Amazon; Antarctica; the Appalachian Mountains; downtown St. Louis, Missouri; Lincoln, Nebraska; Malta; Manhattan, New York City; Middle East; Philadelphia, Pennsylvania
Primary MOS: Interrogation
Secondary MOS: Helicopter pilot
Appearance: No one knows what he looks like;

A black, cable-knit sweater and a black version of his previous division's helmet; a black helmet with a red faceplate; a gray shirt with blue vest and black diagonal straps; black gloves; blue pants with red stripes; black holster and boots. 1991: Black helmet with red faceplate; gray shirt with blue vest and black diagonal straps; black gloves; blue pants with red stripes; black holster and boots
- *Accessories:* Rifle with a claw at the end; Version 3: Pistol, two knives
- *Abilities:* Baritone voice; Copter pilot; Disguise; High tech helmet (see below); Intimidating interrogation techniques; Kidnapper; Qualified Expert Operator: Battle Copter
- *Conditions:* Easily knocked out by punches to the face; Mysterious past; Rumor: Former head of security for a deposed Third World dictator; Rumor: Renegade clinical psychologist; Rumor: Former IRS investigator; Reputation: Intimidating interrogation techniques; Romantically linked with teammate Munitia
- *Quote/Motto:* "Of course, I could simply hurt them until they talk, but it's so much more amusing to twist their minds until all they want to do is tell me every single secret they know." "We think Interrogator has a voice modulator/synthesizer built into his helmet that works in conjunction with a trance-inducing LED display. His subjects listen to his soothing baritone voice, stare at the flashing lights, and before they know it, they're spilling secrets. We suspect that he also uses such sophisticated 'toys' as a stress analyst, a retinal dilation sensor, and other instruments that would add up to a reliable lie detector of sorts."
- *Notes:* During the Scorched Earth campaign, Black Out, Grim Skull, Incision (Aleph), Interrogator, Munitia, and Vector are stationed in Antarctica to guard and launch a nuclear bomb. Interrogator and the other members of The Plague were presumably captured or killed during a battle in the Appalachian Mountains.

Iron Grenadier Elite Trooper

Series: Twenty-four (2008)
Real Name: Various
Place of Birth: Various
Gender: Male and female
Service Branch: M.A.R.S. ground forces
Security Clearance: 9123-IG service
Faction(s): Iron Grenadiers heavy weapons support team
Stationed: Castle Destro
- *Accessories:* Ammo chain, bayonet rifle with folding stock, belt, bipod, depleted turnbinium ammo backpack, pistol, sash, scabbard, submachine gun, sword
- *Abilities:* Heightened endurance; Qualified Weapon Expert: Thermo-Reactive Anti-Armor Assault Cannon; Spread chaos among the enemy; Tenacious; Undermine the authority of the enemy
- *Preferred Weapon:* Thermo-reactive anti-armor assault cannon
- *Conditions:* Distinctive Feature: Mean

Iron Grenadiers

Series: Seven (1988)
Alias/Variations: Destro's Elite Troopers; the Grenadiers; the Hard Corps; the Nameless Legion, the Stainless Steel Brigade
Place of Birth: Various
Gender: Various
Service Branch: M.A.R.S. ground forces
- *Purpose:* Private army owned and maintained by Destro. The Grenadiers are composed of his castle guards, personal bodyguards, and mercenaries. The Grenadiers tend to be better motivated, especially in financial concerns as the elite officers each have a share in Destro's weapons sales.
- *Leader:* Destro; Voltar, acts as the field commander
- *Members:* Annihilators (elite troopers); Darklon (Destro's cousin and ruler of Darklonia); Ferrets (operators of the D.E.M.O.N. tanks); Iron Grenadiers (the basic infantryman had a uniform similar to the original Cobra troopers but with an all-black color scheme and full face mask); Metal-Head (anti-tank specialist); Nullifiers (pilots of the A.G.P. [Anti-Gravity Pod] flight vehicle); T.A.R.G.A.T.s (Trans-atmospheric rapid global assault troopers, soldiers trained for high-altitude combat); Undertows (Specialist: Underwater combat); Wild Boars (operator of the Razorback assault vehicle)
Stationed: Castle Destro
Primary MOS: Infantry
Secondary MOS: Terrorism
- *Appearance:* Black-crested helmet; red face mask; black jacket with gold strap, buttons, and left wristband; black gloves; black pants with red belt and kneepads; black and red boots

Accessories: Saber with long chain, submachine gun, sword, translucent laser pistol with a trapezoidal muzzle; Uzi with attached stock

Abilities: Highly trained commando; Mercenary; Qualified Weapons Expert: Small arms, explosives; Qualified Expert: Hand-to-hand combat; Sales and marketing; Terrorism

Conditions: History of turning on their superiors

Quote/Motto: "Imagine the slickest used car salesman you've ever met. Now imagine that he's also the trickiest accountant in the world. Got that? Try to picture what he would be like if that guy was also a highly trained commando with expertise in explosives, small arms, and hand-to-hand combat. Top it off with the fact that no other mercenary group in the world wants them because of their history of turning on their superiors. That's what an Iron Grenadier is…."

Iron Klaw

Series: One (1995); twenty-nine (2013)
Alias/Variations: Count Rani
Real Name: Count Otto Von Rani
Place of Birth: Kalistan
Gender: Male
Grade/Rank: S.K.A.R. leader
SN: H2JK30JQ
Faction(s): S.K.A.R.
Primary MOS: Dictator
Secondary MOS: Strategy and tactical warfare
Appearance: Black bodysuit, skull-like mask, silver piping and trim, black boots and gloves
Accessories: Bandoliers, beret, claws, missile launcher; missiles, sword, two pistols
Abilities: Acting; Contacts: Decepticons; Contacts: Consortium of villainous folk; Dictator; Leader of Eastern Europe's Kalistan; Leader of S.K.A.R. (Soldiers of Kaos, Anarchy, and Ruin); Leadership; Majority shareholder of I.R.O.N.; Paramilitary commander; Politician; Strategic mastermind
Conditions: Abuses power; Bad to the bone!; Costumed villainous sort; Fascination and respect for Genghis Khan; Lacks restraint; Motives are unclear; Nefarious; Plans to rule the world; Power-hungry; Pretends to be nice and benevolent; Rules by fear; Rumor: Assassinated the royal family of Kalistan
Quote/Motto: "I will watch as all others fail, and I will be victorious!"
Notes: A character in the Transformers Universe, it is unknown if he is an ally or adversary of Cobra.

Joe-Bob

Series: Twenty (2004)
Real Name: Winston P. Smith
Place of Birth: Auburn, Alabama
Gender: Male
Faction(s): Dreadnok recruit
Appearance: Purple mask, gray vest, green beard, gray pants, brown boots
Accessories: Rifle, shotgun
Abilities: Clever; Contacts: To keep him out of jail; Intrepid; Wealthy family
Conditions: Bully; Hates Beach Head; Sneaky; Starts fights with anyone for any reason
Quote/Motto: "Vengeance is best served when the other guy isn't looking."
Notes: Otis, Vance, Billy-Bob, Cletus, and Roscoe are his cousins. All six cousins are identical in appearance.

Juanita Hooper

Gender: Female
Grade/Rank: Major
Faction(s): Cobra
Appearance: Short brown bobbed hair, green army uniform, heavy build
Notes: This is an alias used by the Baroness. The purpose of this disguise was to infiltrate the Relay Star storage facility and plant a M.A.S.S. homing device on a satellite so Cobra could steal it giving them the ability to use the M.A.S.S device on any object, any place on Earth. It is unknown if a real Major Hooper exists.

Kwinn

Series: Twenty (2004)
Alias/Variations: Tracker Kwinn
Real Name: Jesse Kwinn
Place of Birth: Kotzebue, Alaska
Gender: Male
Faction(s): Mercenary
Notably Served At: The frozen north; Sierra Gordo
Primary MOS: Mercenary
Secondary MOS: Tracker
Appearance: An atypical Inuit male, he is uncommonly large in both height and girth (6'10", 260 pounds), though not musclebound. His skin tone was yellowish and his eyes dark brown. His coarse black hair was cut close to his scalp, and his eyes had slight folds. Kwinn dressed appropriately for the weather conditions. Normally, he wore a brown-yellow shirt, the same color shorts, and dark brown

boots. Around his neck, he always wore a necklace of weasel skulls.

Accessories: Ammo belt, backpack, belt, Browning .50-caliber machine gun with a tripod, Nitsiq spear, pick, revolver, rifle, shotgun, sled dog; submachine gun, three-piece bear trap, tripod, ulu, vest, weasel skull necklace

Abilities: Contact: C.I.A., Contact: Cobra; Contact: Destro; Contacts: KGB; Contact: MI6; Contacts: Mossad; Expert marksman; Hand-to-hand combatant; Heightened strength; Language Skill: Proficiency in eight languages (including English, French, Russian, Finnish, and German); Language Skill: Proficiency in three Inuit dialects; Mercenary; Qualified Weapons Expert: Belt-fed, air-cooled .30-caliber machine gun; Resists interrogation; Resists pain; Skilled hunter; Skilled survivalist; Skilled tracker

Conditions: Admires bravery and ingenuity; Always completes the job; Calm; Deeply spiritual; Deeply vengeful; Distinctive Feature: Belt-fed, air-cooled .50-caliber machine gun; Distinctive Feature: Weasel skull necklace; Encourages fair play; Makes overtures to spirit animals and totems; Never lies; Shows mercy if the contract allows; Stoic; Strict code of honor

Quote/Motto: "The man who whips a dog will pull his own sled someday...." "You're so lucky I'm a civilized man." "Spirit of the Otter, help me dive deep.... Spirit of the Bear, give me strength to open this door ... and Spirit of the Weasel, give me counsel to outwit this Dr. Venom!"

Notes: Ghost Bear is his son. Dr. Venom shot Kwinn in the back, killing him; however, the live grenade Kwinn was holding at the time fell and rolled toward Dr. Venom where it exploded, killing him.

Lamprey

Series: Four (1985); nineteen (2003)
Real Name: Various
Place of Birth: Various countries
Grade/Rank: E-4 (1985); O-3 or equivalent
Service Branch: Cobra Navy; specialize in underwater and sea environments
Faction(s): Cobra, Eel unit
Primary MOS: Hydrofoil pilot
Secondary MOS: Cobra Frogmen (Eels)
Appearance: Black shoes, silver jacket with light blue life jacket and gloves; silver mask with black raised visor and light blue faceplate; silver pants with light blue belts (1985). Blue belts, blue helmet with red faceplate, blue life jacket and gloves, bright orange jacket, bright orange pants, brown shoes (1991).

Accessories: Included with the Moray, gray rifle with strap; 1991: Black backpack with short antenna on top, black bayonet rifle, black laser gun, black sniper rifle, black submachine gun

Background Information: The training program takes place in warm, shark- and pirate-infested waters off tropical islands and in the dark, frigid depths of the Arctic Circle.

Abilities: Adept in all marine environments; Amphibious assault specialists; Elite Cobra naval troopers; First-class divers; First-class swimmers; Former Eel; Formidably equipped; Heightened reflexes; Hydrofoil pilots; Qualified Operators: Hydrofoils, all types of submarines; Top physical condition; Underwater demolition specialists

Conditions: Carefully chosen; Rigorously trained; Voracious determination

Quote/Motto: "G.I. Joe team—you better have that second cup of coffee to stay on your toes when the Cobra Lamprey troopers are around!" "Let's face it, a G.I. Joe submarine can usually outshoot and outmaneuver anything in the water. But if a squad of Lampreys uses its lasers to fuse the gun barrels and seal the torpedo hatches, that boat hasn't got a chance. It makes you wonder who's really got the advantage." "You always have to be at the top of your game in any nautical environment. Make one bad choice or stupid move, and you're fish food. The ocean takes no prisoners, and neither do we."

Notes: Their purpose is to protect and defend the criminal organization's coastal and underwater stations. The Lamprey are elite Cobra naval troopers; only the Moray are considered higher.

Laser Viper

Series: Nine (1990)
Real Name: Various
Place of Birth: Various
Service Branch: Special weapons development
Faction(s): Cobra
Primary MOS: Laser trooper
Secondary MOS: Infantry
Appearance: Black face mask, shirt, and pants,

all with a red crisscross pattern; gold chest armor, gloves, and belt pockets; black boots

Accessories: Backpack with swivel cannons and control arm; control arm (attaches to the backpack), face mask with visor; helmet with visor, two hoses, two laser guns (attaches to the backpack), two standard short black hoses

Abilities: Covert operations specialists; Hand-to-hand combat; Heat-generated weapons systems specialists; Infra-red laser weapon technology specialists; Knowledge Skill: Laser optics, Laser trooper; Master's degrees in mechanical engineering

Conditions: Underestimated; Highly competitive among each other

Quote/Motto: "If you're lucky enough to get close enough to peel off a shot at me, then you're close enough for me to make it overly hot for you." "Don't underestimate the Laser-Vipers. You might get the impression that all they do is shine flashlights and spot targets, but that's not the case. These guys can sit well outside the range of your weapons and drop a world of hurt down on your head within seconds! If you're lucky enough to sneak in close to get a shot at them, you're also close enough for them to make it overly hot for you!"

Notes: Laser weapons are only effective at short ranges because of the amount of energy lost through atmospheric dissipation. The primary function of a Cobra Laser Viper on the battlefield is "target illumination" for other Cobra Viper units. They shoot their beam on the target and then send a heat-seeking, anti-tank missile or guided bomb that follows the beam to the target.

Lt. Clayton W. Moore

Real Name: Clayton W. Moore
Place of Birth: Detroit, Michigan
Gender: Male
Grade/Rank: 0-2 (Equivalent)
Service Branch: Shock Viper commander
Faction(s): Cobra
Notably Served At: Rocky Mountains
Primary MOS: Heavy weapons
Secondary MOS: Anti-armor specialist
Appearance: African American; black hair; blue Shock Viper uniform with black bandoliers, gloves, and boots; wore a standard Cobra trooper outfit minus the face mask
Other Known Appearances (Cartoon): Appeared without shirt and helmet (as did Dusty) when fighting in an arena to settle their first dispute
Accessories: Helmet, missile launcher, missile, rifle; 2007: Helmet with logo, machine gun, cylindrical spring-loaded missile launcher with grip at the bottom, thick spring missile with fins on the tip
Abilities: Former gang member; Knowledge Skill: Tactical vulnerabilities; Heightened intelligence; Heightened strength; Natural leadership; Personal arsenal of anti-armor weapons; Shock Viper commander; Street smarts; Tough; Tenacious
Conditions: Jealous of Dusty; Rival to Dusty
Quote/Motto: "It doesn't take much finesse to rally my troops for global carnage."

Machete

Gender: Male
Faction(s): Dreadnok
Appearance: Black hair and soul patch; black bomber jacket, pants and boots; dark brown holster; green shirt
Abilities: Shooting
Conditions: Distinctive Feature: Shotgun with bayonet
Notes: Machete is a Dreadnok from the *Sigma 6* series; he is exclusive to the television series.

Madame Veil

Alias/Variations: Madame Vail
Real Name: Unknown
Place of Birth: Unknown
Gender: Female
Appearance: Old woman; short gray hair
Abilities: Contact: Cobra; Cosmetics tycoon; Facial transference machine; Fashion mogul
Conditions: Aging tycoon; Desperately desiring eternal youth; Vain
Notes: The facial transference machine, also known as the beauty transference device, drains away a young women's youth and beauty and transfers it to Madame Veil. Doctor Mindbender designed and sold it to Madame Veil through Extensive Enterprises. When the Joes destroyed the device, her face transformed to a hideously scarred and disfigured visage.

Major Bludd

Series: Two (1983); mail-in exclusive
Alias/Variations: Prototype name was Major Chill

Real Name: Sebastian Bludd
Place of Birth: Sydney, Australia
Gender: Male
Grade/Rank: O-4 (Major)
Faction(s): Cobra, Iron Grenadier
Notably Served At: Australia; Borovia; Cobra Island; Europe; Italy; Scotland; Sierra Gordo; Springfield; Turkey; Washington, D.C.
Primary MOS: Terrorist
Secondary MOS: Weapons and tactics
Appearance: Black helmet, eyepatch, and mustache; brown shirt and pants with green pads and stripes on legs; black vest, boots, and bionic right arm; dog tags on his chest
Accessories: Missile backpack, rocket launcher
Background Information: Trained in Australian Special Air Service; served in the French Foreign Legion
Abilities: Contact: Criminals; Contact: KGB Agent Colonel Nikita; Contact: Revolutionaries; Contact: Terrorists; Cybernetic right arm; Follower: Tomax; Follower: Xamot; Former Australian Special Air Service; Former French Foreign Legion; Hobby Skill: Writing poetry; Professional Skill: Arms dealer; Professional Skill: Assassin; Professional Skill: Blackmailer; Professional Skill: Hijacker; Professional Skill: Mercenary; Qualified Proficient: Every form of infantry weapon in current use; Qualified Weapons Expert: All NATO and Warsaw Pact small arms; Sky diving; Swimming; Tactics; Terrorist; Toughness
Conditions: Cobra Commander will not trust or hire him; Constantly submitting bad poetry to leading literary reviews; Distinctive Feature: Australian accent; Momentarily distracted when surprised in combat; Only loyalty is to money; Reputation: International soldier of fortune; Seeks revenge against General Rey (for cutting off his hand); Served time in Blackwater Prison; Served time in Fort Leavenworth (two years); Treacherous; War Criminal: Libya; War Criminal: Rhodesia; Will turn on his employers if he finds a better opportunity
Quote/Motto: A poem: "When you're feeling low and woozy | Slap a fresh clip in your Uzi! | Assume the proper firing stance | And make the suckers jump and dance! (from *The Attica Gazette*)." This was the only poem he ever had published; it appeared in a mimeographed quarterly called *The Attica Gazette*. Another poem he penned: "A mercenary's job is a heartless one | I'm a soldier for hire, like a pawn-shop gun | My ruthless tactics keep you on your toes | 'Cause I fight 'em all, whether friends or foes!" From his prototype dossier: "Subject received initial military training in the Australian Special Air Service and served with that unit in South East Asia. Later joined the French Foreign Legion seeing action in Algeria."

Mara

Real Name: Mara (surname unknown)
Place of Birth: An unnamed "hard luck" neighborhood
Gender: Female
Service Branch: Cobra Navy
Faction(s): Cobra, Eel
Appearance: Long black hair; blue skin
Background Information: Mara was one of the first tests of a Cobra experiment to integrate fish DNA into a human.
Abilities: Breathes water; Cobra Eel; Mermaid
Conditions: Former Cobra soldier; Distinctive Feature: Gills; Distinctive Feature: Blue skin; Cannot breathe air; In love with Shipwreck; Mermaid
Quote/Motto: "There are no friends in Cobra—only convenient alliances. They're all cannon fodder when it suits Cobra Commander. I learned that the hard way."

Metal-Head

Series: Nine (1990)
Alias/Variations: Heat-Round, Salvo, Squash-Head Harry, Tank-Buster, Tank-Zapper
Real Name: Stuart A. Finley
Place of Birth: Annapolis, Maryland
Gender: Male
Service Branch: Army
Faction(s): Cobra, Iron Grenadiers
Notably Served At: Cobra Island, the Battle of Benzheen
Primary MOS: Anti-tank specialist
Secondary MOS: Hockey fight analyst
Appearance: Black hair and goatee; red and yellow goggles; red shirt with black vest, armbands, and gloves; light gray straps and belt; black pants and boots with red padding, and light gray kneepads
Accessories: Helmet covering scalp and back of neck; small, H-shaped frame backpack with attached twin missile launcher with small radar dish; small pistol with tiny magazine and sight; two missile boxes attaching to legs; six stubby missiles; two standard short hoses

Abilities: Anti-tank specialist; Battle ready; Booby-trap battlefield tactics; Double agent (spying on Cobra Commander for Destro); Ordnance specialist; Professional Skill: Hockey fight analyst

Conditions: Adrenaline junkie; Dimwitted; Disquieting stare; Laughs with maniacal joy in combat; Maternal grandmother disappointed in him; Romantic interest in Susan Winters (his and Gridiron's high school sweetheart); Sanity in question; Thinks of nothing but battle; Unhinged

Quote/Motto: "The real targeting computer is upstairs in his brain, and it doesn't have an 'off' switch. This guy is so wrapped up with his work that even when he sits down for dinner he's preparing for battle. He tests his visual acquisition sensors by locking onto the mash potatoes as they are passed from one end of the table to the other. He calculates wind deflection by observing how the steam rises off the meatloaf. He even measures the diameter of the green peas, seeing them as micro-targets. If he looks you straight in the eye, you'll feel as if you have a bullseye on your forehead."

Notes: He is frequently partnered with the Dreadnok, Gnawgahyde. His voice-activated weapons command system is built into his blast suit. He makes visual contact with the target, lets the computer "read" the range and plot the trajectory, waits for the green light to flash, and then yells "bang" to complete the firing sequence. There is also a male Joe member with the name Metalhead as well as one named Salvo.

His beloved maternal grandmother is so disappointed in her grandson that when she learned the truth about his career, she went to G.I. Joe and told them everything she knew; she even became a reservist. She has an accent and wears a worn Russian uniform.

Mistress Armada

Alias/Variations: Candy
Real Name: Lillian Osborne
Gender: Female
Faction(s): Cobra, Iron Grenadiers
Primary MOS: Special air service
Appearance: African American, straight black hair, goggles, form-fitting body armor
Background Information: Former member of the British Army
Abilities: British Army Training; Contact: Alexander McCullen; Leadership; Weapons master; Special air service;
Conditions: Braggart; Openly flirts with Destro; Relentless flirt; Romantically linked with Laird Alexander Destro
Notes: Mistress Armada was shot and killed by Baroness.

Monkeywrench

Series: Five (1986)
Alias/Variations: Monkey Wrench; Prototype names were Blaster, Boom-Boom, Frag-Head, Hang-Fire
Real Name: Bill Winkie
Place of Birth: Rhyl, North Wales (prototype card read: Belfast, North Ireland)
Gender: Male
Faction(s): Dreadnok
Notably Served At: Australia; England; New Jersey; Sierra Gordo; Wales
Primary MOS: Explosives
Appearance: Red hair and beard; silver sunglasses; open red vest; grenades diagonally across chest; black gloves; blue jeans with a black belt, holster, and boots; dark blue patch on the right leg and red cloth tied around both legs
Other Known Appearances (Cartoon): Brown vest; thicker hair than on the figure
Accessories: Trident harpoon rifle
Background Information: Born on November 5, Guy Fawkes Day; his only records are "The 1812 Overture," "The Anvil Chorus," and "Wipeout"
Abilities: Contacts: Obscure terrorists; Demolitions expert; Explosives expert; Knowledge Skill: Explosive devices; Qualified Operator: Ferret, Swampfire
Conditions: Crude, anti-social behavior; Distinctive Feature: Cockney accent; Obsessed with explosives; Pariah in his hometown; Rude
Notes: Tomax was able to eliminate those Cobra considered loose ends and he was executed during a raid on a G.I. Joe prison facility. His death was the trigger that caused Zartan to defect from Cobra and aid the Joes during World War III.

Motor Viper

Series: Five (1986)
Alias/Variations: Cobra STUN Driver, Motor-Vipers; Python Motor Vipers, Stun Driver, Stun Pilot

Real Name: Various
Place of Birth: Various
Service Branch: Cobra Army
Faction(s): Cobra, Perimeter defense forces
Primary MOS: Mechanized infantry
Secondary MOS: Armor
Appearance: Light and dark blue helmet with large silver visor; light blue shirt; dark blue vest with black pipes and blue shoulder guards; black wristbands; dark blue gloves; light blue pants with dark blue panels; black belt and holster; dark blue boots
Other Known Appearances (Cartoon): Visors smaller than on the figure
Accessories: Included with the Cobra STUN; no additional accessories
Abilities: Can drive anything; Disciplined; Educated; Efficient; High-speed pursuit specialists; Highly motivated; Knowledge Skill: Motor vehicles; Patrol; Qualified Expert Operators: STUN; Reconnaissance
Conditions: Distinctive Feature: Uniform; Danger Hounds; High-Speed junkies; Lack ambition; Lack education; Prefer the Python Patrol Stinger jeep; Recon Training; Standard pay
Quote/Motto: "You can run but you can't hide—that's our job!" "As far as we can figure, the Motor-Vipers don't get paid any better than the Ground-Vipers or Sea-Vipers, nor do they receive any special privileges or benefits. They have their own distinctive uniform but it's no flashier than the rest. Why then, would a Cobra volunteer for such an obviously hazardous duty unless it was the danger itself that appealed to him?"
Notes: The file card also mentions Ground-Vipers and Sea-Vipers, two groups that have never been seen or referenced anywhere else. Python Vehicles use a top-secret combination of natural elements in their armor coating, active emitter technology, and experimental plasma stealth to achieve unsurpassed radar deflection and reduced visibility in infrared, visual, audio, and radio spectrums. They also diligently maintain exhaust noise reduction and muzzle suppressors on all on-board weapons, because once someone hears their vehicles or sees where the fire is coming from, their cover is blown!

Munitia

Series: Twenty-five (2009)
Alias/Variations: Cheryl, Ellis, Fronhofer, Janke, Lynne; Sarah, Stratforn, Victoria
Real Name: Unknown
Place of Birth: Unknown
Gender: Female
Service Branch: Cobra army
Faction(s): Cobra, H.I.S.S., and The Plague
Stationed: Cobra headquarters
Notably Served At: The Amazon; Antarctica; the Appalachian Mountains; Lincoln, Nebraska; Malta; Manhattan, New York; Philadelphia, Pennsylvania
Primary MOS: Mercenary
Secondary MOS: CLASSIFIED
Appearance: Black, cable-knit sweater and a black version of her previous division's helmet
Accessories: Goggles, pistol, rifle
Abilities: Ability to guess the actions of others; Bounty hunter; Cool under fire; Cannot be frightened; Detects ambushes; Mercenary; Tank operator
Conditions: Cannot be pleased; Discerning presence (area around her is chilled, face devoid of emotion, predatory stare); Fearless; Reputation: Member of elite death squad known as The Plague; Single-minded passion for devastation and darkness
Quote/Motto: "Emotions make you vulnerable and weak. Stay cool and stay alive."
Notes: She is one-third of a Cobra team calling itself the Hierarchy of Infiltration, Stealth, and Sabotage (H.I.S.S.). The other members are Blackout and Firefly. During the Scorched Earth campaign, Black Out, Grim Skull, Incision (Aleph), Interrogator, Munitia, and Vector are stationed in Antarctica to guard and launch a nuclear bomb. Munitia and the other members of The Plague were presumably captured or killed during a battle in the Appalachian Mountains.

Nemesis Enforcer

Series: Six (1987)
Alias/Variations: Nemesis Immortal
Real Name: None
Place of Birth: Cobra-La
Gender: Male
Grade/Rank: Commander of the guard of Cobra-La
Faction(s): Cobra
Notably Served At: The Himalayas
Appearance: Blank, white eyes; purple helmet and vest with red chest armor; beige sleeves with purple gloves; purple pants with red belt and kneepads; beige holsters; purple boots.

He is seven feet tall, weighs 400 pounds, and is over 40,000 years old. His armor protects against any weapon used by G.I. Joe.

Other Known Appearances: Sunbow's Nemesis Enforcer was quite different from the 1987 design. He had normal eyes, no scales on his armor, bare upper arms, and large talons extending from his gloves. These differences carried into the 2008 version, where he had only the large bat wings and not the tentacles.

Accessories: Tentacle backpack, wing backpack. 2008: Bio-tech armored vest with a diamond-shaped medallion, bio-tech backpack with slots for wings, eight-tentacle backpack, pair of large bat-like wings for a backpack, tech belt with engraved tentacles

Abilities: Ageless; Bat-like wings for flight (24-foot span); Combat (uses wings); Deflection (with wings); Right-hand man of Golobulus; Stealth; Scythe-like blades on forearms; Superhuman strength; Towering stature; Tentacles (eight)

Conditions: Enigmatic; Fiercely loyal to Golobulus; Hibernates periodically; Raised by Golobulus; Rarely speaks; Soulless

In the Transformers Universe: Appearance of a shriveled, desiccated corpse when hibernating (can be awakened from hibernation and restored to vitality with blood); Must carry out the will of his master; Communicates in animalistic growls; Compelled to obey the individual whose blood awakened him; Created by Golobulus from corpses in a fluid-filled pod

Quote/Motto: "He can glide silently and land without a sound. He is the other presence in the pitch-black room. He is the lurker in the dark, just outside your bedroom window. He rattles the garbage cans and makes the floor creak. He is the dread that stands behind you in the dark and dares you to turn and face him." "Nemesis Enforcer? Golobulus must be ticked if he's sending you after me, you rotten slab of leftovers." Quote given by Joe Colton.

Notes: Nemesis Enforcer met his fate at the hands of Sgt. Slaughter, who threw him into a pit; its walls were lined with spikes. Unable to fly because Slaughter had broken one of his wings, he fell to his death. In the Transformers continuity, he was slain by Pythona, who stabbed him in the back. In the Hasbro comic continuity, Nemesis was killed when Falcon ordered a Tomahawk to fire missiles at him.

Neo-Viper

Series: Eighteen (2002)
Real Name: Various
Place of Birth: Various
Grade/Rank: Officer and better
SN: 1005-NV
Service Branch: Cobra Army
Faction(s): Cobra, Crimson Neo-Vipers, Nano Vipers, and Neo-Viper Commandos
Primary MOS: Specialized infantry
Secondary MOS: Basic infantry
Appearance: Gray flared helmet with black mask; silver shirt and pants with gray armor and black gloves, belt, and boots; large blue Cobra emblem on the chest
Accessories: Two rifles, six missiles
Abilities: Camouflage; Commando; Deep battle tactics; Enhanced with nanomites; Heightened reflexes; High-tech weapon-systems management; Infantry; Independent thinking; Initiative; Qualified Expert Operators: Ringneck; Survival experts
Preferred Weapon: M.A.R.S. Industries D57-A extreme environment tactical rifle
Conditions: Aggressive; Attentive to detail; Cold-blooded commandos; Daring; Distinctive Feature: Scar in the shape of a small cobra's head; Distinctive Feature: Sneak up on the enemy from the left side; Ferocious; Hated by Frostbite (they destroy unspoiled tundra lands to set up bio-research laboratories); Heightened strength; Heightened speed; Practical; Sneaky; Trustworthy; Wary; Willing to tactically retreat
Quote/Motto: "Nothing makes our day like watching the G.I. Joe team roll right past us while we are under cover and camouflaged. Especially when we call artillery in on them!" "The G.I. Joe teams are no match for us because they'll be freezing in their tracks while we're doing marathons on the ice."
Notes: Troops are equipped with armored climate-control suits enabling them to function efficiently in extreme environments. Nanomites remove the sense of self-preservation and pain and make them completely obedient to Cobra. Each subject was injected with 1000 milliliters of nanomite solution, which left a scar in the shape of a small cobra's head. After injection, the nanomites rewire the central nervous system. Neo-Vipers constitute the main ground force of Cobra's army.

Neurotoxin

Series: Twenty (2004)
Alias/Variations: Cobra Sand Scorpion leader
Real Name: Unknown
Place of Birth: Unknown
Gender: Male
Grade/Rank: Captain; Sand Scorpion leader
Service Branch: Cobra army
Faction(s): Cobra
Notably Served At: The Coffin, prison in Greenland; Mexico
Primary MOS: Captain/extreme desert operations
Secondary MOS: Infantry
Appearance: Scales along the side of his body
Accessories: Rifle, scorpion (that doubled as a backpack), two claws
Abilities: Ambush; Desert fighter; Heightened charisma among his troops; Powerful
Conditions: Brandishes weapons; Disdain for his appearance; Over-aggressive; Particularly irritable; Wants to revert to human form
Notes: He was hand-picked from the Cobra Sand Vipers to have his DNA combined with a scorpion to produce a more effective warrior. Completely buried in the sand, he waits patiently in ambush, sensing the approach of a victim by feeling vibrations through the packed desert floor. Then, he erupts from his burrow, attacking. After his capture, he was held in the maximum security prison, The Coffin, located in Greenland, and was one of several operatives who escaped during a raid led by Tomax.

Night Adder

Series: Twenty-five (2009)
Real Name: Unknown
Place of Birth: Unknown
Gender: Male
Grade/Rank: Officer status
SN: 3388-NA
Service Branch: Cobra security
Faction(s): Cobra
Stationed: Cobra base
Appearance: High black combat boots; dark blue tactical pants, black armored top, full-face helmet with glowing red eyes
Accessories: Dog with chain, knife, pistol, shotgun, tactical vest. Some figures came with blue tattoos while others had black tattoos.
Abilities: Cobra security protocol; Enforces highest levels of protection; Professional Skill: Security officer; Trained attack dog
Preferred Weapon: M.A.R.S. Industries D57-A extreme environment tactical rifle
Conditions: Feared by fellow officers; Ruthless

Night Creeper

Series: Nine (1990)
Real Name: Various
Place of Birth: Various
Faction(s): Night Creeper mercenaries
Notably Served At: Worldwide
Primary MOS: Field intelligence
Secondary MOS: Covert operations
Appearance: Black skullcap; orange blindfold; shirtless; black straps with orange grenades and knife; black wristbands; orange pants with black stripes and black boots
Other Known Appearances (Cartoon): Night Creeper Leader in the DiC cartoon wears a costume similar to the other Night-Creepers but with his face partly uncovered
Accessories: Barbed sword, backpack, crossbow, kris sword
Abilities: Almost impossible to catch; CEO assassination specialist; Covert operations; Equipped with cutting-edge technology; Field intelligence; Hi-tech ninjas; Hostile takeover specialists; Martial arts experts; Professional Skill: Assassin; Professional Skill: Corporate mercenary; Professional Skill: Spy; Professional Skill: Swiss banker
Conditions: Enemy of Ninja Force; Preference for electronic stealth and infiltration technology; Reputation: Cunning manipulators; Reputation: Experts in five martial arts forms
Quote/Motto: "Like a fierce, dark cloud, we appear and rain misery over all!" "All evidence seems to indicate that the Night Creepers have the drive and scruples of a Wall Street stock manipulator, the lethal skills of a master martial artist, and the stealthy talents of a cat burglar. To make matters worse, they're backed by the latest and most sophisticated anti-detection and weapons technology in the world! It's as if Attila the Hun had a black belt, an MBA, and was armed with lasers." "We move like shadows on a moonless night, enhanced by the elegant sophistication of electronic devices that shut down layers of protective technology and leave us a clear path to our goal."
Notes: Night Creepers are a syndicate of hi-tech ninjas and corporate mercenaries hired by Cobra as spies and assassins. They handle Cobra's bankroll, as well as the

organization's most dangerous assassination missions. Night Creepers prefer laser-cut carbon-fiber-composite weapons to ancient weapons. They are not united by blood or history; they are interested in profit. They contract their services to criminal organizations or individuals who meet their excessive fees. Their leader is named Aleph (Night Creeper Leader; Incision).

Night Creeper Ninja Clan

Purpose: "The Night Creeper forces are a super-secret group of high-tech ninjas who have had a long-standing contract with Cobra to handle high-risk field intelligence operations and covert infiltration. They are extremely crafty, well-motivated, and have abnormally high pain tolerances, which makes them hard to predict, hard to stop, hard to knock down and keep down. If you took a ruthless person, trained them for ten years in five forms of martial arts, and then equipped him with all the most advanced electronic stealth and passive sensor technology you may have an approximation of an ordinary high-tech ninja. Once you strip away all his scruples, morals, and innate feelings of common decency, then you have a Night Creeper. When they aren't participating in missions, the Night Creeper ninjas are accountants who are kept busy creating new tax shelters for Cobra." From the file card

Accessories: Single-sheath backpack; sword; Wet Suit disguise (helmet; scuba vest with tubing; two flippers).

Quote/Motto: "There is no place you can hide where we can't find you, no fortress that can keep us from getting to you, and no armor to protect you once we are there."

Notes: They wear silver face masks; blue shirts and pants with silver armor on the chest, gloves, and thighs; and black kneepads.

Night Stalkers Commander

Series: Twenty-three (2007)
Alias/Variations: Cobra officer
Real Name: Rebecca M. Bristo
Place of Birth: Perth, Australia
Gender: Female
Grade/Rank: O-3 (Equivalent)
Service Branch: Cobra Army
Faction(s): Army
Primary MOS: Covert operations
Secondary MOS: Rotary/fixed-wing pilot
Appearance: Blonde hair pulled in a ponytail; full-body black body armor, white Cobra insignia on chest; white band on helmet, white piping on shoulders, white trim denoting kneepad
Other Known Appearance: On her file card, she is depicted as a redhead.
Accessories: Helmet, knife, stand; two different types of riles
Background Information: Served in the Australian Army
Abilities: Battlefield adaptability; Command; Edged weapons expert; Extraction of special operation targets; Firearms expert; Infiltration; Leadership; Pilot; Quick; Self-sufficient; Stealth; Tactician: Hit-and-run infiltration
Conditions: Constantly pushes the limits of her team; Distinctive Feature: Recognizable body armor; Has Cobra Commander's attention; Micromanages every mission; Personally responsible for team's success; Reputation: Commands a hand-picked all-female unit; Reputation: Dishonorable discharge for staging a mercenary coup for Cobra
Quote/Motto: "Our silence can be lethal!"
Notes: This fifth version of the Cobra Officer was released at the International G.I. Joe Con 2007 in Atlanta, Georgia. The boxed set, named "Tanks for the Memories," included Clutch, Doc, Grunt, Lt. Clayton Moore, Rock 'n Roll, Sgt. Flash, Sparks, Zap, the Cobra Officer, and six Cobra Troopers.

Night Stalkers Shock Troops

Series: Twenty-three (2007)
Alias/Variations: Cobra trooper
Real Name: Various
Place of Birth: Various
Gender: Female
Service Branch: Army
Faction(s): Cobra
Primary MOS: Covert operations
Secondary MOS: Reconnaissance
Appearance: Hair pulled back into a ponytail; black bodysuit, red Cobra insignia on the chest, red piping on kneepads, shoulders, and wrist; red belt buckle
Accessories: Helmet, knife, rifle, stand, two stick grenades
Background Information: Works best behind enemy lines
Abilities: Avoid traditional detection methods; Escape!; Improvise orders; Infiltration;

Knowledge Skill: Restricted areas; Quick; Recognize key documents; Stealth; Well-trained; Utilized battlefield to their advantage

Conditions: Despise working with Lt. Clayton Moore; Light body frame; Reputation: Part of a special all-female unit; Ruthless; Under armored; Under equipped

Quote/Motto: "We arrive right after the SHOCK and leave just before the AWE!"

Notes: The figure was released with three different hair colors: blonde, brunette, and redheaded.

Ninja B.A.T. (Battle Android Trooper)

Alias/Variations: BAT, B.A.T.; B.A.A.T (Battle Armored Android Trooper), Cobra B.A.T.
Place of Birth: Created for the Cobra Organization by Doctor Mindbender
Gender: Android
Service Branch: Cobra army
Faction(s): Cobra, under the command of Storm Shadow
Primary MOS: Extreme combat shock trooper
Secondary MOS: Support ninjas for Storm Shadow
Appearance: Gray, robotic humanoids with large blades on their forearms; Cobra emblem on their chests; exposed electronics in their chest cavity for easy battlefield maintenance. The right forearm could be equipped with a flamethrower, laser cannon, gripper claw, or standard robotic hand.
Other Known Appearances (Cartoon/Comic): The Jungle B.A.T. features green camouflage fatigues and additional jungle combat–themed accessories. The Arctic B.A.T. is mostly white with pixelated-looking gray camouflage on his uniform.
Accessories: Gun, robotic sword, removable chest plate, two daggers
Background Information: Disposable brute strength of the Cobra Army
Abilities: Arms extend an abnormal length; Built-in weaponry (claws, knives, pistols, swords); Cheap and easy to replace; Difficult to stop; Grapple; Highly advanced android; Programmed for martial arts combat; Powerful fighters; Strong; Unrelenting onslaught
Conditions: Cannot be reasoned with; Cobra infantry don't like to be on the battlefield with them; Does not discriminate well between targets; Does not react well to changes in field conditions; Tends to burst into flames when hit from behind; Never question orders; Never shirks its duty; Never surrenders; Will shoot anything that moves
Notes: The B.A.T.s provide disposable brute strength to the Cobra army.

Olga

Real Name: Olga Rose
Place of Birth: Russia
Gender: Female
Grade/Rank: Corporal
Service Branch: USSR Army
Faction(s): Russian military
Appearance: Blue eyes; blonde hair cut in men's military style; Russian uniform; wears a pistol on her hip
Abilities: Command; Intimidation; Language Skill: English
Conditions: Cruel
Notes: She oversaw the capture of several Joes and had them interrogated. When she determined they knew nothing, she ordered their execution; before orders could be fulfilled, the Joes rallied and escaped.

Otis

Series: Twenty (2004)
Real Name: Theodore I. Smith
Place of Birth: Auburn, Alabama
Gender: Male
Faction(s): Dreadnoks
Primary MOS: Mastermind
Appearance: Purple mask; white hair and beard; red vest with black knife and holster; black wristbands; red and white camo pants with black belt and holster; black and brown boots
Accessories: G-36 assault rifle; shotgun
Abilities: Leadership; Mastermind; Professional Skill: Firearm manufacturing business; Wealthy family
Conditions: Appetite for mayhem; Infatuation with power; Outcast in hometown; Seeks revenge on Beach Head; Used to getting things "his way," no matter the consequences
Quote/Motto: "I love the smell of burning tires in the morning."
Notes: Cletus, Vance, Billy-Bob, Joe-Bob, and Roscoe are his cousins. All six cousins are identical in appearance. Otis is considered to be their leader.

Over Kill

Series: Nineteen (2003)
Alias/Variations: Overkill (1992); The Eliminator

Real Name: Robert Skelton
Place of Birth: Unknown
Gender: Male
Grade/Rank: B.A.T. Leader
Service Branch: Cobra Army, Coil Army
Faction(s): Cobra, The Coil
Stationed: His lab in the underground Cobra base
Notably Served At: The Arctic; Badhikistan; Cobra Island
Primary MOS: B.A.T. Commander
Secondary MOS: Operate the destructive Cobra Earthquake battle vehicle
Appearance: Blue-green segmented shirt and pants under black body armor on chest, shoulders, and forearms; black grenade belt and knee-high boots
Other Known Appearances (Cartoon/Comic/Movie): Depending on the comic, cartoon, toy, or movie version and where they are in the storyline, Over Kill is anywhere from mostly cyborg to a full-blown robot-looking cyborg.
Accessories: Claw attachment on right hand, hand-held red rifle/cannon. Version 2: Smooth, flared helmet with Cobra emblem; one shoulder pad; thick waist belt with circular buckle; knife with a curved, textured hilt and J-shaped Quillen; machine gun arm with a magazine; knife arm with serrated blade
Background Information: Cobra Commander's idea was to add a voice synthesizer program to Over Kill to belt out demoralizing slogans at deafening volumes (*Sigma 6*).
Abilities: Chest cannon; Command of a small army of mindless robots; Cyborg: Infrared scanners; Cyborg: Integral body armor; Cyborg: Self-contained breathing unit; Cyborg: Targeting computer hard-wired between his right eye and trigger finger; Cyborg: Vision enhanced with image intensifiers; Cyborg: Wireless modem implanted in his brain; Eliminator Chip: Heightened strength, heightened speed, and heightened intelligence
In the *Sigma 6* comic: Cobra's chief scientist; Free will; Highly Intelligent
In the CGI movie version: Lab assistant to Doctor Mindbender
Conditions: Gives the B.A.T.S. secret names; Grudge against Tunnel Rat; Has favorite B.A.T.S who get special attention; If ever defeated in combat, will beg to be killed; In Cobra Commander's good graces; Overly sentimental about the B.A.T.S.; Protective of the B.A.T.S.; Reputation: Infamous SAW viper; Reputation: Killed Joes Crank Case, Doc, and Heavy Metal; Sees the B.A.T.S. as individuals
In the CGI Movie: Belief: He and B.A.T.s are better candidates to rule the world; Looks down upon "Organics"; Repeats the end of his sentences in a manic tone of voice
In the *Sigma 6* comic: Devious; Periodic half-hearted attempts for a robot revolution
Quote/Motto: "Of course I have feelings. They may be enhanced digitally, but they are still feelings!"
Notes: There are two different characters known by Over Kill; both are the leader of the B.A.T.s. Overkill (one word), an experimental prototype B.A.T. with an advanced computer system and tactical logic programs, was too expensive for mass production. A soulless automaton, Overkill is frequently referred to as a "he."

Over Kill (two words) is a cyborg who volunteered for the experiment; more than 50 percent of his body was replaced. His name references his impressive body count: he killed four Joes. Recruited by Serpentor for The Coil, Over Kill was executed during Tomax's raid on The Coffin, a prison facility.

His cyborg package includes but is not limited to: hidden leg-based flamethrower; infrared night scope eye; telescopic analyzer eye; mind control, memory drain unit; two .50-caliber machine guns revealed by opening his chest plate; oxygen regulator mask; psychic sensor backpack; shin-based fuel porta-packs; sophisticated strength activation system in arms; techno-cerebral intelligence; and turbo hydraulic legs.

Overlord

Series: Nine (1990)
Alias/Variations: Nowhere Man; Braco Dracommen, Cobra Khan, Carbo Medmornac
Real Name: Mikhail Derenko
Place of Birth: Russia
Gender: Male
Grade/Rank: General; Serpentor's field commander
Service Branch: Cobra Command
Faction(s): Cobra, Coil, the Jugglers, former CIA, former Hammer Team, and former Russian Spetsnaz
Notably Served At: Afghanistan; Cobra Island; Duke's secret base in Iceland; Tokyo, Japan

Primary MOS: Coil General
Secondary MOS: Conspiracy; Bureaucrat
Appearance: He has the face of a Fred and wears battle armor with a helmet keeping his face hidden and a deadly claw weapon attached to his arm. He has black slicked-back hair; silver monocle; gold face mask; orange vest with gold shoulder armor and black gloves; gold pants with a red belt; and black padded waist piece.
Accessories: Slightly crested helmet; two short, webbed claws attaching to wrists
Abilities: Battle armor; Bureaucrat; Charismatic; Conspiracy; Contacts: CIA; Contact: Firefly; Contact: General Gibbs; Contacts: the Jugglers; Contacts: Spetsnaz; Former CIA; Former Hammer Team (a U.S. covert ops unit); Former Russian Spetsnaz commando; Professional Skill: Mercenary; Qualified Expert Operator: Dictator (attack tank/hovercraft); Recruiting Expert; Serpentor's field commander
Conditions: Advocates traditional Cobra values; Disgruntled member of Cobra; Elderly mother; Power-hungry; Rumor: Former Crimson Guard; Watched by the Jugglers
Notes: Overlord murdered Chuckles. While in a remote base in Iceland attempting to murder Duke, Overlord was killed in an explosion set and detonated by the mortally wounded Joe operative Scanner. Since two of his suggested code names were anagrams of "Cobra Commander," it may eventually be revealed that Overlord was Cobra Commander looking to reclaim his title.

Overlord Vector B.A.T.

Real Name: Vector plus a numeric designation
Place of Birth: Created for the Cobra Organization by Doctor Mindbender
Gender: Robot
Service Branch: Cobra Air Force
Faction(s): Cobra, B.A.T.s
Notably Served At: The Alaska pipeline
Primary MOS: Battle Android Trooper Assault
Secondary MOS: Battle Android Trooper Transport
Appearance: 25 feet in length and about 15 feet in height, the vehicle looks like a sci-fi dragon capable of carrying a vehicle as large as a H.I.S.S. in its mechanical claws. The vector is light blue with a long, serpentine body fully articulated, gray talon claw-like feet, and gray turbines under its tail for rocket propulsion. It has red, glowing, lifeless optics, which give visuals in three spectrums. On its forepaws and shoulders rests a pair of .50-caliber machine guns.
Background Information: Disposable brute strength to the Cobra army
Abilities: Aerial maneuvers; Claws; Flying B.A.T.; Gatling guns; Missiles
Notes: In the Transformers Universe, Vectors are flying B.A.T.s, under the command of Over Kill. Originally there were 13 Vectors, but currently only three remain: numbers 4, 6, and 11. Number six (identifying as female) is the "alpha" serving as the current Overlord Vector; Four is her acting second in command.

Overlord Virus B.A.T.

Place of Birth: Created for the Cobra Organization by Doctor Mindbender
Gender: Robot
Faction(s): Cobra
Notably Served At: Japan
Primary MOS: A ninja-type B.A.T.
Secondary MOS: Backup for Storm Shadow
Appearance: B.A.T.
Background Information: Disposable brute strength for the Cobra Army
Abilities: Almost Invincible (under the influence of Power Stone); Guardian of Destro's Romanian Cobra base
Conditions: Under the influence of Power Stone
Notes: Power Stones are a highly dense form of energy. Some have been mined off the coast of Guam. They are mysterious natural stones with amazing technological powers that both Cobra and G.I. Joe are on the hunt for.

Overlord Vortex B.A.T.

Gender: Robot
Faction(s): Cobra
Appearance: A single red eye, two laser-firing arm cannons, and tank-like treads for feet
Abilities: Armored metal hide; Two laser-firing arm cannons
Conditions: Distinctive Feature: Single red glowing eye; Tank treads for feet
Notes: Appears briefly in the Transformers Universe storyline

The Plague Troopers

Service Branch: Cobra Army
Faction(s): Cobra
Notably Served At: Antarctica; the Amazon; the Appalachian Mountains; Lincoln,

Nebraska; Malta; New York City; Philadelphia, Pennsylvania

Appearance: Members of The Plague wore a black, cable-knit sweater and a black version of their previous division's helmet.

Conditions: Distinctive Feature: Attack from high ground; Distinctive Feature: Will not intentionally engage without the upper hand

Notes: The Plague is Cobra Commander's attempt to duplicate the success of G.I. Joe by forming his own equivalent team of specialists, drawn from the various Cobra forces. The Plague comprises: Bayonet (Snow Serpent), Blackout (former Joe), Body Bags (Range-Viper), Gallows (S.A.W.-Viper), Grim Skull (Sand Viper), Guillotine (Eel), Incision (formerly known as Aleph, excommunicated Night-Creeper), Infrared (Crimson Guard), Interrogator, Munitia, Vanguard, Vector (Laser-Viper), and Velocity (A.V.). Rip It and Sky Creeper were under consideration for the group but failed the evaluation—they had questions about their orders, and even though they performed the missions successfully, they were executed on the flight back to base. After numerous conflicts with the Joes all over the globe, The Plague was either captured or killed during the battle in the Appalachian Mountains.

Professor Apple

Alias/Variations: Agent Jones; Crimson Guardsmen Jones; Jones
Real Name: Professor (first name unknown) Apple
Place of Birth: Unknown
Gender: Male
Grade/Rank: Cobra scientist and Crimson Guardsman
Service Branch: Cobra army
Faction(s): Cobra
Stationed: A house in Staten Island, New York
Primary MOS: Terrorist
Secondary MOS: Geologist
Appearance: Blue eyes, gray hair with white streaks at his temples; 5'9", over 200 pounds; crimson jacket with silver cuff stripes over a white T-shirt, adorned with silver medals and a silver Cobra sigil; crimson trousers with silver side stripes; black leather boots, gloves, and belts; and a crimson helmet with a black faceplate
Accessories: AK-47, bayonet, helmet, semi-automatic pistol

Abilities: Applied science; Contacts: Cobra; Contacts: Crimson Guard; Crimson Guardsman; Demolitions; Detective; Espionage; Geology expert; Highly skilled Cobra operative; Intelligence; Knowledge Skill: Firearms; Martial artist; Mastermind; Poses as a mundane citizen; Sabotage specialist; Scientist; Small arms

Conditions: Daughter: Candy Apple; Loving father; Physically out of shape; Reputation: Creator of Cobra Island; Radical ideas; Supremely smug; Zealous Cobra operative

Notes: Professor Apple loves his daughter; the only thing that could cause him to betray Cobra would be the organization putting her in danger. He was killed in a battle between Storm Shadow and Rip Cord; he was aboard a Firebat awaiting launch when the vehicle exploded.

Pythona

Series: Thirty-two (2016)
Place of Birth: Cobra-La
Gender: Female
Grade/Rank: Royal Messenger of King Golobulus and Harbinger of Destruction
Faction(s): Cobra, Cobra-La
Notably Served At: The Himalayas
Primary MOS: Emissary/herald
Secondary MOS: Assassin
Appearance: Purple eyes with snake-like slits; bald except for dark green ponytail; 5'9", 125 pounds
Accessories: Cloak, ponytail, tentacles
Abilities: Access to anything in the Cobra-La arsenal; Assassin; Assortment of bizarre techno-organic weapons and gadgets; Beautiful; Cult-like followers; Hand-to-hand armed; Hand-to-hand unarmed; Heightened intelligence; Heightened reflexes; Infiltration expert; Member of the elite ruling warrior caste; Poison-tipped claws; Professional Skill: Emissary for the Kingdom of Cobra-La; Stealth
Conditions: Burning hatred of humanity; Disquieting aura; Distinctive Feature: Animalistic and alluring; Distinctive Feature: Pale skin; Distinctive Feature: Strange eyes; Distinctive Feature: Strange attire; Femme fatale; Haughty demeanor; Regal demeanor; Romantically linked to Serpentor; Sense of compassion for humans; Subject of bio-genetic manipulation; Taunts her captives
Quote/Motto: "Prepare for eternity!"

Rampage

Series: Thirteen (1996)
Real Name: J. Remington III
Place of Birth: Unknown
Gender: Male
SN: 06TYJF59
Faction(s): G.I. Joe
Primary MOS: Arms dealer
Appearance: Wears high-tech armor in battle that has guns on it varying from a chain gun to rocket launcher
Abilities: Black market dealer; Controls of a small Third World nation; Operates legitimate business fronts; Professional Skill: Arms manufacturer; Professional Skill: Businessman; Transformation: Grotesque, devilish, green-skinned creature; Tycoon; Wealthy
Conditions: Greedy; Power-hungry; Seeks to eliminate Iron Klaw; Seeks to seize control of S.K.A.R.
Notes: He is S.K.A.R.'s primary weapon supplier. It is unclear if his ability to transform into that creature is because of science or the supernatural.

Range Viper (individual)

Real Name: Keith B. Holland
Place of Birth: Simpson Desert, Australia
Gender: Male
Service Branch: Cobra Range Vipers
Faction(s): Cobra
Primary MOS: Long-range recon
Secondary MOS: Wilderness survival: Desert
Appearance: Tan armored shirt and pants with Cobra emblem on left breast; black boots; pouch belt, bandoliers; full helmet with large green "eyes" and a wide "toothy" grin
Accessories: Backpack, grenade launcher and chamber, mortar, mortar shell, short hose
Abilities: Ambush; Knowledge Skill: Australian Outback; Range Vipers skillset; Survival expert; Wilderness Survival: Desert
Conditions: Anti-social; Enjoys remote locations; Grudgingly accepts aid; Orphan; Sole survivor of a long-range recon team
Quote/Motto: "No one enters my territory and leaves alive!"

Range Vipers

Series: Twenty-one (2005)
Alias/Variations: Range-Vipers, Cobra Wilderness Trooper
Real Name: Varies
Grade/Rank: E-4, Operative
Service Branch: Cobra ground forces
Faction(s): Cobra infantry
Notably Served At: Alcatraz; Cobra base; Cobra Commander's broadcast facility; Cobra's jungle base, guarding an occupied dam; Lapland; the Millard Fillmore Memorial; rocket base command center, Tokyo; volcano base
Primary MOS: Long-range recon
Secondary MOS: Survivalist
Appearance: Turtle green armored shirt and pants with Cobra emblem on left breast; black boots; pouch belt, bandoliers; full helmet with large green "eyes" and a wide "toothy" grin
Other Known Appearances (Cartoon): In the animated commercial, they had larger eyes, blue teeth, and white ammo belts
Accessories: Cylindrical mortar shell with cap; gas mask; knife with diamond-shaped blade and pegs on cross guard; large square back pack with engraved grenades and grooves across middle; multi-shot grenade launcher with square trigger guard and removable round 11-grenade chamber, short, handheld mortar; short hose
Abilities: Combat expert; Hit-and-run raid experts; Infantry; Qualified Operator: Avalanche, craft turret, H.I.S.S. II, motorcycle, Paralyzers, Rages; Resist pain; Survival Skill: Live off the land; Survival Skill: Long-term operations in unfriendly territory; Survival Skills: Wilderness
Preferred Weapon: Assault rifle
Conditions: Only equipped with uniforms and basic weapons; Propensity for violence
Quote/Motto: "We don't care who we shoot, as long as we get to shoot at someone or something. It's a real party when a G.I. Joe patrol comes by. Otherwise, it becomes pretty boring." "Range Vipers are favorites of the Cobra High Command since they are so inexpensive to sustain. Once they're in the field, they don't cost anything to feed, clothe, and arm. Range Vipers don't care who they shoot, as long as they shoot at someone or something! That's why Cobra High Command makes sure they stay out in the bush!"
Notes: These men are recruited from the most extreme of wilderness enthusiasts with a propensity for violence. Body Bags is a Range-Viper assigned to The Plague.

Raptor

Series: Six (1987)

Alias/Variations: Gos, Peregrine, Skree
Real Name: Unknown
Place of Birth: Unknown
Gender: Male
Faction(s): Cobra
Notably Served At: New York City; secret lab in Denver, Colorado; San Francisco, California
Primary MOS: Falconer
Secondary MOS: Accountant
Appearance: Brown bird-head helmet; black face paint around eyes; no shirt; red medallion; feathers on shoulders; orange-brown pants; black belts with silver falcon buckle; brown gloves and bird-foot boots with feathers; 2017: tan harness, a red whistle and chain, a tan backpack mount, four tan wing segments, a black revolver, a brown staff, a brown and tan falcon, a brown hood for the falcon
Accessories: Falcon; wing cape/backpack
Abilities: Avian husbandry: Falcons; Avian training; Computer hacking; Contact: Crimson Guardsman Fred VII; Falconer; Followers: Rookery of falcons; Hobby Skill: Poaching; Knowledge Skill: Bird calling whistles techniques; Kinship with his feathered minions; Professional Skill: Tax consultant
Conditions: Distinctive Feature: Dresses like a falcon; Eccentricities: Talks to his birds; Obsessed with avian blood sport; Rambles on about his birds; Yuppie
Quote/Motto: "Fly hard, attack swiftly, make no apologies!"
Notes: He has bred his falcons to be large and vicious with sharp beaks and talons. The birds are trained to attack humans and steal jewels. Raptor is not delusional; he dresses like a giant falcon to calm his birds. Raptor was buried alive in a landlocked freighter under a volcano on Cobra Island by Cobra Commander; he died of food poisoning.

Razorclaw

Series: Twenty (2004)
Real Name: Unknown (Andrew D. Meyers)
Place of Birth: Unknown
Gender: Male
Grade/Rank: Leader of the Cobra Razor Troopers
Service Branch: Feral berserker
Faction(s): Cobra, Cobra Razor Troopers, and V-Trooper
Primary MOS: Feral berserker
Secondary MOS: Infantry
Appearance: Gray, light brown hair, blue eyes. Red and black body armor with a gray belt
Accessories: Helmet, pistol, and rifle; the two blades on the arms are not meant to be removable
Abilities: Cobra feral berserker; Fights multiple targets; Infused with tiger DNA; Instinctive combat skills; Knowledge Skill: High-tech weapons; Resists pain; Retractable claws; Vicious and sneaky tactics
Conditions: Lost his memories to feral berserker process; Ruthless; Tiger thoughts and urges; World is a haze of red, unrestricted anger
Notes: The feral berserker process was a procedure conceived and performed by Doctor Mindbender. Razorclaw isn't "deployed" into an area of operation; he is "unleashed." In the IDW Universe, Razorclaw is one of the crazed residents of the Cobra-La installation for unfit and unstable agents deemed valuable to Cobra R&D.

Red Ninjas

Series: Twelve (1993)
Alias/Variations: Red Ninja Viper
Real Name: Various/unknown
Place of Birth: Various
Service Branch: Mercenaries working for Cobra Commander
Faction(s): Cobra, Ninja Force
Stationed: Mountaintop dojo
Notably Served At: Cobra's Silent Castle in Trans-Carpathia
Primary MOS: Battle Ax vehicle operator
Secondary MOS: Assassins
Secondary MOS: Cobra elite ninja masters
Appearance: Blue mask; red vest with blue straps; orange right armband; blue and purple wristbands; black pants with red boots and kneepads
Accessories: Battle Ax vehicle. Carded equipment: Armored shin guards, baseball grenades, battle-ax, four-point shuriken throwing stars, nunchaku power-point defense weapon, standard issue Red Ninja battle uniform, sword blocking firearm guard, toriko canister explosives
Abilities: Assassination; Covert operations; Knowledge Skill: Arashikage fighting techniques; Knowledge Skill: Cybernetics, explosives, and firearms; Martial arts; Mid-air battles experts; Ninja masters; Ninjutsu; Professional Skill: Mercenaries; Qualified Expert Operators: Battle Ax vehicle; Storm Shadow's bodyguards; Zip-line experts

Conditions: Can be bought; Cannon fodder; Feared ninja warriors; Followers of Red Ninja Master (Firefly); Mysterious; Renegade members of the Arashikage clan; Reputation: Fight like sharks in a feeding frenzy; Reputation: Most feared ninja warriors since the fifteenth century; Ruthless; Will switch sides if offered more money by the other side
Quote/Motto: "We'll spin 'n' chop our enemies fasters than frogs in blenders!"
Notes: Red Ninjas are a toned-down imitation of the ninja sect the Hand from Marvel Comics. The major difference is that the Hand is a nihilistic death cult involved in the supernatural (worshiping a demon and using magic).

Red Scream

Real Name: Commander Roston
Place of Birth: Unknown
Gender: Female
Service Branch: American military
Faction(s): Red Scream
Primary MOS: Anti-globalist terrorist
Secondary MOS: Undercover operations
Appearance: White hair, blue eyes; red bodysuit
Abilities: Access to Joe files; American military officer; Terrorist; Undercover operations
Conditions: Anti-globalist; Seeks to destroy the Inter-Alliance (the Joe-verse version of the United Nations); Seeks to discredit the Joe team through use of imposters
Notes: Other Red Scream members are Dela Eden, Wilder Vaughn, and Artur Kulik.

Red Shadows

Purpose: This group attempted to destroy both Cobra and G.I. Joe. They are dedicated to replacing the current world order with a technocratic paradise of Wilder Vaughn's own design.
Leader: Wilder Vaughn
Members: Artur Kulik, Dela Eden, Red Scream, Skeletron, and nameless fanatical others known as the Red Shadows

Repulsor

Series: Thirty (2014)
Alias/Variations: Sludge-Slinger
Real Name: Frederick M. Townsend
Place of Birth: Wallingford, Vermont
Gender: Male
Grade/Rank: O-3 (Captain), Commander of the Toxo-Vipers
Service Branch: Director of Security at Cobra Industries
Faction(s): Cobra
Stationed: Cobra Industries
Primary MOS: Security director
Secondary MOS: Tactical advisor
Appearance: Wears the last remnants of the Sludge-Viper battle suits
Accessories: Backpack, a dog named Dawg, helmet, hose, pistol, rifle, shotgun, tanks that fit into the backpack, vest
Abilities: Advisor and right-hand man to Cesspool; Animal Companion: Dawg; Director of security for Cobra Industries; Military experience
Conditions: Cruel and severe taskmaster; Inseparable from Dawg; No regard for his soldiers; Soft spot for Dawg; Would do anything to protect Dawg
Quote/Motto: "I'll give you one chance to live, but you won't like the aftereffect."
Notes: His job at Cobra Industries is to oversee all laboratory facility activities as well as protect all production services from curious authorities. He uses his Toxo-Vipers to deploy Compound Z on specific target locations. Dawg was accidentally killed by Outback and was brought back to life by his grieving master. He has exposed ribs and a partially fleshless tail; this dog has been ravaged by the effects of Compound Z.

Rip It

Series: Sixteen (2000)
Real Name: Fred T. Booth III
Place of Birth: Fall River, Massachusetts
Gender: Male
Grade/Rank: O-1 (Equivalent) Commander of Cobra's H.I.S.S. (High-Speed Sentry) tank division
Service Branch: Cobra operative
Faction(s): Cobra
Notably Served At: Lincoln, Nebraska
Primary MOS: Heavy equipment operator
Appearance: Blue helmet with black goggles and red face mask; blue shirt with black chest panel and red insignia on chest; red wristbands and black thigh-high segmented boots; red belt and blue pants
Accessories: Shotgun
Abilities: Analyzes and negotiates battlefield problems; Golf expert; Heavy equipment

operator; Knowledge Skill: Tracked vehicles; Qualified Expert Operator: H.I.S.S. III; Talented

Conditions: Always follows orders; Belief: Destroy or be destroyed; Fearless; Frequently in a bad mood; Lacks patience; May take matters into his own hands; Mean; No allies (even in Cobra); Quick to anger; Vicious; Wages private battles

Quote/Motto: "The Cobra blue paint job is an improvement, but I would have used black—it just looks MEANER!"

Notes: Rip It was considered for membership in The Plague but failed the evaluation for questioning an order even though he followed it flawlessly. He was shot and thrown out of a helicopter by Black Out and Guillotine.

Ripper

Series: Four (1985), twenty (2004)
Alias/Variations: Dreadnok Ripper
Real Name: Harry Nod
Place of Birth: Grim Cape, Tasmania
Gender: Male
Faction(s): Dreadnok
Notably Served At: Blackwater Prison; Cobra Island; Washington, D.C.
Primary MOS: Edged weapons and cutting tools
Appearance: Black Mohawk and beard; red sunglasses; ripped sleeveless green camouflage with a gold knife; light blue jeans with a black belt, holster, and boots
Other Known Appearances (Cartoon): Yellow leopard-print vest with grenade and knife matching the figure's; gold medallion around his neck; glasses almost always silver instead of red
Accessories: Assault rifle with large bayonet/metal splitter; "Jaws of Life" cutting tool; hydraulic hose; power pack backpack with removable frame
Background Information: Spent time in the Australian military
Abilities: Affinity for motorcycles; Basic grunt; Heightened intelligence; Knowledge Skill: Correctional facilities; Knowledge Skill: Edged weapons and cutting tools; Knowledge Skill: Prison life; Leadership; Numerous side businesses (legitimate and illicit); Professional Skill: Accountant; Professional Skill: Criminal; Qualified Operator: Chameleon, FANG, Ferret, the RAM, Stinger, Swampfire, Water Moccasin; Safecracker; Wealthy

Conditions: Afraid of Zartan; Appetite for destruction; Detests the niceties of civilization (except motorcycles); Distinctive Feature: Cockney accent; Greedy; No aspirations; Poor hygiene; Propensity for violence; Superstitious

Quote/Motto: "Lucky for me that silly new logo is growing on the other Dreadnoks—I copyrighted it!" "There's nothing like it in the whole world! Destruction and wreckage!" "There are devils in Tasmania and Ripper is probably the meanest of them all." Quote taken from an unnamed G.I. Joe member.

Notes: He was one of the three Dreadnoks—with Buzzer and Torch—who traveled to the United States with Zartan, who had begun working for Cobra.

The action figure for Ripper does not have the swivel-ball neck most other 1985 characters possess.

Road Pig

Series: Seven (1988)
Alias/Variations: Dreadnok Road Pig
Real Name: Donald DeLuca
Place of Birth: Goblu, Michigan
Gender: Male
Faction(s): Dreadnoks
Stationed: Jersey Shore, New Jersey; Broca Beach
Notably Served At: Cobra Island
Appearance: White flat-top hair with red stripe; no shirt; black left glove; red anarchy tattoo on left shoulder; black pants with brown spiked codpiece; silver boots
Accessories: Cinderblock on a long handle; flat, spiked wrist shield; shoulder armor; small crossbow attaching to the wrist
Background Information: Dishonorably discharged from the Cub Scouts
Abilities: Brute strength; Extortionist
Conditions: Antisocial behavior; Belief: Smashing things is the solution to all of life's problems; Decided he is Zarana's bodyguard; Easily angered; Gross looking; Loves Zarana; Low-life; Profoundly ugly; *Rare medical condition; Smells terrible; Vexatious wanderer
Quote/Motto: "I think, therefore, I smash!"
Notes: Road Pig has an extensive arrest record: speeding, reckless endangerment, littering, assault, grand theft auto, usury, felony spitting, petty bribery, and passing stopped school buses at high speeds.

*He has a rare split-personality disorder, which he exhibits through two identities: Road Pig and Donald. Road Pig is his stupid and violent side, while Donald is intelligent, speaks poetically and properly, and possess a large vocabulary. He seems to switch between these personalities at a moment's notice, sometimes mid-sentence. Both identities remain extremely dangerous and are in love with Zarana.

Rock Vipers

Series: Nine (1990)
Alias/Variations: Cobra Rock Viper; Rock-Viper (1990)
Real Name: Various
Place of Birth: Various
Faction(s): Cobra
Primary MOS: Mountain assault specialists
Secondary MOS: Infantry
Appearance: Dark red helmet with green visor; black mustache and goatee; beige shirt and pants with black urban camo; black vest with dark red straps; dark red wristbands, belt, holsters, and kneepads; black gloves and boots. Gold helmet with red visor; black mustache; black shirt and pants with a red criss-cross pattern; black vest with gold straps; gold wristbands, belt, holsters, and kneepads; black gloves and boots
Accessories: Backpack, grappling hook with cord; laser pistol; machine gun
Abilities: Climbing; Experts at climbing treacherous terrains of rock, snow, and ice; Grenade launcher experts; Infantry; Mountaineering; Vertical assault
Preferred Weapon: LR-V long-range rifle
Quote/Motto: "We can climb mountain crags as easily as you stroll across a deserted street!" "On the day of graduation from the training program, candidate Rock-Vipers are dropped from helicopters onto a 500-foot, sheer-sided mesa. They are outfitted with 250 feet of rope and informed only 50% will graduate upon completion of this final test," implying the solution is to shoot one of your classmates and take his rope. Because suggesting such a thing was too violent for the era, a line was added: "It doesn't take long for them to figure out the only way they will get down the mesa is to slide down the rope and pray they land in a soft pile of dirt at the bottom!"
Notes: Wear non-slip, camo-traction suits and are equipped with rocket-assisted, tungsten steel grappling hooks and megatensile-strength rappelling ropes

Roscoe

Series: Twenty (2004)
Real Name: Maximillian Q. Wesson
Place of Birth: Auburn, Alabama
Gender: Male
Faction(s): Dreadnok Recruit
Primary MOS: Weapon maintenance for Dreadnoks
Appearance: Purple mask; pink hair and beard; blue vest with black knife and holster; black wristbands; blue camo pants with black belt and holster; black and brown boots
Accessories: G-36 assault rifle; shotgun
Abilities: Wealthy family; Weapon maintenance
Conditions: Air of superiority; Abused by the Dreadnoks; Despises having to use "silly" code names; Longstanding hatred of Beach Head; Unresolved jealousy (due to Beach Head's success); Unpredictable
Quote/Motto: "I'll break more than just your pride!"
Notes: He uses Dreadnoks' connections in Cobra to get close to Beach Head. Vance, Joe-Bob, Cletus, Billy-Bob, and Otis are his cousins. All six cousins are identical in appearance.

"Rowdy" Roddy Piper

Series: Twenty-three (2007)
Alias/Variations: Rowdy
Real Name: Roderick George Toombs Piper
Place of Birth: Glasgow, Scotland
Gender: Male
Grade/Rank: Trainer for the Iron Grenadiers
Faction(s): Destro
Stationed: Castle McCullen, Scotland
Primary MOS: Combat Training Instructor
Secondary MOS: Special services (bagpipe player)
Accessories: Helmet, jacket, kilt
Background Information: Trained in the Royal Regiment of the Scottish Army, graduated with top honors
Abilities: Close combat fighting; Destro clan member; Hybrid martial arts; Mercenary; Naturally talented; Offensive tactical skills; Professional Skill: Senior drill instructor; Qualified Weapon Expert: Explosives; Qualified Combat Expert: Hand-to-hand; Qualified Expert: Small arms

Conditions: Aggressive; Argumentative; Distinctive Feature: Kilted uniform
Quote/Motto: "Sooner or later, everybody pays the piper!"

Rugrat

Real Name: Unknown
Place of Birth: Unknown
Gender: Male
Grade/Rank: 3—Dreadnok
Faction(s): Dreadnok
Notably Served At: Los Angeles, California
Primary MOS: Wrestling
Secondary MOS: Demolitions
Appearance: Diminutive, thin, wears a large purple top hat and sunglasses
Abilities: Demolitions; Wrestling
Conditions: Diminutive

Sand Scorpion

Series: Twenty (2004)
Real Name: Varies
Place of Birth: Various; Doctor Mindbender's lab
Gender: Male and female
Service Branch: Army
Faction(s): Cobra
Primary MOS: Elite desert trooper
Secondary MOS: Infantry
Accessories: Black rifle; chest harness with water-squirting tail; two claws that could be worn over his hands or attached to the back of the harness
Abilities: Ambush; Breathe under the sand; Effective troops; Fierce warrior; Heavily armored; Wilderness Survival: Desert
Conditions: Distinctive Feature: Scales on their bodies; Fast; Fierce; Irritating and uncomfortable to breathe in the sand
Notes: All Sand Scorpion troops are hand-picked from the Cobra Sand Vipers to have their DNA recombined with scorpions to produce a more effective warrior. They are the products of a secret program run by Doctor Mindbender. Completely buried in the sand, they wait patiently in ambush; sensing the approach of a victim by feeling vibrations through the packed desert floor, they erupt out of their burrows to attack, with bio-mechanical scorpions mounted on their backs to slash with razor-sharp claws and spit venom. Breathing in the sand is irritating and uncomfortable, so Sand Scorpion troops come out of the sand in a bad mood and are ready to fight anything in front of them. They are formidable opponents best dealt with from a distance with a laser-guided missile.

S.A.W. Vipers (Semi-Automatic Weapons) Vipers

Series: Nine (1990)
Alias/Variations: Cobra S.A.W.-Vipers; was C.L.A.W.-Viper (Cobra Light Automatic Weapons)
Real Name: Various
Place of Birth: Various
Gender: Various
Service Branch: Cobra Army
Faction(s): Cobra, Cobra demolitions team
Notably Served At: Benzheen; Trucial Abysmia
Primary MOS: Squad automatic weapons
Secondary MOS: Heavy machine gunners
Appearance: Gold helmet with silver visor and black microphone; black shirt with a red crisscross pattern; red vest and gold armbands and gloves; red pants with gold boots and leggings; black belt
Accessories: Ammo belt; S.A.W.-Viper backpack; S.A.W.-Viper mini-gun and bipod
Abilities: Demolitions; Heavy gunners; Infantry; Qualified Weapons Experts: Modified mini-chain gun (see below)
Preferred Weapon: Gyro-stabilized, cryogenically cooled mini-chain gun, scoped with an infrared night-vision, auto-ranging, optical sighting system. It is a highly accurate, low-malfunction machine gun, and the barrel will not burn out during intense rapid-fire bursts. It also has a sound suppressor, a flash inhibitor, and a powerful image intensifier. Targets never hear or see it coming.
Conditions: Primarily used to provide cover fire for Crimson Asp
Quote/Motto: "You won't even know I've shot at you until you hear the sonic boom from the bullet whipping past your ear." "We will mow you down before you even hear the sonic boom of our bullets!"
Notes: The original S.A.W.-Viper, Robert Skelton, was recruited by The Coil during Serpentor's return to power in the second Cobra Civil War. Skelton volunteered (with the promise of an extra two months' pay) to execute the Joe prisoners, Doc, Thunder, Crankcase, and Heavy Metal. Later, when he was gravely injured, he was rebuilt as the cyborg Over Kill.

Scalpel

Series: Nineteen (2003)
Real Name: Andrew R. Walker
Place of Birth: Death Valley, California
Gender: Male
Service Branch: Cobra medic
Faction(s): Cobra
Notably Served At: Brooklyn, New York; Cobra Island; Cobra medical facility in Hawaii; the Coffin
Primary MOS: Medic
Secondary MOS: Infantry
Appearance: Yellow hair; blue-green jacket and pants; white chest panel with black straps and silver medical tools; gold right armband; black gloves; blue-green pants; white boots and kneepads with red Cobra emblems
Accessories: AK-47, detachable wrist-mounted surgical saw, hood with T-shaped cut-out for face, knife, shoulder pads with Cobra emblems, T-shaped visor attaching to hood, two carry hooks
Background Information: Received his medical degree through the mail from a small college that advertised on the back of a magazine
Abilities: Contact: Criminal family in Brooklyn; Doctor; Medic; Infantry; Professional Skill: Plastic surgeon
Conditions: Distinctive Feature: Nervous giggle when he's working; Enjoys his work; Grudge against Sergeant Hacker (reasons he won't reveal); In it for the money; Joined Cobra to work on exotic injuries/wounds; No bedside manner
Quote/Motto: "Unlike most medical practitioners, my patients never ask me if it is going to hurt. They know it is going to hurt."
Notes: Interestingly, his patients have a high survival rate. He was held in the maximum security prison called The Coffin, located in Greenland, and was one of several operatives who escaped during a raid led by Tomax.

Scar Face

Series: Twenty-four (2008)
Alias/Variations: Scarred Cobra Officer
Real Name: Unknown
Place of Birth: Unknown
Gender: Male
Grade/Rank: Officer
Service Branch: Cobra army
Faction(s): Cobra, Destro
Notably Served At: Coney Island, New York; San Francisco, California; Sierra Gordo; Washington, D.C.
Primary MOS: Espionage
Secondary MOS: Infantry
Appearance: Blue and black helmet, yellow and silver web gear, a black rifle, a black and silver knife
Abilities: Courier for Cobra Commander; Knowledge Skill: Intelligence community; Knowledge Skill: Day-to-day functions and routines of Cobra; Professional Skill: Chauffeur; Professional Skill: Secretary
Conditions: Cowardly; Dark and dangerous past; Distinctive Feature: V-shaped scar from his forehead to the tip of his nose; Infected by Dr. Venom's Toxin; Leery of working for Cobra; Little more than an errand boy; Mysterious; Other loyalties, possibly to Destro
Quote/Motto: "So, the mighty Destro thinks he's gonna fix my wagon, huh? Well, I've got something for him...." "Scar-Face is my Trojan horse and he will enable me to destroy G.I. Joe headquarters...."
Notes: He was used as a "biological time-bomb" to infect the G.I. Joe team with a deadly toxin invented by Doctor Venom. Scar-Face was killed when explosive charges destroyed G.I. Joe headquarters and he was trapped inside; few mourned his loss.

Scrap-Iron

Series: Three (1984)
Alias/Variations: Mech; Timothy P. Janes
Real Name: CLASSIFIED
Place of Birth: Providence, Rhode Island
Gender: Male
Grade/Rank: Cobra High Command member
Faction(s): Cobra, Destro, and the Phoenix Guard
Notably Served At: Battle of Springfield; Cobra Island; New Moon, Colorado
Primary MOS: Armored vehicle destroyer
Secondary MOS: Experimental weapons
Appearance: Black helmet and visor; a blue shirt with open collar; blue pants; dark red vest, belt, holster, and boots; black gloves and kneepads; red Cobra insignia on the right shoulder
Accessories: RAR pistol (with angled handle); missile system with remote activator, six-piece black missile launcher; two red missiles
Background Information: His prototype file card reads: "It is believed that [he] was a designer for Destro's armaments company who

worked himself up to being a field representative and product demonstrator."

Abilities: Anti-armor specialist; Fanatical about his job; Focus on the objective; Knowledge Skill: Cobra operations; Professional Skill: Product designer for Destro's M.A.R.S. company; Professional Skill: Weapons officer onboard the Cobra space shuttle; Qualified Weapons Expert: Experimental weapons; Remote-launched laser-guided weapons technology specialist; World-class armaments designer

Conditions: Argumentative; Hates imperfection; Loves to blow things up; Methodical; Obsessive-compulsive need for perfection in his designs; Precise

Quote/Motto: "Scrap-Iron is methodical and precise. Imperfection in any form repels him. Perhaps that's why he wants to blow up the world." An excerpt from his personality profile: "Scrap-Iron is excruciatingly methodical and precise. There is no margin for error in his universe. Imperfection in any form repels and disgusts him. Perhaps that's why he wants to blow up the world."

Notes: Scrap-Iron and other Phoenix Guards were arrested and are in custody. Weapons he designed are categorized beyond the "smart" stage and are known by the nomenclature "brilliant" (current state-of-the-art Mil-Tech terminology).

Secto-Viper

Series: Seven (1988)
Real Name: Various
Place of Birth: Various
Gender: Male and Female
Service Branch: Cobra navy
Faction(s): Cobra
Stationed: Cobra Island
Primary MOS: Amphibious operations
Secondary MOS: Marine surveillance
Appearance: Black face mask; black shirt under yellow diving suit and gloves; orange tubing on chest; black padded codpiece and black cuffs over yellow boots
Accessories: Clear dome helmet; futuristic laser pistol with a fin on top
Abilities: Amphibious Operations specialists; Deep sea divers; Knowledge Skill: "Soft" points and areas of vulnerability; Knowledge Skill: Amphibious landing craft currently in use; Knowledge Skill: Assigned sector of shoreline; Qualified Expert Operator: Bugg; Unique marine surveillance specialists

Conditions: Constantly on patrol; Overzealous; Too conscientious

Quote/Motto: "Secto-Vipers are too conscientious. They're always speeding over the dunes or creeping about under the surf. Off-duty Cobra personnel can't spread a towel on the beach to catch some rays without being reduced by an overzealous Secto-Viper looking to make brownie points with his superiors. Not the greatest thing in the world for morale!"

Sergeant Major

Series: Twenty-eight (2012)
Alias/Variations: Sergeant Major Duncan
Real Name: Alastair Thomas Duncan
Place of Birth: Callander, Scotland
Gender: Male
Grade/Rank: Company Sergeant Major (WO2)
Service Branch: M.A.R.S. ground forces
Faction(s): Iron Grenadiers
Stationed: Castle Destro
Primary MOS: Leader of the Iron Grenadiers/Company Sergeant Major
Secondary MOS: Drill instructor
Appearance: Red beret; long coat with red trim and a red Iron Grenadiers armband; black pants and footwear
Accessories: Rifle, sash, sword, sword guard, two pistols
Abilities: Aide-de-camp; Company Sergeant Major of Destro's Castle; Destro's right-hand man; Destro's trusted assistant, driver, and bodyguard; Highly efficient; Warrant officer
Conditions: Extremely loyal; Fair but firm; Tolerates no dissent
Quote/Motto: "Never disappoint Laird Destro."
Notes: Directly responsible for all matters concerning the deportment, discipline, and morale of the unit. He enforces Destro's orders fairly but firmly, and tolerates no dissent, lest the Iron Grenadiers break down into another backstabbing Cobra unit. As the troops are already motivated by wealth and rewarded accordingly, punishment for disobedience is swift and final.

Sergeant Major is not a rank in the British Army and Royal Marines: it is used in the title of various appointments held by Warrant Officers. In particular, the Regimental Sergeant Major (RSM) (WO1) is the senior warrant officer in a battalion or regiment. The Company Sergeant Major (CSM) (WO2) is the senior warrant officer of a company.

Serpentor

Series: Five (1986)
Alias/Variations: Prototype names were Cobra Rex, King Cobra, Rama Set, ZoR. "Serpy" is the nickname occasionally used by Zartan and Zarana to mock the Cobra leader.
Place of Birth: Doctor Mindbender's lab in Springfield
Gender: Male
Grade/Rank: Cobra Emperor
Faction(s): Cobra
Notably Served At: Battle of Springfield; the Pit; Sierra Gordo
Primary MOS: Cobra Emperor
Appearance: Black hair; gold scaled snake-head helmet and uniform with yellow mouth and central chest padding; green serpents on shoulders; green gloves, belt, and leg padding
Other Known Appearances (Cartoon): Dark green cape; uniform has darker green detail and wider segmented chest padding. The commercial animation for Serpentor showed red trim on his hood, arms, and legs. He also had the voice of an aged man in spite of his youthful physique.

The Hasbro mail-in version has many differences from the retail version. On the figure's chest, the snakes have curved tail tips; the chin has visible mold separation; the quality of plastic used is inferior and brittle; the yellow paint is a noticeably lighter shade. Occasionally, the neck of the figure is painted yellow. The snake accessory also came in an array of colors: brown, gold, gold-brown, and translucent green.
Accessories: Cobra cowl; cobra (in one of four colors); decorative ceremonial dagger with segmented handle; golden cobra-hood backpack; green cloth cape
Abilities: Allies: Doctor Mindbender; Allies: Tomax; Allies: Xamot; Charismatic; Diplomat; Financial acumen; Followers: His troops; Heightened intelligence; Heightened strength; Knowledge Skill: G.I. Joe Organization; Leadership; Orator; Political intrigue expert; Propaganda expert; Qualified Expert Operator: Air Chariot, Moray, Night Raven; Tactician; Wise
Conditions: Ambitious; Clone; Daring; Generous to his friends; Implanted loyalty to Cobra; Implanted memories; Intolerant of cowards; Revels in battle; Ruthless; Seeks to defeat his enemies; Seeks world conquest; Severe disciplinarian; Temperamental

In the cartoon: Impatient; Unstable; Unwilling to receive advice

Quote/Motto: "Serpentor … is that my name? I seem to remember … others…." "His eyes have seen the legions of Rome trample the Gauls and Nervii into the dust. His hand lifted the horse-hair baton that signaled the first charge of the Carthaginian armored elephant phalanx. His ears have heard the rattle of French cuirassiers on the streets of Moscow. But it is his mind we must fear the most. The thoughts of the Cobra Emperor have not drifted from global conquest since the reign of King Solomon…."
Notes: Serpentor is a composite clone created from the DNA of Adolf Hitler, Alexander the Great, Attila the Hun, Benito Mussolini, Cyrus the Great, Erik the Red, Erik the Batterer; Francisco Franco, George S. Patton, Genghis Khan, Geronimo, Grigori Rasputin, Hannibal, Henry V of England, Ivan the (Terrible) IV of Russia, Karl Marx, Julius Caesar, King Takshaka, Leonidas King of Sparta, Mao Zedong, Montezuma, Moctezuma II, Napoleon, Nebuchadnezzar, Rasputin, Rip Cord, Sennacherib, Simón Bolívar, Sgt. Slaughter, Solomon, Storm Shadow, Ulric the Batterer, Vlad the Impaler, Xanoth Amon-Toth, and "dozens more." Doctor Mindbender was unable to obtain the DNA of Chinese military genius Sun Tzu.

During his experiments to create Serpentor, Doctor Mindbender created 10 other cloned bodies whose "ages" were not accelerated. Though Cobra Commander ordered the children to be disposed of, Doctor Mindbender secreted them away.

Serpentor was shot between the eyes with an arrow by Zartan during the Cobra Civil War. Doctor Mindbender preserved his body in the island's land-locked freighter, hoping to find a way to revive his creation, but the body was believed lost when the true Cobra Commander returned and buried it under tons of rock.

Calling themselves The Coil, Cobra agents still loyal to Serpentor recovered his body and continued to preserve it, hoping to someday revive their leader. A few years later, they were successful. Serpentor was alive again, and he and The Coil began gathering other loyal former Cobras, creating an army in secret. Doctor Mindbender has since been brought back to life as a clone. While in hiding, through his dreams he began to realize he had a psychic link to the clone children. He and three of the children waited for Serpentor to reveal himself to the world. When the government moved the remaining children, Serpentor and The Coil attacked. Serpentor grabbed Daemon by the throat and broke his neck, killing him. Mikhail Derenko became Serpentor's second-in-command, taking the name Overlord. Serpentor staged an assault on the world. Battle between The Coil, the Joes, and Cobra raged. In the battle, Serpentor was presumed dead, but a nearly lifeless body was recovered by Overlord, who had been hired by the Jugglers. Gibbs placed Serpentor's body in a tank like the one he had been born in and began trying to modify his DNA and reprogram him.

Shadow Strike

Series: Twenty-one (2005)
Real Name: Unknown
Place of Birth: Unknown
Gender: Male
Service Branch: Cobra Army
Faction(s): Cobra
Primary MOS: Infiltration
Secondary MOS: Ninja
Appearance: Red ninja outfit
Accessories: Two knives
Abilities: Corrupts an organization from within; Detects personal weakness in others; Distinctive Feature: Arashikage clan markings on his right arm; Heightened movement; Infiltrator; Martial arts; Ninja; Spy
Conditions: Belief: He is above clan loyalty; Looks down on team actions; Lone wolf; Opportunist; Patient; Values individual actions
Quote/Motto: "I am a blade of grass pushing against a rock until the stone splits. That which appears harmless can destroy a mountain with time and perseverance."

Shary Wingfield

Series: One (1982)
Real Name: Sharon Wingfield
Gender: Female
Grade/Rank: Lieutenant
Service Branch: Militia
Faction(s): Cobra, Strike First
Stationed: Montana
Primary MOS: Strike First lieutenant
Appearance: Long blonde hair
Abilities: Aide to Vance Wingfield
Conditions: Concern for the welfare of Strike First members and their families; Realizes her husband is insane; Resents the U.S. government; Son: Tyler; Taken in by Vance Wingfield's rhetoric; Wife of Vance Wingfield
Notes: Shary appears in the comics. She shoots her husband in the back just before he was about to shoot the wife of a Strike First member. Years later, her son Tyler would pick up his father's mantle and attempt to release the Death Angel virus. To save the world, Shary shoots her son, also in the back.

The Silencer

Series: Thirteen (1996)
Real Name: CLASSIFIED
Place of Birth: CLASSIFIED
Gender: Male
Service Branch: Mercenary
Faction(s): Freelance mercenary
Notably Served At: South America
Primary MOS: Sharpshooter
Appearance: Slicked back black hair, red goggles, black trench coat
Background Information: Former member of the U.S. Special Forces
Abilities: Custom glove*; Custom trench coat; Custom motorcycle; Embraces modern technology and new devices; Marksmanship; Mercenary
Conditions: Blames Ballistic and Julia Rossi* for his injuries and fate; Distinctive Feature: Scar on his face above his eye; Highly completive; Knowledge Skill: SKAR; Often works for SKAR; Reputation: Expert marksmanship; Loves motorcycles; Reputation: One of the best snipers Special Forces ever had; Rivalry with Ballistic (G.I. Joe); Rumor: Shooting hand has a tremor; Seeks revenge against Ballistic; Sore loser; Wanted for attempted murder
Notes: The Silencer takes the rivalry far more seriously than Ballistic ever did, up until the night Silencer tried to murder him in his sleep. Silencer was court-martialed and thrown out of the military for his behavior.

*Julia Rossi, a young ballistics expert, is his ex-girlfriend. She designed a prototype weapon that Silencer stole after they broke up; it exploded on him when he tried to assassinate Ballistic.

His custom glove has two functions: it steadies his sometimes-shaky hand and acts much like a high-powered taser. The trench coat acts as a sound suppressor; it somehow silences all noise around him, making it easier for him to sneak up on people.

S.K.A.R.

Alias/Variations: Soldiers of Kaos, Anarchy, and Ruin

Purpose: Soldiers of Kaos, Anarchy, and Ruin, a.k.a. S.K.A.R., is a multi-faceted organization; however, the militant terrorist wing was the only aspect of it truly explored. The organization is much larger than it appears. S.K.A.R. is an Illuminati-like organization seeking to destroy the Inter-Alliance (United Nations) as it is a threat to their efforts to control the world. S.K.A.R. has an active recruiting campaign in place around the world, seeking to bring those disaffected with the current world order into the fold. They also have extensive connections to several syndicates the world over, including the Tongs. While the organization is supposed to be secret, many members of the American military and Inter-Alliance are well aware of its existence, although the extent of their knowledge is not revealed.

Leader: Iron Klaw, Count Otto Von Rani

Members: Steel Raven (Klaw's right-hand woman); Inferno, Rampage, Wreckage, and countless S.K.A.R. Soldiers (robotic foot soldiers). The Silencer is not a member but a freelance mercenary who frequently works for S.K.A.R.

Notes: S.K.A.R. was also indirectly referenced in several Transformers comics.

Skeletron

Real Name: Unknown
Place of Birth: Unknown
Gender: Unknown
Grade/Rank: Elite Operative
Faction(s): Red Shadow
Primary MOS: Military strategy
Secondary MOS: Pilot
Appearance: Skeletal head, skeleton-like limbs; red humanoid torso
Abilities: Command; Leadership; Fixed-wing pilot
Conditions: Distinctive Feature: Skeleton with a red trunk; Fights in the field of combat; Unknown who or what he is
Notes: Skeletron is the ultimate blank slate. Released as part of the Action Force line in the UK, it was only available as a mail-in and was never offered on a card. As such, there are no details available about the character via file card bio or comic appearance.

Skull Buster

Series: Eighteen (2002)
Real Name: Albert F. Packer
Place of Birth: Donner Pass, California
Gender: Male
Grade/Rank: Range-Viper Commander
Service Branch: Cobra Army
Faction(s): Cobra
Notably Served At: A deserted island in the wilds of Namibia
Primary MOS: Tactical tracking operations
Secondary MOS: Wilderness survival instructor
Accessories: Ammunition belt, backpack, bola, grenade launcher with drum clip, helmet, machine gun with bipod, pistol, shoulder holster, spear
Abilities: Evasion skills; Excels at improvising weapons; Infantry; Hunting; Lives off the land; Operations commander; Survivalist; Tactical tracking operations; Wilderness Survival: Inhospitable locales; Wilderness survival instructor
Conditions: Embraced the life of a survivalist; Fears imprisonment; Grew up neglected; Imagines himself the ultimate alpha predator; Rumor: Human bones with teeth marks on them in his locker; Worked up the ranks; Vicious
Quote/Motto: "Any wimp with a scout handbook, a Swiss army knife, and a compass can survive." "I hope we run into some G.I. Joes soon, I'm feeling hungry for a fight!"
Notes: He was held in the maximum security prison called The Coffin, located in Greenland, and was one of several operatives who escaped during a raid led by Tomax.

Sky Creeper

Series: Ten (1991)
Alias/Variations: Nightwing, Sky Skull
Real Name: Brad L. Cooper
Place of Birth: Pueblo, Colorado
Gender: Male
Grade/Rank: Air Recon leader
Service Branch: Cobra Air Force
Faction(s): Cobra, Night Vultures
Notably Served At: Lincoln, Nebraska
Primary MOS: Air Recon leader
Secondary MOS: Criminal operations
Appearance: Yellow helmet and goggles; a blue-green shirt with yellow straps and gloves; black pants with yellow belt and leggings; black boots

Accessories: Hang glider, pistol with scope and distinct trigger but no trigger guard
Abilities: Aerial reconnaissance; Commander of the Night Vultures; Contact: Fence; Professional Skill: Criminal; Professional Skill: Theft and robbery; Qualified Expert Operator: Glider
Conditions: Known Criminal; Specializes in robbing rooftop restaurants
Quote/Motto: "Swoop in, swoop out, and fence the goods before the mark knows they're gone." "Sky Creeper is not a glider enthusiast who happens to be a criminal; he's a criminal with an interest in gliders so long as they help promote his illicit activities. He is not at all enraptured by the glider's graceful lines, fluid controls, or birdlike feeling of oneness with the sky. His only concern is whether it will carry enough loot and still avoid radar detection."
Notes: Recruited by the Dreadnoks while in prison. Sky Creeper was considered for membership in The Plague but failed the evaluation.

Slash

Series: Twenty-one (2005)
Real Name: Unknown
Place of Birth: Jonestown, Guyana
Gender: Male
Faction(s): Cobra; Ninja Force
Stationed: Cobra Citadel in Trans-Carpathia
Notably Served At: Millville
Primary MOS: Swordsman
Secondary MOS: Espionage
Appearance: Gray bodysuit, red gi with a white strip and Cobra emblem; black boots, headband, belt, and gloves; prefers wearing an uwagi bearing Cobra's emblem over ninja garb
Accessories: Carrying case, two-piece staff, two sword halves
Abilities: Ambush; Heightened strength; Highly graceful; Mercenary, Ninja; Qualified Operator: Cobra Parasite; Sword master
Conditions: Behaves politely with Slice in a humorous way; Cold and calculating; Distinctive Feature: Wields twin dao broadswords; Distinctive martial arts style; Exiled by his clan for numerous crimes; Frequently partners with Slice; Former mental slave of Firefly; Lacks humanity; Lacks the silent, subtle ways of the ninja; Laughs at wrong things
Quote/Motto: "I am a living weapon, the sole reason for my existence is to cut and slice. I am a sword without a scabbard, and I am always thirsty."
Notes: Recruited into Cobra by Storm Shadow, he frequently partners with Dice. In the IDW Universe he killed Snake Eyes's students, including Dojo, Banzai, Nunchuk, T'Gin Zu, and T'Jbang under orders of Raja Khallikhan. He is not to be confused with Colonel Slash.

Slice

Series: Eleven (1992)
Alias/Variations: Cobra Slice
Real Name: Unknown
Place of Birth: Jonestown, Guyana
Gender: Male
Service Branch: Cobra ninja
Faction(s): Cobra
Primary MOS: Cobra ninja swordsman
Secondary MOS: Espionage
Appearance: Net-shaped mask; Four-point quick-flick throwing star, Full face cloaking mask; Jab hook heavy sword; Ninja leather shin guard; Super slash stiletto, Wide butterfly battle knife; two cloth ribbons attached to his right hip
Accessories: Ax, bisento spear, butterfly knife, heavy sword, hooked sword, two double-sided knives
Abilities: Ambush; Frequently works with Slash; Heightened strength; Qualified Operator: Cobra Parasite; Qualified Weapons Expert: All edged weapons, explosives, small handguns; Supreme swordsman
Conditions: Behaves politely with Slash in a humorous way; Distinctive Feature: Attacks from behind; Distinctive Feature: Sword attack copies the attack patterns of the Scorpions; Lacks the silent, subtle ways of the ninja; Reputation: Considered Cobra's supreme swordsman; Renegade of the Arashikage clan
Quote/Motto: "I fear no mortal man in face-to-face combat, but my sword cuts easiest from behind!"

Snow Serpent

Series: Four (1985)
Alias/Variations: Cobra Snow Viper
Real Name: Various
Place of Birth: Various countries
Gender: Male
Grade/Rank: E-4
Service Branch: Cobra Army

Faction(s): Cobra
Stationed: Graduate of six-month cold weather course; Graduate of Eel School; Graduate of Ice-Viper program; Graduate of Techno-Viper program
Notably Served At: Action Force Apogee Base, Greenland; Norwegian Arctic Circle
Primary MOS: Cold weather environment operations
Secondary MOS: Polar infantry
Appearance: 1985: Black face mask, blue backpack straps, blue belt, blue boots, blue goggles, off-white helmet, off-white snowsuit, red Cobra insignia on left arm, white-furred collar, white-furred gloves; 1991: Brown belt, brown boots with yellow fur, brown gloves, brown straps, purple face mask, white helmet, white pants, white shirt with furred chest and wrists, yellow furred goggles with red eyepiece; 1993: Black belt, black boots with white fur, black eyepiece, black gloves, black helmet, black straps, blue pants, blue shirt with white furred chest and wrists, red face mask, white-furred goggles
Other Known Appearances: Overstock of this action figure was sold at the 1992 G.I. Joe convention; it was misnamed "Cobra Snow Viper."
Accessories: 1985: AK-47, Anti-tank EK-99 missile with stand, parachute pack, snow shows, survival pack; 1991: Large, rectangular purple frame backpack with hole for missile launcher; purple snowboard, short spring-loaded missile launcher with handle and scope trigger; two standard short black hoses, white missile (original sculpt), white wrapped machine gun with scope and sloped magazine, white wrapped pistol with scope and peg for hose; 1993: Black submachine gun
Abilities: Airborne operations under Arctic conditions; Anti-tank procedures; Kayaking; Skiing; Survival Skill: Artic
Conditions: Reputation: Arctic Specialist branch of the Eels
Quote/Motto: "If the Eels are the elite of Cobra's naval branch, then the Snow Serpents are the best of the best. How else could you characterize an individual who would parachute onto an ice floe in sub-zero temperatures and then be prepared to march 50 miles with full field pack, assault rifle, and anti-tank weapon?" Quote taken from an unnamed G.I. Joe member.
Notes: The Two-Headed Serpent, a Cobra splinter faction, also has Snow Serpents in the Himalayas.

Snow Wolf

Series: Twenty (2004)
Alias/Variations: Snow Wolf troopers
Real Name: Varies
Place of Birth: Various; Doctor Mindbender's lab
Gender: Male and Female
Service Branch: Army
Faction(s): Cobra, V-troops
Stationed: The Arctic
Primary MOS: Polar sentry
Secondary MOS: Infantry
Appearance: White arctic bodysuit, gray-furred boots, gray-furred gloves, gray ski mask with black re-breather and goggles
Accessories: Silver assault rifle, silver pistol, silver submachine gun, white cloak
Abilities: Expert marksmen; Heightened endurance; Heightened strength; Hybridized DNA of Arctic wolf; Immune to the effects of the cold; Pack Mentality; Swimming; Traverse icy terrain
Conditions: Complacent and listless in warm weather; Despise fire; Distinctive Feature: Travel in packs; Feral, Heightened aggression; Subjected to a grueling and dangerous training program; Unpredictable
Quote/Motto: "The enemy cannot escape, the elements cannot hide them—or stop us."

Star-Viper

Series: Seven (1988)
Alias/Variations: Jolt-Head; Star Viper
Real Name: Unknown
Place of Birth: Unknown
Gender: Male
Service Branch: Cobra Air Force
Faction(s): Cobra
Notably Served At: Cobra Island; the Pit III
Primary MOS: Stellar Stiletto pilot
Secondary MOS: Jet fighter pilot
Appearance: Black insectoid helmet with red visor; black flight suit with gold X-shaped straps and gloves; black boots
Accessories: None
Abilities: Aeronautical engineering; Heightened tolerance for g-forces than other Strato-Viper; Professional Skill: Test pilot; Qualified Expert Operator: Stellar Stiletto; Qualified Operator: Cobra Strato-Viper with an

electro-magnetic shunt surgically implanted in the right side of the brain; Shunt gives heightened senses; Shunt gives heightened reflexes; Shunt gives an advantage in high altitude dogfights

Conditions: Arrogant; Brave; Calculating; Craves recognition; Daring; Generally disoriented between missions; Generally distracted between missions; Heightened vanity; Not popular amongst other Cobras; Precision oriented

Quote/Motto: "Star-Vipers are exceedingly dangerous in action! They routinely execute fast maneuvers with insect-like efficiency. However, they are referred to as 'Jolt-Heads' by their fellow Cobras and are known to be distracted and generally disoriented between missions."

Steel Cobra

Series: Twenty-seven (2011)
Alias/Variations: Cobra de Aco (Brazil)
Real Name: Unknown
Place of Birth: Unknown
Gender: Male
Service Branch: Cobra army
Faction(s): Cobra, Python Patrol
Stationed: The Brazilian Amazon
Primary MOS: Laser weapons specialist
Secondary MOS: Infiltration
Appearance: Black body armor with large yellow areas; Cobra emblem in red on the chest; The word "Estrela" is inscribed in raised letters on the figure's back.
Accessories: Belt, backpack, laser rifle
Abilities: Calculated strategist; Oversees Cobra's Python Patrol facility in the Brazilian Amazon
Conditions: Boastful egotist; Clashes with superior officers; Distinctive Feature: Wears unique helmet and notoriously garish body armor; Grating personality; Incredibly conceited; The most feared operative of Cobra Command; Others refuse to work with him; Obsession with Claymore causes him to lose his tactical advantage; Proud; Seeks revenge against Claymore
Quote/Motto: "The man that can stop me has yet to be born!"

Steel Raven

Series: Fourteen (1995); thirty-three (2017)
Real Name: Unknown
Place of Birth: Unknown
Gender: Female
Grade/Rank: OF-1 (Lieutenant)
Faction(s): S.K.A.R.
Primary MOS: Infantry commander
Secondary MOS: Interrogation
Appearance: Black hair (originally brown); Commander uniform with hat, eyepatch
Accessories: Coat, data pad, hat, rifle, two pistols
Abilities: Chief interrogator; Commands all special forces operations; Delegates tasks and missions assigned by Iron Klaw; Force to be reckoned with; Handpicks each recruit; Instruction; Interrogation; Logistics; Oversees the morale, professional development, and welfare of soldiers under her command; Oversees training; Recruitment
Conditions: Brutal medieval methods; Fanatically committed to the ultimate destruction of the existing world powers; Follows orders without question; Joined S.K.A.R. as a pre-teen; Lost left eye; Reputation: Most dangerous woman alive; Rumor: Lost eye saving Iron Klaw's life; Steadfastly loyal to her commander
Quote/Motto: "The only true test of loyalty is through your sacrifice!"
Notes: Her toy was released years after her appearance, accounting for her series listing two years.

Stiletto

Real Name: Paithoon Kwaigno
Place of Birth: Hua Hin, Thailand
Gender: Female
Grade/Rank: E-5
SN: 414-33-PK72
Service Branch: Cobra Army
Faction(s): Cobra
Notably Served At: Alejandro Selkirk Island, Chile; Casamance, Senegal; Gotland, Sweden; Cobra Island; Flores, Indonesia; Kersab, Trucial Abysmia; Laos; the Pit; San Francisco, California
Primary MOS: Covert operations
Secondary MOS: Infantry
Appearance: Long black hair kept in a tight single braid; dead left eye, ugly scar running from the white streak of hair on the top left side of her face, down over her left eye, nostril, lip, ending on her chin; black thigh-high boots, green pants, black corset, maroon chest armor, black short-sleeved shirt, bright blue scarf
Accessories: Dragunov, machine gun, pistol, two hooked knives—katana and tonto—and sheath for each

Abilities: Contact: The Plague; Contact: Whisper; Covert operations; Demolitions; Extensive military training; Heightened battle skills; Highly skilled with bladed weapons; Infantry; Infiltration; Knowledge Skill: Cobra Commander; Knowledge Skill: Missing persons; Personal agent of Cobra Commander; Professional Skill: Bodyguard (to Felix "Mercer" Stratton); Qualified Weapons Expert: Bladed weapons; Qualified Weapons: Most NATO and Warsaw Pact small arms; Research: Missing persons; Special forces training; Tracking

Conditions: Ambitious; Distinctive Feature: Facially disfigured; Grudge against Serenity; Mysterious Past; Openly covets the Baroness's position; Torture survivor

Notes: Stiletto is undercover for Cobra in the G.I. Joe ranks. There is another Cobra member with the code name Stiletto; she works directly for Cobra Commander.

Storm Rider

Series: Twenty-six (2010)
Real Name: Unknown
Gender: Male
Faction(s): Cobra
Appearance: Short Mohawk; black shirt, gray cargo pants, black biker boots, black biker gloves
Accessories: Bandana, pistol
Abilities: Born to ride!; Knowledge Skill: POPS-2 pneumatic oscillating pressure-spike weapon system; Professional Skill: Custom motorcycles; Professional Skill: Bike-mounted weapons; Qualified Expert Operator: Doom Cycle; Qualified Expert: Brawler, martial artist

Storm Shadow

Series: Three (1984)
Alias/Variations: Cobra do Gelo (Brazil); Cobra de Hielo (Argentina); Ghost Shadow; Ninja-Ku (Argentina); Phoenix Master; Satan (Argentina); Sombra (Spain); Sombra Blanca (Mexico); Thomas M. Arashikage (2004); Tomisaburo Arashikage; Tommy Yureikage; Young Master
Real Name: Thomas "Tommy" S. Arashikage (1997)
Place of Birth: Fresno, California; San Francisco, California; St. Louis, Missouri (sources conflict)
Gender: Male
Grade/Rank: CLASSIFIED (E-8 Master Sergeant; only listed with a rank while a member of the Joe team)
SN: CLASSIFIED
Service Branch: Army; Ninja Force (G.I. Joe) Cobra Urban Strike; Cobra Ninja Strike Force
Faction(s): Cobra, G.I. Joe 1988, Ninja Force 1992 (Leader), Shadow Ninjas 1994, and Sound Attack (Leader)
Notably Served At: Battle of Benzheen; Borovia; Cobra's Arctic Base; Cobra Island; the High Sierras; Hong Kong; Manhattan; Millville; New Moon, Colorado; Southeast Asia; Tibet; Trans-Carpathia; Vietnam
Primary MOS: Assassin, sabotage; covert operations (sources conflict)
Secondary MOS: Intelligence; martial arts instructor (sources conflict)
Appearance: Japanese American with black hair and dark eyes. 1984: white face mask, short-sleeved tunic, wrist wraps, pants, and boots; black diagonal strap; red Cobra insignia on left chest.

1988: white ninja suit with hood and face mask, all with dark gray urban camo; dark gray rope across chest; red tattoo on right forearm; white boots. 1992 Ninja Force: black helmet and face mask with cloth hood; green shirt and pants with black stripes; black straps, gloves, belt, and boots. There were 50 different versions of Storm Shadow created for retail.

Other Known Appearances: White uniform with a long jacket (*G.I. Joe: Reloaded* Universe)
Accessories: 1984: bow, katana sword, quiver-backpack with engraved arrows, small nunchuks, wakizashi knife; 1988: Black, three-tined claw attaching to the wrist; high-tension Yumi bow with telescopic sights and sculpted arrows; large, square backpack with clips on the side for sword; sword with ribbed hilt; Ninja Force 1992: Sword with a long hilt and thick, curving blade; nunchuks
Background Information: Began career in mainstream U.S. intelligence groups (*G.I. Joe: Sigma 6*); Ranger School; Served on long-range recon patrol (LRRP); Served in U.S. Army special operations; He traces family history through 30 generations of assassins.
Abilities: Apprentice: Junko Akita; Arashikage martial arts; Bodyguard and mentor to the Baroness (*G.I. Joe: Retaliation*); Covert ops counterintelligence expert; Eighth-degree

black belt in several martial arts; Followers: Highly trained support troopers (*G.I. Joe: A Real American Hero*); Followers: Ninja B.A.T. support troopers (*G.I. Joe: Sigma 6*); Heightened reflexes; Heightened resistance to pain; Heightened speed; Instruction: Intelligence; Knowledge Skill: Billy; Knowledge Skill: Cobra operations; Language Skill: Korean; Martial arts instructor; Martial arts specialist; Professional Skill: Assassin; Professional Skill: Bodyguard; Professional Skill: Ninja; Qualified Weapons Expert: Longbow, katana, nunchaku, shuriken; Sabotage; Stealth; U.S. Army special operations; Undercover sabotage operations specialist

Conditions: Belief: Beyond redemption (*G.I. Joe: Renegades* Universe); Belief: Will somehow set things right; Blames Snake Eyes for the downfall of the Arashikage ninja clan (*Sigma 6*); Bloodlust (*G.I. Joe: Resolute* Universe); Brainwashed to believe G.I. Joe and Snake Eyes were his enemies (*G.I. Joe: Sigma 6*); Cousin of Kimi Arashikage (Jinx, *G.I. Joe: Renegades* Universe); Distinctive Feature: Paired with his sword brother, Snake Eyes; Distinctive Feature: Tattoo of the *I Ching* named *jì jì* ("Already Fording"); Distinctive Feature: White uniform and mask; Enemy of Quick Kick (Sunbow Universe); Enemy of Spirit (Sunbow Universe); Family in Japan; History with Snake Eyes (back to childhood); Hunted by Red Ninjas; In love with Junko Akita; Loyal only to Cobra (Sunbow universe); Periodic hallucinations and visions of devils once freed of Cobra's brainwave scanner; Reputation: Cobra Commander's ninja bodyguard; Respects Snake Eyes's abilities and skill; Rivalry with Snake Eyes (*G.I. Joe: Resolute* Universe); Traitorous half-brother: Snake Eyes (*G.I. Joe: Reloaded* Universe); Watched by Shipwreck

Quote/Motto: "The great ninja assassin clans disappeared a hundred years ago. If they were wiped out, nobody took the credit for it and if they're still around—who are they working for?" "Will my past ever stop catching up to me?" "Tommy's unpronounceable name? It translates directly into English as 'Storm Shadow.'" Said of him by Stalker.

Notes: Currently, Storm Shadow is on reserve status. Conflicted in loyalties between Cobra, G.I. Joe, and his blood brother, Snake Eyes, Storm Shadow has changed sides several times. The duo has been everything to each other from the bitterest of enemies to the most loyal of friends, who would fight and die for each other. He was trained by his estranged uncle, the Hard Master. In the DiC universe, Storm Shadow claims he only joined Cobra to find out who had dishonored his ninja clan.

Strato-Viper

Series: Five (1986)
Real Name: Various
Place of Birth: Various
Faction(s): Cobra, Air-Viper
Stationed: Cobra Island
Primary MOS: Cobra Night Raven S3P Pilot
Secondary MOS: Infantry
Appearance: Black and red helmet with silver visor; dark gray flight suit with a red vest and black wristbands and leg coverings; silver kneepads; black and red boots
Other Known Appearances (Cartoon): Neck and chin uncovered below helmet; light gray gloves
Accessories: Included with the Cobra Night Raven S3P; no additional accessories
Abilities: Best of the best; Contemptuous view of the Star-Vipers; Double or triple salary; Fixed-wing rating up to four engines; Heightened resistance to hypoxia, hyperventilation, and other decompression sicknesses; Heightened strength; Highly skilled; Pilot; Professional Skill: Air-Viper; Qualified Operator: Night Raven spy plane; Security clearance
Conditions: Extreme arrogance; Hated by fellow Cobras; Hated by the Star-Vipers; Reputation: Best secret agents in the world
Quote/Motto: "To qualify as a Strato-Viper, a candidate must first be an Air-Viper with 1500 hours logged in flight time. He must have a fixed-wing rating of up to four engines, combat experience, an impeccable security clearance, and be willing to undergo the surgical procedure necessary to make him more resistant to hypoxia, hyperventilation, and other decompression sicknesses that can affect a pilot above Armstrong's Line (63,000 feet)."

Strike First

Purpose: To train for the inevitable World War Three, to survive, and to rule over the aftermath. Their base of operations is located in the wilderness of Montana. They are funded by Cobra.
Leader: Commander Vance Wingfield

Members: Shary Wingfield, second in command; a small army of followers

Swamp Rat

Series: Twenty (2004)
Alias/Variations: Various
Real Name: Varies
Place of Birth: Various; Doctor Mindbender's lab
Gender: Males
Service Branch: Army
Faction(s): Cobra, V-Troop
Notably Served At: Sewer systems and wetlands
Primary MOS: Wetland infantry specialist
Secondary MOS: Scrounger
Appearance: Bald with a brown and gray bodysuit with black banding, brown gloves, black face mask re-breather, and holsters; Brown belt and gray knee pads
Other Known Appearances: Versions 2 and 3 are the same sculpt, but with different color bodysuits
Accessories: Brown helmet, cape, and tail that attaches to the cape; black rifle, two knives
Abilities: Contortionist; Escapology; Fighting Style: Frenzied resistance; Hiding; Immune to most diseases; Infiltration; Iron stomach; Knowledge Skill: Sewer systems; Sabotage; Stealth; Survival Skill: Fetid, stagnant water
Conditions: Inadequate combat troops
Quote/Motto: "Nasty traps they set for us, and electrified fences—but none of that can keep us from creeping in and gnawing through their walls."
Notes: All Swamp Rats are either volunteers or captured civilians who were transformed by the Venom serum.

Swamp Viper

Series: Nineteen (2003)
Real Name: Various
Place of Birth: Various
Service Branch: Cobra army
Faction(s): Cobra
Stationed: Cobra Island
Primary MOS: Amphibious assault troopers
Secondary MOS: Infantry
Appearance: Black helmet with silver face shield; gray shirt with a blue vest; black gloves and belt; gray pants with blue waist and boots
Accessories: Backpack, flamethrower, machine gun, rifle, submachine gun
Abilities: Amphibious assault troopers; Elite troopers; Jungle assault expert; Knowledge Skill: Canals and swampland; Knowledge Skill: Cobra Island fauna; Knowledge Skill: Cobra Island flora; Knowledge Skill: Cobra Island; Marine; Qualified Operators: Fangboat; Stealth; Tropical battle tactics; Wilderness Survival: Cobra Island; Wilderness Survival: Jungle; Wilderness Survival: Swamps
Preferred Weapon: D57-A Extreme Environment Tactical Rifle
Conditions: Distinctive Feature: M.A.R.S. Industries D57-A Extreme Environment Tactical Rifle; Live for the thrill of capturing invaders; Ruthless adversaries
Quote/Motto: "I will not take any chances; I've personally selected a detachment of the most ruthless Swamp Viper members to accompany me during my meeting with Black Dragon on Anaconda Beach." Quote by Cobra Commander.
Notes: They wear fully protective uniforms with oxygen re-breather units built into their bulbous helmets.

Tele-Viper

Series: Four (1985)
Alias/Variations: Estrela (Brazil, 1991), Python Tele-Viper; prototype name was Tele-Wraith
Real Name: Various
Place of Birth: Various
Gender: Male
Grade/Rank: E-4
Service Branch: Cobra Army
Faction(s): Cobra
Notably Served At: Australian Outback; Gulf of Arabia; Himalayas; Italy; London; Milleville; Silent Castle
Primary MOS: Communications
Secondary MOS: Electronics
Appearance: 1985: Black belt with purple pockets, blue helmet with mics, blue pants, blue short-sleeved shirt, purple padded vest, red Cobra insignia on left arm; silver goggles; 1989: Black boots, dark gray padded vest, pants with light gray crisscross pattern, red belt, red goggles, yellow and black helmet with mics, yellow short-sleeved shirt; 2003: Black belt with red Cobra logo, blue padded vest, dark gray pants, dark gray short-sleeved shirt, gray helmet, olive drab boots, silver goggles; 2004: Black and gray belt, black boots, brown padded vest, gray helmet with black Cobra logo, gray pants, gray short-sleeved shirt, silver goggles; 2005: Black boots, dark blue helmet with Cobra logo,

dark blue pants, dark blue short-sleeved shirt with orange cuffs, purple belt, purple padded vest, silver goggles; June 2008: Black belt and boots, dark blue helmet, short-sleeved shirt, arm bracers, and pants, silver goggles; December 2008: Arctic Communications Specialist Cobra Tele-Viper: black belt, black gloves, gray blue helmet and pants, gray boots, gray parka with furred collar, red Cobra logo on left arm

Accessories: 1985: Communipac, hose, VS-11 scanner; 1989: Black backpack, black scanner pistol, long black hose; 2003: Black shotgun, black silencer pistol, gray shoulder-mounted antenna on C-shaped mount, gray walkie-talkie with short antenna, large graphite mic bent at wide angle; 2004: Black shotgun, black silencer pistol, gold antenna, gold walkie-talkie, gray mic; 2005: Black backpack, black mic, black shotgun, black silencer pistol, black walkie-talkie; June 2008: Black Cobra figure stand, purple open vest with quilted pattern on shoulders; December 2008: Arctic Communications Specialist Cobra Tele-Viper: black antenna, black Cobra figure stand, black knife with silver blade, black radio, black radio, blue backpack with tan rope, blue computer with gray keys and hinged legs, gray rifle

Background Information: Graduate of Viper School; The helmets and web gear are advanced and equipped with the latest technological advantages. The collective file card information includes built-in microminiaturized equipment, FM receiver with automatic frequency control, GPS receiver, high-speed burst microwave transceiver, LED readouts on their visors, low-speed recording decks for ultra-high speed burst transmissions, random series digital encryption module, receivers, third-generation passive jamming devices, transceivers, VHF and laser signal units, and voice synthesizers. Additionally, each Tele-Viper carries a multi-shot grenade launcher and a suppressed submachine gun.

Abilities: Cryptography; Electronics; Knowledge Skill: Latest technology in radio telecommunications; Professional Skill: Radio Telecommunications Operators; Radio and satellite communications specialists; Telemarketing

Conditions: Frequently combat ionospheric disturbances; Not respected by other members of Cobra; Visors flash words on them for anyone to see; Work in extremely harsh environments

Quote/Motto: "Half of our job is to provide clear communications up and down the Cobra chain of command. The other half of our job is to degrade or completely jam all G.I. Joe communications!" "It's almost impossible to stay undetected as long as this guy is in the field! As soon as your position is discovered, you might as well 'call it a day' because he is going to radio in for an air strike on your location before you can get away! Once he has you, he has you!" Quote taken from an unnamed G.I. Joe team member.

Notes: All high-end Cobra command personnel have a Tele-Viper trooper assigned to them as their personal link to headquarters and as a bodyguard.

   This action figure was the first Cobra to have the suffix "Viper" added to its name. Although this figure does not come with a weapon, the VS-11 hand-held scanner is equipped with a "microwave beam and laser."

   It is believed that off-duty Tele-Vipers work as Cobra telemarketers to sell pirated technology.

Thrasher

Series: Five (1986)
Alias/Variations: Bruno La Crosse, Dreadnok Thrasher, Dreadnok Thunder. Prototype names: Bash McFeral, Basher, Cruncher, and Mean-Streak
Real Name: Bruno LaCrosse
Place of Birth: Brussels, Belgium
Gender: Male
Faction(s): Dreadnoks
Notably Served At: Australian desert; Wales
Primary MOS: Thunder Machine operations/demolitions
Secondary MOS: Civil disturbance
Appearance: Black hair with green stripes; gray chest armor over torn green shirt; gray and black gloves; dark gray pants with a black belt and thigh coverings; silver boots and kneepads
Other Known Appearances (Cartoon): Lighter gray armor; more green coloration in his hair; smaller head
Accessories: Included with the Dreadnok Thunder Machine; spiked lacrosse stick
Background Information: According to his prototype dossier card, he was "spoiled rotten

as a child by his nice middle-class parents in their nice middle-class neighborhood. He was never disciplined, since that might 'stifle energies he might need later in life.' He was never denied anything he asked for even though he had bad luck with pets and all his playmates were mysteriously accident prone." After his parents were crippled in the car wreck that may or may not have had something to do with Thrasher's repair work on the brakes, the "wild child" wandered into the swamps, where he could do what he wanted to living things and inanimate objects alike. "It was in the swamps where he met up with Zartan and the Dreadnoks and was welcomed into the fold...."

Abilities: Auto mechanic; Demolitions; Qualified Operator: Swampfire, Thunder Machine; Unique vehicle creations

Conditions: Braggart; Boaster; Civil disturbance; Spoiled rotten as a child; Sociopath

Quote/Motto: A quote taken from his prototype Peer Personality Profile, given by a fellow unnamed Dreadnok member: Thrasher "derives a slight sensation, which almost registers as pleasure, on his primitive central nervous system from inflicting misery and suffering on sentient beings. He doesn't like you, either!"

Tomax

Series: Four (1985)
Alias/Variations: The Crimson Twins or Crimson Guard Commanders; Tovam (original Sunbow animation name)
Real Name: CLASSIFIED; Tomax Rogue
Place of Birth: Corsica
Gender: Male
Service Branch: Cobra Crimson Guard (Commander)
Faction(s): Cobra
Stationed: Cobra Island
Notably Served At: Africa; Algeria; Angola; Battle of Benzheen; Bosnia, Lebanon; Sierra Gordo; Sierra Leone Diamond Wars; South America; Springfield, USA; Trucial Abysmia; Zurich
Primary MOS: Crimson Guard Commander
Secondary MOS: Finance
Appearance: The mirror image of his brother except for a scar on Xamot's face and that Tomax wears his silver shoulder guard on his right; Brown hair parted on the right side, red jacket with black collar, gloves, and belt; red pants with black boots; Reddish-brown hair parted on the right; a blue sleeveless shirt with silver collar and red sash diagonally across chest; silver Cobra insignia on the left side of chest; silver armor on right shoulder; black gloves; blue pants with silver and red belt and boots; silver and red Cobra symbols above red kneepads; 2002 action figure is similar in appearance to the 1985 figure but has darker coloration and a faint scar; June 2002: A G.I. Joe convention exclusive, red hair, red vest and pants, black sash across the chest, black gloves, silver Cobra insignia on his left chest; 2003: Double breasted red coat and pants, black gloves and boots, red-brown hair; 2005 Toys "R" Us exclusive: Double breasted blue coat and pants, blue-silver boots, brown hair; 2008: Blue vest with silver trim, silver Cobra insignia on left chest, blue pants, tall silver boots with red kneepads, black gloves, brown hair; 2009 International G.I. Joe Convention: Black gloves, unkempt brown hair, gray boots with white Cobra kneepads, red pants, red vest with silver Cobra insignia on left chest; In the Sunbow animation, except for animation errors, Tomax wore mirror opposite of the 1985 action figure uniform.

Accessories: 1984: Pistol, sky hook and string with Xamot; helmet with visor; April 2002: Black pistol and silver skyhook; June 2002: Knife, submachine gun; 2003: Black, gray, and red helmet; 2005 Toys "R" Us exclusive: Battle stand, knife, rocket pistol, submachine gun; 2008: Display stand, red and silver sash, rifle, silver shoulder pad; 2009: International G.I. Joe Convention: Black and silver sash, red display stand, rifle, silver shoulder pad, submachine gun

Background Information: Served with the Foreign Legion

Abilities: Advisor to Cobra Commander; Banker; Business Cover: The Arbco Brothers Circus; Command; Contact: Zurich bankers; Contact: Zurich banks; Contacts: Corporations all over the world; Contacts: Governments all over the world; Demolitions; Disguise; Espionage; Feels whatever is happening to his brother; Financial art of war; Followers: Legions of followers; Former Foreign Legion; Heightened intelligence; Heightened physical condition; Infiltration; Knowledge Skill: Commerce; Knowledge Skill: Finance; Knowledge Skill: Foreign Legion protocol; Knowledge Skill: Global law specialist; Knowledge Skill: Law; Mercenary skills;

Military advisor; Only the Finest!; Private corporation: Extensive Enterprises; Professional Skill: Corporate law specialist; Professional Skill: International finance specialist; Propaganda specialist; Qualified Operator: Helicopters; Sabotage; Telepathy with brother; Unofficial bodyguards to Cobra Commander; Wealthy
Conditions: Extremely vain; Finishes brother's sentences; Greedy; Manipulative; Obsessive drive to locate the perfect diamond; Ruthless tendencies; Sticks to a rigorous training schedule; Sulks when he doesn't get his way; Too smart to be a soldier; Wilderness Survival: African Bush; Will not take orders from others
Quote/Motto: "In capable hands, the briefcase can be as effective as a blade." "How do we weasel through this without having anything foul-smelling stick to us?" "Our greed is deadlier that your weapons."
Notes: Extensive Enterprises is an international company involved in legitimate businesses, which provides a cover for the twins' various illegal operations.

Tombstone

Series: Thirty-two (2016)
Real Name: Unknown
Place of Birth: Unknown
Gender: Male
Grade/Rank: Field Commander for the Cobra Viper corps
Service Branch: Cobra Viper corps
Faction(s): Cobra
Primary MOS: Psychological operations
Secondary MOS: Intelligence
Appearance: African American, bald, heavily armored tactical vest
Accessories: Armored vest, four rifles
Background Information: Cobra trooper who has been through the wringer
Abilities: Battlefield tactician; Engenders deep loyalty among Cobra troops; Field commander for the Cobra Viper corps; Heightened intelligence; Highly competent; Highly skilled; Immune to mind tricks; Immune to phantom terrors; Knowledge Skill: Cobra operations; Psychological manipulator; Psychological operations; Psyops commander
Conditions: Blind in his right eye; Distinctive Feature: Scar over right eye; Heightened tactical leadership; Mysterious; Reputation: Strikes fear in the hearts of his enemies
Notes: He is equal in leadership and skills to Duke.

Torch

Series: Four (1985)
Alias/Variations: Dreadnok Torch
Real Name: Tom Winken
Place of Birth: Botany Bay, New South Wales
Gender: Male
Faction(s): Dreadnoks
Notably Served At: Australia; Blackwater Prison; Cobra Island
Primary MOS: Chops stolen cars
Appearance: Brown hair, sideburns, and mustache; red headband; black sunglasses, spiked collar, and open vest; skull necklace; dark gray right armband and gloves; light blue jeans with dark gray holsters and boots; silver chain belt and boots
Other Known Appearances (Cartoon): Redder hair with a full beard; beige boots and leg straps
Accessories: BP-47 fuel-tank backpack with hole for cord; acetylene cutting torch and cord
Background Information: Remanded to borstal reform school at age 14; escaped and went to sea in the Merchant Marines, where he learned to use a cutting torch
Abilities: Contact: the Melbourne Maulers Motorcycle Club; Former member of the Melbourne Maulers Motorcycle Club; Merchant marine; Professional Skill: oxy-acetylene torch operator; Qualified Operator: Chameleon, FANG, Ferret, Swampfire; Safecracker; Scavenges the swamps for fun and profit
Conditions: Afraid of Zartan; Bursts of sudden and unexpected violence; Can be convinced to disobey Zartan; Distinctive Feature: Cockney accent; Illiterate; Loves tearing things apart; Loves violence; Unrepentant thug; Unknown depth to his stupidity
Quote/Motto: "He is an illiterate, unrepentant thug whose penchant for sudden and unexpected violence is matched only by the utter depths of his stupidity." Quote by an unnamed G.I. Joe team member.
Notes: He was one of the three Dreadnoks—with Buzzer and Ripper—who traveled to the United States with Zartan.

Torquemada Paine

Place of Birth: Unknown
Gender: Male
Grade/Rank: Torturer
Faction(s): Cobra, the Baroness's torturer
Notably Served At: Cobra Consultant Building, New York City

Primary MOS: Interrogation expert
Secondary MOS: Torturer
Appearance: Bald, black rubber overalls, thick elbow-length rubber gloves, black goggles
Abilities: Incredibly muscular physique; Skilled torturer with knives
Conditions: Deranged; Distinctive Feature: Rubber daddy; Distinctive Feature: Uses knives to torture his victims

Toxo-Vipers

Series: Seven (1988)
Alias/Variations: Gas-Viper, Heavy-Breathers, Stinkbugs
Real Name: Various
SN: 6513
Service Branch: Army
Faction(s): Cobra
Notably Served At: The Arctic
Primary MOS: Hostile environment infantry
Secondary MOS: Infantry
Appearance: Purple face mask; purple pants with black boots; purple shirt with blue-green mechanisms on chest; red gloves
Accessories: Black backpack with vents and twin gas canisters; full-head environmental helmet with red mouthpiece; short black rifle with two grips and box-like muzzle; yellow visor with blue-green trim
Background Information: Their objective is to enter the battlefield and create a foul environment to cause the enemy to retreat or put them at a severe disadvantage.
Abilities: Knowledge Skill: Hazardous substances
Conditions: Disparaging nickname: Leaky Suit Brigade; Not a position to aspire to; Reputation: Unit is filled with the most discipline-challenged troops; Weapons are toxic
Quote/Motto: "Needless to say, being a Toxo-Viper is not something a Cobra trooper aspires to be. In fact, the assignment is meted out as punishment for major offenses. The mere threat of being transferred to the 'leaky suit brigade' is enough to keep even the most obstreperous troops in line."
Notes: Their suits are cheaply made, mostly airtight, and resistant to many solvents.

Undertow

Series: Nine (1990)
Alias/Variations: River-Rats, Submarauders
Real Name: Various
Place of Birth: Various
Faction(s): Cobra, Iron Grenadiers
Primary MOS: Frogman
Secondary MOS: Hostile environment
Appearance: Green face mask; a red shirt with gray chest panel and green padding; black air tank; green gloves; gray pants and boots with green kneepads and black knife on left ankle
Accessories: Barracuda, facemask with a single red eye, sled with two handles and tab for torpedo, standard short hose, torpedo, trident, two flippers with grills on toes
Abilities: Experienced divers; Strong swimmers; Willing to swim in the foulest water environment imaginable; Wilderness Survival: Hostile environments, e.g., Polluted harbor bays, industrial wastewater, and the sewers
Conditions: Avoided because of what they will swim through
Quote/Motto: "Undertow will swim through anything! You definitely don't want to get in a fight with one of these slimy characters, especially if you have any open cuts and haven't had a tetanus booster recently. Your best bet is to run away and throw grenades from behind cover!"
Notes: Their loyalty was changed to Cobra Command in some of the universes. They wear non-corrosive, near-hermetically sealed wetsuits and undergo special anti-infection shots giving them some immunity from all but the strongest pathogens.

Vance

Series: Twenty (2004)
Real Name: Cornelius E. Smith
Place of Birth: Auburn, Alabama
Gender: Male
Faction(s): Dreadnok Recruit
Appearance: Purple mask; brown hair and beard; blue vest with black knife and holster; black wristbands; blue camo pants with black belt and holster; black and brown boots
Accessories: G-36 assault rifle; shotgun
Abilities: Carousing, Drinking; Knowledge Skill: Drinking games; "Right-Hand Maniac" to the Dreadnok
Conditions: Always in trouble; Antithesis of Beach Head; Bad boy biker; Completely out of control; Disappears when there is work to be done; Ill-mannered; Reputation: Last to leave the bar at night, first one there in the morning; Never follows the rules; Plays unfunny practical jokes; Self-destructive; Starts fights then sneaks out

Quote/Motto: "I'm bad to the bone, baby! That's why I'm the Dreadnoks' favorite!"
Notes: Cletus, Otis, Billy-Bob, Joe-Bob, and Roscoe are his cousins. All six cousins are identical in appearance.

Vance Wingfield

Series: One (1982)
Alias/Variations: Commander Wingfield
Real Name: Vance Wingfield
Gender: Male
Grade/Rank: Commander
Service Branch: Militia
Faction(s): Cobra, Strike First militia group
Stationed: Montana, USA
Notably Served At: Various theaters of war
Primary MOS: Leader of the Strike First militia group
Appearance: Insanely long and curled handlebar mustache
Background Information: Former U.S. Marine and Navy SEAL team member; After a training accident, he became paranoid and was discharged on psychological grounds.
Abilities: Contact: Cobra (finances and equipment); Contact: Various survivalist groups; Expert marksman's rating; Followers: Small army of followers; Former U.S. Marine; Former SEAL; Highly trained in all aspects of combat; Instruction; Leadership; Trainer for Cobra troopers; Visionary
Conditions: Belief: His organization will rule after the Great War; Distinctive Feature: Long and curled handlebar mustache; Distrusts the government; Families of his recruits against him; Harsh training methods; Paranoid; Predicts a global war; Seeks to drop a nuclear bomb on Russia; Son: Tyler; Takes extreme measures; Wanted by NATO; Wife: Shary; Willing to start "the war" if no one else will
Notes: Vance appeared in the comic. His Strike First militia group, located in Montana, is a Cobra training facility. His wife shot him and left him for dead. He returned using M.A.R.S. technology to pull satellites from orbit and collide them with cities on Earth, killing thousands of innocent civilians in Chicago and Silicon Valley.

Vanguard

Alias/Variations: Nick Bailey
Real Name: Nicholas M. Bailey
Place of Birth: Savannah, Georgia
Gender: Male
Grade/Rank: Sergeant or lieutenant, sources conflict
Service Branch: Snow Serpent
Faction(s): Cobra, The Plague
Stationed: Cobra headquarters
Notably Served At: The Amazon; Antarctica; the Appalachian Mountains; Darfur; Lincoln, Nebraska; Malta; Manhattan, New York City; Philadelphia, Pennsylvania; Somalia
Primary MOS: Ranger
Appearance: Black, cable-knit sweater and a black version of his previous division's helmet
Background Information: Top of his class in the Army Ranger school
Abilities: Former Army Ranger; Infantry; Sharpshooting
Conditions: Radical worldview; Stands against laws that disregard injustice; Young ("just a kid")
Notes: He was personally recruited and influenced by Cobra Commander himself. During the Scorched Earth campaign, Bayonet, Body Bags, Gallows, Guillotine, Infrared, Vanguard, and Velocity are stationed in Antarctica to guard and launch a nuclear bomb. Vanguard and the other members of The Plague were presumably captured or killed during a battle in the Appalachian Mountains.

Vapor

Series: Nine (1990)
Real Name: Unknown
Place of Birth: Unknown
Gender: Male
Service Branch: Cobra Air Force
Faction(s): Cobra
Primary MOS: Cobra Hurricane V.T.O.L
Secondary MOS: Fighter pilot
Appearance: Robotic helmet with red eyes; gray shirt, black diagonal straps and Cobra emblem on chest; red backpack straps; black gloves; gray pants, red waist piece, holster; black boots
Accessories: None
Abilities: Cybernetic enhancement*; Heightened targeting ability (for 30 minutes); Qualified Expert Operator: Cobra Hurricane V.T.O.L.; Tactical fighter pilot
Conditions: After 30 minutes of cyber-usage, he experiences debilitating headaches and vision problems; Aspires for the reputation

of "One of Cobra's Best Pilots"; Without the cyber-ware, he is an average pilot

Quote/Motto: "Vapor is an unbeatable sky warrior for the first half-hour of an engagement, then he becomes debilitated by excruciating headaches and vision failure caused by a massive overload in the image-processing centers in the brain. What makes him truly dangerous is his uncanny ability to knock out almost every enemy fighter in the air during that half-hour before he blacks out!"

Notes: *The cybernetic implant gives a direct connection between the pilot's optic nerve and the vehicle's targeting computer; it also broadcasts directly inside the pilot's helmet. It is linked to voice-activated weaponry. After 30 minutes of use, the pilot will experience debilitating headaches and suffer vision problems. According to the *G.I. Joe: America's Elite* #25, Vapor was meant to be a unique character.

Vector

Real Name: Unknown
Place of Birth: Unknown
Gender: Male
Service Branch: Laser Viper
Faction(s): Cobra, The Plague
Stationed: Cobra headquarters
Notably Served At: The Amazon; Antarctica; the Appalachian Mountains; Lincoln, Nebraska; Malta; Manhattan, New York City; Philadelphia, Pennsylvania
Primary MOS: Offensive laser weapon system
Secondary MOS: Infantry
Appearance: Black, cable-knit sweater and a black version of his previous division's helmet
Abilities: Knowledge Skill: Laser weaponry; Knowledge Skill: Targeting systems; Knowledge Skill: Weapon systems; Modifies his equipment; Scientist; Technical engineer
Conditions: Rumor: Destro tried to recruit him or purchase his technology for M.A.R.S.
Notes: During the Scorched Earth campaign, Black Out, Grim Skull, Incision (Aleph), Interrogator, Munitia, and Vector are stationed in Antarctica to guard and launch a nuclear bomb. Vector and the other members of The Plague were presumably captured or killed during a battle in the Appalachian Mountains.

Velocity

Real Name: Unknown
Place of Birth: Unknown
Gender: Male
Service Branch: Cobra Air Force
Faction(s): Cobra, The Plague
Stationed: Cobra headquarters
Notably Served At: The Amazon; Antarctica; the Appalachian Mountains; Lincoln, Nebraska; Malta; Manhattan, New York; Philadelphia, Pennsylvania
Primary MOS: Pilot
Secondary MOS: Infantry
Appearance: Black, cable-knit sweater and a black version of his previous division's helmet
Accessories: Personal Jetpack System Foxbat*
Abilities: A.V.A.C. Pilot; Qualified Expert Operator: Firebat, jet packs; Well-liked by the Plague
Conditions: Climbed through the ranks; Considers being in The Plague the ultimate challenge; Friendly personality; Reputation: Best Pilot in Cobra (second to Wild Weasel); Reputation: Highest-paid pilot in the A.V.A.C. ranks of Cobra; Sense of humor
Notes: *Foxbat is an advanced portable jetpack made of super-light carbon fiber, equipped with an array of sensors and radars integrated with the suit and helmet to provide a complete scan of the battlefield.

During the Scorched Earth campaign, Bayonet, Body Bags, Gallows, Guillotine, Infrared, Vanguard, and Velocity are stationed in Antarctica to guard and launch a nuclear bomb. Velocity is shot down and killed by Black Out on Guillotine's orders.

Venomous Maximus

Series: Twenty (2004)
Alias/Variations: V-Troops (Venomized Troopers) Overlord
Real Name: General Hawk
Place of Birth: Doctor Mindbender's lab
Gender: Male
Service Branch: Cobra Command
Faction(s): Cobra
Notably Served At: South America
Primary MOS: V-Troops commander
Secondary MOS: Military commander
Appearance: Humanlike face and skin tone with prominent fangs; orc-like
Accessories: Cape, knife, war hammer staff; Version 2: Fang Blade staff
Abilities: Command; Hand-to-hand armed: Massive war hammer; Heightened strength; Knowledge Skill: Insider knowledge of G.I. Joe; Linked to his troops through some sort

of animal connection; Military commander; Monster; Strong-willed; V-Troops commander; War hammer mastery

Conditions: Ambitious; Bloodlust; Brutal; Cold and calculating mind; Condition is reversible; Detached from humanity; Difficult to control; Distinctive Feature: Wields a massive war hammer in battle; Feral savagery; Monster; Reptilian focus; Savage; Seeks to overthrow and rule Cobra

Quote/Motto: "No one can stop me. I will control all of Cobra and destroy the G.I. Joe team completely."

Notes: He is the venomized form of General Clayton Hawk Abernathy created by Doctor Mindbender. He is genetically connected to his V-Troops, forming an unbreakable bond of command and loyalty.

Viper Agent

Series: Two (1983); five (1986)
Alias/Variations: Cobra Viper; Python Viper; Crimson Viper; Crossing Guard Viper (due to the brightness of their vests)
Real Name: Various
Place of Birth: Various countries
Gender: Male
Grade/Rank: E-4 or equivalent
Service Branch: Cobra Army
Faction(s): Cobra
Stationed: Worldwide
Notably Served At: Worldwide
Primary MOS: Infantry trooper, infantry
Secondary MOS: Various/pending
Appearance: Multi-layered body armor and wraparound helmets with built-in radio telecommunications gear; carry multi-burst laser pistols, commando rifles, and grenade launchers; blue helmet with black goggles and silver faceplate; blue shirt and black vest with red straps; red gloves; blue pants with a black belt and red stripes on the sides of legs; black boots. All Vipers are issued a combination assault rifle/grenade launcher, the rifle part of which can function as a short-burst assault weapon, a sustained fire cover support weapon, or a long-range sniper rifle with an advanced light-intensification night vision telescopic sight with a built-in rangefinder. Multi-layer body armor and wraparound acrylic/composite helmets with built-in RTO gear are standard issues.
Other Known Appearances (Cartoon): White lenses on goggles; red pockets on shoulders

Accessories: Backpack (with engraved canteen and two grenades) with small Cobra emblem on back; two-handled assault rifle/grenade launcher with a small scope; 1986: came with a field pack and RDT-7 assault rifle with grenade launcher
Background Information: Graduate of Viper School
Abilities: Fight hard; Demolitions experts; Infantry soldiers; Martial arts; Pilot; Qualified Operators: Attack glider; Qualified Weapons Experts: All NATO and Warsaw Pact small arms; Qualified Weapons Experts: Dragunov (SVD) sniper's rifle, machine pistol, Skorpion (VZOR61), Uzi submachine gun, M-16; Ready at a moment's notice; Sabotage
Conditions: Crave material wealth; Crave power; Cruel; Envious; Formidably equipped; Greedy; Highly motivated; Highly trained; Looked down upon by the elite Cobra groups; Nameless, faceless legions of Cobra; Need to prove rottenness gets the job done; Reputation: Backbone of the Cobra legions; Seek higher-level training; Seek to be noticed; Think of themselves as a biker gang with the most technologically advanced "Hogs" on the planet
Quote/Motto: "Cobras swear absolute loyalty to their fanatical leader.... Cobra Commander. Their goal ... to conquer the world for their own evil purpose!" "G.I. Joe team be warned! We have more weapons and more guts than you could ever hope to have." "If you want to get anywhere in Cobra, you have to start out as a Viper. That's the bottom of the pyramid and serving in the Cobra infantry is a small price to pay to gain access to the glittering prizes at the top. Cobra doesn't reward success with parades and medals. They offer material wealth, power, and an outlet for the terrible urges that drive the greedy, the envious, and the cruel. If that doesn't make a Viper a dangerous opponent, nothing does!"
Notes: A Viper is the code name given to a large majority of the soldiers/troops in the Cobra Organization; for the most part, the code name Viper is followed or preceded by their area of expertise. The first figure to receive the designation Viper was the Tele-Viper (Cobra Communications) in 1985. Since then, Cobra Troops, including drivers/pilots, have had the Viper code name attached to their area of expertise. Until 1986, the Cobra Soldier was the infantry trooper for Cobra; then Hasbro released the Cobra Infantry trooper, code name Vipers. In the G.I. Joe mythos, they are the

bottom of the totem pole, the start for every Cobra agent.

Viper Officer

Series: Thirty (2014)
Real Name: Various
Place of Birth: Various
Grade/Rank: Leaders of the Cobra Viper troopers
Service Branch: Cobra Army
Faction(s): Cobra, Cobra Viper Troopers
Stationed: Worldwide
Notably Served At: Worldwide
Primary MOS: Infantry
Secondary MOS: Sabotage
Appearance: Gray full-body padded armor; red vest, full helmet with gold face cover; black boots and gloves
Accessories: Backpack, pistol, rifle, submachine gun, vest
Abilities: Better pay; Command; Highly trained for battle; Heavily equipped; Leadership
Conditions: Find pleasure in causing mayhem; First in line to do the dirty jobs; Seek promotions and rewards

Voltar

Series: Seven (1988)
Alias/Variations: Field Marshall Null; Graf, Lord Kondor, Madagascar
Real Name: Unknown
Place of Birth: Unknown
Gender: Male
Grade/Rank: O-7 General
Service Branch: Army
Faction(s): Cobra, Iron Grenadiers
Notably Served At: Worldwide
Primary MOS: Mercenary commander
Secondary MOS: Infantry commander
Appearance: Gold helmet with red eyepiece; black hair and beard; a fuchsia shirt with gold armor straps; black gloves; fuchsia pants with gold belt, holsters
Accessories: Backpack with handle and long, thick antenna; futuristic submachine gun with trigger guard, angled magazine, and sound suppressor; black vulture*
Abilities: Animal Companion: Vulture; Bucks the odds; Command; Contact: Destro; Contact: Iron Grenadiers; Contacts: Military dictatorships; Contacts: Provisional governments; Contacts: Revolutionary councils; Followers: Mercenaries; Foresees long-term results; Heightened tactical ability; Knowledge Skill: Armaments; Knowledge Skill: Geography; Knowledge Skill: Supply lines; Knowledge Skill: Troop disposition; Knowledge Skill: Vehicles; Knowledge Skill: Weapons; Knowledge Skill: Weather conditions; Leadership; Sees the big picture
Conditions: Confronts poachers; Hunted by Oktober Guard; Hatred for Muskrat (G.I. Joe); Reputation: Destro's general; Never looks back; Reputation: Can pull victory from imminent defeat; Reputation: Extremely success mercenary commander
Quote/Motto: "Winners never look backward!"

"He has that quality I admire most in a general. You know that Napoleonic anecdote? The Marshalls of France were extolling the tactical prowess of a certain young commander. The Little Corporal cut them off tersely, 'All very well and good, but tell me one thing; is he LUCKY?'" Quote by Destro.

Notes: *It's possible his pet is not a vulture but a condor. In fact, until shortly before release, he was going to be called Lord Kondor. Voltar was buried alive in a landlocked freighter under a volcano on Cobra Island by Cobra Commander; he died of food poisoning.

Vypra

Series: Fifteen (1998)
Real Name: CLASSIFIED (Ann A. Conda)
Place of Birth: New Orleans, Louisiana
Gender: Female
Service Branch: Cobra Army
Faction(s): Cobra, Ninja Cobra Strike Team
Primary MOS: Intelligence
Secondary MOS: Martial Arts
Appearance: Small and slight build; black mask; black and blue shirt and pants; black belt, gloves, and shoes
Accessories: Backpack; naginata staff; two swords
Abilities: Intelligence; Knowledge Skill: Swamps of New Orleans; Martial Arts; Qualified Expert Operator: Rattler 4-WD
Conditions: Likes the Cobra organization; Mean; Nasty; Regards soldiers as wimps; Reputation: Rose through the ranks; Reputation: Not to be underestimated; Uncontrollable
Quote/Motto: "Where does Cobra FIND people like this? Vypra looks small and slight, but she drives the Rattler like she's in a monster truck show. The only thing more dangerous than her driving skills are her fighting techniques. She's one of the nastier threats to

come out of Cobra's rank and files in recent years." Quote is taken from General Hawk's files.

Notes: The Threat Matrix lists her as "In Custody"; then her name was on the list of escapees due to Tomax's raid on the Coffin.

There are three different Cobra agents with the name Vypra. However, eventually the code name Vypra became a generic troop builder title.

Vypra Courier

Series: Thirty-one (2015)
Real Name: CLASSIFIED
Place of Birth: CLASSIFIED
Gender: Female
Grade/Rank: Courier
Faction(s): Cobra
Primary MOS: Mercenary
Secondary MOS: Intelligence Courier
Appearance: Black hood, belt, gloves, boots, dark blue bodysuit
Accessories: Monitor, rugged computer case with removable HK MP5K with suppressor, sheath backpack, two katana blades, two submachine guns
Abilities: Knowledge Skill: Bypassing security systems; Lacks information leverage; Numerous false identities; Stealth; Unlimited access: Cobra motor pool; Uses deceptive attire
Conditions: Audacious; Bold; Reputation: Loose cannon; Under- or over-performs to keep people guessing her range of skill and ability; Tenaciously defends her secretive background; Willingly uses high power weapons/explosives
Quote/Motto: "No enemy shall stay me from a swift delivery guarantee!"

Vypra, twins

Series: Twenty (2004)
Alias/Variations: Guardians of the Sacred Forge
Real Name: Unknown
Gender: Females
Faction(s): Cobra
Stationed: Sacred Temple and Weapons Forge at the base of Mount Fuji
Primary MOS: Martial artist
Secondary MOS: Ninja guardian
Appearance: Red hood, red shirt with a gold dragon on the left side, red pants, red slippers
Accessories: Skirt, set of nunchuks, sword
Abilities: Beautiful; Heightened ninja skills

Conditions: Lethal; Loyal to Arashikage Forge; Reputation: Guardians of a Sacred Temple and Weapons Forge at the base of Mount Fuji
Quote/Motto: "The sword in the ninja. Respect and honor the place from which your heart and soul were born."
Notes: This is the code name for the twin daughters of the Arashikage legendary swordsmith Onihashi, who creates his weapons in an ancient forge hidden in a sacred mountain (Mount Fuji).

Whisper

Alias/Variations: Cobra Whisper
Real Name: Unknown
Place of Birth: Unidentified South American island fishing village
Gender: Female
Service Branch: Cobra Army
Faction(s): Cobra, The Coil
Primary MOS: Assassination, silent weapons
Secondary MOS: Covert operations
Appearance: Dark-skinned, shoulder-length black hair; traditional blue Cobra uniform
Background Information: Trained by elite of Cobra operatives
Abilities: Accomplished martial artist; Covert operations; Disguise; Expert in sound-suppressed weapons; Hand-to-hand armed specialist; Personal assassin for Cobra Commander; Qualified Weapons: Knives, pistols, submachine guns, swords; Sabotage
Conditions: Belief: G.I. Joe is the reason she is an orphan; Hates G.I. Joe; Sense of isolation; Seeks revenge on former G.I. Joe leadership; Thirst for revenge

Wild Weasel

Series: Three (1984)
Real Name: CLASSIFIED
Place of Birth: CLASSIFIED
Gender: Male
Service Branch: Cobra Air Force
Faction(s): Cobra
Stationed: The Coffin prison facility, Greenland (escaped)
Notably Served At: The Florida swamps; Punta del Mucosa; the bush wars of South America and Africa; suburban New Jersey
Primary MOS: Ground support pilot
Appearance: Red flight suit with a helmet hiding his face; red helmet with black goggles; red jacket with a blue shirt and white insignia

on right shoulder; red pants with white maps on thighs; black straps, belt, gloves, and shoes
Accessories: Included with the Cobra Rattler vehicle
Abilities: Ace pilot; Ground support pilot; Knowledge Skill: Close support aircraft; Knowledge Skill: ECM Pods; Knowledge Skill: Jury-rigged civilian conversions; Knowledge Skill: Laser-guided missiles; Knowledge Skill: State-of-the-art flying machines; Qualified Expert Operator: Rattler Pilot
Conditions: Arrogant; Boring conversationalist; Distinctive Feature: Speech consistent with mouth injury; No friends in Cobra; Natural troublemaker; Never been seen outside of his flight suit; Only talks about jets and motor parts; Practical joker; Rivalry with Ace; Reputation: Back shooter; Reputation: Best pilot in Cobra; Reputation: Fights dirty; Thinks everyone avoids him because they fear him; Wild and unpredictable
Quote/Motto: "There's no place where G.I. Joe can run or hide when I'm flying above them!" "He may be a back-shootin', low down snake in the grass, but the boy can fly like nobody's business. You gotta respect the skunk for that! Hey—what did Voltaire say? To forgive our enemies their virtues—that is the greater miracle." Quote taken from a transcript given by G.I. Joe team member Wild Bill.
Notes: Phoenix Guard member Halo is actually Wild Weasel. He was held in the maximum security prison called The Coffin, located in Greenland, and was one of several operatives who escaped during a raid.

Wilder Vaughn

Real Name: Wilder A. Vaughn
Place of Birth: CLASSIFIED
Gender: Male
Service Branch: Red Shadows Commander
Faction(s): Red Shadows
Primary MOS: Long term strategy
Secondary MOS: Command
Background Information: : Trained by British Intelligence
Abilities: Contact: Joe Colton; Command; Intelligence operative; Long term strategy
Conditions: Callous; Dedicated to replacing the current world order with a technocratic paradise of his design; Reputation: One of the most dangerous men in the world; Ruthless; Sees society as decadent; Well-intentioned extremist

Quote/Motto: "Vaughn's a man with long-term aims. Not for him the quick fix of a bomb or an assassination. He deals in years, not weeks, and plans meticulously. He's patient and careful because he knows that what he does will ultimately be inevitable."

Wraith

Series: Twenty-four (2008)
Alias/Variations: Mercenary Wraith
Real Name: Charles Halifax
Place of Birth: Unknown, probably France (Lyon, France)
Gender: Male
Grade/Rank: CLASSIFIED
Faction(s): Cobra
Primary MOS: Sabotage, Espionage
Secondary MOS: Covert operations
Accessories: Backpack, battle armor, flip-up facemask, FN P90 submachine gun
Abilities: Covert operations; Espionage; Expert marksman; Mercenary; Personal equipment: Stealth assault suit; Qualified Weapons Expert: Wrist-mounted lasers, various guns, combat knife; Skilled fighter; Skilled spy
Conditions: Doesn't care about causes, sides, right, or wrong; Not a merc for money; Seeks to foster chaos, kill, and fight
Quote/Motto: "Do you ever get the feeling that someone is watching you, even when no one is in sight? That creeping feeling on the back of your neck could be telling you that I am next to you, ready to strike."
Notes: His stealth assault suit—stolen from the Chinese Government—makes him virtually invisible; the only flaw in the suit is that an outline of Wraith can be seen if he moves too fast. He was killed by the Baroness during her mission of revenge on all that had wronged her in the past. The Wraith suit then fell into the hands of the Red Shadows, reportedly the suit's original designers.

Wreckage

Real Name: Eric Alexander
Gender: Male
Faction(s): S.K.A.R.
Primary MOS: Cyborg super-soldier
Background Information: Former soldier in U.S. military; served with Freight
Abilities: Belief: The military made him a monster; Heightened resilience; Heightened strength; Still friends with Freight (who

is trying to help him discover the truth); Super-soldier

Conditions: Angry with the U.S. and the Joes; Prone to fits of rage; Seeks revenge against Iron Klaw (when he learns the truth); Subjected to cybernetic experimentation

Notes: He was captured and held as a prisoner of war in South America; there, he was experimented upon in an early attempt by Iron Klaw to create a cybernetic super-soldier. There is also a Joe who uses the code name Wreckage.

Xamot

Series: Four (1985)
Alias/Variations: "The one with the scar on his cheek"; "the slightly unhinged one"; the Crimson Twins or Crimson Guard Commanders; Tovam
Real Name: CLASSIFIED (Xamot Rogue)
Place of Birth: Corsica
Gender: Male
Service Branch: Cobra Crimson Guard (leader)
Faction(s): Cobra
Stationed: Cobra Island
Notably Served At: Africa; Algeria; Angola; Battle of Benzheen; Bosnia, Lebanon; Sierra Gordo; Sierra Leone Diamond Wars; South America; Springfield; Trucial Abysmia; Zurich
Primary MOS: Crimson Guard Commander
Appearance: Brown hair, red jacket with black collar, gloves, and belt; red pants with black boots; silver shoulder guard on his left
Accessories: Pistol; Shared the sky hook and string with Tomax; helmet a with visor
Background Information: Served with the Foreign Legion
Abilities: Advisor to Cobra Commander; Banker; Business Cover: The Arbco Brothers Circus; Command; Contact: Zurich bankers; Contact: Zurich banks; Contacts: Corporations all over the world; Contacts: Governments all over the world; Demolitions; Disguise; Espionage; Feels whatever is happening to his brother; Financial art of war; Followers: Legions of followers; Former Foreign Legion; Heightened intelligence; Heightened physical condition; Infiltration; Knowledge Skill: Commerce; Knowledge Skill: Finance; Knowledge Skill: Foreign Legion protocol; Knowledge Skill: Global law specialist; Knowledge Skill: Law; Mercenary skills; Military advisor; Only the Finest!; Private corporation: Extensive Enterprises; Professional Skill: Corporate law specialist; Professional Skill: International finance specialist; Propaganda specialist; Qualified Operator: Helicopters; Sabotage; Telepathy with brother; Unofficial bodyguards to Cobra Commander; Wealthy

Conditions: Distinctive Feature: Scar on his face; Extremely vain; Finishes brother's sentences; Greedy; Manipulative; Obsessive drive to locate the perfect diamond; Ruthless Tendencies; Sticks to a rigorous training schedule; Sulks when he doesn't get his way; Too smart to be a soldier; Wilderness Survival: African Bush; Will not take orders from others

Quote/Motto: "In capable hands, the briefcase can be as effective as a blade."

Notes: Extensive Enterprises is an international company involved in legitimate businesses, which provides a cover for the twins' various illegal operations.

It is never mentioned in cannon how Xamot received his facial scar.

Zandar

Series: Five (1986)
Alias/Variations: James Nurss; Zack; various aliases
Real Name: Zachary (surname unknown)
Place of Birth: Unknown; possibly London, England
Gender: Male
Faction(s): Dreadnoks, works almost exclusively for Cobra
Stationed: Dreadnoks' main compound in the Florida Everglades
Notably Served At: Broca Beach, New Jersey; Cobra Island; Florida swamps; Jersey swamps
Primary MOS: Camouflage
Secondary MOS: Covert movement
Appearance: Punk appearance with orange hair, a blue bandana, earrings, red facial markings, a shirtless torso with jagged tattoos, and a torn pink neckerchief that resembles Zarana's torn pink shirt
Accessories: Barbed gun with scope, grenade quiver
Background Information: "He was the kid who never got noticed. Teachers forgot he was there and never called on him. Nobody that has ever met him can remember what his voice sounds like. His anonymity was no accident. He worked at it all through his

formative years and after he grew up ... he got even better at it!"

Abilities: Camouflage; Change skin color; Concealment; Covert operations; Difficult to keep track of; Disguise expert; Hidden cache of gold; Hide; Knowledge Skill: New York City sewer system; Knowledge Skill: New York City telephone system; No one seems to notice him; Professional Skill: Real estate scams; Professional Skill: Semi-legitimate telemarketing business; Silent weapons expert

Conditions: Ambitious; Belief: Zartan is ignoring him; Belief: Zartan is leaving him behind as Dreadnok becomes more successful; Brother of Zartan and Zarana; Grim; Growing resentment towards Zartan; Hunted by Storm Shadow; Knowledge Skill: Swamps; Mysterious; Silent; Spy for Coil; Spying on Cobra; Wilderness Survival: Swamps

Quote/Motto: "They should never have let those Dreadnoks into the organization! They give international terrorism a bad name!" Quote taken from random, unnamed Techno-Viper.

Notes: Sibling of Zartan and Zarana

Zanya

Series: Twenty-seven (2011)
Real Name: Zanya (surname unknown)
Place of Birth: Chicago, Illinois
Gender: Female
Grade/Rank: Dreadnok Member
Faction(s): Dreadnok
Appearance: Green dreadlocks and lips, torn black shirt, green pants, black combat boots
Accessories: Pistol, rifle
Abilities: Can handle opponents twice her size; Disguise; Knowledge Skill: Florida Swamps; Knowledge Skill: Dreadnok lifestyle; Marksmanship; Professional Skill: Underground Streetfighter; Streetwise; Thief
Conditions: Defiant; Never gives an inch; Never knew father growing up; Raised by angry, bitter mother; Tough; Tenacious

Zanzibar

Series: Six (1987)
Real Name: Morgan Teach
Place of Birth: Cayman Islands
Gender: Male
Faction(s): Dreadnok
Primary MOS: Pirate
Appearance: Black hair with ponytail and mustache; gold eye patch; a torn olive-green shirt with gray shoulder armor; gold wristbands and gray gloves; blue and white camo pants with a black belt and an olive-green codpiece; purple cloth around left leg; black boots

Accessories: Gun with a trapezoidal barrel, no trigger guard, and angled grip; long, barbed spear; pistol; sledgehammer; spear

Abilities: Conman (stocks and bonds); Natural talent for vehicular engineering; Professional Skill: Banditry; Professional Skill: Extortionist; Professional Skill: Freelance pirate; Professional Skill: Hijacking; Professional Skill: Pickpocket; Professional Skill: Pirate; Professional Skill: Smuggler

Conditions: Bizarre; Despicable; Detested by other Dreadnoks; Fancies himself a globe-trotting rogue, a romantic mercenary, and a modern-day swashbuckler; Idiosyncratic; Overplays the role of pirate; There isn't anything wrong with his eye

Quote/Motto: "It's a pirate's life for me!"

Zarana

Series: Five (1986)
Alias/Variations: Friday, Heather, Jharna ("Mountain Stream"), Sgt. Carol Weidler, Dr. Deborah Karday, Phoenix Guard member Friday, and many more too numerous to list
Real Name: Zoe (surname unknown)
Place of Birth: London, England
Gender: Female
Faction(s): Dreadnoks
Stationed: Florida
Notably Served At: Australia; Broca Beach, New Jersey; Chicago, Illinois; Cobra Island; Florida swamps; New Jersey swamps; Sierra Gordo
Primary MOS: Infiltration
Secondary MOS: Espionage, assassination
Appearance: Caucasian female with a pink mohawk, a pink torn half shirt, blue jeans, red knee pads, black boots, black gloves, and red belt
Other Known Appearances: The early version of the action figure is sculpted wearing gold earrings.
Accessories: Backpack, shotgun with a circular saw blade attached at the end
Background Information: Taken from the prototype dossier: "Zarana could have had a brilliant career on the professional stage if her evil nature hadn't been so strong. She's cruel to animals, cuts ahead on lines, and never leaves a tip. She posed as an oral hygienist for

six months on one assignment armed only with a reel of poisoned dental floss." [crossed out by author, Larry Hama: "…and terminated her victim by swabbing his gums with poison."] She escaped dressed as a granny lady holding onto a walker right past the cops and into a cab. The cabbie remembered her. She didn't leave a tip."

Abilities: Can change the color of her skin; Close ally of Cobra Commander; Command; Cunning mind; Expert at disguise; De facto leader of the Dreadnoks; In charge of the Chicago chapter of the Dreadnoks; Knowledge Skill: Swamps; Knowledge Skill: New York City sewer system; Knowledge Skill: New York City telephone system; Knowledge Skill: Cobra operations; Leadership; Mistress of makeups and masks; Professional Skill: Assassin; Professional Skill: Real estate scams; Professional Skill: Semi-legitimate telemarketing business; Survival Skill: Swamps; Talented Actress

Conditions: Ambitious; Antagonistic relationship with the Baroness; Belief: The "Rightful Heir" to the Dreadnoks; Cruel; Fearless; Former aspiring actress; Greedy; Hunted by Storm Shadow; Mysterious; Sadistic nature; Sibling of Zartan and Zandar; Risk taker; Selfish; Star-crossed romantic attraction to Mainframe

Notes: Phoenix Guard member Friday is Zarana.

Zartan

Series: Three (1984)
Alias/Variations: Too numerous to list
Real Name: Unknown
Place of Birth: Unknown, possibly Nice, France
Gender: Male
Service Branch: Mercenary
Faction(s): Dreadnok
Stationed: Dreadnoks' main compound in the Florida Everglades
Appearance: Red-brown cowl; black face paint around eyes; bare torso; black shoulder armor, gloves, belt, and boots; red-brown pants; 1993: Orange mohawk; orange face paint around eyes; black closed sleeveless biker jacket and right glove; gloveless left hand; dark purple belt and boots; green pants; 2002: trademark hood and an open-vested shirt; 2004: ski cap, face markings; 2007: "Toxic" purple uniform, and green highlights
Accessories: Included with the Chameleon Swamp Skier; 1984: Hinged backpack for his mask; bearded mask disguise; pistol with trigger guard and angled handle; clear chest panel and thigh pads; pistol, a chest shield, two knee pads, a face mask, backpack. He also came with a sheet of heat-sensitive stickers to be placed on the chest piece and each thigh pad. The stickers turned maroon when cold, aqua at room temperature, and blue when hot; 1993: Range plastic tree with a bow, long and short swords, sickle, pair of knives
Background Information: European Military Academy Training (probably Saint-Cyr)
Abilities: Acrobatics; Archery expert; Assassin; Close combat expert; Command; Contact: Cobra Commander; Contact: Destro; Contortionist; Disguise expert; European military academy training; Former apprentice of the sword master Onihashi; Hologram generators in his suit; Hypnosis; Illusions; Impersonate to a physical and vocal likeness; Knowledge Skill: Dreadnoks culture; Knowledge Skill: Holograms (Marvel Comics Universe); Knowledge Skill: Hypnosis (Marvel Comics Universe); Knowledge Skill: Illusions (Marvel Comics Universe); Knowledge Skill: Swamps; Leader of the Dreadnoks; Leadership; Linguist (more than 20 languages and dialects); Make-up and disguise expert; Martial arts expert; Master of disguise; Master of holograms (Marvel Comics Universe); Mercenary; Practitioner of mystics martial arts; Qualified Expert Operator: Chameleon; Skin can alter to blend with the environment; Ventriloquist; Wilderness Survival: Swamps
Conditions: Ambitious; Hunted by Storm Shadow; Less involved with the Dreadnoks; Medicine keeps his mental state stable (known only by his siblings and daughter); Mysterious; Paranoid schizophrenic; Preoccupied with killing Storm Shadow; Protective of sister, Zandar; Raised in an orphanage; Reputation: Better archer than Storm Shadow; Reputation: Delivered the killing blow to Serpentor during the Cobra Civil War; Reputation: Finest archer in the world; Rumor: A hidden cache of gold; Rumor: Worked with the Dreadnoks; Sibling of Zandar and Zarana; Slight Australian accent
Notes: The Dreadnoks were originally a biker gang of Zartan and three additional members (Buzzer, Ripper, and Torch) hailing out of Australia. They relocated to America

and began to expand, having a chapter in every major city and several in Europe. Due to increasing G.I. Joe pressure, they eventually abandoned the Florida base and moved the operation to Toronto, Ontario, Canada.

The genetic mutation that gave Zartan the ability to change skin color was present in not only the action figure line but in the Sunbow animation. However, the Marvel Comics described his ability as being rooted in hypnotism and holographics. The name Zartan is an anagram for Tarzan.

Zeus B.A.T.

Place of Birth: Created for the Cobra Organization by Doctor Mindbender
Gender: Robot
Grade/Rank: Mega BAT
Faction(s): Cobra
Notably Served At: Megalo City
Background Information: Disposable brute strength to the Cobra Army
Notes: See Battle Android Trooper (B.A.T.). Zeus's AI is run by the captured Spud.

Index

Bold indicates main entries

Abernathy, Clayton M. 83, 92, 126, 251
Abutre Negro 59, 114, 181
Ace, Version 2 28
Ace 1 27
Action Force 21, 22, 28, 35, 36, 37, 39, 40, 42, 43, 45, 49, 65, 72, 76, 78, 84, 87, 89, 90, 91, 93, 96, 107, 109, 110, 112, 113, 115, 116, 123, 130, 133, 139, 145, 146, 154, 155, 156, 161, 168, 170, 176, 185, 195, 238, 240
Action Force Parachute Regiment 123
Action Man 21, **28**, 109, 110
Action Marine 13
Action Pilot 13
Action Sailor 13
Adams, Paige 105
Adcox, David 104
Admiral Dyson 92
Adventure Team 77
Aero-B.A.T. **181**
A.G.P.-Anti-Gravity Pod flight vehicle 124
Aguia Commando **28**, 114
Air Chariot 236
Air Commandos **28**, 52, 139, 146
Air Devils **182**, 146
Air-Driver Swamp Vehicle 196
Air Raid **29**, 45, 139
Air Raid 2 29
Air-Vipers 182
Airborne 24, 28, **29**, 30, 108, 139
Airborne 2 30
Airtight 24, **30**, 33
Airwave 24, 29, **30**, 31, 54, 139
Aisha 31
Akita, Junko **92**, 152, 242, 243
Alabama 38; Auburn 38
Alaska 44, 75, 215; Galena 75; Juneau 44; Kotzebue 215
Albatroz **31**, 114, 139
Aleph 179, 189, 209, 212, 214, 220, 223, 227, 250
Alexander, Daniel R. 165
Alexander, Eric 254
Alexander McCullen **182**, 219
All-Terrain Dinosaur Reconnaissance Vehicle 62
Alley Viper **183**

Alpine 24, **31**, 38, 154, 159
Altitude 22, 23, 29, 30, **32**, 74, 139, 154
Amalgamated Super-Conductor Corporation 202
Amber 32
Ambush 24, **32**, 38, 60, 62, 79, 114, 128
AMP TS DSR-1 100
Animated Series 20, 38, **176**
Annihilators 214
Ansatsusha 33
Anti-Venom Task Force 30, **33**, 50, 67, 97, 109, 124
Aqua Trooper 116
Ar Puro 30, 159
Arashikage, Kimi 91, 153, 243
Arashikage, Thomas "Tommy" S. 25, 82, 92, 151, 153, 242
Arashikage Clan **33**, 34, 43, 82, 92, 112, 144, 157, 179, 230, 237, 239
Arashikage Martial Arts Academy 25, 47, 64
Arbco Brother Circus 246, 255
Arboc, William "Billy" 33, 41, 43, 48, 144, 152
Arctic Attack Force **33**, 59, 147, 154
Arctic Circle 143, 216, 240
Argen Seven 103
Argentina 103, 116, 134, 160, 193; Buenos Aires 103, 116, 160, 193; San Luis 134
Arizona 74, 101, 146; Grand Canyon 74, 146; Phoenix 101
Arkansas 51, 88, 162; Helena 162; Little Rock 51; Quitman 88
Arkoma Technology 142
Arlington National Cemetery 34, 38, 43, 44, 54, 58, 72, 93, 94, 102, 104, 117
Armadillo 24, **33–34**, 127
Armadillo vehicle 67, 73, 85, 94, 124, 129, 140
Armbruster, Brad J. 27
Armbruster, Wendall L. 28
Arndt, Philip W. 74
Artur Kulik **183**, 230
Asa Negra **183**, 187
Ashiko 25, **34**

Asimov, Yuri Ivanovich 88
ASP 124, 233
Assault Team Beta 164
Atlantic City Freeway Battle 122
Austin, Aaron B. 22, 27, 71, 76, 92
Australia 43, 62, 67, 119, 139, 202, 228; Alice Springs 62, 67, 119, 139, 202, 218, 223, 228; Exmouth, WA 62; Perth 224; Queenstown 139; Sidney 202; Simpson Desert 228; Snowy River 119; Sydney 43, 218
Autobots 8, 72, 104, 156
AVAC (Air-Viper Advanced Class) 182, **184**
Avalanche **34**, 38, 53
A.W.E. Striker 31, 55, 56, 61, 67, 68, 73, 80, 84, 94, 100, 114, 124, 130, 134, 201
Ayvazyan, Varujan 156

Backblast 24, **34**, 37, 169
Backstop 25, **35**
Bacus, Kirk 105
Badducci, Wallace J. 148
Badger 37
Badhikistan 69, 181, 188, 195, 225
Baikun, Joseph R. 106
Bailey, Nicholas M. 249
Balboa, Rocky 125, 187
Balducci, Ralph 111
Ballistic **35**, **157**, 237
Bama, Rando 117
Bambi 23, **36**
Banzai 25, 33, **36**, 48, 111, 239
Barbecue 24, 30, **36**, 68, 140
Barbieri, Frank 161
Barney, James J. 78
Baron Ironblood 176, **184**, 185, 192
Baroness 6, 16, 20, 49, 50, 78, 81, 82, 110, 116, 131, 150, 153, 177, 178, **185**, 197, 200, 201, 206, 209, 215, 219, 242, 247, 254, 257
Barracuda 37
Barrel Roll 24, **37**, 45, 158, 189
Barricade 24, 33, **37**, 123, 124
Bases and Holdings 25, **179**
B.A.T.s 46, 143, 152, 176, 179, 181, **186**, 210, 212, 224, 225, 226, 243, 258

259

Index

Battle Action Force 22, 28
Battle Android Trooper (B.A.T.)
  186, 202, 224, 226, 258
Battle Android Trooper (B.A.T.)
  Generation 2 186
Battle at the Statue of Liberty 136
Battle Ax vehicle 229
Battle Commanders 37
Battle Copter 28, 102, 214
Battle Corps 27, 34, **37**, 38, 47, 54,
  56, 57, 60, 61, 67, 71, 72, 75, 80,
  89, 90, 93, 95, 96, 99, 101, 108,
  109, 112, 124, 134, 143, 147, 165,
  166, 167, 168, 204
Battle-Flash 67
Battle in the Gulf of Mexico 59
The Battle of Benzheen 33, 34, 35,
  38, 42, 43, 44, 59, 63, 83, 93, 94,
  101, 104, 118, 142, 151, 164, 167,
  168, 218, 242, 246, 255
Battle of Cobra-La 100
Battle of Springfield 39, 120, 129,
  180, 234, 236
Battle of the Great Flood of 2011
  50
Battle of the Statue of Liberty 100,
  146
Battle Wagon 32, 111, 144
Battleforce 2000 34, **38**, 42, 44,
  53, 59, 63, 64, 70, 94, 104
Bayonet 186–187, 189, 207, 210,
  213, 227, 249, 250
Bazooka 24, 31, 32, 37, **38**, 40, 159
Beach Head 22, 37, **38**, 39, 110, 119,
  147, 154, 159, 187, 192, 215, 224,
  2323, 248
Beaver 39
Beck, Aron 68
Belgium 129, 145, 245; Bruges 129;
  Brussels 145, 245
Benjamin, Joseph M. 128
Bennet, David J. 40
Benzheen 33, 34, 35, 38, 42, 43, 44,
  54, 59, 63, 64, 68, 69, 77, 83, 93,
  94, 101, 103, 104, 118, 119, 127, 140,
  142, 152, 153, 154, 167, 168, 218,
  233, 242, 246, 255
beryllium steel 201
Beuke, Anthony 143
Big Bear 39, 40, 90, 91, 112, 127
Big Ben 40, 90, 91, 105
Big Boa 126, **187**
Big Brawler 24, **40**, 159
Big Lob 25, **41**, 119
Biggles-Jones, Sidney 201, 202
Billy Arboc 33, **41**, 43, 48, 144, 152
Billy-Bob 187, 192, 203, 215, 224,
  232, 249
Billy the falcon 146
Binder, Brian 202
Biologico 41
Biomassa 41, 104
Biosfera 42, 142
B.J.'s exclusive 61
Black, Lester 86
Black Dragon 42, 157
Black Dragon Leader 42, 188
Black Dragon, Organization 42,
  188, 244

Black Dragon, spy organization
  warlord **188**
Black Dragon Trooper 188
the Black Major 45, 176
Black Out 37, 45, **188**, 189, 205,
  209, 212, 213, 214, 220, 231, 250
Blackstar 189
Blackstar; the individual **189**
Blackwater Prison 39, 136, 190,
  218, 231, 247
Blades 42, 163
Blais, Robert M. 56
Blanchet, John 161
Blast-Off 25, **42**, 106
Blast-Off 2 43
Blaster 38, **43**, 219
Blind Master 33, **43**, 91, 92, 111
Blinken-Smythe, Richard 190
Blizzard 24, **43**, 44, 53, 159, 169
Blockbuster 38, 168, 169
Blocker 38, **44**
Blowtorch 24, 28, 44, 45
Bludd, Sebastian 218
Blue Ninjas 41
Blue Ridge Marauders 1
Body Bags 187, **189**, 207, 210, 213,
  227, 228, 249, 250
Bombardier 45
Bombstrike 25, 37, **45**, 158, 189
Bon Appetit 45–46
Bongo Bear 48
Booth, Fred T. III 230
Borovia 41, 43, 101, 112, 116, 129,
  151, 166, 180, 218, 242
Boulder 46, 138
Bouvier, Jean-Luc 37
Bowman, Thomas S. 101
Boyajian, Gregory B. 140
Boyce, John 137
Bozigian, H. Kirk 13
Bradley 110
The Brainwave Scanner 41, 185,
  203, 243
Brawler (vehicle) 64, 242
Brazil 70, 145; Altamira 70; Sao
  Paulo 145
Breaker 6, 20, 28, **46**, 47, 56, 57,
  67, 70, 72, 115, 117, 148, 170
Breckinridge, Matthew Harris
  158
Brekhov, Ivan Nikolevich 58, 88,
  111, 112, 121, 152, 153
Brewi, David X. 58
Brian Hassell 189
Bristo, Rebecca M. 223
British Action Force 35
Brittany "Bree" Van Mark 97
Broca, Fred 92, 93, 205, 206, 207
Bronson, Caleb and Sarah 124
Brown, Eliot 70
Buckingham, Charles Richard
  49
Budo 23, 25, 33, **47**, 90, 91, 92
Bugg (vehicle) 235
Bullet-Proof 23, 37, **47**, 67
Bullhorn 24, **47**, 48, 114, 128
Burn Out 190, 203
Bushido 24, 36, **48**, 111
Buzzer 190, 203, 231, 247, 257

California 25, 32, 41, 43, 47, 52, 53,
  57, 60, 64, 72, 91, 92, 94, 99, 100,
  110, 111, 115, 116, 117, 118, 121, 125,
  134, 138, 141, 147, 148, 152, 155,
  159, 162, 170, 195, 197, 200, 206,
  211, 229, 233, 234, 238, 241, 242;
  Boulder Creek 99; Burlingame
  148; Cambria 32; Chula Vista
  134; Coronado 53, 57, 60, 110, 118,
  162, 165, 197; Death Valley 234;
  Donner Pass 238; Fresno 47, 152,
  242; High Sierras 25, 141, 152,
  159, 200, 206, 242; Lodi 72; Los
  Angeles 41, 91, 100, 116, 117, 138,
  147, 155, 170, 195, 211, 233; Malibu
  125; Roseville 92; Sacramento
  47; San Diego 52; San Francisco
  25, 41, 43, 47, 64, 94, 111, 115, 152,
  229, 234, 241, 242; Stockton 121;
  Walnut 32; Watts, Los Angeles
  116, 117
Camp Lejeune 95, 96, 132
Campbell, Grant J. 49
Canada 29, 39, 89, 110, 165, 200,
  258; Caughnawaga 29; Ontario
  39, 200, 258; Pikangikum 200;
  Qikiqtaaluk 89; Toronto 110,
  165, 258
Candy Apple 48, 123, 144, 227
Cannonball 25, **48**
Captain Bulgakov 167
Captain "Eagle" Buckingham 49
Captain Skip 45, **49**, 91, 170
Carday, Deborah 40
Castle Destro 55, 180, 185, 201,
  214, 235
Cataclysm (submarine) 200
Cayman Islands 204, 256
Cesspool 190, 191, 230
Chameleon 24, **49**
Chameleon (vehicle) 49, 231, 247,
  257
Chance 24, **50**, 154
Chaplain's Assistant motor pool
  25, 55, 62, 63, 67, 135, 168
Charbroil 25, 33, **50**, 110, 154
Checkpoint 25, **50**
CheyTac Intervention LRRS 100
Chile 150, 241; Alejandro Selkirk
  Island 150, 241
China 116, 169; Canton 116;
  Urumqi, Xinjiang 169
Chop Shop 191, 203
Chuckles 24, 49, **51**, 81, 92, 110,
  119, 226
Circuit (Cybertronian) 83
Cissarovna, Anastasia 185
CLAW (vehicle) 185, 201
CLAWS Commander 191
Claymore 23, **51**, 61, 96, 101, 146,
  166, 241
Clean-Sweep 51, 52, 68
Cletus 188, **191**, 203, 215, 224, 232,
  249
Cloak of the Chameleon 82
clone children 195, 236
Cloudburst 25, 29, **52**
Clutch 20, 24, **52**, 53, 55, 65, 106,
  154, 223

Index

Clyde 192
Clyde the boar 208, 258
Cob, Reginald 122
Cobra A.D.D.E.R.S. 182
Cobra Castle 131
Cobra Choir and Glee Club 191
Cobra Citadel 180, 185, 200, 239
Cobra Civil War 123, 178, 180, 195, 233, 236, 257
Cobra CLAWS 59
Cobra Command 13, 18, 28, 71, 173, 174, 175, 176, 178, 179, 180, 181, 185, 188, 192, 225, 241, 245, 248, 250
Cobra Commander 6, 7, 20, 21, 22, 34, 41, 43, 44, 84, 94, 101, 104, 110, 138, 150, 161, 166, 173, 174, 175, 176, 178, 181, 185, 187, 188, 192, 193, 194, 195, 196, 197, 198, 200, 201, 203, 205, 206, 207, 210, 218, 219, 226, 229, 234, 236, 242, 244, 246, 247, 249, 251, 252, 253, 255, 257
Cobra Consulate 129, 180
Cobra Crimson Guard Immortal 213
Cobra Emperor 76, 208, 236
Cobra Headquarters 185, 186, 189, 194, 207, 209, 212, 213, 220, 249, 250
Cobra High Command 176, 228, 234
Cobra Island 33, 35, 36, 39, 40, 41, 51, 58, 62, 65, 69, 72, 77, 80, 87, 93, 95, 101, 102, 104, 105, 106, 112, 114, 115, 116, 119, 120, 123, 134, 135, 136, 138, 140, 142, 143, 146, 147, 149, 151, 153, 160, 161, 162, 163, 164, 165, 167, 168, 169, 170, 175, 180, 182, 183, 185, 187, 190, 191, 192, 194, 195, 196, 198, 199, 200, 201, 203, 204, 206, 207, 208, 210, 211, 218, 225, 227, 229, 231, 234, 235, 240, 241, 242, 243, 244, 246, 247, 252, 255, 256
Cobra Mantis 186
Cobra Moray 94
Cobra Mortal 193
Cobra Mortal 2 193, 194
Cobra Officer 194, 223, 234
Cobra Soldier 194, 218, 251
Cobra Vipers 102, 105, 179
the Coffin 126, 166, 168, 191, 193, 196, 197, 202, 204, 205, 211, 222, 225, 235, 238, 253, 254
The Coil 51, 58, 178, 180, 195, 196, 225, 226, 233, 236, 237, 253, 256
The Coil High Command Players 195
Colby, Everett P. 93
Cold Front 24, 53
Cold Shot 25, 53
Coleco 126
Collins, Sean 81, 92, 93
Collins, Wade 92, 206
Colombani, Cyril 138
Colombia 156; Bogota 156
Colonel Brekhov 53, 88, 111, 112, 121, 152

Colonel Courage 23, 31, 37, **54**, 144
Colonel Nikita 218
Colonel Slash 196, 239
Colorado 43, 57, 83, 92, 101, 107, 111, 146, 152, 158, 167, 188, 206, 208, 229, 242; Denver 43, 83, 101, 111, 122, 206, 229; Devil's Thumb 122; New Moon 57, 92, 107, 129, 152, 158, 167, 188, 234, 242; Pueblo 146, 238
Colton, Joseph B. 76, 77, 86, 93, 145, 221, 254
Comandos Em Acao 70
Comandos Heroicos 103, 122, 134, 148, 160, 161
Combat Pay dollars 75
Combat Support Troop (Company) 112
Compound Z 230
Conda, Ann A. 252
Connecticut 30, 153, 160; Bridgeport 166; Hartford 153; New Haven 30
Connors, Charles Theodore 139
Conquest X-30 (vehicle) 140, 141
Cookie 25, 154
Cool Breeze 54, 90, 169
Cooper, Brad L. 100, 238
Copperhead 196, 197
Corey, Max W. 87
Corsica 246, 255
Cortez, Brigid 145
Costello, Ian M. 34
Council of Worlds 83
Countdown 23, 54, 148
Courtney Krieger and Project: Runway 83
Cover Girl 24, 55, 158
Coyote (vehicle) 65, 124
Craig, Jodie 135
Crankcase 55, 56, 63, 86, 158, 233
Crawler (vehicle) 82, 83
Crazylegs 47, **56**, 57, 67, 70, 110, 117
Crecelius, Spencer D. 158
Crimson Asp 233
Crimson Guard 69, 131, 179, **197**, 204, 206, 207, 213, 226, 227, 246, 255
Crimson Rain 25
Crispo Paine 197
Croc Master 198
Cross Country 24, 38, 47, **56**, 57, 67, 70, 117, 154
Cross Hair 25, **57**, 110, 159, 191
Crossfire 24, **57**, 127
Crowther, Thurston 76, 92
Crusher 198, 203
Crystal Ball 76, **198**
Cuba 143
Cunningham, Michael 50
Curtis Letson 57, 107
Cutter 25, 28, 38, **57**, 58, 67
cyborg 41, 124, 125, 128, 196, 225, 233, 254
Czechoslovakia 58; Prague 58

D-Day 58, 131
Daemon 58, 71, 237

Daina 58
D'Alleva, Vincent A. 190
Damien 110
Dan 193
Darkened Room 82
Darklon 199, 214
Darklonia 142, 199, 200, 214
Dart 24, 59
David, Brian R. 43
Dawg 108, 109, 230
Daystar 11
Decepticons 8, 104, 138, 215
Decimator 199
Dee-Jay 33, 59
Deep Sea Defender 116
Deep Sea Diver 116
Deep Six 25, 28, 30, **59**, 60, 68
Defiant (vehicle) 54, 82, 101, 115, 256
Dela Eden 95, **199**, 230
De La Vega, Jocelyn 74
Delgado, Hector X. 134
Delisi, Samuel C. 66
DeLuca, Donald 231
Demolishor 200, 203
D.E.M.O.N. (vehicle) 214
Denver School of the Blind Master 111
Depth Charge 25, **60**
Derenko, Mikhail 81, 195, 196, 225, 237
Desade Paine 200
Desert Patrol Squad 32, **60**, 68, 80, 129, 141, 147, 156, 164
Desert Wolf 60, 138
Destro 6, 20, 33, 55, 78, 95, 115, 125, 176, 177, 178, 179, 180, 183, 185, 186, 192, 195, 199, 200, 201, 207, 214, 216, 219, 2323, 234, 235, 250, 252, 257
Destro XXIV, James McCullen 178, 200
DEVGRU (vehicle) 83
Devilfish (vehicle) 61, 96, 100, 132, 134, 143, 157, 166
Devil's Due 20, 58, 119, 129
Dial Tone 24, 38, 47, 51, **60**, 96, 101, 128, 144, 146, 159, 166
Dial Tone 2 61–62
DiC Universe 153, 243
Dice 201, 239
Dictator (vehicle) 226
Diesel, Omar K. 74
Digger 24, **62**, 139
dimantium metal 151
Dino Hunters 32, **62**, 100
Dirk Manus 104
Doc 23, 28, 56, **62**, 63, 86, 153, 158, 168, 170, 223, 225, 233
Doc 2 63
Dr. Adele Burkhart 63, 97, 209
Doctor Biggles-Jones 201, 202
Doctor Cassandra Knox 202
Doctor Mindbender 7, 69, 76, 165, 176, 178, 181, 186, 195, **202**, 203, 210, 212, 217, 224, 225, 226, 229, 233, 236, 251, 258
Doctor Venom 203, 234
Dr. Venom's Toxin 234

Index

Dodger 24, 38, **63**, 64, 144
Dogfight 23, **64**
Dojo 24, 25, 33, 43, **64**, 111, 239
Dolphin 28, **64**, 170, 171
Domestic Operations Agency 92
The Dominator tank 38
Donahue, Charles 53
Donahue, Greg M. 46
Donald 232
Doom Cycle 242
Double Blast 24, **65**, 124
Double Clutch 52, **65**
Downtown 25, **65**, 66
Dragonfly (vehicle) 36, 67, 94, 117, 129, 147, 164, 167, 201
Dragonsky 58, **66**, 112
Dreadnok cycle 96
Dreadnok Recruit 187, 191, 215, 232, 248
Dreadnok Thunder Machine 245
Dreadnoks 90, 132, 178, 179, 180, 190, 191, 195, 196, 197, 198, **203**, 208, 211, 224, 231, 232, 239, 245, 246, 247, 249, 255, 256, 257
Dremmler, Wolfgang 131
Drop Zone 24, 29, 30, **66**, 139
Drug Elimination Force 8, 47, 57, 67, 99, 108, 109, 135
Drukersky, Stepan 88
Dube, Robert D. 126
Dubosky, David D. 54
Duggleby, Wilmer S. 82
Duke 11, 22, 28, 31, 33, 38, 47, 55, 56, 57, **67**, 69, 70, 73, 76, 81, 83, 84, 88, 105, 110, 117, 123, 129, 131, 132, 133, 135, 138, 139, 142, 144, 148, 151, 154, 159, 226, 247
Duncan, Alastair Thomas 235
Duque (Duke) 159
Dusty 24, 60, **67**, 68, 113, 114, 128, 142, 159, 217
Dynamite 68, 131
Dynamo Sports Club 121

Eaglehawk Helicopter 97
Ear That Sees 82
Earth Defense Command 104, 105
Earthquake (vehicle) 211, 225
Eastern Siberia 208; Chuchki Peninsula 208
Eco-Warriors 36, 41, 42, 52, **68**, 72, 113
Eden, Dela 95
Eels 204, 216, 240
Effects 24, **68**, 148
Eliminator (vehicle) 38, 44
Ellesmere Island Research Base 89
Ellison, Luke 121
el Shafei, Tariq 107
Elsund, Lars 84
Emirate of Benzheen 54
Enemy Leader 173, 192, 193
England 40, 45, 49, 51, 55, 65, 69, 70, 72, 83, 85, 87, 89, 95, 97, 109, 118, 122, 123, 125, 130, 135, 140, 142, 151, 165, 167, 168, 190, 195, 244, 255, 256; Avonmouth, Bristol 151; Basildon in Essex 87; Bath 89; Birmingham, Somerset

72; Bracknell, Berkshire 70; Brixton, London 123; Burford 40; Cambridge 190; Coalville 45; Glastonbury, Somerset 69; High Wycombe, Buckinghamshire 142; Hull, East Riding of Yorkshire 167; Lincoln, Lincolnshire 72; Liverpool, Merseyside 85; London 45, 55, 95, 109, 118, 123, 130, 135, 140, 168, 195, 244, 255, 256; Luton, Bedfordshire 65; Manchester 51, 123, 135; Middlesex 49; Penrith, Cumberland 122; Streatham, London 95; Torquay 165; Truro, Cornwall 125; Warminster, Wiltshire 83; Wimborne, Dorset 97
Enterprise City 196, 204
Escorpiao Voador 68, 114, **204**
Eugene 185
Evac 23, **68**, 154
Extensive Enterprises 111, 179, **204**, 206, 217, 247, 255

Faceless Master 33, 204
Faces 24, **69**, 70
Fairborn, Marissa 25, 73, 95, 104, 105
Faireborn, Dashiell R. 72
Faireborne, Dashiell R. 72
Falcon 22, 23, 46, 47, 56, 57, 67, **69**, 70, 74, 92, 110, 117, 119, 133, 144, 154, 155, 221
Falcon Glider 36, 61, 80, 94, 96, 100, 130
Falcone, Vincent R. 69
FANG (vehicle) 167, 185, 201, 231, 247
Fangboat 244
Fardie, Don G. 57
Faria, Jason A. 135
Fast Draw 25, **70**, 118
Father Cobra 33
Feedback 70
Felino 25, **70**, 159
Felix, Dwayne A. 118
Felix, Lynton N. 139
Felton, Joseph 119
Fer-de-Lance, Louisiana 80
Feral Berserker 229
Ferreira, Stephen A. 48
Ferret (vehicle) 219, 231, 247
Fetzer, Scott 157
5th SFGA "Blue Light" counter-terrorist unit 69
Filbert, Darren K. 79
Finback (dolphin) 60, 68
Fine, Seymour P. 130
Finley, Stuart A. 106, 218
Firebat (vehicle) 184, 201, 227, 250
Firefly 33, 61, 81, 93, 111, 112, 141, 151, 183, 188, 195, 201, **204**, 205, 212, 220, 226, 239
Firewall 58, **71**, 101
Flag points 173
USS *Flagg* 27, 46, 50, 58, 61, 71, 93, 96, 100, 101, 140, 141
Flagg (1) 71

Flagg (3) 71
Flagg, James Longstreet III 22, 27, 37, 71, 72, 133, 135
Flagg, Lawrence J. 71
FLAK (vehicle) 39
Flak-Viper 205
Flak-Viper Nostaw 205
Flak-vipers 205
Flash 6, 20, 24, 28, **72**, 148, 154, 223
Flint 22, 30, 38, 68, **72**, 73, 78, 95, 104, 110, 124, 132, 133, 138, 159, 201
Florida 42, 44, 114, 139, 170, 198; Big Cypress Swamp 114; Cape Canaveral 114, 170; Key West 114; Kissimmee 198; Panama City 42; Pensacola 139; Tampa 44
Folger, William P. 161
Footloose 24, **73**, 127, 140
Forasteiro 112, 159
Forca Eco 41, 42
Ford, Jerome 134
Foreign Legion 205, 218, 246, 255
Forrest, Brian C. 165
Forrest, Brian M. 165
Fort Benning, Georgia 29, 31, 38, 39, 67, 73, 100, 139, 141, 147, 197
Fort Bliss, Texas 68, 113
Fort Bragg, North Carolina 31, 55, 57, 115, 141, 163
Fort Dodge, Iowa 56
Fort Holabird, Maryland 94, 147
Fort Hood, Texas 149
Fort Huachuca, Arizona 33, 129, 158, 188
Fort Knox, Kentucky 38, 53, 75, 136, 149
Fort Leonard Wood, Missouri 81, 150
Fort Lewis, Washington 83, 94, 131
Fort Meade, Maryland 41
Fort Riley, Kansas 107, 188
Fort Rucker, Alabama 165, 169
Fort Sill, Oklahoma 149
Fort Wadsworth, New York 25, 39, 50, 55, 62, 67, 83, 85, 92, 95, 112, 122, 123, 128, 137, 146, 160, 170, 200, 206
Fox Hunt 73
France 31, 56, 130, 254, 257; Grenoble 31; Lyon 254; Nice 257; Rouen 56; Strasbourg 130
Frankel, Andrew 137
Frankenstein, Victor 212
Fred I 205, 206
Fred II 92, **206**
Fred VII 206, 229
Fred LXV 207
Fred Series 48, 92, 197, **207**
Fred's Garage 206
Fredwick 213
Freedom (eagle) 146
Freefall 24, **74**
Freestyle 23, **74**, 110
Freight 74, 157, 254
Freisov, Andrei 66
Freistadt, Eric W. 135, 171

Freistadt, Mark W. 135
the Fridge 24, **74**, 75
Fritz, Karl W. 99
Frostbite 21, 24, 38, **75**, 159, 169, 221
Frusenland 34, 35, 38, 42, 44, 59, 63, 94, 104

Gabriel, Ophelia 81, 112
Gaines 108
Gallows 187, 189, **207**, 210, 213, 227, 249, 250
Gambello, Anthony S. 72
Garbage O's 204
Garcia, Alejandro 99
Garrido, Hector J. 68
Gaucho 75, 170
Gears 23, 25, **76**, 148
General Abernathy 83, 92, 126
General Austin 22, 27, 71, **76**, 92
General Crowther 76, 92
General Curtis 92
General Gibbs 92, 226
General Harring 92
General Hollingsworth 22, 87, 92
General Iron Bear 111, 207
General Malthus 92
General Mayhem 66, 111, **207**
General Philip Rey 76, 198
General Ryan 92
General Winters 92
Georgia 129, 223; Atlanta 129, 223
Germany 30, 44, 46, 95, 131, 212; Berchtesgaden 95; Lauingen, Bavaria 212; Leipzig, Austria 44, 131; Munich 30, 46
Ghana 199; Atebubu 199
Ghost Bear 207, 216
Ghost jet (vehicle) 94
Ghostbusters 156
Ghostrider 23, **77**
Ghoststriker 38
G.I. Jane 77
G.I. Joe 77
G.I. Joe: A Real American Hero 20, 22, 143, 152, 168, 243
G.I. Joe: America's Elite 199, 250
G.I. Joe and the Action Force 28
G.I. Joe Con 223
G.I. Joe Extreme 13, 157
G.I. Joe Kindle Worlds Fan Vote 150
G.I. Joe Reinstated 20
G.I. Joe Resolute 27, 153, 243
G.I. Joe Stars cereal 148
G.I. Joe: The Movie 21, 69, 86, 176
G.I. Joe: The Rise of Cobra 8, 61, 62
G.I. Joe II: The Revenge of Cobra 20
Glenda 78, 82, 118, 129
Gnawgahyde 198, 203, **208**, 219
Goggles, Gary 137
Goldfine, Lloyd S. 48
Golobulus 21, **208**, 221, 227
Gonsalves, Blain M. 94
Gonzalles, Chio 75
Gonzalles, Rico 75
Goren, Chuck X. 160
Gorky 33, **78**, 112

Gorky, Mikhail P. 78
Grand Slam 20, 24, **78**, 79, 138
Graves, Robert W. 80
Greece 149; Salonika 149
Green, Elijah F. 54
Green Ridge 204
Greenland 44, 90, 132, 134, 135, 240; Apogee Base 90, 240; Thule 44, 132, 134, 135
Greenshirt 50, 57, 70, **79**, 92, 103, 147, 158, 189
Greer, Carl W. 23, 62
Greer, Carla P. 63
Gregor 208, 209
Grid-Iron 24, 32, **79**, 95, 114, 128, 139
Griffith, Charles L. 65
Grill 79, 131
Grim Skull 189, **209**, 213, 214, 220, 227, 250
Gristle 209
Grizzly (vehicle) 110
Groen, Christopher R. 162
Grogan, Steve 38
Ground-Vipers 220
Grunbach family 213
Grunt 6, 20, 24, 28, 73, **80**, 110, 130, 148, 155, 223
Guderian, Sherman R. 85
Guillotine 187, 189, 207, **209**, 210, 213, 227, 231, 249, 250
Gung Ho 7, 22, 28, 38, 60, **80**, 81, 105, 110, 138, 154, 197

Habershaw, Mark 154
Hacker 24, **81**, 101, 106, 234
Halifax, Charles 254
Hama, Larry 18, 19, 126, 162, 257
Hammer Team 81, 92, 93, 195, 196, 225, 226
Hammerhead (vehicle) 199
Hannibal 195, **210**
Hanrahan, Timothy P. 44
Hard Drive 24, **81**
Hard Master 33, **82**, 141, 144, 153, 243
Hardball 24, 35, **82**, 118, 123
Hardtop 24, **82**, 83, 115, 159
Hardy, William S. 167, 168
Harpoon 83, 157
Hart-Burnett, Alison R. 94
Hart-Smyth, Alison R. 94
Hasbro 8, 9, 11, 13, 14, 16, 75, 84, 104, 148, 194, 221, 236, 251
Hasbro Direct Pack 194
Hasbro mail-in 84, 236
Hashtag 83
Hasle, David K. 127
Hassell, Brian 189
Haun, Julie 92, 107
Hauser, Aisha 31
Hauser, Carl 67
Hauser, Conrad S. 67
H.A.V.O.C (vehicle) 51, 56, 61, 67, 84, 101, 117, 124, 132, 134, 139, 143
Hawaii 90, 129, 155, 162, 234
Hawk 20, 22, 24, 25, 37, 54, 70, 71, **83**, 84, 87, 92, 93, 126, 128, 129, 131, 132, 133, 138, 139, 141, 148, 150, 151, 154, 162, 166, 196, 250, 251
Hawkwind 84
Head Banger 84, 131
Headhunter B.A.T.s (Headhunter Battle Android Troopers) 210
Headhunter Elite Urban Crime Guards 210
Headhunter Guardians 210
Headhunter Vehicle Operators 210
Headhunters 207, 209, **210**, 211
Headman 8, 67, 210, **211**
Headman's Narcotic Guard 210
Heart-Wrencher 203, **211**
Heat Viper (High Explosive Anti-Tank) Viper 211
Heather 206, 207
Heavy Assault Squad 67, 79, **84**, 124, 141
Heavy Duty 24, **84**, 85, 124, 132, 138, 148, 151
Heavy Metal 56, 63, **85**, 86, 117, 158, 225, 233
Heavy Water Trooper 212
Hector Ramirez 86
Helix 25, **86**
Hep Cat 86, 131
Her Dolls! 128
Hi-Tech 22, 24, 64, **87**, 138
Himalayas 180, 194, 208, 220, 227, 240, 244; Cobra-La 21, 69, 91, 100, 163, 165, 176, 198, 208, 220, 227, 229
Hinton, Marvin F. 123
H.I.S.S. 127, 185, 205, **212**, 226, 228, 230, 231
H.I.S.S. II 127, 128
Hit and Run 24, **87**, 110, 131, 159
Hoffman, Susan 155
Holland, Keith B. 228
Hollingsworth 22, 87, 92
Hollow Point 87
Honda Lou West 88
Horror Show 40, **88**, 112
Hoslinger, Philip M. 37
Hot Jets 88, 89
Hot Seat 24, **89**
Hotwire 51, **212**
Hurley, Matthew 106
Hurricane V.T.O.L. (vehicle) 249
Hyata, Ryjui 92
Hyde, Clyde 208

Iannotti, William V. 114
Ice Cream Soldier 24, 38, **89**
Ice Storm 25, **89**
Iceberg 24, 38, 75, **90**, 143
Iceland 48, 129, 147, 196, 225, 226; Reykjavík 129, 147
Idaho 31, 129, 160; Boise 160; Snake River Plain, Minidoka 31
IDW 27, 61, 104, 123, 129, 197, 229, 239
Illinois 41, 47, 74, 75, 77, 79, 82, 85, 125, 130, 134, 136, 137, 141, 148, 197, 204, 249, 256, 257; Chicago 41, 47, 55, 75, 77, 82, 85, 125, 130, 136, 137, 141, 148, 204, 249,

256, 257; Downers Grove 74; Evergreen Park 79; Great Lakes 134, 197; Peoria 55
image comics 20, 129
Incision 179, 189, 209, **212**, 213, 214, 220, 223, 227, 250
Indiana 63, 73, 161; Fort Wayne 161; Gary 73; South Bend 63
Indiana, Elwood G. 55
Inferno 90, 138, 213, 238
Inferno, S.K.A.R. 213
Infrared 187, 189, 207, 210, **213**, 227, 249, 250
Inglesen, Sven 63
Inhumanoids 86
Intelligence Support Troop (Company) 112
Inter-Alliance 230, 238
International Action Force 40, **90**, 146
International G.I. Joe Convention 246
Interrogator 116, 189, 209, **213**, 214, 220, 227, 250
USS *Intrepid* 93
Invasion of Springfield 146, 149, 163
Iowa 42, 56, 81, 86, 87, 104, 168; Cedar Rapids 12, 68; Clarinda 86; Emmetsburg 81; Fort Dodge 56; Ida Grove 104; Riverside 42; Sioux City 87
Ireland 59, 94, 115, 130, 219; Belfast 219; Cork, Eire 59, 94; Dublin 94, 115, 130
I.R.O.N. Army 128
Iron Bear 91, 111
Iron Grenadier Elite Trooper 214
Iron Grenadiers 140, 152, 179, 180, 183, 199, 200, 201, 207, **214**, 218, 219, 232, 235, 248, 252
Iron Klaw 117, 151, 157, 213, **215**, 228, 238, 241, 255
Iron-Knife, Charlie 146
Italy 29, 36, 46, 60, 94, 109, 134, 144, 185, 218, 244; Carcare 144; Luca 185; Milan 46, 60; Naples 29, 36; Venice 134

Jamaica 62, 117, 209; Black River 117; Kingston 62; Montego Bay 209
Jammer 91, 147, 170
Janack, Diana L. 58
Japan 33, 47, 82, 90, 125, 129, 144, 152, 153, 163, 170, 186, 196, 204, 225, 226, 243; Osaka 47; Tokyo 225; Yokosuka 152, 163
Jazz (Autobot) 104
Jeffries, Jonas S. 77
Jem 86
Jem and the Holograms 86
Jesso, Kyle A. 47
Jinx 24, 33, 41, 43, 47, 49, 70, **91**, 92, 119, 141, 153, 159, 243
Jivoin, Jerome T. 156
Joe-Bob 188, 192, 203, **215**, 224, 232, 249
Joe's "Americana Museum" sub-base 115

Johnson, Chad M. 159
Johnson, Don 69
Johnson, Edward T. 197
Jones, Ayana 105
Jones, John-Edward O. 32
Jones, Walter O. **190**
Jonestown, Guyana 239
Jordan, Jesse E. 81
Juanita Hooper 215
the Jugglers 76, 87, **92**, 195, 196, 210, 225, 226, 237
Julia 120
Julia Rossi 36, 237
Julie Haun 92, 107
JUMP (vehicle) 30, 46, 67, 73, 84, 90, 97, 100, 103, 117, 124, 129, 147, 148, 149, 167, 170
Junko Akita 92, 152, 153, 242, 243
Junkyard 28, 33, 38, 67, **106**, 109, 140, 159, 190
Junkyard II 109

K9s for Warriors 1
Kaeru, N. 34
Kalistan 215
Kamakura 24, 33, 41, 81, **92**, 138, 141, 154, 196, 206
Kansas 36, 55, 57, 72, 98, 107, 188; Kinsley 57; Lawrence 55; Pittsburg 36; Wichita 72, 98
Kassels, Marcus 184
Katzenbogen, David L. 38
Kavanagh, Jason 103
Kayapo, Joao 70
Kaye, Kevin M. 84, 86
Keel-Haul 22, 26, 38, **93**
Kelly, Gabriel A. 36
Kenner 14, 104
Kentucky 30, 50, 53, 158; Fort Knox 53; Lexington 50; Louisville 30, 158
Kessler, William (Billy) 150
Kibbey, Alvin R. 46
Kickstart 24, **93**
Kiley, Thomas P. 104
Killer W.H.A.L.E. (vehicle) 57, 58
King, James R. 64
King, Owen S. 142
Kiwi 93
Klas, Nicholas D. 82
Knockdown 38, **94**
Knox, Cassandra 186, 202
Koga Ninja Clan 204
Kojima, Minami 170
Koskov, Ivan 127
Kranseler, Larry M. 167
Krieger, Ariana 55, 83
Krieger, Courtney A. 55, 83
Krimov, Anatoly Fydorovich 121
Kulik, Artur M. 183, 230
Kunitz, David F. 113
Kwaigno, Paithoon 150, 241
Kwinn 185, 203, 208, **215**, 216
Kwinn, Jesse 208, 215
Kwinn, Jesse, Jr. 208

LaCarr City 46
Lacefield, Jeff 58
LaChance, Michelle 71

LaCrosse, Bruno 245
Lady Jaye 24, 73, 78, **94**, 95, 104, 110, 124, 128, 139, 201
LaFitte, Etienne R. 80
Lamont 84, 167
Lamprey 216
Lane, David S. 155
Langdon, Lance M. 60
Langdon, Nick H. 60
LaQuale, Sam 159
Larivee, Thomas J. 153
Larkin, Barbara 131
Laser Viper 216, 217, 227, 250
La Tene, Erika 49
Latimer, Paul 154
Lavigne, Christopher M. 95
Law and Order 95, 119
Lazy Sue (starship) 104
LCV Recon Sled (vehicle) 30, 56, 61, 73, 84, 94, 96, 97, 101, 117, 129, 130, 143, 147, 166
Leaky Suit Brigade 212, 248
Leatherneck 25, 38, 51, 61, 81, **95**, 101, 112, 128, 130, 131, 138, 146, 165, 166
LeClaire, Daniel M. 119
Ledger 22, 27, **96**
Ledger, Warren D. 96
Lee, Jason B. 141, 204
Lee, Kang Chi 42
Lee, Nicky 164
Lee, Leonard J. III 166
Legend of G.I. Joe 13
Leialoha, Edward W. 162
Letson, Curtis 57, 107
Leviathan 96
Levin, Robert A. 35
Lewinski, David P. 87
Lifeline 21, 24, 33, 38, **96**, 97, 110, 153, 159
Lifeline 2 97
Lift-Ticket 24, **97**, 154, 168
Lightfoot 25, **97**, 98, 110, 154
Ligotke, Nolan M. 89
Link 25, **98**
Listen 'N Fun 163
"Live the Adventure Assignment II" 115
Lockdown 98 138
LOCUST (vehicle) 88
Lombardi, Andy 126
London, Robbie 118
Long Arm 24, 38, **99**
Long Range 24, **99**, 138
Long Range 2 99
Lord Kondor 252
Louisiana 80, 81, 108, 252; Dubach 108; Fer-de-Lance 80; New Orleans 252; Thibodaux 108
Low Light 24, 62, **100**, 140, 154, 165
Lowdown 22, **100**, 154
Lt Clayton W. Moore 217
Lunartix Empire 148
Lyndon, Terrence 79

MacArthur, Ito S. 116
MacBride, Cooper G. 100, 165
MacBride, Una 165

Index

Mace 24, 38, **101**
Machete 203, **217**
Madame Veil 165, **217**
Magda **101**, 166
Maine 34, 142; Bangor 142; Madawaska 34
Mainframe 25, 51, 61, 71, 96, **101**, 102, 146, 166, 257
Major Altitude 22, **102**
Major Barrage 50, **102**
Major Bludd 62, 71, 76, 110, 120, 150, 195, 203, 211, **217**
Major Hooper 215
Major Storm **103**
Makepeace, Philo R. 33
Malenkiy, Evaldas 103
Malyenkiy **103**
Mangiaratti, Thomas P. 99
Mangler **103**
Manleh **103**, 147
MANTA (vehicle) 94
Manta-Ray raft 38
Mara 25, 134, **218**
Marauder (vehicle) 38, 64
Marina 206
Mariner 83, **104**
Marissa Faireborn 25, 73, 95, **104**, 105
M.A.R.S. 178, 182, 183, 200, 201, 202, 214, 221, 222, 235, 244, 249, 250
Mars Harring 196
Marseille, France 37
Martelle, Jane Ann 77
Marujo 134, 159
Marvel Comics Universe **18**, 27, 55, 80, 125, 147, 174, 180, 257
Maryland 29, 59, 94, 218; Annapolis 29, 218; Baltimore 59, 94
M.A.S.K. **104**, 163
Massachusetts 36, 44, 54, 57, 62, 63, 94, 98, 137, 144, 159, 167, 168, 190, 191, 202, 230; Boston 36, 44, 54, 202; Brockton 57; Clarksburg 98; Concord 62, 63; Douglas 159; Everett 144; Fall River 230; Hingham 137; Martha's Vineyard 94; Newton 167, 190; Northhampton 168
Matt Trakker 104, 163
Mauler M.B.T. Tank 85
Maverick 38, **104**
Max the bobcat 145, 146
Mayday 23, 25, **104**, 157
Mayday 2 105
Mayhemovski, Vladimir P. 207
McCarthy, David B. 44
McConnel, Craig S. 125
McCoy, James 196
McDaniel, Walter A. 85, 117
McDonald, Jim 168
McLaren, Jamie Hugh 96
McLaughlin, Sean C. 137
McMahon, Aaron 32
Mean Dog (vehicle) 168
Med Alert 24, **105**
Mega-Marines 43, 52, 80, **105**, 106
Mega-Monsters 43, 105, 106

Megalo City 186, 258
Megatron 8, 138
the Melbourne Maulers Motorcycle Club 247
Melendez, Rafael J. 170
Melnitz, Janine 156
Menninger, Edward J. 34
Mercer 22, **106**, 133, 150, 242
Metal-Head 106, 201, 214, **218**
Metalhead 106, 156, 157, 219
Metz 153
Metzger, Wendell A. 95
Mewett, Cliff V. 30, 54
Mexico 36, 44, 59, 75, 94, 99, 152, 190, 196, 206, 222, 242; *Distrito Federal* 75; Gulf of Mexico 36, 59, 94, 190, 196, 206; Mexico City 75; Monterrey 99
Meyers, Andrew D. 73, 229
Michaels, Leonard 130
Michigan 135, 147, 217, 231; Dearborn 135; Detroit 147, 217; Goblu 231
Mikhail Derenko 81, 195, 196, 225, 237
Miles 213
Millard Fillmore Memorial 228
Miller, Michelle 110
Millman, Peter R. 145
Millville 109, 125, 146, 152, 164, 167, 180, 200, 201, 239, 242
Minnesota 38, 50, 58, 87, 149, 163; Blackduck 50; Duluth 149; Hibbing 38, 163; St. Paul 87; White Earth Indian Reservation 58
Mirage 25, **106**, 107, 158, 169, 189
Misha **107**, 112
Mississippi 85, 123, 124; Biloxi 85, 123, 124
Missouri 43, 67, 145, 152, 213, 242; Kirkwood 43; St. Louis 67, 145, 152, 213, 242
Mr. Clancy **107**, 151
Mistress Armada 183, 195, **219**
MOBAT (vehicle) 149, 159
Mondale, Calvin 91
Monev, Archibald 203
Monkeywrench 204, **219**
Monolith Base 181, 192
Monstructor 169
Montalvo, Jose 83
Montana 91, 130, 237, 243, 249; Geraldine 130
Moondancer 28, **107**
Moore, Clayton W. 217, 223, 224
Moore, Harlan W. 143
Moray (vehicle) 94, 195, 216, 236
Morelli, Jack S. 60, 62
Morelli, Jill S. 61
Moreno, Dillon L. 169
Morera, Jason 68
Morgan, Gareth 65
Morgan, Mark, Jr. 114
Morris, Earl S. 47
Morris, Lamont A. 84
Morrone, Joseph A. 76
Motor Viper **219**
Mouse 25, **108**

Mouse 2 **108**, 131
Mount Fuji 253
Mudbuster (vehicle) 38
Mudfighter (vehicle) 64
Mulholland, Brian K. 40
Mullighan, Jane 78
Munitia 189, 205, 209, 212, 213, 214, **220**, 227, 250
Muskrat 24, 38, **108**, 110, 131, 252
Mutt 24, 28, 33, 38, 67, **108**, 109, 140, 159, 190
Mutt and Junkyard 28, 33, 38, 67, **108**, 190

nanomites 221
NASA 7, 43, 54, 89, 139
Nash, Clifton L. 90
Natale, Gregory M. 44
Natalie Poole 22, **109**
NATO 249
Nebraska 95, 186, 188, 189, 207, 209, 213, 220, 227, 230, 238, 249, 250; Lincoln 186, 188, 189, 207, 209, 213, 220, 227, 230, 238, 249, 250; Stromsburg 95
Nemesis Enforcer **220**, 221
Neo-Viper 75, **221**
Netherlands 162, 166; Eindhoven 166; Rotterdam 162
Neurotoxin **222**
Nevada 27, 67; Las Vegas 67, 158
New Hampshire 44, 51; Wolfboro 44
New Jersey 52, 54, 65, 99, 109, 135, 168, 202, 219, 231, 253, 256; Amalgamated Super-Conductor Corporation 202; Asbury Park 52, 65; Broca Beach 47, 52, 125, 168, 180, 185, 207, 231, 255, 256; Elizabeth 52; Giant Stadium 99; Iselin 109; Jersey Shore 231; Montclair 135; Plainfield 54; Ridgewood 202
New Mexico 100, 145, 146; Albuquerque 145; Crosby 100; Taos Pueblo Reservation, Taos 146
New South Wales 247; Botany Bay 247
New York 26, 31, 34, 36, 40, 48, 57, 74, 77, 81, 82, 85, 91, 94, 97, 98, 99, 100, 104, 105, 111, 117, 118, 128, 129, 141, 144, 145, 149, 157, 164, 189, 190, 195, 197, 200, 203, 206, 207, 209, 213, 220, 227, 229, 234, 247, 249, 250, 256, 257; Albany 128; Brighton Beach 105; the Bronx 74; Brooklyn 85, 111, 117, 164, 203, 234; Catskill 190; Coney Island 234; Cooperstown 82; Flushing 99; Hartsdale 36; Hollis, Queens 48; Long Island 31, 57; Manhattan 136, 189, 207, 209, 113, 213, 220, 249, 250, 256; New York City 34, 40, 77, 91, 98, 100, 164, 167, 170, 171, 180, 185, 186, 197, 200, 257; Oyster Bay, Long Island 31; Shea Stadium 99; Somers 157; Spanish Harlem

34, 141; Spring Valley 97; Staten Island 26, 48, 200, 206, 227; Yonkers 81
New Zealand 38, 57, 93; Auckland 38, 57; Christchurch 93
Night Adder 222
Night Blaster 110
Night Boomer 110
Night Creeper 179, **222**, 223, 227
Night Creeper Ninja Clan 223
Night Creepers 179, 201, 213, **222**, 223, 227
Night F.L.A.K. 110
Night Force 56, 69, 74, 98, 108, **110**, 112, 115, 122, 135, 142, 145, 164
Night Fox 25, **110**
Night Raider 110
Night Raven (vehicle) 94, 119, 182, 185, 203, 236, 243
Night Ray (vehicle) 110
Night Rhino (vehicle) 68, 114
Night Scrambler (vehicle) 110
Night Shade (vehicle) 110
Night Stalkers Commander 223
Night Stalkers Shock Troops 223
Night Storm (vehicle) 110
Night Striker (vehicle) 110
Night Vultures 181, 238, 239
Nightingale 24, 110
Nightstalker 110
Ninja B.A.T. (Battle Android Trooper) 152, **224**, 243
Ninja Cobra Strike Team 252
Ninja Force 34, 36, 48, 64, 91, **111**, 129, 141, 152, 157, 160, 222, 229, 239, 242
Nod, Harry 231
North Carolina 1, 56, 69, 127, 163; Fayetteville 69; Greensboro 1, 56; Raeford 127
North Dakota 100, 165; Bismarck 100, 165
Norway 63, 143; Tronsk 63
Norwegian Arctic Circle 240
Nostaw, Shane R. 205
Nowhere Man 195, 196, 225
Nullifiers 214
Nunchuk 24, 33, 110, **111**, 112, 239

O'Flaherty, Patrick Liam 115
O'Hara, Shana M. 129
Ohio 32, 37, 50, 55, 58, 65, 69, 77, 79, 80, 89, 120, 123, 139, 154, 158, 188; Cincinnati 37, 58, 120, 139, 158, 188; Cleveland 65, 69; Columbus 80, 123; Dayton 65, 154; Delhi Hills 32; Elyria 89; Parma 69; Springboro 50; Warren 79; Warrenton 55
Oklahoma 66, 97; Lawton 97; Poteau 66
Oktober Guard 16, 39, 40, 53, 54, 58, 66, 78, 88, 89, 91, 103, 107, 111, 115, 121, 127, 136, 137, 151, 169, 207, 252
Old Clyde's 192
Olga 224
Olliestan 92, 99

Onihashi 160, 253, 257
Operation Dragonfly 21
Operation: Lady Doomsday 135
Operations Support Squadron 112
Ophelia 81, 112, 141
Ophelia Gabriel 112
Optimus Prime 104, 208
Oregon 60, 61, 129; Eugene 60, 61; New Moon 129
Orozco, Sofía 86
Ortiz, Armando M. 110
Osborne, Lilian 219
Otis 188, 192, 204, 215, **224**, 232, 249
Outback 24, 38, 110, **112**, 159, 230
Over Kill 224, 225, 226, 233
Overlord 51, 129, 138, 186, 195, 196, **225**, 226, 237, 250
Overlord Vector 186
Overlord Vector B.A.T. 226
Overlord Virus 186, 226
Overlord Virus B.A.T. 226
Overlord Vortex 186
Overlord Vortex B.A.T. 226
Owens, Cory R. 98
Owens, Robert D. 102
Ozone 24, 68, **113**, 148

P-40 Warhawks 128
pacifist 62, 63, 97, 145
Packer, Albert F. 238
Pago Pago, Samoa 120
the Paine Brothers 185
Paolino, Michelino J. 69
Paquette 25, **113**
Paquette, Jeffrey 113
Paralyzers 228
Parasite 205, 239
Parker, Blaine L. 101
Patagonia 55
Pathfinder 24, 32, 48, 79, **114**, 128, 139, 154
Patriot (vehicle) 54, 107, 137, 152
Patrulha Do Ar 28, 31, 68, **114**, 139, 181, 204
Patrulheiro da Selva 120
Payload 23, 83, **114**, 115, 148, 154
Pennsylvania 60, 71, 91, 98, 113, 125, 137, 149, 169, 186, 189, 207, 213, 220, 227, 249, 250; Allentown 169; Philadelphia 186, 189, 207, 209, 213, 220, 227, 250; Pittsburgh 60, 71, 125, 137, 149; Three Mile Island 113
Perlmutter, Stanley R. 109
Perry, William 74, 75
Persuader (vehicle) 35
P.E.T.S. (Primal Emergency Tactical Squad) 135
the Phoenix Guard 141, 185, 197, 204, 234, 254, 256, 257
Phones 115
Pidel, Martin A. 81
Pile Driver 111, 157
Pincus, Floyd R. 82
Pine, Albert M. 31
Piper, Roderick George Toombs 232

the Pit 1 25
the Pit 2 27
the Pit 3 27
the Pit 4 27
the Plague 119, 186, 187, 189, 207, 209, 210, 212, 213, 214, 220, 226, 227, 228, 231, 239, 242, 249, 250
the Plague Troopers 210, **226**
plasmatox 190, 191
Polar Battle Bear 94, 129, 143, 164
Polly the parrot 134, 135
Poole, Natalie 22, 109
Power Station Alpha 94, 131
Power Stone 186, 226
Prater, Thomas K. 2, 4
President Freedlowe 197
Price, Daniel W. 52
Professor Apple 227
Provost, Michael A. 89
Provost, Philip M. 51
Prudence, Dwight M. 156
Psyche-Out 24, 110, **115**, 144, 159
Pulaski, Ralph W. 149, 150
Pulver, Hedda L. 116
Pulverizer (vehicle) 38, 147, 208
Punta del Mucosa 35, 253
Pyre, Kidwell 213
the Python Patrol 123, 180, 194, 196, 197, 220, 241
Pythona 221, **227**

Q-Force 109, **116**
Quarrel 24, **116**, 129, 170
Quebec 29, 35; Montreal 35
Quick Kick 32, 47, 56, 57, 67, 70, **116**, 117, 153, 243
Quick Stryke 117, 157
Quintesson Invasion 69

Ragan, Tom-Henry 89
Rages (vehicle) 228
Rainone, Joseph R. 157
Raja Khallikhan 239
RAM (vehicle) 94, 124, 128, 129, 147, 231
Ram, Chuck 52
RAM Cycle (vehicle) 67
Rambo 126
Rambo: The Force of Freedom 126
Ramirez, Hector 86
Rampage 85, **117**, 228, 238
Rampart 25, 82, **117**, 118
Range Viper (individual) 32, 227, 228
Range Vipers 189, **228**
Rank and File 179
Rapid Deployment Force 70, **118**, 122
Rapid-Fire 24, **118**
Raptor 206, **228**, 229
the Rattler 185, 201, 252, 254
Raven 119
Rawhides 21, 41, 91, 95, **119**
Razor-Blade helicopter 38
Razor Troopers 229
Razorback (assault vehicle) 88, 214
Razorclaw 229
A Real American Hero 6, 20, 21, 22, 143, 152, 168, 243

Index

Recoil 24, **119**
Recondo 24, 28, 80, **119**, 120, 138, 145, 159
Red Devils 123
Red Dog 24, **120**, 133
Red McKnox 120, 157
Red Ninja Master 201, 230
Red Ninjas 25, 153, 157, **229**, 230, 243
Red Scream 183, **230**
Red Shadows 28, 82, 95, 118, 163, 176, 184, 185, 187, 189, 192, 199, **230**, 254
Red Spot 24, **120**
Red Star 112, **121**
Red Zone 25, **121**
Redmack 24, **122**, 134, 161
Reel FX 39
Relay Star 215
Remington, J. III 228
Remus, Robert Rudolph 132
Renegade 123
Renwick, Richard 63
Repeater 24, 70, 110, 118, **122**
Republic of Baranique 55
Repulsor 230
Reservist 11, 35, 41, 79, 83, 92, **122**
Rey, Philip A. 76, 77
R.H.I.N.O. 49
Rhode Island 27, 45, 48, 59, 64, 76, 77, 89, 93, 99, 102, 103, 113, 122, 126, 140, 154, 160, 234; Central Falls 77; Cranston 45, 48; Cumberland 77, 122; East Greenwich 126, 160; Newport 93; North Kingstown 113; Pawtucket 89; Providence 27, 48, 59, 64, 103, 140, 234; Rumford 102; Smithfield 154; Warwick 99, 102; Westerly 76
Rice Krispies 97
Rich, Kenneth D. 115
Riley, Thomas P. 65
Rip Cord 24, 28, 48, **123**, 227, 236
Rip Cord 2 123
Rip It 189, 227, **230**, 231
Ripper 204, **231**, 247, 257
Ritchie, Michael P. 120
Rivera, Joseph A. 93
Rivera, Roberto K. 198
Rives, Jean-Paul 133
Road Pig 187, 204, **231**, 232
Roadblock 16, 24, 28, 33, 37, 38, 61, 84, 107, 110, **123**, 124, 148, 154, 159, 171
Roberts, George A. 144
Robo-J.O.E. 33, 76, **124**
R.O.C.C. 138
Rock 'N Roll 6, 19, 20, 24, 83, **125**, 143, 144, 148, 223
Rock Vipers 232
Rocky 125
Rocky Mountain Line 47
Rocky Mountains 112, 122, 217
Rogers, Danimal J. 209
Rogue, Tomax 246
Rogue, Xamot 255
Rollbar 25, **126**
Rook 25, 121, **126**

Roscoe 188, 192, 204, 215, 224, **232**, 249
Rose, Olga 224
Rossi, Thomas R. III 59
Rostoff, Grigori Ivanovich 39
Roth, Edward J. 169
Rotweiler, Herbert J. 42
"Rowdy" Roddy Piper 23
Rudat, Ronald 68
Rugrat 204, **233**
Rumbler 24, 33, 34, 57, **126**, 127
Ruslan 112, **127**
Russia 6, 39, 66, 75, 78, 81, 88, 90, 91, 94, 107, 121, 127, 151, 191, 224, 225, 236, 249; Archangel 39; Arkhangelsk 78; Kalinigrad 127; Leningrad 88; Moscow 66, 151; Saint Petersburg 91; Smolensk 107
Russo, Alexander P. 140
Russo, Michael P. 64

Sabre Squadrons 112
S.A.F. (Special Action Force) 45, 91, 116, 146
Salindra 156
Salviatti, Albert 35
Salvo 24, 25, 114, **127**, 128, 218, 219
Samurai Smash 111
Sand Razor (vehicle) 68
Sand Scorpion 222, **233**
Sanders, Bradley J. 41
Sanderson, Morris L. 108
Sandstorm 25, 68, **128**
Sao Cristobel 33, 97, 100, 108, 119, 135, 146, 199
Sao Paulo 145
SAS Force 28, 145
Sasaki, Teiko 156
Satin 128
Savage 13, 24, **128**, 131, 157, 251
Savage, Robert S., Jr. 128
Savage Eagles 59, 68, 79, 84, 87, 156
Savannah, Georgia 249
Saw Viper 196, 207, 225
S.A.W. Vipers (Semi-Automatic Weapons) Vipers **233**
Scalpel 234
Scanner 129, 135, 226
Scar Face 234
Scarlett 6, 11, 18, 20, 22, 28, 41, 60, 60, 67, 111, 123, **129**, 130, 138, 141, 142, 147, 148, 154, 186
Schnurr, Kurt 30
Schrage 88, 136, **130**, 148
Sci-Fi 24, 42, **121**
Scoop 25, 100, **130**, 131
Scorched Earth campaign 187, 189, 207, 209, 210, 213, 214, 220, 249, 250
Scotland 41, 49, 73, 94, 96, 112, 135, 168, 183, 185, 200, 218, 232, 235; Bantor 73; Callander 200, 235; Edinburgh 49; Glasgow 96, 232; Loch Lomond 168; Midland Valley 183; Stirling 112
Scott, Brent 87
Scott, Bryan 87

Scott, Eric U. 168
Scott, Greg D. 124
Scotty 197
Scout 131, 170
Scrap-Iron 48, 144, 195, **234**, 235
Screaming Eagles 108, 128, **131**
Sea Skimmer 116, 155
Sea Titan 138, 151
Sea-Vipers 220
Sean (Kamakura) 24, 33, 41, 81, **92**, 138, 141, 154, 196, 206
Sears Exclusive 194
Sear's Holiday Wish Book 161
Secto-Viper 235
Selina 131
Selkirk, Stuart R. 112
Senator Barbara Larkin 131
Sgt. Hacker 24, 81, 101, 234
Sergeant Major 235
Sgt. Redmack 24, 122, 134, 161
Sgt. Savage 13, 24, 59, 68, 79, **128**, 131, 157
Sgt. Slaughter 9, 25, **132**, 133, 139, 221, 236
Sgt. Slaughter's Renegades 132, **133**, 156
Sgt. Topson 161
Serpentor 7, 21, 58, 77, 115, 176, 178, 181, 192, 195, 196, 203, 206, 208, 210, 225, 227, **236**, 237, 257
Seward, Farley S. 75
Shadow Ninjas 141, 152, 242
Shadow Strike 237
Shah, Farooq 147
Shannon, Carl G. 50
S.H.A.R.C. 59, 60, 90
Shark 133
Sharp 25, **133**
Sharp, Warwick J. 133
Sharpe, Dexter 133
Shary Wingfield 237, 244
Shaz 25, **133**, 134
Shimik 122, **134**, 161
Shipwreck 25, 38, 55, 128, **134**, 135, 138, 153, 218, 243
Shockwave 24, 67, 70, 110, 118, 129, **135**, 138, 167
Shooter 135, 145
Short Fuze 6, 20, 110, **135**, 136, 148, 154, 156, 157, 169, 171
Shrage 112, **136**
Siberia 66, 183, 202, 208; Irkutsk 183
Side Track 24, **137**
Side Track 2 137
Sideswipe 25, **137**
Sierra Gordo 33, 35, 39, 53, 54, 58, 80, 87, 88, 98, 100, 104, 107, 115, 120, 123, 125, 129, 130, 135, 137, 144, 147, 152, 153, 162, 164, 167, 170, 185, 200, 203, 215, 218, 219, 234, 236, 246, 255, 256
Sierra Leone Diamond Wars 246, 255
Sightline 24, **137**
Sigma 6 22, 46, 60, 90, 92, 98, 99, 138, 151, 152, 153, 164, 176, 217, 225, 242, 243
Sikorski, Victor W. 97

the Silencer 36, **237**, 238
Silent Backslash 160
the Silent Castle 41, 180, 229, 244
Silver Mirage 30, 36, 67, 94, 96, 97, 101, 117, 129, 130, 134, 158, 167, 170
Singh, Aruna 83
Siobhan 129
Six, Robert M. 30
S.K.A.R. 90, 117, 157, 170, **213**, 215, 228, 238, 241, 254
Skidmark 230, **238**
Skoog, Tormod S. 163
Skull Buster 238
Sky Creeper 189, 227, **238**, 239
Sky Hawk (vehicle) 30, 46, 62, 67, 73, 94, 129, 139
Sky Patrol 28, 29, 30, 31, 32, 66, 68, 114, **138**, 139, 148, 181, 204
Sky Raven (vehicle) 139
Sky SHARC (vehicle) 139
Sky Striker (vehicle) 29, 94, 129, 134
Sky-Sweeper 38, 94
Skydive 24, 29, 30, 138, **139**
Skylar, Edward J. 148
Skymate 29, **139**
Skyraider 139, 140
Skystorm X-Wing Chopper 169
Skystriker 23, **140**, 159
SkyStriker (vehicle) 30, 67, 124, 167, 185, 201
Skywatch 105
Slash 196, **239**
Slaughter's Marauders 36, 73, 94, 100, 109, **140**, 146
Sleeping Phoenix 82
Slice 33, 239
Slipstream 23, 119, **140**, 141
the Slugger (vehicle) 158
Smith, Cornelius E. 248
Smith, Jacques-Peter 39
Smith, Theodore I. 224
Smith, Winston P. 215
Smithers, Matthew W. 165
Snake-Eater 141, 204
Snake Eyes 6, 8, 11, 20, 24, 33, 41, 43, 60, 61, 81, 82, 84, 86, 92, 93, 111, 112, 128, 129, 138, **141**, 142, 144, 147, 148, 153, 159, 163, 169, 179, 185, 196, 198, 200, 206, 208, 243
Snapdragon 25, **142**
Sneak Peek 25, 68, 110, **142**, 153, 159
Sneak Peek 2 143
Sneeden, Wayne R. 38
Snow Cat (vehicle) 36, 67, 73, 75, 84, 94, 124, 143, 169
Snow Job 24, 28, **143**
Snow Serpent 33, 186, 187, 227, **239**, 249
Snow Storm 24, 38, **143**
Snow Viper 239, 240
Snow Wolf 16, **240**
Soft Master 33, 64, 82, **144**
Sonar Officer 115, 116
Sonic Fighters 60, 64, 69, 95, 125, **144**, 164, 170
Sonic Force 38, 63

Sound Attack 60, 61, 81, 124, 141, 152, 166, 204, 242
South Carolina 75, 101, 132, 165; Aiken 75; Myrtle Beach 165; Parris Island 101, 132
South Dakota 48; Sioux Falls 48
Southeastern Insurance Group 51
Space Force 28, 43, 84, 89, 93, 107, 139
Space Shot 23, **144**, 148
Space Vehicle Launch Operator 83
Spain 44, 57, 94, 109, 152, 162, 170, 242; Madrid 162, 170
Sparks 25, 71, 135, **144**, 223
Sparrow Hawk 145
Sparta 55, **145**, 236
Spearhead 110, **145**, 146
Special Action Force 42, 49, 65, 91, 109, 116, **146**
Special Anti-Terrorist Squad 37
Special Counter-Terrorism Unit Delta 128
Special Mission: Brazil (boxed set with cassette) 51, 60, 61, 95, 96, 101, 128, 146, 166
Special Ops Hammer Team 196
Spengler, Egon 156
Spirit 24, 29, 41, 90, 91, 138, 140, **146**, 153, 154, 163, 216, 243
Spitfire 24, **146**
Springfield 36, 39, 41, 67, 72, 76, 94, 95, 120, 123, 129, 134, 136, 144, 146, 149, 162, 163, 167, 170, 174, 180, 181, 185, 192, 200, 203, 204, 206, 218, 234, 236, 246, 255
Spud 186, 258
Spy Troops 16
Stalker 6, 20, 22, 28, 29, 33, 36, 37, 38, 60, 67, 92, 131, 141, **147**, 148, 153, 154, 159, 161, 169, 179, 206, 243
Stall, Alyssa Renee 45
Stall, Dwight E. 37
Stanley 147
Stantz, Ray 156
Star Brigade 54, 67, 68, 76, 83, 85, 113, 114, 124, 125, 130, 144, **147**, 200, 201
Star-Viper 203, **240**
Starduster 24, **148**
Starfighter jet 130
Stars and Stripes Forever 23, 46, 80, 125, 129, 141, 147, **148**, 158
Static Line 24, 29, 30, 139, **148**
Steam-Roller 25, **149**
Steel Brigade 25, 50, 121, 126, **149**, 214
Steel Cobra 241
Steel marauder (vehicle) 93
Steel Raven 238, **241**
Steeler 20, 23, 110, 131, 136, 145, **149**, 150, 154, 170, 185
Steen, Edwin C. 96
Steinberg, Lance J. 52, 65
Stevens, Scott 77, 198
Steyr Scout Tactical (vehicle) 100
Stiletto 25, **150**, **241**, 242
Stinger (vehicle) 73, 201, 231
Stingray (vehicle) 133

Stitches 24
Stone 138, **150**, 157, 163
Stone 2 151
Stone 3 151
Stone, Geoffrey IV 151
Stone, Daniel Will 151
Stone, Skip A. 57
Storm Rider 242
Storm Shadow 25, 26, 33, 35, 41, 43, 58, 61, 64, 82, 92, 111, 117, 141, 142, 144, 146, 147, 150, **151**, 153, 157, 159, 160, 179, 186, 193, 206, 213, 224, 226, 227, 236, 239, **242**, 243, 256, 257
Stormavik 88, 112, **153**
Strato-Viper 119, 240, **243**
Stratton, Felix P. 106, 150, 242
Strawhacker 153
Strawhacker, George 153
Stretcher 25, 114, **153**
Strike First 237, **243**, 249
Strike Team: Alpha 38, 50, 67, 80, 97, 124, **154**, 162, 167
Strike Team: Bravo 52, 69, 72, 92, 129, 136, 147, 149, **154**
Strike Team: Charlie 31, 32, 50, 56, 98, 100, 114, 115, 146, **154**, 168
STUN (vehicle) 94, 203, 219, 220
Sturgis, Scott E. 129
Sub-Zero 23, 33, 53, **154**
Sunbow 20, 27, 39, 46, 58, 69, 94, 124, 133, 134, 143, 153, 176, 185, 243, 246, 258
Super Trooper 24, **154**
Supreme Leader 42, 188, 196
Sure Fire 23, **155**
Surfer 155
Susan Hoffman 155
Swamp Cruiser (vehicle) 196
Swamp Rat 16, **244**
Swamp Skier (vehicle) 49, 257
Swamp Skimmer (vehicle) 108
Swamp Viper 244
Swampfire (vehicle) 51, 90, 219, 231, 246, 247
Swansea, Wales 163
Swanson, Robert G. 103
S.W.A.T. 135
Sweden 84, 150, 161, 241; Gotland 150, 241; Malmö 161; Stockholm 84
Swilley, Earl-Bob 127
Switch Gears 25, 60, 156
Switzerland 116, 185; Interlaken 116
Swordfish 115

Tadur, Ronald 114
Tadur, Ronald W. 67
Taeko 156
Taggart, Greg 43
Talbot, Lincoln B. 98
Tall Elk, Jimmy 59
Tall Sally 156, 157
Talltree, Franklin E. 29
"Tan Grunt" 80
Tank 131, **156**
"Tanks for the Memories" 223
Taputapu, David 120

Index

T.A.R.G.A.T.s 214
Tasmania 231; Grim Cape 231
Tatsuwashi 93
Taurus 25, 133, **156**
Teach, Morgan 256
Team Extreme 35, 42, 74, 83, 104, 106, 107, 117, 120, 128, 136, 151, 156, **157**
Tele-Viper 244, 245, 251
Tennessee 46, 70, 105; Collierville 70; Gatlinburg 46; Nashville 105
Terror Drome 184
Texas 68, 90, 95, 102, 113, 167; Brady 167; Brownsville 90; Fort Worth 68; Houston 95; Victoria 102
T'gin-Zu 25, 111, **157**, 239
Thailand 150, 241; Hua Hin 150, 241
Therien, Jeffrey R. 122
3rd Armored Division 53
Thomas, Benjamin R. 29
Thomas, David O. 56
Thomas, Theodore M. 160
Thomas, Theodore N. 160
Thompson, Jeffrey D. 42
Thomas Stall 57, 92, 107, **158**
Thrasher 204, **245**, 246
Thunder 56, 63, 86, **158**, 233
Thunderwing 24, **158**, 159
Tiger Claw 25, 33, 141, **159**
Tiger Force 31, 38, 40, 44, 57, 60, 61, 67, 68, 70, 72, 75, 82, 87, 91, 96, 109, 112, 113, 115, 120, 124, 140, 142, 147, **159**, 163, 167, 168, 170
Timber 141, **159**
T'jbang 33, 111, 112, **159**, 239
TNT 160
Tollbooth 24, **160**, 161
Tomahawk 23, 83, **161**
Tomahawk (vehicle) 51, 84, 94, 97, 116, 117, 130, 167, 221
Tomax 179, 191, 193, 195, 197, 202, 204, 205, 211, 218, 219, 222, 234, 236, 238, **246**, 255
Tombstone 247
Ton Up 28, **161**
Toner, Daniel T. 139
Topside 25, 114, **161**
Topson 46, 122, 134, **161**
Torch 204, 231, **247**, 257
Torngark, Sukko 200
Torpedo 25, 28, 60, 154, **162**, 190
Torquemada Paine 247
Toss 'n Cross (vehicle) 160, 161
Toulouse, France 44, 133
Townsend, Frederick M. 230
Toxo-Vipers 230, **248**
Toys "R" Us 18, 60, 96, 101, 146, 246
Tracker 157, **162**, 163, 170
Trakker 24, 104, 162, **163**
Trakker, Matt 104
Trans-Carpathia 40, 80, 92, 94, 129, 141, 152, 180, 183, 185, 200, 201, 229, 239, 242
Transformers 8, 19, 33, 69, 86, 100, 104, 110, 111, 124, 156, 169, 192, 215, 221, 221, 226, 238

Travalino, Robert J. 36
Tree, Connor D. 45
Trench, Percy R. 62
Triple 'T' 132
Tripwire 24, 28, 159, **163**, 164
Trooper 164
Trubble Bubble (vehicle) 117, 132, 185, 201, 203
Trucial Abysima 47, 50, 54, 55, 56, 57, 62, 67, 69, 70, 98, 103, 115, 116, 117, 150, 158, 168, 196, 233, 241, 246, 255
the Trucial States 31
Tucaros 89
Tunnel Rat 24, 60, 85, 110, 119, 123, 124, 131, 138, 144, 159, **164,** 225
Turkey 45, 85, 125, 156, 218; Istanbul 45, 85, 156
Twenty Questions 86
22nd Regiment of the British Special Air Service 40
the Two-Headed Serpent 194, 240
Tyler 237, 249

Ukraine 53, 121, 207; Kirovograd 207; Odesa 53, 121
Una 128
Una Macbride 165
Undertow 61, **248**
Unicron 208
Updraft 24, 102, **165**
Ursula 109
Utah 27, 34, 35, 39, 50, 55, 62, 67, 83, 85, 95, 112, 122, 123, 127, 128, 137, 140, 146, 149, 150, 160, 162, 164, 168, 170; Provo 140

V-Troop 244
V-Trooper 229
Valor vs. Venom 16
Van der Burgh, Pieter 145
Vance 188, 192, 204, 215, 224, 232, **248**
Vance Wingfield 237, 243, **249**
Van Eyck, Frits 166
Vapor 249, 250
Vaskovia, Artur 91, 111
Vaughn, Wilder A. 254
Vector 38, 189, 209, 213, 214, 220, 227, **250**
Velocity 187, 189, 207, 210, 213, 227, 249, **250**
Veloz, Flecha 146
Venkman, Peter 156
Vennemeyer, David 102
Venom serum 244
Venomous Maximus 250
Verdi, Alessandro D. 144
Vermont 57, 143, 230; Manchester 51; Rutland 143; Wallingford 230
Viper Agent 251
Viper Officer 252
Virginia 48, 71, 72, 85, 93, 106, 117, 127, 165; Alexandria 71, 127; Charlottesville 93; Fort Belvoir 85, 117; Norfolk 165; Quantico 48; Richmond 106; Virginia Beach 71
Voltar 108, 214, 252

von Clausewitz, Carl 121
Von Rani, Otto 215, 238
Vypra 252, 253
Vypra Courier 253
Vypra, twins 253

Wade, Jared 50
Wales 65, 91, 219, 245; Cardiff 65, 91; Rhyl 219; Swansea 163
Walker, Andrew R. 234
Walters, Scott 93
Warden, John 48
Washington 27, 28, 83, 96, 106, 118, 119; Molson 106; Seattle 27, 28, 96, 118; Tacoma 83; Vashon Island 119
Washington, DC 76, 93, 101, 131, 136, 154, 162, 185, 200, 218, 231, 234; Pentagon 76, 93, 101, 131, 136, 154, 162
Water Moccasin (vehicle) 67, 196, 231
"The Weather Dominator" 128
Weems, Wallace A. 123
Weidler, Carol 102, 256
Wesson, Horatio T. 187
Wesson, Maximillian Q. 232
Wesson, Terrance W. 191
West Virginia 106, 137; New Manchester 137; Spencer 106
Wet Down 22, 154, **165**
Wet Suit 25, 38, 51, 61, 96, 101, 128, 130, 138, 146, 162, **165**, 166, 223
Wheels 166, 170
Whipple, Hoxworth 155
Whisper 150, 242, **253**
Whitcomb, Averill B. 149
White, Bill 57
The White Clown 101, **166**
White Eagle, Lori Ann 111
White Eagle, Temera 110
Whiteout 24, **166**
Wichita, Kansas 72, 98
Wide Scope 25, **167**
Wild Bill 24, 38, 154, 159, **167**, 168, 254
Wild Bill, Action Force 168
Wild Weasel 250, **253**, 254
Wild West Haulin' 88
Wildcard 25, 154, 157, **168**
Wilder Vaughn 183, 200, 230, **254**
Wilkinson, Lonzo R. 147
William Penny Laboratory 45
Williams, Ross A. 108
"Willie" Suarez, Guillermo 143
Willoughby, Malcolm R. 59
Windchill 24, 38, **168**, 169
Windmill 169
Wingfield, Sharon 237
Wingfield, Vance 237, 243, **249**
Winken, Tom 247
Winkie, Bill 219
Winter Operations 34, 75, 106, 136, 141, 147, 154, **169**
Winters, Susan 219
Wisconsin 30, 78, 119, 126; Chippewa Falls 78; La Crosse 126; Lake Geneva 30; Wheaton 119

Wolkekuck-Uckland 147
Wong 112, **168**
Wong, Wen-Yun 169
World War III 46, 60, 79, 90, 98
Wraith 23, 122, **254**
Wreckage 25, 159, **169**, 170, 238
Wyckoff, Tommy 1, 4
Wyoming 112, 124; Big Piney 112; Casper 124

Xamot 179, 195, 197, 204, 218, 236, 246, **255**
"XTERMIN8" 118

Yuki 170

Z Force 28, 46, 49, 63, 75, 91, 115, 116, 131, 149, 162, 166, **170**
Zachary 255
Zandar 76, 195, 196, 204, **255**, 257
Zanya 204, **256**
Zanzibar 204, **256**
Zap 6, 20, 24, 41, 81, 85, 144, 148, **170**, 171, 223
Zarana 102, 187, 188, 204, 231, 232, 236, **256**, 257
Zartan 25, 43, 49, 82, 84, 178, 179, 195, 196, 201, 203, 211, 219, 231, 236, 246, 247, 256, **257**, 258
Zeddemore, Winston 156
Zeus 186, 191
Zeus B.A.T. 258
Zoe 25, 256
Zubenkov, Misha L. 107
Zullo, John 51

www.ingramcontent.com/pod-product-compliance
Lightning Source LLC
Chambersburg PA
CBHW060338010526
44117CB00017B/2873